# THE CONSTITUTIONAL HISTORY
# OF MODERN BRITAIN
## SINCE 1485

*by*

### SIR DAVID LINDSAY KEIR
FORMERLY MASTER OF BALLIOL COLLEGE, OXFORD

### NINTH EDITION

### ADAM & CHARLES BLACK
### LONDON

A. AND C. BLACK LIMITED

4, 5 AND 6 SOHO SQUARE LONDON W.I

FIRST PUBLISHED (1485–1937) 1938
SECOND EDITION 1943   THIRD EDITION 1946
REPRINTED 1947 AND 1948
FOURTH EDITION 1950
FIFTH EDITION (1485–1951) 1953
REPRINTED, WITH SLIGHT REVISION, 1955
SIXTH EDITION 1960
REPRINTED 1961
SEVENTH EDITION 1963
EIGHTH EDITION 1966
NINTH EDITION 1969
REPRINTED 1975

© 1969 A. AND C. BLACK LIMITED


SBN 7136 0939 7

PRINTED IN GREAT BRITAIN BY
REDWOOD BURN LIMITED, TROWBRIDGE AND ESHER

# NOTE TO THE NINTH EDITION

THE need for this new edition has given me an opportunity both of making a number of minor but necessary amendments and of touching on two topics of major importance. A previously brief reference to the Franks Report has been much extended: and a first mention appears of the newly created office of Parliamentary Commissioner. In other respects, the recent and rapid processes of constitutional change at home and overseas seem still to belong to current politics and not yet to history.

D. L. K.

OXFORD *July* 1968

# PREFACE TO THE FIRST EDITION

THE constitutional development of Britain and the British Commonwealth imposes on its historian a twofold task. His first duty must be to describe the structure and working of the main organs of government during the successive stages of their growth. Second, but not less imperative, is that of interpreting their evolution with reference to the political and social conditions and the currents of thought and opinion by which it has been determined. British institutions are the product of long and varied experience in the art of government; their historical study demands, more than that of any other system, a clear understanding of the needs they have been devised to fulfil and the forces from which they have drawn vitality. In this volume an endeavour has been made, so far as limits of space allow, to show how government has been conducted by living and changing communities of men sharing a common political tradition.

For this purpose some sacrifice of detail has been inevitable. The loss will, it is hoped, be largely compensated by recourse to the references provided in the footnotes. These are in the main intended to be bibliographical, and to enable the student to see where ampler information is most readily available. Wherever possible, the most easily accessible reference has been given, and the fullest use made of the works of accepted authority, the standard collections of documents, and the monographs and periodical literature which the ordinary student may be expected to consult and to find at his disposal in a well-equipped library. The path from these towards the great store of materials for constitutional history amassed in printed collections of original sources lies invitingly open for the student who has opportunity to follow it. In the first instance, however, this book is meant to find its place in a more general course of reading, and to permit the study of the constitution to be combined, as it should be, with that of cognate historical processes.

The writing of these pages has put me under obligations which it is pleasant to record. My thanks are due to the Warden and

Fellows of All Souls College for so generously granting me special facilities for work in the Codrington Library, and to the Sub-Librarian, Mr A. Whitaker, and his assistants for their constant and ready help. A similar debt is owed to the staff of the Public Record Office; and here I have in particular to mention the kindness I received from the late Mr J. R. Crompton, who gave me his expert guidance in using to advantage the archives of which he had so unique a knowledge. Among colleagues and friends in Oxford, Mr Kenneth Leys has rendered me invaluable service by criticising and commenting in detail on the greater part of my work. Mr R. B. Wernham, Mr R. Pares, and Mr G. D. H. Cole very kindly read and advised me on the extensive portions which I submitted to their judgment. To Professors Powicke and Holdsworth I am indebted for opportunities of utilising writings of their own at that time still unpublished. On special points, Sir William Beveridge, Master of University College, Mr C. R. Cheney, Mr F. H. Lawson, Mr J. P. R. Maud, and many other friends have ungrudgingly given me the assistance I sought. Mr A. F. Wells's minute and scrupulous revision of the closing chapters aided me greatly in matters of style and wording. Finally, I have to express my gratitude to Mr E. Lipson for the care and vigilance with which he read the proofs, and for a large number of most helpful suggestions. How much I owe to the counsel and the criticism here acknowledged will, I trust, be evident in the following pages. For their defects I am of course alone responsible.

D. L. K.

OXFORD
*September* 1938

# CONTENTS

## ABBREVIATIONS

The following abbreviations have been employed in citing the periodicals most frequently referred to:

E.H.R.    *English Historical Review*
L.Q.R.    *Law Quarterly Review*
Hist.     *History*
B.I.H.R.  *Bulletin of the Institute of Historical Research*
C.H.J.    *Cambridge Historical Journal*
A.H.R.    *American Historical Review*
J.M.H.    *Journal of Modern History*

With regard to each of the above, the numeral preceding the abbreviation indicates the number of the volume, that following the abbreviation indicates the page.

The *Transactions of the Royal Historical Society* are referred to by the abbreviation *T.R.H.S.* In this case the preceding numeral indicates the series number, those which follow indicate the volume and the page.

# THE CONSTITUTIONAL HISTORY
# OF MODERN BRITAIN

## CHAPTER I

### THE FOUNDATIONS OF MODERN ENGLISH
### GOVERNMENT

i

CONTINUITY has been the dominant characteristic in the develop- *Continuity* ment of English government. Its institutions, though unprotected *and change* by the fundamental or organic laws which safeguard the "rigid" *in English constitu-* constitutions of most other states, have preserved the same general *tional de-* appearance throughout their history, and have been regulated in *velopment* their working by principles which can be regarded as constant. Crown and Parliament, Council and great offices of state, courts with their judges and magistrates, have all retained, amid varying environments, many of the inherent attributes as well as much of the outward circumstance and dignity which were theirs in the medieval world of their origin. In no other European country is the constitution so largely a legacy from that remote but not unfamiliar age. Yet continuity has not meant changelessness. Ancient institutions have been ceaselessly adapted to meet purposes often very different from those for which they were originally intended, and have been combined in apparent harmony with newer organs of government devised to meet requirements which have manifested themselves only as society has developed the intricate patterns of its modern life. The very flexibility of the constitution has ensured that the process of modifying and adding to it has involved no sudden and capricious breach with the past. In the English constitution, to adapt a picturesque phrase, the centuries have "given one another rendezvous."[1] Some of the institutions of former days have from time to time been swept away. But their disappearance has generally been preceded by atrophy, and their end has been painless. The destruction of living and working parts of the constitution has been rare. Even more subtle have been the changes, in their nature less easy to follow, in the unwritten customs and understandings—the "conventions of the constitution" as they have been termed—which supplement the strict letter of constitutional law. These too have been profoundly altered from age to age. The assumptions made in the sixteenth century had in the eighteenth long since ceased to be accepted. In the nineteenth century, those of the eighteenth were dissolved away. Whatever has been their form, they have always been reinterpretations, under changed circumstances, of principles inherent in the constitution, and they have lain within the very logic of constitutional growth. Neither in its formal and legal, nor in its informal and practical aspect, has English government at any stage of its history violently and permanently repudiated its own tradition.

*The New Monarchy*    At no point in that history is it more necessary to remember how it has combined permanence with flexibility than at the accession of the Tudor dynasty. This event has often been regarded as marking a transition, in the sphere of government as in other spheres of national life, from medieval to modern England, and from one system of government to another radically dissimilar from it. It is sometimes admitted that the transformation may have begun in the reign of Edward IV, but whether this be accepted or denied, the rule of the Tudors and of their Stuart successors to 1641 has been invested with unique constitutional attributes and described by the term "New Monarchy". It has been suggested that the "New Monarchy" began and ended with fundamental change in the structure and working of government, that its rise involved the rejection of principles hitherto regarded as axiomatic, that its fall meant their revival, and that while it existed they were in abeyance. It is thus represented as a kind of constitutional hiatus.

[1] Applied to the history of English law by J. S. Mill, *Dissertations and Discussions*, i. 369.

It repudiated the past, and was itself to be repudiated by the future.[1]

This catastrophic view of its history cannot be accepted. Yet *Its dis-* those who have held it have not done so without justification. *tinctive* The main features of the "New Monarchy" are distinct and *features* impressive. It concentrated authority, diffused during the Middle Ages among a multitude of holders, lay and ecclesiastical, in the grasp of the Crown. The independence of the feudal aristocracy and of the Catholic Church was destroyed. As the medieval immunities which had impeded its action were reduced, the executive arm of government, lately dilatory and ineffective, became summary and severe. In the fifteenth century, and indeed throughout the Middle Ages, the constitutional defect most often complained of had been "lack of governance". Under the "New Monarchy" the danger most apparent was that the royal authority should be transformed into a personal despotism, unrestricted by legal rules. As it gathered power into its hands, the monarchy ceaselessly enlarged the sphere of its activity. In medieval times the subject might have few dealings with the Crown unless he happened to hold land directly of it, or to be a party to proceedings before the royal courts of justice. Contact with it could now no longer be avoided. Royal control was widely extended over the social and economic affairs of the nation at large, which were brought under increasingly minute regulation. Nor did that control confine itself to material affairs. The intellectual convictions of each individual, the most intimate scruples of his conscience, became the subject-matter of royal inquisition and coercion. As every aspect of national life provided new material for the activities of the government, its machinery was overhauled and modernised. Old institutions were renovated, new institutions developed by their side. In the King's Council there centred a powerful executive system which likewise possessed legislative and judicial functions. The authority of the central government was strongly asserted in the domain of local administration. The King's Council threw off satellites such as the Council of the North and the Council of Wales and the Marches, and drew into its orbit a host of local officials, of whom the

---

[1] The views expressed by J. R. Green, *Short History of the English People*—in which the term "New Monarchy" was first used—282-3 (ed. 1874).

most important were the sheriff and the Justices of the Peace. This governmental system called for expert advisers, administrators and lawyers, and a staff of men so qualified made its appearance in the service of the Crown both in the sphere of domestic government and in that of foreign affairs, in which developments of the same swift and complex character were for the first time turning diplomacy into a regular profession and creating a network of international relationships, conducted by permanent embassies such as had been unknown in medieval life.[1] The ablest minds of the age thus enlisted themselves among the King's servants, and magnified the sovereignty of which they were the instruments.

*New conception of sovereignty*    These transformations, indeed, could hardly come about without causing profound changes in the whole conception of royal authority. The monarchy, raised in isolated splendour above the mass of its subjects, claimed from them obedience to a degree never demanded heretofore. Medieval kings had exercised a variety of powers. They were feudal suzerains; within the feudal organisation they were holders of great fiefs like the Duchy of Lancaster; and, besides being lords or overlords of land, they were political sovereigns directly in contact with subjects to whom they were feudally unrelated. The "New Monarch" unified and simplified his position. The relative importance of his feudal attributes diminished.[2] His political sovereignty was overwhelmingly emphasised. This latter aspect of kingship was fortified by the absolutist principles of Roman law, which civil lawyers had never ceased to inculcate, and which now began to acquire wider currency as the revival of Roman jurisprudence in continental countries affected English legal and political thought.[3] Even more profound were the results which followed from the ecclesiastical revolutions of the sixteenth century. Attributing to the Crown power over the minds and consciences of every estate of its subjects, of a kind which no medieval ruler could conceivably have claimed, the age which worked out the conception of royal supremacy over the Church made the last and greatest contribution to the develop-

[1] B. Behrens, *Origin of the Office of English Resident Ambassador*, 4 *T.R.H.S.* xvi. 161.

[2] On the continuing use of the feudal attributes of the New Monarch see Miss H. M. Cam, *The Decline and Fall of English Feudalism*, 25 *Hist.* 216.

[3] On the Reception of Roman Law, see F. W. Maitland, *English Law and the Renaissance*, and W. S. Holdsworth, *History of English Law*, iv. 217 ff.

ment of the modern doctrine of sovereignty. The position asserted for the Crown during this period came naturally to be expressed in terms which emphasised its monopoly of power, the essentially derivative nature of all other lawful magistracies, the lack of legal restraints on royal action, and the divine sanctions by which it was upheld.

These considerations make it only too easy to regard the "New Monarchy" as something abnormal and exceptional. The revolutions with which it began and ended, as well as the qualities which marked its ascendancy, have tended to obscure the essential facts that the "New Monarchy" grew naturally out of the system which preceded it and transmitted an enduring legacy to that which arose on its overthrow. The foundations of modern English government were already laid when the House of Tudor came to the throne. The edifice of later ages embodies much of their handiwork. *Continuity preserved*

The revolution which made Henry VII king in August 1485 was an event of political rather than constitutional significance. It placed the destinies of England in the hands of the ablest ruler she had had since Edward I. But it involved no revision of the constitution. The organisation of government remained unaffected by a change which to contemporaries must have seemed only another phase in the dynastic struggles between the Houses of Lancaster and York which had periodically convulsed the country during the preceding thirty years. Nor was any new principle invoked in support of kingly power, the theoretical basis and claims of which remained substantially unaltered. Henry VII inherited a system of government based on the work of his predecessors. Under the dynasty of Lancaster that system had collapsed, owing to a combination of adverse circumstances, chief of which had been the poverty of the Crown, prolonged foreign war, and the personal misfortunes of the reigning house. In these circumstances the Lancastrian period had inevitably turned into one of aristocratic rule, which the more vigorous kings of the House of York had only partly succeeded in bringing to a close. Yet the fifteenth century, so disturbed in its political life, was an age of continuous constitutional development. The main organs of government, Crown, Council, and Parliament, central and local administration, and courts of justice had retained their characteristic attributes *Existing structure and principles of government maintained* throughout, and only awaited the coming of a prudent, resolute, and far-seeing line of kings for their revival and effective working. Henry VII's reign is as much a postscript to the Middle Ages as a prelude to the "New Monarchy." The beginnings of Tudor rule do not take the form of a breach with the past, nor of sweeping constitutional innovation, but of a determined and successful attempt to make existing institutions yield their proper results. Its ideal was an efficient central administration controlled by a strong and wealthy royal house.

*Conditions favouring revival of royal authority*    The difficulties of this task must not be underrated. The first of the Tudor house succeeded to a burdensome heritage. The government he assumed was financially weak, and its prestige and authority had suffered by the mistakes and calamities of his predecessors. The century which was wearing towards its close had been one of aristocratic domination and aristocratic turbulence. Violence, disorder, and the perversion of justice had deeply affected all ranks of the nation. Yet the outlook was not without hope. The civil wars of the preceding generation had seriously impaired the wealth and power of the great landowning families. Influential baronial houses had lost their leaders on the battlefield or the scaffold; successive confiscations of the lands of those who had supported the losing side in wars of many vicissitudes had diminished and broken up their estates. Meanwhile other classes, less concerned in the conflict, had been swiftly advancing towards political predominance. There was another England in the fifteenth century besides that of the great baronage. In the cities and seaports of the south and east an urban patriciate of traders and moneyed men had gained steadily in material resources.[1] From their ranks there was being drawn a new order of minor landowners into whose possession the estates of the older territorial families came by purchase or foreclosure. These newcomers were speedily assimilated with, and fortified, the class of country knights and squires whose fortunes were being likewise established by the commercial prosperity of the age. The connexion, always intimate, between the men of moderate property in town and in country was drawn ever closer. These two elements in society had many objects in common, the first of which

[1] See C. L. Kingsford, *Prejudice and Promise in Fifteenth-Century England*, 63, 70, 121 ff. Town and country alike gained from the growing wool-trade.

was the restoration of regular and effective administration and of peace and plenty. Their loyalty and co-operation was the prize awaiting any dynasty of rulers which could show vigour, good sense, and the will to be obeyed. Lacking the political traditions of the great aristocracy, they were content to allow the Crown the fullest control over the central government, and to second its efforts locally as Justices of the Peace or officers of the shirelevy or in other subordinate positions of authority. From among them were drawn the most competent and devoted servants of the Tudor sovereigns at home and abroad. The Tudor House of Lords gradually recruited from this source a new nobility, closely bound to the Crown by ties of loyalty and interest more compelling than any the older aristocracy had ever known. The Tudor House of Commons was filled with men similarly permeated by a sense of partnership and co-operation with the dynasty which expressed and made effective their ruling prejudices and desires.

This dependence on the co-operation of the middle class of pro- *Limita-* pertied men was the fundamental political characteristic of Tudor *tion on royal ab-* rule, and deeply affected its constitutional nature. The Tudors *solutism* never developed a professional and salaried bureaucracy wholly amenable to their own direction and command. The service they obtained was loyal, zealous, efficient, and reasonably honest and disinterested, and came to be dignified, as the sixteenth century advanced, with a spirit of generous obligation towards the common weal which owed much to the influence of classical literature and thought. But, in the last resort, that service was voluntary and incapable of rigid enforcement. If it were to be withheld, it was not easy to see what substitute the Crown could devise in its place. Tudor rule was unsupported by any standing professional army. The military system depended in effect on the same co-operative principle as civil government. Nor did the Crown possess sufficient means of constructing and maintaining any system, whether civil or military, which could be held entirely at its own disposition. The corollary of this tendency to surrender government into the hands of the monarchy was that the monarchy was expected to meet its responsibilities from its own resources. When these proved inadequate, the propertied classes showed some reluctance at coming to its aid in Parliament, and were stubborn in their refusal to do so otherwise. Inherited from the past, like every other element of

Tudor rule, were Parliament and the courts of Common Law, and the principles which they expressed and which were accepted as binding by King and people alike, that the rights and property of the subject were at the King's disposal only by virtue of popular consent. Here was a sure defence which the subjects of the Tudor monarchy never abandoned, and behind which they sheltered when demands were made that they should assume larger financial burdens for the support of the Crown, even when the increased liabilities of the central government made it ever more difficult for the King to defray its expenses out of his own pocket, and when the rapid decline in the value of money, due at first to the debasement of the currency and later to the influx of silver from America, increased the amount of the payments the Crown had to make, while its revenue failed to rise in proportion. The political alliance on which Tudor rule was based therefore necessarily limited its independence of action, impeded its development into a personal despotism, and trained in the business of the State a class which, were its loyalty to be extinguished and its co-operation with the Crown turned into opposition and hostility, might well prove equally invincible in the rôle of antagonist as it had been indispensable in that of partner.

ii

*Succession to the throne*    The first business of the new dynasty was to seat itself securely on the throne. For this purpose possession was nine-tenths of a law of succession which was exceedingly indefinite and uncertain.[1]

*Nature of the Tudor title*    The Tudor dynasty could appeal neither to the theory of a hereditary right which had been the basis of the Yorkist claim, nor to the statute law on which a Lancastrian claim in the right line might have been maintained had there been one in existence. At Bosworth, where Richard III had been slain and his crown immediately assumed by the victor, Henry VII became at least *de facto* king. His first Parliament enacted that the inheritance of the Crown, with all the pre-eminence and dignity royal, was, rested, and remained in the person of "our new sovereign lord King

---

[1] Discussed in S. B. Chrimes, *English Constitutional Ideas in the Fifteenth Century*, 22 ff. See also K. Pickthorn, *Early Tudor Government, Henry VII*, 2-5.

Henry" and in the heirs of his body, perpetually so to endure.[1] Here is no assertion of hereditary right, and indeed there could hardly have been such a claim. Nor is there, in precise words or by necessary intendment, the creation of a title to the throne based on parliamentary enactment, still less any reference to election. So far as Henry VII was concerned the statute merely recognises a fact. The only principle which it seems to suggest is that the right of his heirs to succeed to his Crown had been placed on a statutory foundation, which, implicitly at least, excluded any title derived from heredity alone.

The assertion or reassertion of this principle must, however, have *Dynastic* remained barren but for the ruthlessness and success with which *position of* the Tudors removed all actual or potential competitors. Henry VII's *the early* marriage to Elizabeth of York in the year after his accession and *Tudors* coronation, while it contributed nothing to his own title, transmitted to his descendants the strongest of the legitimist claims and united the White Rose with the Red. Yet there were plenty of possible pretenders, besides the imposters Simnel and Warbeck, to the throne he had won. The blood of the Yorkist claimant of 1460 flowed in the veins of several great families of early Tudor England. It proved a fatal legacy. One grandson, Edward, Earl of Warwick, was executed with Warbeck as a traitor in 1499. Although Henry VIII's title was never in much danger, Warwick's sister Margaret, Countess of Salisbury, suffered the same fate in 1541, as had her son Henry, Lord Montague, three years earlier. Three other grandsons of York, descended through his daughter Elizabeth, wife of John de la Pole, Duke of Suffolk, perished in battle or on the scaffold in the forty years after 1485.[2] A great-grandson, Henry, Marquis of Exeter, went to the block in 1539. Another great-grandson, Henry, Earl of Surrey, met the same death in 1547. Even so remote a connexion with the Plantagenet line as that possessed by Edward Stafford, Duke of Buckingham, descended in female line from Edward I, may have helped to bring about his judicial murder in 1521. The Tudors were always acutely aware of rivals near the

---

[1] A. F. Pollard, *Reign of Henry VII from Contemporary Sources*, I, 11-12. G. R. Elton, *The Tudor Constitution, Documents*, 4.

[2] These were John de la Pole, Earl of Lincoln, who fell at Stoke (1487); Edmund de la Pole, Earl of Suffolk, executed in 1513; and Richard de la Pole, killed at the Battle of Pavia (1525).

throne. Their success in consolidating their position was but little due to its strength on either statutory or legitimist grounds. It was obtained by a remarkable combination of energy, caution, and unscrupulousness. To Henry VII, in whom these qualities were clearly embodied, the attributes of kingship were, notwithstanding his dubious title, fully conceded. His recognition as king freed him, as a man, from his attainted past.[1] He acquired in its fullness the royal Prerogative—the mass of powers, rights, and immunities which distinguished a king from a private individual. In him was centred that popular belief in the sanctity and the miraculous powers of kingship which had always been connected with the royal office. Into his hands fell all the property, and the dues payable from the property of the subject, which formed the estate of the Crown. All that kingship implied was Henry's, to make of it what use he could.

*Financial recovery*
　　The essential prerequisite for the effective exercise of royal authority was the improvement of the Crown's financial position. Personal factors excluded, the chief reason for the decline of the monarchy during the fifteenth century had been its chronic poverty, accentuated by war expenditure in France for which its income proved insufficient, and which had to be met partly by the alienation of Crown lands and other capital resources. The cessation of the war in 1453 might have proved, but for the domestic troubles which followed it, the first stage in financial recovery. That process had begun during the reign of Edward IV, the first sovereign since Richard II to leave a surplus in his treasury. Its continuance, by methods which closely resemble those of Edward IV, was one of Henry VII's principal tasks. The sources from which the "ordinary" revenue of the Crown—that is, revenue not provided by occasional parliamentary grant—was derived yielded increasingly plentiful supplies.

*Crown Lands*
　　These sources comprised in the first place the lands belonging to the Crown in its own right, or to the King as Prince of Wales, Duke of Lancaster and of Cornwall, Earl of Chester and of Richmond,—all of which, supplemented by a large resumption, were assured and reserved to Henry by his first Parliament. To these lands were added the estates of persons attainted for their support of Richard III. With all exceptions made from these resumptions

[1] Pollard, *Henry VII*, I, 10-11. Chrimes, 35, 51. Pickthorn, 16.

and forfeitures, the gains of the Crown were substantial. Henry and his line may be regarded as the ultimate beneficiaries of all the acquisitions made by the Houses of Lancaster and York. During his reign more still was added by way of forfeiture, resumption, or escheat to the Crown, as, for example, by the forfeiture of Sir William Stanley and the escheat of the Duchess of York's estates in 1495. The lands of the King not only increased in extent, but improved in value through better administration. Deducting all administrative and household expenses, the net yield of the Crown estates themselves rose from £3764 in 1491 to £25,145 in 1504. That of the Duchy of Lancaster estates rose from £666 in 1488 to £6566 in 1508.[1]

A second source of revenue was the feudal dues of the Crown *Feudal* —from wardships and reliefs, the profits of marriage, and very *dues* occasionally from an aid such as was exacted (or, more accurately, compounded for) in 1504 on the occasion of the marriage of the King's elder daughter, Margaret, to James IV, King of Scots, and the knighting of his elder son, Arthur.[2] Every care was taken to ensure that land held directly from the Crown should not escape these burdens, and the numbers of persons on whom they fell was increased by frequent resort to distraint of knighthood. The military obligations of tenants-in-chief were revived. Analogous fiscal rights belonged to the Crown with regard to the temporalities of vacant bishoprics and abbacies, which were administered by royal officials and handed over to their new holders on payment of a fine.[3] In the same category, again, fell the rights of the Crown to purveyance and pre-emption, which, notwithstanding frequent attempts to limit them by statute, still enabled royal officers to requisition goods and services for the king at arbitrary prices and often with little chance that they would be paid for.

The judicial system provided a third source of income. The *Profits of* payment of fees, the imposition of fines, the grant of pardons, *justice* even the promise of royal favour in judicial proceedings, were all utilised as means of profit, and the activities of the Common Law

[1] F. C. Dietz, *English Government Finance, 1485-1558*, 25-7. Pickthorn, 15-17.
[2] See J. R. Tanner, *Tudor Constitutional Documents, 1485-1603*, 600 ff., and Elton, 133-4: J. Hurstfield, *Revival of Feudalism in Early Tudor England*, 37 *Hist.* 131, and W. C. Richardson, *The Surveyor of the King's Prerogative*, 56 E.H.R. 52                                                            [3] Dietz, 31.

courts were coming to be supplemented by the judicial work transacted with similar or even more substantial financial results by the Council and the courts derived from it.[1]

*Customs*      The most lucrative sources of permanent revenue have still to be dealt with. The customs on wool, hides, cloth, and leather, the duties of tunnage and poundage on other exported and all imported goods, became the King's for life in virtue of the combined effect of the statute of 1275 which had granted the ancient customs to the Crown and a grant made by Henry's first Parliament, and repeated to each of his successors until it was withheld from Charles I.[2] Henry's pacific foreign policy, his maintenance of internal order, his commercial agreements with foreign states and encouragement of trading enterprise by loans created conditions in which the customs revenue rapidly expanded. Before his accession it had fallen to £20,000 yearly. During his first ten years it rose to an average of almost £33,000, and thereafter to over £40,000.[3]

*Balance of*   Taking all revenues regularly received by the Exchequer, the
*revenue*      increase during the reign was from about £52,000 to about
*and ex-*      £142,000.[4] It is not therefore surprising that, accompanied as this
*penditure*    increase was by improvement in financial administration and a vigilant scrutiny of expenditure, the Crown began to balance its accounts within five years of Henry's accession, or that after ten years there begins to be evidence of an annual surplus. The monarchy had at this point achieved complete financial independence. In fact as well as in theory the normal income of the King, from sources which were in effect entirely under his own control for life, proved itself adequate for the normal needs of government. Only the outbreak of war, or chronic maladministration, could disturb this position and make it necessary to have recourse to extraordinary sources of revenue, such as supplementary grants by Parliament, borrowing, the levy of gifts from the subject under the name of benevolences and the exaction of forced loans.

         During his early years, before his financial position had

[1] Dietz, 42 ff.; A. P. Newton, *King's Chamber under the Early Tudors*, 32 E.H.R. 364.

[2] See Elton, 50-51, for the grant made to Henry VIII.

[3] Dietz, 25. These figures refer of course to the sums for which the customs were farmed. Elton, 48-50.          [4] Dietz, 86.

improved and while he was embarrassed by disaffection at home *Other* and endeavouring to meet commitments abroad, he had not been *sources of* so fortunate. Borrowing was difficult while the new dynasty's *revenue* chances of survival were still problematical. Forced loans of small amounts had been imposed in 1486 and 1489,[1] and Henry's punctual repayment of these and of others negotiated by agreement enhanced his credit. In 1491 he availed himself of the popular feeling in favour of the intervention which he was reluctantly undertaking on the side of Brittany against the French Crown to demand a benevolence.[2] In 1495 a similar course was approved by Parliament.[3] War was apt to demand ampler provision. For this purpose Parliament was the necessary instrument, though there may have been at least some legal authority for the proposition that for a defensive as distinct from an offensive war, the subject was bound, even without his own consent, to aid the King not merely with his person but with his goods.[4] Parliament provided taxes for the defence of the realm after Simnel's rising in 1487. It did the same in 1489 for the defence of Brittany. In 1496, the Scottish war produced a supply of £160,000.[5] This grant—unlike that of 1489—yielded a large profit to the King, whose preference for diplomatic rather than military effort in conducting his foreign relations restricted his war expenditure to insignificant dimensions. The balance of income and expenditure was never during Henry VII's reign deranged, as under the Lancastrians, by profitless military adventures. Yet it must always be remembered that the financial stability of the Tudor monarchy was only to be maintained so long as his methods were followed. Less careful watch over income and expenditure, inefficiency and corruption, increasing governmental responsibilities, war, and a decline in the value of money, all might, and under Henry VIII and Wolsey did destroy the solvency which he painfully but precariously achieved.

Financial recovery was thus accomplished by the skilful utilisa- *Constitu-* tion of familiar and accustomed means. There was, so far as the *tional* sources of revenue were concerned, no real innovation. Such a *aspect of* position as the monarchy had now achieved had always been *financial* *recovery*

---

[1] Dietz, 52.      [2] Dietz, 56.      [3] Pollard, *Henry VII*, i. 48-50.
[4] This may perhaps be inferred from the words of Chief Baron Fray, quoted by T. F. T. Plucknett in *Tudor Studies* (ed. R. W. Seton-Watson), 20, 23. It was to be essential to the decision in the *Ship-money Case* (1637).
[5] Dietz, 58. Pollard, *Henry VII*, i. 27-39.

constitutionally within the reach of Henry's predecessors, and Edward IV had actually attained it. The maxim that the King should live of his own, which had been regarded as fundamental in the Middle Ages, was fulfilled in practice. Its corollary, that all other levies on the subject's property must be a matter of parliamentary consent, was not denied, and such occasional expedients as forced loans and benevolences were hardly regarded as infringing it. If Parliament, as a consequence, were less frequently summoned, no violence was done to constitutional principle. A king who conducted his government without convoking Parliament to provide extraordinary supply was doing what was politically popular and constitutionally unobjectionable.

*Extra-ordinary supply*

For extraordinary expenses recourse to Parliament was generally unavoidable. Though Henry VII had made such recourse only six times in his reign of twenty-four years, Henry VIII's wars with France and Scotland obliged him to seek supply in 1512, 1514, 1515, and 1523. Parliamentary grants were apt to create troublesome opposition and delay, and to come in much too slowly. But even more difficulty was created by attempts to impose non-parliamentary taxes such as the Amicable Grant which Wolsey required in 1525 for war purposes. Clergy and laity united in opposition to an innovation—"worse than the taxes of France" —by which "England should be bond and not free". There was indeed no machinery for enforcing payment, and the scheme was dropped.[1]

*Tenths and fifteenths*

Recourse to Parliament for "extraordinary" supply was at best a not wholly satisfactory expedient. The "tenths and fifteenths" by which the taxes normally imposed were given had become obsolete relics of the past. Originally assessed each time the grant was made, on the basis of a tenth of the movable property of persons within the royal demesne or in a borough, and a fifteenth on that of persons residing elsewhere, they had been fixed in 1334 in a form which had become permanent, and had been attached to lands and tenements rather than movable property. Henceforth these grants were mere repetitions of a standard payment which amounted to less than £40,000.[2] Incapable of increase, it was none the less capable of diminution,

[1] Dietz, 94-5.
[2] E. Lipson, *Economic History of England: Middle Ages*, 7th edn., 606. Dietz, 14-15. Elton, 55-7.

as units of assessment fell into decay and could not meet their obligations, and it gradually sank to about £32,000, a sum bearing no real relation to the taxable capacity of the country. Administratively, such taxes had the disadvantage that their collection fell into the hands of persons appointed by members of Parliament and not by the Crown.[1]

These defects naturally suggested the desirability of experiments *Subsidies* in alternative methods of taxation. Several had been tried in the fifteenth century, but their failure is evident from the fact that none was ever tried twice. Henry VII shared the ill-success of his predecessors when for the tax of 1489 he resorted to a levy on income and movables, to be imposed by royal commissioners.[2] In 1512 a graduated poll-tax, assessed on individuals according to their social status, likewise miscarried.[3] In 1514 however, a new form of tax appeared which was destined to endure for one-and-a-half centuries. The "subsidy" involved taxation of wages, personal property, and rents, and was assessed by royal collectors. Flexible at first, the subsidy gradually became rigid, as each was based on its predecessor, and levied at the rate of 4s. in the £ on land and 2s. 8d. on personal property. Though no standardised collective yield was ever fixed for the subsidy it became difficult to expand. Names dropped out of the subsidy books and adding new ones was difficult. By the end of the sixteenth century a subsidy, originally yielding £100,000 and sometimes more, had become a fiscal expression denoting about £80,000.[4]

Financial independence was the necessary basis of efficient *Executive* executive action, and here again the work of Henry VII is dis- *officials* tinguished mainly by its skilful utilisation of existing institutions *and de-partments* —the great officers of state and their departments, and the King's Council. All of these were essentially outgrowths of the royal household. No line could be drawn between the private and the public business of the King. But some of the offices of state had,

1 J. R. Tanner, *Tudor Constitutional Documents, 1485–1603*, 603. The unproductiveness of the tax might be compensated for by the grant of more than one tenth and fifteenth. But the inequality of incidence and the defects of collection remained.

2 K. Pickthorn, *Early Tudor Government: Henry VII*, 21.

3 Tanner, 606.

4 Tanner, 604. It is to be noted that the term "subsidy" also applied to the much older grants of customs on wool and leather, and to that on cloth imported by unprivileged foreigners.

owing to the more distinctively governmental nature of their functions, become detached from the Household within which others remained. In the first category could be placed the Chancery, presided over by the Chancellor, the Privy Seal office under a Keeper of the Privy Seal, and the Exchequer, with its Treasurer and a Chancellor of its own. Naval and military organisation, such as they were, fell under the control of a Lord High Admiral, and of a Master of the Horse and a Master of the Ordnance. More specifically domestic were the offices of Treasurer and of Comptroller of the Household, Chamberlain, and Steward. All these latter officials might have seats in the Council, and the absence of any fundamental distinction between public and domestic offices is shown by the development of the King's Chamber under Henry VII in order to handle large sums arising from loans, Crown lands, judicial profits, customs, and even on occasion parliamentary grants, which were thus withdrawn from the control of the Exchequer.[1] By an equally informal process, the functions of the Exchequer for purposes of accountancy were later in part transferred by the King's personal action to a Court of Surveyors.[2]

*The King and his servants*    The motive force behind the administrative departments was the King's command. They all existed to give effect to his will. The officials who presided over them were appointed and dismissible by him. Each was charged with the fulfilment of the royal pleasure within his own appropriate sphere. In certain departments the process by which the King's will was expressed had become highly formal. In the Chancery it involved the authentication of royal acts, such as charters, writs, letters patent and letters close, by the affixing of the Great Seal. Equally formal, though less important, was the use of the Privy Seal, which had gained in consequence during the Middle Ages as the use of the Great Seal became too cumbrous for day-to-day governmental needs. The Privy Seal had become specially connected with financial business, as a warrant for payments from the Exchequer. For those from the Chamber a mere personal order from the King was enough.[3] Indeed, as the more ancient methods of ex-

[1] Newton, 32 *E.H.R.* 348. W. C. Richardson, *Tudor Chamber Administration*, 159 ff.    [2] Pickthorn, 26-7. Elton, 134.

[3] Newton, 369, points out that signed warrants began later to displace verbal orders. The latter remained, however, a possible procedure until in Mary's reign

pressing the King's command had become formalised, others more personal had been introduced in their place. The Privy Seal itself had originally been devised in order to give prompter effect to his individual action. As the Privy Seal followed the Great Seal in becoming formal, it came to be supplemented by the Signet and even by the royal sign-manual. In an age when government was expanding swiftly, great consequence attached to those officials to whom the royal command was transmitted most directly and in the least technical manner. The most important of these was the Secretary, who provided the simplest of all channels for communication of the royal pleasure.[1] Unlike the Chancellor the Treasurer and other officials holding offices of ancient origin whose action was confined within rigid limits, expressed by the commissions by which they were appointed and the procedure which their acts must follow, the King's Secretary was free to enter every new branch of royal administration as it developed, and assume, under the direct supervision of the monarch, a growing control over diplomatic negotiations, trade and commerce, and social and economic problems arising within the kingdom, as these questions increasingly occupied the attention of government. It was in the second half of the sixteenth century that the Secretary rose to the first rank among the King's servants. His existence, and with it his potential importance, are all that need be observed during these early years. Under Henry VII the office was already held by men of standing.[2]

Since the reign of Edward III the Council had fallen increasingly under the control of great magnates, and under the House of Lancaster its composition had been predominantly aristocratic. In this it had reflected the real and growing consequence of the baronage in the medieval state.[3] The consequences had been unfortunate, for a body so composed had proved itself to an alarming degree faction-ridden and inefficient, incapable of directing foreign war with success or of maintaining order at home. This

*Composition of the Council*

---

a reorganised Exchequer once more resumed full financial control (Newton, 350).

[1] On the origin of this office, see F. M. G. Higham, *Principal Secretary of State*, 10-22. J. Otway-Ruthven, *The King's Secretary*, 7: Elton, *The Tudor Revolution in Government*, 31-2.   [2] Tanner, 203.

[3] B. Wilkinson, *Studies in the Constitutional History of the Thirteenth and Fourteenth Centuries*, 137.

aristocracy was now impoverished, weakened, and discredited. Edward IV had led the return towards a more official and efficient type of Council,[1] composed in fact as well as in theory of royal nominees. Where his Yorkist predecessor had pointed the way the first Tudor followed. The composition and work of the Council under Henry VII and his successor are not easy to trace. The records of conciliar proceedings, if they ever existed, are missing between 1460 and 1540. A register known as the Book of Entries, begun under Henry VII, has subsequently disappeared, and is now known only through the survival elsewhere of excerpts from its contents.[2] The available evidence is too meagre for any systematic account to be given of conciliar activities. But it seems clear that the Tudors inherited and perpetuated a Council emancipated from aristocratic predominance. Its members were, in the main, men of the middle class, professional government servants of a type which was to become increasingly familiar in the sixteenth century. Henry VII's chief advisers— Morton, Fox, Warden, Bray, Lovell, Poynings, Empson, Dudley —were ecclesiastics, knights, and lawyers. The Crown had won the contest over the composition of the central organ of government. The victory was not wholly due to its own action. It was the natural result of the decline of the baronage in a world undergoing profound social and economic change. Members of the older aristocracy were seldom found at the Council board, and such peers as for the future the King chose to summon were mostly of new creation. Great ecclesiastics were still important members, but the ecclesiastical element in governmental service was already less important than in the Middle Ages, and was soon to decline still further. The composition of the Council, in short, reflected that social class which was to prove itself the most devoted and efficient support of the new dynasty. The number of councillors was fluctuating and indeterminate. But the exact size of the Council is of little importance. Persons whom the King desired to consult, or whose services he intended to use, were sworn of his Council, and assumed the duties of giving him advice and of keeping secret the deliberations in which they participated. Men might, moreover, be summoned to the Council

[1] J. F. Baldwin, *King's Council in the Middle Ages*, 422-4 ; J. R. Lander, *The Yorkist Council and Administration*, 72 E.H.R. 27.
[2] Baldwin, 437.

who had not been sworn of it. The attendance of members was irregular. The King might summon whom he pleased, and summon them when and where he pleased.[1]

The most essential, as it was certainly the most ancient, function *Functions of the Council* of councillors was to give counsel to the King. It was the King who sought it, for such purposes as he wished, and it was for him to decide what action, if any, should be based on the advice which was tendered to him. During the long ascendancy of Wolsey, as later under Thomas Cromwell, the advisory functions of the Council were practically superseded by the action of a single great minister.[2] It would be a misconception, however, to regard the Council as only a body of counsellors. However large or small may have been the number of members present at its meetings, they had something like a corporate existence, and were capable of transacting a variety of types of business. The Council did more than merely advise the King and his ministers. It had long possessed judicial powers. If on the whole its attempts to obtain an appellate jurisdiction were frustrated by Parliament and the Common Law courts, it developed an original jurisdiction which Parliament had sometimes denied and sometimes recognised.[3] It also exercised legislative functions, in the issue of ordinances and proclamations, and it constantly gave orders on matters of administrative detail. Its meetings were presided over, in the King's absence, by a Lord President of the Council, whose office can be traced back to 1496, though the extreme informality of his appointment, by royal word of mouth alone, indicates the degree to which the Council, even in its most formal aspect, was subjected to the King's personal control.[4] Its proceedings were recorded by a clerk, whose existence can similarly be traced in Henry VII's earliest years as king, and the continuous existence of whose office dated from 1405. It had long since acquired a headquarters, in the room styled the Star Chamber, within the Palace of Westminster.[5]

[1] Pickthorn, *Henry VII*, 28-30. D. M. Gladish, *The Tudor Privy Council*, 11-13. W. H. Dunham, 58 *E.H.R.* 301, and 59 *E.H.R.* 187. The present state of knowledge is surveyed by Elton, in *The Tudor Constitution, Documents*, 87-93.

[2] Pollard, *Council, Star Chamber and Privy Council under the Tudors*, 37 *E.H.R.* 360.

[3] Holdsworth, i. 487, 490. The real objection was to the Council dealing with cases cognisable in the Common Law Courts, rather than to its acting where the Common Law provided no remedy. It had been prevented from dealing with cases involving title to freehold and with treason and felony.

[4] Baldwin, 445.          [5] Baldwin, 356. Pollard, 37 *E.H.R.* 516-18.

*Organisa-*
*tion of the*
*Council*

The action of the King strongly pervaded the whole existence and activity of the Council. It was his authority, rather than its own, that the Council exercised. Wherever the King was, there the Council must be. Thus there was always a Council at the Court, a Council in attendance on the King. At the same time, however, it was impossible, since the Council had so much regular business of a governmental and judicial nature, and a home of its own to transact it in at Westminster, for all its members to follow the King in his movements from one royal residence to another. Certain councillors were therefore taken with the King in his progresses, while others remained behind to deal with routine work. Such an arrangement was necessary with a constantly migrating Court. It can be observed in and even before the reign of Henry VII,[1] and in 1526 Henry VIII issued at Eltham an ordinance designed to ensure the attendance on his person of a fixed quota of councillors.[2] It may be inferred from this ordinance that the practice was for those councillors who held offices of state to be kept in attendance on the King, both as advisers and as instruments for the fulfilment of royal commands. This subdivision of the Council was in the highest degree informal. It did not indicate any permanent cleavage of the Council into two distinct bodies. Councillors passed freely from one panel to the other. Both dealt with much the same concerns. They constantly corresponded with one another, and when the King returned to Westminster the two parts of the Council merged, and—frequently under his own presidency—sat in the Star Chamber, to despatch any appropriate business, not necessarily judicial in nature. Nevertheless those councillors attendant on the King naturally derived advantage from this fact, and their colleagues in Westminster very properly deferred to their instructions.[3]

*Jurisdic-*
*tion of the*
*Council*

While there is no question of a formal separation between these two bodies of councillors, the practical consequence followed that those who attended the King were primarily concerned with political deliberation and with carrying out the King's instructions, while those in the Star Chamber dealt chiefly with judicial affairs, although the Council with the King had equal judicial

---

[1] Baldwin, 444. The work during the reign of Henry VII of a small body of counsellors "learned in the law", which was purely judicial in nature and fixed at Westminster, is described by R. Somerville in 54 *E.H.R.* 427.

[2] Elton, 93-4; Newton, *Tudor Reforms in the Royal Household*, in *Tudor Studies*, 240-44.          [3] Baldwin, 448.

power and used it. The increase in the judicial activities of the Council is one of the first important developments of Tudor rule. During the unquiet fifteenth century, and even earlier, the need for more effectual means of restoring order and ensuring the due performance of justice had been a perennial problem. In this respect the Common Law courts had betrayed the most serious defects, from which the jurisdiction of the Council was immune. Unlike the Common Law courts, the Council dealt with offences not in the places where they had been committed, but centrally, where the local influences which had impeded justice, overawing or corrupting juries, witnesses, parties, sheriffs, and even judges could not come into play. It dispensed with the jury. It evaded the Common Law rule against the use of torture. It collected information through its own subordinate officials, and by written depositions taken in privacy, and not through evidence given and tested in open court. It could place accused persons on oath, and lead them to incriminate themselves on their own admissions, and indeed without their being aware of the precise charges to be brought against them. The most potent procedural device employed by the Council for this purpose was the writ sent out under the Privy Seal.[1] Issued without registration or enrolment, and thus easily kept secret, this writ had never been easy to subject to constitutional checks. The recipient was not required to meet any precisely formulated accusation, but to attend before the Council, and answer concerning certain causes there to be laid before him. Disobedience was dealt with by reinforcing the writ with a subpoena, contempt of which was punishable by imprisonment at the Council's discretion. The legality of this whole procedure was perhaps doubtful. Statutes of earlier times had forbidden the issue of writs of Privy Seal in derogation of Common Law. But it had been legalised by statute in 1453, and, although the statute had lapsed in 1460, it had nevertheless been treated during the reign of Edward IV as though it were still in force.[2]

Thus armed, the Council was ready to undertake the task of *The Act* repressing violent and powerful evil-doers. The law for this *of 1487*

[1] Baldwin, 289; Holdsworth, i. 489.
[2] Baldwin, 291; I. S. Leadam, *Select Pleas in the Court of Star Chamber* (Selden Society), Introduction, lx. For the writ *certis de causis*, see Holdsworth, i. 661.

purpose was sufficiently strong and needed little amplification, though in 1504 the statutes against livery and maintenance passed in the fifteenth century were supplemented by another making bonds between lords and retainers illegal.[1] What was needed was not the enactment of new but the enforcement of existing law. By the punishments it could inflict, as well as by the procedure it followed, the Council was well fitted for its task. Though medieval Parliaments had succeeded in preventing it from taking cognisance of cases involving the title to freehold, and of cases of treason and felony, so that it could not take away freehold property or inflict the death penalty, it wielded the scarcely less formidable weapons of mutilation, branding, imprisonment, and the imposition of exorbitant fines. In 1487 a statute defined its judicial function more closely.[2] Part of its jurisdiction—in cases of livery and maintenance, riots and unlawful assemblies, bribery of jurors, abuse of power by sheriffs—was placed in the hands of the Chancellor, Treasurer, Keeper of the Privy Seal (or any two of them), with a bishop and a temporal lord of the Council, and the Chief Justices of King's Bench and Common Pleas. The legal effect of this statute has been much debated, but it can hardly have been intended to supersede or even to limit the jurisdiction of the Council as a whole, and in the result it did not do so. The Act seems to have attempted to ensure the attendance, for the purposes it contemplated, of a prescribed panel of members, and to remove any doubt as to the legality of their proceedings, without prejudicing the powers of the Council in general to deal with these or other offences which could be brought with its competence.[3] A similar statutory committee was established in 1495 when certain members of the Council were empowered to deal with charges of perjury and other offences and inflict punishment.[4] Neither enactment abridged the judicial position of the Council or placed it on a basis limited by statute. Its jurisdiction continues to be an emanation of the royal Prerogative, and does not become the creation of an Act of Parliament.

While the Council in Star Chamber was not a different tribunal from the Council with the King, the regularity and the specialised

[1] Elton, 34-7.        [2] Elton, 78. Pollard, *Henry VII*, i. 55-6.
[3] Holdsworth, i. 493-4; Baldwin, 437-42; C. L. Scofield, *The Court of Star Chamber*, 9 ff.; Pickthorn, *Henry VII*, 47, 145; Pollard, 37 *E.H.R.* 520 ff.; C. H. Williams, *The So-called Star Chamber Act*, 15 *Hist.* 129. Elton, 163-5.
[4] *Statutes of the Realm*, ii. 589.

nature of the work done there inevitably tended to create a dis- *Council* junction between two judicial aspects of the same body. In 1494 *and Star* a distinction is noted between the sessions of the Council and *Chamber as courts* those of the Star Chamber.[1] In 1500 the Star Chamber is first referred to by name in legal proceedings.[2] In 1504 comes its first mention in a statute.[3] Although the Council with the King retained and exercised judicial powers, it began to some extent to differ from the Star Chamber. It did not, as the Star Chamber did, include the judges, and, unlike the Star Chamber, which came to sit publicly and only during the law terms, it sat in private and all the year round.[4] The Star Chamber, being pre-eminently the judicial side of the Council, came to include persons whose advice on political matters the King could hardly need, but whose legal knowledge was of value. Gradually there came into existence a body of persons known as "ordinary" councillors, a term which first occurs under Henry VIII.[5] Though not usually summoned to meetings of the Council with the King, they were nevertheless sworn of the Council. Their membership might be no more than a complimentary dignity, or a gage of fidelity and service. So far as they were efficient, they seem to have discharged services of a technical kind—receiving petitions, conducting examinations, and carrying out similar routine duties.[6]

The emergence of a distinction, however imperfect, between *Court of* Council and Star Chamber, is only part, though the most im- *Requests* portant part, of a great development of the structure of the Council in early Tudor times. The committees of 1487 and 1495 were constituted by statute. The same could be done by the personal authority of the King. About 1493 Henry created a committee to entertain the complaints of poor men.[7] With such business, dealt with by a procedure analogous to but simpler and less expensive than that of the Chancellor in dealing with petitions for equitable remedy where the Common Law was defective,[8] the Privy Seal was already connected, and it came naturally into the care of the Keeper of the Privy Seal. Under

---

[1] Scofield, 27. But compare Tanner, 252-3.
[2] Polland, 37 *E.H.R.* 530.          [3] Scofield, 27-8.
[4] In this capacity, it came to be known as the Council Table. Tanner, 253.
[5] Baldwin, 450-51.
[6] For a review of the present state of the questions raised in this paragraph, see Elton, 158-63.
[7] I. S. Leadam, *Select Cases in the Court of Requests* (Selden Society), Introduction, xi. Elton, 190.          [8] See below, 26.

Henry VIII the committee, at first attendant on the King, became a permanent court, sitting in the White Hall of the Palace of Westminster, conducted by royal officials, and styled the Court of Requests. By the middle of the century professional judges known as Masters of Requests were assuming control of its business.[1]

The Marches of Wales

The needs of government in the remote and lawless districts of the West and North led to further extensions of conciliar activity by bodies kept in subordination to the Council itself. In the Marches of Wales, the semi-independent feudal organisation which had been created while the frontiers of English power were being advanced against the native rulers had become an anachronism. Its military side had relapsed into insignificance, and the great fortresses of South Wales were already falling into decay. They were outlived by a governmental system within whose multitudinous units the King's writ did not run and the place of the English Common Law was taken by the "custom of the Marches".[2] In the fifteenth century, however, a profound change, portending the future union of Wales with England, had transformed the relations of Marcher Wales with the Crown. The Marcher lordships had begun to fall into its hands. Those of Lancaster had come in with the accession of that dynasty to the throne. The lordships belonging to the Earldom of March were acquired on Richard III's death in 1485. Henry VII obtained the Earldom of Pembroke on the death of his uncle, Jasper Tudor, in 1495. In the same year the forfeiture of Stanley as a supporter of Warbeck involved the lands of his family in Denbigh. Later, in 1521, that of Buckingham gave to the Crown the lordships of Brecon and Newport. By the third decade of the sixteenth century the Crown had gained the greater number of the lordships of the Marches.[3] The ancient Marcher families, where they still survived, had shrunk to unimportance, and the Welsh blood of the new dynasty made it the heir to ancient loyalties. Under Henry VII a new governmental organisation begun in the Marches by Edward IV became better defined. Royal commissions were

[1] Holdsworth, i. 412-14.
[2] Holdsworth, i. 121; C. A. J. Skeel, *The Council in the Marches of Wales*, 6-10; P. Williams, *The Council in the Marches of Wales under Elizabeth I*, 6-11; T. B. Pugh, *The Indenture for the Marches*, 71 *E.H.R.* 436. The six counties forming the Principality of Wales—Anglesey, Flint, Merioneth, Carnarvon, Cardigan and Carmarthen—had a separate judicial organisation.    [3] Skeel, 290-93.

granted to members of the household of Arthur, Prince of Wales, for particular purposes within the Marcher lands and the four adjoining English counties of Salop, Hereford, Worcester and Gloucester. After his death in 1502 this organisation was transformed into a Council of the Marches.[1] In 1525 Henry VIII. appointed various persons to attend his daughter, the Princess Mary, during her residence in the Marches and to be commissioners for administrative and judicial purposes.[2] Ludlow, the main centre of their activities, developed something of the importance of a political capital, housing a corps of officials and frequented by a swarm of litigants and attorneys.

In the North the problem was more difficult. Like the Welsh *The North* Marches, the North was a highland region where means of com- *Parts* munication were few and difficult, and the population was scanty, poor, unprogressive, attached to old customs and allegiances, and wedded to the practice of arms. No peaceable middle class existed, as elsewhere in England, to form a counterpoise to the great aristocratic houses and to the warlike inhabitants of the remote valleys and mountain fastnesses which owned their lordship. What really differentiated the northern from the Welsh border was, however, the fact that it still constituted a frontier against the Scots. The three northern shires of Northumberland, Cumberland, and Westmorland formed a military area under the Warden (or Wardens) of the Marches, established in 1309.[3] The defensive problems of the North made it difficult for the Crown to reduce these districts to complete subordination, nor did any fortunate series of accidents occur to bring the principal northern fiefs into the hands of the Crown, and if the great honours and liberties of the earlier Middle Ages had passed away, the offices created by the Crown for the defence and administration of the North fell into the hands of local magnates.[4] Richard III, both before and after his accession, had endeavoured to set the affairs of the North on a firmer basis by an organisation of his ducal household for governmental purposes, analogous to that inaugurated in the Marches of Wales.[5] The Tudors were not immediately able to build on the foundations he had laid.

---

[1] Skeel, 31.                                              [2] Skeel, 49.
[3] R. R. Reid, *The King's Council in the North*, 24.      [4] Reid, 22.
[5] Reid, 59. Elton, 200-1: for a brief account see F. W. Brooks, *Council of the North*.

The North was solidly Yorkist in sentiment, and rose against Henry VII in 1487 and 1489. In the latter revolt the Earl of Northumberland, King's Lieutenant in the North, was slain. Thereafter the King devised a dual system, civil and military, for the government of the North. Both needs had to be provided for, but the attempt to relate them satisfactorily proved difficult. Until 1525 a King's Lieutenant generally conducted the government of the North parts, assisted by a Council exercising both civil and criminal jurisdiction. This arrangement left the military organisation, subject at times to his supervision as Warden-General, to the Wardens of the Marches themselves. By that date the dual system had collapsed. Henry VIII restored unified control under his natural son, Henry Fitzroy, Duke of Richmond and Somerset, with the help of a Council wielding administrative and judicial powers over all the five northern counties except Durham.[1] The experiment did not succeed. Military and civil administration once more fell apart, and the jurisdiction of the Council was restricted to the shire of York.[2] The government of the North was on the eve of the Reformation still an unsolved problem.

*The Court of Chancery* Cognate with the jurisdiction of the royal Council was that exercised by the Chancellor.[3] Originally the head of the King's secretarial department, and custodian of the Great Seal by which royal instruments were authenticated, he had soon established a special connexion with the issue of writs initiating judicial proceedings. Thus he was largely concerned with ascertaining the extent to which the law administered by the royal courts of justice was efficient and satisfactory. Where it proved defective it became his function to deal with the petitions for redress sent up to the King by suitors who could find no appropriate remedy at Common Law, or found that the only remedy available failed to do substantial justice. His duty was reinforced by the obligation falling on him as an ecclesiastic (which most Chancellors were) to act as "Keeper of the King's Conscience" and to advise the King when his conscience was troubled at the failure of the courts to remedy the wrongs of his subjects. The work of the Chancellor in devising remedies in such cases was done either alone or in

---

[1] Reid, 108.  [2] Reid, 109.

[3] See Holdsworth, i. 395-404; and Wilkinson, 196 ff., for the earlier history of this office.

the Council. As it might be left to the Chancellor himself to act, his department, originally secretarial, began to develop some of the attributes of a court. By the end of the fifteenth century the Chancery in this capacity is becoming clearly distinguishable from the Council on the one hand and from the courts of Common Law on the other. The Chancellor had begun to formulate rules applicable in his court, to which the term "equity" was to be attached. With the development of substantive rules came that of a specific procedure, which in its flexibility strongly resembled the procedure of the Council itself.

### iii

It is difficult to exaggerate the importance and the results of *Com-* that development of jurisdiction which marked the history of the *plexity of* Council and its offshoots during the opening years of Tudor rule. *the judicial* *system* The Council thrust an ever-increasing control into the affairs of English society. Yet it was only part of the whole judicial organisation of the land, and its existence did not threaten with extinction the other jurisdictions which had come down from the past. English legal history had been characterised by their multiplicity and complexity, and the English judicial system comprised a large variety of courts—central courts, local courts, and courts of special jurisdiction. Into this system the Council in its judicial capacity could be easily fitted, nor was there any immediate reason for conflict with its partners, though such a conflict was brought nearer as its judicial functions expanded.

The great potential rival of the Council—even if the days *The Com-* of their rivalry lay in a remote future—was the great trinity of *mon Law* *courts* Common Law courts, the King's Bench, Common Pleas, and Exchequer. During the Middle Ages these courts had achieved a nearer approach to centralising justice in the Crown than had been accomplished in any other European state. Their authority pervaded the greater part of the country and reduced most inferior jurisdictions to their control. Though restricted in scope and highly technical in content and process, the Common Law was capable, in the hands of the able succession of judges who administered its rules, of being developed to meet the needs even of a society in such rapid transition as that of the Tudor age. Its decisions had been recorded in a unique series of law reports, the Year Books, which demonstrated its procedure and its principles over a period of more than two centuries.[1] Its traditions were safeguarded by the powerful corporations known as the Inns of Court, by which its learning was transmitted from one generation to another of legal practitioners.[2] In an age when elsewhere in Europe the jurisprudence of the Middle Ages was showing itself unadaptable to changing conditions and was yielding before a "Reception" of Roman Law, the English Common Law and its exponents were to demonstrate a native strength which ensured the preservation of its insular predominance.[3]

*Their position under the early Tudors*    The Common Law courts had lately passed through a period from which their approaching decline might perhaps have been augured. Their failure to do justice adequately during the fifteenth century necessitated the emphasis which the first two Tudor sovereigns placed on the judicial competence of their own Council. Moreover, the technicality which the Common Law had developed, or into which it had been forced, during the Middle Ages, had evoked in the Chancery a judicial activity, supplementing and correcting its deficiencies. The "equity" dispensed by the Chancellor in civil cases might, like the "criminal equity" of the Star Chamber, be regarded as a competitor with the Common Law.[4] But the great courts established at Westminster still remained an imposing fabric of judicial organisation and power. In their darkest days they had not lacked great judges and learned lawyers. The rules of Common Law covered a vast area of English life, even if it was becoming an open question whether Common Law or Conciliar jurisdiction would have the main hand in the legal development of the future.

*The Common Law courts and the Crown*    King's Bench, Common Pleas, and Exchequer had long been separate courts, each with its own staff of judges and its own records. Four judges sat in each, a Chief Justice and three puisne judges in the King's Bench and in the Common Pleas, a Chief Baron and three ordinary barons in the Exchequer. Judges were appointed by the Crown, those of the King's Bench and Common Pleas during the King's good pleasure, those of the Exchequer

---

[1] Holdsworth, ii. 532 ff. See generally, W. C. Bolland, *The Year Books*.
[2] Holdsworth, ii. 484 ff.; iv. 263 ff.
[3] Holdsworth, iv. 252-9, 285-6. Elton, 5 *T.R.H.S.* vi. 78.
[4] Why this did not happen is suggested by Elton, *Documents,* 151.

during their good behaviour.[1] In practice judicial tenure was secure, and remuneration largely independent of the Crown, in that judges derived more from fees than from their official salaries. In any case, the Common Law in which judges were bred and in which—except for the Exchequer barons—they must have reached the degree of Serjeant-at-law before being eligible for appointment to the Bench, preserved, by its insistence on the principle that government must be conducted according to law, an independence of temper which prevented undue subordination to the executive. It should, however, be added that contact between the Crown and its judges was close and that the judges reckoned themselves very fully its servants. They advised as to the drafting and the effect of legislation, answered questions addressed to them by the executive, and on assize acted as political as well as judicial representatives of the central authority.[2]

Besides fulfilling their duties in the superior courts the judges of King's Bench and Common Pleas proceeded at intervals on circuit through the country. For this purpose they were armed with a variety of commissions, which in their collective effect invested their holders with powers almost co-extensive with those which they exercised in the courts at Westminster.[3] Commissions of oyer and terminer, of gaol delivery, and of the peace conferred criminal jurisdiction. The commission of assize conferred civil jurisdiction, further amplified by authority to hear cases at *nisi prius*. The commissions of general eyre out of which in the twelfth century the whole system of itinerant justice had grown were now obsolete. Yet the connexion between justice and administration established by the general eyre had been perpetuated. The judges of assize fulfilled the double function of unifying the law by applying the same system both in the superior courts and in those which they held on circuit, and of maintaining a close connexion between law and administration by their superintendence of subordinate governmental activities. Notwithstanding the supplementary check on local authorities provided by the Council and its offshoots, the Common Law judges were by no means excluded, either in the superior courts or on circuit, from dealing with cases in which questions relating to the exercise of governmental authority arose.[4] Too much em-

*Justice and administration*

---

[1] Tanner, 342.  
[3] Holdsworth, i. 668-70.  
[2] Holdsworth, i. 272.  
[4] Holdsworth, i. 231.

phasis can hardly be laid on the fact that Tudor rule, even when most nearly absolute, did not rest on the denial of the principle that the acts of government, like those of private persons, ought to be regulated by law. The Common and statute law remained an essential foundation of the Tudor state.

*Jurisdiction in error*

The same important conclusion is suggested by the process governing the correction of errors in the courts of law. It may first be noted that, before giving a decision on a case, the judges of any one of the three superior courts could refer it for discussion to an assembly in which they met their colleagues of the other two courts in the Exchequer Chamber. The action of this body was purely consultative. It pronounced no decision but gave guidance to the court from which the matter had been referred.[1] In this aspect the Exchequer Chamber did not provide judicial review. A statute of Edward III had, however, set up a court of the same name to review errors in the Court of Exchequer, which was thus able to deny to the King's Bench any authority to reverse its decisions.[2] Elsewhere the King's Bench had full power of judicial review. The decisions of the Common Pleas and of all inferior courts could be brought before it. It is obvious that a further question arises here—that of providing a tribunal to review the decisions of the King's Bench itself. The Common Law judges and Parliament combined to uphold the sole authority of Parliament to do so, and repudiated the claims of the Council to exercise an appellate jurisdiction. Practical difficulties arose from the infrequency with which Parliament met during the later fifteenth century, and indeed during most of the sixteenth.[3] But the point of principle involved was never abandoned, and the superior courts, where the law was administered, and Parliament, where it could be corrected by judicial process as well as changed by statute, stood together to prevent the Council from fully asserting its supremacy in the judicial system and treating the Common Law courts as its inferiors.[4]

*Local Courts*

The supremacy of the Common Law courts had left little

---

[1] M. Hemmant, *Select Cases in the Exchequer Chamber* (Selden Society) Introduction, xix. Before 1579 only the Chief Baron, of the Exchequer judges, sat in the Exchequer Chamber.   [2] Holdsworth, i. 242.

[3] Holdsworth, i. 370, n. 2, points out that only three cases are recorded in Elizabeth's reign as coming to the Lords on writ of error.

[4] For writs of error, see Holdsworth, i. 654-5.

vitality in the ancient local courts. The shire courts had long since fallen into decay and the sheriff had become since 1444 a merely annual officer. The sheriff's tourn through the hundreds of his shire was likewise obsolescent. Local criminal jurisdiction in respect of cases not sufficiently important to be reserved for the judges on circuit had been placed in the efficient hands of the Justices of the Peace.[1] Their duties had been created and developed by fourteenth-century statutes. They were chiefly concerned with the maintenance of peace and order, and were theoretically competent in their quarter sessions to try and punish persons indicted by a jury of any crime save treason. Serious cases were in practice referred by them to the justices of assize. They could deal with the official conduct of subordinate functionaries such as mayors, constables, gaolers, and even sheriffs. In petty sessions of two or three justices they could punish misdemeanours. Individual justices were charged with the duty of seeing to the apprehension of offenders, and issued warrants to constables for this purpose. They were appointed and dismissible by the Crown, on the nomination of the Chancellor, were to be qualified by holding land to the assessed value of £20, and were unpaid except for certain inconsiderable fees. The Commission of the Peace enlisted the services of the country gentry and men of property in the administration of justice. It is to be observed that they were recruited from the same class as supplied the majority of members of the Commons, and that Parliament ceaselessly added to their duties by statute. A dual control was exercised on them from above, both by the Council and by the Common Law courts. Conciliar control over them was limited from a practical if not from a legal point of view by their being essentially not professional servants of the government, but unpaid amateur judges and administrators whose service was in the last resort voluntary and unenforceable. Moreover, they were not simply agents of executive power, but magistrates whose supreme duty was to conform with and carry out the law.

A similar history of decay can be recorded of the great franchises *Franchisal* and immunities of medieval times within which, by royal grant, *courts* judicial authorities were created outside the sphere of the Common Law courts. The King himself possessed such an immunity from

---

[1] For their early history, see C. A. Beard, *The Office of the Justice of the Peace in England*, 52-70. For their commission, see Holdsworth, i. 670-1.

the Common Law in the Forest courts.[1] A statute of 1327 had fixed
the limits of the royal forests, and within these limits they still remained. The unpopular and oppressive jurisdiction of their courts
had been abridged by statute and restricted through the growth
of control by the Common Law judges.[2] Of the franchises held
by private owners, some of the greatest, such as the Duchy of
Lancaster and the Earldom of Chester, had fallen in to the Crown.
Though preserving their own organisation, separate from that
of the kingdom at large, these latter had ceased to possess any
true independence. The duchy lands of Lancaster remained
distinct from the Crown estates, and had their own criminal and
civil jurisdiction, reinforced by Henry VII with a new equity
court, the Court of Duchy Chamber, but the courts at Westminster corrected the errors of the palatine courts.[3] Those of the
Earldom of Chester fell under the same control.[4] The palatinate
of Durham, held by the bishop, in whose nomination the Crown
had an important influence, similarly maintained its own judicial
identity, but it was closely connected with the kingdom, and the
Durham courts were subject to the authority of the King's Bench
and of Parliament.[5] Thus, unlike the Marches of Wales, the pala-
tinates developed a law which was much the same as that of the
kingdom, and palatine jurisdiction represented a purely formal
survival.

*Minor franchises*    Apart from these great franchises, the country abounded in
minor immunities. Their owners possessed the right to hold the
court of a hundred, or to exercise the powers of a sheriff's tourn
in what was known as a court-leet.[6] These possessed more vitality
than the courts of shire and hundred. Yet their importance lay
rather in the administrative than in the judicial sphere. Losing
jurisdiction to the royal courts and the Justices of the Peace, these
courts, with the manorial courts-baron and courts-customary with
which they were connected by their history though not in their
origin, concerned themselves with the conduct of details of local
rural organisation and estate management, petty offences such as

---

1 In a few instances a forest had been alienated to a subject. G. J. Turner,
*Select Pleas of the Forest*, Introduction, i.
2 Holdsworth, i. 103-4.
3 Holdsworth, i. 115-16.   Pickthorn, *Henry VII*, 53-4.
4 Holdsworth, i. 119-20.
5 Holdsworth, i. 111. G. T. Lapsley, *The County Palatine of Durham*, 210 ff.
6 W. O. Ault, *Private Jurisdiction in England*, 3-6, 88. Holdsworth, i. 135-7.

trespass and assault, the enforcement of dues and small debts, and transfers of land, though here and there they provided a framework of government for boroughs springing up on manorial estates.

Boroughs generally are to be classified with holders of franchises. In some instances the borough enjoyed the right to hold a court-leet for itself, though this tended to give place from the middle of the sixteenth century to courts of petty or even quarter sessions held by the mayor and other borough officials as Justices of the Peace, sometimes wholly independent, sometimes subordinate to the county justices. By their charters boroughs generally obtained a jurisdiction over civil cases. But every borough, whatever the degree of judicial organisation it obtained, was from the beginning within the sphere of the Common Law courts and the law they laid down.[1] *Boroughs*

Mention of another group of minor courts will serve to amplify, though not to complete, a survey of the innumerable jurisdictions which covered early Tudor England. The tin-miners in Devon and Cornwall possessed courts known as Stannary courts, for the enforcement of their own customs, with jurisdiction over cases not affecting life and limb or the ownership of land within the areas assigned to them, but again subject to the control of the courts of Common Law.[2] *Stannary Courts*

Besides local courts, there existed a number of courts administering a special jurisdiction over cases which for some reason lay outside the scope of the Common Law. Commercial affairs had given rise to a separate Law Merchant. A Court of Admiralty which had originated in the fourteenth century to deal with maritime cases, after suffering a decline in the fifteenth, now profited from the revival of royal authority under the Tudors and from their special interest in maritime affairs.[3] This jurisdiction, however, expanded slowly. It was regarded jealously by Parliament, and by the Common Law courts, which were annexing the affairs of internal trade from local merchant courts, and disliked seeing foreign trade removed from their ambit.[4] *Courts of special jurisdiction*

---

[1] Holdsworth, i. 141.

[2] G. R. Lewis, *The Stannaries*, 87. The Star Chamber also asserted the right to hear appeals from the Stannary Courts. Holdsworth, i. 158-61.

[3] R. G. Marsden, *Select Pleas in the Court of Admiralty* (Selden Society), i. Introduction, lvii. The revival of royal interest preceded the advent of the Tudors. See W. Senior, *Admiralty Matters in the Fifteenth Century*, 35 L.Q.R. 298.

[4] Holdsworth, i. 539 ff. 569 ff.

*Court of the Constable and Marshal*   The same attitude was shown with regard to the judicial authority exercised by the Constable and Marshal. These great military officers of the Crown had assumed power to maintain discipline among troops on active service. Medieval statutes had attempted to restrain the further growth of a jurisdiction which was essentially summary and drastic.[1] It was uncertain how far these officials could assert authority over civilians while war was raging within the realm. If such a jurisdiction was not definitely illegal, it was certain that only the existence of war and the interruption of the normal course of justice could lead to such a supersession ot the safeguards provided for the subject by the procedure of the Common Law.

*Review of the judicial system*   In review of the judicial system of this period, it may be said that its fundamental characteristic was the historic supremacy of the Common Law courts. Their jurisdiction had spread to almost every part of the realm. Even if they did not exercise it directly, owing to the existence of local and special courts, they were in the commanding position of being able to prescribe the limits and review the errors of other courts. Potentially, their most serious rivals were the Council and its offshoots. There was some prospect of English law, like that of continental states, becoming subdivided into two compartments, the one—administered by conciliar courts—dealing with questions in which the interests of government were specially involved, while the other—administered by the Common Law courts—was confined to cases of a mainly private nature.[2] The Common Law courts had not, however, been warned off the field of government, and the oversight of governmental acts was still within their competence as well as that of the Council. Allied with them was Parliament, defender of their jurisdiction against its rivals, and standing like them for the principle that government was a matter of law and not of arbitrary power. The future rôle of the Common Law courts was, however, not easily to be predicted. To the minds of many men, as the sixteenth century advanced, the principle of subordinating the action of the Crown to the rule of law seemed antiquated. The first requisite of society must be the development

---

[1] For examples, see Holdsworth i. 574, *n*. 4, 5, 6.
[2] For this tendency in France, see J. S. C. Bridge, *History of France*, v. 34 ff. 75 ff. Compare Holdsworth, iv. 166.

of a vigorous and untrammelled royal authority, and the doctrines of sovereignty enunciated by Roman lawyers appeared more in harmony with modern conditions than the restrictive notions of a monarchy limited by law which formed the legacy of medieval legal thought.[1]

### iv

It will by now be evident that the local administration of Tudor England was really a function of its judicial organisation. To make a separation between them, even for purposes of exposition, is to distort the nature of Tudor government. But to modern eyes, if not to those of the early sixteenth century, administrative as well as judicial duties were performed by the local governmental authorities already referred to. The courts of the shire, the manor, and the franchise were administrative as well as judicial bodies, and dealt with their administrative duties under judicial forms. Loss of judicial power had indeed relegated many of them almost entirely to the conduct of administrative business, though what they did might be of very minor importance. The Justices of the Peace, on the other hand, were adding to their judicial functions an increasing number of powers of an administrative character. They exercised some control over wages and prices, endeavoured to prevent profiteering in foodstuffs and other necessaries, examined the by-laws of gilds, supervised weights and measures, and regulated apprenticeship and the supply of agricultural labour.[2] They were the instruments by which royal control over the social and economic life of the nation was extended and made closer and more detailed. The machinery for the maintenance of the peace fell into their hands. Every hundred possessed its high constable, every parish its petty constable. These officials were in effect unpaid and service was compulsory. Their appointment rested, except within leet jurisdictions, in the hands of the Justices of the Peace.

Local government imposed its obligations on men of even lower rank than the well-to-do landowners who served as Justices of the Peace. Any man might find himself compelled to serve in such

*Intercon-nexion of jurisdiction and ad-ministra-tion*

*The Justices of the Peace*

*Juries*

---

[1] See, generally, F. le V. Baumer, *The Early Tudor Theory of Kingship*, especially pp. 153 ff.

[2] Beard, *Office of the Justice of the Peace in England*, 58 ff.; Holdsworth, iv. 134.

inferior offices as that of constable. Any man might be summoned to serve on a jury. The grand jury indicted offenders, the petty jury dealt with the question of their guilt or innocence, though, unlike its modern counterpart, it relied as much, if not more, on its own knowledge of the facts as on evidence placed before it during the trial, and was therefore subject to a degree of pressure from the court which was in later ages to seem intolerable. At this stage, however, it was doubtless necessary in order to restore the proper working of the jury system. Failure to convict might even lead to the jury being attainted—a process attended by serious penalties, and a means of redress open not only to the Crown but to disappointed private litigants. Besides the risk of attaint, the jury was subject to punishment by the judge, and might in the last resort be disciplined by the Council.[1]

*Administrative procedure*    In dealing with their administrative duties the Justices of the Peace naturally had recourse to the machinery through which they worked for judicial purposes. Their duty was essentially to punish breaches of the law rather than to give orders for it to be carried out. Administration was therefore done under the judicial forms of presentment and indictment for neglect or misbehaviour in carrying out the law, and it became deeply impregnated with judicial characteristics. Like local jurisdiction, local administration was committed to amateur and unpaid officials whose main obligation was to fulfil the law rather than the orders of the central government, and whose affinities were strongest with the Common Law courts and with Parliament. Tudor administration depended on their co-operation. If that were withheld, it was in danger of collapse.

*Military organisation*    Military service was likewise organised on a mainly local basis. Tudor rule was unsupported by any large professional army. The outbreak of foreign wars necessitated the enlistment of mercenaries, and the raising of troops within the realm by contract with persons prepared to raise, officer, pay, and equip regiments of their own.[2] The Crown had a number of permanent garrisons in such fortresses as Calais and Berwick, a small cavalry force of gentlemen pensioners, an infantry force of yeomen of the guard, and a train of ordnance under a Master-General, whose office, dating from 1483, was of very recent origin. On these foundations

---

[1] Holdsworth, i. 341 ff.
[2] C. W. C. Oman, *Art of War in the Sixteenth Century*, 285, 288.

no attempt to erect an arbitrary despotism could be made. Otherwise the armed strength of England, such as it was, existed in two forms. One was the feudal levy, now antiquated and useless. The other, representing a principle originating in the Anglo-Saxon period, took the form of shire-levies, pressed for service by virtue of the obligation at Common Law of every subject to bear arms in defence of the realm or to provide those who served with coat-and-conduct money. These contingents were in practice embodied by the issue of commissions of array to persons of importance to muster and exercise all men within their counties capable of bearing arms.[1] A force like this, composed of and commanded by men who were merely amateurs in the art of war, could never become efficient and was sometimes not even wholly dependable, and its usefulness was further diminished by the doubt which arose as to the liability of levies to serve outside the limits of their own county.

The naval forces of the country were, though to a less extent, *Naval* local in character. In medieval times, liability to provide con- *organisa-* tingents of ships for the King's service had been imposed, as a *tion* species of feudal obligation, on the Cinque Ports. As these ports fell into decay it was placed on other maritime towns. A royal navy was indeed coming into existence in the sixteenth century. Henry VIII was keenly interested in the construction of ships of war. But the King's ships were not numerous, and naval campaigns still required the provision of important local contingents of merchant vessels.[2] Here again, the Crown might find itself seriously handicapped by the subject's refusal to co-operate with it.

v

The Council and its satellites, the Common Law courts, the *Parlia-* Justices of the Peace were the day-to-day working organs of *ment : fre-* Tudor government, and the normal forms with which the exercise *quency and* *duration* of royal authority was vested. But the powers of the Crown must for certain purposes be displayed in a still more august guise. It

---

[1] Pickthorn, *Henry VII*, 75.
[2] C. S. Goldingham, *The Navy under Henry VII*, 33 E.H.R. 475. See also Holdsworth, *Power of the Crown to Requisition Ships*, 35 L.Q.R. 12.

was in Parliament that they attained their zenith. Only in this capacity could the King impose extraordinary taxation on his subjects, or make changes in the law affecting their rights. Parliamentary action was rather the medicine of the constitution than its daily food. Recourse to Parliament was not frequent under the first two Tudor sovereigns. Henry VII summoned six Parliaments in the first thirteen years of his reign, and only one thereafter. Six years elapsed between the end of his last Parliament in 1504 and the meeting of the first of his son's reign in 1510. After a series of annual Parliaments between that date and 1515, an interval of eight years occurred before Parliament was again summoned in 1523, and a further intermission of six years followed its close. Individual Parliaments normally had no long life. Continuation from session to session was exceptional, although the last Parliament of Edward IV had held the unprecedented number of seven. Sessions were short, varying from a fortnight to a little over two months, with an average of about four weeks.[1] Under such conditions it was difficult for Parliament to assert or be given a regular place in the mechanism of government. In a sense it was an occasional expedient, though this description does not imply any minimising of its majesty and power. The authority of the Crown did not constantly need to be raised to the level which it reached in Parliament. The nation had no desire to find itself frequently summoned to give the King its advice, and, what was more important, to fill the royal exchequer by additional grants from its own purse. It was true that fourteenth-century statutes requiring an annual session of Parliament were still part of the law, but political morality was not outraged by their non-observance, and their existence was tacitly passed over.

*Its relation to the Crown*  Lack of continuous life, and consequent changes of personnel prevented Parliament from forming an independent tradition and conceiving of itself as either a constant ally or a constant critic of the Crown. While asserting with decision that its consent was necessary to the imposition of new taxes, it was content to leave the King in possession of those which the law in any case assigned to him. He might make what he could out of his ordinary revenue, and spend it as he liked. Only infrequently had Parliament ever

[1] For details, see *Interim Report on House of Commons Personnel and Politics* [1932: Cmd. 4130].

claimed the right to control the expenditure even of taxes voted by its own authority. New legislation, though it might originate in petitions from Parliament, was largely though not wholly initiated and framed by the King and his advisers, and Parliament, while preserving its right to initiate if need be, and in any case to advise and consent, would not have demurred to the withholding of royal assent from measures which the King did not approve—a course which, however, he never found it necessary to follow—nor to the existence of a royal prerogative to make new rules by proclamation, to dispense with the requirements of statutes, and to pardon offences. Only rarely, so far as is known, did it exhibit much interest in the policy which the King saw fit to adopt, and it showed no desire whatever to wrest the conduct of government from his hands. It was the King's business to govern the country. For this purpose Parliament might, if it chose, find additional financial supplies, or extend the field covered by statutory enactment. It could give advice, it might occasionally offer criticism, and perhaps even manifest open dissatisfaction, as it did in 1523 over the waging of futile campaigns in France while the Scottish Border was neglected.[1] Thus far it could go, and no further, although in the not very recent past it had, by the process of impeachment—in which the Commons acted as accusers and the Lords as judges—been bold enough to attack the unpopular ministers of ineffectual kings. Under the Tudors this attempt to impose on ministers a responsibility towards the nation as well as the Crown was to fall into disuse. The facts as well as the theory of government were against its revival. When ministers fell from power, as did Empson and Dudley—arrested, tried, and executed after Henry VIII's accession—it was only because the royal protection was withdrawn from them.[2]

In its origin, Parliament had been essentially an extension of the royal Council. For certain purposes, the most important of which was deliberation on the public affairs of the realm, but which also *Structure of Parliament* included the grant of additional financial supply, the Council had met in a greatly expanded form. The King was attended not only by the great officers of state and other permanent councillors, but

[1] Speech of Thomas Cromwell (perhaps never actually delivered) in R. B. Merriman, *Life and Letters of Thomas Cromwell,* i. 30 ff.

[2] D. M. Brodie, *Edmund Dudley,* 4 *T.R.H.S.* xv. 133.

also by the estates of the realm—clergy, Lords, and Commons. The conjunction of the estates of the realm with the Council in an assembly possessing plenary authority to legislate, tax, and judge was the essence of a Parliament in the later Middle Ages.[1]

*The two* Parliament was already divided into two Houses. In one House
*Houses* sat the King's officials, councillors, and judges, the magnates summoned to Parliament in their personal capacity as "peers of the realm", and the great ecclesiastics, archbishops, bishops, and abbots. In the other House sat the representatives of the Commons of the realm, as organised in their local communities of shire, city, and borough. The separation of the two Houses had at least a "locative" sense. The upper House sat in the Parliament House in the Palace of Westminster. The lower House sat outside the precincts of the Palace, using either the chapter-house or the refectory of Westminster Abbey. But the term "House" as applied to the Commons was beginning to take on an institutional sense as well. "House" meant not only a place of assembly, but a body accustomed to meet there.[2] Doubtless this idea had reached only a rudimentary stage. No records survive of the actual proceedings of the House within its own walls. There was no clerk to keep such a record, though the Clerk of the Parliament kept Rolls of Parliament recording what was actually transacted in the Parliament House, and these gradually merged in the early sixteenth century into the Lords' Journals.[3] There were as yet no Commons' Journals. An under-clerk told off to attend the Commons, whose office was ultimately to develop into that of Clerk of the House, probably did no more than register attendances and help to draft petitions. There was no need for more, for the proceedings of the Commons were not strictly proceedings in Parliament. The Commons appeared only at the opening ceremony, to hear the business of the Parliament explained by the Chancellor and to present the Speaker who was to act as a channel of communication between them and the King, and at the close, to announce the decisions they had taken. Nor did the representatives of shires and boroughs invariably vote together. Nevertheless, rudimentary as it still was, something like a House of Commons existed.

[1] Chrimes, 125-6, 140.                [2] Chrimes, 126-30.
[3] See Pollard, *Authenticity of the Lords' Journals in the Sixteenth Century,*
3 *T.R.H.S.* viii. 28.

The "Houses" were thus more than mere places of assembly. *The Lords* They were organised bodies, of whose structure and functions some description can be attempted. The spiritual and lay magnates summoned to early Tudor Parliaments may have numbered at the most rather under a hundred. The number of spiritual lords was practically constant. There were the two archbishops, nineteen bishops, and thirty abbots or less. The number of lay lords in attendance fluctuated owing to minorities, extinctions, and new creations, but tended to range from forty to fifty. There may generally have been a slight preponderance of the ecclesiastical element, which would have possessed a decisive majority but for the steady decline during the later Middle Ages in the number of abbots who sat in Parliament. It was to be of great importance in the sixteenth century that the spiritual lords should have so diminished in number as to be capable of being outvoted. It is equally, perhaps more, important that the Upper House, spiritual and temporal elements alike, formed one body and not two, in which majority rule prevailed.[1]

While the nature of the qualification possessed by ecclesiastics *Lordship* was obscure, and it is probable that they were not summoned as *of Parliament* barons but sat in their spiritual capacity, the theory had begun to prevail that holders of lay baronies were entitled to attend, and that their right was inheritable. In the earliest period of parliamentary history the Crown had summoned whom it would. Its weakness in the later Middle Ages had provided an ample opportunity for the lay magnates to insist on a theory of peerage, and to impose themselves on the King as advisers. Edward IV and Henry VII had repelled this invasion so far as membership of the Privy Council was concerned. It succeeded with regard to those who, not being members of the Council, were summoned to Parliament. Gradually there was defined a ring of hereditary councillors of the Crown with a permanent right of summons. The corollary was to exclude from this assembly all persons not so qualified, which in practice meant non-baronial Privy Councillors and judges. When this process was completed—and it was still incomplete—a House of Lords was the result. But the gain made by the Lords was not of high importance. The great families of the past were dwindling in number. The Crown could

[1] Pollard, *Evolution of Parliament*, 75-6. Pickthorn, *Henry VII*, 90-93.

2a

create new peerages, the holders of which were closely bound to it by loyalty and interest. Moreover, the ecclesiastical lords were at all times largely appointed by royal influence, and the Reformation, while eliminating the abbacies, was to give the Crown undisputed control over episcopal elections.

*Composition of the Commons*

The composition of the Commons in this period is not easy to determine, since from 1477 to 1529 there is only one list of members, that of 1491. The number of counties represented, each returning two members, was constant at thirty-seven. The number of boroughs, likewise returning two members each, fluctuated, though there may have been slightly over one hundred. It depended on whether the Crown or its officer the sheriff thought fit to require representatives to be sent, and sometimes on the ability of a borough to avoid or buy itself out of the duty. In all, therefore, the House of Commons must have numbered rather less than three hundred members.[1]

*Electorate and elections*

In the counties the electorate had been defined by statute in 1430. The franchise was restricted to freeholders having tenements to the annual value of forty shillings. In the boroughs the franchise varied widely—as did the municipal history of the boroughs themselves, with which the franchise was connected. Each town had made its own electorate. Sometimes the municipal authorities kept the right of voting to themselves, elsewhere it belonged to the holders of lands by burgage tenure, or to all householders, or such householders as paid local rates known as *scot and lot*. In general, the tendency was to restrict the franchise, as municipal government itself was being restricted, to an oligarchy of well-to-do traders. Recent royal charters incorporating boroughs and bringing their representatives into the Commons had vested the right to vote in relatively few persons. In both counties and boroughs the method of election was, except for the barest framework of rules laid down by statute, left to the discretion of the local authority. All returns were made through the sheriff, to whom the writs for both county and borough elections were addressed, and disputed returns were dealt with by the King with the Lords or judges. There is some evidence of influence being exercised on elections both by local magnates and by the Crown,[2] but representation was

---

[1] Tanner, 514. Pickthorn, 96.
[2] E. and A. Porritt, *The Unreformed House of Commons*, i. 21-2, 367-71.

ceasing to be a matter of indifference to the constituencies, and the Commons cannot be regarded as a servile instrument of royal policy or aristocratic power.

The law required knights and burgesses to be resident within *Qualifica-* the constituencies they sat for, but this requirement was falling *tions of* into desuetude. So also was the rule that shire members were to *members* be "notable esquires and gentlemen", though the practice perhaps did not seriously vary from the law. The House tended to be a body of landowners or merchants, with an infusion of lawyers, to whom a seat was a valuable adjunct to their legal business. On the whole there was little anxiety as yet to obtain a seat in the Commons for its own sake, if here and there cases can be seen where rival candidates were in the field, and inducements to elect were being offered, if only in the simple form of promises to forgo the wages to which knights and burgesses were by law entitled.[1]

In the House the county members, while considerably less *Functions* numerous than those of the boroughs, possessed a decided ascend- *of the* ancy, explicable easily enough on the ground of their tradition of *Commons* political service and their superior social status. No burgess was elected Speaker until 1533. But to suggest comparison between the rôles of knights and burgesses is to run the risk of exaggerating both. The Commons no doubt had their recognised functions in Parliament. They were necessary parties to the enactment of statutes. The preambles to Acts from 1485 onward recited their assent with that of the Lords.[2] Bills, however, were generally introduced on governmental initiative, even if petitions from the Commons (occasionally drafted in the form of a bill, providing a ready-made answer to a petition) sometimes provided a starting-point for legislation, especially such as issued in private as distinct from public Acts, *i.e.* those concerned not with the general affairs of the realm but with the affairs of individuals or particular groups of individuals. The King sometimes amended bills by inserting provisions after they had passed through Parliament.[3] The completeness of his control is shown by the fact that Henry VII never had to withhold assent from a bill. In matters of finance the Commons had a more important share. From the reign of Henry IV

[1] Porritt, i. 155. Pickthorn, 105.        [2] Chrimes, 104.
[3] Pollard, *Evolution of Parliament*, 130; *Henry VII*, i. 16-17.

they had asserted that grants of extraordinary supply to the Crown must originate with them. Acts granting supply had ceased to be enacted by each estate imposing a tax on itself, and had become collective, applying to all types of property save that of the Church. Both the authority of the Lords, and the influence of the Crown over the Commons, stood at a lower point in the matter of taxation than in legislation.

*Parlia-*   In yet another way the still inchoate nature of the House of
*mentary*   Commons can be demonstrated. Its members, being engaged on
*privilege*   the King's business in his highest court, were under his protec-
tion and enjoyed certain immunities. They were exempt from the jurisdiction of other courts. One member, Strode, suc- cessfully claimed in 1512 that he should be released from the imprisonment inflicted on him by a Stannary court in retaliation for his introduction of a bill regulating the privileges of tin-miners.[1] Members and their servants were immune during the session of Parliament from arrest on account of debts and other civil pro- cesses, but not on criminal charges. No privilege could yet be enforced by the action of the House itself. It had no servants of its own, and no jurisdiction by which it could act. The Speaker, through whom its privileges have subsequently been asserted, was still, and was long to remain, rather the servant of the Crown than of the House itself.[2] Freedom of speech within the Commons was perhaps to be inferred from the fact that their proceedings took place outside the Parliament House, and would not be noticed elsewhere, yet instances of its violation had occurred in the fifteenth century, and at best the privilege could only be asserted by the complaisance of the King. It was not formally claimed by the House, though More as Speaker in 1523 made an elaborate request for it.[3] Nor could the Commons protect it by their own authority.

*Jurisdic-*   The Lords, on the other hand, had a jurisdiction of their own.
*tion of the*   Impeachment, as already said, had fallen into disuse. But Lords
*Lords*   of Parliament indicted of treason or felony could claim the privi- lege of trial by their peers. The House was entitled to act as a tribunal for the review of errors in the Common Law courts, even

---

[1] Tanner, 555, 558.   [2] P. Laundy, *The Office of Speaker*, 153-9.
[3] J. E. Neale, *The Commons' Privilege of Free Speech in Parliament*, in *Tudor Studies*, 267. Tanner, *Constitutional Documents of James I*, 382. Pickthorn, 109-14.

if this jurisdiction was ceasing to be exercised.[1] It could, moreover, enforce its parliamentary privileges by its own action.

## vi

It is now time to draw together these various aspects of early Tudor government, and relate them to one another as a systematic whole. In its essence Tudor government was government by the King, yet it involved no repudiation of the constitutional traditions of the English State. The King's acts were acts done by virtue of the legal authority which was his. There was no search for restrictive principles to be applied against the Crown. The main danger was not that its action would be too strong, but that it would, like that of the Lancastrian sovereigns, be too weak. Such restrictions on royal authority as existed were inherent in, and accepted with, the system of government which the Tudors inherited, and within which they began their work. Their vigorous rule reorganised every part of it, but destroyed none save those representing authorities other than their own. Royal authority, however, appeared in many different forms. To a large extent it comprised personal and discretionary powers. It was for the King to appoint and dismiss his ministers and all royal officials. He could issue to them instructions which they were bound to fulfil, order the expenditure of revenue, much of which he enjoyed in his own right, as he saw fit, and intervene in the course of justice by using his dispensing power and power of pardon. The royal Council became once more a body of royal nominees, advising the King, conducting his affairs, and acting in conformity with his will. Among its functions it possessed, with little or no doubt as to their legal validity, powers to legislate, to supervise administration, to organise national defence, to regulate social and economic affairs, to exercise a jurisdiction supplementing that of the courts of Common Law. To this extent, and it was a large extent, Tudor government was based on personal absolutism. If the right of *property* belonged to the subject, the right to *govern* belonged as plainly to the Crown.[2]

Yet this is but one half of the truth. For certain purposes the

*The Crown in early Tudor government*

---

[1] Holdsworth, i. 371-5.
[2] C. H. McIlwain. *Growth of Political Thought in the West*, 373.

*The limits on royal power* law required that royal authority must be carried on in conformity with rules which the King by his personal act was wholly unable to change. His power to do justice, while a residue of it survived in the Council and even in himself, had largely been made over to the courts in which the Common Law was administered. The rules of the Common and statute law formed a legal framework within which the royal power itself must move even if it enjoyed some freedom of action outside it. Thus the law, though it permitted a wide and indefinite discretionary power to the Crown, formed the true basis of the State. This fact invests Parliament with an importance which might perhaps not be inferred from the infrequency of its meeting, the extent of its subjection to the Crown, the inchoate character of its organisation, and the rudimentary nature of its procedure. The making of a statute was undeniably the act of the King himself, to which Lords and Commons did but consent : yet without that consent the King could not make a statute, nor do the things which a statute enabled him to do. There was no doubt of the ultimate superiority of a statute to a proclamation or ordinance. The most that the King could do with it was, within limits, to dispense with its penalties in a particular case. Its ambit extended throughout the realm. It could, to an uncertain extent, abridge the King's discretionary power. It could override the Common Law itself, much though judges disliked the idea, and could do the same with other systems of law such as the Law Merchant, and perhaps even some parts of the law of the Church. The only limit to the supremacy of a statute, except for the existence of the Canon Law, was that a subsequent statute might repeal it. Men might, as in the Middle Ages, conceive of law as something fundamental, existing in its own right, inviolable by any human enactment. But the supremacy of law was in England coming to mean the supremacy of statute, and its power of effecting whatever change those who made it desired.[1] The time was close at hand when this formidable instrument of power was to be bent to tasks which no legislature in Christian Europe had yet attempted.

[1] See Chrimes, 269 ff., and Pickthorn, 133 ff., for detailed discussion of the whole question.

# CHAPTER II

## THE CONQUEST OF THE CHURCH

### i

THE strongholds of aristocratic power were decaying in later *The* medieval England. Those of the Catholic Church stood to all *Church in* appearances still intact. Throughout the land, cathedral and parish *later* church, abbey and priory, college, hospital and almshouse raised *England* their carved and jewelled fabrics of masonry and glass. Abundant revenues maintained the majesty of the Church. Its prelates ranked among the wealthiest of the King's subjects, and in their palaces surrounded themselves with households comparable to those of the foremost lay magnates. The six hundred or so monastic houses held about one-tenth of the land of England.[1] Some districts seemed almost wholly given over to great ecclesiastical lordships. With its feudal revenues the Church often possessed also the profits of leet and franchise, toll, market, and fair. The secular clergy of inferior rank, though they included many impoverished priests unprovided with benefice, usually enjoyed the tithes to which the law entitled them, the income from their glebelands, and fees and offerings from the faithful in respect of their spiritual ministrations to the living and the dead. Shrines enriched by the offerings of a millennium of Catholic piety had become treasuries of precious things. More important even than the material wealth of the Church was its sway over the minds and consciences of men. Its sacraments mediated the grace of God to mankind; exclusion from its fold meant after death an extremity of torment which painted wall and window displayed with dreadful impressiveness to the eyes of ignorant and illiterate worshippers. Combining, as they did, control over the material wealth of this world and the treasures awaiting the faithful in the next, the clergy pervaded with their influence every aspect of medieval life. The education

[1] A. Savine, *The English Monasteries on the Eve of the Dissolution*, 83, 97.

of the young, charitable relief to the poor and aged, care of the
sick, hospitality to the traveller, all served to strengthen with ties
of respect and affection the hold of the Church over the lay society
which it was divinely appointed to serve.

*Its auto-*
*nomous*
*character-*
*istics*

Churchmen, like other men, were the King's subjects. Nor could
he be indifferent to the place they held within his realm. A learned
class, and for long the only learned class, they had served the
Crown as officials, judges, and councillors. To the close of the
Middle Ages an ecclesiastic normally held the office of Chancellor.
Prelates sat in the Council, and sometimes constituted a majority
of the Upper House of Parliament. As holders of fiefs and franchises they had a part in local administration. The obligations of
feudal military service, such as they were, fell on ecclesiastical as
on lay tenants-in-chief. The Church in Convocation levied taxes
on its revenues when the Crown sought for extraordinary supply.
Yet churchmen, though the King's subjects, were not like his
other subjects. Theirs was a dual allegiance. They were members
not only of the English State, but of an international organisation,
transcending all national boundaries and centring in the See of
Rome. In this capacity they formed a body of persons clearly
marked off from the secular world by their ordination. They both
wielded and obeyed an authority which did not emanate from
the Crown, and was exercised through institutions wholly
different from those which carried on the royal government. By
her own authority the Church conferred orders and admitted to
monastic vows, setting men apart for the fulfilment of duties
and the acceptance of a discipline which she alone prescribed. By
the same authority she defined the content of her belief and the
nature of heresy, the form of her ritual, and the rules necessary to
the spiritual and moral health of her faithful children in the world.
Her control over clergy and laity alike was made effective by
tribunals of her own, those of the archdeacon and bishop in each
diocese, the Canterbury Court of Arches and the York Chancery
for the archdioceses, from which lay an ultimate appeal to the
Papal Curia. By papal enactment and by the legislation of the two
Convocations of Canterbury and York, a law was laid down which
was not the law of England, but the Canon Law of the Church,
owing nothing for its validity to royal action or consent, though
it might, in certain cases and circumstances, be recognised and

enforced by the Crown. Ecclesiastical administration lay in the hands of an episcopal hierarchy in whose appointment the Church enjoyed, formally at least, complete independence of choice, and whose members on their appointment took a dual oath of fidelity first to Pope and then to King. The Church in England was not a national institution save in the loosest sense. It comprised two provinces of the Catholic Church, linked by the somewhat informal bonds which united Canterbury and York. Visible and permanent proof of papal supremacy over it as a whole was provided by the legatine commissions, implying the formal delegation of papal powers, granted to the Archbishop of Canterbury as *legatus natus*, and occasionally to a special envoy sent directly from Rome and commissioned as *legatus a latere*. The term *Ecclesia Anglicana* had sometimes been used by medieval ecclesiastical writers to describe the Church in England. Except in so far as York tended to follow examples set by Canterbury, it had hardly more than a merely geographical significance. It implied no disjunction from other provinces of the Church, and no local ecclesiastical immunity, such as was connoted by the Gallican Liberties in France, from full papal control. The Pope was supreme legislator, administrator, and judge. The independence of the Church in England from the English Crown, so far as it extended, meant and depended on its complete subjection to Rome.

Under Henry VIII the authority of the See of Rome over the provinces of Canterbury and York was rejected. The result was not the establishment of a Church henceforth independent alike of papal and royal supremacy, but of one wholly subordinated to the Crown. The *Ecclesia Anglicana* was in fact proved to possess no independent authority capable of being asserted apart from that of the Papacy. Severed from Rome, its two provinces were organised by the Crown as a national Church, of which the King became Head in a sense to which no explicit limitation applied except such as he chose to formulate. Its government, its belief, its ritual, its jurisdiction were settled for it by the Crown. This change was so far as possible disguised by a plausible, though fallacious, appeal to history and law, and by the restriction to a minimum of alteration in the organisation of the Church, its creed, and its ritual. The Crown attempted to make innovation acceptable

*Revolutionary results of the rejection of Roman authority*

by maintaining at least the appearance of continuity. At later periods in the history of the English Church some of its historians have, for wholly different reasons, likewise sought to prove that continuity has in every essential respect been unbroken. Such ideas, while their applicability to the history of religious experience and its expression, or to the transmission of spiritual authority, need not be denied, can have little or no meaning for the historian of the constitution. For him the Reformation, despite all the efforts of King or churchman to suggest otherwise, must be regarded as a revolution.

*Novelty of the royal supremacy over the Church*    Herein lies the fundamental difference between the restoration of royal authority in civil government and the assertion of royal supremacy over the Church. The powers of the Tudor monarchy in the former sphere were not different in kind from those belonging to its predecessors, though they were raised to an immensely higher level. The reduction of the Church to dependence on the Crown involved the assumption of a wholly new kind of power. Hitherto there had been no question that the Church in England was actuated by an essentially independent authority. Disputes had arisen as to its limits. But while its limits might be doubtful, no one contradicted the principle that within them the Church was autonomous. Henry VIII repudiated that principle. Notwithstanding his appeal to law and history, what he asserted for the Crown went far beyond anything that could be deduced from these sources. He possessed himself of a sovereignty which none of his predecessors had ever supposed he had a right to, and which intruded itself into spheres of human action and thought that they had never invaded.

*Not based on ecclesiastical consent*    The change was not accomplished by any agreement or concordat recognising the inherently different natures of lay and ecclesiastical power. It was done against the will of the Church, though the King found it politic to seek for the acquiescence of the clergy so far as it was obtainable, and was not wholly unsuccessful in so doing. The theory on which royal action proceeded implied no necessity for such consent. The independence of the Church was no longer accepted. Henry's action was based on the assumption that the Crown's authority in Parliament was illimitable. The assumption, so far as it implied a legal right to destroy the autonomy of the Church, was unfounded. That it was successfully made and given effect to constituted a new departure in the history of the Church, of the Crown, and of the Parliament in which its new sphere of action was claimed.

Swift and radical as the revolution was, it did not come entirely *Relations* without preparation or warning. Neither in practice nor even in *of Crown* theory had the medieval Church denied all forms of royal control *and* *Church* over its affairs. Lay and spiritual authorities were conceived of as *in the* working in different spheres, but not as necessarily antagonistic to *later* one another; rather, indeed, as fulfilling different but complement- *Middle* ary functions. To the Church kingship was a consecrated office, *Ages* and its duties included the protection of religion. It was not easy to fix the true limits of the power of intervention here implied, and while in theory any interference on the King's part with concerns which the Church claimed as its own might have been resisted as usurpation, in practice no frontier was clearly drawn, nor were attempts at delimitation frequent. The Crown, while insisting on its competence to deal with certain questions affecting the Church which related to public order and private property, enunciated no broad and sweeping claims to an ecclesiastical supremacy. Crown and Church became accustomed to living in an atmosphere of convenient if not very logical compromise. This is not surprising, for the King and his officials and judges were loyal sons of the Church, while the clergy were also loyal subjects of the Crown and fulfilled many duties in that capacity. Laymen of all degrees were within the sphere of the Canon Law. Ecclesiastics similarly lived within that of the Common and statute law of the realm, expecting its protection, and for that reason submitting themselves to its restrictions. The Papacy acquiesced in this ill-defined but workable compromise, even though it necessarily fastened a certain degree of royal control over the Church in England. Acquiescence was easy, for no point of principle arose.

Royal participation in the affairs of the Church was therefore *Royal* not inextensive. In form, the rights of the Church to make its *control* *over elec-* own canonical elections were respected. In practice, elections to *tions* bishoprics, except when appointment arose from papal provision, could be made only on receipt of the King's *congé d'élire*, and the person to be elected was named in letters of recommendation which accompanied its issue. The King's share in elections was restricted not by the rights of the cathedral clergy, but by the authority asserted by the Pope to provide to vacant benefices. At Common Law the right to present to a benefice was a form of lay property, protected by the royal courts. Legislation of the fourteenth century vindicated the rights of patrons by statutes of Provisors, and imposed penalties by statutes of Praemunire on persons who invoked papal authority in order to oust the jurisdiction of the King's courts in such cases. But in practice this legislation was seldom invoked. Papal provisions continued. They could conveniently be utilised by the King, who found no great difficulty in inducing the Pope to provide his own nominees. The interests of both could be harmoniously adjusted if both were content to treat the question as one of expediency.

*Ecclesiasti-*     In matters of ecclesiastical jurisdiction there was a similar asser-
*cal juris-*   tion of royal control. Ecclesiastical courts dealt with a twofold
*diction and*
*its limits*   subject-matter. Certain cases belonged to them *ratione personae*, certain others *ratione causae*. In the former category fell cases of felonies committed by persons in orders, which included not only holy orders but the minor orders possessed by many individuals connected in one capacity or another with the Church. In the latter fell a miscellaneous assortment of cases affecting clergy and laity alike, such as heresy, moral offences, matrimonial cases, and succession to personal property both under last wills and testaments and also in the event of intestacy. In all these, courts Christian possessed considerable independence. For example, the statute *de Heretico Comburendo* of Henry IV assumed their right to initiate and conduct heresy trials, the lay power inflicting on the heretic the penalty of death by burning. Elsewhere, however, the professional interest of the royal judges—who after the thirteenth century had generally been laymen—led them to impose considerable limitations on ecclesiastical jurisdiction. The Common Law courts jealously retained questions relating to real property, including advowsons, and even acquired jurisdiction over frankalmoign tenures, originally left to the ecclesiastical courts. They defeated all attempts by the Church to invade the realms of contract and of civil liability for wrong. In restraining the criminal jurisdiction of the Church, they had, by Henry II's defeat over the Constitutions of Clarendon, irretrievably lost the principle at issue. Yet their failure was in detail not complete. Even where

the immunity—termed benefit of clergy—did exist, it could be curtailed. It had in the first instance to be asserted before the royal courts, which turned the simple principle which it expressed into a highly complicated mass of rules. In cases of treason, a few other serious crimes, and the numerous minor offences called mis-demeanours, clergy could be pleaded only after conviction. The royal courts decided what persons were entitled to it.[1] Statutes of Henry VII withdrew benefit of clergy from persons in minor orders who committed a second offence, and from persons guilty, even for the first time, of certain offences.[2]

Somewhat analogous to benefit of clergy was the right of *Sanctuary* sanctuary, by which lay fugitives from justice could take refuge on sacred soil, and on confessing their guilt before a coroner and taking an oath to abjure the realm were allowed to proceed to a specified port and go abroad, though in some sanctuaries perma-nent protection was available. Here again restriction was imposed. In *Humphrey Stafford's Case*, 1486, the royal judges held that sanctuary afforded no protection in cases of treason. It was laid down that usage alone could not create sanctuary, which must be based on royal charter, and must have been recognised in general eyre. Papal bulls aided the Crown in ridding the realm of these colonies of wrongdoers. For instance, royal officers who invaded sanctuaries were freed from the threat of excommunication. Sanctuaries thus came more closely under at least the supervision of the royal courts.[3]

To some extent such processes could be regarded as a natural *Anti-* concomitant of the general increase of monarchical power, and *clerical* could be carried on with the approval of churchmen who re- *sentiment* cognised that certain of the Church's attributes related to an antiquated and less orderly state of society. Obviously there must be limits to the degree of this clerical acquiescence. Among the laity, however, a temper was developing which was ready to sup-port the widest claims the Crown cared to advance against the independence of the Church. Heresy, anti-clericalism, and even anti-papalism had manifested themselves at earlier stages in English

---

[1] For an account of benefit of clergy before Henry VII's accession, see C. B. Firth, *Benefit of Clergy in the time of Edward IV*, 32 *E.H.R.* 175.

[2] Tanner, *Tudor Constitutional Documents*, 14. Pollard, *Reign of Henry VII*, iii. 197, 199.

[3] I. D. Thornley, *The Destruction of Sanctuary*, in *Tudor Studies*, 182 ff.

history. Under the stimulus of the Renaissance and Reformation they now appeared with increasing strength, particularly in London and the South and East, where intellectual and material advance had been most rapid. Only, however, if animated by the spirit of nationalism would the vague anti-clericalism of the age, and its still vaguer tendencies to intellectual and religious heterodoxy, be transformed into a revolutionary force, bent not on restricting but on abolishing papal authority and ecclesiastical independence. If that were to happen, the compromise and uncertainties which obscured the relations of Church and State would prevent the more timid from seeing how far they were going, and provide the more clear-sighted, resolute, and unscrupulous with plausible justifications for change.

*Its prevalence among the governing class*    Among the laity, those most inclined to attempt the assault on the Church were precisely those most strongly entrenched in the Tudor governmental system. Men of property, intelligent, ambitious, and acquisitive, turned greedy eyes on its accumulated wealth, sometimes incompetently administered by ecclesiastics, often administered and virtually owned by lay landlords who were tempted to transform *de facto* into *de jure* ownership.[1] Lawyers, servants of the Crown, and local officials regarded with impatience the archaic privileges and powers which made of the clergy a caste invidiously distinguishable from the rest of the King's subjects. All classes, even the poorest, suffered from the exactions of the priesthood and the penalties inflicted by courts Christian. It was difficult to discern, except in the backward North, where the social conditions of a former age still survived, any element likely to rally to the Church in a conflict with the Crown. There is force in the suggestion that the fall of the medieval aristocracy had left that other great pillar of the medieval order, the Church, isolated in a new world where potential enemies abounded and surviving friends were few. The administration of the State, both central and local, had passed to a class whose attitude towards the Church was ambiguous. In Parliament a new nobility was entering the Upper House, and in the Commons the preponderance of members representing the populous and wealthy districts of the South and East instilled into that body a temper from which the Church could augur little good.

[1] Savine, 253-60.

Indications of this temper were not wanting. The limitation of *The dis-*
benefit of clergy by statute has already been noted, and in 1515 a *putes of*
temporary Act passed for this purpose three years earlier came up *1515*
for renewal. Debates took place in a stormy atmosphere. A London
merchant, Richard Hunne, had been found hanged in the Bishop
of London's prison, to which he had been committed to await
trial for heresy.[1] His friends and sympathisers suspected that he
had been murdered by the bishop's officers, and that his heresy
consisted in his refusal to pay a mortuary fee to a priest on the
death of his child, and in having taken out against him a writ of
praemunire.[1] A coroner's jury found that Hunne had been murdered. The bishop's court condemned him posthumously as a
heretic. That the Commons sympathised with the anti-clerical
feeling of London seemed to be shown by their sending up bills
for the relief of Hunne's relatives, which the Lords, with their
dominant ecclesiastical vote, refused to pass.[2] Feeling was exacerbated by the issue of a summons to Dr. Standish, Warden of
the Greyfriars in London, to answer in Convocation for his advocacy, in a debate before the King, of restrictions on benefit of
clergy. Constitutionally, a stalemate resulted. The Act of 1512 was
not renewed. No effect was given to a petition of the Commons
for statutory restrictions in the fees demanded by the clergy for
administering the sacraments. Standish, on the other hand, escaped
ecclesiastical punishment. But the King had listened to arguments
in which the clergy had exalted their privileges and defended the
authority underlying them against any other, while the judges had
held that the whole Convocation was guilty of a breach of the
praemunire statute, and that the King could hold a Parliament
and exercise its full authority without the participation of the
spiritual lords.[3]

The lesson cannot have been lost on the government. Although *Beginnings*
the King took an early opportunity of getting Standish promoted *of the*
to the diocese of St. Asaph, his chief minister, Wolsey, looked on *Reforma-*
the events of 1515 with different eyes. He advised Henry to hasten *tion*
the dissolution of the Parliament, had only one more summoned
during his thirteen remaining years in office, and allowed eight

[1] On praemunire, see Tanner, 18 n. i.
[2] For this case, see E. Jeffries Davies, *Authorities for the Case of Richard Hunne*,
30 *E.H.R.* 477. Pollard, *Wolsey*, 32 ff., A. Ogle, *The Tragedy of the Lollards'
Tower*, and S. C. F. Milson, *Richard Hunne's Praemunire*, 76 *E.H.R.* 80.
[3] Pickthorn, *Early Tudor Government, Henry VIII*, 114-17.

years to elapse before doing so. During those years events deeply charged with significance for English history took place on the Continent. Luther's protest—Henry's reply to which earned for him the title of "Defender of the Faith", conferred by Pope Leo X—was followed by his expulsion from the Roman communion, and by the adoption of the Lutheran Reformation in many German states and in the Swedish kingdom. These defections had involved the extension of royal or princely authority over the Church, the extinction of ecclesiastical privilege, and the confiscation of ecclesiastical property. The echo of this convulsion reached England, mingling with the murmurs of complaint and criticism against the Church already audible there. Among English ecclesiastics there were feeble attempts at reform, but, as is common enough in periods of crisis, the tendency was to emphasise and concentrate authority and means of defence. Wolsey, Archbishop of York in 1514, Cardinal in 1515, became *legatus a latere* in 1518, to the supersession of all other ecclesiastical authority within the realm, including that enjoyed by the Archbishop of Canterbury as *legatus natus*. In 1515 he had become Chancellor. He therefore united in his own hands supreme authority in both Church and State.[1] It was a unique but essentially insecure position, combining as it did functions and duties which might in the issue prove incompatible.

*The "divorce" question*

Their incompatibility was demonstrated when the King sought for a dissolution of his marriage with Catherine of Aragon. As a royal official, Wolsey was bound in duty to the King to promote a transaction in which as an ecclesiastic he was bound to defer to an external authority. He did what he could. As legate he summoned Henry, with his own consent and in strict privacy, to answer the charge of living with his deceased brother's wife (May 1527). He devised the plan of obtaining full papal jurisdiction to decide on the validity of Henry's union. A mission to Rome obtained the grant of a legatine commission to Wolsey and Cardinal Campeggio, the absentee Italian bishop of Salisbury and "Protector" of the English Church, for the purpose of hearing the case. But the commission was not a "decretal" commission. It did not preclude the revocation of the matter to Rome. The legatine court opened in May 1529. Its proceedings were inconclusive. In

---

[1] On Wolsey's position, see Pollard, *Wolsey*, 215-20.

July, it was adjourned, never to sit again.[1] As servant of the Pope, Wolsey was powerless to pronounce that decision which he sought as servant of the King. In August the Pope suspended the hearing and evoked the case to Rome, where it was certain that the decision must be adverse to the King, since the Pope was a virtual prisoner in the hands of Catherine's nephew, Charles, Holy Roman Emperor and King of Spain. Wolsey's attempt to unite in his own hands the discrete authorities of King and Pope had failed. The King resumed that which derived from himself, and paralysed that which did not. In October, Wolsey was commanded as Chancellor to surrender the Great Seal, and as legate was indicted and found guilty in the King's Bench of breach of the statute of Praemunire.[2] The spiritual authority emanating from Rome could no longer be permitted to a subject. It was to be annexed by the Crown. Only thus could the conflict of jurisdiction be ended.

For Henry now found himself where many of his subjects had been—entangled in a jurisdiction which admitted no superior within his realm. The manifold grievances of common men found an echo in the heart of the King. This particular grievance was not his alone. His desire to annul his marriage with Catherine and espouse Anne Boleyn was a matter of public as well as private concern. Succession to the throne hung on the sickly life of his one legitimate child, the Princess Mary. The national feeling necessary to transform vague anti-clericalism into active anti-papalism could readily be kindled by the notion that a foreign tribunal, whose decisions were liable to perversion by the power of Spain, alone stood between the nation and the maintenance of the Tudor succession. Thus reinforced, the passions, both honourable and base, which had manifested themselves in 1515 only awaited liberation by the Crown to discharge their destructive energy. The moment had now come. Henry's face was set against the Papacy. New ministers and councillors, hostile to Rome and to the Church, took up the policy against which the Cardinal's influence had so long prevailed. In the administrative system, in the courts of justice, among the Lords and Commons of the land, their allies awaited the signal to move. It was in

*Appeal to the nation against the Papacy*

[1] On these proceedings, see G. Constant, *La Réforme en Angleterre*, 25-34.
[2] For a discussion of the procedure followed, see Pollard, *Wolsey*, 242-52.

Parliament, the great reserve engine of power in the constitution, that this accumulated force could be invested with the forms and sanctions of the law. On August 9, 1529, writs for a new Parliament had gone out. On November 3 the Reformation Parliament assembled.

ii

*Character of the Reformation Parliament*    The life of this Parliament was unprecedentedly long. Its predecessors had, with few exceptions, dispersed after a single session, and that a brief one. The Reformation Parliament continued to sit at intervals until 1536, the longest duration yet recorded.[1] It might be inferred that the government found it an usually pliant and even servile body. Such an inference would be highly dubious, though in the opinion of at least a few contemporaries it was composed of men "bribed and gained over in favour of the King", "King's servants", and "not only heretics, but also such as he [the King] and his counsel were persuaded to malign the clergy and their wealth". Royal influence was used to promote the return of knights and burgesses likely to support the new trend of royal policy. Aristocratic influence was enlisted for the same purpose.[2] Yet it cannot be shown that either attained unaccustomed dimensions whether in 1529 or the by-elections of later years. Even had the King foreseen in 1529 the lengths to which he was ultimately to invite Parliament to go—which is improbable—he would still have had good reason to permit the House of Commons to reflect as faithfully as possible the sentiment prevailing among the classes and communities from which it was drawn, and on whose co-operation his own power in the last resort depended, for only thus could the pace at which it was safe to advance be accurately determined.

*Royal influence on the Reformation Parliament*    The same comment applies to proceedings in Parliament as to the elections which created it or supplied its vacancies. It was undoubtedly dominated by the King and his ministers. Their personal presence bore on the course of debate. Procedure, parti-

---

[1] For details, see *Interim Report on House of Commons Personnel and Politics*.
[2] Pollard, *Henry VIII*, 252-5; H. A. L. Fisher, *Political History of England, 1485-1547*, 292-3; Constant, *La Réforme en Angleterre*, 14-15; Pickthorn, *Henry VIII*, 129-32.

cularly in the Commons, was not sufficiently developed to enable the Houses to assert independent control of what took place within their walls. The government not only drafted the bills in which legislation was embodied, but also inspired the petitions for ecclesiastical reform which such legislation purported to satisfy. In all this, however, there was nothing unusual. Moreover, just as evident as the pervasive influence of the government is the fact that the Commons had a mind of their own. There were criticisms of the King's policy, opposition to bills, divisions in the House, amendments and withdrawals of proposals emanating from official sources.[1] In short, the Reformation Parliament was an assembly thoroughly characteristic of the age and the society which produced it, and reflecting its diversity of opinion. For the issues were not clear and simple. Sympathy with Catherine, which was widespread, did not necessarily imply support of papal jurisdiction, and on the other hand, a convinced papalist might yet hope that the King would get his marriage annulled.

The Pope, even if he had evoked the case, had not yet pronounced on it, and the Parliament of 1529, though recognised to have been summoned to deal with "the enormities of the clergy", did not in its earliest legislation invade any really new ground. *Early legislation against the Church* Mortuary fees, the abuse of which had been the occasion of *Hunne's Case*, were limited. A scale of fees was prescribed for the probate of wills in ecclesiastical courts, and sanctuary was again regulated. Another statute imposed stricter conditions on the holding of pluralities, penalised non-residence except in certain defined cases, and prohibited spiritual persons from taking lands and tenements to farm. Against the Papacy this last statute contained a veiled threat, for it invalidated papal dispensations for non-residence, and penalised persons who sought them.[2] The bill passed the Lords only after a conference in the Star Chamber in which the temporal lords sided with the Commons against their spiritual colleagues, who had already manifested their dislike of the Probate bill. The relative weight of clerical and anti-clerical opinion was not meantime to be further tested. In December 1529 Parliament was prorogued until February 1531.

The interval was occupied with negotiations which made it evident that no satisfactory decision could be hoped for from the

---

[1] Pickthorn, *Henry VIII*, 171, 172, 182, 203, 249.     [2] Tanner, 13.

*The prae-munire proceed-ings* Papacy regarding the King's marriage, and that the King must fall back on national support. The transactions of 1529 had shown that the clergy were plainly the least reliable element, and before Parliament assembled they had been cowed by the same means as had struck down the ecclesiastical power of Wolsey. In December 1530 the Attorney-General brought in the King's Bench a praemunire against the clergy as a whole, on the ground of their admission of Wolsey's legatine authority.[1] There was no thought of opposition. The Convocations of Canterbury and York purged their offence by fines of £100,000 and £18,000 respectively. Even so, the King's acceptance of this atonement was made conditional on his being recognised as "singular protector, only and supreme lord, and, so far as the law of Christ allows, also Supreme Head of the English Church and clergy".[2] The habits bred in an atmosphere of compromise made it difficult for churchmen to delimit the respective spheres of King and Pope. Some progressive spirits were genuinely inclined to the view that the Church should yield to the Crown on points no longer defensible either on grounds of national well-being or corporate interest, though they would still have limited the royal supremacy to the temporal affairs of the clergy.[3] But no one, with whatever degree of precision he viewed the issues involved, was likely to venture on prolonged debate with the King as to the exact limits of the royal headship and the "law of Christ". Further ecclesiastical resistance was improbable now that over the clergy there hung the dread shadow of praemunire. If acceptance of a legatine authority exercised with the King's consent constituted a breach of the statutes, it was difficult to avoid the conclusion that whatever the King should in future choose to regard as an offence of this kind would be similarly treated.[4]

*Parlia-mentary attack re-sumed* Convocation being reduced to submission, it now remained to mobilise the anti-clericalism of Parliament, and give it a more definitely anti-papal bias. When Parliament reassembled, to deal in the first place with the business of giving statutory effect to the King's pardon to the clergy for their unlawful recognition of Wolsey's commission, and add a free pardon to the laity as well,

[1] Pickthorn, *Henry VIII*, 157.
[2] Wilkins, *Concilia*, iii. 275. For a discussion of the Submission of the Clergy, see G. R. Elton, *King or Minister?*, 39 *Hist.* 225-8.
[3] F. M. Powicke, *The Reformation in England*, in *European Civilisation*, ed. E. Eyre, iv. 392.     [4] Tanner, 20.

the King's case was laid before it.[1] Clerical opposition, thwarted in Convocation, tried to raise its head in the Lords. There, however, the ecclesiastical estate was submerged. It had no separate existence from the House of which it formed a part. Overriding its opposition, the majority of both Houses delivered their second assault.

The "Supplication against the Ordinaries", presented to the King on March 18, 1532, was doubtless officially inspired.[2] Its text had been carefully revised by Cromwell. Yet the grievances it recited *The sub-mission of the clergy* were familiar enough. Orthodoxy being first vindicated by an expression of concern at the multiplication of heretical books, their vogue was attributed to the discontent caused by the conduct of ecclesiastics, who without royal consent made laws in Convocation inconsistent with those of the realm, vexatiously cited laymen before Church courts and even out of their own dioceses, exacted excessive fees and imposed undue delays in legal processes, and in other minor ways behaved tyrannically. An ably-drafted answer defending the independent legislative authority of Convocation was laid before Parliament by the King with unmistakable signs of his disapproval.[3] A second answer expressed very clearly the extent to which progressive churchmen were prepared to go in accepting the implications of royal supremacy. Though defending the Church's independent legislative power, which Kings, including Henry, had always recognised, it offered to submit existing ecclesiastical law, save in matters of faith and morals, for royal approval, and, with the same reservation, not to legislate in future without royal consent.[4] Surrender soon followed. In May 1532, only one bishop dissenting, the Canterbury Convocation undertook not to legislate without royal consent, and to submit existing laws to the censorship of a commission of sixteen members equally drawn from the Upper and Lower Houses of Parliament and sixteen clergy. Those which received the approval of a majority were, with the King's assent, to remain valid.[5]

The legislative power of Parliament was shaking off an ancient rival. In 1532 the direction in which it was to be exercised was *The first Act of Annates*

[1] Tanner, 16.

[2] H. Gee and W. J. Hardy, *Documents illustrative of English Church History*, 145-53; Elton, *The Tudor Constitution, Documents*, 324-6. The question is further discussed in articles by Elton in 67 *E.H.R.* 507 and J. P. Cooper, 72 *E.H.R.* 616.

[3] Gee and Hardy, 154-76.    [4] Wilkins, *Concilia*, iii. 753.

[5] Gee and Hardy, 176-8. This surrender was accompanied by the resignation of Sir Thomas More, who had succeeded Wolsey as Chancellor.

shown by enactments further limiting benefit of clergy, and prohibiting undue citations to ecclesiastical courts. These were on
familiar lines. The path led over the frontier of an unknown
land in the Act of Annates, and Parliament followed it only
hesitantly. It had, however, been skilfully chosen. Annates, the
payment to the Pope of the first year's income of newly-appointed
archbishops and bishops, were of no great antiquity. A statute of
Henry IV had endeavoured to restrict such payments and had
referred to them as "a horrible mischief and barbarous custom".
To this temper the preamble of the bill appealed. The enacting part abolished such payments in future and declared
that the consecration of archbishops and bishops should be valid
even if annates were not paid.[1] Doubts as to the complete servility
of Parliament are suggested by the process of its passage into law.
Although in the Upper House only one lay peer joined in the
unanimous opposition of the spiritual lords, opposition showed
itself in the Commons, where a division had to be taken. The
threat to papal authority implied by the bill seemed alarming to
the minds of many members.[2]

*Its im-
mediate
intention*

The Act of Annates is best regarded as a weapon intended to
strengthen the King's hand in his negotiations with the Pope. It
deprived the Pope of a lucrative source of revenue, and enabled
Henry to increase the pressure on him by the use of a respiting
clause under which the King was enabled to defer its operation
for a year, pending further attempts at agreement.

*Henry's
marriage
dissolved*

When that date came, the crisis had reached its height. In
November 1532 the Pope prohibited the King from putting away
Catherine and remarrying. The King defied the prohibition. In
January 1533 he secretly married Anne Boleyn. In September her
child, the future Queen Elizabeth, was born. Some tribunal within
the realm must meanwhile be devised with competence to annul
the former marriage. Archbishop Warham, persisting in his
objection to all that the King had done and proposed, had died in
August 1532. The Pope, still uncertain of Henry's ultimate purpose, issued the bulls necessary for the institution of Thomas
Cranmer as his successor. In March 1533 he was consecrated,

---

[1] Elton, 341-4.
[2] It is possible that opposition was stimulated by fear lest the Emperor
should close the Flanders wool market.

surrendering to the King, however, the bulls relative to his appointment, and asserting that nothing in his oath to the Pope should impede his duty to the Crown, or towards the reformation of the faith or the government of the English Church.[1] In May the new archbishop sat at Dunstable as "most principal minister" of the King's "spiritual jurisdiction within this our realm" to decide Henry's case against his marriage with Catherine, which was pronounced null from the beginning, and the marriage of Henry and Anne valid.[2] In July both decisions were condemned at Rome. Cranmer and his colleagues at Dunstable were excommunicated, and so also, with a suspension until September, was the King. In November the sentence against him was published.

The issue was at last fairly joined. Against the exclusive juris- *The Act* diction of the Papacy there was now asserted the exclusive *in Restraint of Appeals* jurisdiction of the Crown. It was asserted in Parliament, by the Act *Appeals* in Restraint of Appeals,[3] passed, though against opposition, with a rapidity which suggests how acute was the sense of national crisis which dominated the minds of Englishmen in 1533. The preamble to the Act declared the realm of England an empire governed by one head and king. His subjects formed one body-politic "divided in terms and by names of spiritualty and temporalty", and bore to him, next to God, "a natural and humble obedience". Two jurisdictions, spiritual and temporal, governed all their affairs, but both were subordinate to the King, who had "entire power . . . to render and yield justice and final determination to all manner of folk . . . in all causes . . . without restraint or provocation to any foreign princes or potentates". The Act enacted that all causes by royal consent and the law of the land belonging to the ecclesiastical courts should be "determined within the King's jurisdiction and authority". Appeal from the inferior ecclesiastical courts lay to that of the archbishop, and in cases affecting the King to the Upper House of Convocation.

This Act is the decisive instrument in the destruction of Roman *Its effect* authority. But it is more than that. It rudely denies the conception, which some progressive churchmen were prepared to admit, of an *Ecclesia Anglicana* freed from Roman jurisdiction to resume a primitive independence. Ecclesiastical authority was to have no

---

[1] Pickthorn, *Henry VIII*, 194-5.          [2] Pickthorn, *Henry VIII*, 208-9.
[3] Elton, 344-9.

autonomous quality. It was to be drawn from the Crown and exercised in conformity with the laws of the realm. What these were to be was a matter for decision by Parliament and the royal courts. No doubt the medieval conception of the essential unity of society under its dual hierarchy of officials, ecclesiastical and lay, was preserved. Society was, however, to be dominated by one supreme authority, that of the Crown, and subjected to a single law, that of the State, in which ecclesiastical rules were only one and that an essentially subordinate element. The ramparts of the Church were down. Royal authority swept into the breaches and occupied its new position in strength.

*Later*
*legislation*    In 1534, a second Act of Annates (the first had been made effective by royal patent in the previous July) prohibited papal nomination to bishoprics, renewed the prohibition against the payment of annates, and empowered the King, in default of election by chapters, to appoint by letters patent.[1] First-fruits and tenths of benefices were annexed to the Crown.[2] Another Act made it illegal to seek licences and dispensations from Rome, and to pay Peter's Pence (a tax of one penny on each hearth paid to Rome since Anglo-Saxon times) or other moneys levied by papal authority.[3] Dispensations issued before March 1533 were to stand only if consonant with English law. Their future issue by the Archbishop of Canterbury was limited by the necessity for the consent of King and Council to any intrument not warranted by custom.[4] A Heresy Act repealed Henry IV's *De Heretico Comburendo*, and while retaining trial by ecclesiastics and punishment by the lay power in the accustomed way, deprived ecclesiastics of the initiative in prosecutions and placed it in the hands of laymen.[5] Another Act put in statutory form the submission of the clergy in 1532,[6] the effect of which was now more than ever complete since Convocation in March 1534 had by a large majority repudiated papal jurisdiction.[7] In its second

---

[1] Elton, 349-51.    [2] Tanner, 37-9.    [3] Elton, 351-5.

[4] E. F. Churchill, *Dispensations under the Tudors and Stuarts*, 34 *E.H.R.* 409. Tanner, 35.

[5] The King was given power to suspend or repeal this Act by letters patent, such appeal to have the same effect as though made in Parliament. This is an interesting early example of the grant of statutory powers of legislation to the Crown (see p. 524 below). Similar powers were given to Henry in 1543 by the Act for the Advancement of Religion.

[6] Elton, 347-9.    [7] Gee and Hardy, 251-2.

session of 1534, Parliament passed the Act of Supremacy.[1] Its form is merely declaratory. The royal supremacy is now an axiom. The clergy have accepted it. Their reservation "so far as the law of Christ allows" is omitted. The King is accepted as "only supreme head in earth of the Church of England" with all powers and profits pertaining to that position, and in particular the right to use all jurisdiction for the repression of error, heresy, and other offences as any spiritual authority had ever lawfully possessed.

It now remained to gain national acceptance for the sum of destructive change which this torrent of legislation had effected. Submission was singularly complete. The Convocations, universities, cathedral chapters, minor clergy and the mass of the laity manifested little opposition. Even the monastic houses, the least national element in Tudor society, did not resist the current, except for protests by some of the more ascetic communities. The penalties of recalcitrancy were terribly severe. Two statutes of 1534 imposed on all subjects an oath abjuring all authority save the King's and engaging to maintain the statutory settlement of the succession made in the first of the two, by which the marriage with Catherine was declared invalid, and that with Anne accepted as lawful. Refusal to take it was punishable as misprision of treason, by imprisonment and loss of goods, while words denying the King's title became punishable as treason.[2] Here, indeed, were "windows let into men's souls" such as Elizabeth was later to refuse to open. What they revealed in the souls of most men were the confusion and the failure to see clear principles which were so typical of the age. It was not so with all. The Carthusian priors of London would not "consent or believe" that the King was Head of the Church, and in May 1535 they suffered the death of traitors.[3] Equally clear was the position taken up by John Fisher, Bishop of Rochester, and the ex-Chancellor, Sir Thomas More. In April 1534 they had refused to take the oath regarding the succession and were thrown into the Tower. Both would swear to the succession. Neither would do so in the prescribed form. They were therefore attainted for misprision of treason under the Succession Acts. While they lay in prison the Supremacy Act was passed. In June 1535 Fisher was indicted for treason. He

*Enforcement of the anti-papal statutes*

---

[1] Elton, 355-6.     [2] Tanner, 382-9.     [3] Pickthorn, *Henry VIII*, 258.

3

had apparently, when in the Tower, expressly denied the royal supremacy. He was found guilty by a jury, condemned, and executed. More's trial followed at once. He was charged with a similar formal denial, which he did not admit, maintaining that he had observed silence on the point. Like Fisher, he was found guilty. He suffered the same fate. Before his judges he plainly put the principle animating his conduct. The Act of Parliament on which he was charged was repugnant not only to unrepealed statutes but to the law of God and the Church. In this appeal to a fundamental law limiting the legislative capacity of the Crown in Parliament there is reflected the last ray of an expiring luminary by which generations of men had guided their course. The fellow-subjects and fellow-churchmen of the martyrs forsook the star to which they had been constant and turned their faces towards the new lord of the ascendant.[1]

*Nature and application of the royal supremacy*    During the remaining twelve years of Henry's reign the implications of that ascendancy were worked out. The Crown fixed its grasp on ecclesiastical property, administration, and law, defined the content of belief, and settled forms of ritual. Its action was very far from being solely entrusted to ecclesiastics to carry out. These no doubt had their place. The Church was compliant. Its organisation was left substantially intact, though deriving its animating principle from the Crown. But Henry was not content to act solely through ecclesiastical means. The supervisory functions of the Council, the legislative powers of Parliament, the administrative authority of a royal Vicar-General, the layman Thomas Cromwell, were exercised to more decisive purpose than those of Convocation, episcopate, or courts Christian. It may be admitted that the royal supremacy did not expressly connote a *potestas ordinis*—an authority for certain purposes which only the possession of holy orders could confer. It was only a *potestas jurisdictionis*. Such a jurisdiction could, however, be pushed far beyond questions of property, of discipline, and of morality, and be thrust into the inner sanctuaries of religious conviction and Christian conscience. It seems idle to attempt to discover any true limitations on the extent of the Crown's spiritual claims, or any principle prescribing the

[1] For the attitude of Fisher and More, see Constant, 125-31, 141-52; R. W. Chambers, *Thomas More*, 300-305, 319-20, 327, 332, 336-41; Elton, 238-9; Tanner, 433-9; Pickthorn, *Henry VIII*, 260-63; Baumer, 162.

appropriate channels of its activity. The Church lay within the uncovenanted mercy of her Supreme Head.

The quality of that mercy was speedily manifested in its dealings *Confisca-* with ecclesiastical property. This had always been the Church's *tion of* most vulnerable point. Schemes for the expropriation of the *ecclesi-* Church had been mooted in the fourteenth century and a number *property* of alien priories were dissolved in the fifteenth. The idea of spoliation was therefore not new. It was suggested to Henry by Cromwell when the Reformation Parliament began. Somewhat later, a plan for the complete confiscation of all ecclesiastical property came under consideration. Archbishops and bishops were to be allotted fixed stipends, the residue being annexed by the Crown.[1] This sweeping programme was dropped. Monastic property was alone marked for destruction. The attack fell on a part of the Church already far gone in decay. Diversion of monastic revenues, with papal consent, had begun before there was any question of a breach with Rome. No need for papal consent now subsisted. In 1532 Christ Church, Aldgate, the affairs of which were hopelessly embarrassed, set the example of voluntary surrender to the Crown.[2] In 1534 the small order of Friars Observant was dissolved by royal authority. In January 1535 Cromwell, as Vicar-General, was empowered to hold a general visitation of churches, monasteries and clergy. The reports of his agents, which presented a gloomy picture of monastic discipline, came before Parliament in 1536.[3] Statutory authorisation was given for the dissolution of all monasteries with less than £200 annual revenue, with a dispensing power to the King to save such as he chose.[4] After the Pilgrimage of Grace, a rising caused at least partly by popular opposition to the dissolution of the monasteries, the spoliation was extended. Some abbeys, implicated in the movement, had their abbots attainted and their property confiscated in consequence. Others were terrified into

---

[1] Fisher, *Political History of England*, 345.
[2] E. Jeffries Davis, *The Beginnings of the Dissolution*, 4 *T.R.H.S.* viii, 127 ff. For earlier suppressions, see G. Baskerville, *The English Monks and the Suppression of the Monasteries*, ch. iv.
[3] For the visitation of the monasteries, see Baskerville, ch. v; Pickthorn, *Henry VIII*, 272-4; Constant, 85-92.
[4] Elton, 374-8. The Act was soon followed by the appointment of local commissions to inquire and report to the Crown on the monasteries involved.

an ostensibly voluntary surrender. In 1539 Parliament gave authority for the destruction of all remaining houses.[1]

*Disposal of monastic property*   The wealth of the monasteries fell in the main to the Crown. Its immediate gains were enormous. The sale of movables realised about one-and-a-half millions sterling. Revenues from land amounted to about £100,000 annually, impropriated tithe brought in about one-third as much. Yet from all this the Crown gained no large permanent endowment. Monastic revenues were often heavily encumbered, and many laymen retained what was already in effect their own. Moreover, and most important of all, the Crown after a very short delay began the process of sale. By the end of Henry's reign, only one-third of the monastic lands still remained to the Crown, usually as lessor at a moderate reserved rent. The rest had been sold for a total of £800,000, which was treated as income and expended on war with France. The true gainers were the landed and moneyed class and not the King. The Crown, which might have endowed itself, had endowed its partners instead. Receipts by the Crown from monastic sources did not exceed £66,000 of true annual income, though for many years the total was swelled by sales of property used as revenue.[2]

*The Crown's ecclesiastical revenues*   The revenues derived from first-fruits and tenths were valued with those of the monasteries by commissioners—appointed in 1535 under the Act annexing them to the Crown—the results of whose investigations were embodied in the *Valor Ecclesiasticus*.[3] From this source an income was derived which amounted to £70,000 annually. In all, the ecclesiastical revenues of the Crown may have reached about £136,000, a sum which equalled its ordinary income before the Reformation, but might well have been much greater. To deal with these revenues it became necessary to establish special courts. Confiscated monastic property came under the jurisdiction of a Court of Augmentations, created by statute in 1536, and later suppressed and re-erected by royal prerogative.[4] A similar organisation was created in 1540 by the statute establishing the Court of First-Fruits and Tenths.[5]

---

[1] Tanner, 63-7. Elton, 380-82.

[2] On the financial results of the Dissolution, see Pickthorn, *Henry VIII*, 377-84; Fisher, Appendix ii.

[3] On this document, see A. Savine, The *Valor Ecclesiasticus*, in *Oxford Studies in Social and Legal History*, i.

[4] Tanner, 336-9.          [5] Tanner, 340. Holdsworth, iv. 271.

Yet the true life of a religious communion does not depend on *Royal* the integrity of its property, and more striking illustrations of the *adminis-* dependence to which Henry VIII had reduced the Church must *trative* be sought elsewhere. Its organisation was in his hands. Episcopal *control* appointments were under his practical, though not fully under his formal control. He was authorised to make a scheme for new dioceses by a statute of 1539.[1] The new bishoprics of Gloucester, Peterborough, Oxford, Bristol, Chester (and for a time West-minster), owed their existence to royal fiat. Their holders unques-tionably sat in the Lords in their spiritual capacity and not as holders of baronies. Convocations met only by royal summons. They were presided over by the King's Vicar-General or his deputy, their legislation took effect only with royal assent. Besides the legislation of Convocation, royal Injunctions on points of disci-pline and worship prescribed a law for the Church to follow.[2] The courts Christian exercised a jurisdiction which the law of the land could freely modify and which applied less the Canon Law than the "King's law in ecclesiastical causes".[3] Parliament defined the prohibited degrees in matrimony, and reconstituted a commission to revise the Canon Law. The teaching of the Canon Law in the universities was prohibited. In its place was elevated the Civil Law of Rome with all its magnification of princely power.[4]

The royal supremacy did not confine itself to merely external *Royal* points of order and discipline. The beliefs to be held forth and *authority* professed by the English Church were settled by royal authority. *over* It was still the duty of the Defender of the Faith to defend ortho- *doctrine* doxy. His doctrinal views had hitherto been impeccable. The government had issued a proclamation against heretical books in 1530; unauthorised translations of Scripture had been burned, heretics imprisoned or sent to the stake. 1534 had seen a new Heresy Act.[5] In 1536 Henry charged Cranmer with the pre-paration of a statement of the doctrine to be received by the Church. In July the work of the Archbishop was presented to Convocation. It could be regarded as a response to a petition regarding sixty-seven specified errors and abuses presented by the Lower House of Convocation to the Upper. But it did not fully

[1] Tanner, 68-9.
[2] For the Injunctions of 1536 and 1538, see Tanner, 93-4; Gee and Hardy, 269-75.
[3] Holdsworth, i. 595-6.
[4] Holdsworth, iv. 232-4.
[5] Pickthorn, *Henry VIII*, 230-32.

reflect the orthodoxy which had inspired the complaint. Only three of the sacraments were pronounced necessary—baptism, the eucharist, and penance—the other four being passed over in silence, though Catholic doctrines of transubstantiation, penance, good works, the use of images, the invocation of the saints, and purgatory were substantially retained. Theologically, the Ten Articles made little change. Institutionally, they expressed the new principle of royal supremacy. Their title ascribed their authorship to the King. By his authority they were enforced. Royal Injunctions bade the clergy read and comment on them periodically.[1] In the following year, after long discussions in a conference of theologians commissioned by Cromwell as vicegerent of the King's spiritual authority, the *Godly and Pious Institution of a Christian Man*, known familiarly as the *Bishops' Book*, was published. The King, who had actively participated in its preparation, issued it without reference either to Convocation or Parliament.[2] An English version of the Bible, prepared by Cromwell's order, was by royal Injunction of 1538 directed to be placed in every parish church, though not till 1544 did Cranmer's English Litany make the first formal change in ritual.

*Parlia-mentary authorisa-tion of belief*
Still concerned to establish and enforce uniformity of belief, the King brought the question before Parliament in 1539. The Six Articles obtained the approval of Convocation; but what made them operative was a statute, "so spiritual that . . . none shall dare say, in the blessed sacrament of the altar doth remain either bread or wine after the consecration".[3] Conformity to their rigidly orthodox doctrines was enforced by Parliament, though Parliament did not actually formulate their statement of belief, which owed most perhaps to the King's ability to confound opponents with God's learning. Heresy became a criminal offence by the law of the land, executed by lay tribunals. The royal arm did not use the "whip with six strings" with any great vigour. The rest of the reign witnessed little systematic persecution, though the Act of Six Articles was followed by other statutes aimed at the same formal purpose. In 1543 a new exposition of doctrine, based on the *Bishops' Book*, was issued under the name of the *Necessary Doctrine and Erudition for any Christian Man*, known commonly as

---

[1] Constant, 247-8, 258-60.        [2] Constant, 262.
[3] Quoted by Pickthorn, *Henry VIII*, 406. For the statute, see Elton, 389-92.

the *King's Book*. Though prepared under Henry's supervision and approved in Convocation, it was confirmed by Act of Parliament.[1]

This increasing tendency to introduce parliamentary authority into the actual exercise of the royal supremacy complicated the position considerably. The royal supremacy, without ceasing to be essentially personal, and to be exercised on many occasions through ecclesiastics, was finding another method of expressing itself. Doubtless Parliament was used not to define, but merely to protect, true Christian belief. So long as Henry lived it could not attempt more. But a foundation was being laid for wider claims. In Parliament, the King had asserted his ecclesiastical supremacy. There he had now begun to exercise it. In future, it might well be maintained that he could exercise it nowhere else. He had united spiritual to temporal authority. Both might pass under the same control and be exercisable in Parliament alone. *Implica-tions of parlia-mentary interven-tion*

### iii

On Henry's death in 1547 the royal supremacy passed into the hands of a nine-year-old King. The actual exercise of authority was soon vested in the hands of Edward VI's uncle, Somerset, as Protector. There could be no difficulty about the Protector's exercise of temporal powers. It could, none the less, be disputed whether such an official, possessing none of the sacred attributes of monarchy, could validly use the royal supremacy over the Church. It was contended, amid the whirl of ecclesiastical change which the new reign brought, that the King could alone use this power, that all that was done in pursuance of it until he could exercise it for himself lacked validity, and that until he came of age further advance was impossible. No attention was paid to such arguments. The royal supremacy of the Church was conceived of as not only inherent in the new King notwithstanding his minority, but as capable of exercise forthwith in his name.[2] It was to this extent further de-personalised. *Royal supremacy under Edward VI*

The manner of its exercise emphasised the essential dependence

---

[1] Constant, 273-7.

[2] Tanner, 100. But compare J. A. Muller, *Stephen Gardiner and the Tudor Reaction*, 164-5.

*Further
subjection
of the
Church to
lay control*
of the Church on the Crown. Ecclesiastical authority was deemed to have ceased with the demise of the Crown, and had to be renewed by the issue of fresh commissions.[1] An Act passed in the first Parliament of the reign abolished the system of episcopal election by *congé d'élire* and substituted for it a simple scheme of appointment by letters patent.[2] Only ecclesiastics specifically empowered by the King were allowed to exercise spiritual jurisdiction, and this was frequently overridden by the action of special royal commissions. Process in the ecclesiastical courts was taken in the King's name. It is not too much to say that bishops were treated merely as heads of the ecclesiastical department of state, subject to the control of the Privy Council, which could summon them to answer before it for failure to do their duty and inflict on them suspension, imprisonment, or deprivation.[3] Towards the end of the reign one bishopric was suppressed and one dismembered.[4]

*Conciliar
and parlia-
mentary
action in
ecclesiasti-
cal affairs*
More than ever were Erastian principles in the ascendant. Henry had often appeared to act in and through the officers and assemblies of the Church. Edward VI's government seemed to disregard them, and chose Parliament as the instrument of its action. The tendency manifested since 1539 was thus continued and emphasised. Royal Injunctions might serve in 1547 to enforce, in a general visitation, the duties of preaching, teaching, using the English Litany, reading the Gospel and Epistle, administering poor relief, and keeping a parish register.[5] The government did not merely intend to keep the ecclesiastical organisation going. It intended to change the direction in which it was to move. Administrative action sufficed to stay religious persecution under the statutes of the previous reign. When change had been decided on, Parliament was employed to carry it out.

*Earliest
Edwardian
Legislation*
The earliest legislation of Edward VI's first Parliament repealed the Six Articles and all the statutes punishing heresy or restraining

---

[1] G. W. Child, *Church and State under the Tudors,* 111.

[2] The preamble to this Act and a brief note of its provisions are printed by Child, 351-2.

[3] J. Gairdner, *History of the English Church from Henry VIII to Mary,* 247-8, 258-60, 270-72, 284-7, 295-6, 301, 307.

[4] Durham was dismembered on the deprivation of Bishop Tunstall, 1553, and Gloucester suppressed, as Westminster already had been in 1550. Durham and Gloucester were restored under Mary.        [5] Tanner, 100.

the free reading and exposition of Scripture.[1] With the Six Articles disappeared governmental sanction for such beliefs as the invocation of saints and prayers for the dead. The endowments of chantries and gilds associated with these practices, menaced with confiscation in 1545, were now seized for the Crown.[2] Gild endowments were already being diverted to secular purposes before the Reformation. The Act of 1547 was so drafted as to protect endowments thus used, and those applied to education and charity. Only endowments devoted to the maintenance of religious rites were intended to lie within its scope; but clumsy and rapacious administration of its provisions caused funds which might have continued to serve socially beneficent purposes to pass into the hands of persons already enriched by the spoliation of the monasteries. The end of the Six Articles, moreover, opened the way for innovation in doctrine and ritual. The removal of constraint reduced the Church to a chaos in which priests and parishes did much as they liked. Convocation expressed the desire to permit to the laity communion under both kinds and to remove the laws prohibiting clerical marriage. It was by Parliament and Council that the changes were effected. Statutes dealt with communion in 1548 and clerical marriage in 1549.[3] In 1548 the Council ordered the removal of images and the disuse of candles, holy water, and other aids to devotion. It constituted a committee of clergy to draw up an English communion service supplementing but not excluding the Latin rite. The use of the new order was enforced by proclamation. There followed a complete new service-book in English, laid before Parliament in 1549. It is doubtful whether this work was ever seen or approved by Convocation. What is certain is that this first Book of Common Prayer became a schedule to an Act of Parliament. Its use was prescribed by the Act of Uniformity of that year.[4] Ecclesiastical approval is probable enough. Twelve bishops voted for the Book in the Lords, and only eight against. Clerical opposition could, however, have made no difference. It no longer lay with the clergy to determine the

[1] Tanner, 402.
[2] Elton, 383-5.
[3] Child, 347-51, 354-5. See also Gee and Hardy, 322-8, 366-8.
[4] Elton, 392-6.

form of their worship with its doctrinal implications. Detailed arrangements for the manner in which the communion service was to be conducted were laid down by order of the Council. The Act of Uniformity penalised, with fine for the first and imprisonment for any subsequent offence, priests who refused to use the new Book, though imposing no punishment on laymen who absented themselves from the services of the Church.

*Changes under War- wick's govern- ment*

The government of Warwick which thrust Somerset out of office in October 1549 soon manifested proclivities even more radical than those of the Protector. It may be an open question how far the changes in ritual effected by Somerset had expressed the mind and will of a majority of the clergy. There is no question that those now begun expressed those of a minority. Nine out of fourteen bishops present in the Lords voted for a bill for drawing up a new Ordinal, or book of ceremonies for ordination, but a majority voted against that for destroying all service-books save Henry VIII's Primers and the Book of Common Prayer. So also the bishops opposed a bill appointing a commission to revise the Canon Law—which did not, however, succeed in completing its task. Their own bill for restoring episcopal authority failed, while Parliament gave statutory force to the new Ordinal beforehand.[1] The Council appointed the commissioners who drew it up, and imprisoned and deprived the bishops who declined to accept it. It was in vain that bishops Day of Chichester and Heath of Worcester urged again the argument that the Council could not validly exercise the royal supremacy. Radical bishops such as Ridley, Latimer, and Hooper seconded the government loyally by setting an example of the conversion of altars into communion tables which the Council enforced on their more backward colleagues.[2]

*The Second Prayer Book*

In 1552 the progress made since 1549 was again summarised by statute. Cranmer in 1550 brought before Convocation the project of revising the Prayer Book. There followed merely an inconclusive debate. Thenceforward the archbishop acted alone, and revised the Book in a distinctively Protestant sense. At the end of 1551 the Council decided to submit his Book to Parliament. The second Act of Uniformity, passed in 1552, did not, like the first, append the second Prayer Book as a schedule to itself, but did

[1] Gairdner, 278.                    [2] Tanner, 115.

treat it—for all its departures from Catholic doctrine—as a mere explanation and perfecting of its predecessor, and place it under the protection of the former Act.[1] It added, however, new clauses compelling the acceptance of the Book by the laity. It is therefore the first in the long series of recusancy Acts. Like the new Ordinal of 1550 the Prayer Book received statutory sanction. The Council itself took a hand in the formulation of Anglican ritual, ordering, while the Book was still in the hands of the printer, the insertion of the Black Rubric directed against the adoration of the sacred elements.[2]

Ritual by its very nature implied certain theological beliefs. *The* But more still was done to settle doctrine by lay authority. The *Forty-two* Ten Articles and the Six Articles had been earlier efforts in this *Articles* direction. In 1553 a new collection, the Forty-two Articles, based on a code already in use by Cranmer, was published by the Council under royal authority alone, and accompanied by a mendacious statement that it had been approved by Convocation.[3]

To a King incapable of personally exercising the royal supremacy *Royal* over the Church, there succeeded a Queen who conscientiously *supremacy* repudiated it. Yet it was by law attached to the Crown she had *under* inherited, and she found it a convenient means of restoring *Mary* deprived bishops such as Gardiner, Heath, and Day, and of silencing their opponents, though she dispensed with it in official documents when she could. By no act of her own, however, could she disburden herself of this intolerable legacy, and restore the Catholic faith and papal authority which had been destroyed. Only in Parliament could the revolution be undone. Every step taken towards that end strengthened the presumption that Parliament was conjoined in the exercise of the royal supremacy. Parliament had vindicated it for the Crown. Parliament had shared in its exercise. It was now to be invited to destroy its own handiwork. What it had destroyed, it might with the same authority rebuild. In the end, it must seem that the royal supremacy was not to be exercised by the monarch as he saw fit, and with equal validity through whatever means he chose, but in Parliament above all, and essentially.

[1] Tanner, 117-20.
[2] Pollard, *Political History of England, 1547-1603*, 70. As revived under Elizabeth, the Book omitted the Rubric.     [3] Gairdner, 311.

*The first stage of repeal*

The process of restoring the old order in the Church was certainly not carried out in a way determined by the Supreme Head. Mary's first Parliament indeed repealed all the ecclesiastical legislation of Edward VI's reign, and effected a return to the position at Henry VIII's death.[1] Worship and doctrine were thus established according to the practice of 1547, but no punishment was annexed to non-attendance at the services of the Church. The penalties for denial of the royal supremacy were repealed. The title itself was not abolished. There was no restoration of papal authority. The Queen's legitimacy was based not on the validity of her mother's marriage, but on statute.[2] Parliament made it clear that no proposal for the restoration of ecclesiastical property would obtain its sanction.

*The second stage of repeal*

The second Parliament of the reign, in April 1554, made the same lesson plain. The programme of the government could not be forced through in its entirety. Bills against heresy were lost. The clergy petitioned for the revival of ecclesiastical jurisdiction. They met with no success. The third Parliament, meeting in November of the same year, yielded more ground. Subject to understandings that nothing would be attempted toward the restoration of confiscated ecclesiastical property, it petitioned for and obtained absolution for the schism into which the kingdom had fallen.[3] It revived the heresy statutes.[4] It repealed all the ecclesiastical legislation of Henry VIII since 1528, safeguarding, however, the rights of owners of property taken from the Church and the jurisdiction of the Common Law with regard thereto, and retaining the 1529 Acts against probate and mortuary fees. The Queen alone returned secularised property to the Church. Only Westminster, Sion, Smithfield, and Greenwich,[5] of all the dissolved monasteries, resumed their life.

*The Marian persecution*

The use to which the Church put its restored authority was to lead Parliament to repent what it had done. The revival of the heresy statutes took effect on January 20, 1555. The Church had already subjected religious suspects to examination. On January 20 the papal legate, Cardinal Pole, issued a commission for their trial, which began on January 28. Common and statute law alike

---

[1] Tanner, 121-2. Gee and Hardy, 377-80.    [2] Tanner, 123-4.
[3] Gee and Hardy, 385-415.    [4] Gee and Hardy, 384; Tanner, 124-5.
[5] Baskerville, 266-8.

bound the secular arm to carry out the sentence of the spiritual courts, and Canon Law denounced excommunication against the lay officer who declined to do his duty. Under Mary it was not likely that vigour would be wanting. On February 4 the first victim perished at the stake. For some weeks the attack fell principally on the clergy. In March it extended to the laity. During the rest of the reign some three hundred heretics suffered death by burning, including Cranmer, who as metropolitan was reserved for papal condemnation, and bishops Ridley and Latimer. Pole was enthroned in Cranmer's place.

Persecution was stayed during the session of Mary's fourth *The atti-* Parliament, from October to December 1555, which manifested *tude of* its attitude towards the Church by denying to the government *liaments later Par-* the authority it sought for restoring first-fruits and tenths to Rome. Its utmost concession was that tenths were to be paid by ecclesiastics to the legate for the use of the Crown, to which lay impropriators of benefices were to continue to pay direct.[1] Parliament was dissolved in December 1555, and the intermission lasted rather more than two years, to January 1558, when the last Parliament of the reign held the first of its brief and barren sessions. Neither of these two last Parliaments showed a very friendly spirit towards Church and Crown. Having armed the Church with its ancient jurisdiction under a Queen anxious to support it by the secular arm, Parliament had to remain a helpless spectator of the results. Only if, as in 1529, the Crown reversed its policy could it again interfere.

The course of Mary's reign from the end of 1555 to her death *The* in 1558 made it certain that an anti-Roman and anti-clerical lead *reaction* from a new sovereign would meet with an overwhelming *against the Marian* response. Public feeling, shocked by the horror of the persecution, *policy* resentful of the subordination of English to Spanish interests which the Queen's marriage to Philip of Spain entailed, and humiliated by the consequent loss of Calais, developed a spirit dangerously like that of 1529. As in 1529, Parliament would concentrate and express it. Translated into action, it would move more swiftly and radically than in 1529, since the path of ecclesiastical revolution was now a familiar one, and the goal could easily be defined by reference to points attained in the past. All that was needed

[1] Pollard, *Political History of England*, 146.

was a government prepared, as in 1529, to make a reversal of policy.

*Position at the accession of Elizabeth*    The accession of Elizabeth in November 1559 seems to reproduce the situation of exactly thirty years before. Mary, like her mother, had come to be identified with a discredited Church and an intolerable foreign interference in national affairs. The child of the Boleyn marriage represented the causes of insular independence and the subjection of the Church to national control. The situation was not, however, reproduced precisely. Where Henry had had to deal with a Church divided in opinion and uncertain as to the limits of royal supremacy, Elizabeth faced a Marian Church resolute on principle and courageous in its own defence. Where Henry had had to gauge the dubious temper of his subjects and accommodate his advance to what was gradually seen to be possible, Elizabeth could feel no such hesitancies. A second breach with Rome, a second subjugation of the Church, each more swift, more clearly conceived, more radical than the first, was the policy she must personally incline to, since it was to be presumed that in the eyes of rigid Catholics she was a heretic, the issue of an adulterous marriage, and a usurper of the throne.[1] It was also the policy which her subjects must expect of her. The hesitancies of her reign were to be of a different sort. Parliament, which had seen its competence so illimitably extended in the sphere of religion, which had been the instrument of so much change in every department of ecclesiastical affairs, was in the unseen future to be capable of defining the nature of the national Church on lines very different from those which the sovereign personally preferred, and the Queen might refuse the path on which her subjects invited her to enter.

*The beginnings of Elizabethan ecclesiastical policy*    The future, however, was unseen and remote. For the moment the urgent need was to oust alien authority over the Church, restore the royal supremacy, and re-erect the settlement of religion which Marian legislation had swept away. Though an order issued on the day when Elizabeth's accession was proclaimed forbade alteration of the religious usages then in force, prosecutions for heresy abruptly ceased. The ritual used in the royal chapel and at

[1] Catholic opinion regarding Elizabeth may be studied in C. G. Bayne, *Anglo-Roman Relations, 1558–1565*, 20 ff.

the coronation connoted Protestant views.[1] The Council with which she surrounded herself balanced advisers of various opinions, but Archbishop Heath was the only ecclesiastic, and he soon ceased to attend. Religious policy was to be shaped by cool and prudent laymen whose essentially secular and political outlook, devoid of profound religious conviction, characterised the Queen herself.

The Parliament of January 1559 was no more a packed body than that of 1529—no more, indeed, than its own immediate predecessors.[2] The Commons, dominated as ever by members for the southern and eastern boroughs, were an average assembly of the period, somewhat clearer as to their immediate purpose than most had been, but not otherwise very dissimilar. Marked differences revealed themselves between the Lower House and the Upper. Nine bishoprics were vacant. Not all of the other Marian bishops were present, but those who did attend held the proxies of the absentees. Supported by a group of temporal lords, the doomed Church made a valiant struggle against its own extinction. A bill reviving the royal supremacy and the Edwardian Acts of Uniformity passed rapidly through the Commons. It was wrecked in the Lords, where the Edwardian Acts were removed from its scope, and the title of Supreme Head left to the Queen's discretion. Meanwhile the Canterbury Convocation had reaffirmed the central dogmas of Catholicism regarding the mass, Roman supremacy, and the incompetence of the lay power to deal with matters of faith. The Commons retaliated by seeking to repeal penalties for the use of the 1552 Prayer Book, and to restore that Book and the Acts of Uniformity as well. In these circumstances the government changed its tactics. The official programme was divided into two parts. A bill re-establishing royal supremacy in which the Queen was styled "supreme governor as well in all matters ecclesiastical as temporal" passed the Commons, was amended in the Lords, and became law. A separate Uniformity bill, restoring the 1552 Prayer Book, similarly passed the Commons, but was nearly rejected in the Lords. The spiritual lords were solid against both bills. On the latter they mustered with

*Parliamentary nature of the settlement*

---

[1] For a full discussion of the significance of Elizabeth's coronation rite, see C. G. Bayne, *The Coronation of Queen Elizabeth*, 22 E.H.R. 650 ff.

[2] The composition of this Parliament is analysed in detail by C. G. Bayne, *The First House of Commons of Queen Elizabeth*, 23 E.H.R. 455, 643. See also J. E. Neale, *Elizabethan House of Commons*, 286, and *Elizabeth I and her Parliaments*, i. 38-40.

lay support eighteen votes against twenty-one. Only the absence of four churchmen from the House decided the issue. The determination of the Marian bishops deserves to be recorded. Only one of this resolute group of men subsequently conformed. Resistance was stubborn among cathedral clergy, though only about two hundred of the parochial clergy were deprived. More clearly and unmistakably than ever before was it made evident that the ecclesiastical revolution could not be regarded as the work of the Church itself.[1]

*Prayer Book reissued*    The Prayer Book of 1552, now issued with revisions, henceforth determined the ritual of the Church. It was not the work of Convocation to revise or authorise it. The revising committee of clergy, from whatever source it derived its authority, got none from that body. Parliament, if it did not draft the revisions, had no hesitation in discussing the Book. The whole process of change embodied in the Acts of Supremacy and Uniformity was parliamentary. It shows no trace of ecclesiastical independence or initiative.

## iv

*The Act of Supremacy*    On the twin pillars of the Acts of Supremacy and Uniformity the Elizabethan Church was erected. Its nature and history necessitate an examination of their main provisions.[2] The Act of Supremacy begins in declaratory form. It treats the royal supremacy as an ancient authority of the Crown, recovered by the legislation of Henry VIII, and now once more restored after being resigned by Mary. Mary's statutes were repealed, and a series of specified statutes of the reigns of Henry VIII and Edward VI were revived. The Act of Supremacy of Henry VIII was not among these, but all foreign authority was abolished from the realm. All spiritual jurisdiction heretofore lawfully exercised within it was annexed to the Crown for ever. The Crown was empowered to issue commissions from time to time to exercise such authority. All ecclesiastics, lay officials, and persons in receipt of stipends from the Crown were required to take an oath of supremacy (extended by

[1] For a fuller account of these parliamentary proceedings, see H. Gee, *The Elizabethan Clergy and the Settlement of Religion*, ch. i; H. N. Birt, *The Elizabethan Religious Settlement*, ch. ii.

[2] See J. E. Neale, *The Elizabethan Acts of Supremacy and Uniformity*, 65 E.H.R. 304, and *Elizabeth I and her Parliaments*, i. 51 ff.

a statute of 1563 to every person in orders, graduates of universities, schoolmasters, lawyers, officers of courts of law, sheriffs, and members of the House of Commons), accepting the Queen as "only supreme governor of this realm and all other of her Highness' dominions and countries, as well in all spiritual and ecclesiastical things or causes as temporal", promising to her faith and true allegiance, and repudiating all foreign jurisdiction and authority. Penalties were annexed to refusal to take the oath. Defence of any foreign jurisdiction was punishable on a scale by which a second offence was a breach of praemunire, and a third became treason.[1]

The Act of Uniformity restored the Prayer Book of 1552, *The Act* enjoined its use in all cathedrals, parish churches, and chapels, *of Uni-* penalised clergy who refused to use it or spoke in derogation of it *formity* and others who caused any unauthorised ritual to be followed, interrupted services where it was used, or showed disrespect of it. Attendance at parish churches was commanded on Sundays and holy days, under penalty of one shilling for each offence. Bishops and other ecclesiastical judges were to enforce the Act by spiritual censures. Temporal penalties were enforceable by judges of assize, and by local magistrates in places which the judges did not visit.[2]

This settlement presents certain obvious points of difference *Nature* from that made by Henry VIII. The title of "Supreme Head" is *of the* abandoned. "There's a great difference", observed Selden over *royal* half a century later, "between head of the Church and supreme *supremacy* governor. . . . Conceive it thus, there is in the Kingdom of England a college of physicians: the King is supreme governor of those, but not head of them, nor president of the college, nor the best physician."[3] How far was such a distinction drawn at the time? It was emphasised by the Queen herself in Injunctions issued in 1559. She denounced the suggestion that the oath of supremacy implied acceptance of an "authority and power of ministry of divine service in the church". It meant only "under God to have the sovereignty and rule over all manner of persons born within these her realms". That, she asserted, was all that her father had claimed.[4]

---

[1] Gee and Hardy, 442-58; Prothero, *Statutes and Constitutional Documents, 1558-1625*, 1-13; Tanner, 130-35.
[2] Gee and Hardy, 458-67; Prothero, 13-20; Tanner, 136-9.
[3] Prothero, 412.          [4] Prothero, 189.

If these latter words were true, however, her supremacy was the same as his, the Crown stood in 1559 just where it had stood in 1535, and the change of style made no difference, for Henry VIII had never claimed the *potestas ordinis.*

*How far different from that of Henry VIII*

It is, moreover, to be observed that the Act giving effect to the submission of the clergy, revived by the Act of Supremacy, contained mention of the headship, and grounded it on the law of God. It is therefore at least arguable that "Supreme Head" and "Supreme Governor" meant the same thing. What that thing was ought to be gathered from the interpretation placed upon it by Henry himself, as well as by his daughter's reassuring explanation. While it is true that he had not asserted himself to be a priest or to be the source of sacerdotal authority, his use of the *potestas jurisdictionis* had made the distinction between the two powers somewhat unreal. The King had never administered a sacrament, but he had prescribed what sacraments were to be administered. Without claiming to be the source of the Church's teaching authority, he had largely determined what it should teach. His was no mere external control, administrative and judicial, over the organisation, property, and judicial competence of the Church. It was a control over its mind and spirit as well as over its body. There seems no reason to suppose that, for all the change of title, the supremacy resumed by Elizabeth connoted anything less.[1]

*Method of its exercise*

It is the method of its exercise that counts. With Henry that had been a matter mainly of personal choice. He acted indifferently with ecclesiastical and lay advisers, relying in the last resort on that knowledge of "God's learning" in which he had been bred, and which he had so masterfully displayed. Such a part could hardly be played by a woman, and by a woman who, like Elizabeth, had little interest in theology and was fundamentally indifferent to religion. On its external side, the royal supremacy presented a simple and easy task. The election of bishops, the work of Convocation, the taxation of the clergy, their payments by way of annates and first-fruits, and the activity of ecclesiastical courts, resumed, on the whole, the aspect they had presented in Henry's later years. It was otherwise with matters of ritual and dogma. In these, Elizabeth did not, and could not, resume her father's freedom of action and amplitude of authority. Except for the English Litany, the ritual of the Church

[1] The whole question is discussed in E. T. Davies, *Episcopacy and the Royal Supremacy in the Church of England in the XVI Century.*

with its doctrinal implications was based not on that existing under Henry VIII, but on that of Edward VI's last year. It was contained in a schedule to an Act of Parliament, the amendments to which had been discussed in a subsequent Parliament. Authority to determine the nature of heresy was limited by the Act of Supremacy itself. Parliament declared that nothing was to be adjudged heretical unless it had been declared so by Scripture, or by any one of the first four General Councils of the Church, any subsequent General Council whose decision was supported by Scripture, or Parliament itself, provided that Convocation assented to its decision.[1] While the structure and working of ecclesiastical organisation could be regarded as having been fully re-committed to the Crown by statute, and left to royal management as in the days of Henry VIII, it was not so clear that the Crown possessed a similar plenitude of power regarding ritual and dogma. On these questions, the settlement of 1559 was not Henrician but Edwardian, based on the work not of a Supreme Head exercising personal control, but of a Parliament which had entered the field in the reign of a minor incapable of retaining that sole, individual, and virtually limitless power which the will and intelligence of his masterful father had annexed. Moreover, it was probable that, should the Crown's control over the external organisation of the Church be employed as a barrier against further advance towards changes in ritual and dogma, or used to effect changes which Parliament could not approve, a House of Commons more radical than the Crown would attack that control and insist on its own competence to deal with questions even of external organisation. If that were to happen, the hierarchy, the diocesan system, ecclesiastical discipline, the authority of Convocation and courts, would all alike be in peril. It would rest with Parliament to say whether they should remain or perish.

The atmosphere of Elizabeth's earlier years as queen presaged *Imposi-* no such conflict. The Crown, Parliament, the bishops, and the *tion of the* *Eliza-* majority of the nation except in the conservative North, all moved *bethan* in harmony. In 1559 a visitation, largely carried out by laymen, *settlement* imposed the Oath of Supremacy and the Book of Common Prayer,[2]

[1] Act of Supremacy, cl. xx; Prothero, 12.
[2] Gee, 40-6, 96-102. The commissioners' proceedings in the province of Canterbury are described by C. G. Bayne, *Visitation of the Province of Canterbury, 1559,* 28 E.H.R. 636.

and endeavoured to give effect to a series of royal Injunctions, dealing, for example, with the prohibition of processions and of the use of images and relics, clerical marriage, public worship, and—potentially the most important question of all—ecclesiastical vestments, which were to be the same as those worn in the last year of Edward VI.[1] As the Marian bishops, the most obstinate opponents of the new order, were deprived for refusal to take the Oath of Supremacy, a new episcopate, composed largely of men of definitely Protestant convictions, was elected and consecrated in their stead. The difficulty arising from the omission of the Act of Uniformity to revive the Ordinal of 1550 was overcome by a royal dispensation to confirm the consecration of Parker, the new Archbishop of Canterbury.[2] It became the task of the new bishops to enforce conformity, to issue successive documents of instructions for the maintenance of ecclesiastical order as now reformed, to draft, though not to impose, statements of belief, and to ordain new clergy as quickly as possible to serve the parishes under their supervision, many of which were destitute of pastors. The commissioners appointed by the Crown under the Act of Supremacy in July 1559 supplemented the labours of the bishops by enforcing the Acts of Supremacy and Uniformity and executing royal orders on points of detail.[3] By the combined action of Crown and Parliament, Council, ecclesiastical commissioners, and episcopate, a prolonged and largely successful attempt was made to unify the religious life of the nation in a State Church, independent of Rome but subject to the Crown, into whose fold the mass of the laity could without violence be shepherded. Administration was tolerant and lenient. It was sought rather to regulate conduct than conscience.

*Catholic recusancy*    Conduct and conscience are not, however, thus easily separable. Leniently as it might be administered, the law underlying the Elizabethan settlement had to enforce at least a minimum standard of external conformity. Many of the Queen's subjects could not bring themselves to conform even to that minimum standard, though the majority did. There was not wanting in any district

[1] Prothero, 188.

[2] W. H. Frere, *History of the English Church in the Reigns of Elizabeth and James I*, 47; Birt, 243.

[3] Prothero, 227-32; Tanner, 367-72; R. G. Usher, *Rise and Fall of the High Commission*, 27.

of England a handful of resolute spirits who determined to follow the lead of the Marian bishops. In the North and North-West, under the influence and protection of great aristocratic families who held fast to the old faith, they were so numerous that strict enforcement of the law was impossible. In varying strength, therefore, Catholic recusancy continued to exist. It was impossible that it should become a constitutional opposition. Ousted from office under the Crown and from the House of Commons by the operation of the Oath of Supremacy, Catholic recusants were denied constitutional means of expressing their dissent. As a body, they could at most seek to profit by the lenient administration of the law, pay their recusancy fines,[1] and strive to maintain the faith by maintaining side by side with the State Church an unofficial and inconspicuous sectarian organisation. Many, uncertain as yet how the Papacy would treat the Queen and the Anglican Church, were content to render a hesitant conformity. Little or nothing occurred to affect further the legal position of Catholicism in England until 1569. Then the North and North-West, still the home and hope of English recusancy, rose in rebellion under the Earls of Northumberland and Westmorland. The presence of Mary Queen of Scots, now a refugee after Langside, inspired in many the ambition of having her declared Elizabeth's successor, or even of placing her on the throne. In Rome, the inflexible Pius V was making up his mind to pronounce definitive sentence against the heretic Queen. Elizabeth's case was tried at Rome, and the Bull *Regnans in Excelsis* (February 1570) pronounced and published sentence of excommunication and deposition against her.[2] In 1571 came the Ridolfi Plot for her dethronement.

These events, associating Catholicism with treason, inaugurated against the unhappy recusants, most of whom were far enough removed from being traitors, a flood of penal statutes which, gathering momentum as it ran, drove its torrential course for the rest of the reign and extended throughout the whole of the succeeding century. To be reconciled to Rome or introduce or attempt to

*Recusancy laws*

---

[1] W. P. M. Kennedy, *Fines under the Elizabethan Act of Uniformity*, 33 E.H.R. 526-8, concludes that on the whole an attempt was made regularly to impose recusancy fines on both Catholics and Protestants who absented themselves from their parish churches.

[2] Prothero, 195-6 (Latin version); Tanner, 144-6 (English translation).

give effect to the bull became in 1571 treason in principals, misprision of treason in their confederates.[1] From 1573 began the English missions of priests from the refugee seminary of Douai, moved in 1578 to Rheims with a daughter college at Rome. Against these devoted men Council and episcopate directed their fullest rigours. In 1577-8, three Douai missionaries suffered the death of traitors. For each diocese in England lists of recusants were compiled. In 1581 during the mission of the Jesuits Campion and Parsons, Parliament enacted that those who were reconciled or caused others to reconcile themselves to Rome were traitors. The saying or hearing of mass was penalised by fine and imprisonment, mere recusancy by the enormous fine of £20 monthly.[2] In 1581 Campion and other martyrs perished. The government tried leniency so far as it could. But in the atmosphere of Spanish and Catholic plotting which soon enveloped the country, Parliament sharpened the law further, and made it treasonable for seminary priests to remain in England, felonious to maintain them, and treasonable in English subjects educated abroad to fail to return and take the Oath of Supremacy.[3] About 1591 persecution reached its height. In 1593 recusants were ordered to remain within five miles of their homes on pain of banishment, and persons suspected of being Jesuits or seminary priests could be imprisoned until they submitted to examination.[4] In sum, the Elizabethan legislation excluded Catholics from public office, the House of Commons, the universities, and the professions; made the presence of their priests treasonable, attendance at Catholic worship a felony, and mere absence from Anglican worship punishable by a fine so heavy as to crush any Catholic family of wealth and influence on which the government chose to inflict it.[5] Catholicism was probably rescued from extinction by the missionaries, but it survived only as the creed of a disheartened and powerless minority, denied the protection of the law, powerless to alter it, and condemned to passive acceptance of its disabilities, save where it involved itself in conspiracies as detestable to most Catholics as to their triumphant persecutors.

---

[1] Prothero, 60-63; Tanner, 146-50.     [2] Prothero, 74-6; Tanner, 152-4.
[3] Gee and Hardy, 485-92; Prothero, 83-6; Tanner, 154-9.
[4] Gee and Hardy, 498-508; Prothero, 92-3; Tanner, 159-63.
[5] Sir J. F. Stephen, *History of the Criminal Law*, ii. 484-6.

The dissent of Protestants presented an essentially different *Constitu-*
problem, not merely religious and political, but constitutional as *tional*
well. Protestantism was heavily armed with power. In Convoca- *Protestant*
tion, even among the bishops themselves, in Parliament, in *radicalism*
Council, in offices under the Crown, and in local government,
men qualified for authority by their acceptance of the statutes of
1559 were in a position from which they could hope to determine
the practice and doctrine of the Church to which they adhered.
If the harmony which at the outset governed the relations of
Crown, Parliament, Council, Church, and courts were to be disturbed, the very nature of the royal supremacy might come into
question. Catholic recusants could have no theory of the royal
supremacy save that it could have no valid existence. Protestants,
accepting that supremacy, might find themselves forced to define
it more closely than had yet been attempted. Two conflicting views
were obviously possible. One was that the Crown's supremacy
over the Church was entirely different in kind from its authority in
secular affairs. Parliament had restored and recognised it, but the
Crown, once in possession, could use it out of Parliament, through
ecclesiastical means exclusively, and without any reference to
Parliament except such as it chose to make. The other was that
there was no constitutional difference between the authority of
the Crown over the Church and any other department of royal
power. It was vested in the Crown by Parliament; it could be
controlled by Parliament; it could in the last resort be abridged
and restricted by Parliament, even in opposition to the Crown.
One view accorded the Crown the initiative and the choice of
means in the exercise of the royal supremacy. The other deprived
it of the initiative, transferred the initiative to Parliament, and
made the royal supremacy essentially no longer personal but
parliamentary.[1] The only conception there was no room for in the
constitution was that the Church possessed an authority independent alike of Crown and Parliament.

The difficulties which were henceforth to attend the exercise of *Its*
the royal supremacy gradually revealed themselves as the reign *demands*
progressed. It was far from easy for the Crown to work even

[1] The question how far the ecclesiastical supremacy was royal, and how
far it was shared by Parliament, was the cause of doubts as to the ambit
of the suspending and dispensing powers, reflected in the *Case of the Seven
Bishops*, (p. 266 below). There Powell, J. held that there was no difference
between the suspending power in ecclesiastical and in any other causes.

through ecclesiastical channels. Purged of the Marian bishops and the recusant clergy, the reformed Church, reinforced by new blood, advanced pretensions to regulate its affairs by its own action. Bishops like Grindal of London, Cox of Ely, and Pilkington of Durham, and an active minority, at least, of the clergy, looked forward to a reformation along more radical lines, and influenced by continental practice.[1] Almost at once the controversy as to ecclesiastical vestments, already raised by Hooper as Bishop of Gloucester in Edward VI's reign, again broke out. With it questions arose on such points as the position of the altar, kneeling at communion, the observance of holy days, the use of the cross in baptism and of the ring in marriage. Claims to innovate by ecclesiastical authority in these and similar matters were made in the first reformed Convocation of the reign in 1563.[2] Both bishops and lower clergy pressed for change, and Grindal was of opinion that "it can be done in the synod". On a division, the reformers won by forty-three to thirty-five. When proxies were counted, the decision was reversed by the narrowest of majorities—fifty-nine to fifty-eight. The forms prescribed by the Prayer Book had been thus barely saved. A body of Thirty-Nine Articles of doctrine, based on the Forty-Two of Edward VI, was compiled and issued. A draft scheme for the administration of ecclesiastical discipline over both clergy and laity was likewise discussed, but came to nothing. Parliament, sitting at the same time, was more preoccupied with repressing recusants than supporting reformers, and misliked clerical proposals to enforce attendance at church and to augment poor benefices. If the attitude of Parliament was as yet unhelpful, that of the Crown was positively hostile to further reform. Changes repudiating the Catholic tradition and emphasising the Protestant character of the Church were antipathetic to the Queen and her lay advisers. Thus in 1565 the government ordered the bishops to take united action in maintaining ecclesiastical discipline. Reluctantly they obeyed. In March 1566 the main points of the government's demands were embodied in *Advertisements* issued by Parker, Archbishop of Canterbury, prescribing rules as to preaching, vestments, kneeling at communion, and the like.[3] Importance chiefly attached to the use of vestments. Many men could not regard these as matters of indifference. To use them was

---

[1] See W. M. Southgate, *The Marian Exiles and the Influence of John Calvin*, 27 *Hist.* 148.          [2] Prothero, 191; Tanner, 164-5; Frere, 98-9.
[3] Gee and Hardy, 467-70; Prothero, 191-4.

to assert for the clergy sacerdotal functions which were thought inconsistent with Protestant principles. Thus the enforcement of the *Advertisements* led to resistance, to deprivations, and, before long, to the formation of congregations worshipping in defiance of the law, outside the communion of the English Church. In June 1567 a "conventicle" was for the first time broken up and its members arrested and punished. Meanwhile within the Church there remained many merely outward conformists, men of less tenacity of character and greater respect for authority, but eager none the less to work for further reformation by synodal action. Puritanism had appeared in both its separatist and its Anglican forms.

The years 1566-7 are a constitutional divide. The episcopate, *Enforce-* after its early hesitation, was beginning to align itself with the *ment of the* Crown and become the instrument of royal authority rather than *govern-* of the Church's will. Unlike so many of the inferior clergy, it *policy* ceased to put forward serious claims to ecclesiastical independence. Though the Roman objection to Anglican orders had hardly yet been formulated, the bishops found in the royal supremacy their surest defence against imputations on the validity of their position. They were from now on to shelter themselves under that authority against reformers who sought to impugn episcopal government and enable the Church, through unconstrained synodal action, to declare its own will in matters of ritual and belief. Supplementing the unenthusiastic labours of the bishops, those of the commissioners, preponderantly laymen, appointed under the Act of Supremacy, helped to extinguish the idea of an autonomous Church.

Against this alliance of Crown, Council, and episcopate, it *Parlia-* was, however, possible to appeal to a Parliament less adverse to *mentary* reform. As opposition to the royal policy was silenced in Con- *of the* vocation, Parliament began to intervene in the ecclesiastical sphere. *reformers* In 1566 several bills on ecclesiastical matters were introduced into the Commons.[1] One, giving statutory force to the Thirty-Nine Articles, got to the Lords before it was stopped by the Queen's intervention. In 1571 parliamentary encroachment on the royal supremacy was renewed in a bill for reformation of the Book of Common Prayer which the Commons in vain sought the Queen's leave to proceed with.[2] A bill giving statutory force to the

---

[1] Frere, 132-3.     [2] Frere, 161; Tanner, 565-7.

Thirty-Nine Articles once more passed the Commons.[1] Five others embodying the aims of the reforming party came into debate, though the opposition of the Lords and the Queen prevented any important legislation from resulting. An Act requiring clerical subscription to the Articles indeed obtained the royal assent; but these had meanwhile been amended by the action of Convocation alone.[2] The plan of legalising a code of Canon Law by parliamentary authority again came to nothing. A now docile Convocation issued a collection of canons on ecclesiastical discipline, which, possessing no basis in statute, and lacking even royal assent, offered an easy mark to the attacks of lawyers and parliamentarians at a later date.[3]

*The growth of opposition*

Like the wearing of vestments and the use of the Prayer Book, the enforcement of subscription to the Articles encountered stubborn opposition, and led to numerous further deprivations, including, of course, cases of Catholic as well as Protestant dissent. In 1572 the reformers in the Commons, stimulated during the session by an able though venomous Puritan *Admonition to Parliament*, again intervened with a bill for rites and ceremonies to supersede the Prayer Book.[4] Again the Queen's prohibition against the discussion of ecclesiastical affairs cut short their debates. The government spurred on the bishops to more rigid enforcement of the Act of Uniformity and to suppression of the *Admonition*. Meanwhile opposition to the Crown's ecclesiastical policy showed itself both inside and outside the Church. Within, the practice of "prophesyings"—unauthorised meetings for prayer and exposition of Scripture—seemed to be growing, and some of the bishops regarded it with a lenient eye.[5] Even more dangerous was the tendency for an informal Presbyterian organisation to introduce itself. Grindal, translated from York to Canterbury as Parker's successor in 1575, proved an uncompliant instrument of royal policy, and during his period of office a privately compiled *Book of Discipline* provided a pattern for non-episcopal organisation within the Church.[6] Outside the Church, numbers of harried and embittered dissenters, including some of the ablest and best as

[1] Frere, 162.        [2] Prothero, 64-5.        [3] Frere, 165-8.
[4] Prothero, 198-9. See also A. F. Scott Pearson, *Thomas Cartwright and Elizabethan Puritanism*, 58 ff.        [5] Scott Pearson, 156 ff.
[6] Scott Pearson, 257. It is to be noted that Elizabethan Presbyterianism was mainly of a local parochial type (Scott Pearson, 76).

well as some of the most ignorant and most factious of Englishmen, carried on an impoverished and insecure existence, hardly likely to breed wise heads or generous hearts. The founders of English separatism—men like Robert Browne and Robert Harrison —believed in ending wholly the dependence of the Church on the State, and in "reformation without tarrying for any".[1] If they did not look to Parliament, Anglican Puritans did.

The Parliament of 1576 again entered the lists with a bill for *The reforming ecclesiastical discipline. But the Queen's statement that government's* it was for the bishops to consider the matter brought it to an end.[2] *success* In 1581 the Commons, joined by the Lower House of Convocation, sought for redress of grievances arising out of ecclesiastical discipline. Again the Queen warned the Commons off the field.[3] The prolonged controversy was now beginning, in some measure, to turn in her favour. On Grindal's death in 1583 she at last got at Canterbury a man after her own heart. John Whitgift, the new archbishop, was to give the Church twenty years of resolute government. His hand, strengthened by disciplinary Articles approved by the Crown, fell heavily on the nascent presbyterian organisation within the Church, and on irregularities in worship.

Extending beyond the action of Whitgift and the bishops, *The High* the campaign for conformity was waged by the commissioners *Commission* appointed under the Act of Supremacy. Delegation of the ecclesiastical jurisdiction of the Crown had been made under Henry VIII to Cromwell as Vicar-General, but this delegation to one person was not repeated, bodies of commissioners being appointed under Edward VI and Mary, in 1547, 1551, and 1557. The functions of these early commissioners were not defined by statute but by the terms of their commissions from the Crown. Differing in this respect from its predecessors, the first commission of Elizabeth, issued in 1559, was grounded on statute. Nineteen commissioners were appointed, any six of whom could act, provided one were of a named quorum, composed of two bishops, one royal official, and two lawyers. Similar commissions were issued in 1562, 1572, and 1576.[4]

What was thus established was primarily a body exercising

---

[1] Scott Pearson, 213.     [2] Prothero, 209.     [3] Prothero, 210.
[4] For earlier commissions, see Usher, 20-31, 42-6, 52 ff. For the forms of Elizabethan commissions, see Prothero, 227-40.

*Its juris-* administrative jurisdiction, or rather a series of such bodies
*diction* appointed from time to time. Their business was to remove dis-
obedient clergy, coerce dissent among the laity, punish offences
against the Articles, and exercise a censorship over the press. But
the line between administrative and private jurisdiction was hard
to draw. The commissioners came to deal with disputes and
petitions, and to create a procedure for dealing with them.
Insensibly they developed the formalities of a court. From 1570
they became known as the Court of High Commission, and stood
forth as a tribunal independent of other courts and of the Privy
Council. In this form, the Court of High Commission, reconstituted in 1583, supplemented the work of ecclesiastical courts in
the work of coercion. It was pre-eminently an instrument of State,
exercising the ecclesiastical jurisdiction of the Crown in first
instance, while appellate jurisdiction over ecclesiastical courts
proper was entrusted to the High Court of Delegates.[1] Much
objection was taken to its inquisitorial procedure, and above all to
the oath *ex-officio* by which the accused was compelled to answer
incriminating interrogatories addressed to him by his judges.[2]
Cecil himself protested to Whitgift against this practice, but the
archbishop had his way.[3]

*The*         Cecil's was not the only criticism which was disregarded. The
*decline of* Commons petitioned in favour of deprived ministers in 1584, and
*opposition* tried again to alter the ritual of the Church by statute, but got
only a royal reprimand for answer.[4] Another attempt to modify
discipline and worship was made in a sweeping bill introduced by
the radical leader Cope in 1587.[5] Again the Queen suppressed discussion, and reiterated the principle that the amendment of the
Church belonged to herself and the clergy. By this time she had
thoroughly tamed the episcopate and Convocation. Radicalism
within the Church was subsiding. Outside the Church, Separatism
developed views violently repudiating royal supremacy in any
shape or form, denying the authority of any secular power in the

---

[1] For the Court of Delegates, see Holdsworth, i. 603-5. The evolution of the
Commission is fully dealt with in Usher, ch. iii-v, and there is a short account
in Holdsworth, i. 605-7.

[2] M. H. Maguire, *The Oath ex-officio*, in *Essays presented to C. H. McIlwain*,
199.                                         [3] Prothero, 213-14; Tanner, 373-4.

[4] Prothero, 215 ff; Tanner, 191-4.

[5] Tanner. 570-2.

affairs of the Church, and repudiating the idea of a single all-embracing national Church. Such views went far beyond the point up to which parliamentary support was forthcoming, and Separatism was further discredited by the virulence of the tracts emanating from *Martin Marprelate* in 1588.[1] Parliament itself legislated in 1592 against sectaries, the sectarian leaders Barrow and Greenwood, with Penry, the principal author of *Marprelate*, suffered death, and many of their followers only escaped punishment by flight. The interest of the Commons in the fortunes of the radicals within the Church tended to wane. Though in 1589, 1593, 1597, and 1601 efforts on their behalf were renewed, the Queen persisted in her steadfast refusal to allow the Commons any initiative in matters affecting her ecclesiastical supremacy, and had her way.[2] The supporters of the more extreme Protestants remained an ineffective minority.

Here matters rested at the end of her long reign. Coercion seemed to have done its work. Crown, hierarchy, and Convocation stood together. Parliament had effected nothing. It would be unfair to contend that conformity was solely the product of coercion. A generation was now growing up to which the Elizabethan Church was not a mere enforced compromise, born of political necessity, and maintained by the coercive power of the State, but a true expression of the prevailing religious sentiment of the nation. They began to find a warrant for it in Scripture, in Christian history, and in the nature of human society. Such views were brilliantly set forth in Hooker's *Ecclesiastical Polity*. Thus there was instilled into the Anglican Church a conception of its own position which, if not wholly justified by its past, was to inspire and consecrate its future. Its claim to be national and comprehensive was not unreal. It gave expression to the feeling of national unity and patriotism which flowered in the Elizabethan age. Familiar and beautiful forms of worship endeared its services to those who administered and those who heard them. The royal supremacy, maintaining a Church system become congenial to the majority of the clergy and the mass of the nation, might well, if preserved in its Elizabethan form, be successfully defended.[3]

*Situation at the close of Elizabeth's reign*

[1] Extracts printed by Tanner, 195-6.     [2] Frere, 277-85.
[3] Hooker's position is given detailed examination in F. J. Shirley, *Richard Hooker and Contemporary Political Ideas.*

# CHAPTER III

## THE ZENITH OF THE TUDOR MONARCHY

### i

*External emergencies* THE government of England after 1529 was developed under the impulses of emergency and achievement. The emergency was mainly, though not wholly, to be ascribed to the religious revolution. By the twice-repeated breach with Rome, England became an outlaw from Catholic Europe. In 1535 a bull of excommunication was published against Henry VIII, and Catholic princes were invited to co-operate in invading his country and restoring it to the Roman obedience. In 1570 Elizabeth incurred the sentence pronounced by *Regnans in Excelsis*. The threat was always more alarming in appearance than in reality. Combined action by the great continental reigning houses of Hapsburg and Valois was paralysed by an inveterate mutual enmity which proved the salvation of England. No invading force from Spain ever set foot on English soil. For a moment, France seemed to present a greater danger. Until 1560 she had, as Spain never had, a client-state in the British Isles. United to France by the ties of the "Auld Alliance" and since 1548 by the marriage of the Dauphin Francis to Mary Queen of Scots, great-granddaughter of Henry VII and therefore in 1559 the strongest Catholic claimant to Elizabeth's throne, the Scottish kingdom seemed to present, as under Henry VIII, a valuable base of operations against schismatic England. The death of Francis dissolved the personal union. Even before then, the "Auld Alliance" was obsolescent and discredited. A nationalist and Protestant opposition faced Mary on her return to Scotland in 1561. By 1567 she was a refugee in England, her claims to the Crown of which now became a subject of merely speculative interest to foreign Catholics. From 1567 to 1581 a series of Protestant regents, closely linked with the English government, ruled in the name of her Protestant son James VI, who, on assuming the reins of government for himself, was careful not to imperil his claim to the English throne by too obvious association with England's Catholic enemies. In Ireland alone did a foreign invader ever violate the island territories of the English Crown after the breach with Rome. Yet the nightmare of foreign invasion perpetually hung before the eyes of the English government and the mass of its subjects. It led to a resort to extraordinary and even desperate measures for ensuring public safety, and to acquiescence in a system which might often strain the letter of the law.

For the peril from without was accompanied by much more *Internal* real perils from within. Attachment to the ancient Church was *emergencies* widespread. Sometimes it assumed the formidable guise of armed risings, as in the Pilgrimage of Grace in 1536, the revolt of Devon and Cornwall in 1549, and the rebellion of the northern earls in 1569. The final failure of armed opposition inaugurated a series of plots aimed at dethroning Elizabeth and setting up the Queen of Scots in her stead. Mary's marriage to the Duke of Norfolk and her elevation as Queen, or at least the settlement of the succession on her children by this marriage, were among the objects of the northern leaders in 1569. Elizabeth's deposition and Mary's accession and marriage to Norfolk were aimed at in the Ridolfi Plot of 1571. The '80's were a decade of terror. Plots for Mary's release and the Queen's assassination multiplied. National resentment led in 1584 to the formation of a voluntary Association pledged to withstand and avenge attempts against her. In the following year Parliament legalised the Association, authorised the creation of a special commission to condemn participants in conspiracies or invasions, and excluded from the succession persons participating in such enterprises or in whose interest they might be formed. The execution of Mary in 1587 after trial by an extraordinary commission for complicity in Babington's plot, and the failure of the Armada in the next year, dissipated the peril without altogether allaying the national panic it had aroused. A taint of conspiracy and treason still clung to the Queen's Catholic subjects at the end of her reign.

Religion did not stand alone as a cause of the insecurity which *Economic* troubled the mind of that age. It was a period of rapid and often *and social* ruthless social and economic changes. The level of prices was *problems* rising for ill-understood reasons connected mainly with the influx of precious metals to Europe from South America, while the government's resort from time to time to debasements of the currency exacerbated the evil. Townsmen suffered from the dislocating affects of the increased use of capital in industry. Countrymen were the victims of an analogous process in agriculture. Enclosures of arable or common land for sheep-farming drove the rural population from their ancient homes. Charitable endowments which might have served to relieve distress had been confiscated. The problem of poverty presented itself sharply to a society hitherto content to leave it to the Church. It got unsympathetic treatment from a Parliament representing mainly the propertied classes. "Valiant beggars" threatened the maintenance of local order. In 1549 the government of Edward VI had to suppress an agrarian rebellion led by Robert Kett in Norfolk, and ramifying through almost the whole of southern England. Social grievances contributed to the discontent enlisted by movements not ostensibly social in their aims. The destruction of an ancient system of property and of the vested interests it had sheltered beset with perennial difficulties a government sometimes not unresponsive towards the grievances of its subjects.

*Achievements of the later Tudor period*

Ringed about with foreign enemies, threatened at home by religious and social discontents, England of this age resembled a beleaguered city, part of whose inhabitants cannot be trusted. Yet such a picture would if unrelieved be too dark. The shores of the island realm remained inviolate. No prolonged foreign war drained its wealth and blunted its enterprise from Elizabeth's accession to the days of the Armada. Its overseas commerce, in large part a preserve of foreigners during the Middle Ages, was, as the sixteenth century advanced, captured and developed by Englishmen. While the Merchant Adventurers ousted the German Hanse from control of North European trade, new companies were chartered by the Crown to deal with Muscovy (1555), the Baltic (1579), the Levant (1581), and the East Indies (1600). Maritime enterprise bred a race of hardy and ambitious seamen, and enriched the land which sent them forth. The Narrow Seas maintained a valuable fishing industry. The Arctic was furrowed by the keels of the earliest English whalers. But it was the limitless expanse of the great oceans which fired the imagination of sixteenth-century English seafarers. Early dreams of a North-East or a North-

West Passage to the Indies faded, and Englishmen set themselves to combat the pretensions of Catholic Spain and Portugal to a monopoly of the "New World called America". Piracy and slave-trading gave place to efforts for the more desirable gains of permanent overseas settlement. The earliest attempt to found a colony on the American mainland occurred in the reign of the Virgin Queen after whom it was named.

New wealth was created at home as well as abroad. London was *Prosperity* becoming a money market where the operations of government *of later* could be financed. New industries both extractive and secondary *Tudor* were planted, sometimes with the assistance of religious refugees *England* from the Continent. The manufacture of soap, glass, salt, alum, and saltpetre, to take only a few examples, obtained the direct encouragement of the State. While enclosure led to maldistribution of wealth between classes, it enriched the total national productivity. New landowners, if more rapacious than the old, were more efficient in the exploitation of their estates. Wool was the product of greatest value, but tillage was improved by men anxious to swell their rent-rolls, who sunk capital plentifully in fencing, draining, and stocking their land. Opulent manor houses and town residences testified not only to the wealth but also to the cultivated taste of the ruling classes of England. The prolonged though precarious peace which Tudor England won for herself nurtured almost every form of artistic, literary, and intellectual achievement. Colet, More, Grocyn, and Linacre had planted the seeds of the English Renaissance while the century was young. In the succeeding age, enriched meantime by the work of Ascham, Surrey, and Wyatt, it blossomed in the achievements of Spenser, Shakespeare, and the Elizabethan dramatists. The Renaissance meant more than merely the perfecting of expression in art and letters. Conjoined with the influence of a Reformation which, in its better aspects, set before its adherents a singularly elevated type of Christian character and dignified anew the commonest occupations of mankind, it helped to create a new conception of human excellence. The chivalric tradition in education mingled with ideals borrowed from the highest thought of antiquity. Courtesy and breeding shewn forth in external behaviour, proficiency both in bodily exercises and in polite accomplishments, were blended with a keen and delicate sense of duty towards the State to form

4

that happy combination of qualities which the Elizabethan aristocracy and gentry at their best strove to attain. Newcomers into
the caste found its ideals and obligations clearly reflected in the
education, the tastes, and the pursuits which it followed. That
co-operation of the subject with the Crown on which Tudor
government rested gave constant opportunity for the exercise, as
servants of the Crown, members of Parliament, and magistrates,
of the capacities of a ruling class which conceived of itself almost
as a Platonic aristocracy.[1]

*Constitu-*     Both the emergencies which beset Tudor rule in this period and
*tional*     the prosperity and glory it gave to its subjects have to be borne in
*nature of*
*later*     mind when any attempt is made to pronounce on its general
*Tudor*     character or investigate the details of its structure and working.
*rule*     It was, even when most rigorous and authoritative, much more
than a brutal dictatorship created by fear and governing by force.
Henry VIII and his children were never mere lawless tyrants, and
the common description of their rule as the "Tudor despotism"
seriously obscures its true nature. It is of course evident that
under their sway the arm of government was immensely
strengthened, and royal action in the public interest often passed
beyond the still indeterminate frontiers of the law. The Council,
its offshoots, and the Court of High Commission, reinforced by
occasional extraordinary tribunals, and forming a vastly extended
executive system, acted as the mainspring of government. Law
was plentifully laid down by royal proclamation, the boundaries between which and the law laid down by Parliament and
known to the Common Law courts were far from easy to define.
Proclamation acquired for a time and for certain purposes the
force of statute. Statutes themselves conferred on the King authority to suspend or amend their terms, even had he not possessed
analogous powers by Prerogative. Trade, industry, and the press
fell beneath the control of the Crown. Within uncertain limits,
the Crown could even affect the property of the subject, as for
example by impositions, benevolences, forced loans, ship-money,

---

[1] For this aspect of Tudor society, see F. Caspari, *Humanism and the Social
Order in Tudor England*, ch. i. It need hardly be added that Renaissance influence had its less attractive aspects. See R. B. Merriman, *Life and Letters
of Thomas Cromwell*, i. 85-7; E. R. Adair, *William Thomas*, in *Tudor Studies*,
155. Reference may also be made to D. M. Brodie, *Edmund Dudley*, in
4 *T.R.H.S.* xv. 133. A recent study of the "new men" has been made in
W. G. Zeefeld, *The Foundations of Tudor Policy*.

and the grant of charters and monopolies. Its police powers included those of arbitrary arrest, detention, and examination of suspects. Torture was used to extort evidence, and a formidable and effective spy-system, delation and domiciliary visits threw their shadow over the private affairs of men. The courts emanating from the Council freely employed inquisitorial processes alien to the Common Law and doubtfully valid by statute. In times of crisis the subject lost his legal rights completely and fell under the control of military men exercising martial law. The executive dominated local government and thrust its influence into Parliament, striving to ensure satisfactory results at elections, creating new constituencies, examining returns, manipulating parliamentary procedure, suppressing unwelcome debate, intimidating truculent members. The legislative functions of Parliament were debased to the tasks of condemning the King's suspected enemies or even his profitless servants to the penalties of attainder, and of enabling him to repudiate his debts or to cover royal acts which outraged justice with a cloak of legality.[1] Tudor government undeniably wore a dictatorial, harsh, and remorseless aspect. It put reason of State above the letter of the law and rated the public interest, real or alleged, immeasurably higher than the rights of the subject. The case is not really altered much by the argument that the majority of the nation acquiesced in the resort to arbitrary rule. That argument, moreover, valid enough as far as it goes, fails to cover all the facts of Tudor government. For while it is true that the Tudor executive possessed itself of authority of every kind, it did not monopolise the exercise of power within the system which it controlled. Tudor government meant not only the development of the Council and its offshoots, but also of Parliament, which increased its activity, enlarged its competence, added to its privileges, and formalised its procedure. It meant also the development of local administration in the hands of the Justices of the Peace. In a word, it implied an insistence both on the personal and conciliar authority of the Crown, and on the necessary co-operation of the subject. Virtually unarmed, and inadequately supplied with money, the Tudors had to depend on and actively to promote such co-operation. Royal authority and popular consent were, as always, combined as the

[1] Pickthorn, *Henry VIII*, 137-9.

fundamental principles of the English State. Its organisation gave effect to both. The constitutional arrangements of the past were not destroyed to make room for a nakedly personal rule. But the conventions which surrounded them were changed. In the later Middle Ages constitutional ideas had emphasised the existence of parliamentary and legal checks on the Crown. The conventions which prevailed in the sixteenth century favoured the ascendancy of the Crown in government. Yet they never implied that the Crown could for every purpose stand or act alone. And if much that the Crown did was of doubtful legality, it is to be remembered that the frontiers between law and discretionary power were very imperfectly defined.

*Import-*
*ance of co-*
*operation*
*and consent*
　　The Tudor State therefore continued, constitutionally as well as politically, to rest on the consent and co-operation which underlay its creation. The Englishmen who rallied to the Crown against emergencies at home and abroad, and felt for it the loyalty which national achievement quickened into an obedience at once humble and proud, did not thereby surrender to a despotism. In its service they preserved the system of government inherited from the past. The system, in its essentials, continued not only unimpaired, but strengthened, while elsewhere in Europe systems similarly fashioned during the Middle Ages atrophied and perished, leaving the sole exercise of political power to centralised absolute monarchies.[1]

ii

*The*
*Crown*
　　In any detailed description of a constitution which laid so much emphasis on the personal authority of the sovereign, it is natural to begin with the position of the monarch himself. From him the powers of government are derived. In strict law kingship is perpetual. The King never dies. There is merely a demise of the Crown to a successor, in whom authority is immediately perfect without even an instant of intermission, and the incapacity of the monarch necessitates recourse to statute, for it is unknown to Common Law. In practice this conception is not fulfilled, nor has it been until very recent times. In the sixteenth century and long afterwards, the King's decease automatically brought

[1] Holdsworth, iv. 165-7.

government to a standstill. Parliament, if in existence, was dissolved. Officials, judges, and—after the breach with Rome—even bishops, found their authority terminated and had to seek new commissions. The King had an unfettered discretion in making appointments. He personally transacted much of the business of government, had a large degree of freedom in choosing the means by which his will was put into effect, and consulted his councillors as much or as little as he wished. His personal action was all-important. Under Edward VI, a minor, it was the weakness of Somerset's position that he was no more than a Protector, and the strength of his rival Warwick that he induced the King to shake off the control of his Council and act as though he were of full age.

A kingship controlling government in this highly personal *The* fashion had to be vigilant in its own protection, safeguard its *succession* position by grounding it firmly in the law, and look for the aid *to the* *throne* of its subjects in securing its tenure of the throne. The succession to the Crown in the days of the Tudor dynasty was never secure. After the death of Arthur, Prince of Wales, in 1502, the future Henry VIII was the sole surviving male heir of the royal line. Henry VIII's three legitimate children died without issue. Throughout Elizabeth's long reign, the throne hung on the chances of a single and oft-endangered life. Potential claimants with pedigrees extending back to the Houses of York and Plantagenet had awakened the jealous anxiety of her father. Others, of Tudor lineage, faced her sister Mary and herself. Mary's title was disputed in the name of Lady Jane Grey, great-granddaughter of Henry VII through his youngest child, Mary, wife of Charles Brandon, Duke of Suffolk, and the right of her elder sister, Lady Catherine Grey, was, though less seriously, advanced against Elizabeth during her earlier years as Queen. More dangerous were the claims derived from Henry VII through his elder daughter, Margaret Tudor, married in 1504 to James IV, King of Scots. From this first marriage of Margaret, Mary Queen of Scots traced her descent. On her subsequent marriage to Archibald Douglas, Earl of Angus, could be founded a title inherited by Henry, Lord Darnley. The marriage of Darnley and the Queen of Scots united these two claims for a moment, and transmitted them to their child James VI. After Mary's execution in 1587, Darnley's niece, Arabella Stuart, took her place in

Catholic dreams of dynastic change in England. Elizabeth kept her unmarried, and even under James I, her marriage in 1610 to William Seymour, a descendant of the Suffolk line, led to her lifelong imprisonment in the Tower.

*Title to the throne*    It was insufficient for the Tudors to rely on the magic of legitimacy. Nor, indeed, could either title or succession be defined and secured on that principle alone. The right of Edward VI was as fully indisputable as that of his father, for both Catherine of Aragon and Anne Boleyn were dead when Henry married Jane Seymour. But the position of Edward's half-sisters Mary and Elizabeth was far from clear, and had already needed regulation by statute. The Succession Act of 1534 had vested the succession in the children of Henry and Anne, thereby excluding Mary.[1] An Act of 1536 declared the marriages with Catherine and Anne alike void and their offspring illegitimate, thus excluding both half-sisters, and vested the succession in the issue of Henry and Jane. As no such issue yet existed, Henry was empowered to appoint his own successor by letters patent or by will, and to nominate a Council to guide him if he were under age on his accession.[2] In 1544 a final Succession Act recited the King's statutory authority to devise the Crown by will, and enacted that, failing other issue of himself or Edward, the throne was to go, under conditions to be laid down by Henry, first to Mary and her heirs, and then to Elizabeth and hers.[3] In 1546 Henry made his will. It left the Crown to Edward and his heirs, then to Henry's heirs by his present or any subsequent marriage, then to Mary provided she did not marry without the consent of the Council appointed for Edward's guidance, then to Elizabeth similarly, then to the heirs of the Suffolk line, and then to the next rightful heirs.[4] The intention to exclude the Scottish line is evident. It can be argued that these statutory regulations of the succession, the authority given to Henry VIII to devise the Crown by will, and his use of it to defeat the strongest legitimist claim, constitute a successful assertion of the principle that Parliament is competent to regulate the succession and establish the title to the throne.

Such a view must be received with caution. Henry VIII's will,

[1] Elton, *The Tudor Constitution, Documents,* 6-12.
[2] Tanner, 389-95.                                   [3] Tanner, 397-400.
[5] Pickthorn, *Henry VIII,* 534-7.

statutory though its force was, had little effect either on the How far governmental system of Edward VI or on the succession to the based on throne. On Henry's death, the Council in which he had vested statute the government appointed Edward's uncle Hertford, raised to the dukedom of Somerset, to be Protector of the Realm, and was reconstituted as a Council by the young King.[1] Henry's elaborate arrangements for the succession produced equally little ultimate effect. So far as his own children were concerned, the succession indeed followed the prescribed order. Edward's attempt to imitate his father and devise the Crown by will, but without statutory authorisation, to Lady Jane Grey and her heirs, was condemned because of its repugnancy to statute by the lawyers called in to draft it.[2] Yet it was hardly in order to vindicate a statutory title that the country rejected Queen Jane and rose for Queen Mary.

Nor can any theory of statutory title be safely inferred from *Dubiety of* Parliament's refusal to permit the coronation of Philip II as King, *Parlia-* or to enable Mary to disinherit Elizabeth and devise the Crown *ment's* by will—which would have involved Philip's accession on her *right to* death—or from its limitation of Philip's powers in that event to the *regulate* exercise of a regency should she leave a child under age.[3] These *the* transactions imply defence of the legitimist principle more plainly *succession* than that of a succession based on statute. On Elizabeth's accession Parliament gave statutory recognition to the Queen's title.[4] In 1571 it affirmed the sufficiency of a statutory title.[5] Yet if such assertions served to defeat the pretensions of any other authority, such as the Papacy, to alter the succession, they did not prove the capacity of Parliament to do so, or to intervene at all without royal permission. In 1563 a petition regarding the Queen's marriage was drawn up in the Commons, approved by the Lords, presented to her, and after some delay encouragingly but evasively answered. In 1566 Parliament took up the problem again. If Henry's arrangements still had force, the right to succeed lay with the Suffolk line. The Queen refused to allow the discussion of their claim—for which the more extreme Protestants were

[1] Pollard, *England under Protector Somerset*, 37. For his position, see J. S. Roskell, *The Office and Dignity of Protector of England*; 68 E.H.R. 228-9.
[2] Pollard, *Political History of England, 1547-1603*, 83-6.
[3] Pollard, *Political History of England*, 119, 148-9, 175.
[4] Prothero, 21-2.          [5] Tanner, 415-16; Prothero, 59.

anxious—soundly rated petitioners who addressed her on the subject of her marriage, and eventually ordered the Commons to suspend debate on the succession.[1] Once more the proceedings ended with vague reassurances on her part In 1568 she disapproved the proposal, which a majority of her Council favoured, to permit the marriage of the Queen of Scots, now a prisoner in England, to Norfolk. On such matters the Queen insisted on making her own policy. In 1578, and again in 1581, she indulged, to her subjects' indignation, in elaborate pretences at courtship with the French prince, Francis of Anjou. By this time her marriage could have no effect on the succession, and Mary's execution rid her of her nearest rival. But in 1593 the Queen insisted on the punishment of members of the Commons who sought to introduce bills regulating the succession.[2] During the whole of her reign, therefore, no statute for such a purpose was passed. The Queen treated the question as lying outside the scope of parliamentary initiative, if not of parliamentary competence. She was succeeded, and must have intended to be succeeded, by James VI of Scotland, whom Henry VIII's will, had it possessed any real force, would have excluded. Legitimism had still a long life before it. Its highest flights were yet to be attained.

*The treason law*

No less acute than the anxieties with regard to the succession were those felt for the security of the monarch himself. Under so highly personal a system of government, the safety of the State was bound up with his own. Crimes against the one must be regarded as crimes against the other. Yet the law of treason, the main bulwark of the King's personal safety, was, in the form in which the Tudors inherited it, singularly out of date. Derived originally from the purely feudal crime of breach of loyalty to an overlord, its archaism reflected the primitive conceptions of the ages during which it had been formulated. In its essence, it implied a personal rather than a political offence—a breach of allegiance to the King by any person born within his dominions. The acts amounting to such an offence had been defined in 1352 by a statute, which laid down three principal and several minor species

---

[1] On the debates of 1563 and 1566, see J. E. Neale, *Parliament and the Succession Question in 1562–1563 and 1566*, 36 E.H.R. 497; *Elizabeth I and her Parliaments*, i. 101 ff., 129 ff.

[2] The proceedings against Peter Wentworth and others are discussed in Neale *Peter Wentworth*, 39 E.H.R. 186 ff.

of treason.[1] The first three comprised compassing or imagining the King's death, adhering to his enemies, and levying war against him. After enumerating other heads the Act went on to state that no offence which it did not specify should be adjudged treason except by the King in Parliament.[2] Offences unspecified in the Act were too numerous for its protection to be complete. The imprisonment and even the deposition of the King were not made treasonable, nor was conspiracy to levy war against him, though it clearly must be made treasonable before it has reached the length of actually levying war. To some extent, the scope of the statute could be widened by judicial interpretation, and acts not mentioned therein could be held to amount to compassing or imagining the King's death.

The most satisfactory means of enlargement was not by this method of devising "constructive" treason, but through supplementary legislation. In the sixteenth century this device, occasionally used in the Middle Ages, was constantly adopted, and extended to offences which were rather directed against the position of the King in the State than against his personal security. The position of a king in *de facto* possession of the throne was in 1495 safeguarded against the claims of a *de jure* pretender by a statute enacting that acts done in obedience to the former could not constitute treason to the latter.[3] After the breach with Rome, setting as it did the claims of papal sovereignty against those of the English allegiance, a succession of statutes threw their protection over the Crown and its lawful authority, whereas former legislation had been largely confined to offences directed against its wearer as an individual. The Succession Act of 1534 made it treason to slander by writing or act the King's marriage with Anne Boleyn or the lawfulness of their children's title to the throne, and misprision of treason to do so in spoken words.[4] A Treason Act of the same year extended the crime to words as well as writings intended to lead to the bodily harm of

*New treason legislation*

---

[1] For the earlier history of the treason law, see Holdsworth, ii. 449-50, iii. 287-93 ; Tanner, 374-7.

[2] The history of this restriction is traced by S. Rezneck, *Parliamentary Declaration of Treason*, 46 *L.Q.R.* 80.

[3] Pollard, *Reign of Henry VII*, ii. 12-13 ; and 7 *B.I.H.R.* 1.

[4] Elton, 11. The treason legislation of 1531-4 is discussed by I. D. Thornley, *Treason Legislation of Henry VIII*, 3 *T.R.H.S.* xi. 87.

the King or Queen or to depriving them of their royal dignity, or representing the King as a heretic, tyrant, or usurper, and to any act intended to take from him control of his armed forces.[1] The Succession Act of 1536 annexed the penalties of treason to words, writing, or acts imperilling the King, or denying the Seymour marriage or the succession based on it; to upholding the former marriages; refusing to take an oath to answer, or having taken it to refuse to answer, questions relating to the Act; and also to words or acts directed against the King's power to regulate the Council of his successor.[2] The Act extinguishing Roman authority in the same year made it treason in ecclesiastical or lay officials, tenants of the Crown, and persons taking orders, vows, or degrees, to refuse an oath upholding the royal supremacy and repudiating that of the Pope.[3] Under these statutes Fisher and More had been the earliest victims. Exeter and Montague in 1538, Cromwell in 1540, and the Countess of Salisbury in the next year were executed on attainders reciting offences which owed to Henrician legislation such treasonable quality as they had. That of marriage without royal consent to the sister, aunt, or niece of the King became treasonable in 1536, and the statute so declaring it led retrospectively to the attainder of Lord Thomas Howard for having contracted himself to a niece of Henry at a time before it became treasonable to do so.[4] Adultery was alleged as the treason of Anne Boleyn and of Catherine Howard—and the associates who died with them—and the attainder of the latter contained a clause making it treason for a woman guilty of unchastity before her marriage to the King to fail to reveal it.[5] The Succession Act of 1543 prescribed a new oath abjuring papal authority, required all officials of Church and State, and any other person who might be called on, to take it under penalty of treason for refusal. Treason likewise attached to written or printed words impugning the statute or anything done by the King under it.[6]

*General character of Henry VIII's treason legislation*

At this point the dreary and bloody catalogue of Henry VIII's treason legislation may be brought to an end. What is most striking in it, apart from its capricious and arbitrary character, is

[1] Tanner, 388-9. Elton, 61-3.  [2] Tanner, 389-95.
[3] Tanner, 48-50, Elton, 356-58.
[4] S. Rezneck, *Trial of Treason in Tudor England*, in *Essays Presented to C. H. McIlwain*, 263.  [5] Tanner, 427.
[6] Tanner, 397-400. Other treason Acts are mentioned by Tanner, 379.

its extremely loose connexion with the principles laid down in 1352, or even their constructive enlargements.[1] Spoken words, written words, even the maintenance of silence, were brought into the category of overt acts.[2] None of the three, and least of all abstention from any utterance whatever, need be regarded as intended to lead to the King's death, deposition, or imprisonment, or to amount to the raising of war against him or to adherence to his enemies. The Acts constitute a clumsy and cruel attempt to superadd to the personal crime of treason a series of political offences denoting at most dissatisfaction with the political and religious structure of the State. They penalised not deeds but opinions. And their conformity to the changeful and revengeful humours of the King raises them, parliamentary in form though they were, to the bad eminence of illustrating the most evil and lawless element in Tudor rule.

The governments of both Edward VI and Mary sought to *Edwardian* return to the inadequate basis of the 1352 Act. Neither was success- *and* ful. In 1547 a new Treasons Act repealed the sanguinary enact- *Marian* ments which had defaced the statute-book during the preceding *statutes* fifteen years, and, with certain additions, restored the pre-existing law.[3] Interference with the succession as laid down by statute and Henry's will, however, remained treasonable, as did deeds and written words against the royal supremacy. The rising of 1549 restored to the list of treasons riots aimed at altering the laws and conspiracies to imprison councillors,[4] and in 1552 the royal supremacy was once more safeguarded by the enactment that to attack it in writing, and, on a third offence, even by word of mouth, was treason.[5] Mary's first Treason Act of 1553 naturally abandoned this ground.[6] An Act of 1555, however, extended treason to the offence of praying that God would shorten the Queen's days, and a later Act again made treasonable the utterance

---

[1] Tanner, 379. The tendency to treat particularly heinous offences as treasonable is shown in the Act of 1531 annexing the penalties of treason to poisoning (Tanner, 381-2). From 1485 to 1603, it has been reckoned, sixty-eight treason statutes were enacted.

[2] For the early history of treason by words, see I. D. Thornley, *Treason by Words in the Fifteenth Century*, 32 *E.H.R.* 556.

[3] Tanner, 401-4. Elton, 64-7.

[4] Holdsworth, iv. 497. Elton, 67-8.

[5] Tanner, 405-6.

[6] Tanner, 406-7. Elton, 69.

of spoken words against the Queen, and extended the treason law to offences against the King-Consort.[1]

*Eliza-bethan treason legislation*    In the emergencies of Elizabeth's reign treason was once more enlarged, though less widely and far less tyrannically than under her father.[2] The Act of Supremacy made treasonable on the third offence the maintenance, by deeds or written or spoken words, of any foreign jurisdiction. Another Act of 1559 enacted that spoken words aimed at the Queen's destruction or deposition, or at raising war against her, or denying her title to the throne, or maintaining that of any other person, should on a second offence become treasonable, and that overt acts or written words directed against her title should be treasonable in the first offence.[3] In 1563 the offence of maintaining Roman authority, if repeated a second time, and a second refusal to take the Oath of Supremacy, became treason.[4] The bull of 1570 resulted in further strengthening of the law. Treason was attached to compassing the Queen's death, wounding, or deposition, levying war against her, moving foreigners to invade the realm, writing or speaking words denying her title, maintaining the rights of another claimant, affirming her to be a heretic, schismatic, or usurper, asserting the right of any person to succeed her, or questioning the authority of statute to settle the succession. Another statute passed at the same time made treasonable the introduction of papal bulls.[5] In 1572 the same penalties were annexed to attempts to deprive her of the armed forces of the Crown, or to liberate persons convicted of treason.[6] In 1581 it became treason to attempt to reconcile the Queen's subjects to Rome, or for any of them to be reconciled.[7] In 1585 the presence of a Jesuit or seminary priest became *ipso facto* treasonable; the Queen's subjects abroad, except Jesuits and seminary priests, were required, when a proclamation for the purpose should be issued, to return and take the Oath of Supremacy, and persons returning without doing so should be adjudged traitors.[8]

*Character of Eliza-bethan treason laws*    It will, however, be observed that Elizabethan legislation, unlike that of Henry VIII, seems to distinguish degrees of gravity in the offences it deals with. In many instances it is only on the offence

[1] Tanner, 407-11. Elton, 69-72.
[2] But compare Rezneck, *Trial of Treason in Tudor England*, 268.
[3] Act of Supremacy, cl. xiv; Tanner, 411-13.        [4] Prothero, 41.
[5] Tanner, 146, 413-17; Elton, 72-6; Prothero, 57-63.
[6] Prothero, 65-7.        [7] Tanner, 152-4; Prothero, 74-6; Elton, 422-4.
[8] Elton, 418; Tanner, 154-9; Prothero, 83-6.

being repeated that it becomes treasonable. Otherwise it may be punishable only as a felony, by such penalties as fine, deprivation, imprisonment, or praemunire. Other cognate offences, as for example, attempts to liberate persons imprisoned on suspicion of being traitors but not yet condemned as such, are in any case treated as felonies. In 1581 the utterance or repetition of slanderous words against the Queen is punishable by fine or imprisonment for the first offence, as felony for the second. Publication of such words in writing is treated as felony.[1] Here, perhaps, may be seen the beginning of an attempt to found a law of sedition as distinct from treason. Such a classification of legal thought advanced slowly. Not until the eighteenth and nineteenth centuries was it to be attained, and then not completely.

Menaced at its most important yet most vulnerable spot, *Procedure* the Tudor State dealt remorselessly with offenders whose acts *in treason* seemed to threaten its own existence with that of its sovereign. *trials* Suspects were treated as public enemies rather than as accused persons to be presumed innocent until proved to be guilty. The prisoner was denied counsel. He was not furnished with a copy of the indictment against him, or of the depositions, or even of the names of witnesses to be called by the Crown. He therefore had no means of knowing the case he would have to answer. He was not always furnished with a list of the jury, and so given an opportunity of considering at leisure how he would exercise his right of challenge. The Crown could compel the attendance of witnesses, the accused could not. At Common Law, only one witness was necessary to prove a criminal act. Moreover, while the Crown's witnesses gave evidence on oath, those for the defence did not, and their evidence was therefore regarded as of inferior value. The evidence of accomplices was admitted without corroboration, and even held to be of special value. Accused persons were not always confronted with the witnesses brought against them, or allowed to cross-examine them. The court itself virtually conducted the case for the Crown, and the accused defended himself as best he could on the spur of the moment.[2] Hard as these conditions were, the legislation of Henry VIII made them still harder. The Crown got power to hold trials in any court, or even

[1] Prothero, 77-80.
[2] On procedure in treason trials, see J. FitzJ. Stephen, *History of the Criminal Law*, i. 350.

by extraordinary commission, and could change the venue to where it pleased. Peers indeed retained the right of trial by their peers: but that was worth little. The right to challenge the jury was permitted only when a juror did not possess the qualifying freehold. The penalties of treason were as barbarous as the form of treason trials. Convicted traitors were, unless some other form of execution was accorded them, hanged, drawn, and quartered. They lost all their chattels, and all their lands in both fee-simple and fee-tail. Their widows forfeited all right of dower. Their children were degraded in blood and lost capacity to inherit.[1]

*Ameliorations under Edward VI*    Only at one point was the procedure in treason trials relaxed in the sixteenth century. The first Treason Act of Edward VI required two lawful and sufficient witnesses instead of only one to testify to each overt act, or individually to two acts of the same kind, and provided that accusations must be made within thirty days of the offence. His second Treason Act required that the witnesses should be confronted by the accused. These mitigations subsisted under Mary, and in one form or another were embodied in Elizabethan statutes.[2]

*Martial law*    The suppression of armed risings was apt to be effected by means as violent as, and even less cloaked with legality than, the methods used against the individual traitor. Possessing neither a standing army nor an adequate police force, the Crown resorted in such emergencies to a virtual outlawry of its subjects, both those implicated in rebellion, and those resident in areas where rebellion broke out or serious discontent was manifest, by the issue of commissions of martial law. Originally intended for the maintenance of discipline in the army, such commissions, with their summary and lawless procedure, were extended to civilians as well. They were employed during the Pilgrimage of Grace, by Mary in 1557, and by Elizabeth in 1589 and 1595. It may be noted that in the latter three cases they could not be justified on the ground that a state of insurrection existed.[3] Any unusual crisis of public order seemed to

---

[1] Tanner, 432.

[2] Tanner, 404, 406, 410, 413, 417; Prothero, 12, 25, 60. Note, however, the discrepancy between the wording of Mary's first and second Treason Acts, and the difficulty it created. S. Rezneck, *Trial of Treason in Tudor England*, 278 ff.

[3] Pickthorn, *Henry VIII*, 355-6; Pollard, *Political History of England*, 166; Prothero, 443-4. E. P. Cheyney, *History of England from the Defeat of the Armada to the death of Elizabeth*, ii. 247.

invoke measures as savage and brutal as those taken against persons who offended against a harsh and illogical treason law. *Salus populi suprema lex* came to mean, as it generally does, no law at all.


### iii


The principal instrument in the King's hands was his Council. *The Privy* Attention has already been drawn to its indefinite composition *Council* and functions, both of which depended on the King's will. These characteristics clung to it throughout the Tudor period, but constant employment by a vigorous monarchy on the regular business of administration and jurisdiction necessarily made it more of a real entity. The office of President became statutory after 1529.[1] The Council could transact business of a routine kind in the King's absence. It began to keep records of its proceedings, a new series of which began in 1540, though not all that was transacted there— especially important business done when the King was present— was placed on its minutes.[2] The rise of Cromwell and his immense activity as an administrator created spheres of authority which the Council might later enter and partly fill.[3] It could begin to direct governmental action on its own authority instead of invoking that of officers of State. Its letters and orders multiplied. It got a seal of its own.[4] The King might carry councillors with him about the country, but a Council, different at least in function from the Star Chamber, sat in London. Ambassadors negotiated with it, and matters of national defence and public safety, together with the supervision of administration and other duties fell into its hands. Of course, a word from the royal mouth, a letter from the royal hand, could stay its activities in mid-career, or prescribe or rescind its action. There is no question of a body so coherent and authoritative as to act otherwise than the King permitted or directed. Yet, with or without the King, the Council

[1] Tanner, 259.

[2] Tanner, 217. On the clerkship of the Privy Council from 1509 onwards, see E. R. Adair, *The First Clerk of the Privy Council*, 39 L.Q.R. 240.

[3] G. R. Elton, *The Tudor Revolution in Government*, 382–97, ascribes to Cromwell the main influence in transforming the King's Household into a real administrative organisation: but the demarcation should not be sharply drawn.

[4] For the Privy Council and its conduct of business, see L. W. Labaree and R. E. Moody, *The Seal of the Privy Council*, 43 E.H.R. 190. The Council got a seal in 1556. The Star Chamber never had one.

was sufficiently definite and formal, and sufficiently concerned with business of its own, to be regarded as much more than a mere casual group of counsellors. It recovered the corporate identity attached to it in the Middle Ages, though to some extent obscured by Yorkist and early Tudor practice. It became a real "Privy Council", though that name was not an exact term, and it is frequently referred to merely as "the Council".

*Other Councillors*    As it resumed this identity, the nebulous group of "ordinary" councillors receded back from the Privy Council proper. There seems to be no such body as an "ordinary" council. "Ordinary" councillors, as legal experts, came to be regarded as "the King's counsel learned in the law", and found their place in the legal hierarchy of the country rather than in its governmental organisation. Similarly withdrawn from the inner circle of Privy Councillors were the staffs of the Star Chamber, Court of Requests, councils of the North and of Wales, and ambassadors, judges, bishops, and other dignitaries whom it was desirable to swear in as councillors, though their duties might make it impossible for them to take any useful part in the Privy Council itself. The needs of local administration, again, made it convenient similarly to attach to the Council gentlemen of rank in the counties, whose position as councillors added to their authority, and their responsibility, for the preservation of peace and the execution of royal commands.[1]

*Size and composition of the Council*    Detaching itself from this series of outer rings of councillors, the true Privy Council comes to stand out with increasing sharpness and definition. The number of persons sworn as members fluctuated widely, but tended to fall as its corporate importance grew, though at times its increased size reflected the need for the Crown not only to have its administrative business done, but to draw into association with it men of different political and religious standpoints, so that the mind of the sovereign should at least be fully informed, if not decisively influenced, by the advice tendered to him. Henry's Privy Council toward the close of his reign comprised nineteen members. By his will he surrounded Edward VI with a body of sixteen, with twelve "assistants".[2] Later in that reign of weak and divided government, the number rose to about forty. About half of these were displaced by Mary, but, relying as she did on support of the most varied kind, she proceeded to

[1] Pickthorn, *Henry VIII*, 21, 463.    [2] Pickthorn, *Henry VIII*, 536.

expand her Privy Council, and at her death the number was again about forty. In Elizabeth's reign, however, the average hardly rose above eighteen, and sank to fourteen or twelve after 1588. More and more the Council became a body of great officers of State, drawing salaries by virtue of the offices which they held.[1]

After the fall of Cromwell, in whose hands several offices were *The* conjoined, departments became dissevered under their own heads. *Secretaries* New business, lying outside the processes of the older departments, *of State* fell in a special degree to the Secretary.[2] Side by side with the more ancient departmental papers—Chancery rolls, Treasury accounts and warrants, Privy Seal writs, and the like—there appeared in increasing volume the letters and papers in which his business was transacted. Foreign affairs, those of Wales and Ireland, defence, public order, all came into his purview. In 1539 increased business led to the appointment of a second Secretary.[3] The Secretaries, entering the Council as full members, rose to a principal rank therein. Under Elizabeth, the Secretaries Cecil and Walsingham were in effect chief ministers of the Crown.[4]

Apart from the work of its individual members, the Council *General* as such was constantly immersed in business of its own. Its multi- *work* farious activities penetrated into every part of the governmental *of the* system. It connected the departments of State, and directed their *Council* work. No principle of "separation of powers" was recognised in its action. It was an instrument of legislation and taxation. It administered, and it supervised the administration of others. It did not omit a general oversight over the Church. It exercised jurisdictions of its own, and watched over jurisdictions exercised elsewhere. It managed Parliament, by influencing elections, scrutinising their results, and directing parliamentary business.[5] It was in fact the regular engine for the conduct of the normal business of the Tudor State. Parliament was the supreme authority. But Parliaments came and went, with their short sessions and long

---

[1] Tanner, 202-4; Gladish, *Tudor Privy Council*, 29.

[2] Elton, *The Tudor Revolution in Government*, 299-304, ascribes the rise of the Secretaryship to Cromwell himself.    [3] Evans, *Principal Secretary of State*, 34.

[4] It follows from what has been said earlier that profound divergences of opinion on questions of policy might divide councillors and even the Secretaries one from another. On this, see C. Read, *Walsingham and Burghley in Queen Elizabeth's Privy Council*, 28 E.H.R. 34, and C. Read, *Sir Francis Walsingham*, i, 266-271, 423 ff. For an interesting account of the duties of the Secretary of State, written by Walsingham's private secretary, Faunt, see 20 E.H.R. 499, and compare Prothero, 166-8, and Elton, *The Tudor Constitution, Documents*, 123-4.    [5] See Holdsworth, iv. 70-105, for a general account of its work.

intermissions, and personnel of various and generally mediocre ability. The Council, always in being and at work, ceaselessly vigilant and active, placed at the Crown's disposal the subtlest intellects and most resolute wills which England produced in her age of crisis.

*Personnel of the Council*

The personnel of the Privy Council well reflects two main aspects of Tudor government; the increasing amplitude of its functions, and its dependence on the services of professional administrators drawn from the rising and capable middle class. Continuous attendance in London or at the Court was well-nigh indispensable, some legal training or diplomatic experience almost equally so. In such a body, neither the old aristocracy nor the Church could have any great part. At the end of Henry VIII's reign only six of his nineteen Privy Councillors were men of title, and of these only Arundel held a peerage antedating the dissolution of the monasteries.[1] Under Edward VI and Mary the aristocratic element increased, but it waned again in the days of Elizabeth. The Church likewise lost its formerly strong representation in the Privy Council. In Henry VIII's closing years the Council included only three ecclesiastics; under Mary the number rose to eight, but under Elizabeth it fell to vanishing-point. From the death of Wotton in 1567 to the appointment of Whitgift as a Privy Councillor in 1586 no ecclesiastic sat at the Council board. It became a body of expert lay administrators. Men of this new type were requisite for the work now falling to the Council. Regulation of the most remote details of national affairs became the object of royal policy, and the Council was there to undertake the task. No complete account of its manifold responsibilities is possible. But some illustration must be attempted of the various functions which, besides its prime duty of informing and advising the Crown, it was called on to perform.

*Legislative work of the Council*

In legislation, the Council formed the appropriate channel for the issue of royal proclamations and ordinances.[2] This prerogative formed an indisputable part of the King's inheritance. Issued under the Great Seal, such instruments were constantly in use to com-

---

[1] Gladish, 37. Note the complaint of the Pilgrims of Grace that the Council was filled with low-born persons, M. H. and R. Dodds, *The Pilgrimage of Grace*, i. 182, and compare Pickthorn, *Henry VIII*, 527, 530.

[2] Holdsworth, iv. 296 ff.

municate the King's commands. In the sixteenth century, when royal control over national affairs was so strongly emphasised, resort to regulations issued in this way was convenient and indeed necessary. The network of control applied by rules of Common and statute law was still slight. Vast new areas of governmental activity presented themselves in which even a skeleton system of rules derived from this source was wholly lacking. To supplement existing law, to create law where none yet existed, became the business of Crown and Council, using for the purpose a prerogative which none denied or was concerned to seek limits for. Streams of proclamations dealt with such topics as foreign relations and commerce, aliens, customs, the army and navy, military and naval supplies, trade and industry, wages and prices, coinage, weights and measures, patents, monopolies, charters, and enclosures of land; enjoined adherence to prescribed religious ceremonies, penalised recusancy and heresy, controlled printing and publication; issued directions relating to public order, dress,[1] food, and even games. New forms of national activity, new problems of national discipline, were caught up as they appeared and annexed to the domain of the Crown's prerogative. Most important of all, perhaps, was the grasp which it at once obtained over the new business of printing and publication, control over which implied control over the expression of public opinion and political and religious criticism.

Printing and publication had been annexed to the sphere of the royal prerogative as soon as they made their appearance. Though sometimes confirmed and extended by statute, censorship of the press and licensing of printers was in no sense a power created by statute. The press was regulated by proclamation. In 1538 a proclamation forbade the import of English books printed abroad, or the printing of books in England except after approval by the Privy Council, or some person appointed by it.[2] Subsequent proclamations fortified this control, held necessary in the interest of the State. Statutes had extended the conception of treason to written words. Proclamations penalised the importation or

*The Press*

---

[1] For legislation, by statute and proclamation, restricting apparel, see W. Hooper, *Tudor Sumptuary Laws*, 30 *E.H.R.*, 433.

[2] Holdsworth, iv. 305-6. For examples of later proclamations on printing, see Tanner, 245-7, 279-84; Prothero, 168-72; Elton, *The Tudor Constitution, Documents*, 105-7, 179-84.

printing of treasonable, seditious, or heretical works, ordered the destruction of the books themselves, forbade unlicensed printing, formed printers into a monopolistic company of stationers, gave its officers power of search for unlicensed presses, required recognisances from printers and booksellers, limited printing to London and the university presses of Oxford and Cambridge, and gave power to the High Commission to grant licences to newly admitted members of the Stationers' Company.

*Legal force of proclamations*
The exact legal quality of proclamations was not altogether easy to define. It may be said that they were reckoned of inferior force to statute or Common Law, but proclamations commonly rather thrust themselves into the interstices of existing law or advanced beyond any area it yet covered than attempted to cut across its web. They were in many respects a valuable complement to it. Coming into existence by a far readier and simpler process, they proved an apter instrument of regulation. They were by their very nature more flexible, and could deal with points of minute detail with an efficiency otherwise impossible. They possessed a temporary character, and it was indeed supposed that in the last resort they must lapse with the life of the sovereign who issued them unless expressly renewed by his successor.

*The Statute of Proclamations*
Whether they required the actual consent of the Council is uncertain and perhaps unlikely. Of the two hundred or so proclamations issued by Henry VIII, only thirty-six purport to have been made in this way.[1] It is likely that at some stage in their drafting they at least came before the notice of the Council, and formed the subject of discussion. But their nature remained doubtful, and, in view of their rapid multiplication, uncertainties as to the method of their enactment and the authority attaching to them were bound to cause some questioning. In 1539 a bold and skilful attempt to settle doubtful points was made by statute. The preamble to the Statute of Proclamations makes it clear that it was not aimed, as has sometimes been asserted, at annihilating the difference between statute and proclamation, and giving the force of statute to any proclamation the King might choose to make. Proclamations, it is stated by the statute, have not been duly obeyed, as they should be, in view of emergencies suddenly arising which may preclude the making of a statute. It is

[1] Gladish, 95.

therefore provided that the King, on the advice of his Council, or the greater part of them, may issue proclamations having the full force of law. These are to be published in a prescribed manner, the King may direct Justices of the Peace to see to their execution, and offenders against them may be punished by specified members of the Council, sitting as a board. There are clear limitations to the authority thus conferred. Neither Common Law nor statute can be infringed by a proclamation. Rights of property in general are preserved. The breach of a proclamation cannot be made a capital offence. Besides these specific limitations, the whole tenor of the statute bears witness to its acceptance of the legislative supremacy of Parliament. There may be, it is admitted, doubts about the validity of a proclamation. There can be none about that of a statute. It is for the law made in Parliament to cure the defects inherent in laws made out of Parliament. In this famous Act of 1539, the so-called *Lex Regia* of England, there was no surrender of the commanding position won by statute law. It was a statesmanlike attempt at definition. Its absolutist appearance led, however, to its repeal at the beginning of Edward VI's reign. With its repeal, the relation of proclamations to the law relapsed into an obscurity which, becoming only darker and more irksome with the passage of time, was to beset with difficulties the path of politicians and lawyers under the early Stuart kings.[1]

*Fiscal powers of the Council* In matters of taxation the powers of the Crown in Council were necessarily of a more limited kind. There could be no paltering with the fundamental rule, based on Common Law and frequently reinforced by statute, that no tax could be laid on the subject without his consent, and that Parliament was the only place where such consent could validly be asked or given. Yet there might be some doubt as to what exactly constituted a tax. The problem was economic as well as political. It was an indisputable part of the Crown's prerogative that it could regulate external trade in what it deemed to be the national interest. Trade as a whole with certain countries, certain branches of any trade, might thus be subjected to total or partial suspension. Participation in foreign trade might with equal validity be confined to an

[1] On the Statute of Proclamations, see Holdsworth, iv. 102-4; E. R. Adair, *The Statute of Proclamations*, 32 *E.H.R.*, 34; Elton, *The Statute of Proclamations*, 75 *E.H.R.* 208.

incorporated group of traders, and "interlopers" prohibited from engaging therein.[1] Governmental supervision of trade, assumed to aim at the greatest advantage for the nation, inevitably implied a power of regulation. Various means of regulation existed. Additional duties might be so levied as to act as restrictions on the flow of goods. Henry VIII had been empowered by statute to levy them. There was also a prerogative to do so. Thus Mary in 1557 set a duty on exported cloth and imported wines and in 1558 imposed fixed duties on imported French wine and exported beer, and discretionary duties on other imported goods. Elizabeth added to the number of royal impositions.[2] Conversely, trade might be stimulated by the grant of exclusive privileges to inventors and *entrepreneurs* engaged in new manufactures at home.[3] By these methods of levying impositions and granting patents and monopolies, financial profit accrued to the Crown. Were such financial returns really a form of tax? It was uncertain who bore them. It could be argued that where a merchant bought goods subjected to an imposition (and no one obliged him to do so) he found it already burdened with the additional charge, which he might if he chose pass on to the consumer, whom again no one obliged to buy. Similarly, the payment made to the Crown for the grant of a monopoly need not be considered a tax, but a return for the grant of privileges and protection which the Crown undertook in the national interest to bestow. It put into the grantee's pocket far larger sums than he handed over to the Crown, and left him far more than he could have gained in face of free competition. Nor could the consumer feel aggrieved if he got—as he might, even if he usually did not get—a superior product at a lower price, or one he would not otherwise have got at all. The revenues accruing from impositions and monopolies could therefore be regarded as mere by-products of undoubted prerogative powers, and as not infringing the vested right of the subject in his own property.

*Forced loans and benevolences*   The same argument could be used in defence of other methods of raising extra-parliamentary revenues. Forced loans, attempted

[1] For a discussion of the incorporation of companies for overseas trade, see C. T. Carr, *Select Charter of Trading Companies* (Selden Society), Introduction, xiv-xx; W. R. Scott, *Joint Stock Companies*, i. 8-15.
[2] Holdsworth, iv. 336-8.   [3] Carr, lv-lxv.

without much success in 1525 and 1528, were not infrequently
resorted to later. In 1542 a sum of over £112,000 was thus raised,
under promise to repay.[1] Such promises might prove empty, yet
the promise of repayment removed these contributions out of the
sphere of taxation. Enjoined by writs under the Privy Seal, they
were addressed by the Tudors to their wealthier subjects in order to
meet financial stringency and provide against national danger. They
were usually unpopular. Mary's forced loan in 1557 aroused much
resistance, and proceedings had to be taken by the Council both
against collectors who had failed to bring in enough and con-
tributors who had refused to pay. Rigorous enforcement, however, raised £109,000 in 1558.[2] Benevolences—hardly to be
distinguished from forced loans if the latter were not repaid,
and illegal by a statute of Richard III—were from time to
time extorted by the Tudors. In 1545 and 1546, for example,
Henry VIII raised two sums of £120,000 thereby.[3] Like forced
loans, however, they did not obviously fall into the category of
taxation, since in form they were voluntary gifts to the Crown
by the well-to-do.

The plea of national defence, often used to justify recourse to *Contribu-*
benevolences and forced loans, applied to other forms of demand *tions to*
on the subject's purse. Licences could be sold to persons giving *national defence*
them leave to absent themselves from military service. The obligation to assume knighthood (the military obligations of which had
long been translated into terms of money with the other feudal
incidents) could be extended by distraint of knighthood. Naval
service was similarly treated. Originally owed by seaports, it was
coming in the later sixteenth century to be imposed on coastal
districts generally, and even on adjoining inland regions. Towns
so far from the sea as Shrewsbury and Halifax were required to
undertake it, usually on the plea of maritime towns which desired
to spread their burdens. From the nature of the case they could
do so only by payments of money. The Council undertook the
business of deciding who should pay, how the payment was to

[1] Dietz, *English Government Finance*, 164-5.
[2] Tanner, 624-5. For Elizabeth's forced loans, see Cheyney, *History of
England from the Defeat of the Armada*, ii. 218-23.
[3] Dietz, 166-7. In Pollard, *An Early Parliamentary Election Petition*, 8 B.I.H.R.
158, it is suggested that a benevolence might cost a small borough less than the
amount of its members' wages and expenses.

be distributed, and how it should be enforced. Thus there developed a system of ship-money supervised by the Council.[1]

*Economic regulation*    Legislation and taxation were occasional, though not infrequent, duties. Administration was a day-to-day occupation. The Council was there to carry out the law and to make sure that other officials carried it out. The rules which it enforced were partly derived from the statute-book, partly from the direct orders of the Crown or its own authority. Statutory legislation, like proclamations, became more and more copious as the State extended the ambit of its interference. Within it came the organisation of trade, industry, and agriculture, the relations of master and man, apprenticeship and conditions of work, food supply and prices, poverty and pauperism, the repression of disorder, the maintenance of religious uniformity, and a whole catalogue of topics which reflect the development and complexity of society in this new age.[2] Pursuit of the mercantilist ideal of basing political power on a regulated national economy involved wholesale intrusion by the State into commercial affairs. External trade was controlled largely by prerogative powers. Though the establishment of new industries was generally, if not always, left to the prerogative action of the Crown, by the issue of patents and monopolies, internal trade required large recourse to statute. For this purpose, statutory powers were conferred on local officials, or on craft gilds, and the rules of the latter were subjected to disallowance by the judges. Particular industries, especially those essential to national defence, received encouragement. Shipping and the fishing industry—the latter benefiting from the enactment of a political Lent—the manufacture of gunpowder and metal, the cultivation of flax and hemp, all came into this category. Statutes dealt with the import and export of precious metals, and of manufactured commodities and raw materials, such as wool, leather, and copper. A great statute of 1563 regulated apprenticeship to trades in order to promote adequate training,[3] and other

---

[1] On this topic, see A. H. Lewis, *A Study of Elizabethan Ship-money*; Holdsworth, 35 *L.Q.R.* 12, and *H.E.L.* vi. 49–50. During the battles with the Armada the English fleet comprised 34 Queen's ships and 134 merchantmen (M. Oppenheim, *Royal Navy and Merchant Navy under Elizabeth*, 6 *E.H.R.* 465).

[2] For a general account of Tudor statutes of this kind, see Holdsworth, iv. 326 ff.

[3] Tanner, 502–6; Prothero, 45–54.

statutes sought the same end by setting up standards to which manufacturers must conform. In the domain of agriculture, statutes dealt with the prevalent evils of enclosure and de-population, and aimed specially at the maintenance of sufficient tillage to ensure the national food supply, though such Acts were difficult to apply since the interests of the ruling class were so often opposed to them. Enclosure for tillage was more favourably regarded by sixteenth-century statutes. The Statute of Apprentices sought to ensure an adequate supply of farm labour. Since the prime object of government was to ensure that the nation was properly fed, it sought to control the level of prices, to prevent profiteering, and to adjust wages to the cost of living.[1]

If wages were regulated, work might be made compulsory, and there was no question of leaving either entirely to free contract. *Social legislation* Those who could not or would not work presented a special problem. In former times, hospitals and almshouses, monasteries and gilds had done useful work in relieving the destitute, but this organisation had been destroyed and its endowments confiscated. The State now had to deal with a problem which its own rapacious action had greatly accentuated. The earliest Tudor statutes pre-scribed punishment for the able-bodied vagrant, and left the im-potent poor to beg in their place of residence.[2] More important was the legislation, beginning in 1536, which worked out the principles that the duty to contribute to poor relief is one owed to the State, that the parish should, under the supervision of the Justice of the Peace, imposed in 1563, be the local unit of rating for this purpose, that it must maintain its own impotent poor, that their children must be taught a trade, that work must be found for and enforced upon persons able to do it, and that those who refused it must be punished. From Edward VI onwards parishes were allowed to rid themselves of poor persons who had not obtained a "settlement" by residence. Those they had to maintain were to be at the charge of the parish if they were impotent. There was no compulsory rate for poor relief until 1572, but only a system of voluntary contributions, never very effective. The injunction to provide work was not properly carried out, except by local experiments such as the Bridewell in London,[3] until in 1576 the legislature

---

[1] For examples of these statutes, see Prothero, 45-54, 93-6.
[2] Tanner, 473-9.     [3] S. and B. Webb, *The English Poor Law*, i. 49-50.

enacted that the Justices of the Peace were to arrange places where materials could be got together on which to set the able-bodied poor to work. The sturdy vagabond was the object of brutal punishment—in 1547, slavery, and death for a third offence. In 1572, after this Act had been for some time repealed, death was re-enacted as the penalty for the third offence. The Act of 1576, referred to above, provided for the institution of "houses of correction" for the punishment and employment of vagabonds. In 1601 a comprehensive poor-law, summarising the advances thus far made, was placed in the statute-book. Relief of the impotent poor, and provision of work for the able-bodied, were in each parish entrusted to the church-wardens and overseers of the poor. Rates were to be levied for this purpose. Begging and vagrancy were penalised. Almshouses and hospitals were to be maintained, out of the rates, by the Justices of the Peace.[1]

*Enforcement of statute law and royal orders*

It is obvious that such enactments provided an ample field of work for the administrative authorities of the country. It was one thing to put them in the statute-book, another to get them enforced. Responsibility for this lay ultimately with the Council. Statute law might often have remained a dead letter but for the vigilance of the Council to see that it was carried out. Apart from this, which alone might have fully occupied the Council, it was ceaselessly employed in giving effect to orders coming from the Crown or devised by itself. For these purposes it acted as a board, or set up committees of its members or commissions including persons who were not Privy Councillors.[2] Only under Edward VI was there a committee of councillors charged with supervision of its business as a whole. Committees were essentially *ad hoc* groups of councillors, dealing with particular pieces of business—finance, victualling, munitions, garrisons, the navy, and such questions. Letters and directions to officials of every description poured forth from the Council office. Its records turned more and more into letter-books, preserving actual instructions given, whereas originally they had rather been minutes of business considered and decided. Special commissions were similarly of an *ad hoc* type—to deal with local grievances or technical problems.[3]

[1] For this series of statutes, see Tanner, 479-81, Prothero, 41-5, 67-72, 72-4; Tanner, 481-4, 484-94, Prothero, 96-105.
[2] Tanner, 221-5; Holdsworth, iv. 67-8.     [3] Holdsworth, iv. 68-9.

They were part of a general process by which the sixteenth-century Council, like the twentieth-century departments of State, availed itself of the knowledge and services of persons specially qualified to direct it in matters requiring unusual and intimate knowledge.

With administrative duties went police powers for the pre- *Police* servation of public order and security. It was the business of the *powers of the* Council to issue passports, maintain vigilant watch for suspected *Council* political offenders, secure their persons, examine them, extort evidence and confessions. Commitment of suspects to prison without trial, and perhaps without any intention to bring them to trial, was a regular procedure of the Council,[1] and prisoners so detained seemed to have no safeguard by Habeas Corpus. This power, while necessary to public safety, since it could be used to nip conspiracies in the bud, and keep under control persons as to whose guilty intention there could be no moral doubt but might be no sufficient legal proof, was liable to abuse, and in 1591 the Common Law judges were invited to pronounce on its limits.[2] There are two records of this opinion and they unfortunately do not coincide; but even if the version more favourable to the rights of the subject be adopted, it is very far from establishing the right of a prisoner committed by royal order or by the Council to regain his liberty if not brought to trial.

Chief of the local authorities supervised by the Council were *Wales and* the special local councils already existing in the Marches. The *the Marches* government of Wales underwent an entire revolution under Henry VIII which in time was to make the existence of the Council of Wales superfluous and irksome. A union of Wales, Principality and Marches alike, with the kingdom of England was accomplished. An Act of 1536 formed in addition to the existing counties of Wales the five new counties of Monmouth, Brecon, Radnor, Montgomery, and Denbigh, annexed to the new counties or to neighbouring English counties one hundred and thirty-seven Marcher lordships, subjected Welshmen as well as Englishmen to English law, thereby suppressing the "custom of the Marches", made English the legal language, and provided for the representation of Wales in Parliament.[3] In 1543 another Act subtracted Monmouth from Wales and added it to England, created the two

---

[1] Tanner, 233-4.            [2] Holdsworth, v. 495-7; Prothero, 446-8.
[3] Holdsworth, i. 122-3.

new counties of Glamorgan and Pembroke, and established in each county a county court and a sheriff, coroners, Justices of the Peace, quarter sessions, hundreds, and tourns. Judicially, Wales was divided into groups of three shires, under a Court of Great Sessions, above which lay a jurisdiction in error belonging to the King's Bench and the Council of Wales.[1]

*The Council of Wales*  This latter body was recognised by the Act of 1543, and its jurisdiction confirmed as hitherto exercised. In Wales, as in England, there now co-existed courts administering the Common and statute law, and a court exercising the Prerogative. Feudal and franchisal courts, hitherto the great rivals of the Crown, sank to the same insignificant level as in England. At first there was room in Wales for both Common Law and a prerogative jurisdiction. The two, though partly coincident, were not competitive, and their judicial personnel to some extent was the same. As the Council, especially under the energetic presidency (1534–40) of Rowland Lee, Bishop of Chester, achieved its task of reducing Wales to order, it was inevitable that the possibility of a conflict of jurisdictions should arise; and apart from Wales, the Marcher shires of England came to dislike their subjection to an extraordinary authority.[2]

*The Council of the West*  In the South-West an ephemeral court of the same nature, styled the Council of the West, existed from 1539 to 1547. With a jurisdiction extending over the four counties of Cornwall, Devon, Somerset, and Dorset, it exercised much the same powers as the Star Chamber. But it lacked the solid foundations of the other provincial courts, and, in face of a local opposition it could not overcome, the Crown was obliged to let it lapse, and to leave the relatively tranquil South-West under the remoter control of the Star Chamber and the Common Law courts.[3]

*The Council of the North*  In fact, the strongest and most permanent need for a provincial court of this type was found in the North. The period before the Pilgrimage of Grace had witnessed a number of experiments, none very successful, in providing for the needs of a region which besides being remote, inaccessible, and turbulent, remained, as the

---

[1] Holdsworth, i. 123-5; P. Williams, *The Council in the Marches of Wales under Elizabeth I*, 21-8. The King was given statutory authority to amend this act, and to make laws for Wales. This power was abolished by statute in 1624.                                         [2] Williams, 197 ff.

[3] On this body, see Skeel, *The Council of the West*, 4 *T.R.H.S.* iv. 62; J. A. Youings, *The Council of the West*, 5 *T.R.H.S.* x. 41, has added greatly to our knowledge of this Council.

Welsh March did not, a military and political frontier. Faced by the Pilgrims of 1536, the northern administration had shown itself powerless. Some of its members demonstrated their local patriotism by siding with them. When the rising had been suppressed the government of the North had to be remodelled. Completely detached from dealings with the royal household and estates, it became the supreme administrative and judicial authority for the five northern counties of York, Durham, Northumberland, Cumberland, and Westmorland, and the principal channel of communication between the Crown and its subjects in the North.[1] To this Council may be ascribed the credit for the relative tranquillity of the North between the Pilgrimage of Grace and the rising of 1569. Under Elizabeth it superadded to its criminal and equitable jurisdictions the functions of what was virtually a northern court of High Commission.[2] Its task in the Catholic and conservative North was difficult. Attachment to the ancient Church, and to great landed families which, unlike those of the Welsh Marches, were still wealthy and powerful, was there still a dominant force. The failure of the northern earls in 1570 opened a new chapter in its history. Reinvigorated by the Earl of Huntingdon, who became President in 1572, its vitality persisted to the end of the century and into the next.

The actual frontier remained organised on a military basis in *The Northern Marches* the West, Middle, and East Marches. From 1541 control in time of war was exercised by a Lieutenant, in peace-time by Wardens who were directly responsible to the Privy Council. The Wardens, commissioned by the Crown, saw to the defence of their districts, concluded truces and concerted other measures with the Scottish Wardens for the maintenance of order, and judged and punished offenders in Warden Courts.[3] In the Warden Courts the ordinances of the Lieutenant and Wardens were applied, with the ancient customs of such local towns as Berwick and Carlisle, and rules, special to the district as a whole, constituting what were known as "March treasons". On "days of truce" the English Wardens met their Scottish colleagues, mixed juries of English and Scots were

[1] The condition of the North during the later sixteenth century is discussed by R. R. Reid, *Political Influence of the North Parts under the later Tudors*, in *Tudor Studies*, 208.
[2] Reid, *Council of the North*, 194, 211; but compare 158, 171.
[3] D. L. W. Tough, *Last Years of a Frontier*, 160-3.

empanelled, and an attempt was made to settle private international disputes.[1] The jurisdiction of the Wardens was never very effective in these international questions nor even in domestic affairs, but it was at least more so than that of Common Law courts of the North.

*Other units of local government*

The Northern Marches, retaining their exceptional character, and the Welsh Marches, tending to lose theirs, constituted special areas of Tudor administration. The Privy Council retained supreme authority there, but devolved its work on the local Councils which have been described. Over the rest of England it remained in direct contact with the actual administrators of the shire and the borough. These did not cease to be in principle self-directing authorities, armed with considerable discretionary power, and bound to obey the law rather than the executive commands of the central government. Yet the Council gave to their proceedings its closest attention, and linked itself with them through the Justices of Assize and by the newly instituted Lords-Lieutenant.[2] Lords-Lieutenant were appointed by Henry VIII to supervise the local military organisation of the realm. Under Edward VI, Mary, and Elizabeth, their position was confirmed by statute. By the end of the century their appointments, at first temporary, were becoming permanent. Themselves often Privy Councillors, they were expected, besides performing their military functions, to help the Council in the appointment of local officials, report on their doings, and obtain information for the Council on local affairs. The Council could also act for itself. It heard complaints against sheriffs, Justices of the Peace, and mayors, administered to them praise or reprimand, dealt with their election and removal, regulated their organisation and procedure, and where necessary reinforced their authority, heard and decided disputes between one authority and another, and defined the extent of their respective areas.[3] The care and attention bestowed on these local concerns, sometimes of the most trifling nature, by men on whose shoulders rested the gravest business of the State is an illuminating illustration of the infinite capacity for detail which was an essential

[1] Tough, 136-45.
[2] On this office, see G. Scott Thomson, *Lords-Lieutenant in the Sixteenth Century*. A commission is printed by Prothero, 127.
[3] Holdsworth, iv. 77-9.

part of the genius for government shown by the chief servants of the Tudor monarchy, and lays bare some of the secrets of their amazing success.

It was above all to the work of the Justices of the Peace that *The* the attention of the Council was turned. Tudor statutes increased *Justices of* their judicial and police functions. Under Mary and Elizabeth they *the Peace* were as individuals empowered to order rioters to disperse and arrest persons who refused to obey. They assumed as individuals a power to order arrest on suspicion, with what legal basis is not clear. Two or more justices could punish rioters and deal with persons who tried to avoid paying taxes. The collective sessions of the Justices of the Peace were beginning to undergo a substantial change of organisation. Judicial business was being separately classified from administrative business. The ancient procedure of indictment and presentment was ceasing to be the business of the inhabitants at large and was left to the constables. Administrative business was dealt with by the justices alone without the help of a jury.[1]

Administration was in fact becoming a principal part of the *Their* work of the justices. The execution of "stacks of statutes" as well *adminis-* as administrative instructions from the Council was piled on their *trative* shoulders. A single justice could entertain complaints, to be dealt *duties* with in sessions, about the upkeep of roads.[2] He could assess rates, if officials whose duty it was omitted to do so. He could send to the house of correction persons refusing to work, authorise begging, certify the loading and unloading of corn, see that the provisions of the laws relating to industry were kept, fine for non-attendance at church, and report the possessors of Roman Catholic aids to devotion. Two or more justices could appoint overseers of the poor, supervise the expenditure of overseers and churchwardens, assess rates, bind apprentices, license ale-houses, make regulations in time of plague.[3] Three or more justices had powers in relation to bridges, hospitals, sewers, gaols, weights and measures, manufactures, popish books and popish recusants.[4] In their collective sessions, the justices had still wider powers of rating and hearing

[1] Holdsworth, iv. 148.
[2] For the administrative powers of the single justice, see Holdsworth, iv. 139-40. Prothero, index, 481, *tit.* Justice of the Peace, gives an excellent classified series of references to the statutory powers of the Justice of the Peace at this time.
[3] Holdsworth, iv. 141-2.        [4] Holdsworth, iv. 142.

appeals regarding rates fixed by others, licensing, fixing wages, and poor relief.[1] It was the multiplication of these duties that led to the beginnings of severance between their judicial and their administrative sessions. A statute of 1541 attempted to regulate this division. It was repealed in 1545, and the justices were left to devise means of holding periodical meetings in order to carry out their statutory administrative duties. Too much ought not to be read into this division. It must always be remembered that administrative business was still conducted by officials who were primarily judicial, who are also occupied with judicial affairs, and who brought to the conduct of administration an outlook which was judicial rather than merely administrative.[2]

*The parish*   Their organisation remained surprisingly rudimentary: they were directly aided only by a *Custos Rotulorum*, a Clerk of the Peace, and one or two clerical assistants employed by him.[3] As executors of their orders, there were only the officials of hundred and township and other ancient local sub-divisions. The requirements of the sixteenth-century poor-law, however, added another to these areas. As a unit of civil government, the parish begins its history only after the Reformation. The medieval parish had been a purely religious organisation, on which the State imposed, and could impose, no duties. Its inhabitants, meeting in the church, appointed the churchwardens, supervised the affairs of the parish, and imposed a Church rate. Above it stood the ecclesiastical courts. It was much concerned with material things —the management of property, the upkeep of buildings, and the sale of produce. But since it was primarily ecclesiastical, the Common Law courts had not reduced it to the insignificance of other local authorities, and it remained active and vigorous. Tudor legislation seized on it as the instrument of poor relief. Its rating function, originally based on voluntary contributions, was later applied to the levying of obligatory contributions enforced by the ecclesiastical courts, and finally, in 1572, to imposing a compulsory rate. Overseers were appointed by this latter Act. Thus the parish developed a civil organisation easily capable of being

---

[1] Holdsworth, iv. 144. Tanner, 500-501, 502, 506-7. For an example of wage assessment, see B. H. Putnam, *A Kent Wage Assessment of 1563*, 41 *E.H.R.* 270-3. E. M. Leonard, *A Fifteenth-Century Assessment of Wages*, 13 *E.H.R.* 299, quotes an even earlier case. See also 9 *E.H.R.* 310.    [2] Holdsworth, iv. 135-7.

[3] Holdsworth iv. 149-50; Tanner, 459-60; Elton, *The Tudor Constitution, Documents*, 451 ff.

turned to other objects—the upkeep of highways and the like. Parish officials and rates were used for these purposes. Officials belonging to earlier units of local government were drawn in —the hayward or neat-herd from the manor, the ale-conner and scavenger from the leet. Over the parish officials the vestry, probably narrowing to a select body of well-to-do parishioners, supervised parish affairs subject to the scrutiny of the Justices of the Peace.[1]

The parish was not the only part of the organisation of the *Oversight* Church to be drawn into close contact with the secular administra- *of ecclesi-* tion. It was impossible to leave to unsupported ecclesiastical action *administra-* the maintenance of that religious uniformity which was regarded, *tion* not incorrectly, as essential to the safety of the State. The Privy Council addressed itself to bishops on the state of their dioceses, supervised the ecclesiastical courts, and called for returns of recusants and sectaries.[2] The Church became accustomed to having its organisation used for the purposes of the State, and an alliance was slowly forged between the lay and ecclesiastical powers which for centuries was to impress its peculiar stamp on the working of local administration.

To make its action effective, the Council had to use inde- *Council* pendent coercive authority. It could not be obliged invari- *and Star* ably to have recourse to the machinery of the Common Law. *Chamber* Such a judicial authority the Council inherited. In the sixteenth century it was fully developed. The Star Chamber specialised in this work. In addition the Council itself, wherever it happened to be, dealt with judicial duties, though as it was heavily burdened with non-judicial work it naturally left the bulk of its judicial business, particularly that of a routine character, to the Star Chamber. Star Chamber was turning into a true court, and practitioners were beginning to compile reports of cases heard before it.[3] Its relations with the Council are not easy to define, and the difficulty is increased by the Council's practice of meeting occasionally in the Star Chamber for non-judicial functions. There the sovereign or the Chancellor would explain the policy of the government to councillors and judges, issue orders, carry out annually the trial of the pyx by which

[1] Holdsworth, iv. 151-63; Tanner, 508-10.    [2] Holdsworth, iv. 81-3.
[3] Holdsworth, v. 162-3.

5

the fineness of currency was tested. By the end of the century the rule was that any Privy Councillor might sit in the Star Chamber working as a court, accompanied by such lords, judges, and bishops as the sovereign or the Chancellor might choose to summon. The sovereign never appeared. Judges always did. The statute of 1487 was not regarded as limiting either its composition or its powers.[1]

*Star Chamber procedure*

Procedure developed on lines already indicated in their general form. Process, whether initiated by the Crown's attorney or by a private litigant, began with a bill setting forth complaints which brought the case within the competence of the court. The defendant was summoned by subpoena, confronted with the bill, and required to answer it. On his answer, the plaintiff might base further interrogatories. Witnesses were then examined similarly. So far the case had been conducted by officers of the court. It was now ripe for the court itself. If a defendant made an admission, even though not on oath, before an official of the court, he could be directly brought before the Star Chamber, by what was termed *ore tenus* procedure, to make his defence and receive its sentence. Sometimes a statutory penalty existed. In default of one, the court devised sentences of fine, damages, imprisonment, mutilation, pillory, whipping, and humiliating punishments such as riding a horse with one's face to the tail.[2]

*The Court of Requests*

As in the Star Chamber, an intense activity prevailed in the sixteenth-century Court of Requests. Restitution of property, fulfilment of contracts, non-payment of debts, disputed accounts, enclosure quarrels, were all brought to the Masters of Requests at Whitehall. Constitutionally this court was in a weaker position than the Star Chamber. Its members were not Privy Councillors and its powers were recognised by no statute. Yet their functions were long immune from being challenged on legal grounds, and like the Star Chamber it was a popular and frequently-invoked court.[3]

---

[1] Leadam, *Select Cases in Star Chamber* (Selden Society), ii., Introduction, xxxii.; Holdsworth, i. 500. The King's presence was not entirely a fiction. A seat was always reserved for him. Later, James I is recorded to have sat at least twice (Holdsworth, i. 500 *n.* 2).

[2] Holdsworth, v. 178-84; Scofield, *Star Chamber*, 73-9; Tanner, 256. Elton, 169-70.

[3] I. S. Leadam, *Select Cases in the Court of Requests* (Selden Society), Introduction, xv-xvii; Tanner, 299-302. Occasionally a Master of Requests followed the Court with the sovereign, Holdsworth, i. 414.

Less intimately connected with the Council, but lying within *Courts of* its general sphere, were the Courts of Chancery and of Admiralty. *Chancery* The former, though sitting at Westminster Hall, was not a *Admiralty* Common Law court, and its influence lent weight rather to the conciliar and prerogative elements than to the Common Law elements in the English legal system. Intermittent strife existed between it and the Common Law courts, but the dignity and traditions of the Chancellorship and the Chancellor's connexion with the Common Law judges prevented, so far as the sixteenth century was concerned, any really deep cleavage.[1] The Court of Admiralty, sitting not at Westminster but at Southwark, exercised by royal commission the jurisdiction attached to the office of Lord High Admiral in cases of loss of ships and goods, piracy, contraband, and prize, and matters arising in tidal waters, on the high seas, and in lands oversea.[2]

Thus the judicial system was becoming highly complex. The *Complex-* courts of Common Law found growing up beside them courts *ity of the* using jurisdictions which threatened to trench on their domain, *judicial* and inevitably limited their expansion. Some co-ordinating *system* authority was necessary and was provided by the Council. Besides controlling its own satellites, such as the Councils of the North and of Wales, it distributed business among courts generally, gave instructions as to their hearing, rebuked judges whom it considered to have acted unwisely, and watched the behaviour of juries. The writ *de non procedendo rege inconsulto* gave it a powerful instrument for defeating the claims of particular courts to jurisdiction over matters which it desired to withhold from their competence.[3]

iv

English law was being fed from many sources. It was enacted *Complex-* by statute and proclamation, and created by judicial decision *ity of the* in numerous different courts. Parliament and the Common *law* Law courts had no monopoly. The period can be regarded as one in which their ascendancy was in some danger. Beyond the area

[1] Holdsworth, iv. 277.     [2] Holdsworth, i. 546-7, 549, 550-51, 552-3.
[3] Holdsworth, i. 658, iv. 83-5, v. 439-40.

covered by statute, proclamations were laying down an intricate network of rules. Co-ordinately with the Common Law courts, the decisions of Prerogative courts were shaping large departments of judge-made law.

*The Statute of Uses*

In one notable respect Parliament recovered for the Common Law a sphere in which its control was seriously diminishing. Land had been passing out of Common Law jurisdiction through the creation of uses, by which land and other forms of property could be conveyed by their legal owner to the use of another, who enjoyed the benefit of the endowment without being subjected to the Common Law rules attaching to legal ownership. These devices had been largely employed in the Middle Ages. They enabled land to be devised by will, and unincorporated bodies to become virtual owners of property. The Common Law framed no rules regarding uses, and Chancery stepped into the breach by developing an elaborate jurisprudence which tended to convert them into outright ownership, without the restrictions which Common Law imposed on legal owners. The creation of uses, convenient though it was, led to serious hardships. The King suffered the loss of his feudal rights, which could not be enforced regarding land thus held. Other men suffered too, by the resort to uses in order to defeat the law against mortmain, the claims of creditors, and the rights of purchasers. After a series of unsuccessful attempts, a statute aimed at removing these grievances was enacted in 1536. Its main effect was to convert existing uses affecting land into legal ownership, with all its capacities and incapacities at Common Law. The King gained by the recovery of his feudal dues.[1] Landowners, whose dissatisfaction at the loss of the right to convey land by will was reflected in the demands of the Pilgrims of Grace, were conciliated by the recovery of that power in the Statute of Wills in 1540, which, with safeguards for the King's feudal rights, allowed land held by socage to be devised without restriction, and land held by knight-service to be devised as to two-thirds.[2] The Common Law courts gained by the arrest of the tendency to subject real property to equitable jurisdiction.

The gain of the Common Law courts was considerable. Yet

[1] On the Statute of Uses, see Holdsworth, iv. 449-65; Pickthorn, *Henry VIII*, 283-5.   [2] Holdsworth, iv. 465-7; Pickthorn, 440.

their rivals all were active and powerful. Relations with them *The*
were on the whole harmonious. In many respects the stimulus of *Common*
their competition was good for the Common Law. It was com- *Law and*
*its rivals*
pelled to modernise and elaborate its procedure and its rules, both
of which were defective and antiquated. It had to strive to bring
up to date its law of real property, civil wrongs, contract, personal
property, and commercial cases.[1] It cannot, however, be said that
its position was secure. It had triumphed over medieval competitors. It was by no means certain even to hold its own in the
sixteenth-century world. A new age had brought demands which
it did not completely supply. Its rivals did so, for order was better
kept, the need for new rules of law to govern a more complex
social organisation met. Their summary procedure offered a
striking and welcome contrast to the formalities, the delays, the
expense, and the failure to do substantial justice, which too often
attended Common Law litigation. Above all, in an age when the
interests of the State were peremptorily, and with general acceptance, asserting their paramount claims, the Common Law was
proving singularly deficient in any acute sense of their importance.
Its doctrines regarding such offences as conspiracy and defamation, for example, lagged behind those of the Star Chamber.[2]
At Common Law, conspiracy was primarily an attempt against
the administration of justice between party and party, and not
a criminal offence. Libel was an offence against the party
injured, and him only. The Star Chamber punished conspiracy
as criminal, and so also seditious libels against the government and libels on private persons which were likely to provoke
a breach of the peace. The proceedings of the Prerogative courts,
in short, were instinct with the sense that certain acts must be
penalised on grounds of public policy, that the interests of the
State demand their repression. The Common Law was hampered
by its lack of any such strong sense. Its political tradition was the
medieval conception of the supremacy of law in the State and
over the State. That conception was in danger of being regarded
as out of date. Medieval rules imposing restrictions on the action
of the Crown seemed mere antiquated lumber to keen modern
minds which exalted above all things the power of an efficient,
powerful, and well-advised monarch. The Common Law might,

---

[1] Holdsworth, v. 412-23.     [2] Holdsworth, v. 203-12.

if these fashionable opinions triumphed, be relegated to deciding ordinary cases of crime and civil disputes where no public interest was specially involved. A distinction, already becoming evident on the Continent, might be accepted in England also, between public and private law. Were it to be worked out, the Common Law courts would be ousted from their ancient control over governmental acts. There was a real risk that the Common Law judges would surrender to the dominant current of opinion, and confine themselves to the performance of humbler functions. It is to be remembered that they were royal officials, holding office at the Crown's good pleasure, that like other men they felt the force of the new ideas, that they were uncertain of the applicability of the constitutional theories to be inferred from the crabbed and obscure learning in which they were bred, and that the limits of their jurisdiction did not rest with themselves to fix, since the Council acted as a *tribunal des conflits*. Their surrender might well mean the end of the principle that government, like private concerns, was subject to the Common and statute law and not a matter of arbitrary power. The notion of the sovereignty of law was ceasing to be fashionable. In the sixteenth century, that of an illimitable legislative power was coming to be axiomatic. If the Common Law courts were silenced on matters of government, and relegated to dealing with private affairs, it would be possible to assert that sovereignty lay in the Crown alone. They did not consent to this fate, nor did the Tudors seek to impose it on them. So long as a Tudor monarch sat on the throne the Common Law courts were not in serious danger of exclusion from the sphere of government, and retained their ancient control under its accustomed forms. The unique genius of that dynasty blended them in a harmonious union with every other institution of which it made use. Deriving powers from prerogative, statutes, and Common Law, the Tudors preserved with the ideas of public interest connoted by the first those of private rights connoted by the other two. They did not overtly claim that sovereignty resided in the King alone. It was even admitted that a still higher capacity existed in the King than that of purely personal or conciliar action. Royal powers rose to their zenith in Parliament. Thus was kept open the possibility that the King's powers in Parliament could override his powers out of

Parliament. Parliamentary sovereignty as well as personal auto-
cracy could be derived from Tudor principles of government.
If the former prevailed, the government would be based on law,
and not on arbitrary power. For Parliament was a legislative body.
Its will could be expressed only by statutes. To subject government to restrictions imposed by statute, to enlarge its powers only
by means of statute, was to conform to the Common Law tradition of the ultimate supremacy of the law in the State and to
prefer the freedom of the individual to the efficiency of government, and private rights to an arbitrary conception of public
interest, or perhaps to identify the two, and make the preservation
of private rights the main object of the constitution. Essentially,
therefore, the causes of the Common Law courts and of Parliament were bound up together. If Common Law judges hesitated,
weakened, and gave way, Parliament would raise up and support
their drooping hands. If it could not maintain the supremacy of
law in government by peaceful means, it would ultimately do so
by violence, overthrow and destroy the government of Crown
and Council and the prerogatives which that system employed,
govern for itself, and in the end rebuild the State on lines of its
own. For these gigantic and unforeseen tasks it was in this period
being slowly prepared.

v

Recourse to the authority of the Crown in Parliament is a *The*
fundamental characteristic of Tudor rule and the supreme illus- *Crown in*
tration of the co-operation of sovereign and subject on which it *Parlia-*
rested. It was the instrument by which the religious revolution *ment*
was accomplished, and this achievement was the most notable
chapter which had ever been inscribed in the history of Parliament,
since it involved the rejection of a limit to parliamentary competence which had hitherto been unquestioningly accepted.
Panoplied in parliamentary authority, the Crown triumphantly
met and overthrew every force which denied its supremacy within the domain hitherto monopolised by the ecclesiastical power.
Nothing here, however venerable and sacred, could protect
itself against a statute of the realm, or impose any limit on parliamentary intervention. Even within its own undoubted domain of

secular affairs, parliamentary activity was stimulated to an unprecedented extent, and sometimes, as, for example, in Acts enabling the
King to repudiate his debts, and arranging and altering the succession to the throne, in an entirely arbitrary manner, with a disregard
of the claims of morality and conscience almost as striking as its
violation of spiritual independence. Relying as they did on the
strength of this mighty engine of sovereignty, the reigning
dynasty naturally emphasised its power and dignity, and did
everything to promote the efficiency with which it performed
the tasks they set it.

*Relations of Crown and Parliament*   Parliament was nevertheless an engine held in reserve, for
particular and important affairs. It assembled only occasionally,
when a royal summons wakened it into life. Its constitutional
significance is therefore not to be measured in terms of the
frequency or duration of parliamentary sessions. If that test were
applied, the results would be unimpressive. Moreover, Parliament
still remained, largely because it met so seldom and dispersed so
soon, a somewhat raw and amateurish body. Its members lacked
knowledge and experience of the kind which professional servants
of the Crown necessarily acquired. It therefore usually accepted
official direction, and moved whither the Crown would. It was
slow to assert an initiative, to criticise or impede the conduct of
government, still hesitant and uncertain as to its own precise
position even where it felt emboldened to express an independent
view. But the experience which it gained by being used as the
supreme instrument of royal power gradually trained its members
in the business of the State, and, combined with their experience
in local affairs, converted them into a body capable of asserting a
necessary, and ultimately a dominant, place in the constitution.

*The House of Lords*   The House of Lords under the Tudors was on the whole a
complaisant body, "sprung from the willow rather than the oak".
Both spiritual and lay lords were closely bound to the Crown.
The former had shrunk in numbers, and fallen into a position
of complete dependence. By the dissolution of the monasteries
about thirty abbots ceased to form part of the Upper House, and
the addition of five or six new bishoprics was only a meagre
compensation for that loss, which permanently destroyed the
once even balance between lay and spiritual peers. Moreover,
the breach with Rome had given the Crown complete command

over the composition of the episcopate. The composition of the lay peerage was less subject to royal control. Writs of summons were issued by the Chancery with an almost unbroken regularity which suggests that the Crown's power of withholding them was practically extinct.[1] New peerages could of course be created, but this was not frequently done. The number of lay lords qualified to sit averaged about fifty throughout the century, rising only to sixty at its close.[2] Royal influence over the Lords was secure enough without resorting to the devices of packing it with new peers, and denying writs of summons. Peers whose attendance was not desired might receive intimation that they would do wisely to absent themselves, or that their failure to appear would be acquiesced in.[3] More effective still was the bond of interest which united to the Crown lords whose fortunes had been founded on the spoils of the religious revolution. A loyal and serviceable new nobility had come into being. The ancient aristocratic houses which rivalled the Crown had been struck down. Even the ancient degrees of dignity within the peerage almost ceased to exist. From 1554 to 1572 Norfolk was the only dukedom in England, and after the Duke's execution the dignity was not again revived for half a century. One marquisate, that of Winchester, alone maintained another link with former days of aristocratic pre-eminence and pride.[4]

At one point only was the connexion between the Crown and the Lords being relaxed. The emergence, among the lay lords, of the principle of a hereditary right of summons and the consequent creation of a defined lay peerage, involved the exclusion from the Upper House of royal officers who in earlier times had sat there, as being, like the Lords, counsellors of the Crown.[5] Of these the Chancellor was the most important, but with him were other officials and councillors, judges and lawyers unqualified by peerage. Writs of summons went out to them all, and a statute of 1539 regulated their precedence, though adding that if below the rank of baron they could have "not interest to give any assent or dissent" in the proceedings of the House.[6] This gave

*Development of theory of peerage*

1 Pollard, *Evolution of Parliament*, 296.
2 Pollard, 100, 106, 302-3.       3 Pollard, 101.
4 Pollard, 173 *n*.               5 Pollard, 311.
6 On the summons to the Lords of others than spiritual and temporal peers, see F. M. G. Evans, *Writs of Assistance*, 36 *E.H.R.* 356. For their position in the

effect to the rigid theory of peerage which had been evolved, and relegated non-baronial members of the House to the status of mere assistants, valuable no doubt in helping with the business of the House, yet without the right to vote. So far as the Chancellor was concerned, the position was sometimes rectified by his being created a peer. This practice, though not uncommon, was not to become regular until 1705. Nothing was done for the others. Law officers and judges found their appropriate sphere rather in the courts than in Parliament. Privy Councillors were, if below baronial rank, to find theirs in the Commons.[1] It is a clear indication of the growing importance of that body in the sixteenth century that Privy Councillors should seek to obtain election to it, and their presence added still further to its dignity and authority.[2]

*The House of Commons*    The sixteenth century proved a more important chapter in the history of the Commons than in that of the Lords. Its membership increased in numbers, and election to it was more keenly sought for and more highly prized. Its procedure became better defined, its privileges were amplified and made capable of enforcement by the independent action of the House itself. Both processes were promoted by the systematic recording of its business begun in 1547 in the Commons' Journals.[3] In the Journals, the first scanty entries, mainly heads of bills introduced, gradually developed into elaborate statements of action taken, inquiries made, and orders given by the House in the conduct of its affairs. Here, and not by reference to other authorities, the House began to find the true basis of its procedure and the foundation of its privileges, both individual and corporate. These indications of autonomy reinforced the need, already evident on more general grounds, for the Crown to attempt to make its influence felt over the election of members and the use to which they put their powers.

*New Constituencies*    The membership of the House was added to both by statute and by prerogative. Under Henry VIII the union with Wales added fourteen county and thirteen borough members, two of

House see Holdsworth, *Rise of the Order of King's Counsel*, 36 L.Q.R. 212; Pollard, 292.
[1] Pollard, *Evolution of Parliament*, 247, 290.
[2] Cheyney, *History of England from the Defeat of the Armada*, ii. 185.
[3] On the early Journals, see J. E. Neale, *Commons' Journals of the Tudor Period*, 4 T.R.H.S. iii. 136.

each sitting for the county and the borough of Monmouth. The inclusion of Chester in 1543 added two county and two borough members. These creations were made by statute. Royal writ added five more boroughs and raised the number of members to 334 at the close of Henry's reign. Creations of new borough constituencies by prerogative were freely made by his successors. Edward VI added twenty-four, Mary twenty-one, and Elizabeth thirty. By the close of the century these new one- or two-member borough constituencies had raised the membership of the House to 467.[1]

The object of the government in forming these constitu- *Purpose of* encies may have been to increase the number of seats where it *these* could either directly control the elections or at least make sure *additions* that members were returned who would support its policy. This may well have happened in the royal duchy of Cornwall, where six constituencies were added by Edward VI and twelve by Elizabeth, and in the Catholic and conservative shire of York, where ten were created by Mary. But the initiative in adding to the number of constituencies did not always come from the government. A desire to obtain representation is also evident. During this period no borough ceased to send members, and attempts were made to gain the right to do so. Newark petitioned unsuccessfully for separate representation, and schemes, equally fruitless, can be seen for the representation of the universities.[2] No doubt there were instances where places of little or no importance were enfranchised, and must have been "rotten boroughs" from the beginning.[3] It was not invariably the Crown that gained thereby. With all the royal influence which prevailed in Cornwall, the county was not remarkable for the number of royal nominees and officials which it returned, and even under Elizabeth Cornish members—such as the brothers Peter Wentworth, member for Tregony from 1576 to 1583, and Paul Wentworth, member for Liskeard from 1572 to 1583—were remarkable for the independence of their attitude towards the Crown and their resolute vindication of the authority of the

---

[1] Porritt, *Unreformed House of Commons*, i. 373-6, 425; Pollard, *Evolution of Parliament*, 158-9, 162, 273. Calais sent burgesses from 1536 to 1558. See H. F. Chettle, *The Burgesses for Calais*, 50 E.H.R. 492.
[2] Porritt, i. 2, 6, 99.          [3] Porritt, i. 375.

House in which they sat. It seems probable that in many cases the addition of new boroughs, where it could not be justified by their rising wealth and importance in an age of increased commercial prosperity, gave recognition to the political consequence of landed proprietors into whose hands the return of borough members could be entrusted with a feeling of safety which subsequent events did not always justify.

*Sixteenth-century elections*    Men were in fact now eager to sit in the Commons. Elections were keenly and not too scrupulously fought, between candidates whose rivalry was not so much based on political differences as on personal and family contests for ascendancy in local affairs.[1] Counties were torn by the feuds of great landlords and their supporters. Elections were accompanied less by attempts to enlist the support of an informed public opinion than by dubious tactical devices like moving the poll to unaccustomed places and misusing the authority of sympathisers in official positions. Sheriffs and mayors could pervert the election and falsify the return, and commissioners of array could hold over opposition voters the threat of being drafted into the army. The bribing of a mayor by the successful candidate at Westbury was confessed before the Commons in 1571, and led to restitution of the bribe being ordered and a fine imposed on the corporation.[2] Anxiety to obtain a seat was beginning to create a market in boroughs. In 1594 the Lancashire borough of Newton was sold by its proprietors the Laytons to the family of Fleetwood.[3] The sense that constituencies and votes were saleable properties may have had much to do with the desire shown by boroughs to obtain the right to return members of their own.

*Disuse of payment of members*    This right, while acquiring additional value, was ceasing to be burdened by the financial obligations of former times. Men anxious to be elected were prepared to pay their own expenses, and to undertake not to require payment of their wages by their constituents. Even in the fifteenth century instances of such bargains had occurred. A statute of 1544, applying to the new Welsh constituencies the scale of wages payable in England, was the last legal recognition of the ancient practice.[4] It was already

---

[1] For an account of electioneering tactics, see Neale, *Three Elizabethan Elections*, 46 E.H.R. 209, and his *Elizabethan House of Commons*, 246 ff. Also Cheyney, ii. 179-81.

[2] Tanner, 526-7; Prothero, 132.    [3] Porritt, i. 97.    [4] Porritt, i. 105.

breaking down. Counties and boroughs found men of wealth ready to serve them gratuitously. Under these conditions, the old requirement that knights and burgesses must be "dwelling and resident" in their constituencies ceased to be regarded. The House of Commons lay open to men of property in money or land. Thus the social distinction between county and borough members came to be obscured. The House acquired a more aristocratic or at least oligarchical character, which was further emphasised when a resolution of 1549 abolished the rule disqualifying the eldest sons of peers from membership of the Commons.[1]

The chief gainers from these changes were the landed class. But they did not wholly monopolise membership. Merchant cities, like London and Bristol, returned their own townsmen as members, and opulent individuals of the same type were returned by similar constituencies, such as Coventry and Leicester, whether resident there or not.[2] Lawyers securely established themselves in the House, membership of which could be combined with the professional duties which in any case required their presence in London. They were doubly valuable to the Commons, in helping to elaborate their procedure and privileges, and in forging a personal link between the House and the courts of Common Law which reinforced the common interest already binding these two institutions together in matters of constitutional principle.[3] Equally important, though far less numerous, as an element in the Commons were the officials and Privy Councillors who, ousted from the Lords as being of less than baronial status, found their natural, and only possible, places in Parliament as members of the Lower House. Such notable figures as Thomas Cromwell and William Cecil sat continuously there until raised to the peerage. With officials of high rank sat a number holding inferior positions under the Crown, which in Elizabeth's first Parliament is said to have reached seventy-five, or about one-fifth of the whole.[4] The presence of this element was not wholly welcome either inside or outside the House. Its influence, alleged to be predominant, had been complained of at the time of the Reformation

*Personnel of the House*

---

[1] Porritt, i. 123; Tanner, 596. Confirmed in 1576, when the son of the Earl of Bedford succeeded his father as a member of the Commons, Prothero, 131. Sheriffs and mayors were, as returning officers, excluded from election by statutes of Henry VIII. On the social composition of the House, see Neale, *The Elizabethan House of Commons*, 301 ff.

[2] Porritt, i. 519.     [3] Holdsworth, iv. 174.     [4] Bayne, 23 *E.H.R.* 681.

Parliament. The Pilgrims of Grace had petitioned against it. In 1555 the Commons debated, but threw out, a place bill disqualifying for election "any stipendiary, pensioner or official, or any person deriving profit in any other way from the king and royal council, and being dependent on them".[1] There were, however, as all subsequent experience was to prove, disadvantages as well as advantages in excluding this official group from the House, and their presence came to be acquiesced in. Among them the Privy Councillors formed a small but highly important element. Sitting together near the Speaker and in constant consultation with one another, taking a leading part in debate, trying to head their fellow-members off courses likely to be disapproved by the Crown, serving on committees of the House, taking the initiative in choosing the Speaker, they formed a kind of embryo ministry acting as spokesmen for the government and explaining its policy, though they did not always act in unanimity with one another, nor did they by any means invariably succeed in persuading the House itself.[2]

*Govern-*
*mental*
*control*
*over the*
*Commons*
The government's control over the Commons was indeed always uncertain, and generally inferior to that which it exercised over the Lords. There was undoubtedly interference with elections. Both Henry VIII and his successors, and their Councils and ministers, recommended—either in general terms, or with reference to individual cases—the kind of persons whom the government desired to have returned.[3] Directions, which the Council's intimate knowledge of local affairs qualified it to issue, were addressed to constituencies, to returning officers, to magnates whose influence would be decisive.[4] In all these there was as much of persuasion as of command, and the persuasion did not necessarily prevail. Occasionally the Council might intervene over a disputed election return. But it is only rarely, as in 1539, that there is evident any unusual degree of electoral manipulation

---

[1] Pollard, *Political History of England*, 148.

[2] W. Notestein, *Winning of the Initiative by the House of Commons*, 18-28; Cheyney, ii. 185-7.

[3] Porritt, i. 371-8; Gladish, 110. Pollard, *Thomas Cromwell's Parliamentary Lists* (9 *B.I.H.R.* 42) attributes to Cromwell the origin of the policy of influencing by-elections in the Crown's interest.

[4] Tanner, 519-26; Gladish, 110-13. But compare Cheyney, ii. 173-5, 260.

by the Crown.[1] The House of Commons was not, nor was it intended to be, a mere automatic register of its wishes. To say this is not to underrate the extent to which the Crown directed its proceedings. After the middle of the century the Commons were brought within the precincts of Westminster Palace itself, where the chapel of St. Stephen, now vested in the Crown by a statute suppressing free chapels, was fitted up for the use of the members and served them for almost three centuries.[2] Here, or in neighbouring chambers of the Palace, the Commons were more under the immediate eye of the government, and might on occasion find themselves confronted by the sovereign in person, though this practice, followed by Henry VIII, was less easily kept up by the child and the two female sovereigns who succeeded him. The House was always subject to official direction in one way or another. Except for the Speaker it had no officers of its own, since its Clerk and its Serjeant were royal officers lent to it for the session. The Speaker was in effect a royal nominee, though formally elected by the House. His election was moved by an official, he drew a salary from the Crown and held grants of lands and offices. He received instructions from the Crown as to the conduct of business, and was the servant of the Crown rather than of the House over which he presided. In his hands lay the order and conduct of business. His powers could be, and indeed were intended to be, used to thwart attempts by the House to initiate discussion or action on topics regarding which authority to initiate, or even to act at all, was reserved to the sovereign personally.[3] Should admonition be insufficient, the sovereign could intervene to suppress turbulent members and unwelcome debates. In the last resort, if royal efforts to check the passage of measures failed in both Commons and Lords, the royal assent to legislation might be refused. Thus in 1571 the Queen refused assent to a bill imposing fine and forfeiture on persons who refused to take communion. In 1598 she refused assent to no less than ten bills which had passed both Houses during the session.[4]

[1] Merriman, *Life and Letters of Thomas Cromwell*, i. 253.
[2] See W. Jay, *The House of Commons and St. Stephen's Chapel*, 36 E.H.R. 225.
[3] Tanner, 527-9, 569, 572; Prothero, 115, 116, 118, 120, 125, 126; Porritt, i. 436, 482-3. Neale, *The Elizabethan House of Commons*, 354-63.
[4] Neale, *Elizabeth I and her Parliaments, 1584-1601*, 363-7.

In secret conference with their advisers, the Tudor sovereigns decided, in the "robing room" adjacent to the Parliament Chamber, whether to utter the ancient formula "le roy le veult" which alone gave force to a bill and transformed it into a statute.

*Limits of royal influence*

Though accepting a position of subordinate partnership, the House was far from servile. It was an elective assembly and had to be treated as such. The art of political management was requisite for successful dealing with it, and management had its limits. Tudor Houses of Commons could be fractious and obstructive. Even the Reformation Parliament, so often stigmatised as servile, showed its dislike of the Act of Annates of 1532, the Treasons Act of 1534, and the earlier drafts of the Statute of Uses. Its successor, the Parliament of 1539—the elections to which had been subjected to unusual interference—was with difficulty induced to pass the Statute of Proclamations. Under Edward VI, Northumberland failed to dominate Parliament, and it rejected bills drawn up by the King himself. Mary met with opposition regarding the succession question, the heresy laws, and the treason laws. In 1555 a bill for restoring first-fruits and tenths was carried only by the device of locking the Commons in until they passed it. A few days later the manœuvre was repeated, but this time by the opposition in order to defeat a government bill for seizing the property of refugees.[1] Even the reign of Elizabeth, the classic example of the Tudor harmony between Crown and Parliament, affords illustrations of the need for managing Parliament, and especially the Lower House. For example, in 1566 the succession question and the attempted imposition of the Thirty-nine Articles by statute led to parliamentary proceedings which the Queen intervened to stop.[2] In the same Parliament the royal grant of monopolies was challenged. In 1571 the Commons again attempted ecclesiastical legislation, and Strickland, a leading radical, was summoned before the Council to explain his trespass on the Prerogative.[3] In 1572 discussion of the reform of the Prayer Book led to an order by the Queen prohibiting the introduction of ecclesiastical bills unless "the same had first been considered

---

[1] Pollard, *Political History of England*, 146, 147.
[2] Pollard, 264; Tanner, 560-62.
[3] Tanner, 565-7.

and liked by the clergy".[1] The same answer was returned to the Commons when they petitioned in 1576 for amendments in ecclesiastical organisation.[2] Again in 1581, 1584, and the last Parliaments of the reign, similar conflicts occurred between the Crown and the radical group in the Commons. The interest of the majority of the members in ecclesiastical questions may not have been strong enough to induce them to enter on any long and violent contest with the Crown, and probably waned in the closing years of the reign. The Queen's marriage became a matter of little importance. Her obstinate refusal to allow her successor to be nominated ultimately prevailed. But financial questions were always pregnant with trouble. In 1598 the Commons petitioned against the abuse of monopolies, and the Queen in promising redress was careful to add words safeguarding her Prerogative.[3] In 1601, to avert the danger that they would bring in a bill on the subject, the Queen, besides promising redress through her minister Robert Cecil, personally reassured the House of her intention to introduce reform by prerogative action.[4]

Though it would be an exaggeration to say that these instances of conflict reveal the presence in Tudor Parliaments of a formed opposition, and the desire to conciliate Parliament did not lead to weakness, consummate skill in parliamentary management was essential to the success of Tudor government. Particularly was this necessary in dealing with the Commons, which had the power of the purse. War naturally forced the Crown to rely on extraordinary supply. Remarkable as was Henry VIII's success in raising extraordinary taxation, it failed to provide adequately for his military requirements. The campaign of 1544, for example, estimated to cost £250,000, actually needed £650,000, and at the end of his reign he bequeathed to his successor an intolerable burden of debt, impaired credit as a borrower, and a debased currency.[5] The wars of Edward VI added a further expenditure of nearly £1,400,000.[6] The reign of Mary, though marked by attempts at retrenchment and reform, made the position little better. Elizabeth, cautious and parsimonious as she was, had to

*The Commons and finance*

---

[1] Prothero, 120; Tanner, 568. On this occasion the objectionable bills were impounded by royal order. [2] Prothero, 209.
[3] W. R. Scott, *Joint Stock Companies*, i. 105 ff.; Carr, *Select Charters of Trading Companies*, Introduction, lxv. [4] Prothero, 116; Tanner, 576.
[5] Dietz, 155, 158. [6] Dietz, 182.

provide for the expenses of suppressing the rebellion of 1569, and for the external emergencies of 1559–63 in Scotland and France, and 1585–1603 in the Netherlands. Above all, Irish expenses mounted from less than a million before 1588 to three and a half millions from that date to 1603.[1] What was still more significant was that the ordinary peace-time expenditure of the Crown under Elizabeth was on a scale which necessitated parliamentary grants to an average of twenty to thirty thousand pounds a year. Even with this help, supplemented by the sale of capital assets, such as Crown lands to the value of £372,000, which naturally involved a shrinkage of income, she never achieved a surplus after 1590, and died £400,000 in debt.[2] At its best, Tudor government was not incapable of prudently managing its finances. Reforms were made in the Royal household.[3] New financial courts appeared, such as the Courts of Surveyors, of First-Fruits and Tenths, and of Augmentations, and a Court of Wards and Liveries was set up in 1540 and amplified in 1542, to deal with the King's feudal revenues.[4] The farm of the customs was wholly reorganised. But the problem of maintaining solvency, however resolutely it was met, was insoluble in this age of rising prices and stationary or diminishing income. Nothing could long delay the time when the Crown must depend on Parliament for paying its way. The chief redeeming feature was that the Commons as yet showed no inclination to convert their control of supply into an instrument of attack on the Crown. Loss of financial independence endangered the very foundation of personal rule, and made the need to manage Parliament peremptory.

*Parliamentary privilege*    Consciousness of the care which must be taken not to arm the Houses with rights which might be turned against the Crown governed the attitude of the Tudor sovereigns towards the assertion of their privileges. To promote privileges which enhanced the status and efficiency of the parliamentary instrument which they chose to use was an obviously wise policy. It would be unwise to permit the assertion that privileges were valid against the sovereign. Privileges applied only against other persons. To enforce them, the Houses were permitted to act as courts exer-

[1] Dietz, *English Public Finance, 1558–1640*, 37, 93.    [2] Dietz, 113.
[3] Described by A. P. Newton, *Tudor Reforms in the Royal Household*, in *Tudor Studies*, 231. See also Elton, *Tudor Revolution in Government*, 375 ff.
[4] Tanner, 336–41; J. Hurstfield, *The Queen's Wards*; and H. E. Bell, *Introduction to the History and Records of the Court of Wards and Liveries*.

cising an independent jurisdiction. Thus in *Ferrers' Case* (1543) where one of the burgesses for Plymouth was arrested on account of a debt for which he had become surety, the Commons, deciding to act directly through the Serjeant-at-arms, and not indirectly by seeking a writ of privilege from the Chancellor, liberated their member and punished those responsible for his imprisonment, and did so with the King's full approval.[1] Recourse to writs of privilege occurred in later cases, but in 1593 in *Fitzherbert's Case* the House itself investigated the arrest of a member, though it laid down that the privilege of freedom from arrest did not apply to an outlawry at the suit of the Crown.[2] In 1587 it had held in *Martin's Case* that the "reasonable time" during which its member enjoyed the protection of the privilege extended at least twenty days before the opening of the session, but it inflicted no punishment on the person who had caused his detention.[3] In the Upper House *Lord Cromwell's Case* (1572) asserted that freedom from arrest, violated in this instance by an injunction of the Court of Chancery, belonged to peers from "time out of memory".[4] The privilege of both Lords and Commons of immunity from arrest on civil process rested, like that of immunity from jury service and from being called as witnesses, on the principle already laid down in *Strode's Case*, that attendance in the High Court of Parliament took priority of any obligation owed to any other jurisdiction. By the end of the century even the Star Chamber had admitted the principle, though it had not been explicitly accepted by the Court of Chancery. It was extended to members' servants, whose service was deemed necessary to their masters while Parliament was in session. In 1576 *Smalley's Case* concerned a borough member's servant who had been arrested by the City authorities in London. The House found he had fraudulently procured his own arrest to evade a debt. It did not, however, remand him to the same custody, but ordered him to the Tower by its own authority. In 1584 *Digges' Case* involved the liberation by the Lords of a gentleman in the service of the Archbishop of Canterbury.[5] This privilege, if too widely

---

[1] Tanner, 580-83. Elton, *Documents*, 267 ff.
[2] Tanner, 588; Prothero, 127.    [3] Tanner, 587; Prothero, 127.
[4] Tanner, 583-4; Prothero, 126; Elton, 270-71.
[5] Tanner, 583-4; Prothero, 128; Elton, 271-2. On the extension of privilege to members' servants, see A. S. Turberville, *The Protection of Servants of Members of Parliament*, 42 *E.H.R.* 590.

extended, might lead as in *Smalley's Case* to serious abuse. In granting it the Queen in 1559 added words of caution, bidding the Houses take heed "that no evil-disposed person seek of purpose that privilege for the only defrauding of his creditors and for the maintenance of injuries and wrongs".[1] The warning was needed. Injured creditors might be solely dependent for redress on such measures as the Houses might choose to take, or an action against the gaoler from whose custody the debtor had been removed. Abuses of privilege struck deep root. The Crown's financial rights were alone secure against the privilege of freedom from arrest on civil process, and its authority to repress disorder was vindicated by the exception from the cover of this privilege of the offences of treason, felony, and breach of the peace.

*Jurisdiction of the Houses*
The same principle holds with regard to the jurisdiction which the Houses acquired over persons, whether members or not, who disturbed their proceedings or showed contempt of their authority. Members of the Commons were fined for absence without leave. Arthur Hall, member for Grantham—whose servant Smalley was —suffered in 1581 fine, imprisonment and expulsion for a libel on the House and the Speaker arising out of *Smalley's Case*.[2] Dr. Parry, another member, was in 1584 imprisoned, censured, and finally expelled for the violence of his language against a bill dealing with Jesuits and seminary priests.[3] Outsiders were restrained from molesting or assaulting members, and in 1585 a London currier named John Bland was fined for showing contempt of the Commons by asserting that "curriers could have no justice in this House".[4] Had the privilege of ordering their own proceedings been given effect to logically and completely, the Houses alone would have had exclusive control of everything short of treason, felony, or breach of the peace which occurred inside their walls. In practice their control was limited by that of the Crown. Nowhere is royal control more evident than in the extent of their freedom of speech.

*Freedom of speech*
This privilege, originally of no great extension, had been strongly insisted on by Henry VIII in face of papal protests against the proceedings of the Reformation Parliament. Thus

---

[1] Tanner, 552.
[2] Tanner, 592-3; Prothero, 131-2; H.Wright, *Life and Works of Arthur Hall of Grantham*, 68 ff.     [3] Tanner, 593-4.     [4] Tanner, 594-5.

stimulated, it became a matter of formal request at the opening of Parliament in 1541.[1] In 1559 it was granted subject to the condition that members be "neither unmindful nor uncareful of their duties, reverence, and obedience to their sovereign".[2] The privilege had limits. Topics touching on the Prerogative were excluded from its protection. It was not that the Crown would have no discussion of them. This restriction would have been equally profitless to the Crown and irritating to the Houses. But leave to introduce such topics must come from the Crown. It was natural that some members at least should seek to enlarge the scope of their privilege, as Paul Wentworth did in the debate on the succession in 1566, as Strickland did in 1571 with regard to the ecclesiastical supremacy, and as Yelverton did at the same time in his contention that "all matters not treason, or too much to the derogation of the imperial Crown, were tolerable there, where all things came to be considered of".[3] Elizabeth would not admit these pretensions. In 1571 Strickland was restrained from attending the House. In 1587 the Queen forced the House to abandon Cope's bill and book, and Peter Wentworth was committed to the Tower.[4] The same fate befell the religious radical Morice in 1593. Peter Wentworth's final attempt in the same year to raise the succession question led to his lifelong imprisonment.[5] It is true that the House was sometimes with the Queen, and punished factious members or left them to the Queen without protest, and also that proceedings ending in imprisonment by the Queen and Council resulted from proceedings outside rather than within the House.[6] Even so, it seems plain that freedom of speech in Tudor Parliaments was a privilege held on a precarious tenure.

If the gains of Parliament were limited, they were none the *Procedure* less considerable. The Houses were sufficiently in control of their own affairs to regulate much of their procedure, which began to

[1] Tanner, 551.                              [2] Tanner, 552.
[3] On the debate of 1571, see Tanner, 566; Prothero, 119-20; Neale, *Peter Wentworth*, 39 *E.H.R.* 38-41. For the term imperial Crown, see W. H. Dunham, *The Crown Imperial*, in *Parliamentary Affairs*, vi, 199.
[4] Neale, 39 *E.H.R.* 49; Tanner, 571.     [5] Neale, 39 *E.H.R.* 191; Tanner, 565.
[6] In 1576 Peter Wentworth was sent to the Tower by the House's order (Neale, 39 *E.H.R.* 45). His imprisonment in 1593 appears not to have been due to words spoken in the House (39 *E.H.R.* 195). For a general discussion of the question, see Neale, *Commons' Privilege of Free Speech in Parliament*, in *Tudor Studies*, 257. The limitation placed on free speech by the Lord Keeper in 1593 (Prothero, 124) is now said to be apocryphal, Neale, 31 *E.H.R.* 128.

assume something of its modern aspect.[1] Members of the Commons paid to the Speaker the deference due to a skilled and experienced moderator of their proceedings. The Clerk having read the Litany, the Speaker began each day's proceedings with the prayers which had become customary since the Reformation. To him members had to curtsey on entering or leaving the Chamber, to him their speeches were addressed, and under his authority the Clerk who kept the Journals and the Serjeant who executed the orders of the House did their work. The members met each morning at half-past eight, and attendance was compulsory on pain of a fine of fourpence to the poor-box. Only from the Speaker could they get leave of absence. The proceedings of each session began, as at the present day, with the reading of a formal bill of the House's own choosing, to indicate its right to consider matters not submitted to it by the Crown. Most bills received three readings in the Commons, though more might be given in the Lords. A committee stage followed by a report stage intervened between the first and second, or the second and third readings, the latter practice being commoner. Divisions were taken, though the procedure on division was only gradually being elaborated. When in 1593 the division was taken by the "Noes" leaving the House, the procedure had to be explained from the Chair.[2] Disagreements between the two Houses were coming to be dealt with by means of messages and conferences, the latter practice being apparently introduced in 1554.[3] By 1597 it had become settled. From the outside world the Commons were beginning to isolate themselves. Strangers were excluded, members warned not to divulge proceedings. Some kept unofficial records. But publication of debates or division lists was unknown. No doubt there were breaches of secrecy, yet officially Parliament was as secret as the Privy Council.[4]

*Committees*    Committees were still select bodies, meeting elsewhere in the Houses, as, for example, in the Inns of Court or the Guildhall. There was as yet no committee of the whole house, but small

---

[1] Porritt, i. 490 ff., 529 ff., 542; Holdsworth, iv. 174-8.
[2] Tanner, 547; Porritt, i. 535.    [3] Porritt, i. 557, 561.
[4] Tanner, 591; Porritt, i. 584. But this did not prevent members from subsequently giving information as to parliamentary proceedings to their constituents. Porritt, i. 257-8; see also Pollard, *Evolution of Parliament*, 301; Cheyney, ii. 207.

bodies of members dealt with particular topics.[1] One of the most important dealt with privileges generally, and speedily laid hold of a new one—that of determining disputed election returns. The practice had long been to make returns into Chancery and have them scrutinised by the Lords or judges. The Commons had, however, begun to examine for themselves the qualifications of their members. In 1553 they had decided that Dr. Nowell, prebendary of Westminster, was incapable, being a member of Convocation, of sitting for the Borough of Looe which had elected him to the House.[2] In 1571 they examined the return for Westbury. In 1581 and 1584 they appointed committees to examine the returns generally. In 1586 they insisted, in face of the Queen's expostulation that the matter belonged to the Chancellor and the judges, on quashing a doubtful election in Norfolk and ordering a new one to be held, and asserted that this privilege belonged to themselves.[3] In 1589 a standing committee of privileges was created, and from 1593 jurisdiction over returns was made over to this body.[4] The historical and legal basis of this jurisdiction was more than doubtful. Its constitutional importance in eliminating royal influence from elections was immense.

It is not easy to see the evolution of Parliament in the sixteenth *Position of* century in its true proportion. Its authority is enlarged in a *Parliament in* revolutionary fashion. There seems to be nothing that it cannot do. *the Con-* It gives visible and formidable evidence of the popular support *stitution* on which the Tudor relied, and its majesty is enhanced by their constant use of its powers. Its privileges are extended, its power of vindicating them is increased, its procedure elaborated. Its management required the greatest care and dexterity on the part of the government, and it could on occasion prove stubborn, refractory, and wilful. Yet it has always to be borne in mind that royal authority is its motive force, and that without that vital principle of life the great machine lies inert. Parliamentary action is a function of monarchy. To act without the King, to coerce his action, prescribe his policy, and hold his ministers accountable before Parliament, does not enter any man's mind. The King

---

[1] Pollard, *Evolution of Parliament*, 334 n.; Porritt, i. 531.
[2] Porritt, i. 125; Tanner, 596.
[3] Tanner, 596; Prothero, 130.
[4] For the history of this question, see Porritt, i. 7; Tanner, 595; Cheyney, ii. 201-2; L. O. Pike, *Constitutional History of the House of Lords*, 285.

may, and for some purposes must, act in Parliament. He may also, and generally does, act out of Parliament. Whether in or out of Parliament, his is the dominant figure in the constitution.[1] The Crown is the governor of the realm, the soul and expression of national unity, the object of loyalty and obedience, the centre of command. Kingship is conceived of in mystical fashion; and the King as "anointed to be a defence unto the people . . . by all Godly and politic means to seek the good of the commonwealth. By his great travails, study, and labours, they enjoy not only their lives, lands, and goods but all that they ever have besides, in rest, peace and quietness."[2] It is not surprising that while the amplitude of his power in Parliament is strongly insisted on against any rival authority, it is not so clearly conceived of as superior for all purposes to the action he might take out of Parliament. The duality of these two functions is not very distinctly apprehended at the close of the Tudor period, and the Tudors never laid any emphasis on it, acting as they did indifferently through one or another organ of government without dogmatising on the supreme efficacy of one mode of action over another. It was, however, inevitable that an attempt to classify on a theoretical basis should be made. The discretionary powers of the Crown, exerted outside Parliament, not contained in the sum of statute and Common Law, and forming, at least to some observers, the fundamental fact in English government, attracted to themselves the term "Prerogative"—used in earlier ages almost exclusively with reference to the King's peculiar property rights, or at most to the total sum of powers which made up kingship, whether they were discretionary or not. In contrast to these, the King's "ordinary" power, exercised through bodies like Parliament and the Common Law courts, might well appear to occupy a somewhat inferior position.[3] Could Parliament abridge the Prerogative? Could the Common Law courts prescribe its limits? It must be confessed that the authority of either to do so was doubtful. Under the Tudors both had been tactfully but firmly warned off, by prohibitions of debate, by *rege inconsulto* writs, when they seemed to approach what might be regarded as the most vital and essential attributes of royal power. The sixteenth-century cult

[1] R. W. K. Hinton argues in *The Decline of Parliamentary Government*, 13 C.H.J. 116, that the ideal of a non-parliamentary government was gaining ground at the beginning of the seventeenth century.

[2] Quoted by C. H. McIlwain, *High Court of Parliament*, 337-8.

[3] Holdsworth, iv. 203-8.

of monarchy safeguarded its inner sanctuary from rash assault. It
revived the distinction, rejected in the Middle Ages, between the
King's natural and politic capacities, conceived of him in the
exercise of his kingly functions as impeccable as well as immortal,
and committed to his unerring and unchallengeable authority the
vast sum of powers which an able line of sovereigns, ruling cap-
ably and prosperously through difficult and perilous years, had
managed, had indeed been compelled, to acquire.[1] If the King were
tempted to rely on his "absolute" power under the Prerogative,
rather than on his "ordinary" powers under Common and statute
law, who was to say him nay?

Yet the path towards a personal absolution was not clear. The *Duality of*
Tudors indeed hardly ventured, or wished, to set foot on this *royal*
*authority*
tempting but perilous declivity. If the constitution, from one *under the*
point of view, could be interpreted as an instrument of absolute *Tudors*
power, it preserved principles which were with difficulty to be
reconciled with that theory. So far as these were effective, government must be a matter not of discretionary power alone, but of
"absolute" and "ordinary" powers combined in a union which
the Tudors contrived so carefully that none saw the joints in
their flawless handiwork. To break this union, to set royal action
in Council and Star Chamber above royal action in Parliament
and the Common Law courts and the use of Prerogative above
that of "ordinary" power—which no Tudor ever attempted—was
to repudiate constitutional tradition, ignore constitutional convention, and attempt the impracticable as well as the unwise. For,
however acquiescent the Parliaments, judges, and servants of the
Tudor monarchy had been, they had done little to weaken and
much to nerve the opposition to be offered to the Crown by a
later and more stiff-necked generation of the Lords and Commons
of England.

---

[1] It ought, however, to be added that, as the personal action of the
monarch became increasingly formalised, the institutions it was embodied
in aroused jealousies which purely personal action would not have inspired.

# CHAPTER IV

## THE DECLINE AND FALL OF CONCILIAR
## GOVERNMENT, 1603–1660

i

*Law and
convention
in Tudor
govern-
ment*
TUDOR government had been highly successful in combining the
principles of royal authority and popular consent. Both indeed
were essential to the Tudor constitution. Yet neither contained
within itself the whole system, or could assert ultimate superiority
over the other, and in practice the two principles, antithetical
though they were, seldom came into conflict. Tudor government,
in fact, reposed on a tacit understanding that neither would be
pressed to an extremity. While avoiding any attempt to use their
Prerogative so as to reduce government to mere arbitrary power,
the Tudors had nevertheless not allowed it to be cramped by an
over-rigid legalism. They claimed for the Crown a sphere of action
extending far beyond that created for it by the rules of Common
and statute law. Outside the law they asserted a wide and indeterminate liberty of action for the public good. Their claim
was not new or improper, for this liberty of action was part
of their inheritance of authority. Yet their energetic application
of discretionary power undeniably gave the constitution a bias
towards absolutism, manifested by changes not so much in the
structure of government as in the conventions which underlay
its working, and which, unlike those of the fifteenth century,
emphasised the discretionary powers of government more than
its subordination to legal restraints.

*End of the
emergency
period
(i) the
succession*
Constitutional conventions, being the product of opinion,
must change as the circumstances which mould that opinion alter.
Such an alteration of circumstances attended, and in some measure
even preceded, the advent of the Stuart dynasty to the throne in
1603. The perils and splendours of the sixteenth century had
created a unique partnership between Crown and people, in which

predominance was strongly asserted by the one and unhesitatingly accorded by the other. However potent such memories were, it could not be assumed that the constitutional understandings they had formed would subsist when they had become merely memories. The dawning seventeenth century was not an age of ardours and endurances, but of security, ease, and plenty. The succession to the throne presented little anxiety. No opposition was offered to the claim of James I. Notwithstanding the will of Henry VIII, nothing was heard of the rights of the Suffolk line, now represented by Lord Beauchamp, who in any case was doubtfully legitimate by birth and insignificant in position and character.[1] The feeble and ill-contrived "Main Plot", in which Raleigh was implicated, demonstrated the absence of serious support for Arabella Stuart, and her marriage to Beauchamp's son, William Seymour, in 1610, only led to her life-long imprisonment. James's unopposed accession, in breach of an arrangement based on statutory powers, may well have seemed to others, as it did to himself, the vindication of the claims of legitimacy and the fulfilment of a divine purpose. With three children born to a King still only in early middle life, there was little likelihood of a failure of the dynasty.

The Crowns of England and Scotland were henceforth united *(ii) the* in that of Great Britain, from which the ruling house now took *international* its title, and the existence of an independent and perhaps hostile *situation* government seated within the same island ceased for a century to haunt the imagination and inspire the fears of Englishmen. In the same month that saw the unopposed accession of the Stuarts came news of the final collapse of the rebellion in Ireland which, patronised by Spain and the Papacy, had overcast the last years of the preceding reign. Four years later on the flight of the Earls of Tyrone and Tyrconnel, Ulster was planted with English and Scottish colonists. In August 1604 war with Spain was ended by the Treaty of London. The Papacy, already in friendly intercourse with James before his accession, fully accepted his establishment on the English throne. The "Bye Plot" of 1603 in which a handful of Catholics proposed to seize the King and extort from him a promise to relax the recusancy laws was

[1] For the Act recognising the succession, see Tanner, *Constitutional Documents of James I*, 10-12. See also S. T. Bindoff, *The Stuarts and their Style*, 60 E.H.R. 192.

revealed to the government by the archpriest Blackwell, whom
the Pope had appointed to administer the Catholic body in
England. Thus secured against external enemies and domestic
disaffection, the government entered upon a period of unaccustomed tranquillity. Friendship with France was sealed by the
Treaty of Hampton Court in 1603. The treaty with Spain in the
following year naturally involved withdrawal from support of
the insurrection against Spain in the Netherlands, where the sole
English responsibility henceforth was to maintain control over
a number of "cautionary towns" pledged to Elizabeth by the
rebels. With the truce of 1609 between the Spanish Crown and
the revolted provinces, international tranquillity was almost
unbroken until the Bohemian rising of 1618.

*Com-
mercial
prosperity*　With the return of peace, the tide of commercial enterprise
flowed in increasing volume. A golden stream of Oriental trade
was anticipated from the newly founded East India Company. The
hitherto fruitless attempts to colonise Virginia were successfully
resumed. In 1606 the Old Dominion received its first charter,
and in 1607 the pioneer settlers founded at Jamestown the first
of English cities on the American continent. By 1640 colonies had
been established in New England and Maryland, and in the islands
of Bermuda, St. Kitts, and Barbados. Overseas trade prospered at
a rate presently to be revealed in rising receipts from customs.
Agriculture and industry throve with the increasing application
of capital and the progress of technical improvement. The
serenity of urban and rural life, the patiently-husbanded countryside with its pleasant manors and villages, the well-built towns,
all reflected, as did the advance in the intellectual and cultural
accompaniments of a rich and gracious civilisation, the opulence
and energy of the nation over which the new dynasty had been
called to rule, and the security of a settled social order in which
the political storms of the future were not to reawaken the discontents of the past.

*Constitu-
tional
implica-
tions of
these
changes*　Abler men than the first two Stuart kings might well be excused
for failing to read aright the significance in constitutional terms of
this transition from an age of stress and achievement under a native
dynasty to one of ease and enjoyment under their alien successors.
The position obtained by the Crown in the sixteenth century was
bound to be re-examined and re-stated. Even Elizabeth had in her

last years found Parliament refractory and critical. Her prerogatives, particularly regarding monopolies, had been called in question. It had been with increasing difficulty that Privy Councillors maintained their ascendancy. Government bills had failed. Others disapproved of by the government passed the two Houses and had to be stifled by refusal of the royal assent.[1] Though spiritually isolated amidst a new and unfamiliar generation, she had yet shown, in her famous "Golden Speech" to her last Parliament, that the instinctive sense by which the dynasty had so long been able to combine persuasion and command in dealing with its subjects still evoked the ancient and steady response.[2]

A successor cast in the same mould might have surmounted the *Personal* difficulties she had momentarily dissipated. It was the misfortune *qualities of* of the first two Stuart kings and of their subjects that they were *James I* poorly qualified even to attempt the difficult task of working out *Charles I* fresh constitutional understandings. James I, though not an old man, for he was only thirty-seven at his accession, was unfortunately an old king, a king almost since his birth, and had personally ruled his northern kingdom for the preceding score of years. He had a fully developed theory of kingship, already expounded in his *True Law of Free Monarchies*, and inclining towards a conception of enlightened absolutism.[3] Notwithstanding his practical experience of government, it was from books rather than men that his knowledge of the world was derived. Like many men of dogmatic temper, he disliked dogmatism in others, and found it as hard to appreciate the stronger points in his opponents' case as to recognise the weaker points in his own, or to credit his critics with upright intentions. But he was good-natured and peaceable, and had a large share of that mixture of common sense and timidity which induces a man to abandon untenable positions, though seldom at the right moment nor in the most graceful way. His second son, Charles, who became heir to the throne in 1612 on the death of his elder brother Henry, had not been bred for kingship. It was the Church which evoked his deepest emotions, which shaped his ideas on monarchy. Even less than his father was he fitted to control a difficult period of transi-

---

[1] W. Notestein, *Winning of the Initiative by the House of Commons*, 22-3.

[2] Tanner, *Tudor Constitutional Documents*, 577-8; Cheyney, *History of England from the Defeat of the Armada*, ii. 305. J. E. Neale, *Elizabeth I and her Parliaments*, finds less contrast between the earliest and the last years of her reign.

[3] Extracts printed by Prothero, *Constitutional Documents*, 400-401, and Tanner, *Constitutional Documents of James I*, 9.

tion. He inherited his father's distrust of opposition, but not his genial if slightly ridiculous amiability, and with greater inflexibility of temper had considerably less ability to see facts as they were and accommodate his conduct to them. Thus his greater steadiness of purpose was offset by larger ignorance of the men and the problems with which he had to deal. The sincere religious convictions which governed his life, while they shaped a private character of singular purity and simplicity, led him into dilemmas of public conduct from which a baser man would have escaped. To defend the royal authority committed to him became a sacred trust. James might regard the Divine Right of kingship only as a convenient dialectical device, but to Charles it was an imperative principle of action. No obligation inconsistent therewith which he might be obliged to assume could be binding on his conscience. It is not surprising that adherence to this principle should, in combination with the reticence of his slow and mistrustful nature, fasten on him the reputation of being evasive and untruthful.

*Their opponents* Nor were the opponents who faced the first two Stuarts any better qualified than they to contribute effectively to the difficult task of re-stating the conventions of the constitution in terms appropriate to a new era. The peace and plenty of the dawning seventeenth century bred men of arrogant and self-confident temper, impatient of control and distrustful of authority. Political opposition to Stuart rule was largely based on self-interested motives.[1] The propertied classes who dominated Parliament and local administration showed repugnance towards the development of a centralised government which might challenge their own predominance. They were particularly opposed to the policy by which the Crown sought to maintain social justice by such measures as the prohibition of enclosures, the restriction of commercial competition, and the enforcement of the Elizabethan code of economic regulation and poor-relief. Above all, they were reluctant to assume the additional financial burdens imposed by the rising cost of government in an age in which the level of prices was still rising while the yields of fixed revenues and even of parliamentary grants were both falling.[2] It was no longer possible

[1] A discussion on the significance of the rise of the Tudor and early Stuart gentry was begun by L. Stone's article, *The Anatomy of the Elizabethan Aristocracy,* in 18 *Economic History Review,* 1.

[2] On the disparity between the assessments for taxes and the real wealth of the taxpayers, see Cheyney, ii. 237-45.

in the early seventeenth century that the King should "live of his own" and the history of early Stuart government is largely concerned with the unavailing attempts of an impoverished government to bring home to its subjects the duty of providing adequately for its reasonable requirements. Attacks on individual ministers such as Buckingham or Strafford were not inspired solely by disinterested motives. Criticism of their policy was envenomed by personal jealousies and not redeemed by the ignorance, rancour, and impracticability which too often informed it. Nor were the common lawyers, such as Coke, who opposed the Crown animated any more than their parliamentary colleagues by constitutional scruples alone. Personal and professional rivalries mingled their baser alloy with the metal of their resistance. Religious zeal, which can be regarded as the most sensitive emotion of the age, came by degrees to dignify opposition to the Crown with finer attributes and to unite with the propertied classes other elements in English society whose material interests, had they alone been consulted, would more naturally have attracted them to the support of a paternalistic government. The claims of conscience entered strongly into theories of political obligation. Yet on the tongues of many who sought to arouse against the Crown the forces of religious zeal or prejudice, that appeal must seem merely disingenuous though skilful propaganda. The political failure of the Stuarts may be read in the process by which they allowed such opponents to win the support of moderate opinion.

The constitutional historian need not take sides in the political *Divergent* and religious controversies of the age. It is enough to note that *interpretations* the reigning house and its opponents alike proved destitute of *of the* the gifts of intellect and character which would have made a *constitu-* gradual adjustment of constitutional ideas possible. With a doc- *tion* trinaire obstinacy in which neither side was inferior to the other, each gave exclusive and intolerant emphasis to those elements in the constitution which best suited its own purpose. The nature of the Tudor constitution, with its skilful combination of organs and principles of government between which existed a latent antagonism, provided both with abundant material. The Crown could rely on its prerogatives to legislate by proclamation, to impose financial burdens on the subject out of Parliament, to appoint and dismiss ministers, conduct administration and provide for national defence, to dispense justice outside the Common Law courts, remove judges from the bench, exercise the royal supremacy in ecclesiastical matters without reference to Parliament, and summon and dispense with Parliaments at discretion. It could point to the acceptance of royal control over elections and parliamentary business and of royal limitations on parliamentary privilege. Its antagonists could adduce oft-repeated affirmations of the illimitable authority which the Crown possessed in Parliament alone, the necessary superiority of statute to any other form of legislation, the sole competence of Parliament to grant extraordinary supply, the statutory foundations of the ecclesiastical supremacy and the fundamental character of the Common Law.[1] They could contend that the customary request for the confirmation of parliamentary privileges was a mere polite formality and that privileges were valid even against the Crown. More boldly still, they could attack ministers not only through the use of attainder, but by reviving the antiquated procedure of impeachment, now obsolescent by a century and a half of desuetude. There was much bad law and worse history in the appeals which each side made to the constitutional practice of the past. Each side had a case, and the Crown at most points the better case. The case of each was imperfect, because the case of neither was complete. Each disregarded the inconvenient weaknesses of its own position, or, admitting them, strove with much tortured argument to deny their relevance.

*Funda-*
*mental*
*problems*
*raised*

This resort to a harsh and literal interpretation of the constitution—with perversions where necessary—proved, as it always must, a thoroughly vicious and destructive process. The Tudor system was not devised to withstand such strains. Unable to agree amicably as to the working of their government, men began to debate its very foundations. At the outset there may indeed have been little desire anywhere to effect serious structural alterations in government. Problems arose which brought such a prospect closer. Was the King's discretionary power derived from and limited by the law, or altogether beyond its confines? Could it be abridged by statute, or must statutes be construed so as to leave it intact? Could he compel the Common Law courts to abandon jurisdiction when matters affecting his Prerogative came in ques-

---

[1] For a criticism of the view that a belief in "fundamental law" characterised seventeenth-century thought, see J. W. Gough, *Fundamental Law in English Constitutional History*, 56 ff.

tion, or at least to admit their incompetence to impose limits on it? Was the exercise of prerogative powers, particularly those contained in the royal supremacy over the Church and in the conduct of foreign policy, wholly beyond parliamentary control? Did parliamentary privilege, and especially that of free speech, exist as of right, or solely by royal grace? Debate on such matters, as to which constitutional doctrine was uncertain and much might be said on both sides, imperilled the whole fabric of government. · Both the Crown and the opposition, driven into an unyielding defence of imperfectly defensible positions, soon put themselves hopelessly in the wrong. Admitting that the King might impose financial burdens by Prerogative in order to regulate trade or provide for defence, it none the less did not follow that he might use this power in order to avoid recourse to Parliament for extraordinary supply. Yet he did so. Admitting that Parliament alone could grant that supply, it did not follow that this power might be used to deprive the King of control over the executive, yet this was what Parliament attempted. These perversions of the constitution, of which both sides were guilty, bred a bitter and uncompromising temper. Because it proved impossible any longer to agree as to how the constitution should be worked, each side strove to alter its structure so as to make its own will prevail. The King, working solely through conciliar means of government, might try to dispense with Parliament and reduce the Common Law courts to impotence, and the constitution to something approaching absolutism. His opponents, on the other hand, might try to deprive him of the power of choosing his ministers and determining his policy, destroy the legislative, fiscal and judical powers inherent in the Prerogative, and reduce the constitution to terms of rigid legalism. The former solution seemed to prevail during the long periods of non-parliamentary government from 1614 to 1621 and 1629 to 1640, the latter when in the revolutionary proceedings of 1640 to 1642 the Long Parliament asserted claims which virtually deprived the King of sovereignty.

Neither solution could prove permanent, since each excluded *The* elements without which the constitution could not subsist. It *break-* was as hopeless for the King to attempt to govern solely by *down* virtue of Prerogative as it was for his opponents to cast out *constitu-* completely the discretionary element from English government. *tion*

The resort to arms in 1642 really settled nothing, and the task of constitution-building had to be undertaken again at the close of the war under conditions made even more difficult by the unsettlement of ancient habits and modes of thought which the convulsion had brought about. Innumerable theories, obstinately defended, as to the purpose and organisation of government challenged the action of any man who undertook to rule. Successive ill-founded and unfortunate experiments at length drove the nation back upon its own constitutional tradition, and led it in 1660 to piece together whatever could be salved of the delicately adjusted system which had broken down between 1603 and 1642. A Crown reinvested at least in its essential prerogatives, a Parliament confirmed in its sovereignty and its privileges, once more appeared as the indelible marks of the English governmental system. But the conciliar authority which had so long held the central position in the State had been irreparably destroyed.

## ii

Parlia-
ment,
courts,
and
Council in
early
Stuart
govern-
ment

The constitutional history of this period of crisis has generally been written with primary reference to the conflicts fought out in Parliament and the courts of Common Law, each of the two forming an arena in which the fundamental problems of English government were laid open to debate. It was in Parliament, and particularly in the Commons, that opposition manifested itself when the discretionary authority of the Crown seemed to have been abused, or diverted in pursuit of what were regarded with more or less justice as wrong or mistaken objects. It was in the courts that the legality and extent of royal powers were examined in the course of litigation. Yet it is well to remember that the centre of government during this period still lay in the royal Council. Parliament was an occasional rather than a regular instrument of royal action, summoned and dismissed at the King's pleasure. James I assembled four Parliaments, in 1604, 1614, 1621, and 1624. The first continued until the end of 1610, but did not meet between July 1607 and February 1610. No Parliament sat thereafter until April 1614, nor from June 1614 to January 1621, nor between December 1621 and February 1624, and the Parliament then summoned stood prorogued for the last ten months of the King's reign. Charles I summoned five Parliaments, in 1625, 1626, 1628, and in 1640, when there were two; but the parliamentary history of his reign is marked by long prorogations as well as by the unprecedentedly long interval between Parliaments which occurred from 1629 to 1640. In all, parliamentary sessions covered less than four-and-a-half of the thirty-seven years elapsing between 1603 and 1640. Unlike Parliament, the courts were in regular session during the law terms. But cases involving problems of governmental authority were by no means of frequent occurrence. The courts, whatever the constitutional views of lawyers might be, had to wait until the Crown or some private litigant set their processes in motion. While, therefore, it was in Parliament and the courts that the great issues were debated and decided, their intervention was infrequent. The business of government out of which these problems arose was conducted elsewhere. The royal household, the Privy Council, the departments of State, the Star Chamber, High Commission, Councils of the North and of Wales continued to perform the main business of the Stuart as of the Tudor State. The collapse and destruction of this powerful engine of government was the principal episode of constitutional history in the first half of the seventeenth century.

During this closing period of its ascendancy, the Council became a *The* more active, and certainly a more numerous and highly-organised *Council* body. Its numbers rose from the twelve or fourteen of Elizabeth's reign to between thirty and forty, comprising the great household dignitaries and officers of State with such other persons as the King's service required or his inclination suggested.[1] In the King's absence the Lord President or—when that office was in abeyance —the Chancellor acted as chairman.[2] The larger size of the Council and the increased number of members who attended its meetings may have led to a certain loss of coherence. Divisions of opinion within the Council possibly contributed to its diminishing hold

[1] E. R. Turner, *The Privy Council, 1603–1784*, i. 72-81; Tanner, *Constitutional Documents of James I*, 128.

[2] James I was seldom present. The office of Lord President was filled only from 1621 to 1631. In the absence of King and Lord President, the Lord Chancellor's name headed the list of members, Turner, i. 101-5. On the procedure of the Council and the duties of the Lord President and Secretaries, see also the document of 1624 printed by H. W. V. Temperley, 28 *E.H.R.* 127.

over Parliament.[1] The formal unity of the Council was nevertheless maintained. Unlike France and Spain, England never developed any series of co-ordinate councils. There was but one, transacting every variety of business, and maintaining its satellites within its orbit of control. This principle, besides applying to the provincial Councils of Wales and of the North, affected the committees of the Council itself. With the expansion of conciliar business, committees became numerous, but they never attained to any independence of the parent body. They were generally appointed *ad hoc* for the transaction of particular pieces of business, they were apt to coalesce with one another, and sooner or later they dropped back into the Council itself where final decisions were taken. One committee deserves special mention—a Foreign Committee which, as it generally comprised all the great officers of State, may be regarded as a forerunner of the Cabinet. The narrowing of the Privy Council into the Cabinet was, however, impossible so long as the ultimate and effective authority was retained by the Council itself.[2] From this body the great officers of State were not yet free to detach themselves in any unofficial or informal way for the conduct of business. At least in the normal routine of administration, it was the Council which set them and their departments in motion.

*Functions of the Council*     The control of the Council over administration was uneven, and naturally depended to a large extent on the personal inclination of the sovereign. He could deal with business in consultation with favourites like the Scotsman, Ker of Fernichurst, or foreigners like the Spanish ambassador Sarmiento. While seeking the advice of his Council, he might dispatch important affairs directly through a few intimate advisers or alone. Such was the case with the conduct of diplomacy.[3] With regard to external commerce and colonisation, lying well within the field of the Prerogative, the Council could develop something like effective supervision.[4] In the absence of any well-developed military administration, the Council necessarily undertook much business connected with national defence. It dealt with the raising, equipment, and

---

[1] Notestein, 36.

[2] Turner, i. 135-7, ii. 183-6, 213-30; Tanner, 129. On the Council and its committees in this period, see also E. I. Carlyle, *Committees of Council under the Earlier Stuarts*, 21 E.H.R. 673.

[3] Turner, i. 141-7, 151, 196-7.     [4] Turner, i. 148, 151-3.

provisioning of the small force of guards and garrisons which constituted the sole standing force of early Stuart times, and paid such attention as it could to the shire-musters which constituted the nation's somewhat ineffective last line of defence. In the war years of 1621–9 it provided—sometimes acting through a Council of War—for the enrolment of troops, if necessary by compulsion, for their organisation, supplies, transport, and pay, and authorised the disbursement of sums by the Treasurer to the Paymaster of the Army.[1] The maintenance of discipline, always difficult in the absence of any proper system of military law, could be enforced by commissions empowering commanders to act by martial law. These commissions, doubtful as their legality was, were on occasion—as in 1621, 1624, and 1628—still more illegitimately extended to confer jurisdiction over civilians as well.[2] The navy, placed under a body of Commissioners in 1618, possessed a less rudimentary departmental organisation than the army, but even here the Council acted with regard to shipbuilding, impressment of men, naval expenditure, stores, and even such detailed and technical points as the movements of ships. In addition, the Council concerned itself with those levies of ships and ship-money which, as in 1619, 1626, and later, were needed to put the naval forces of the country on a war footing.[3]

Like naval affairs, finance was just beginning to develop in the *Financial* Treasury a new departmental organisation destined to carry it *organisa-* out of the sphere of conciliar control. From the time of Eliza- *tion* beth's Treasurer, Lord Burghley, the relations of the Treasury with the Exchequer were in process of change. Too fully occupied otherwise to conduct actual Exchequer routine, he dealt with that office by correspondence and order. This practice was bound finally to lead to the emergence of the Treasury as a separate office, concerned less with the receipt, custody and disbursement of money than with the general supervision of a national scheme of revenue and expenditure, whose orders the Exchequer and the revenue

---

[1] Turner, i. 164-18, 217-19; Prothero, 396; Tanner, 380.

[2] Prothero, 397-9.

[3] Turner, i. 158-9, 162-3, 168-71, ii. 204. On the deficiencies of naval administration under Lord High Admiral Nottingham (Howard of Effingham), and the reforms of 1618, see M. Oppenheim, *The Royal Navy under James I*, 7 E.H.R. 471, and *The Royal Navy under Charles I*, 9 E.H.R. 473.

departments, as they came into being, were expected to fulfil. Nevertheless the financial organisation of the Crown was not yet separated from the Council, whose business it was to plan income and expenditure, and which moreover was used for the actual levying of monies such as impositions, forced loans and ship-money, supervising collectors both of such revenues as these and of sums granted by Parliament, stimulating their efforts and if necessary supporting their authority.[1]

*Social and economic policy of the Council*    Conciliar oversight was maintained over social and economic concerns with a rigour to which has been attributed much of the odium which conciliar government now began to incur. Besides keeping local authorities up to the mark in the administration of the law regarding wages, prices, and poor-relief, and taking measures against enclosures and depopulation—in which respect it was seriously handicapped by having to work through officials who were not its paid subordinates and whose interests often ran counter to the policy of the government—the Council was specially concerned, in an age of expanding commerce and intensified competition, with the supervision of trading companies and patents of monopoly. Efforts thus to regulate trade in the national interest, with which might be associated insistence on royal rights of pre-emption, as a means of forcing prices down,[2] were natural enough as a corollary of the paternalistic functions exercised by the Crown in matters affecting the social and material well-being of its subjects. Ideally, they might be considered as an attempt to protect the poor against the rich; to hold the balance evenly between the producer and the consumer; to safeguard the interests of the small master-craftsman; and to ensure an abundant supply of goods of high quality at a reasonable price. They did in fact impose some control over the predatory landlord and the wealthy capitalist who resented interference with his economic freedom. It hardly appears, however, that the conduct of royal control over economic affairs attained to these lofty heights. The Council, to which consideration of patents of monopoly was assigned, seems to have confined itself to merely approving grants passed by the Treasury and the law officers of

[1] Turner, i. 153-8, 159-62.
[2] Where the Crown was the buyer, at least. But the seller might recoup this loss by charging higher prices to others.

the Crown.[1] Elizabeth indeed had in 1597 promised to have all her grants brought to the "trial and true touchstone" of the law.[2] James began his reign by calling in all patents save those held by companies in order to ascertain their validity, and instructed his Council to enquire into all future grants. The Common Law had indeed a doctrine to lay down regarding monopolies, stated in the case of *D'Arcy* v. *Allen* (1602), where a patent for the sole importation of playing cards was condemned as not being intended to protect a new invention or necessary for the furtherance of commerce, and as inflicting damage on the public.[3] Yet in the grants made by James I little or no regard was paid either to the legality or the expediency of such grants. The main consideration was the financial advantage of the Crown. The creation of monopolies, too often by corrupt means, in favour of financiers and courtiers and with reference to commodities in everyday use or for purposes—such as the licensing of alehouses—the public utility of which was doubtful, created an irritation which led in 1621 to the impeachment of two notorious monopolists, Michell and Mompesson, and in 1624 to the enactment of the Statute of Monopolies, the first statutory abridgement of the Prerogative accomplished since the New Monarchy began.[4]

Ecclesiastical affairs were gradually but not wholly ceasing to concern the Council directly. Dealings with recusants, it is true, remained under its general supervision, exercised over local commissioners or local officials such as the Justices of the Peace, sheriffs, constables, and churchwardens.[5] Ecclesiastical discipline was committed to the bishops, subject to conciliar oversight together with that exercised by the High Commission. The rigid policy initiated by Whitgift as Archbishop of Canterbury was continued by his successors, Bancroft (1604–10), Abbot (1611–33), and Laud (1633–45). A well-drilled Convocation

*Ecclesiastical administration*

---

[1] E. Hughes, *Studies in Administration and Finance, 1558–1825*, 83.

[2] On this point, compare Hughes, 67, and Cheyney, ii. 292.

[3] For a detailed study of this case, see D. Seaborne Davies, *Further Light on the Case of Monopolies*, 48 L.Q.R. 394.

[4] The best opinion is that the Stuart monopolies only did harm, raising prices, lowering quality, and retarding industry. See G. Unwin, *The Gilds and Companies of London*, 327.

[5] Turner, i. 171-2.

seconded their efforts by the enactment of sets of canons, of which the most important appeared in 1604 and 1640.[1] Presiding over the whole system, the High Commission, having parted with its administrative duties of enforcing the Acts of Supremacy and Uniformity, turned itself after 1580 almost completely into a court of justice. Its jurisdiction, partly taken over from the Council, partly created by itself, was both appellate from lower ecclesiastical courts and original. It swiftly developed a wide sphere of competence in matters of defamation, perjury, sexual and other moral irregularities, matrimonial cases, probate and ecclesiastical business, subject to the concurrent jurisdiction for certain purposes and the ultimate control of the Council itself. Its jurisdiction, more equitable at many points than that of the Common Law courts, was in demand among suitors, and it remained a popular court except with regard to its penal jurisdiction, which penetrated into the most intimate details of the personal life of clergy and laity alike, and came, in conjunction with that of the Star Chamber, to be employed in order to repress rigorously any criticism in word or writing of the uses to which the royal supremacy over the Church was being put.[2]

*The religious situation*.    The use of the royal supremacy by James I, and still more by Charles I, aroused an anxiety which proved the closest bond of union among the various classes who were drawn together into opposition to the Crown. In the reign of James I the Anglican Church was beginning to lose its old comprehensive character. The dwindling ranks of English separatism were swelled by renewed deprivations of clergy who, while remaining within the establishment, had scrupled to conform to certain points of ceremonial and to profess literal and entire acceptance of the Articles and the Prayer Book. On the other hand, such hopes as still remained—and they had been temporarily quickened by dissensions among Catholics in Elizabeth's later years—that recusants might in the end be induced to reconcile themselves with the Church were wrecked by the Gunpowder Plot of 1605. With

[1] Prothero, 444-5; Wilkins, *Concilia*, iv. 543-53.; Tanner, 231-43.
[2] Holdsworth, i. 608-9; R. G. Usher, *Rise and Fall of the High Commission*, 100-103. For procedure, see Usher, ch. v. It may perhaps be remarked that the combination with the other powers of the executive of this inquisitorial power into the details of personal life was bound to make its authority intolerable to an increasing number of its subjects.

increasing distinctness there appeared, sharply severed from the Church, groups of irreconcilable recusants and sectaries. Towards these, the Crown and Parliament (the latter in this respect clearly voicing the opinion of the nation) adopted wholly different attitudes. While the Crown persecuted radical Reformers, Parliament showed its antagonism to a policy which engendered schism in the Protestant ranks. The Crown's policy towards recusants, on the other hand, while based on a sensible recognition of the claim of loyal Catholics to be regarded otherwise than as enemies of the State, kindled general suspicion. Abroad, it involved an incomprehensible preference for Catholic alliances, for dynastic unions with the Catholic reigning houses of France and Spain, for friendly instead of hostile relations with the Papacy. Foreign states urged James and Charles to relax the penal laws. James's Queen, Anne of Denmark, became a Catholic, and Charles's French wife, Henrietta Maria, made the Court itself a centre of Catholic revival where conversions became fashionable.[1] A papal nuncio, Panzani, entered England in 1634. It was widely believed that the Crown and the hierarchy intended a reconciliation with Rome.

This belief was unfounded. Yet even under James I, *Opposition* Protestant fervour in the Church was being disciplined into sub- *to the* mission. Conformist ecclesiastics were coming to align them- *Crown's* selves with the King against a Parliament of Puritan sympathies. *astical* In such works as Cowell's *Interpreter*, they elevated the royal *policy* power from which rather than from any principle of ecclesiastical independence they derived episcopal authority, and propounded notions of royal absolutism and passive obedience, and limitations on parliamentary competence and privilege, which could not fail to arouse parliamentary animosity.[2] The situation became worse when, under Charles I, royal patronage was extended to a party inspired by the teaching of Lancelot Andrewes, which seemed to emphasise the Catholic while rejecting the Protestant heritage of Anglicanism. This High Church or "Arminian"[3] party indelibly associated the royal supremacy with

---

[1] Gardiner, *History of England, 1603–1642*, viii. 238–44. The whole question is discussed by A. O. Meyer, *Charles I and Rome*, 19 *A.H.R.* 13.

[2] Extracts printed by Tanner, 12–14, and Prothero, 409–11. See also S. B. Chrimes, *The Constitutional Ideas of Dr. John Cowell*, 64 *E.H.R.* 461.

[3] So-called because of the supposed similarity of Laud's opinions to those of the Dutch theologian Arminius, in whose works the more extreme form of Calvinist doctrine was modified.

Romanising tendencies in the Church. Attempts to impose conformity on the clergy in such matters as vestments and ceremonial; the enforcement, often badly needed, of more orderly and reverent behaviour by the laity in church; greater care in the maintenance of ecclesiastical buildings; and above all, the requirement that the communion table should be railed off altar-wise at the east end of the church—all of which, uninspired in all probability by any desire to insist on their doctrinal implications, characterised the administration of Laud as archbishop—seemed so many indications of a fixed purpose to restore the Anglican Church to communion with Rome.[1]

*The record of conciliar government*   Conciliar government under the first two Stuarts might thus be variously regarded. From one point of view, those years in which it approached its stormy sunset were the golden age in which its ideals were most nearly attained. Save in the decade 1620–30, it maintained external peace. It greatly improved naval defence. After years of effort, royal income and expenditure were balanced without parliamentary supply. The government did its best to maintain social justice. The regulation of wages and prices was enforced, the poor-law was perhaps never better administered.[2] Order and decency were restored in the services of the Church, sacred buildings rescued from improper uses, Christian standards of conduct enforced. Yet it was possible to take a less favourable view of its achievements. It was not easy to reconcile concern for the Protestant cause in the Thirty Years War with a proclivity for Catholic alliances, or sincere attachment to Anglican Protestantism with attempts to relax the penal laws, systematic persecution of Protestant radicals, and patronage of a Romanising episcopate. The policy of regulating trade in the national interest seemed a mere restraint on individual enterprise, and was moreover tainted with the miasma of favouritism and corruption which infected the Court. This atmosphere of decay likewise brooded over the Councils of the North and of Wales.[3] The royal

---

[1] Such doctrinal implications as they had certainly involved a sacramentarian view of the Church, but did not involve any recognition of Roman authority. The distinction was, however, difficult to draw. See E. C. E. Bourne, *The Anglicanism of Archbishop Laud.*

[2] E. M. Leonard, *Early History of English Poor Relief,* 144–64.

[3] On the scandals in the Council of the North after 1612, see Reid, *King's Council in the North,* 378 ff. The Council of Wales seems to have offered

finances were supported by revenues derived from the perversion of prerogative powers, and the naval strength which the Crown contrived to develop under Charles I was based on a judicial decision in the *Case of Ship-Money* which most men regarded as grotesque and dangerous. With all its merits, therefore, the last age of conciliar government only succeeded in awakening an opposition of which Parliament made itself to an increasing extent the authentic representative.

### iii

No intention to deny to Parliament its traditional place in the constitution need be imputed to the first two Stuarts, or to the abler of their advisers. Strong men like Salisbury, Bacon, Middlesex, Buckingham and Wentworth did not fear to meet Parliament, and were confident of their power to maintain it in the ancient relationship with the Crown. Nor did they intend to repudiate the law, for they were confident that the law was on their side. If their rule led to a temporary disuse of Parliament, or to straining of the law by the judges, it was, as they conceived, because their opponents were perverting the proper powers and privileges of Parliament for their own factious and selfish purposes. Their ideal of government was that a well-equipped and vigorous monarchy, aided by wise counsellors, should act disinterestedly, benevolently and effectively for the common good of its subjects, while Parliament should act as its instrument of legislation and supply, and as a means of supplying on public questions an opinion which would at least be duly weighed if not always given effect to. It is impossible not to recognise here an idealised version of the Tudor constitution, perfectly defensible by reference to the standards of the past, and failing only by its decreasing relevance to the circumstances of the present. *The place of Parliament in the constitution*

If the Crown and its servants failed to exhibit the old Tudor gift of combining executive and legislature harmoniously together, the fault was not altogether on their side. James indeed proved unable to dispel, through Elizabeth's wise combination of persuasion *Changed disposition of Parliament*

similar cause of complaint; see Skeel, *Council of the Marches*, 140, and *The Council of the Marches in the Seventeenth Century*, 30 E.H.R. 19. There seems little doubt that both courts had outlived their usefulness.

and command, the parliamentary difficulties which her closing years presaged for the reign of her successor. Over-frequent and generally undignified interventions in parliamentary proceedings blunted the edge of a weapon which she had employed with economy and effect, and a didactic tone more appropriate to a pedagogue than a prince stimulated rather than silenced criticism.[1] Yet, when all allowances are made for the inability of James I to command respect and of Charles I to inspire confidence, and for the incapacity which some of their ministers showed in handling Parliament, it none the less remains true that they had to deal with a very refractory assembly, no longer content to accept guidance and control from the King and his servants.

*The Lords under the early Stuarts*

This disposition existed more strongly in the Commons than in the Lords. In the Lower House the Crown's opponents came to command a working majority, even if it was due to the indifference or timidity which induced less radical men to absent themselves from debates. Among the Lords the regular opposition always remained a minority, never exceeding thirty in number, or about one-third of the peers generally in attendance at the House.[2] The majority were by no means partisans of the Crown, though they included in the bishops a solid block of royalist supporters whose ranks were never broken except in the debates on the Petition of Right.[3] The bishops were not typical of the Upper House. When an individual bishop fell foul of the Commons—as did Thornborough of Bristol in 1604 with regard to Anglo-Scottish union and Neile of Lincoln in 1614 by an attack on their competence to debate matters affecting the Prerogative—the lay peers showed no disposition to support him.[4] The lay peers as a whole sided neither with Crown nor Commons and attempted to preserve in their disputes an independent and mediatorial position for which the non-elective character and the judicial attributes of the House well qualified it. At times the House of Lords of the early Stuarts could show an unaccustomed attitude of hostility towards the Crown, which thus lost direct support in Parliament and indirect support from the exercise of aristocratic influence on the royal

---

[1] Notestein, 32.

[2] C. H. Firth, *House of Lords during the Civil War*, 77.

[3] Firth, 49. The Archbishop of Canterbury and the Bishops of Lincoln and Norwich were for the Petition.      [4] Firth, 36-7.

side in elections.[1] The numerous new creations which increased the number of lords from about sixty on James's accession to about one hundred and fifty on the eve of the Civil War alienated the holders of more ancient peerages, the more so because of the "merchandise of honours" which attended it.[2] In 1626 it was proposed to exclude new-made peers from taking part in the proceedings of the House.[3] Attacks on the privileges of the House could move the peers to unanimous protest. In 1626 and 1642 they even helped to maintain the Commons' privilege of freedom from arrest. With the Commons, the Lords might defend the position of Parliament as a necessary part of the machinery of government. Nevertheless they were not partners of the Commons. On certain topics, such as the financial questions debated in James's first Parliament, they showed themselves ready to take the opinion of the Commons, and anxious to hold conferences instead of merely exchanging messages with them.[4] Yet they showed a natural reluctance to follow the initiative of the Lower House, an elective body whose members possessed only a "private and local wisdom" not fitting them to meddle with great matters of State such as foreign policy. They looked askance at the claims put forward by the Commons to restrict the powers of the Crown, as in the debates on impositions in 1614 and on arbitrary imprisonment in 1627.[5] In short, the Lords strove to act as guardians of the constitution against innovations and encroachment by either Crown or Commons. It was perhaps among them that the will to preserve the ancient form of government remained strongest. This attitude was certain to alienate from them the sympathies of the radical majority in the Commons. The leaders of the Commons worked in concert with the radical minority in the Lords, and the wiser among them saw the need for seeking the support of the majority of the peers so far as possible. In the stormy times preceding the dissolution of 1629, however, the Commons, acting without the Lords' support and at odds with the

---

[1] For an interesting study of the influence of a peer over parliamentary elections in this period, see V. A. Rowe, *Influence of the Earls of Pembroke on Parliamentary Elections, 1625–1642*, 50 E.H.R. 242. The earls shared in the return of about a dozen members. The third earl was the enemy of Buckingham and patron of Eliot.        [2] Firth, 10–15.        [3] Firth, 45.
[4] Firth, 34. But perhaps conferences played into the hands of the government.        [5] Firth, 35, 40, 50–51.

judges endeavoured to combat the Crown alone.[1] In 1640–42 the same situation was reproduced. The Lords were gradually enlisted on the side of reformed monarchy against the pretensions of a revolutionary House of Commons to assert for itself the final authority in the State. With the constitution they had striven to defend, the Lords were shipwrecked in 1642. The minority who adhered to the Commons lingered on as an increasingly insignificant appendage to the popular House until their abolition followed the destruction of monarchy itself in 1649.

*Declining influence of the Crown over the Commons*    The conflict between Crown and Parliament has therefore to be written largely with reference to the attitude of the Commons. Alienation of the elective House, which controlled taxation and was intimately related with local administration and the mass of the electorate, was not seriously compensated for by the neutrality or even the support of an Upper House which in weight of property and influence was far its inferior.[2] From the beginning of James's reign the tendency of the Commons to escape from royal and ministerial control, already visible in the later years of Elizabeth, steadily gathered force. This tendency may in part be ascribed to mere deficiencies on the part of the Crown in the arts of political management. Except in the election of 1614, royal influence over the constituencies does not seem to have been exerted in the accustomed forms.[3] The example of 1614 suggests that such influence was no longer possible. In order to obtain the return of a majority favourable to the government, persons described as "Undertakers" were induced to promote the election of dependable candidates. The odium aroused by this transaction pervaded the proceedings of the 1614 Parliament. It caused the King to disavow all connexion with the "Undertakers" and to refrain from any similar experiment in the future. Equally little success attended the efforts of Charles I to rid himself of opponents in 1626 by nominating them as sheriffs, in which

---

[1] Firth, 54.                              [2] Firth, 31–2.

[3] A number of new constituencies were created by royal charter in the early part of James's reign—Tiverton, Tewkesbury, Evesham, Bewdley, Harwich, Bury St. Edmunds, Oxford and Cambridge Universities. The revival of others, like Ilchester, Pontefract, Amersham, Marlow, and Wendover was brought about by the action of the House itself.—In election cases, the House generally tried to enlarge the franchise. See W. Taffs, 8 *B.I.H.R.* 43, H. Willson, *Salisbury and the Court Party in Parliament*, 36 *A.H.R.* 274, and Lady E. de Villiers, *Parliamentary Boroughs restored by the House of Commons 1621–41*, 67 *E.H.R.* 175.

capacity they would be rendered incapable of election. This device merely cleared the way for Sir John Eliot's still more radical leadership. Opposition leaders, indeed, seem to have had little difficulty in obtaining election, and Court patronage proved no passport to a seat in the Commons.[1]

Another instrument for controlling the Commons was finally lost *Disputed* when in 1604 the House in the *Bucks Election Case* asserted its sole *elections* and exclusive jurisdiction over disputed election returns, which *and freedom* by the proclamation summoning the Parliament of that year *from arrest* had been conferred upon Chancery. The proclamation having disqualified from election persons under the technical disabilities imposed by outlawry, the Chancery quashed the election of Sir Francis Goodwin as knight of the shire for Bucks, ordered a new election, and declared his opponent, Sir John Fortescue, to have been returned. The Commons strongly and successfully repudiated this jurisdiction. In a third contest a new candidate, Sir Christopher Piggott, was duly elected and took his seat. The King got the empty satisfaction of a statute disabling outlaws from being elected in future, but he at once surrendered to the Commons jurisdiction over two other disputed returns, at Shrewsbury and Cardigan.[2] An authority which would have enabled the Crown to control with effect the composition of the Commons was henceforth abandoned. The capacity of the House to act as a court with exclusive jurisdiction over its own members save in cases of treason, felony, and breach of the peace was further asserted in *Shirley's Case* (1604), where a member imprisoned for debt was liberated by order of the House alone and without the issue of a writ of privilege, and those responsible for his detention, including the Warden of the Fleet prison, were committed to the custody of the Serjeant-at-arms. Again legislation dealt with subordinate points by safeguarding the rights of creditors and relieving gaolers from liability in such cases, but the point of principle was secured by the House.[3]

[1] A case in which the influence of the Privy Council was issued and prevailed is discussed by M. D. Bohannon, *The Essex Election of 1604*, 48 *E.H.R.* 395, but the writer contrasts with this election those of 1628 and 1640. For an instance of what appears to be reaction in the shires against court direction, see E. Farnham, *The Somerset Election of 1614*, 46 *E.H.R.* 579. The responsibility of the King for the proceedings of the "Undertakers" is somewhat uncertain, however. Private patronage has been studied by L. Stone, *The Electoral Influence of the Second Earl of Salisbury 1614-68*, 71 *E.H.R.* 384.

[2] Prothero, 280-81, 324, 325-33; Tanner, 202-17.

[3] Tanner, 303-17; Prothero, 320-25, and in 8 *E.H.R.* 733.

*Privy Councillors in the Commons*

The House asserted increasing command over its own business. Resort to the committee system impaired the authority so long exercised by the Speaker under direction from the Crown. The handful of Privy Councillors who sat in James's first Parliament were too few in number and perhaps too deficient in ability to impose their control over procedure and debate. That their numbers were small was not perhaps the King's fault. To sit in the House they had first to obtain election, and the experience of Sir John Fortescue, whose election the House declined to accept in 1604, suggests that this was not perhaps easy. The candidate ultimately elected, Sir Christopher Piggott, was indeed soon conspicuous in opposition. James may have made mistakes. He has been criticised for conferring the Secretaryship of State in 1614 on Sir Ralph Winwood, who had had extensive diplomatic but no parliamentary experience. But it may be doubted whether the failure of the Crown lay merely in the technique of electoral and parliamentary tactics. Its roots lay deeper, and needed the skill of the statesman rather than the arts of the political manager if they were to be dealt with. The Commons were ceasing to be amenable to governmental guidance. In the Parliament of 1614 objection was raised to the influence of Councillors on committees, once accepted as proper and valuable. The House no longer trusted the policy and intentions of these official spokesmen. Behind the defensive positions afforded by their claims to determine their privileges and procedure, they were beginning to organise themselves under leaders of their own choice rather than under the leadership of Privy Councillors, and as opponents rather than allies of the Crown.[1] At first merely obstructive, they later began to aim at imposing on the government a policy of their own. Against the men who were ousting its own servants from ascendancy over the House, the Crown sometimes resorted, as in Elizabeth's days, to measures of coercion. The commitment of opposition leaders was ordered by James in 1614 and 1621 and by Charles I in 1626 and 1629. It was attempted in 1642 against the Five Members. Whereas in the sixteenth century such action had been acquiescently received, in the

---

[1] On the position of Privy Councillors in the early Stuart Parliaments, see Notestein, 27-31; D. H. Willson, 36 *A.H.R.* 279-80, and his *Privy Councillors in the House of Commons, 1604-29.*

seventeenth it was met by a stubborn and unanimous defence of privilege.

The winning of the initiative by the Commons was a long *The* process, extending over the half-century from 1588 to 1642, *Commons'* yet the rapidity with which the House formulated its position *Apology* on James's accession suggests that the process was already far advanced. The session was hardly two months old when the Commons' Apology made explicit those discords between legislature and executive which had so long been latent.[1] In respectful but resolute tones, the House defended the privileges involved in the *Bucks Election Case* and *Shirley's Case*, and to the particular discussion of these points added the fundamental proposition that its privileges were a matter not of royal grace but of inheritance and right. Under the cover of this principle they placed also the privilege of freedom of speech, subject only to the condition that it must be used "with due reverence to the sovereign court of Parliament, that is, to your Majesty, and both the Houses, who all in this case make but one politic body, whereof Your Highness is the head"—a qualification which sensibly alters the traditional meaning of the privilege and increases its efficacy against the Crown.[2] The Apology likewise defended the right of the Commons to control its conduct of business with regard to a projected Anglo-Scottish Union and to the settlement of the revenues arising from pre-emption, purveyance, and feudal incidents, denied to the Crown any right to legislate in ecclesiastical matters except through Parliament, and asserted for Parliament the right to be referred to for the information on which the King based his policy.

Such claims as these invaded a field of action from which *Ecclesi-* the Commons had been repeatedly warned off, and on which *astical* they had lately made little serious effort to encroach. They had *problems:* listened, in the King's opening speech to Parliament, to an exposi- *Millenary* tion of his ecclesiastical policy which cannot have failed to *Petition* arouse their disquiet.[3] The King proposed, on the one hand, the enforcement of conformity on the Puritan clergy within the establishment who had in the Millenary Petition of the previous

---

[1] Tanner, 217-30; Prothero, 286-93.
[2] For the form in which this privilege was requested by the Speaker in 1604, see Tanner, 272-4, and 44 *E.H.R.* 454.    [3] Tanner, 27-30; Prothero, 283-5.

year expressed in moderate and deferential terms the familiar
objections to certain articles of ceremonial, various portions of
the Prayer Book and Articles, abuses such as pluralities and non-
residence, and the undue rigours of the High Commission.[1] On
the other, he held out the prospect of toleration to peaceable
Catholic recusants, though not to their clergy, to whom doctrines
of tyrannicide and of the authority of popes to depose kings were
attributed.

*Depriva-
tion of the
Puritan
clergy*

The royal policy, in both aspects, had already been put into
effect. At the Hampton Court Conference of January 1604 the
Puritans, notwithstanding their repudiation in the Petition of any
objection to the royal supremacy or any adherence to a "popular
parity" in Church government, had been confused by the King
with the theocratic Presbyterians of Scotland, and threatened with
expulsion if they declined to conform.[2] In June Convocation
had denounced excommunication against persons who denied
that Anglican government, ritual and dogma were consistent
with apostolic standards. A royal proclamation gave the Puritans
until November 30 to bring themselves to submission.[3] The
Commons were certain to react against all that the King
intended. Without sympathising with sectaries, they disliked a
policy which turned into sectaries a small and in late years a
dwindling number of Puritan members of the Church, no longer
supported as they once had been by influential patronage at Court.
Wiser men than James and his bishops might have left the
Petitioners unmolested as offering no real danger, and as representing opinions which—since on points of ceremonial they required
not a relaxation in individual cases but the general adoption and
enforcement of relaxed standards—the majority of churchmen
would have found no fault with the King in rejecting. James's hasty
and ill-considered action, which early in 1605 brought about the
eviction of some sixty clergy from their benefices, invested the
Petition with an importance which it did not intrinsically deserve.[4]
As in 1573, the ecclesiastical problem re-entered politics. The

---

[1] Tanner, 56-60; Prothero, 413-16. Examples of the abuses against which
Puritans protested is shown in papers printed by A. F. Peel, *A Puritan Survey of
the Church in Staffordshire in 1604*, 26 E.H.R. 338. The King's initial attitude
towards these complaints was not unsympathetic.
[2] Tanner, 67.                              [3] Tanner, 70-73; Prothero, 420-21.
[4] See R. G. Usher, *Deprivation of Puritan Ministers in 1605*, 24 E.H.R. 242.

Commons, forming themselves into a committee on religion, sent up to the Lords a series of proposals based on the Petition, refused the King's suggestion of a conference with Convocation, and declined to treat with the bishops save as lords of Parliament.[1] Thenceforward the cause of the ejected clergy became that of the Commons, while their conformist opponents supported and were supported by the Crown.

The antagonism of Crown and Commons further declared itself *The* on the Catholic question. James's first efforts to relax persecution *Roman* were countered by the renewal of the recusancy laws in 1604. In the *Catholics* following year, under the panic created by the Gunpowder Plot, this legislation was supplemented by measures enforcing the taking of communion and the celebration of marriages and baptisms under the Anglican rite as well as attendance at church, empowering the Crown to seize two-thirds of the property of recusants, forbidding them to practise as lawyers or physicians, appear at Court, or remain within ten miles of London, and imposing on them a new oath of allegiance repudiating the temporal authority of the Pope.[2] The increase of Catholic disabilities threw an additional strain on the dispensing power, used to relax the rigour of penal statutes which Parliament could not be induced to repeal.

Grave as these religious differences between Crown and *Projected* Commons appeared, it may be doubted whether they attained *union* at this juncture the fundamental importance attaching to them a *with* generation later. Whatever mistrust might be conceived of the *Scotland* King's ecclesiastical policy as creating schism and encouraging recusancy, it did not appear to threaten the essentially Pro- testant character of a Church still worshipping under the forms used in Elizabethan days and strongly influenced by Calvinistic theology. The quarrels of James with his Parliaments arose largely from more material and even sordid considerations. Commercial jealousy, as well as three centuries of national animosity which a mere dynastic union could not cancel out, determined the attitude of the Commons towards the King's well-meant schemes for an incorporating Anglo-Scottish union. James's assumption of the title of King of Great Britain had already aroused criticism. In 1604 his plan for a union was referred to commissioners empowered to

---

[1] Gardiner, *History of England*, i. 179-80; Prothero, 285-6, 289, 290.
[2] Prothero, 256-68.

negotiate with those of the Scottish Parliament.[1] When they reported in 1606, union was wrecked on the refusal of the Commons
to consent to the naturalisation of Scots in England—involving
the correlative right to acquire property there like natural-born
subjects—or to the establishment of commercial equality between
the two nations.[2] The sole result was the repeal of statutes treating
Scotland as a hostile state.[3] It was left for the judges in *Calvin's
Case* (1608) to take the important step of deciding that Scots born
after the Union of the Crowns (the *post-nati*) were to be accounted
natural-born subjects in England.[4]

*The
financial
problem*

Above all, problems connected with the royal revenue seem
to lie at the root of these early difficulties of the Crown with
Parliament. Here again, the opening debates of James's first
Parliament were ominous of later discord. Evils connected with
purveyance and pre-emption, with the jurisdiction of the Court
of Wards, and with the grant of monopolies excited more
interest in the Commons than the need for adequately endowing
the Crown. Abuses doubtless occurred with regard to all three.
Yet it may be suspected that the main object of the Commons
was to escape or impose on others the financial burdens of the
propertied class, and to remove what were considered undue
restraints on private enterprise. The same niggardly attitude
was adopted by the House with regard to financing the
normal requirements of the Crown. On this point they
adhered to the principle that "the King should live of his own".
That was no longer possible. The needs of the Crown increased
as the level of prices rose and the administrative system grew
more complex. Though the normal grant of tunnage and
poundage to the King for life was renewed, his income proved
inadequate to cover his ordinary outgoings. That this was so was
partly attributable to the extravagance with which the Commons
often charged him, and particularly to his reckless grants of
gifts and pensions to courtiers. The economies effected from 1620
onwards indicate that the Commons' complaints were not unfounded, and that James had shown little skill in husbanding his
resources. The fault was not wholly his own. With a family to maintain, he could not hope to restrict his household expenditure to the

---

[1] Tanner, 31-2.     [2] Gardiner, *History of England*, i. 324-38.
[3] Tanner, 38-43; Prothero, 251-2.     [4] Prothero, 446.

modest standard Elizabeth had set. Moreover, even her prudently managed government had had to appeal for supply to every Parliament which met in her reign. Though she had a stronger case to lay before Parliament than James, whose position was not visibly threatened in any quarter, she had not contrived to make ends meet, and had bequeathed to her successor a diminished income and a heavy burden of debt. The government of James I, adding to this debt by a yearly deficit averaging nearly £90,000 from 1603 to 1608 on ordinary expenditure alone without reckoning in extraordinary items not annually recurring, fell rapidly into deeper insolvency.[1]

Towards this problem the Commons showed the profoundest *Parsimony* indifference. In 1603, the supplies granted in 1601 not having fully *of the* come in to the Exchequer, no additional tax was imposed. In *Commons* 1606, after an initial offer of only a little over a quarter of a million, they were induced to grant £390,000, payable by 1610.[2] Meanwhile their attack on revenues derived from feudal dues and other sources threatened still further to impair the King's financial position. It is unnecessary to suppose that they had yet formed any conscious design to deprive the Crown of its control over government and policy by restricting supply. Their attitude was based on an ignorance partly excused by the inability of the government itself to form, or place before them, any clear account of its own liabilities and needs, and on a rooted antipathy to assuming regular financial obligations for the upkeep of government in time of peace when, according to current theory, the King's normal revenues ought to suffice him.

In this dilemma, the Crown naturally sought to exploit every *Financial* source of revenue to which any claim might be asserted. *expedi-* Devices like fines for encroaching on royal forests or for violating *ents of* proclamations against building in London brought in little *the Crown* revenue and created infinite friction. More profitable were new and more advantageous leases of Crown property. Even better were the results achieved by utilising the Crown's victory in the Courts in *Bates's Case* (1606). Several companies had successively been formed to monopolise Levantine trade on payment of an annual sum to the Crown, and when their charters lapsed the

---

[1] Dietz, *English Public Finance*, 122 *n.* 41. By 1608 debt stood at nearly £600,000.        [2] Dietz, 121.

Crown had recouped itself by imposing by Prerogative additional duties on imports. Following Elizabeth's example, James
in 1605 levied such duties on currants. A merchant named Bates
refused to pay them, probably on the ground that they were unauthorised by statute. The Court of Exchequer decided against
him, holding that the levy was legal as incident to the Prerogative to regulate trade, a reasoning approved, so far as it underlay
the decision, by Popham and Coke, Chief Justices of King's Bench
and Common Pleas. But the decision was plentifully overlaid with
*dicta*, treating the question as one of revenue and annexing the
revenues of the Crown to its "absolute" as distinct from its
"ordinary" power.[1] Thus a large opening was made for the
introduction of non-parliamentary taxation. In 1608 Salisbury
as Lord Treasurer used it to embody numerous impositions in
a new Book of Rates. Impositions became an additional and
important element in the fiscal system [2] rather than a device for
commercial regulation.

*The session of 1610*

Parliamentary proceedings in 1610 showed that this innovation
had still further vitiated the relation of Crown and Commons.
By impositions, sales of Crown property, and the enforcement
of arrears due to the Crown, the Lord Treasurer had reduced
indebtedness by two-thirds. He now sought a non-recurrent
grant of £600,000 to complete the process, provide for the navy,
and form a reserve fund, and a permanent annual grant of
£200,000.[3] Coupled with these proposals was the suggestion,
pregnant with future trouble, that in return for financial aid the
Crown would consider fiscal and political concessions. Thus
began that marketing of prerogative powers which characterised
the rest of the Stuart period. Royal prerogatives seemed to become a saleable commodity. The Commons at once improved
their opportunity. The Crown was faced with complaints against
the ejection of clergy, the High Commission, the abuse of proclamations in order to create new offences and impose new punishments, the jurisdiction of the Council of Wales over the English
border counties, and the new impositions.[4] By the negotiations

---

[1] Tanner, 264, 338-45; Prothero, 340-42; D. L. Keir and F. H. Lawson,
*Cases in Constitutional Law* (5th ed.), 78-9.

[2] Dietz, 120. They were reckoned to bring in £60,000 yearly.

[3] Dietz, 134.    [4] Tanner, 77-80, 148-56, 245-7; Prothero, 296-8, 300-307

known as the Great Contract [1] it was proposed to commute the revenues accruing from purveyance and feudal dues, and restrict impositions by statute. There was offered in return an annual payment which the Commons ultimately proposed to fix at £200,000. Since the King was already deriving from these sources, excluding impositions, a net revenue of £115,000, the bargain was from his point of view none too attractive. On their side, the Commons soon repented of having gone so far. In the discontents of this final session, the whole scheme perished and with it the bill on impositions. The dissolution of 1610 left the financial problem unsolved.[2]

Between 1610 and 1614 the position further deteriorated. *The Addled Parliament* Every expedient for improving it—including the sale of the newly invented title of baronet [3]—had been attempted. Yet debt increased as the annual deficit mounted to £160,000, without counting such extraordinary items as the £60,000 spent on the Princess Elizabeth's marriage in 1612 to the Elector Palatine of the Rhine.[4] In 1614 ministers, conscious that Parliament held the key to the situation, once more turned to it with an optimism which the brief and sterile proceedings of the "Addled Parliament" proved to be baseless. That the temper of the House of Commons was animated by other than material concerns was shown when the members received communion at St. Margaret's Westminster instead of the Abbey, "for fear of copes and wafer-cakes",[5] but the main current of debate ran stormily and inconclusively on the themes of impositions, monopolies, and the "Undertakers". Proceedings were dominated not by Privy Councillors but by the old leaders of revolt, now reinforced by newcomers like Eliot and Wentworth. Thus passed away the last chance of amicably readjusting the financial relations of Crown and Parliament under peace-time conditions. It never recurred.[6]

Henceforth, the policy of the government was to rely on its *Financial rehabilitation* own resources rather than on any expectation of parliamentary support. At first the situation seemed more than ever desperate. Salisbury was succeeded as Treasurer in 1612 by a body of commissioners who were at least aware of the facts, even if unable to

---

[1] Dietz, 134-40: Tanner, 345-54; Prothero, 275-6.
[2] Dietz, 140.      [3] Dietz, 148.
[4] Dietz, 156.      [5] Gardiner, *History of England*, ii. 237.
[6] The Addled Parliament has now been fully studied by T. L. Moir in his book bearing that title.

suggest a remedy. Their successor, Suffolk (1614–18), seems to
have been aware of nothing.[1] Debt approached £900,000 in 1618,
and the deficiency on ordinary expenditure was £137,000.[2] A
benevolence of 1614 had failed. Subsequent schemes for raising
money were sterile as they were plentiful. In 1615 the Council
even contemplated a new appeal to Parliament. The need for
such a hopeless experiment was averted by competent administrative action, perhaps to be ascribed to Buckingham, the new royal
favourite who had displaced the incompetent Ker of Ferniehurst,
but more probably to Lionel Cranfield, a London merchant whose
influence can be traced in the management of various branches
of royal finance from 1612 onwards.[3] From 1618 to 1620 drastic
reforms of household and public expenditure were undertaken.
The commissioners appointed to control the navy in 1618 created
a better fleet on a smaller annual income. In 1619 ordinary
revenue for the first time balanced ordinary expenditure and
there was even a small surplus for extraordinaries. In 1620
arrangements for the repayment of debt were resumed.[4]

*Its
dangers*
It now seemed possible that, once his debts were repaid, the
King could hope to govern without Parliament. Yet success had
been attained at a dangerous price. The means by which revenue
had been improved, such as impositions and monopolies, were
certain to provoke bitter conflict with Parliament should it again
be summoned, and Cranfield's economies had raised up for him
enemies who would not help him in face of parliamentary attack.
The Crown's new position, in short, was secure only if the
meeting of Parliament were indefinitely delayed. Such a position
was highly unstable. It was not insured against the greatest risk
of any political system—the risk of war.

iv

*The war
years and
the con-
stitution*
The development of the constitution was determined between
1621 and 1629 by the crisis which emerged from the Bohemian

---

[1] Dietz, 150-53, 165, 170.                    [2] Dietz, 169, 172.
[3] Surveyor-General of Customs, 1613, Master of the Wardrobe, 1618,
Master of the Court of Wards and Commissioner for the Navy, 1619, Privy
Councillor, 1620, created Baron Cranfield and Earl of Middlesex, 1622. For
accounts of his career, see Dietz, 171 ff., and R. H. Tawney, *Business and Politics
under James I.*                                 [4] Dietz, 180-81.

Revolt of 1618. James had wisely declined to countenance his son-in-law Frederick's acceptance of the Bohemian throne. He could not be indifferent to its results. As a man of peace, with ambitions to act in a mediatorial rôle, he endeavoured at first to use diplomatic means alone. His hope that an Anglo-Spanish entente might lead to a negotiated peace was not wholly misplaced. By the end of 1620 it was fading. Frederick was a fugitive both from his usurped kingdom and from his electoral territories, occupied by Spanish and Bavarian forces. The King saw the need for strengthening his hand by an appeal to Parliament. To James and his ministers co-operation with Parliament was still, it is to be remembered, a constitutional axiom, though they had not yet found the terms in which it would work. Hitherto the difficulties which had arisen had been concerned mainly with domestic affairs, and in particular with the problem of the King's peace-time revenues. Since that question seemed to have been successfully solved, it might be hoped that its contentious possibilities were exhausted. Now that war threatened, it was the constitutional duty of Parliament to aid the Crown with grants of extraordinary supply and thus enable it to conduct the necessary military, naval and diplomatic action of the State. To withhold supply, to give it in inadequate measure, to condemn or dictate the purposes for which it was to be employed, would be to wrest government and policy from royal control, and it was not to be thought that Parliament would advance so revolutionary a claim.

Yet this was the line which Parliament (or more accurately, *Renewed* the Commons) followed until the policy of continental inter- *attacks* vention was abandoned in 1629. Before 1621 the Crown had had *by the* no specific continental responsibilities save for the cautionary *Commons* towns, and these had as a financial expedient been sold to the *Crown* Dutch in 1616.[1] The necessity in which the Crown now found itself of framing a foreign policy gave to the Commons their long-awaited opportunity. With regard to continental affairs they professed sympathy for the purposes which inspired its action. But they distrusted its aims, refused to finance its schemes, and tried to force on it a policy of their own devising which was

[1] Dietz, 162-3. They had cost £25,000 yearly to maintain, which was now saved, and were sold for £210,000.

wholly inadequate to the true needs of the situation. Their real interest was to pay off old scores about unparliamentary taxation and conciliar jurisdiction, to attack and overthrow royal ministers, dispute the Crown's ecclesiastical supremacy, even at the cost of impeding the measures which it took in order to support its continental allies. Not until peace was restored in 1629 could the conciliar element in government, impaired in vigour by the impeachment of ministers, and by statutory diminutions of the Prerogative in 1624 and 1628, drag itself out of range of the attacks of its parliamentary partner.

*Failure of the Crown's foreign policy*    The action of Parliament is not without defence. James's proclivity for a Spanish alliance had led him after 1614 to admit the Spanish ambassador, Diego de Sarmiento, Count of Gondomar, to an improper influence over his counsels. To that influence was attributed the national disgrace of Raleigh's execution in 1618. It seemed unlikely that war supplies, if voted, would be used against Spain, which the mass of James's subjects differed from their king in still regarding as the national enemy. The fiasco of Charles's visit to Madrid with Buckingham in 1623 seemed the final and humiliating condemnation of the royal policy and a vindication of the Commons' criticisms. Nor did the French alliance which Charles and Buckingham entered upon in 1625, linked though it was with the treaties of Southampton and the Hague uniting England with Denmark and the Dutch Republic, prove any more fortunate in its results, of which the first was the loan of an English squadron to co-operate with the forces of the French government against the Huguenot rebels of La Rochelle. The record of the Crown's military and diplomatic efforts up to 1629 was indeed unimpressive. A continental expedition under Mansfeld had failed miserably in 1624-5, as did a naval campaign against Cadiz in the autumn of the latter year. The French alliance had worked badly, English command of the sea having generated friction over the seizure of French ships suspected of carrying contraband, so that England drifted into war with France as well as Spain. Attempts to relieve La Rochelle miscarried in 1627, 1628, and 1629. Meanwhile the last English military forces on the Continent had surrendered. The Elector was still a homeless refugee. Denmark, lacking the expected English subsidies, had been overrun, and the progress of the armies of the victorious Counter-Reformation was stayed only by the waters of the North Sea and the Baltic. It would seem that a policy so inept and futile could never have deserved to obtain parliamentary support.

The Crown too had its case. The concern which Parliament *Attitude* during the years from 1621 professed for the cause of continental *of the* Protestantism was shallow. Its failure to issue in action might *Parlia-ment of* have been predicted from the collapse of schemes to help the *1621* Elector by loan or gift before Parliament was summoned. In 1621 Parliament was ready to pass resolutions of sympathy for the King's son-in-law. Confronted with the government's request for an immediate grant of half a million for the armed forces, the Commons replied with two subsidies, amounting to about £160,000, to which a third subsidy was later added.[1] Coupled with these meagre grants, and perhaps as a means of ensuring that they should not in the absence of any effective system of appropriation and audit be diverted to other uses, they put forward demands that James should seek a Protestant marriage for his son, break with Spain and declare war on her.[2] Politically, such counsel was unsound. It forced the King to resort to war when his diplomatic resources were not exhausted and would have been enhanced by an increase in his military strength, and it directed his action against Spain when, as the government was well aware, the chief need was for effective action in Germany. Constitutionally, it was an impertinence. Royal marriages and foreign policy lay within the King's undoubted Prerogative.[3] In these matters the Commons had never been allowed any initiative. As in 1614, the King followed Tudor precedents by coercing the opposition. Its leaders—Southampton in the Lords and Sandys in the Commons—were committed to custody by his order. He announced that he had authority to "punish any man's misdemeanours in Parliament, as well during their sittings as afterwards". An angry interchange of messages, culminating in the Commons' Protestation of November 1621 which asserted that the privilege of freedom of speech within such limits as the House alone could impose existed as of right, and which

---

[1] Dietz, 188.               [2] Tanner, 276-9; Prothero, 307-10.
[3] On this point, see E. R. Turner, *Parliament and Foreign Affairs, 1603-1760*, 34 *E.H.R.* 172-5.

the King himself subsequently tore out of the Journals of the House, brought to an appropriate end a Parliament which for the first time had challenged the Crown's control over powers hitherto regarded as essential to the discretionary authority of kingship.[1]

*Parliament of 1624*

By 1624 the conduct of a successful foreign policy without an adequate basis of parliamentary supply had been proved impossible. A benevolence of 1622 had yielded £116,000, but with customs increased and every source of revenue fully utilised, the annual deficit had risen to £160,000 by 1623, and £371,000 was needed to pay for extraordinary expenditure, mainly in connexion with the continental war. The King was ready to surrender, and even to invite Parliament in 1624 to take into consideration those matters of foreign policy previously withheld from it. No attempt had been made to tamper with elections. The device of sending the opposition leaders Coke and Sandys to Ireland had been considered but laid aside. James and his ministers were indeed prepared to carry out the opposition's favourite plan of a mainly naval war against Spain, while sensibly emphasising the superior claims of the continental theatre of war. At the Commons' request, relations with Spain were broken off. They were allowed to nominate treasurers to control supplies appropriated for the war.[2] But, for the fourfold plan which they put forward— the defence of Ireland and of England, aid to the Dutch, and an expedition overseas—they voted only £300,000, where four times as much would not have been excessive. How feebly they conceived the realities of the situation is expressed in the remark of a member who said, "The Palatinate was the place intended by His Majesty. This we never thought of, nor is it fit for the consideration of the House, in regard of the infinite charge."[3]

*Parliament of 1625*

It might be urged in defence of the Commons of 1621 and 1624

[1] Tanner, 279-89; Prothero, 310-14. The Commons' Debates of 1621 have been edited in seven volumes by W. Notestein, F. H. Relf, and H. Simpson. For a general commentary, see W. S. Holdsworth in 52 *L.Q.R.* 481. Attention is drawn to the development of privilege and procedure, the enlargement of asserted competence, and the numerous grievances regarding administration and justice.

[2] Dietz, 205-8; Tanner, 374-9; Prothero, 278-80.       [3] Dietz, 208.

that they had no real belief in James's warlike intentions. The same cannot be said of their successors of 1625-9. Inspired partly by his own personal feelings, partly by the influence of Buckingham, who had long been eager for war and confident of his ability to dominate Parliament, Charles I prepared elaborate schemes for continental intervention, including a subsidy of £30,000 monthly to Denmark.[1] He was eager for parliamentary support and expected to get it. Only five days after his accession he issued writs for a new Parliament. But for extraordinary supply it offered only two subsidies, about one-tenth of what he needed. With these were associated demands, justifiable enough by the terms of the 1624 grant, for an enquiry into the conduct of Mansfeld's expedition.[2] More serious was an attack, prompted by the grievance regarding impositions, on the King's ordinary revenue. The customary vote of tunnage and poundage for life was replaced by a grant for one year only.[3] The second session of this Parliament, at Oxford, proved the hopelessness of looking for parliamentary help. Criticisms of the government's foreign policy, particularly of the French alliance, were accompanied by an obdurate refusal to provide supply, and had to be terminated by dissolution.[4] Just as from 1603 to 1614 the Commons had refused to finance the Crown's peace-time government, so by 1625 they had refused to finance its extraordinary requirements even for purposes which they had professed to approve.

Moreover, now that the Crown had yielded to, or come to share, Parliament's ostensible enthusiasm for war, the conduct of the war itself became a grievance. To the failure of Mansfeld in 1624 there was added that of the Cadiz expedition of 1625.[5] More concerned to place responsibility for such misfortunes on the King's ministers than to examine its own part therein or to prevent their future recurrence, the Parliament of 1626 delivered fresh assaults on the Prerogative. Both Houses were aggrieved by measures taken by the King against certain of their number. The Earl of Bristol had been forbidden to comply with his writ of summons, and the Earl of Arundel had been

*Parliament of 1626*

---

[1] Dietz, 222.　　　　　　　[2] Gardiner, *History of England*, v. 346.
[3] Dietz, 226.　　　　　　　[4] Dietz, 226-7.
[5] On the administrative conduct of these campaigns, see M. Oppenheim, *The Royal Navy under Charles I*, 8 E.H.R. 467.

committed to custody.[1] Coke and Wentworth, leaders of the opposition in the Commons, had been appointed sheriffs and thereby incapacitated from re-election.[2] Grievances took precedence of supply. Mansfeld's failure, the loan of ships against La Rochelle, maritime quarrels with France, all provided themes for complaint; for a demand, which the King resisted, to investigate the proceedings of the Council of War; and ultimately for a further direct attack, by the impeachment of Buckingham, on the principle that ministers were solely responsible to the King.[3] The King's attempt to coerce the managers of the impeachment, Eliot and Digges, caused the Lords to rally to Digges's defence and obtain his liberation on the ground that he had not uttered words imputed to him by the King. The Commons, disregarding the King's assertion that Eliot's offence had been committed out of Parliament, declined to go on with business until Eliot also was set free. Both Houses were unanimous in protesting against the threat that the King would do without Parliaments altogether.[4]

*Extra-parliamentary taxation*

After a dissolution, forced on the King as the sole means of saving his minister, the attempt to wage war without Parliament was disastrously resumed. In 1625 levies of troops had been raised in the counties. In 1626 and 1627 a demand was made on maritime districts for ships or ship-money. Sale of Crown lands was again resorted to. Efforts were made to raise money by free gift and by a forced loan. Tunnage and poundage, unauthorised by Parliament, was levied by Prerogative.[5] By various means, about one million pounds was raised in the year ending at Michaelmas 1627. All this was at a disastrous political cost, which could be redeemed only by successes which the King never achieved. Resistance to the forced loan of September 1626 was countered by numerous dismissals of Justices of the Peace. The Stuarts were now faced by the risk, inherent in the Tudor system, that unpaid

---

[1] Firth, 44-5; S. R. Gardiner, *Constitutional Documents of the Puritan Revolution*, 44-6.

[2] One of the six members appointed sheriffs, Coke, was actually returned for Norfolk, and the Commons allowed him to take his seat. See H. Hulme, *The Sheriff in the House of Commons*, 1 *J.M.H.* 367.

[3] For a full account of the parliamentary proceedings of 1626, see H. Hulme, *The Leadership of Sir John Eliot in the Parliament of 1626*, 4 *J.M.H.* 361.

[4] Firth, 46-7.

[5] Gardiner, *Constitutional Documents*, 46-57; Dietz, 228-33, 235-7.

administrators would refuse to execute the Crown's orders. The names of persons who declined to pay were certified to the Privy Council. Many were pressed for military service. Some were imprisoned by order of the King. In the *Five Knights' Case* (1627) the King's Bench—previously tuned by the dismissal of Chief Justice Crew—held on the authority of the judges' opinion of 1591, and on considerations of public policy which made such a power requisite to the safety of the State, that an imprisonment *per speciale mandatum domini regis* but without cause shown was not bailable.[1] Whatever the legal merits of the judgment, it entirely omitted to reckon with the difference between the troubled sixteenth century when such a power readily obtained its sanctions in public opinion and the circumstances of the present when it seemed merely a convenient device for coercing the King's critics and opponents.

Beyond this forced loan the government's financial measures *Martial* hardly extended. Schemes for debasing the coinage, for levying *law* an excise, and for imposing ship-money generally over the kingdom were all abandoned.[2] Financial stringency led naturally to other embarrassments. Unpaid and ill-disciplined soldiers and sailors, enlisted for the expeditions of 1624 and later years, had to be compulsorily billeted, for there was no money to hire quarters for them. Their relations—and those of the miscellaneous fringe of civilians who attached themselves to the forces—with the general civil population involved the issue of commissions of martial law conferring summary jurisdiction over soldiers and civilians alike, though the legality of their issue within the realm and in time of internal peace was not easily justifiable.[3]

It was with such grievances rather than the fate of La Rochelle *The* and the crisis of Protestantism in Germany that the Parliament of *Parlia-* 1628 was concerned. A grant of five subsidies—about one-third *ment of* of what the King needed, though it is proper to add that neither *1628-9* his policy nor his financial needs were laid in detail before the Commons—was agreed to in principle, but no date was fixed for its imposition.[4] Redress was to precede supply. The attack

[1] Gardiner, *Constitutional Documents*, 57-64; Keir and Lawson, 79-80.
[2] Gardiner, *History of England*, vi. 138, 235, 238; Dietz, 234, 244.
[3] Gardiner, *History of England*, vi. 156.
[4] Dietz, 246; Gardiner, *History of England*, vi. 250.

on Buckingham was laid aside in favour of a more thorough-going assault on the whole system of discretionary powers which, from the Commons' point of view, had thus been perverted. It was decided to proceed by petition. To this—though, as the King made plain, not to a bill—a favourable answer might be returned before the grant of supply was made. Moreover, assuming as it did that the matters contained in it were well grounded in law, it would be as authoritative for the judges as a statute. This procedure would, in addition, help to unite those who had hoped for a statute and those who would have preferred to depend solely on the King's word.[1] The result was the Petition of Right, reciting, and condemning as illegal, the practices of forced loans, arbitrary imprisonment, and compulsory billeting of troops, and the issue of commissions of martial law. After an attempt to save his Prerogative by returning an evasive answer, the King gave way, assented to the Petition, and got his subsidies. Even the acceptance of the Petition did not satiate the Commons. A renewal of Buckingham's impeachment was threatened, and it was contended that the levy of tunnage and poundage by prerogative was illegal under the Petition of Right, though that document had in fact made no mention of it.[2] During the prorogation by which the King temporarily ended the deadlock, Buckingham was assassinated, and his war policy met with its final failure at La Rochelle. It was now discarded, and the Crown, no longer needing extraordinary supply, could look forward to dismissing Parliament and returning to the normal peace-time system of government through Council alone.

*The attack on monopolies*    That system had not survived the stress of the war years unimpaired. The Commons had throughout the whole period been unmistakably bent on utilising the opportunity of inflicting on it as much damage as possible. The Prerogative had been ceaselessly assailed. In 1621 the attack had fallen on the monopolies which had become a favourite device of governmental finance. Impeachment, disused throughout the Tudor period, was revived in order to strike down the monopolists

[1] See E. R. Adair, *The Petition of Right*, 5 *Hist.* 99. The discussions leading to the adoption of procedure by petition are outlined by H. Hulme, *Opinion in the House of Commons on the Proposal for a Petition of Right*, 50 E.H.R. 302.
[2] Gardiner, *Constitutional Documents* 73.

Michell and Mompesson with a sentence of degradation from knighthood, fine and imprisonment. Their patent, derived though it was from an ancient prerogative, was resolved by the House to have been bad in law.[1] In 1624 the prerogative to grant monopolies was restricted by a statute forbidding their issue except to cities and boroughs and to trading companies, saving to individuals only the right of an inventor to the protection of a patent for twenty-one years, and subjecting the legality of monopolies to the Common Law jurisdiction.[2]

Impeachment, revived against monopolists, had also been applied to ministers of the Crown. That of the Lord Chancellor, Bacon, in 1621 was founded on his conduct not as a minister but as a judge.[3] The charges laid against him for accepting presents from parties engaged in Chancery litigation were not highly culpable by the relaxed standards of the age, nor could it be proved that his acceptance of these gifts had in any way influenced his decisions. His fall is remarkable, therefore, as an illustration not so much of the punishment of administrative wrongdoing or judicial corruption as of the destruction of that immunity—save from an attainder consented to or even inspired by the King in Tudor times (as against Empson, Dudley, or Cromwell)—which had so long protected the royal ministers. James's offer that Bacon should be tried by a special commission was rejected. He was required to dismiss a competent and trusted servant, whom the Lords declared incapable of seat in Parliament or office under the Crown. He was impotent except to use his prerogative of pardon to alleviate the sentence of fine and imprisonment which completed his Chancellor's overthrow.[4] In 1624 impeachment fell on the Lord Treasurer, Middlesex, on charges of malversation. His antipathy to continental commitments did not win for him the sympathy which might have been expected from the Commons, and his rigid economies had lost him friends at Court. The King did what he could, but again he failed to protect a valuable servant from a sentence similar to that inflicted on Bacon.[5] Buckingham's foolish encouragement of the resort to impeachment in this case was

*Impeachments of Bacon, Middlesex and Buckingham*

---

[1] Tanner, 322-4.  [2] Tanner, 269-72; Prothero, 275-7.
[3] The administrative duties of the Chancellor in the early seventeenth century are described by J. S. Wilson, 6 *B.I.H.R.* 33. See generally, Holdsworth, v. 231 ff.  [4] Tanner, 324-34.  [5] Tanner, 334-5; Dietz, 209-13.

7

visited on himself in 1626. Here the issue on point of Prerogative
was graver. The charges against Buckingham, apart from an
absurd assertion that he had tried to poison the late King, were
all in respect of acts done or ordered by Charles—grants of titles,
offices and emoluments, and measures taken in connexion with the
war. James might find it impossible to defend the judicial corruption of Bacon or the administrative corruption of Middlesex, if
indeed there had been any. Charles could hardly avoid vindicating
the principle that for administrative conduct in itself legal, no
matter how mistaken or unfortunate, ministers were answerable
to himself alone. And if this issue were not implicit in the impeachment itself, it was made so by the Commons' direct demand
for Buckingham's dismissal.[1]

*Parlia-
ment
and the
Catholics*

At yet another point the Commons had profited by the opportunities of these years to assail the Prerogative. Their zeal for
religion inspired an attack on the King's ecclesiastical policy.
The Parliament of 1621 found it easier to demonstrate its Protestant sympathies by demanding the enforcement of the penal
laws than by supplying soldiers and ships to the Crown. The
Commons assumed the right—renouncing it to the Lords, who had
as little title to it as they—to punish an elderly Catholic gentleman
named Floyd, who had expressed his satisfaction at the successes
of his co-religionists in Bohemia in terms which, however indis-
creet, were in no way a contempt of either House. Their victim
suffered fine, branding, pillory and imprisonment by order of the
Upper House.[2] In 1624 the Houses petitioned that no negotiations
for the Prince's marriage should include any undertaking to relax
the penal laws, but the King included, and his son consented to,
a bargain of this nature in the marriage treaty with France in that
year, and in December proceedings against recusants were suspended. Nemesis came early in the reign of Charles I. In 1625
parliamentary petitions against recusants again appeared, and the
King was involved in a dilemma between the undertakings he had
made towards France and the assurances he gave to Parliament.

*The King
and the
Arminian
clergy*

At this point anti-Roman feeling was being quickened by a sharp
anxiety about the bearing of the King's ecclesiastical policy on the
character of the Anglican Church itself. The ecclesiastical petition

---

[1] The documents relating to Buckingham's impeachment are printed by
S. R. Gardiner, *Constitutional Documents*, 3-44.        [2] Tanner, 319-21.

of 1625 included a clause in favour of ejected ministers and the remedy of abuses in the Church.[1] While the Commons, as always, were no supporters of toleration or separatism, they were becoming uneasily aware that the complaints of radical Protestants were justified by tendencies perceptible in that element of the Anglican clergy who had the largest share in the King's confidence—a confidence which they repaid by strenuous support of the Prerogative and attacks on parliamentary privilege. From 1624 to 1628 a series of books—such as Montagu's *New Gag for an old Goose* and *Appello Caesarem*, and Cosin's *Book of Devotions*— emphasised the Catholic element in Anglicanism, while sermons by Dr. Mainwaring before the King and Dr. Sibthorp as assize preacher at Nottingham in 1626 enunciated strongly the duty of non-resistance.[2] Archbishop Abbot was no upholder of High Church or "Arminian" doctrines, but his influence was waning before that of such bishops as Laud who were ready to permit their expression. The King's own attitude was indicated by the protection which he threw over Montagu and others against parliamentary attack.[3]

The accumulated discontents of the war years flared up once again in the session of 1629. The Commons contended that *Dissolu-* the Petition of Right had been violated by the continued levy of *tion of* tunnage and poundage without parliamentary grant. They com-*1629* plained of the growth of Popery and Arminianism.[4] In a final disorderly scene, the Speaker, Finch, was held down in his chair while resolutions condemning the levying and payment of tunnage and poundage and the recent innovations in religion were put to the House, the adjournment of which was followed by a dissolution.[5] The protagonists of revolt had overreached themselves. The Commons were unsupported by the Lords. Eliot, as their leader, had gone far beyond the point aimed at by moderate men like Wentworth who now went over to the Crown, or even the future leader of the Long Parliament, Pym. It is probable that they had forfeited such hold as they had ever possessed on public opinion in the country. Their views as to the bearing of the

---

[1] Gardiner, *History of England*, v. 344.
[2] Prothero, 437-9; Gardiner, *History of England*, v. 352, 354, vi. 206, 208; vii. 9; *Constitutional Documents*, 78-9.
[3] It may be added that Montagu was given the bishopric of Chichester in 1628.
[4] Gardiner, *Constitutional Documents*, 70-73, 77-82.
[5] Gardiner, *Constitutional Documents*, 82-3.

Petition of Right on the levying of tunnage and poundage had been rejected by the judges of the Court of Exchequer.[1] Notwithstanding the demands they had asserted to control the composition and policy of the King's government, they had proved themselves destitute of the ability and judgment requisite to the successful conduct even of opposition. From a political point of view their recklessness provided the King with his best chance of making purely conciliar government once more effective. The chance was lost. His rule from 1629 to 1640 turned moderate men against him, and restored to his more extreme opponents their lost ascendancy.

v

*The return to conciliar government*

From 1629 to 1638 conciliar government once more had a respite from ordeal by battle. Without violating either law or convention, it could dispense with Parliament. Some of Charles's advisers, such as the Lord Treasurer Weston, had conceived a strong antipathy to Parliaments, natural enough in his case since his impeachment had been proposed in 1629. But Parliaments were now no longer required. For peace-time purposes the Crown needed only the normal peace-time organisation of government. The law provided all that the Crown could want. It would be the mete-wand of royal action. A royal declaration issued after the dissolution made a well-reasoned appeal to the nation against Parliament, on grounds both of law and policy which were not easily to be refuted.[2] To Wentworth and other ex-members of the opposition such as Noy, who became Attorney-General, the monarchy as restricted by the Petition of Right now presented a constitutional ideal to be preferred to that implied by the ungovernable proceedings of the lately dissolved House of Commons. At some future date a Parliament prepared to resume its historic relationship with the Crown and renounce its pretensions to usurp control over government and policy might once more be readmitted to a share in the constitution. In the meantime the King's administration, conforming strictly to the letter of the law, would resume its benevolent task of promoting national well-being. Similarly the ecclesiastical supremacy, like-

---

[1] Gardiner, *History of England*, vii. 61.    [2] Gardiner, *Documents*, 83–99.

wise rescued from violent encroachment, would be applied by the hierarchy to suppress sectarian controversy and infuse reverence and dignity into the services of the Church, and ultimately utilised to bring the Churches of England and Scotland into conformity. Bishops such as Laud, and Juxon who succeeded him in London, would as Privy Councillors and officials, endeavour to purify finance by their services at the Treasury, and strive to raise conciliar control generally to the highest point of efficiency and public utility. Vigorous, economical and disinterested administration, relying on the legal and financial resources which the constitution provided, was at least the ideal of the system which Wentworth and Laud in their correspondence referred to as "Thorough".[1]

Its rigid dependence on the strict letter of the law cannot be too strongly insisted on. The law justified both the positive action of the government and its coercion of opponents. What the law allowed was in the first place for the courts of Common Law to say. By this date the courts were clearly, and to a large extent quite properly, arrayed on the side of the King. Resistance to the Crown by the judges had never been strong. The explanation is only partly to be found in their dependence on the executive, commissioned as they were (save in the Exchequer) *durante beneplacito regis*. Doubtless they were for this reason prepared to abandon to the Crown an extensive and ill-defined discretionary power, and to drop rivalries with conciliar courts which threatened the position of the King and Council as a *tribunal des conflits*.[2] But, unlike Parliament, they were concerned only with the legality and not with the policy of governmental acts. The legal rules which they administered, and—again unlike Parliament—could not change, usually told strongly on the side of the King. Except for the cases in which Coke was concerned as Chief Justice, there was, from *Bates's Case* to the *Case of Ship-money*, an uninterrupted current of judicial decisions in the King's favour, none of which was obviously and indefensibly wrong.

The sole exception to this general tendency for the Common Law judges to support the Crown is provided by the career of

*Its reliance on the letter of the law*

---

[1] For the state of administration under Charles I, see G. E. Aylmer, *The King's Servants*, 13 ff.

[2] In 1603 it was laid down that the Council ought not to intervene in cases depending in other courts. But it frequently moved other courts to action or stayed their processes. See E. F. White, *The Privy Council and Private Suitors*, 34 E.H.R. 588. This restriction did not apply to cases where a matter of public concern was raised.

Common Law Courts and Prerogative jurisdiction

Sir Edward Coke.[1] The most learned lawyer of his day, and already Speaker of the Commons and Attorney-General before his appointment in 1606 as Chief Justice of Common Pleas, Coke brought to the bench a fierce and masterful spirit which seems to justify the observation that the King was "probably inclined to rebel rather against the yoke of the lawyers than against that of the law".[2] The Common Law judges of Coke's time, though constant to the principle that government ought to be according to law, were not likely to challenge the legal basis of conciliar government, for they were, as *Bates's Case* showed, very uncertain of the limits between law and Prerogative. They were, however, becoming more acutely sensitive than in earlier years to conflicts of jurisdiction. In Elizabeth's later years they had begun to quarrel with the High Commission, the Court of Requests, the Council of the North, and that of Wales so far as it claimed jurisdiction over the English border shires. Under James I rivalry became acute with the Chancery.[3]

Conflicts with the High Commission

Since the arbiter of such disputes was the King, resolute defence of their own jurisdiction by the Common Law judges might lead them into conflict with the Crown. Into this conflict Coke entered. To some extent his resolute will bore his colleagues with him. Before becoming a judge, he had inspired the judges' answer to complaints by Archbishop Abbot against the use of writs of consultation and of prohibition by the Common Law courts as a means of arresting proceedings in the High Commission, now no longer popular as it once had been with common lawyers as a restraint on the ecclesiastical courts. In 1607 the Common Law courts and the High Commission came into opposition in *Ladd's Case* and *Fuller's Case*.[4] Ladd, impleaded in the Norwich diocesan court for attendance at a conventicle, was imprisoned by the High Commission for perjury in the lower court and refusal to take the *ex-officio* oath. Upon his appeal to the King's Bench the judges decided, on a strict interpretation of the Act of Supremacy of 1559, that since ancient ecclesiastical jurisdictions conferred no power to fine or imprison save for heresy or schism, the High Commission which

---

[1] For an account of his life, see Holdsworth, v. 425 ff.

[2] Gardiner, *History of England*, ii. 39.

[3] Holdsworth, i. 414-15, 460-61, 511, 610-11. In 1607 the criminal jurisdiction of the Council of Wales was abolished. See also Reid, *King's Council in the North*, 343 ff.    [4] Gardiner, *History of England*, ii. 36-8.

now wielded such jurisdictions could have none either. *Fuller's
Case* turned on the imprisonment by the High Commission of
Ladd's counsel in the King's Bench proceedings on account of
words he had used implying denial of the High Commission's
jurisdiction. The King's Bench, at first inclined to defend Fuller,
gave him up on the technical point that the charge against him was
one of schism. In both cases the King tried to act as arbiter. In
both his right to do so was rejected by Coke, who again in 1609
informed the King that his duty in all such cases was to uphold
the Common Law. In 1610 *Chauncy's Case* raised the same
issues as Ladd's.[1] James's hope that the rival courts would live
together "like brothers, in harmony" remained unfulfilled.

To the King such questions were at first not much more than *Constitu-*
tiresome technical quarrels between jealous and predatory lawyers. *tional*
Coke invested them with greater consequence. For him they *bearing of*
involved the assertion of the supremacy of the Common Law, *these*
—which might be held to have a firm basis in medieval books and *conflicts*
precedents—and the reduction of the Prerogative from an unlimited
discretionary power to a mere department of the Common Law,
peculiar and exceptional no doubt, but known and limited. Thus
in the *Case of Prohibitions* (1608), he denied the authority of the
King to hear cases in person.[2] In the *Case of Proclamations* (1610) he
and his colleagues, replying to questions from Lord Salisbury,
denied that proclamations could create new offences or make
offences punishable by Star Chamber which were not so before.[3]
In 1613 they were invited to intervene against the jurisdiction of
commissioners appointed to reform abuses in the navy, with
power to "give due order for the punishment of offenders".[4] Any
jurisdiction outside the Common Law which tried to compete
with it, any right in the Crown to set limits to Common Law
jurisdiction, to lay down the rules which the judges were to
apply, or even to consult them extrajudicially, whether as a body
or individually, was denied by the intractable Chief Justice.[5] His

[1] Tanner, 147-8; Holdsworth, v. 431.
[2] Keir and Lawson, *Cases in Constitutional Law*, 108; Tanner, 186-7. Compare R. G. Usher, *James I and Sir Edward Coke*, 18 E.H.R. 664.
[3] Keir and Lawson, 110; Tanner, 187-8.
[4] Gardiner, *History of England*, ii. 187-91.
[5] On extrajudicial consultation, see Holdsworth, v. 438. Also Gardiner, ii.
272-9; Tanner, 175, 188-92 (*Peacham's Case*). At this point Coke only objected
to individual consultations; later, even to collective consultations.

example encouraged others. In 1613 a barrister pleading before the King's Bench, of which Coke now became Chief Justice, was bold enough to question the legality of the jurisdiction of the Constable and Marshal. In 1614 the judges declined to express an extrajudicial opinion on impositions.[1]

*Conflict with Chancery*

With the Chancery, which professed a higher doctrine of Prerogative than that derived by Coke from the Common Law, a brisk series of disputes was meanwhile in progress. In *Brownlow's Case* the Chancellor stayed by writ of *non procedendo* the proceedings taken in the King's Bench by a clerk of that court in order to set aside a royal grant conferring on another person the right to prepare certain writs with which he had himself hitherto dealt.[2] In *Glanville's Case* the King's Bench issued a praemunire against a suitor who asked Chancery to set aside a Common Law judgment giving effect to a fraudulent bargain.[3] The final clash came in 1616 in the *Case of Commendams* in which a royal grant to the Bishop of Lichfield enabling him to hold a living in plurality was challenged by the patrons. The King's view accurately expressed the constitutional bearing of the case. "Encroach not", he directed the judges, "on the prerogative of the Crown. If there fall out a question which concerns any prerogative or mystery of state, deal not with it till you consult the king or his council, for they are transcendent matters, and must not be carried away with too much wilfulness, for so you may wound the king through the sides of a private person." Summoned before the King, the judges gave way, and, while deciding against the bishop, did so in words which left the Prerogative intact. The Chief Justice, who alone maintained his opposition, was dismissed in November 1616.[4]

*Eliot's Case*

With his dismissal, opposition from the Bench ceased, though an occasional reminder proved necessary in later years that the judges must be careful not to "check or oppose any points of sovereignty". Thus Crew in 1627, Walter in 1630, and Heath in 1634 were suspended or dismissed. The judgments in *Darnel's Case* and in *Rolle's Case*, in which the judges denied to the plaintiff recovery of

[1] Gardiner, ii. 242.                              [2] Gardiner, iii. 7; Holdsworth, v. 439.
[3] Gardiner, iii. 11.
[4] Gardiner, iii. 13; Tanner, 19, 192-8; Prothero, 399-400; Holdsworth, v. 351, 439-41. It may be added that Coke's dismissal meant that the issue between Crown and Parliament would be decided on political and not legal grounds.

goods seized for non-payment of tunnage and poundage,[1] showed that the courts could be relied on to decide in the King's favour. In these conditions, his officials need have little fear that the legality of their actions would be over-jealously scrutinised. The first test was applied in *Eliot's Case*.[2] Immediately after the dissolution of 1629 a number of members of the Commons, including Eliot, were committed to prison. While some made their submission and were freed, others tested the legality of their detention by writs of habeas corpus. The original commitment had mentioned no specific cause of detention, but in strict conformity with the Petition of Right the return to the writ stated their offence—"contempts of the King and his government, and stirring up sedition". Though it did not expressly appear that the acts complained of had been done in Parliament, the jurisdiction of the King's Bench seemed to have been invoked in a matter of parliamentary privilege. Consulted extrajudicially, the judges hesitated to assume jurisdiction. Required to do so, they offered the prisoners liberation not as of right, but only on condition of good behaviour.[3] Against three of the ringleaders, Eliot, Holles and Valentine, proceedings were taken in 1630 which forced the judges to a still more explicit declaration of their view of the law. On a criminal information in the King's Bench, the Crown dropped all ambiguity as to whether the acts of the accused had been done in or out of Parliament. The prisoners repudiated the jurisdiction, and relied on *Strode's Case* to establish their immunity, but the judges held that it referred only to proceedings by the Stannary Court.[4] All three prisoners were fined and committed to prison, not to be released without acknowledging their fault. None did so. Eliot died in the Tower in 1632; Holles escaped; Valentine, and with him Strode, who had been concerned in the habeas corpus proceedings, had to await the meeting of the Short Parliament before regaining their liberty. Both in the habeas corpus proceedings and in the criminal trial the judges had demonstrated their dependability.

Similar reliance on the strictest letter of the law was shown in

[1] Gardiner, vii. 5-6, 32-3, 58, 61-4. *Rolle's Case* was complicated by his privilege as a member of the Commons.

[2] Gardiner, vii. 77, 80, 90, 96, 111-21; Holdsworth, vi. 38-9, 97-8, 269.

[3] This condition was accepted by none of the prisoners.

[4] If riot in the House was not covered by the plea of privilege, the judges could hardly do other than overrule a general plea to their jurisdiction.

*Revenue*
*Cases*

the financial expedients to which the Crown resorted. In *Chambers'*
*Case* (1629) a merchant who refused to pay tunnage and poundage,
and was fined and imprisoned by Star Chamber, brought an action
in the Exchequer to recover goods distrained from him and to have
the Star Chamber proceedings set aside as unwarranted by the
Act of 1487. The Exchequer, influenced perhaps by the dismissal
of Chief Baron Walter, declined to reverse the Star Chamber
sentence and, avoiding any decision as to the validity of tunnage
and poundage, left the Crown in possession of its revenue.[1]
In 1631 *Vassall's Case* upheld the right of the Crown to levy
impositions.[2] New fiscal devices were similarly accepted by the
judges. Distraint of knighthood was revived, and pronounced
legal by the Court of Exchequer.[3]

*New*
*monopol-*
*istic*
*companies*

In the establishment of new monopolies, the Crown showed
a similar concern to keep within at least the technical limits of
the law. The statute of 1624, in saving the prerogative to make
grants to companies, had contemplated the creation of genuine
commercial undertakings. Groups of speculators were found
ready to undertake the sole manufacture of particular commodities on the usually quite unsubstantial ground that they
involved new industrial processes, promising in return payments
to the Crown which being ostensibly voluntary did not infringe
the law against unparliamentary taxation. In 1632 a soap company
undertook to pay to the Crown £4 per ton on an annual output
of 20,000 tons. In the same year a fishery company and in 1635
a salt company were founded. The Vintners' Company was
induced to pay £30,000 yearly, and unsuccessful efforts were
made to incorporate brewers and maltsters. Legally, these grants
might be defended as intended to regulate trade. In practice,
they were economically inefficient. They alienated the trading
classes from the Crown. And, though of little immediate fiscal
profit to the government, they paved the way for the excise
which was to prove a financial mainstay of the Long Parliament.[4]

*Forest*
*jurisdiction*
*revived*

More doubtfully legal were the attempts made to derive
revenue from the Forest courts. Their obsolescent jurisdiction,

[1] Gardiner, vii. 4-5, 84-6, 114, 168.
[2] Gardiner, vii. 168.                          [3] Gardiner, vii. 167.
[4] On these patents see E. Hughes, *Studies in Administration and Finance*, 71;
W. R. Scott, *Joint Stock Companies*, i. 208 ff. Mr. Hughes observes that in 1626
no objection was raised by the Commons to revenue from this source.

invoked by Laud in 1634 to investigate alleged malpractices by the Lord Treasurer, Weston, was utilised in order to levy fines for encroachments in the Forests of Dean, Epping, Waltham, and Rockingham, and the New Forest. Forest boundaries had been defined by a perambulation of 1297, but this was now set aside, and private rights more than three centuries old were impugned. Like the commercial class, rural proprietors were thus made more than ever hostile to the Crown. Their antagonism was sharpened by the penalties levied by Commissioners of Depopulation for pulling down cottages on their lands. These activities further added to the unpopularity of conciliar jurisdiction and of those who wielded it.[1]

However dubious and indeed dangerous the means employed, *Financial* the Crown was gradually restored to financial solvency. The *recovery completed* reduction of expenditure and the levy of new taxes lowered the annual deficit to £18,000 by 1636 and produced a surplus thereafter. Increased customs revenue was the mainstay of the system, and the impositions which had yielded £54,000 when imposed in 1608 rose to £127,000 in 1638.[2] Internally, the government enjoyed a freedom of action usefully employed in fostering trade during a slump in 1630, in schemes for improvements in such matters as drainage, particularly of the Fens, and otherwise. Conciliar administration now attained its zenith.

In the Church, prerogative government was conducted on *Ecclesi-* what seemed to the ecclesiastical authorities an equally law- *astical policy of* ful basis, but with even less acceptable results. Laud, the *Laud* King's most influential adviser, was no upholder of any theory of the independence of the Church from the State, nor indeed was he much concerned to ground the King's authority on any other basis than the law of the land, for it is to others of the Arminian clergy that we must look for the loftiest enunciations of the pure Divine Right theory then becoming fashionable.[3] His essentially practical mind was bent, if in an irritating and pedantic way, on the redress of what he considered to be abuses

---

1 Gardiner, vii. 363; viii. 86, 282.

2 Dietz, 270, 281, 284 *n.* 18. It was under Juxon's Treasurership that the final improvements were made in the system of declaring certain accounts before the Auditors of the Prests, officials taken over by the Exchequer from the Court of Augmentations in 1560. The most important of these branches of revenue was the Customs. See M. D. George, *Origin of the Declared Account*, 31 *E.H.R.* 41.

3 On the other hand, Laud did maintain the divine right of bishops.

in order and discipline. In effect, this meant the repression of clergy who refused to comply with the ritual prescribed by authority, of laymen who supported them, and of words and writings defending their views or opposing the Arminian party. In his diocese of London he particularly attacked the system by which individuals or corporations maintained Lecturers for preaching duties alone, and his policy was embodied in royal instructions on the subject issued in 1630 to bishops generally. So long as the more moderate Abbot ruled at Canterbury, Laud's activity was mainly restricted to his own diocese, but his succession to the archbishopric in 1633 opened a wider field. In Neile he found a vigorous coadjutor at York. Other sees as they fell vacant were filled with bishops of Laudian sympathies if not always of Arminian opinions. A metropolitical visitation by his Vicar-General from 1633 to 1637 enforced discipline generally.

*Position of the communion table* With much that was necessary and praiseworthy, Laud's reforms included innovations which could not fail to create alarm. Most contentious was the order that communion tables should be placed altar-wise against the east end of the church. Under the Injunctions of 1559 it had normally occupied this position, but had been set east and west in the chancel for the administration of communion.[1] This arrangement, confirmed by Convocation in 1604, was now discarded. No doubt it was inconvenient to move the table to and fro, and irreverence towards it may have been made possible by the practice. Early in Charles's reign, and usually against parochial opposition, a number of clergy had railed the table in permanently at the east. In 1635 Laud imposed the rule generally.[2] While he might regard the matter purely as one of convenience, Protestant conviction was outraged by a change which emphasised the sacrificial nature of the sacrament and the mediatorial functions of the priesthood. Puritan feeling was further offended by an attack on the strict observance of the Sabbath in the re-issue of a Declaration of Sports first set forth by James I, which the clergy were ordered to read, and which encouraged secular amusements after divine service was over.[3]

[1] Gee and Hardy, 440.

[2] For the Privy Council order of 1633 regarding St. Gregory's, London, see Gardiner, *Constitutional Documents*, 103-5.

[3] Tanner, 54-6; Gardiner, *Constitutional Documents*, 99-103.

For the enforcement of the Laudian policy, the High Commission provided a convenient instrument of repression, and its efforts were seconded by the Star Chamber and by a rigid censorship over printing and publication. It is not surprising that the censorship was evaded, and that, as in the days of *Marprelate*, acrimonious. pamphlets appeared, attacking recent innovations and the hierarchical system which made them possible. Three pamphleteers, Prynne, Bastwick and Burton, were in 1637 sentenced by the Star Chamber to pillory, mutilation, fine and life imprisonment, and John Lilburne to whipping, pillory, and imprisonment for the importation of similar works from abroad.

It was natural that this policy, repressing whatever seemed most *Fear of* distinctively Protestant in the Church, should create the belief *Roman tendencies* that its object was reunion with Rome. The offer of a cardinal's hat to Laud, made through the Queen's Catholic entourage, suggests that the Papacy itself thought as much. One bishop, Montagu, did in fact favour reunion. Though Laud himself urged High Commission proceedings against Montagu and rigorous repression of proselytising, the whole tendency of his policy, and the presence of a papal nuncio, Panzani, at Court, aroused a general fear for the future of England's cherished Protestantism. It unified many discordant elements into a national opposition to the Crown and enhanced the influence of religious and political radicals.

Against this combination of fiscal, economic and religious *Ship-* grievances, the Crown could hold out only so long as it had no *money* external responsibilities. But Charles could not exclude the Thirty Years' War from his policy. The insecurity of the Narrow Seas and the need to protect sea-borne trade and the fisheries, to say nothing of his ultimate designs for the restoration of his Palatine relatives, demanded an increase of naval strength. The levy of ships and ship-money, based on earlier practice, was discussed in 1633, and in 1634 writs were sent out to maritime towns and districts. In 1635 they were extended (as had been attempted in 1628) to the kingdom at large.[1] Similar writs went out annually until 1639, and, yielding three-quarters of a million, enabled a new fleet to be constructed, though it accomplished little. The levy on

---

[1] Gardiner, *Constitutional Documents*, 105-8 (writ of 1634); Dietz, 278-81. For the writ of August 1635 (not printed by Gardiner), see 3 *State Trials*, 848.

inland counties evoked much resistance, partly based on no higher ground than dislike of a new system which compelled property to contribute more effectively to national needs. In *Hampden's Case* (1637) a constitutional issue was raised. Hampden had omitted to pay his share of the quota in Bucks, and was proceeded against in the Exchequer. The importance of the case caused it to be referred to the judges in the Exchequer Chamber in order to get a decision strengthening the hands of collectors. It is again to be noted how the Crown sought to vindicate its action by an appeal to the law. It was not disappointed. The judges had already twice pronounced extrajudicially in favour of the legality of the levy, and their second opinion approved the view that the Crown could compel payment. They now decided finally in the Crown's favour. Only two condemned ship-money as illegal. Three others decided for Hampden on the ground that the procedure by which the Crown sought to enforce payment was inappropriate. The remaining seven found for the Crown on all points. Their decision has been much criticised. Yet it is to be remembered that the Crown was not ostensibly seeking to impose a tax by prerogative—and indeed admitted that it could not do so—but merely to enforce a service due from the subject when the realm was in danger; and on this point the Crown's assertion, as Hampden's counsel themselves admitted, was conclusive, whatever the facts might otherwise appear to be. The only way in which they could escape the dilemma thus confronting them was to assert a distinction between an "immediate" danger which compelled the king to act without Parliament and a merely "apprehended" danger—like the present—which obliged him to call one. The judges had only to dismiss this distinction as illogical and impracticable—and it was both—and to construe the statutes against unparliamentary taxation so as to leave intact the prerogatives for national defence—which was not difficult—to arrive directly, and not incorrectly, at a decision for the Crown.[1]

*Opposition to the Crown in Scotland* — Their decision perhaps did the King more harm than good, opening up as it did a prospect of unlimited prerogative taxation on a plea of emergency which could never be rebutted. Though the King employed ship-money *bonâ fide* to provide a fleet, he

[1] Keir and Lawson, 81: for detailed discussion see Keir, *The Case of Ship-money*, 52 *L.Q.R.* 546: and C. Russell in 77 *E.H.R.* 312.

got no credit for upright intention.[1] Local resistance to the
levy, patronised by great men, threatened the breakdown of that
voluntary co-operation on which government depended. But even
the failure of ship-money would not oblige the King to resort to
Parliament. That desperate expedient was forced on him by his
failure to repress a rebellion in Scotland. The northern kingdom
had given little trouble since 1603. Removed from the risk of
aristocratic risings, dominant over Parliament by the device of
committing its authority to a body nominated by the Crown
known as the Lords of the Articles,[2] the King had succeeded in
overcoming the only other organisation capable of resistance, the
General Assembly of the Kirk. James had contrived to super-
impose on the lower Presbyterian courts—the Kirk Session and
presbytery—an episcopal organisation, accepted by the Assembly
in 1610 and by Parliament in 1612. In 1618 he had even obtained
from the former approval of certain changes of ritual by the Five
Articles of Perth, to which there was some clerical and popular
resistance, by no means universal. Under Charles I the conflict
took a new turn. In 1625 he attempted to endow the Church by
a resumption of ecclesiastical property granted to laymen since
1542. While the claim was later compromised, the nobility as
holders of Church lands were henceforth aligned with the King's
clerical and middle-class opponents. Developments from 1629 to
1637 urged all three elements into rebellion. A project for a new
liturgy, prudently dropped by James, was revived, and Laud's
influence was exercised in favour of one based on the Anglican
model. Charles's coronation at St. Giles', Edinburgh, in 1633 was
accompanied by a display of Anglican ritual, and a Scottish statute
conferred on the King an authority over ecclesiastical vestments
which was used to prescribe the Anglican surplice instead of the
Geneva gown. In 1635 a new set of canons for the Scottish
Church, and in 1637 a new Prayer Book on Anglican lines were
introduced by royal authority alone, without either parliamentary
sanction or approval by the Assembly, or even much consultation with the Scottish bishops. The latter meanwhile were being

---

[1] On the collection and utilisation of ship-money, see M. D. Gordon,
*Collection of Ship-money in the Reign of Charles I*, 3 *T.R.H.S.* iv. 141.

[2] On the Lords of the Articles, see R. S. Rait, *The Parliaments of Scotland*,
367-74.

brought, as in England, into offices of State and the Privy Council. Charles thus combined against himself the forces of property, of religious enthusiasm, and of national sentiment.

*The Bishops' Wars*

An absentee King, an unpopular hierarchy, and a Privy Council which did not believe in the policy it was required to enforce, could exercise little control over the tumults which attended the introduction of the new Prayer Book. Weakly consenting to the appointment of commissioners to represent those who opposed the Book, the Privy Council found that it had allowed the creation of a rival government. Committees known as the Tables banded nobility, clergy and people together in March 1638, after a fashion familiar in Scottish history, in a National Covenant "in defence of the King's Majesty, his person and authority . . . and of the true religion, liberties and laws of this kingdom".[1] In November a General Assembly at Glasgow decreed the extinction of episcopacy, and though ordered to dissolve by the King's Commissioner went on to abolish the Service Book, the Canons, and the Articles of Perth. Prompt action by the Covenanters secured control of the kingdom and created an army. Charles had to meet force with force. Thanks to Juxon's efficient management, he had money enough to undertake a campaign.[2] But success was imperative. The Treaty of Berwick in June 1639 did not procure it. The King was required to surrender control over Parliament and Kirk by abolishing the Lords of the Articles and consenting to the abolition of episcopacy. He would do neither, and the renewal of the contest in the Second Bishops' War of 1640 forced him to resort once more to his English Parliament. The Crown had again been forced to undertake war, and this time not a foreign war which could be broken off, but one which entered the kingdom itself and placed on its government a burden under which it broke.

## vi

*War and government, 1640-60*

As between 1621 and 1629, but driven more swiftly and tumultuously by more violent emergencies, English constitutional development from 1640 to 1660 pursued its erratic course under the impulse of war. Not since the close of the Hundred Years' War

---

[1] Gardiner, *Constitutional Documents*, 124-34.   [2] Dietz, 284-7.

had English government been subjected to such acute and continuous stresses as in the iron age which witnessed the Bishops' Wars, the Irish rebellion of 1641, the Civil Wars of 1642 and 1648, the wars of 1649 in Ireland and 1650–51 in Scotland, that of 1652 with the Dutch Republic, and that of 1655 with Spain, and which lived in constant apprehension of the overthrow of government by domestic insurrection or foreign intervention. Under these strains, neither the monarchy nor the parliamentary republic and the military dictatorship which successively took its place managed to survive. The very foundations of government, in whatever form, became impaired during this period of subversion. The original issue might lie between prerogative and parliamentary monarchy, but war engendered republicanism, egalitarian democracy, and conceptions of government which either monopolised it as the preserve of the "Saints" or annihilated it altogether in fantasies of a society organised as a purely religious communion with Christ as King. The period was one of ceaseless experiment with little positive achievement, and its inevitable end was a return to the tradition of rule according to law in place of the armed might which a score of tempestuous years had raised to an intolerable predominance, and to monarchy as the guardian of that law against the forces of anarchy and dissolution. Yet the results were not purely of this negative kind. War had wrecked monarchy of the old conciliar type. It had given experience, confidence and power to a House of Commons which had successfully overthrown a king and governed an empire, and could no longer be excluded from the "mystery of state". It had asserted the predominance of the Lower over the Upper House, revolutionised public finance and taxation, reorganised the navy, created a professional army, and wholly changed the relationship between the administrative system and the legislature. The Restoration of 1660 could be no mere return to pre-war monarchy. The structure and working of the restored system were to bear indelible traces of the ordeal to which English government had been subjected during the vicissitudes of the revolutionary age.

It was beneath the shadow of these imminent storms that the *The Short* Short Parliament was summoned. Even with his previous experi- *Parlia-* ence of opposition in mind, Wentworth, who after eight years *ment* as Lord Deputy of Ireland now returned as Charles's principal counsellor, might well have expected that the Parliament which he advised the King to assemble would show a more friendly spirit than it did. The menace from the Covenanters seemed to justify the King's contention that it was in his subjects' defence as well as his own that he was raising an army, and that supply ought to precede redress.[1] Led by John Pym, the Commons soon made it evident that a Scottish invasion was in their eyes less important than the invasion of English liberties in the name of Prerogative. They turned their attention to violations of their privileges, the levy of customs without parliamentary grant, ship-money and other fiscal abuses, extrajudicial consultations of the judges, the long intermission of Parliament, ecclesiastical innovations, and the pressing of men and supplies for military service; and they resolved that "till the liberties of the House and the Kingdom were cleared, they knew not whether they had anything to give or no".[2] Against the advice of Wentworth, the King attempted to bargain with them over ship-money. The judgment of 1637 was to be reversed by writ of error, on condition of the payment of twelve subsidies. Nothing could have been less likely to placate the Commons than the suggestion that they should pay for an immunity from taxation which, rightly or wrongly, they considered illegal. Their attitude was confirmed by the King's action, which this time Wentworth prompted, in inducing the Lords to vote that supply ought to precede redress. This step was useless since the Lords had no initiative in matters of supply, and harmful since it wounded the Commons once more on a point of privilege. Only among the clergy had the King any effective support. Convocation, which had continued to vote supply throughout the years of personal government, showed its royalist temper by granting six subsidies. Both Houses manifested antagonism to it; and the Lords further expressed their hostility towards the spiritual peers by declaring that their attendance was not necessary to proceedings in the Upper House.[3]

*Its dissolution*  Parliament, as in 1621–9, had proved utterly unresponsive to the plea of national emergency. The Commons even seemed

---

[1] Cobbett, *Parliamentary History*, ii. 532–3.

[2] Gardiner, *History of England*, ix. 108.

[3] Gardiner, *History of England*, ix. 108–9; Firth, *House of Lords during the Civil War*, 66–7.

inclined to side with the Scottish rebels, and allotted a day for debating a Declaration in which their case was set forth. In order to avert the crowning misfortune of a resolution urging him to come to terms, the King dissolved Parliament when its session was only three weeks old, and—for the last time—committed his leading opponents to prison.[1] The Short Parliament had been as brief, and as barren, as that of 1614. But it had revealed the strength and unanimity of the opposition which the King's emergencies were speedily to restore to power.

The failure of Charles's efforts to avert a Scottish invasion in the ensuing months proved that the signal for resistance given by the Short Parliament had been caught up outside. Inadequate financial resources and dependence on unpaid administrative service had always been the weaknesses of conciliar government. They were now fully revealed. Any hope that the nation would respond to the plea which the Short Parliament had disregarded was completely belied. Convocation indeed showed its loyalty, and enacted canons upholding the ecclesiastical innovations and investing with religious sanctions the authority of the King and the subject's duty to obey. These canons further deepened its unpopularity by imposing the *etcetera* oath, in which the clergy, swearing to refuse assent to alterations in "the government of the Church by archbishops, bishops, deacons and archdeacons, *etc.*", were bound to the defence of an ecclesiastical establishment uncertainly defined.[2] From Ireland a parliamentary grant might be expected, and Wentworth spoke in Council of bringing over his Irish army to reduce "this Kingdom", by which he almost certainly meant Scotland. All classes in England except the clergy remained passive. The City refused a loan. Advances from officials and tax-farmers produced a little, but the Irish supply, in Wentworth's absence, fell below expectations. The levy of ship-money and coat-and-conduct money practically ceased, men drafted for service mutinied and killed their officers, and martial law had again to be resorted to. The King's commissions of array provided only an ill-equipped and disaffected force of 13,000 men, less than half the number which in August 1640 the Covenanters poured into the counties north of the Tees. In the following month

*Adminis-trative collapse*

---

[1] Gardiner, IX. 129-30.    [2] Text in Wilkins, *Concilia*, IV. 543-53.

a Great Council of peers at York pledged their personal security for a loan but could render the King no further service than to advise him to summon another Parliament.

*The Long Parliament*    To this assembly the King looked with a renewed hope which was soon undeceived. Though the North might resent the presence of an invading Scottish army and the exactions by which it maintained itself, the remoter South and East felt no such emotions. London in particular showed its antagonism to the Crown by once more refusing a loan and by riots against the High Commission, which Star Chamber timidly left to the City authorities to punish, with the natural result that a grand jury found no true bill. Supported by the financial power and mob violence of the capital, the Long Parliament when it met in November 1640 held a commanding position. By the Treaty of Ripon with the Scots, the King had engaged himself to two-monthly payments of £25,000 on terms which clearly implied parliamentary supply, and which in any case he could not meet except by that means. Moreover, the Scots themselves clearly expected that the guarantee of the English Parliament and not that of the King alone would secure their recent revolutionary gains in religion and government.

*Temper of the Houses*    Charles saw the necessity of surrender before this formidable coalition. Some further restriction of prerogative powers by statute, as in 1624 and 1628, must be expected. He nevertheless supposed that he should himself be judge of the extent of his surrender. The Parliament which faced him was little likely to share his expectation. There had been no time for royal electioneering, and the elections returned "all that had any ways appeared obstinate or refractory to the government".[1] In the Lords a less radical temper prevailed, but the impeachment of the King's ministers left the Royalists there leaderless, so that the well-organised minority carried undue weight.

*Impeachment and attainder of Strafford*    Though the proceedings of the Commons were unregulated and discursive, grievances being raised one after another in an unsystematic way, it was plain that their dominant aim was to effect

[1] Quoted by R. N. Kershaw, *The Elections for the Long Parliament*, 38 E.H.R. 506. This article contains a valuable survey of these electoral proceedings. Even in the royal duchy of Cornwall all but one of the Court candidates were defeated in the two elections of 1640; see M. Coate, *The Duchy of Cornwall, 1640–1660*, 4 T.R.H.S. x. 156. The composition of the Long Parliament has been examined in M. F. Keeler, *The Long Parliament*, and D. Brunton and H. Pennington, *The Members of the Long Parliament*.

governmental change in such directions as they themselves and not the King determined. Their first step was to bring his advisers to judgment. The impeachment of Strafford and Laud, and of Finch and other ship-money judges struck down the King's chief supporters in the administration, the Church, and the courts of law. Against Strafford the main charges were his traitorous endeavours " to subvert the fundamental laws and government of the realms of England and Ireland, and instead thereof to introduce an arbitrary and tyrannical government against law by giving His Majesty advice by force of arms to compel his loyal subjects to submit thereunto . . . and to subvert the rights of Parliament and the ancient course of parliamentary proceedings".[1] More evidently than in any previous impeachment was purely political conduct aimed at and the King's sole control over ministers and policy infringed. At first the Lords went with the Commons, ordering Strafford into commitment even before he was formally charged, and approving the examination of Privy Councillors on oath in connexion with the charges to be brought. Eventually the more judicial temper of the Upper House prevailed. Even if a precise meaning could be attached to the term "fundamental laws", it was impossible to say that their breach conformed to any known definition of treason. Moreover, the evidence for his intention of bringing an army into "this Kingdom"—arbitrarily interpreted to mean England—rested solely on the notes taken by Sir Henry Vane in a debate on Scotland in the Privy Council, and this evidence was unsupported by that of another witness as the treason law required. Thus the Commons dropped impeachment and resorted to attainder.[2] Under pressure of mob violence and fears of a dissolution the Lords acquiesced in this course, and Charles in a disastrous moment of weakness consented to his servant's death.

The initiative now wholly passed to the opposition, for no man *The first* would easily be found to enter on the perilous and insecure path of *legislative* service to the King. From February 1641 the grant of a Brotherly *measure* Assistance of £300,000 attached the Scots more firmly to the Parliament. In the previous month royal assent was given to a bill providing for triennial parliaments, with an assured means of

---

[1] Cobbett, *Parliamentary History*, ii. 737-8.
[2] For the bill of attainder, see Gardiner, *Constitutional Documents*, 156-8.

summoning them even if the King withheld the writs.[1] To provide against premature dismissal, and guarantee its own continued ability to raise money by loan, Parliament next forced on Charles a bill making its dissolution conditional on its own assent.[2] Non-parliamentary taxation was prohibited by an Act against raising customs without parliamentary grant, which granted them to the Crown for a first term of three weeks only; another reversing the ship-money judgment, declaring the levy to have been illegal from the beginning and forbidding its future imposition; and two more limiting the bounds of royal forests and forbidding knighthood fines.[3]

*Destruction of the Prerogative Courts*    No structural changes in government were thus far involved. But in July 1641 a statute abolished the jurisdiction of Star Chamber as unwarranted by the Act of 1487, denied the competence of the Privy Council to adjudicate on the property rights of the subject, and required the Common Law courts to pronounce within three days on the legality of commitments made by its order and challenged by habeas corpus.[4] By the same Act the Council of the North was wholly abolished, and the Council of Wales lost such of its jurisdiction as was analogous to that of Star Chamber. The Court of Requests, not mentioned in the statute, ceased to work on the outbreak of the Civil War. At last the battle of the Common Law courts against rival jurisdiction was won for them by their parliamentary ally, and governmental acts were subjected to their sole jurisdiction.

*Ecclesiastical questions*    Until now the King had irresolutely and passively accepted measures thrust upon him by a unanimous opposition. With regard to ecclesiastical changes, however, his own mind was made up, and theirs divided. His guiding principle, set forth in 1628 in a declaration prefixed to the Articles, was that the ecclesiastical supremacy belonged to the Crown alone, and not to the Crown in Parliament, and that the constituted authorities of the Church formed the sole valid instrument for its exercise.[5] This principle he unswervingly maintained. His opponents had no such unity of purpose. They could agree that toleration was inadmissible, and they insisted remorselessly on the execution of the penal laws.

---

[1] Gardiner, *Documents*, 144-56.    [2] Gardiner, *Documents*, 158-9.
[3] Gardiner, *Documents*, 159-62, 189-97.
[4] Gardiner, *Documents*, 179-86. See also H. E. I. Phillips, *The Last Years of the Court of Star Chamber*, 4 *T.R.H.S.* xxi. 103.
[5] Gardiner, *Documents*, 75; Gee and Hardy, 518-21.

They could agree that the Church was not to be Laudian, for that
led Romewards. They could agree in condemning the canons of
1640. They could agree that the ecclesiastical supremacy should
be brought under parliamentary control. But they could not agree
upon a reformed plan of government and ritual. In the Commons'
debates on petitions presented to the House praying for the Root-
and-Branch extirpation of episcopacy a sharp conflict of opinion
was revealed between those who condemned the episcopal system
as harmful to religion and incompatible with parliamentary
government and those who considered that episcopacy, reformed
and limited so far as necessary, must be preserved.[1] Between the
two extremes, a middle party under Pym showed itself indifferent at first to the precise form by which the Church was
to be governed, provided it were put under lay control and its
Protestant character thereby preserved.

In the Lords a more conservative spirit prevailed on this as on *Formation*
purely political questions. The Lords concurred in the abolition of *of an*
the High Commission by a statute condemning its jurisdiction as *Anglican*
*party*
having exceeded that conferred by the Act of 1559 and prohibiting
the future erection of any like court.[2] They agreed that bishops
should be excluded from civil authority. Yet they would not
tolerate interference with the composition of the Upper House by
the Lower when the Commons tried to incapacitate bishops from
sitting there, nor would they surrender—though they might
desire to reform—episcopacy, nor consent to Puritan innovations
in ritual or alterations in the Prayer Book.[3] When the Long Parliament began its second session in October 1641, the schism
between the Root-and-Branch men and the defenders of episcopacy reappeared. The King's determination to defend episcopal
government and Anglican worship made the Crown the natural
rallying-point for religious conservatives in both Houses and the
nation at large.

---

[1] Gardiner, *Documents*, 137-44; *History of England*, ix. 274-80.
[2] Gardiner, *Documents*, 186-9.
[3] Gardiner, *History of England*, ix. 378; Firth, *House of Lords during the Civil
War*, 93. For the views expressed by the Lords on Church reform, see W. A.
Shaw, *English Church during the Civil Wars and the Commonwealth*, i. 65 ff;
Gardiner, *Documents*, 167-79, 199. The Bishops' Exclusion Bill was part of an
attempt by the Commons to diminish the royalist party in the Lords by eliminating bishops and Catholic peers.

*The
majority
assert
control
over the
executive*

This union was consummated when the Puritan majority tried to wrest control of the executive from the King. That their leaders had such an intention in 1640 is perhaps unlikely. In 1641 they could hardly help asserting it. They were sitting in the shadow of armed force. On their side was the Covenanting army, which might abandon their cause when its own was won. Against them stood the English army, with no cause to love a Parliament which did not pay it but did pay its Scottish antagonists. The English officers twice formed Army Plots for its forcible expulsion. By the autumn of 1641 both armies were disbanded, but the King was in Scotland attempting to raise a following there. Remoter, but not less disquieting, were the Catholic army in Ireland, and the forces wielded by Continental states like France and Holland whose support the King was trying to enlist. If he once obtained superior strength, every gain made since 1640 would be imperilled and revenge exacted for Strafford's death. It was imperative for the opposition leaders to achieve control over government; and the King's appointment of opposition Lords as Privy Councillors and his reported design of conferring office under the Crown on Pym and other leaders in the Commons could only be regarded as attempts to divide their ranks.[1] Already in June 1641 the Houses had accepted Pym's Ten Propositions, which included a demand that the King should put his government in the hands of such as the Parliament could trust.[2] During Charles's absence in Scotland, the appointment of a Council of Defence by Parliament brought the creation of a rival government one stage nearer.[3] In November the final crisis came with the news of the Irish rebellion. An army must be created to repress it. By the Additional Instruction the majority in the Commons formally repeated the demand for authority over the executive.[4] The religious animosities which had now divided the Parliament made the demand no longer unanimous. Defenders of the Church could not permit their opponents to grasp executive power and armed force. The cleavage was demonstrated by the debates on the Grand Remonstrance. As to its recital of the King's

---

[1] Gardiner, *History of England*, ix. 413.      [2] Gardiner, *Documents*, 163–6.
[3] Gardiner, *History of England*, x. 2; *Commons' Journals*, ii. 257.
[4] For the Impressment Act for the Army to serve in Ireland, see Gardiner, *Documents*, 242–5. For the Additional Instruction, see *Lords' Journals*, iv. 431.

misgovernment and the remedial work already done there were no differences of opinion, though the more conservative members deprecated what was in effect an appeal to the people against the Crown.[1] Proposals for further ecclesiastical reform by Parliament aided by a synod of divines, and for control over the ministers of the Crown, broke up the Commons into nearly equal parties, for the Remonstrance was carried by only eleven votes in a House of three hundred.

Constitutionally the King's position was now strong. In refusing *The* to surrender his government to the leaders of a fractional majority *Five* in a Parliament he could not get rid of, he had the support of *Members* most of the Lords and a strong party in the Commons. He represented all that was lawful in Church and State against a revolutionary caucus. His government, as lately reformed, might have been preserved. By a renewed appeal to force he threw it away. His attempt to impeach the five opposition leaders, Pym, Holles, Hampden, Hazelrig, and Strode, for "subverting the fundamental laws of the realm" [2]—an offence of which they were at least as guilty as Strafford and against which no parliamentary privilege would avail—and to arrest them for himself when the House declined to do so, renewed the ascendancy of the opposition and confirmed them in the opinion that they also must appeal to force. Though he dropped proceedings against the five members and accepted the bill excluding bishops from Parliament,[3] the Houses, momentarily united again, pressed on him a bill placing the militia under parliamentary control.

Thanks to the King's mistake, the revolutionary party domin- *The final* ated the situation. When he left London for York, they voted that *cleavage* the kingdom should be placed in a posture of defence. Their Militia Bill became an Ordinance of the two Houses alone (an unprecedented use of the term) enforceable by proceedings for contempt.[4] In June 1642 they drew up Nineteen Propositions, claiming for Parliament the right to nominate councillors, ministers and judges, control of the militia, and the right to reform the Church.[5] This was a virtual declaration of war, to which the King replied by the

---

[1] See W. H. Coates, *Observations on the Grand Remonstrance*, 1 *J.M.H.* 1; text of the Grand Remonstrance in Gardiner, *Documents*, 202-32. For a commentary on it see J. W. Allen, *English Political Thought, 1603–1660*, i. 381-3.

[2] Gardiner, *Documents*, 236-7.      [3] Gardiner, *Documents*, 241-2.

[4] Gardiner, *Documents*, 245-7.      [5] Gardiner, *Documents*, 249-54.

issue of commissions of array.[1] Parliament decided that an army should be raised.[2] Civil war now began.

*The royal govern-ment during the Civil War*  The ensuing four years saw two governments at war within a single State. Both were organised primarily for military purposes. Round the King at Oxford gathered a sketchy administrative system of soldiers and officials to which was added in January 1644 a Parliament of seceders from that of Westminster, whose futile and often embarrassing activities caused the King when he adjourned it in March 1645 to congratulate himself on being "freed from the place of base and mutinous motions—that is to say, our mongrel Parliament here".[3] Incurably deficient in financial resources, the royal government could raise neither loans or taxes effectively, voluntary contributions gradually became exhausted and were replaced by capricious and destructive exactions, recruiting both voluntary and compulsory failed, and in the shadow of military defeat men would no longer risk taking up military, administrative, or judicial service under the Crown.

*The rule of the Long Parlia-ment*  Very different was the development of the revolutionary assembly at Westminster. Detached from the Crown, it extended its control over every branch of government. Its Ordinances became the law.[4] The power enforced by virtue of its privileges seemed limitless and unchallengeable. It imposed over the press a censorship hardly less rigorous than that of Star Chamber. It sequestrated the property of royalists and of the royal family, imposed contributions assessed by commissioners possessing discretionary powers, collected customs, and rounded off its financial system by the levy of an excise in July 1643. By gifts, loans and taxation it maintained a navy costing £300,000 annually and an army costing a million. This army was created and remodelled by Ordinance. The unprofessional trained-bands of the counties were in December 1642 grouped into the Midland, Eastern, and Warwickshire and Staffordshire Associations. In the same way the Parliamentary forces were reorganised

---

[1] Gardiner, *Documents*, 258-61.    [2] Gardiner, *Documents*, 261.
[3] Firth, *House of Lords during the Civil War*, 130.
[4] For examples of this legislation, see C. H. Firth and R. S. Rait, *Acts and Ordinances of the Interregnum*, i. e.g. 12-16, 32, 37, 49, 51, 53, 124 (raising forces and appointing commanders), 16, 38, 40, 47, 69, 77, 85, 145 (taxation), 184 (regulation of the press), 202, 274, 339 (excise), 241, 366 (impressment), 425 (images in churches), 582 (abolition of Book of Common Prayer).

in 1644–5 on a professional basis, the soldiers of the "New Model" army being paid regular though low wages. Members of Parliament were disqualified by the Self-Denying Ordinance from holding military commands save in exceptional cases of re-appointment, the officers becoming a professional body commissioned by the commander-in-chief. Parliament nominated generals such as Essex, Manchester, and Waller, and being in continuous session directed the war at first through a Committee of Safety,[1] and after the alliance with the Covenanters in the Solemn League and Covenant of 1643 by a joint Committee of Both Kingdoms, with executive powers but responsible to Parliament.[2] Parliamentary authority invaded the domain of religion unchecked. In July 1643 an assembly of divines, set up by Ordinance to inform the mind of Parliament on such matters as should be referred to it, met at Westminster. The Solemn League had implied, without directly specifying, the reorganisation of the Church in England—and fantastically enough in Ireland also—on a Presbyterian basis.[3] But English Presbyterianism differed from that of Scotland in its avowed Erastianism and the Westminster Assembly got no power of acting independently of Parliament. In 1645 a Directory of Public Worship prepared by the Assembly was imposed instead of the Prayer Book, and a beginning was made in the reorganisation of parishes on Presbyterian lines, and their grouping into local presbyteries.[4]

Competent and aggressive, the triumphant Parliament seemed to hold the future of English government in its grasp when the royal cause had been lost. Its constitutional ideas had been revealed when on two occasions during the war its terms had been placed before the King. Under the influence of early defeats, it had modified in the Treaty[5] of Oxford the demands of the Nineteen Propositions regarding control over appointments to civil and judicial office.[6] In the Treaty of Uxbridge, the stimulus of victory and the pressure of the Covenanters led a Parliament from which moderates had long since disappeared to go beyond the Nineteen Propositions in claiming control over *Constitutional views of Parliament*

---

[1] Gardiner, *History of England*, x. 209; Turner, *Privy Council*, i. 217.
[2] Gardiner, *Documents*, 271–4; Turner i. 218.
[3] Gardiner, *Documents*, 268.    [4] Shaw, i. 196, 343–56, ii. 1–6.
[5] I.e. negotiations.    [6] Gardiner, *Documents*, 262–7.

peace and war and also to require the King's sworn acceptance of the Solemn League and Covenant.[1] After the war, in July 1646, the Propositions of Newcastle substantially repeated the Uxbridge proposals save as regards peace and war, but demanded authority over the militia for twenty years, a period which would probably exceed that of the King's natural life.[2]

*Parlia-*
*ment and*
*the Army*

By 1646, however, the Parliament was no longer in sole control of the destinies of English government. Apart from the King's inflexible resolve, even in the extremity of defeat, not to surrender the essential prerogatives for which he had fought and was to die, and the indifference to English constitutional principles of the Scots who were bent only on getting royal consent to the Solemn League and Covenant, the Army, standing in a position of growing independence from Parliament since the Self-Denying Ordinance and fortified by victory, was to assert a decisive influence over government during the years between the end of the First Civil War and the Restoration.

*Political*
*Views of*
*the Army*

Failing to come to terms with Charles, the Scots withdrew and handed him over to Parliament. That body was in no strong position. Both Houses had been depleted by secessions to the King. Two hundred and forty-one new members had been returned in by-elections, yet the average attendance in the Commons fell to a hundred or less.[3] The Lords, even more reduced in number and more gravely affected by the Self-Denying Ordinance, had declined further than the Lower House, with which they had become rather unsuccessful rivals than partners.[4] In the Army, meanwhile, constitutional doctrines had been formulated with increasing clarity and on lines very different from those professed by Parliament.[5] Recruited on principles which admitted no distinction between Protestants of all varieties, among whom the Independents or Congregationalists predominated, it would never accept an enforced conformity whether Episcopal or Presbyterian. On this fundamental point officers and men agreed. The rank and file, however, permeated by the influence of the Leveller party inspired by Lilburne, based all

[1] Gardiner, *Documents*, 275-86.  [2] Gardiner, *Documents*, 290-306.
[3] See R. N. Kershaw, *The Recruiting of the Long Parliament*, 8 *Hist.* 169.
[4] Firth, *House of Lords during the Civil War*, 141-3, 147, 153.
[5] Firth, *Cromwell's Army*, 351 ff.; G. P. Gooch, *English Democratic Ideas in the Seventeenth Century* (2nd ed.), 118 ff.

power on democratic consent. The Commons were to them supreme only by virtue of their embodiment of this principle, subject to frequent renewal by popular election, and to the observance of fundamental rights which no authority could invade. The constitutional position of the Lords, whose existence reposed on Prerogative, was wholly repudiated. Though the officers were still mainly adherents of a parliamentary monarchy, it was difficult to see what place the Leveller theory of the rank and file could possibly leave for kingship itself.

Well aware of the Army's constitutional and religious views, *The Heads of the Proposals* the Parliament resolved on its disbandment, and refused to meet its arrears of pay. The Army retaliated by seizing the King. The officers at least still inclined towards a new monarchical constitution. Their views, set forth in July 1647 in the Heads of the Proposals, contemplated limited monarchy, toleration outside an episcopal establishment, and a Parliament fettered by the restrictions of a written constitution, biennial, and founded on a remodelled electoral system.[1]

At this point the King, with disastrous results for himself and *The King's downfall* the monarchy, assumed the position of an arbiter, able to choose between the Newcastle Propositions, the Heads of the Proposals, and the programme of the Scots. All three offers were speedily closed to him. His rejection of the Four Bills, embodying the final demands of Parliament, evoked the rupture of negotiations by the Vote of No Addresses.[2] The monarchism of the army officers, still further attenuated by their conviction that it was necessary to deny to the King any negative voice in legislation, yielded before the republicanism of the Levelling rank and file, expressed in the non-monarchical and anti-parliamentary Agreement of the People.[3] Charles's Engagement with the Scots, by which Presbyterianism was to have a three-years provisional establishment in England, unloosed the Second Civil War, in which the Scots were defeated, the Engagement was wrecked, and republicanism triumphed in the Army.[4] Parliament did what it could to save him by entering upon the Treaty of Newport for concessions

---

[1] Gardiner, *Documents*, 316-26.
[2] Gardiner, *Documents*, 335-47, 353-6.
[3] Gardiner, *Documents*, 333-5. On the series of documents called by this name, see J. W. Gough, *The Agreements of the People*, 15 *Hist.* 334.
[4] Gardiner, *Documents*, 347-53.

as to the armed forces and appointments to office which he was prepared to consider, and an establishment of Presbyterianism which he was not.[1] But Parliament was now helpless. Pride's Purge ejected in December 1648 the Presbyterian supporters of monarchy. The Rump which remained passed an Ordinance for the King's trial by a High Court of Justice. To this illegal tribunal he refused to plead, and by it he was on 27th January, 1649, sentenced to death.[2]

*The Common- wealth*    Government henceforward gave effect, in varying forms, to the constitutional ideas of the Army alone. For practical purposes, this meant the group of officers of whom Cromwell's was the commanding personality and Ireton's the dominant political intellect. Levelling principles, again put forward in 1649 in the Second Agreement of the People, were rigorously suppressed.[3] In the eyes of the military junto with which real power lay, the Commons, purified by Pride's Purge, preserved until 1653 the principle of popular sovereignty in a more innocuous form. By Ordinances of 1649 monarchy and the devitalised and unpopular Upper House were abolished, and England was declared to be a free Commonwealth, governed by "the representatives of the people in Parliament . . . without either King or House of Lords".[4] In this Republic the House of Commons, only about sixty strong but now invested with the style of Parliament, seized every branch of power, and by its abuse of them all demonstrated the urgent necessity for their separation and limitation. Ordinances now became Acts, and the vigour of an uncontrolled unicameral legislature was shown by a Navigation Act, and Acts for setting the poor to work, for repealing the statutes requiring attendance at Church while enforcing Sabbath observance, for punishing various moral offences, and for relieving poor prisoners. Another Act required the use of English in legal proceedings, and a commission for reforming the law was established.[5] While thus labouring to establish a society refashioned by its innovatory zeal, Parliament seized as much as it could of the executive power, commissioning generals and admirals, and annually

---

[1] Gardiner, *History of the Great Civil War*, iii. 472, 474-82.
[2] Gardiner, *Documents*, 357-8, 371-80.
[3] Gardiner, *Documents*, 359-71; T. C. Pease, *The Leveller Movement*, 278 ff.
[4] Gardiner, *Documents*, 384-8.
[5] Firth and Rait, ii. 104, 321, 387, 393, 423, 559.

appointing a Council of State, at first without a president and then with one appointed on a monthly tenure.[1] New commissions were made out to such of the judges as could be induced to accept them. To legislative activities irksome or positively repulsive to the society it controlled, it added financial measures both harsh and unsound. Faced by constant war expenditure, amounting in 1651 to two and three-quarter millions, and unable to borrow adequately, it resorted to renewed sales of Church and Crown lands and to spoliation of the property of Royalists, about seventy of the most prominent suffering in 1651 and nearly seven hundred more in 1652,[2] while others were compelled to "compound for delinquency" by fines. The conduct of administrative business by a Council of State too large and too dependent on Parliament to be effective served only to prove the need for placing legislative and executive power in different hands. Local administration was similarly subjected to close control and to a process of "packing".[3] The worst evils created by the unification of all authority in the Rump showed themselves in the judicial sphere. Apart from the practice of interfering, often with corrupt motives, in the course of justice, Parliament ousted the jurisdiction of the courts when it saw fit. Like the King, three Royalist peers suffered death by sentence of a High Court of Justice in 1649, and all enemies to the Commonwealth were subjected to this tribunal in 1650. By this means Levellers like Lilburne were coerced.[4] After Worcester in 1651 adherents to the cause of Charles Stuart were put under martial law.[5]

Investing itself with the protection of a new treason law,[6] and exacting an oath of fidelity intended ultimately to be imposed on every subject, the vicious and irresponsible tyranny which now masqueraded as parliamentary government showed no disposition to submit to popular control. Proposals for a new Parliament

*Expulsion of Parliament by the Army*

---

[1] Gardiner, *Documents*, 381-4; Turner, *Privy Council, 1603-1784*, i. 245-7.
[2] For the details of the sale of Church lands, see W. A. Shaw, *History of the English Church during the Civil Wars and the Commonwealth*, ii. 210 ff.; G. B. Tatham, *Sale of Episcopal lands during the Civil Wars and Commonwealth*, 23 *E.H.R.* 91. The whole question of the sale of lands is dealt with by W. E. Chesney, *Transference of Lands in England, 1640-1660*, 4 *T.R.H.S.* xv. 181.
[3] Firth and Rait, ii. 319-21.
[4] *Commons' Journals*, vi. 131, 382, 387, 456, 590.
[5] Firth and Rait, ii. 551.
[6] Firth and Rait, ii. 120; Gardiner, *Documents*, 388-91.

were occasionally and tepidly discussed between 1649 and 1652, but they were marked by a visible reluctance to fix any date for dissolution, and by an insistance that all sitting members should be automatically returned and should become judges of the qualifications of newcomers. Against the statute which made the dissolution of the Parliament dependent on its own consent there was no recourse except to violence. When in April 1653 the House suspended consideration of the whole scheme, the Army, at last freed from the claims of the Irish and Scottish campaigns, terminated its deliberations by expelling it.

*The Little Parliament*    The Army leaders were now involved in a new attempt at constitutional settlement. With King, Lords, and Commons successively removed, continuity was entirely broken and constitutional schemes were more than ever based necessarily on first principles. The initial attempt was the narrowest example of Puritan political ideas yet formulated. Rejecting recourse to a new Parliament, for theoretical reasons as well as on the practical ground that acceptance of the principle of popular sovereignty would have infallibly overthrown Puritan government, the Army leaders frankly adopted the conception of rule by an aristocracy of the "godly"—a doctrine held forth in its most extreme form by the Fifth Monarchy party. As actually worked out, it bore but a faint resemblance to the institutions which had been overthrown. A summons issued to Independent congregations by a new Council of State and by Cromwell as General required them to submit lists of persons suitable to serve in a new governing assembly. From these lists the Army officers in Council selected one hundred and twenty-nine English, five Scottish, and six Irish members, who met on Cromwell's order in July 1653 and assumed by resolution the style of Parliament.[1]

*Its failure*    The failure of the "Little" or "Barebone's" Parliament amply demonstrated the impracticability of rule by a Puritan oligarchy. If good, or at least well-intentioned, government could be a substitute for self-government, this assembly, which undertook the codification of the law, the abolition of the Court of Chancery, of presentation to benefices, and of tithe, attempted legislation protecting poor prisoners and mental deficients, set up (as the Rump

[1] Gardiner, *Commonwealth and Protectorate*, ii. 235-43, 256-63, 272-9; *Constitutional Documents*, 405.

had done) commissioners for the probate of wills, and introduced parochial registers of births, marriages and deaths seemed determined to provide it. But good intentions were insufficient to appease the unrest which its reforming zeal created, and godliness proved of no avail to maintain unity of purpose among the "elect" themselves. Party differences in the House led a majority of its members to resign their authority into Cromwell's hands on 12th December, 1653.[1]

Subsequent experiments were characterised by their gradual *The* abandonment of the doctrinaire ideas which had so luxuriantly *Instru-* flourished in recent years, and a corresponding return to the main *ment of* outlines of the historic constitution. The third republican experi- *ment* ment was set forth in the Instrument of Government, drafted by the Army officers in December 1653.[2] In many respects, it was a thoroughly practical document. Substantially modifying, if not wholly abandoning, the doctrine of right of the "elect" to rule, it constructed a scheme embodying the traditional principles of English government, interpreted in the light of recent experience. Warned by the example of the Rump, it set up an independent and strong executive composed of a Protector and Council, both holding office by a permanent tenure, two names to be selected for each vacancy in the latter by the Council itself from a list drawn up by Parliament, the final choice lying with the Protector. The executive was adequately endowed. Reviving the principle that "the King must live of his own", the Instrument gave the government an income sufficient to maintain a military establishment of 30,000 and a fleet, and £200,000 annually for civil government. Control over this vitally important point—the standing forces—was reserved, except during sessions of Parliament, to the Protector. Yet the lessons of 1629-40 were not forgotten. For many important purposes, such as legislation by ordinance, the Protector could act only through the Council, which held the key position in the constitution. Nor could he dispense with Parliament, which must meet at least trienially, and for at least five months. Its approval was required for nominations to the highest administrative and judicial posts, it had sole control over extraordinary supply, and over its enactments, so far as not inconsistent with the Instrument, the Protector

---

[1] For examples of its legislation, see Firth and Rait, ii. 713, 715, 753, 773.
[2] Gardiner, *Documents*, 405-17.

had no negative voice after the lapse of twenty-one days. Behind this unicameral Parliament stood an electorate organised in new-modelled constituencies. A new county franchise, based on the possession of £200 of real or personal property made its appearance in England. Like the Little Parliament, that of the Instrument was an assembly representing all three countries.[1] But it was intended to represent only those classes whose interests or principles might be supposed to attach them to republican rule.

*A written constitution*    Following the historic constitution, the Instrument intended a harmony between executive and legislature, each possessing its admitted sphere of action. Under the monarchy the terms of that partnership had depended on well-understood conventions, which had only slowly ceased to operate. Under the Instrument they necessarily depended on a fundamental or organic law contained in its text. Two interpretations of that text were possible, and there was lacking any tribunal empowered to pronounce with authority in case of dispute. Nor in case of dispute did Parliament prevail, for the Protector's negative voice made his assent necessary to constitutional change. No assembly summoned under the Instrument could fail to resume the struggle for full sovereignty, formerly waged with the Crown, against the Protectoral power set up by a military junto.

*Conflict of Protector and Parliament*    Such was the line naturally adopted by both of the two Protectorate Parliaments. Each prepared a new constitutional scheme. It was in vain that the Protector reminded the Parliament of 1654 that it was bound to accept the validity of the constitution to which it owed its existence, and that the form by which its members were elected expressly denied to them constituent powers. Even after the forcible exclusion of the more extreme members, the remainder occupied themselves with constitutional amendments which, rejecting the distinction drawn by Cromwell between "fundamentals" and "circumstantials", treated the whole Instrument as equally flexible, imposed parliamentary control over election to the Protectorship, over the Council, the revenue, the declaration of peace and war, and above all, over the number of the standing forces and the degree of toleration held out except to Catholics and Episcopalians by the Instrument.[2]

---

[1] Ordinances for union with Scotland and for elections in Scotland, Gardiner, *Documents*, 418-25; for elections in Ireland, 425-7.
[2] On "fundamentals" and "circumstantials", see Cromwell's speech of

On these latter points, the differences between the Protector *Military* and Parliament came to a head and brought about a dissolution. *government* Like Charles after 1629, Cromwell now found that to govern without a Parliament and on a basis which a Parliament had dis-approved was at best difficult and in time of war impossible. The · Instrument rejected, his authority seemed at best only that of a commander-in-chief, subsisting alone in a State whence all other lawful authority had vanished. And the Instrument was ceaselessly challenged. Ordinances issued under it were attacked in the courts. Judges and officials resigned rather than enforce them.[1] After a Royalist rising in 1655, military government under Majors-General had to be superimposed on the system of local government, and the militia they commanded financed by an arbitrary "decimation" on the property of royalists.[2] Finally, war with Spain brought the system to breaking-point. A second Parliament was assembled, and a new attempt made to put the Protectorate on a basis of consent.

Like its predecessor, this body was subjected to a purge of *The* disaffected members. As in 1654, the remainder prepared a new *Humble* constitution, the Humble Petition and Advice, supplemented by *Petition* the Additional Petition and Advice.[3] This time the initiative in *Advice* constitution-building seems to have come from the government itself. The terms of the Petition reflect a growing sense that no con-stitution radically different from that of the past could be main-tained. In asking Cromwell to assume the Crown, the petitioners were seeking to relate with Protectoral government legal concepts drawn from the past, though the difficulties which induced him to refuse it, and to accept instead a power of nominating his successor indicated the impossibility of substituting for the historic kingship a parvenu rule maintained by the sword.[4] The same difficulties appeared in the creation of a second chamber, the "Other House", with members nominated by the Protector.[5] This body, intended

12th September 1654, in Carlyle, *Letters and Speeches of Cromwell*, ed. S. C. Lomas, ii. 381-6. For the constitutional scheme prepared by this Parliament, see Gardiner, *Documents*, 427-47.

[1] Gardiner, *Commonwealth and Protectorate*, iii. 152-5; M. P. Ashley, *Financial and Commercial Policy under the Protectorate*, 55.

[2] On Majors-General, see D. W. Rannie, *Cromwell's Major-Generals*, 10 E.H.R. 471.        [3] Gardiner, *Documents*, 447-64.

[4] Firth, *Last Years of the Protectorate*, i. ch. v-vi.

[5] Firth, *House of Lords during the Civil War*, 249-55.

to prevent direct conflicts between Protector and Commons, and perhaps also to compensate the Protector and the Army for the diminished control which the Petition gave them over the Council[1]—whose members were now to be approved by Parliament and only removable with its consent—speedily proved itself as incapable of succeeding to the position of the Lords as the Protector was to that of the monarchy. The Commons of this Parliament, like their predecessors, ended with a violent attack, directed mainly on the Other House, against the constitution under which they sat.

*The fall of the Protectorate*    The more nearly these constitutions approached the historic model, in short, the less secure was their existence. They forfeited for the republic the support of those to whom the republican principle was paramount, without obtaining the adherence of those who could associate monarchy only with the ancient dynasty and constitution. The anarchy which followed Cromwell's death proved the bankruptcy of all the constitution-making of the years since 1642. Alienating the Army, Richard Cromwell was in April 1659 ousted from the Protectorship to which his father appears to have nominated him.[2] The situation of 1649–52 seemed to return with the recall of the Rump by the Army. But no more than at the earlier period could the Parliament regulate its relations with the Army leaders, nor, even when they again expelled it in October 1659, did any Cromwell arise to make military rule tolerable and invest it with a quasi-legal aspect. By the beginning of 1660 they had come to realise that they could govern neither with the Parliament they had again recalled, nor without it.

*The Restoration*    The ensuing months saw a swift return towards the old order. Under Monk the army of Scotland marched south to Westminster, forced the Long Parliament to readmit the secluded members expelled by Pride in 1648, and induced it to consent to its own dissolution. Here at last was the end of republicanism. The Convention, summoned without royal writ, which now assembled, contained a Presbyterian majority.[3] The situation of 1646–8 thus reappeared, and with it proposals, based on those of

[1] The strength of the Army party in the Upper House was a contributory cause of Richard Cromwell's fall.
[2] See A. H. Woolrych, *The Fall of the Protectorate*, 13 *C.H.J.* 133.
[3] See L. F. Brown, *Religious Factors in the Convention Parliament*, 22 *E.H.R.* 51 for an argument that their majority depended on Independent support.

Newport, for a limited monarchy and a Presbyterian establishment. As in earlier years, monarchy thus refashioned was an idle dream, unrealisable against the will of an army which, so far as it preserved coherence, was turned by Monk into an instrument for erecting a monarchy acceptable to himself. Schemes such as those of 1642–8 were dispelled by his resolve to effect an unconditional return, and by the royal Declaration of Breda, promising the pardon to offenders, safeguards for property, satisfaction of arrears, and liberty of conscience which alone now expressed the mind and purpose of the Army.[1] The position of Parliament was secured by the provision that the settlement was to be subject to its authority. But it was enhanced by none of the powers asserted for it after 1641. The final constitutional device of the Army was to dictate a return to the basis of government existing on the eve of the Civil War.

Thus ended the age of written constitutions, inaugurated by the *End of the* Ten Propositions and ended by the Additional Petition and Advice, *period of written* which had aimed at limited monarchy or republicanism. Such *constitu-* political expedients as written constitutions embodying inviolable *tions* rights, restricting sovereignty, and separating the legislative and executive powers, were henceforth discredited, as were single-chamber legislatures, and direct parliamentary appointment to office. Others, like a united Parliament for the three countries, reform of the franchise, and redistribution of seats, were delayed for nearly two centuries through their premature achievement by the sword. The rejection of republicanism at least had been complete and final. Whether parliamentary, democratic, theocratic, or military, it had met only with failure. A nation profoundly monarchist, anti-democratic, anti-sectarian, and anti-military had preserved, amid the stresses under which successive governments collapsed, the abiding sense that it was to be governed only by an authority based on law and not force, operating by virtue of consent and co-operation, and grounded upon a graded diversity of privilege and duty. It was to be the business of restored monarchy to adapt itself to these fundamentals.

[1] Gardiner, *Documents*, 465-7.

# CHAPTER V

## THE BEGINNING OF PARLIAMENTARY
## MONARCHY, 1660–1714

### i

THE restoration of monarchy in 1660 was essentially a return to government by law. It implied primarily a repudiation of the arbitrary rule by civilian or military juntos, parliamentary or republican, which eighteen years of armed force had imposed on the nation. Equally if less obviously, it implied a repudiation of the arbitrary rule, based on a Prerogative which the law admitted but could not restrict, which had been overturned by the Long Parliament between 1640 and 1642. The edifice of government now re-erected comprised all the statutes limiting the Prerogative which had been validly enacted before the outbreak of the Civil War. Impositions, ship-money, and other taxation derived from the Prerogative remained henceforth illegal. The names of benevolence and forced loan disappear from constitutional history. Apart from his hereditary revenues, the King had no means of financing his government other than those provided, permanently or temporarily, by Parliament. The jurisdiction of conciliar courts survived only in the attenuated form of that still preserved in civil and equitable cases by the Council of Wales until its final abolition in 1689.[1] A proposal mooted in the Lords for the revival of Star Chamber was at once abandoned, and with the Star Chamber the Council of the North and other courts of like nature also vanished. Except for an appellate jurisdiction from courts overseas, the Council had been shorn of its judicial powers, retaining only a power of arresting and examining suspected persons, which was subject to the provision of the Act of 1641 requiring the speedy issue of a writ of habeas corpus in such cases.[2] With the abolition of the conciliar courts,

[1] Holdsworth, *History of English Law*, i. 127.　　[2] Gardiner, *Documents*, 185.

the power of legislating by proclamation, unsupported by any coercive processes save those afforded by the Common Law, was confined within the limits imposed by the *Case of Proclamations*. Arbitrary rule was no longer possible to a king who could neither legislate nor tax out of Parliament, nor do justice outside the courts of Common Law and of Chancery.

A return to the basis of government established by 1642 in- *The* volved, in fact, the acceptance of a system in which the Houses *position of* of Parliament and the courts of Common Law could become *Parlia-* predominant. As vitality departed from the institutions created *ment* by revolutionary experiment, the Houses—those of the Convention transformed into a Parliament by the presence of the King and by a declaratory statute [1]—reappeared in their historic form, and with increased authority. The reform of the franchise and redistribution of seats effected under the Republic, though commended by the new Chancellor, Clarendon, as "meet to be more warrantably made, and in a more auspicious time", were abandoned, as indeed they had been in the elections to the last Protectoral Parliament, summoned by Richard Cromwell, and remained for almost two centuries an ideal towards which no progress was made. The legislative union with Scotland and Ireland was similarly dissolved. Almost as automatically as the Commons, the Upper House, illegally evicted from the constitution in 1649, resumed its accustomed place. The handful of Presbyterian peers who sat in the Convention were gradually reinforced by returning Royalists, including those peers created since 1642 whose right to sit had been rejected in negotiations with Charles I.[2] Only the spiritual lords, disqualified by the Bishops' Exclusion Act of 1642, had to await the passing of a repealing statute of 1661 before re-entering the House.[3] Thus restored to their normal aspect, the Houses found themselves heirs of the gains achieved between 1640 and 1642. They possessed an indisputable sovereignty in legislation and taxation. Even the settlement of religion passed within their all-embracing competence, and parliamentary was in effect substituted for royal supremacy over the Church. It would indeed have been difficult

[1] W. C. Costin and J. S. Watson, *Law and Working of the Constitution*, i. 1.
[2] Firth, *House of Lords during the Civil War*, 282-90.
[3] Costin and Watson, i. 9.

to contend that any topic existed with regard to which they had no authority to act, or must await royal initiative before doing so. The notion of "inseparable prerogatives" so integrally and indefeasibly attached to the Crown that no statute could abridge or destroy them had in almost every possible application sustained fatal injury. If many of the prerogatives of which the radical element in the Long Parliament had sought to deprive Charles I —such as control over the appointment of ministers and judges, over the armed forces, and the like—were no longer assailed, it would none the less be difficult, even impossible, for future kings to deny the right of Parliament to discuss the manner of their use, or for them to call in question such privileges as freedom of speech, to coerce opponents, and to employ other traditional devices for subjecting parliamentary proceedings to royal control. In 1666 the House of Lords reversed on writ of error the decision in *Eliot's Case*.[1] In 1673 the enfranchisement of the city and county of Durham was effected by statute. The King had to desist in face of parliamentary opposition from his attempt to create by Prerogative a new parliamentary constituency at Newark.[2] For the management of future Parliaments a new technique would have to be devised, in which the place of compulsion and fear was taken by patronage, bribery, electoral manipulation, and other forms of influence. Only in such ways would the independence of Parliament be assailable and the constitutional ascendancy of the Crown be preserved.

*The legacy of the revolutionary period*    Moreover the Houses profited, though unequally, by the events which followed as well as those which preceded the rupture between King and Parliament in 1642. Nothing could cancel out the years in which Parliament, severed from and opposed to the King, had conducted the business of the State in its entirety, though it is to be observed that the Lords, declining in authority

---

1 For a discussion of this decision, see *Bradlaugh* v. *Gossett*, in Keir and Lawson, *Cases in Constitutional Law* (5th edn.), 287.

2 Newark was enfranchised by statute in 1677. Porritt, *Unreformed House of Commons*, i. 6, 16, 392. The additions to the membership of the House recorded by Porritt are : under James I, 14 counties and boroughs returning 27 members; under Charles I, 9, returning 18 members; under Charles II, 3, returning 6 members. No borough avoided the duty of sending members after 1614. No new constituency was created in England or Wales after 1677. Petitions for enfranchisement were thereafter addressed not to the King but to Parliament.

after 1642 and abolished after 1649, gained less from this experience than the Commons. The expenditure as well as the raising of revenue, control of the army and navy, domestic administration and foreign policy, the overseas colonies and plantations, had all been brought within the purview of the revolutionary Long Parliament. To preserve these topics as pertaining solely to the "mystery of Kingship" was no longer possible now that the veil which protected them had been rent in twain. Post-Restoration Parliaments might contain no member who had ever sat in the Long Parliament and might regard it as the usurper of a wholly unconstitutional authority. They could not help entering into its illegitimate legacy. Irresponsible and ignorant as their attacks on ministers and their criticisms and demands on points of policy might be, they were committed to a political apprenticeship in the course of which they were slowly to learn the art of successfully conducting government under ministers accountable to themselves as well as to the Crown.

Like the Houses of Parliament, the courts of law found them- *The* selves after 1660 in full possession of long-disputed territory. *Common Law* Their conciliar rivals had been swept away. Large areas of *courts* jurisdiction, within which a reformed jurisprudence had been formulated by conciliar judges, lay open for annexation and development. Jurisdiction of first instance lay under the full control of the superior courts at Westminster. The Lords, defeated in their attempt to enter this field by the decision in *Skinner* v. *The East India Company* (1666), successfully resurrected their appellate jurisdiction, after two centuries of abeyance, by asserting their right to hear appeals from the Court of Chancery in *Shirley* v. *Fagg* (1675).[1] This monopolisation of justice by the superior courts and the Upper House naturally ended the distinction between cases involving "matter of State" and those affecting solely the interests of private litigants which had to some extent characterised English law hitherto. The relations of the government and the subject were left for the courts to determine. No powers could be attributed to the one, no duties imposed on the other, save those which the courts recognised by virtue of either statute or Common Law. English constitutional law was therefore bound, sooner or later, to assume a bias, appropriate to the Common Law tradition,

[1] Costin and Watson, i. 157-63, 167-71; Turberville, in 45 *E.H.R.* 69-71.
8a

in favour of individual rights and property, and on the whole adverse to the claims of the State to a freedom of action determined by considerations of public policy. It must be admitted that something of value was lost when conciliar jurisdiction was overthrown. Apart from the advantages to litigants which it had presented over the unwieldy, technical, and expensive processes of the Common Law, it had stood for conceptions of public good in which the Common Law courts had been signally deficient. Moreover, unlike the conciliar courts, the Common Law courts were only concerned with the fulfilment of legal obligations and not with the execution of a policy. In controlling governmental acts, they were necessarily limited to considering merely the letter of the law, whereas the conciliar courts had, in their best periods, used their power in order to make their own standards of administrative efficiency and disinterestedness prevail over the slackness and selfishness of officials.

*Autonomy of local administration*    The results were to be specially noticeable in the domain of local government. Central control, no longer applicable by a Council deprived of judicial powers, fell in the last resort under the easy-going sway of the Common Law judges, whose unambitious task it was to impose on local officials at least a minimum and literal performance of their Common Law and statutory duties, should any litigant be sufficiently bold, and sufficiently wealthy, to undertake the risks of invoking their jurisdiction. No longer effectively supervised by administrative tribunals, local officials such as Justices of the Peace relapsed after 1660 into two centuries of virtual irresponsibility. A profound harmony reigned between them and a Parliament drawn from the same classes as themselves. By degrees the code of social legislation which it was their duty to enforce fell into desuetude, as the fixing of wages and similar duties were either left unperformed or carried out as magistrates themselves saw fit. The age of paternalistic government closed at the Restoration. Government by the propertied classes in their own interest took the place of government by the Crown in what it held to be the national interest. So far as Parliament bent itself to the task of economic and social regulation, it was not by strengthening administrative control, but by legislative action particularly in the manipulation of tariffs. Internally, the main innovation made by the restored Parliament was the enactment in 1662 of a new Law of Settlement, whereby parishes could deport newcomers within forty days of their arrival unless they could find surety that they would never become chargeable on the parish for poor relief.[1] Though this rigid system was to some extent modified by subsequent statutes, it remained until 1795 possible for the propertied classes on whom the burden of poor-rates fell to relieve themselves by sending poor persons back to their own parishes not because they were paupers but merely because they might become so.

It would thus appear that a return to monarchy, as representing *Changed* the principle of government according to law, confronted the *position of* King with a Parliament, courts of justice, and local administra- *the Crown* tive system all largely independent of royal authority. Unable to finance his government or supplement its authority without parliamentary consent, or to invoke any sanctions for its enforcement other than those afforded by the ordinary courts, the King could never again attempt to govern as his predecessors had done. Nor could he, even in the central administration itself, over which he retained the largest measure of control, work except in some kind of partnership with the leaders of the aristocratic class which dominated English political life for almost two centuries after the Restoration, annexing to themselves the principal offices under the Crown, and—as James II was to find—bringing to a standstill any government which tried to dispense with their co-operation. There could never be a second Stuart absolutism on the model of the first.

Yet, all deductions made, the sum of powers remaining at the *The* King's sole disposition was still large. Abandoning the more *King's* radical claims advanced by the Long Parliament, the Parliaments *powers* of the Restoration period left to him the power of appointing to offices of State, to judgeships, to every place of emolument lying within the vast civil and ecclesiastical patronage of the Crown. Control over the fighting forces was still his. The Cromwellian army, it is true, was speedily disbanded. Satisfaction of its arrears of pay, promised in the Declaration of Breda, was carried out by eleven monthly assessments and a poll-tax yielding

---

[1] Grant Robertson, *Select Statutes, Cases and Documents* (5th edn.), 53-60; S. and B. Webb, *English Poor Law History*, i. 315, 325-8. See also D. Marshall, *The English Poor in the Eighteenth Century*, ch. vi.

£853,000.[1] By February 1661 thirteen cavalry and eighteen infantry regiments and fifty-nine garrisons had been disbanded. A regiment of guards, with a few surviving garrison units, alone remained of the red-coated legions of the Protectorate. The maintenance of military discipline in this small force rested on a prerogative so highly doubtful since the abolition of martial law by the Petition of Right that it is conceivable that the Articles of War issued by the Crown from 1666 onwards may have been wholly illegal.[2] Their validity does not, however, seem to have been challenged, and even if the existence of a standing army tended to become a stock topic of parliamentary complaint under the restored monarchy, circumstances enabled Charles II to add by degrees to the diminutive forces left to him at his accession. The growing royal navy was under his full control, and its development was one of his most serious interests. Naval discipline was placed on a clear statutory basis in 1662.[3] Another Act of the same year confirmed royal control over the militia.[4] The Prerogative further included sole control over the declaration of peace and war, the conduct of diplomatic relations and the making of treaties. Parliament itself depended on the royal will for its existence and validity. An Act for preserving the King's person and government expressly repudiated the doctrine that either House alone, or both Houses together, possessed any independent legislative authority, and thus confirmed to the King that negative voice in legislation which Charles I had defended.[5] A Triennial Act of 1664 made the summons and duration of Parliament a matter of royal discretion by repealing the Act of 1641; and while reiterating the rule that sessions ought to be held every three years provided no particular mechanism for making it effective.[6] Taxation had become subject to exclusive parliamentary control, but the disbursement of revenue was still within the domain of Prerogative. The supremacy of statute over proclamation was assumed, but

---

[1] W. A. Shaw, *Calendar of Treasury Books, 1660-67*, i. Introduction, viii-xiii.
[2] F. W. Maitland, *Constitutional History of England*, 327; C. M. Clode, *Military Forces of the Crown*, i. 55.
[3] Costin and Watson, i. 11-12. The corps of Royal Marines first originated in 1664, but was several times "broke" before its permanent establishment in 1755.
[4] Costin and Watson, i. 17-20; Clode, i. 33-6.    [5] Costin and Watson, i. 5-9.
[6] Costin and Watson, i. 33-4. The principle of frequency was based not on the Act of 1641 but on mediaeval statutes.

statutes remained subject to a prerogative of dispensation, within limits restated on familiar lines in 1674 in the case of *Thomas v. Sorrell*.[1] From the existence of a dispensing power that of a more general power to suspend the operation of statutes altogether might be inferred. And, in criminal cases, the Crown still possessed the prerogative of pardon. As in 1642, a Parliament asserting that there was no law save that known to the legislature and the courts faced a King who reserved to himself all other attributes of sovereignty. The antithesis had at that date led to a complete constitutional breakdown. Under a King of a more supple and adaptable type, schooled by adversity to cultivate patience and wariness, alert to see the strength and weakness of his opponents' position and his own, taking a cool and worldly view of politics, and resolute in defence of no principle save the right of his dynasty to rule, the powers still inherent in the Crown might still be used to safeguard by peaceful means its supremacy in the constitution. Such were the personal qualities which Charles II brought with him to the throne, and by virtue of which he maintained during the first generation of parliamentary kingship an ascendancy sacrificed only by the blunders and misfortunes of his successors.

To consolidate this ascendancy—a model of what kingship *The cult of* might become under the conditions of 1660—the sovereign must *monarchy* learn the art of adjusting the conduct of his government so as to disarm parliamentary criticism and make it acceptable to the governing classes on whose co-operation he was dependent. For an able and resolute King this was no impossible task. In his favour he could capitalise the enthusiasm for monarchy and the detestation of rebellion which in 1660 animated the majority of his subjects. To most Englishmen of that day, the return to monarchy was more than a mere practical expedient for ending the rule of arbitrary power. Hereditary kingship, consecrated by the death of Charles I, miraculously preserved in the person of his son during years of peril and destitution in which friends and

---

[1] Holdsworth, *History of English Law*, vi. 223. Keir and Lawson, 98. Costin and Watson, *The Law and Working of the Constitution*, i. 249-51. The limits were (i) no dispensation could authorise an act *malum in se* (i.e. probably, wrongful at Common Law); (ii) no dispensation could take away the rights of a third party. For other illustrations of the dispensing power in this period, see E. F. Churchill, *The Dispensing Power and the Defence of the Realm*, 37 *L.Q.R.* 412.

resources seemed to have vanished, now appeared to be restored by the manifest purpose of a Providence which had declared itself unmistakably against the shifting and transitory expedients of a temporarily successful rebellion. More explicitly and universally than at any previous era in the history of English kingship were conceptions held forth and accepted of its Divine Right, of the impiety of resistance, and of the subject's duty to render at least passive obedience to royal commands even if he could not conscientiously approve them. In the utterances of Anglican royalists of this period the sentimental cult of monarchy reached its zenith.[1] If the King recovered only an attenuated authority, he possessed it by the most august and sacred of titles. The Act of 1660 for the preservation of the King's person and government, besides making it treasonable to attempt to kill, wound, imprison or depose him, to levy war against him or induce foreigners to invade his dominions, expressly repudiated the Solemn League and Covenant and the obligations it imposed, and denied that resistance to the King could ever be lawful.[2] This condemnation was to be repeated in subsequent statutes. At its face value, it seemed to disarm beforehand any opposition prepared, like that of 1642, to proceed from words to overt action.

*Conditions necessary to the constitutional predomin-ance of the Crown* These theories, it is true, had their limitations, which an intelligent King could observe. Those who professed them were none the less wedded to the system of 1640-42. They rejected any idea of an arbitrary prerogative to legislate, tax, and judge. A King who recognised the legal limits on his authority here involved might nevertheless hope to keep intact his power to conduct his own government and policy, without any risk of its being further invaded, if only he could satisfy the ruling classes that it did not conflict with their own political and religious interests. Carefully managed, the extensive prerogatives still remaining to him could be used to ensure the Crown's supremacy, subject only to occasional reference to a Parliament content with having asserted its sole competence to legislate and tax and averse

---

[1] On this topic, see J. N. Figgis, *The Divine Right of Kings*, ch. viii. But non-resistance was not an Anglican monopoly. See, for the attitude of the Quakers, Gooch, *English Democratic Ideas in the Seventeenth Century*, 273. Bunyan took the same view (quoted by C. H. Firth, *Essays, Historical and Literary*, 137).

[2] Costin and Watson, i. 7.

from encroachments on royal authority which might threaten a
return to the disorders of the past.

The continued ascendancy of the Crown therefore depended on *Organisa-*
its making an effective alliance with the Cavalier and Anglican *tion of the*
gentry and clergy. In a minority in the Convention, the Cavaliers *Cavalier*
triumphed in the elections which returned the "Cavalier Parlia- *domination*
ment" of May 1661. Public opinion, moved by such sectarian
disorders as Venner's Fifth Monarchy rising of the preceding
January, pronounced decisively in favour of royalist conservatism.[1]
Once in power, the dominant party proceeded to organise its
position in Church and State. That penalisation of political and
religious opponents by which the Puritan revolutionaries had
tried to consolidate their sway in recent years offered a model
to which their former victims now faithfully conformed. In this
respect, the Presbyterians who swayed the Convention Parliament
had already afforded an example by their rigour towards all
adherents of the fallen Republic. The Act of Indemnity promised
by the Declaration of Breda assumed, particularly in the Lords, the
character of a bill of pains and penalties.[2] The personal intervention
of the King was needed before the list of proposed exclusions was
restricted to the regicides of 1649 alone, with the single addition
of the able and dangerous republican Sir Harry Vane.[3] In 1661 it
was the turn of the Presbyterians themselves to suffer. They had
failed in the Convention Parliament to implement the promise
contained in the Declaration of Breda of a "liberty to tender
consciences", and had rejected the only alternative—that of a
scheme of comprehension, embodied in a royal declaration of
October 1660—by which Anglicans and Presbyterians could be
combined in a unified national Church, constituted on a basis
of limited episcopacy, along lines suggested by the moderates of
1641.[4] The opportunity never recurred. Animated by detestation
of every species of nonconformity, the Cavalier Parliament, and
particularly the Commons, showed no interest in the project. The
breakdown of the Savoy Conference between the bishops and the
leading Presbyterian divines in the summer of 1661 indicated that

[1] On the composition of the Cavalier Parliament, see W. C. Abbott, *The
Long Parliament of Charles II*, 21 E.H.R. 23-4.
[2] K. Feiling, *History of the Tory Party, 1640-1714*, 98-100.
[3] Son of the Vane referred to above, 213.
[4] Cobbett, *Parliamentary History*, iv. 131-41.

no initiative in its favour need be expected from either Anglican
or Presbyterian clergy.

*The
Clarendon
Code*

The temper of the Cavalier Parliament was soon made plain.
The Commons resolved to take communion under the Anglican
rite, and ordered the Solemn League and Covenant to be burned.
They struck at the main citadels of their opponents' political
strength both in local administration and in parliamentary elections by the Corporation Act, imposing on mayors and other
municipal officers the obligation to take the oaths of allegiance
and supremacy and a further oath of non-resistance, a declaration repudiating the Solemn League and Covenant, and the
duty of taking communion under the Anglican rite.[1] The Act
of Uniformity of 1662 ended the *de facto* establishment of Presbyterianism as the religion of the State, giving anticipatory effect
to a revised Prayer Book not yet published, which, when issued,
proved to have been modified by its Anglican compilers in ways
which no Presbyterian could accept. The use of the Book was
enjoined on all clergy, teachers, and similar persons, who were
further compelled to abjure the Solemn League and Covenant,
and required, if holding ecclesiastical preferment, to accept episcopal ordination if they had not already received it, under penalty
of deprivation.[2] In August 1662 some two thousand clergy were
expelled from their livings. As dissenting congregations formed
about them, penal laws against nonconformists were added to
those against recusants. The Quakers had been attacked by an Act
of 1662.[3] In 1664 the first Conventicle Act prohibited assemblies
for non-Anglican worship of more than five persons not belonging to the same household.[4] A year later the Five Mile Act forbade
clergymen who had not complied with the Act of Uniformity

---

[1] Costin and Watson, i. 15-17. In this Act was rounded off a development in
English municipal government towards the creation of the oligarchically-
governed incorporated borough, begun as early as the fourteenth century,
powerfully stimulated by the Tudors, and owing something to recent republican experiment. Charles himself and his brother after him were to
consolidate, by their later forfeitures and regrants of charters, a system which
survived intact until 1835. See T. H. Sacret, *The Restoration Government and
Municipal Corporations*, 45 *E.H.R.* 232. On the treatment of corporations
between 1640 and 1660, see J. H. Round, *Colchester and the Commonwealth*,
15 *E.H.R.* 641, and B. L. K. Henderson, *Commonwealth Charters*, 3 *T.R.H.S.*
vi. 129.                                    [2] Costin and Watson, i. 20-29.
[3] *Statutes of the Realm*, v. 350.        [4] *Statutes of the Realm*, v. 515.

and preachers who had officiated at conventicles to remain within
five miles of any corporate town or any place in which they had
formerly held a benefice, and further prohibited any person from
teaching unless he had taken the oath of non-resistance.[1]

By these measures—known collectively as the Clarendon Code *Divergent*
—Dissent was visited with political and ecclesiastical disabilities *policies of*
which threatened it with continuing impotence and probably with *Crown and Parlia-*
ultimate extinction. In former times such coercive measures had *ment*
been initiated by the Crown. At this point they were imposed
by the will of Parliament, and against the avowed wishes of the
King and probably of his chief minister Clarendon also.[2] Charles
himself, actuated partly by the prudential desire to avert the rise
of a new sectarian danger, and partly by a real interest in achieving
some measure of toleration within which Catholics could find
shelter, endeavoured to fulfil the policy enunciated at Breda. A
bill enabling him to dispense with the Corporation Act was lost
in the Lords in 1661, and another conferring like power with
regard to the Act of Uniformity was similarly rejected there in
1663.[3] He could not rely on Prerogative alone. To his Declaration
of Indulgence of 1662 suspending all penal laws in ecclesiastical
matters, the Commons rejoined with a resolution that the promises
made at Breda were a mere statement of the King's personal
intention, to which no effect could be given except by statute.[4]
Royal control over religious affairs was fast receding before
Parliament's claim to determine the nature of the ecclesiastical
establishment. The intention of Parliament, unlike that of the
Crown in former years, was not to frame a broadly national
Church. Anglicanism became merely the sect which Parliament
patronised, and membership of the established sect the badge of
political privilege and monopoly. Those who would not conform
might remain outside the pale, condemned to political inferiority
and subject to punitive measures against their attempts to set up
a rival communion.

Between the Cavalier gentry and the clergy of their establish-

[1] Costin and Watson, i. 34-6.
[2] On this, see K. Feiling, *Clarendon and the Act of Uniformity*, 44 *E.H.R.* 289.
[3] Turberville, 44 *E.H.R.* 407; F. Bate, *The Declaration of Indulgence*, 23.
[4] Cobbett, *Parliamentary History*, iv. 260-3; D. Ogg, *England in the reign of Charles II*, 203. Authorship of the Declaration is attributed to Henry Bennet, the future Lord Arlington.

*Alliance of* ment the closest links were forged. In 1661 the repeal of the
*Cavalier* Bishops Exclusion Act restored the episcopate to the Lords and
*gentry and* made them re-eligible as Privy Councillors and administrative
*Anglican* and judicial officers. A subsequent statute restored all ecclesiastical
*clergy* jurisdictions with the specific exception of the High Commission Court.[1] In 1664 an arrangement between Clarendon and
Archbishop Sheldon ended the historic right of Convocation
to grant its own taxes, made the clergy liable to taxation by
Parliament, and granted them the electoral franchise while not
removing their disability to be elected.[2] Locally, the alliance of
squire and parson echoed the grander harmonies which were
being struck between the lay and spiritual chiefs of triumphant
Anglicanism. Lords and Commons, ministers of state and local
magistrates, bishops and clergy, were consolidated into a mighty
vested interest of Tory privilege, monopoly and power, prepared
to defend itself not only against recusants and dissenters but even
against the Crown.[3] A King prepared to enlist its support, and to
adapt himself to its prejudices might, however, utilise it as the
mainstay of a system under which he ruled as well as reigned.

*Origins of* Yet there was another England to be taken into consideration
*the Whig* besides that of the intolerant Cavalier and Anglican. The Restora-
*Party* tion had been accomplished not by Cavaliers but by converted
revolutionaries. The more supple and time-serving of these were
to be found in the ranks of the governing class, outwardly loyal
and conformist, unable inwardly to deny their own revolutionary
tradition. The gentry of the new period often sprang from
families which had borne arms against the King.[4] Moreover
the pages of the Restoration statute book, embodying as they
did many recognitions of the acts performed by revolutionary
governments from 1642 to 1660, bore witness to the necessity of
acquiescing in what could not be undone. When validity was
accorded, pursuant to the Breda Declaration, to legal proceedings of the revolutionary years, transfers of property were

[1] Costin and Watson, i. 13-14. See, generally, Miss A. Whiteman, *The Re-establishment of the Church of England, 1660-3,* 5 *T.R.H.S.* 5, 111.

[2] Many of the clergy voted at the elections to the first Restoration Parlia-ment. Porritt, *Unreformed House of Commons,* i. 3.

[3] The names of Whig and Tory do not become party designations until about 1680, but are here used, for convenience, by anticipation.

[4] It is of course equally true that many Tory families of the later seventeenth century were descended from adherents of the Parliament in the Civil War.

legitimised which incorporated in the propertied class men whose antecedents lay in opposition to the Crown and hostility to the Church. Lands belonging to the Crown, to the Church, and to Royalists who had suffered direct confiscation were restored. Those who had been obliged to make "composition for delinquency" or been otherwise impoverished by revolutionary exactions obtained no such redress.[1] Enriched by this spoil, there entered the ruling class men whose outward acceptance of Divine Right and non-resistance meant little. In the last resort, such notions were to them subordinate to the major proposition that monarchy had been set up again on conditions none the less binding because merely implicit, and that the people retained the right to interpret and if necessary to amend them. Such democratic and contractualist notions of sovereignty were temporarily out of fashion among the ruling class of 1660. A statute of 1662 forbade the presentation of petitions in a tumultuous manner intended to overawe Parliament.[2] A Licensing Act established a censorship of the press.[3] But the political traditions of Puritanism had merely been driven underground. In the nonconformist middle class of London and other towns there existed elements among whom the old ferment still worked. Here were the materials of a future Whig party, aristocratic in leadership, democratic in composition, capable of being organised against the Tory ascendancy and of renewing its former challenge to the Crown. The skill of Restoration Kings was to be tested by their success in maintaining a working partnership with the Tories against the common Whig enemy. Their failure would come when their blundering united these mutually hostile forces against the restored monarchy.

ii

Into these uncharted waters Charles II and his ministers had to guide the restored monarchy. The King himself, and some at least of his younger advisers, were capable of adapting themselves to new conditions as they found them. Older men such as Clarendon, whose careers bridged the period back to 1640, were not. *Constitutional ideas of Clarendon*

[1] Ogg, 161-4.    [2] Costin and Watson, i. 9-10.
[3] Costin and Watson, 1. 29-33. See J. Walker, *The Censorship of the Press during the Reign of Charles II*, 35 *Hist*. 219.

Faithful to the ideas he had maintained in opposition to the Crown up to 1642, and against Parliament thereafter, Clarendon stood for a government in which Parliament alone made the law, and the Courts alone interpreted it, while the King by virtue of the authority which the law attached to the Crown conducted his own government through a strong Privy Council guiding his action as the national interest determined. It was the business of Parliament alone to finance his government. Except for his hereditary revenues, he was entirely to depend on it for permanent or temporary grants of supply. Parliament might offer criticisms, and in an extreme case even impeach a minister, but it trespassed beyond its proper sphere if it sought to dictate to the King what policy he must follow, what executive acts he must perform, what ministers he should employ. Parliament, though a necessary part of the constitution, was, to quote Clarendon's own words, "more, or less, or nothing, as he [the King] chose to make it". A sovereign Parliament was to be balanced by a strong and independent Council. These conceptions revealed the wholly unreal world in which Clarendon and others of like mind were living. Not even the Elizabethan constitution, which he imagined had embodied constitutional ideas like his, had ever worked in the fashion he contemplated. In practice, neither the enfeebled Privy Council nor the aggressive Parliament could be placed in the positions he designed for them. The constitutional history of Charles II's reign is a commentary on the inadequacy and failure of the principles to which Clarendon adhered.[1]

*The Privy Council*  This failure was both administrative and parliamentary. In the first place, government by the Privy Council proved impracticable. As reconstituted by Charles II, that body, comprising both former adherents and former opponents of the Crown, became too large for either unity of purpose or efficiency of action. Rising in membership from twenty-seven at the Restoration to about fifty in later years, it was too unwieldy for the prompt dispatch of business, too divided in opinion and interest to be admitted to the inner secrets of policy. As an entity, it was still concerned with the issue of proclamations and administrative orders, with taking

---

[1] On Clarendon's conception of government, see E. I. Carlyle, *Clarendon and the Privy Council, 1660-67*, 27 E.H.R. 251. His fixity of ideas is shown by his own admission that he was "uncounsellable". Ogg, 150.

measures for public safety, and with supervision over colonial affairs.[1] More important than the action of the Council as a whole was the activity of its committees, which abounded under the Restoration monarchy as under the earlier Stuarts. In the years after 1660, committees existed for foreign affairs, the army and navy, complaints and grievances, and trade and plantations—the latter transformed for a period into a commission including others than councillors.[2] In 1668 it was laid down that all business was first to be considered by the Council, then referred to the appropriate committee, on whose advice the Council was to issue orders to the administrative department concerned.[3] In practice, this cautious and dilatory system proved unworkable.

It was in the growth of the departments rather than of the Privy Council that the line of administrative progress was to lie. The younger generation of officials were impatient of the delay and inefficiency which control of expert administrators by the Privy Council entailed. Their views were congenial to the King, not only because they promoted efficiency but because they meant that he could evade control by the Privy Council and deal directly with departmental heads, as was the practice of the French monarchy, then considered a pattern of well-conducted government.[4] Rather than at the Council board, the government of the State should be centralised in the cabinet of the King, where he could deal informally and confidentially with ministers whom he could trust and with whose co-operation he could govern. This group of departmental ministers included the Secretaries of State, whose business was divided between the Northern and the Southern Departments, diplomatic correspondence with the Northern States of Europe falling to the first, with the Southern States to the second of these. Irish affairs belonged to the Northern Secretary, domestic business was divided between the two. They were jointly concerned with internal order and police and the detention of suspects, and shared in the licensing of books. In the absence of any properly organised military system, they dealt with the issue of commissions, military correspondence and the movements

*The departments of State*

[1] E. R. Turner, *The Privy Council, 1603–1784*, i. 381, ii. 104–7.
[2] Turner, ii. 188–90, 263–71, 320–21; Costin and Watson, i. 318–21.
[3] Ogg, 192.
[4] Carlyle, 27 *E.H.R.* 266–7.

of troops.[1] The Treasury, sometimes under a Lord Treasurer sometimes in commission, endeavoured imperfectly but with some increase of skill to supervise the raising and expenditure of the King's revenues, and came gradually to control a number of subordinate revenue departments.[2] Farming of taxes, though still defended by some experts, fell into disrepute, and by the end of Charles II's reign the raising of taxation had in general been brought under governmental management.[3] The navy was placed in 1660 under the control of the Duke of York as Lord High Admiral. Supplementing his work was that of a Navy Board, comprising a Treasurer, a Controller, a Surveyor and a Clerk of the Acts—the last-named office being held until 1672 by Samuel Pepys—whose members, individually or as a body, supervised naval construction and equipment, recruiting and pay.[4] Military organisation, always more inchoate, involved the co-operation of the Secretaries of State, the Treasury, and a Board of Ordnance reconstituted under a Master-General who by virtue of his office commanded the small regular force of artillery and engineers. There now also appeared a new official, inherited from Protectorate times, and originally private secretary to the commander-in-chief, who was destined, under the title of Secretary at War, to be attached directly to the Crown and charged in particular with the issue of moneys available for the upkeep of the army.[5] In this body of officials, rather than in the Privy Council itself, the actual direction of the executive branch of government was gradually concentrated. Their primary function was to carry out the orders of the King. In proportion as he came to rely on them, and admit the most important of them to his intimate confidence, the control of the Privy Council was bound to recede.

*Ministers and Parliaments* The nature of government after 1660 necessitated some attempt to define the relationship of the King's ministers with

[1] F. M. G. Evans, *Principal Secretary of State*, 125, 131-6, 261-2, 266-7, 323-8.
[2] On the Treasury in this period, see D. M. Gill, *The Treasury, 1669-1714*, 46 *E.H.R.* 600; and *Treasury and Excise and Customs Commissioners*, in 4 *C.H.J.* 94.
[3] Hughes, *Studies in Administration and Finance*, 138-41.
[4] On naval organisation, see J. R. Tanner, *Administration of the Navy from the Restoration to the Revolution*, 12 *E.H.R.* 17, 679, 13 *E.H.R.* 26, 14 *E.H.R.* 47.
[5] Clode, i. 71-8.

Parliament as well as the Privy Council. On this point, it is possible, the King would have been satisfied to act on the lines laid down by Clarendon. But the minister failed to make his principles effective. His conception of the place of Parliament in the constitution inevitably made him a bad parliamentary manager. The interpretations placed upon the Declaration of Breda both by the Convention and the Cavalier Parliament showed how slight was the government's control over the legislature, and Clarendon had little responsibility for the "Code" which bore his name. Under Restoration conditions, a minister could achieve success only by bringing up to date the old Tudor technique of maintaining the hold of councillors and ministers over the Houses, and re-learning the art of parliamentary management. Even to attempt this was outside the range of Clarendon's ideas. The natural result was the repetition of a well-worn theme —short and troublesome sessions of Parliament, long prorogations, attacks on the Prerogative, and finally the impeachment of the minister himself in 1667. The complete separation of executive and legislature was plainly undesirable, even if attainable at all, for it could only lead to a recurrence of the old frictions. If the shock was less violent than under Charles I it was mainly because Clarendon had a less constant master than had Buckingham and was less to be dreaded than Strafford.

Such a system, whether desirable or not, was in fact unattainable because the Crown did not possess, even under peacetime conditions, a revenue sufficient to make it independent of additional parliamentary supply. *The financial settlement* The financial settlement of the Restoration monarchy was the work of the Convention Parliament. Charles II found the Exchequer empty at his accession. He and his household and government were in immediate straits for ready money. Debts due by the republican government were repudiated, but those due by the Crown, incurred under Charles I or in Charles II's earlier years, had to be honoured.[1] Provision had to be made for paying off the Cromwellian army and for a permanent endowment of the Crown. The Convention Parliament, anxious to be rid of the standing army, found no difficulty in raising money for its disbandment. In computing the sum necessary to endow the Crown with an adequate annual income,

[1] Shaw, *Calendar of Treasury Books, 1660–67*, i. Introduction, xv.-xxiv.

it took as a basis the charges of Charles I's administration during the pre-war period, which were estimated at £1,100,000 yearly. It was therefore resolved to provide £1,200,000 to cover those of the new royal government.[1] This estimate, though the work of amateur financiers, may not have been wide of the mark. Where amateurism betrayed itself was in the failure to estimate correctly the yield of the revenues assigned to the Crown. The main pillars of the revenue were the customs, and the excise introduced under the Long Parliament, both of which were granted for life.[2] A hereditary excise was added in lieu of the Crown's feudal revenues, extinguished with the Court of Wards by a statute which re-enacted an ordinance made by the Long Parliament in 1645.[3] The customs and the excises, together with Crown lands and minor sources of revenue, hardly produced in these earlier years so much as £900,000, against an annual expenditure seldom falling as low as £1,300,000.[4] Thus, even in peace time, the Crown must either sell capital assets, borrow, run into debt, or apply to Parliament for help.

*Poverty of the Crown*   All these devices were in fact attempted. Charles paid into the Exchequer the cash portion of his wife's dowry and the proceeds of his sale of Dunkirk to Louis XIV in 1662.[5] He sold Crown lands and rents. Borrowing was difficult for a King who might not be able to repay capital or even meet interest as it became due. For he was not only short of money on his accounts as a whole, but unable to regulate receipts so as to provide cash when it was needed. Tax-farming, moreover, tended to make his solvency depend on that of the capitalists who undertook the farms, and who came badly through times of crisis.[6] The line of least resistance was to allow payments to fall into arrears. This could only end in disaster. Officials, contractors, soldiers and sailors went unpaid, the services suffered thereby, Crown property deteriorated, goods had to be bought at disadvantageous rates when no ready cash was available for their purchase, and government became riddled with inefficiency and corruption.

It need not be supposed that either the Convention Parliament

---

1 Shaw, *C.T.B.* i. Introduction, xxxiii-xxxv; Ogg, 156-9.
2 S. Dowell, *History of Taxation*, ii. 17 ff.
3 Costin and Watson, i. 2-5; Gardiner, *Documents*, 290.
4 Shaw, *C.T.B.* i. Introduction, xxxv; iii. part I, Introduction, xiii, xxxi.
5 G. N. Clark, *The Later Stuarts*, 7-8.       6 Hughes, 157-8.

or its successors intended to keep the Crown poor. Their mistakes, *Its causes* like those of earlier Parliaments, were mainly due to ignorance, *and results* and the Cavalier Parliament improved the King's position by granting him a hearth tax in 1662.[1] The Treasury had not yet developed its later function of offering financial guidance to the Commons, whose estimates of revenue and expenditure were necessarily vague. After 1674, indeed, aided by a large expansion of trade and by the competence of Danby as a finance minister, the Crown's revenues attained about one and three-quarter millions yearly. It was only by accident that the King was so long unable to "live of his own". Yet, whatever cause it be ascribed to, that was his normal condition. It made his position very vulnerable to parliamentary attack, and led to the renewal of the old charges of wastefulness and inefficiency. It sharpened the need for devising new methods of linking the executive with the legislative so as to ensure the predominance of the former.

War, as so often before, subjected the government to strains it *The* could barely withstand. The Dutch War of 1665–7 was popular *demand for* enough with a nation which still regarded the Republic as its chief *appropriation of* commercial and colonial rival, and the Commons granted in all *extra-* about four and a half millions of extraordinary supply.[2] The *ordinary* ill-success of the English campaigns—for which the impoverished *supply* government was not wholly to blame—awakened doubts as to the wisdom of entrusting the Crown with control of such large sums. A new encroachment on the Prerogative followed. The Commons insisted on the appropriation of supply and the rendering of accounts.[3]

Charles's resentment at this intrusion was undoubtedly one *Fall of* of the many causes which led him to abandon Clarendon to *Clarendon* impeachment in 1667. To the King, the minister—besides being an irksome censor of his private conduct—was the exponent of an administrative practice which had failed to justify itself, and of parliamentary tactics which inflicted humiliation on the Crown. To Parliament, he seemed responsible for the misfortunes of the war. When he was dismissed in 1667 the Commons thanked the King for removing him. Notwithstanding the royal assurance

---

[1] On this tax, see L. M. Marshall, *The Levying of the Hearth Tax, 1662–88*, 51 *E.H.R.* 628.         [2] Shaw, *C.T.B.* ii. Introduction, lxiv.
[3] Shaw, *C.T.B.* ii. Introduction, xlii; Costin and Watson, i. 326.

that he would never be employed again, they impeached him for high treason.[1] Once more the unsatisfactory nature of this procedure appeared. None of the miscellaneous charges of political misdoing alleged against him—ranging from the sale of Dunkirk to the raising of a standing army—could be satisfactorily shown to warrant a conviction. In the midst of a wrangle between the two Houses, Clarendon withdrew to an exile to which he was later condemned by statute, and which was to be lifelong.

*The Cabal*   The ministry which succeeded him fared no better, and sustained an even more serious check when tested by the Dutch war of 1672-4. The Cabal, comprising Clifford as Lord Treasurer, Arlington as Secretary of State, and Ashley as Lord Chancellor, and therefore creating an informal inner ring of leading ministers,[2] indicates the tendency to substitute for the Privy Council a group of confidential advisers capable of dealing with government more efficiently and with greater secrecy.[3] Only in the loosest sense, however, did the Cabal represent a "ministry". Its members were linked with the King rather than with one another. Sharing his confidence to an unequal extent, they were therefore not fully in the confidence of one another, and were correspondingly ineffective as a combination.[4] The Cabal was in fact riddled with personal animosities, notably the dislike of Lauderdale and the distrust of Ashley felt by all their colleagues. The principal objects common to this group of ministers were the desire for religious toleration, concern for trade, and hostility to Holland. Though to Clifford and Arlington, unlike their colleagues, toleration meant primarily toleration to Catholics and the Dutch War was in the nature of a Catholic crusade, these three topics were to some extent interconnected. Religious persecution was bad for business, and Holland, the great commercial competitor they all desired to ruin, was thought to owe some of her prosperity to the religious freedom she

[1] Costin and Watson, i. 155-7; C. Roberts, *The Impeachment of the Earl of Clarendon*, 13 *C.H.J.* 1. It may be noted that no impeachment of a minister succeeded during the period from 1660 to 1717. A. S. Turberville, *House of Lords under Charles II*, 44 *E.H.R.* 408-9; J. P. Kenyon, *The Reign of Charles II*, 13 *C.H.J.* at p. 85.

[2] With the addition of Buckingham, who was Master of the Horse, and Lauderdale, Secretary for Scottish affairs. On the members of the Cabal, see Ogg, 327-30.

[3] The word was in common use throughout the seventeenth century and seems to have borne no special significance between 1667 and 1673. See Turner, *The Cabinet Council, 1622–1784*, i. 325-36.

[4] On this point, see W. D. Christie, *Life of Lord Shaftesbury*, ii. 3-4, 54-7.

accorded. Under the Cabal, therefore, the policy of the government turned towards antagonism to the Dutch and an attempt at religious toleration. Between 1668 and 1672 the King, supported by his advisers, broke away from his temporary association with the Dutch in the Triple Alliance, entered in 1670 into the Treaty of Dover with Louis XIV, and on March 17, 1672, declared war on the Republic. Two days earlier, the other half of the government's programme had been revealed in a second Declaration of Indulgence, suspending all ecclesiastical penal laws.[1]

What was miscalculated in this policy was the prospect of *Failure of* obtaining parliamentary support for it. The period during which *its religious* it had been concerted had been marked by two long prorogations *policy* —one from May 1668 to October 1669, and another beginning in April 1671 which was to last until February 1673. As regards the Declaration of Indulgence the attitude of Parliament was hardly to be doubted. Although in 1669 a committee of the Commons had recommended a relaxation of the penal laws against Protestants in the interests of trade, the session of 1670 had placed on the statute book a second and more drastic Conventicle Act, empowering magistrates to break into premises in which it was suspected that illicit religious assemblies were being held.[2] In 1671 the King had been presented with a petition against the growth of popery. When Parliament met in 1673, the Declaration was instantly attacked. Two addresses were drawn up by the Commons, denying the alleged Prerogative to suspend laws. The King was obliged to withdraw the Indulgence and to assent to the Test Act, imposing on all holders of office under the Crown the triple duty of taking the oaths of supremacy and allegiance, receiving communion under the Anglican rite, and declaring disbelief in transubstantiation—this last requirement being one, it was thought, regarding which no papal dispensation could be devised.[3] Obviously the Commons' addresses were a simple expression of opinion, devoid of legal force. The Prerogative to dispense in ecclesiastical matters—though Coke had denied its existence—was not easy to rebut, and indeed might be

---

[1] Costin and Watson, i. 163-6, 324-5; F. Bate, *The Declaration of Indulgence*, 79, attributes the authorship to Clifford.

[2] Costin and Watson, i. 36-9. The bill contained a clause inserted by the Lords and approved by the Commons, giving the King a dispensing power.

[3] Costin and Watson, ii. 39-42.

said to have been fortified by the dispensing power inherited by the Crown from the Papacy a century before.[1] Yet a practical rule was established by the King's surrender against which Charles attempted no appeal, least of all against the Test Act itself.

*Failure of its foreign policy*

A similar if more unexpected misfortune attended the foreign policy with which the Cabal had gone to Parliament. It was reasonable to hope that the Commons, which in 1670 had voted a seven years' tax on wine and vinegar and an income and property tax to yield £800,000 for the Crown's naval programme,[2] would be liberal towards the requirements of the renewed Dutch war. The King's persuasive powers and Shaftesbury's vehemence indeed obtained an initial grant of supply coupled, however, with the Test Act.[3] Commercial jealousy was becoming less potent than concern for religion, aroused by the Declaration and stimulated by York's open adherence to Rome and by negotiations for his marriage to the Catholic princess, Mary of Modena, which might provide the dynasty with a Catholic heir-presumptive. Unknown to Parliament, known indeed only to Charles, to Clifford—a Catholic—and to Arlington—who inclined in the same direction—there had been added to the offensive alliance formed against the Dutch at Dover a number of secret provisions. Charles was to receive a subsidy of £150,000 in addition to that promised by France to support the war efforts of England, avow himself a Catholic at a moment of his own choosing, and receive if necessary French military support to defend his position as a Catholic King. If Parliament was not aware of the full danger, its opposition to what it did know or suspect wrecked the government and its policy. Clifford had been driven from office by the Test. Ashley, denying his own principles, had supported it, and been dismissed from office. Buckingham, at variance with Arlington over the French treaty, but attacked as responsible for it by the Commons, was likewise dismissed soon after. Arlington, against whom an impeachment was begun in the Commons, exchanged his Secretaryship in 1674 for the household dignity of Lord Chamberlain. Only Lauderdale, mainly concerned with Scottish

---

[1] On this point, see E. F. Churchill, *Dispensing Power of the Crown in Ecclesiastical Causes*, 38 *L.Q.R.* 207, 420.

[2] Shaw, *C.T.B.*, iii. Part I. Introduction, xxxiv.

[3] Ogg, 365; Feiling, 149.

affairs, survived the wreck of a ministry neither united in itself nor able to recommend effectively a policy which meant different things to its different advocates. Faced by a Parliament which demanded that he should dismiss his advisers or tried to impeach them, criticised York's marriage, evil councillors, and standing armies, and withheld supply unless the Dutch refused peace negotiations, the King had to give way. The Dutch peace terms were placed before the Houses, and in February 1674 Charles's surrender was consummated by the Treaty of Westminster by which England withdrew from the war.[1]

These formidable blows against the Prerogative demonstrated *Changing* that the temper of Parliament had profoundly changed since at *temper of the* the Restoration the constitution of 1642 had been restored. The *Cavalier* prorogation ending in April 1673 had been the longest in the *Parlia-* reign. The Cavalier Parliament threatened to become as intract- *ment* able as its predecessors of 1614 and 1640. In recent years the Commons had been inclined, like their forerunners, to investigate critically the administration of the Crown, particularly in finance, rather than to lend it support. Their control in 1671 had been strengthened by a resolution formally rejecting the right of the Lords to intervene in financial affairs by amending money bills.[2] Over two hundred of the loyalists of 1661 had in fact for various reasons gone from their ranks.[3] The rate at which seats had been vacated had become specially rapid in recent years. One hundred and thirteen new members had entered during the period of the Cabal. Attendances ruled high, and the government's majorities diminished and disappeared altogether. Both outside and inside the walls of Parliament, an organised opposition was coming into existence, capable of gravely embarrassing the ministry. In its ex-members Shaftesbury and Buckingham, particularly the former, the nascent opposition party found itself provided with leaders.[4]

If the Crown were to retain control, it must find a minister *The* better equipped both as administrator and as parliamentary *adminis-* tactician than any who had yet held office since 1660. Such a *tration of* man was found in Thomas Osborne, a hard-headed Yorkshire *Danby*

[1] Ogg, 384-6.
[2] On the Lords and finance, see Turberville, *House of Lords under Charles II*, 45 *E.H.R.* 63-7.
[3] W. C. Abbott, *Long Parliament of Charles II*, 21 *E.H.R.* 54, 261-3.
[4] See A. Browning, *Party Organisation in the Reign of Charles II*, 4 *T.R.H.S.* XXX. 21.

squire who later advanced through successive stages in the peerage as Viscount Osborne, Earl of Danby, Marquess of Carmarthen, and Duke of Leeds. Primarily, Danby was a capable financial administrator, recommending himself to the King by his ability as well as by his tact and social gifts. Beginning as Treasurer of the Navy, he found a larger field for his abilities as successor to Clifford in the office of Lord Treasurer. Here he inherited a position which recent years of poverty and ineptitude had rendered chaotic. Recurrent deficit on ordinary revenue, the accumulated debt arising from the first Dutch war, and the demands of the second, had led in January 1672 to the Stop of the Exchequer. The Crown, having disbursed a year's income in advance, suspended payment of interest on its debts, and was thus enabled to spend as it came in money which would otherwise have been earmarked to satisfy its creditors.[1] The ready cash thus obtained had enabled the fleet of 1672 to be put to sea. On the return of peace Danby was enabled to resume interest payments, enhancing governmental credit and reducing the rate of public borrowing. Improvement in the collection of revenues had begun when the farming of customs was replaced by State management in 1671,[2] and it now continued. The Crown approached solvency, and the official to whom this recovery was so largely due won a degree of royal confidence which advanced him to the leading place among ministers and presaged the future close association between the Treasury and the premiership.[3]

*Danby and Parliament*
As a parliamentarian, it was Danby's business to organise support for the Crown against the nascent opposition party led by Shaftesbury. The arts of parliamentary management were still embryonic, and the Commons in 1673 had shown their suspicion of royal interference in elections by unseating thirty-six members returned in by-elections held under the Chancellor's writ without direction from the House.[4] To Danby may be ascribed the first

---

[1] See A. Browning, *The Stop of the Exchequer*, 14 *Hist.* 333. Compare Lipson, *Economic History*, iii. 236-7. Mr Lipson dates the Stop in December 1671.

[2] On Customs administration after this date see B. R. Leftwich, *Later History and Administration of the Customs Revenue in England*, 4 *T.R.H.S.* xiii. 187.

[3] On Danby's financial administration, see Shaw, *C.T.B.* iv. Introduction, xvi-xix; v. Part I. xxxv-vi.

[4] Christie, ii. 112-13, 121-6. This controversy settled the right of the House to authorise the issue of writs for by-elections.

systematic and successful effort to evolve a new technique of influence, patronage and bribery in order to win parliamentary support.[1] But he was no mere party manager. He fully shared, and utilised to the Crown's advantage, the prejudices which dominated a majority of the members of both Houses—Anglican intolerance and suspicion of France. In 1675 proclamations forbade conventicles and the hearing of mass.[2] At the same time Danby's policy moved towards aligning England with the Dutch Republic and its allies in their contest with Louis XIV. It was marked by the betrothal of Mary, daughter of the Duke of York, to William of Orange in October 1677, and the negotiations for an Anglo-Dutch treaty which began in the following December.

To some extent the minister succeeded in winning parliamentary confidence. Parliament, it is true, did not sit between February 1674 and April 1675, nor from November 1675 to February 1677, and in 1675 Danby's impeachment had been proposed.[3] Yet supplies were voted in 1677 and again in 1678 for an "actual war" against France. The Commons petitioned for an alliance with Holland and for the reduction of France to the boundaries settled by the Peace of the Pyrenees in 1659.[4] These demands implied the determination of the House, by virtue of its financial supremacy, to bring under its control the Prerogative in foreign affairs and peace and war. It was a power which the King was resolved not to yield. As in 1670–73, there existed side by side with the policy presented to Parliament a diplomacy kept in the King's own hand and inconsistent with that made public. From 1675 to 1678 a series of bargains with Louis bound Charles to neutrality in return for financial aid from France. In the last resort it was the King's policy and not that of Parliament that prevailed. While the Crown was being furnished by Parliament with troops and ships, there was no sign that any breach with France was at hand. Distrust of the minister, skilfully fanned by Louis's subsidies to the opposition leaders, was kindled by the equivocal policy by which Danby armed the Crown with military and naval strength for purposes never undertaken. Suspended between a Parliament whose support he had sought for an anti-French policy, and a King whose action he could not compel in that

*Danby's constitutional dilemma*

---

[1] Ogg, 529. See A. Browning, *Thomas Osborne, Earl of Danby and Duke of Leeds*, i, 167–74, for an estimate of him as party organiser: he does not rate him so high as an administrator, 192–3.    [2] R. Steele, *Tudor and Stuart Proclamations*, i. 437.
[3] Ogg, 531.    [4] Abbott, 21 *E.H.R.* 270–73.

direction, Danby was in an impossible situation. In a later age he would have resigned. In the circumstances of 1678, however, his primary obligation was to the King. His relation to Parliament was casual, secondary and indefinite. Whatever chance he had of combining his divergent rôles was destroyed when Ralph Montagu, ex-ambassador in Paris and now burgess for Northampton, produced in the Commons letters written by Danby urging the renewal of the French subsidy.[1] The letters had been authorised and were initialled by the King. Nevertheless Montagu's revelation of them effectually demolished Danby's parliamentary ascendancy. The Commons impeached him for "traitorously encroaching on the royal power", introducing arbitrary government by raising a standing army, negotiating a disadvantageous peace, and other charges. The Lords refused to commit on the ground that the offences did not amount to treason and the King intervened with a dissolution, and granted his minister, who had now resigned, a pardon under the Great Seal.[2] In the next Parliament the pardon was declared invalid and Danby, though his impeachment was not revived, was sent to the Tower for an imprisonment which was to last five years.[3]

### iii

*The con-stitutional problem after Danby's fall*

Under Clarendon, the Cabal, and Danby, three experiments had now been tried in regulating the relation between the supremacy of the Crown in administration and policy and that of Parliament in legislation and finance. All alike had broken down. The Cavalier Parliament had extended its control over the expenditure of supply, sought to subject diplomacy and the issues of peace and war to its own purposes and tried to assert parliamentary control over the militia.[4] It had attacked and overthrown ministers by impeachment. It had denied to the

---

[1] Ogg, 555, 577-8.

[2] For the articles of impeachment, see Costin and Watson, i. 180-2.

[3] On Danby's impeachment, imprisonment, and release, see A. M. Evans, *Imprisonment of the Earl of Danby in the Tower*, 4 *T.R.H.S.* xii. 105.

[4] Charles refused assent to this bill—one of the two instances of refusal during his reign, Ogg, 456-7. But in 1663 a bill disappeared, and in 1680 one was deliberately omitted, from those awaiting royal assent. See C. E. Fryer, *Royal Veto under Charles II*, 32 *E.H.R.* 103.

Crown any dispensing power in ecclesiastical affairs, and deprived it by statute of the right to employ non-Anglicans in its service. The legislative sterility of its later years had been relieved only by a second Test Act, passed in 1678, debarring all Catholics save the Duke of York from sitting in either House.[1] Whatever advisers the King relied on, all alike seemed unable to protect the Prerogative from renewed assault. Arrayed against one another in Parliament and in the country, two inchoate but formidable parties—the nascent Tory party of Anglican squires, dominant among the landed class, the nascent Whig party, aristocratically led, but mainly composed of Dissenters and conformists of dissenting antecedents, strongest among the moneyed class—engaged in a conflict in which the ultimate prize must be supremacy in the State and even over the Crown itself. Against this danger the King girded himself. Not through detaching government from contact with Parliament, but through utilising the advantages presented by party animosities, the King revealed himself as the ablest politician of his day and of his dynasty and rescued royal authority from the dangers which beset it amid the strife of warring factions.

The temper of Parliament had for many years suggested *The Exclusion Parliaments* ominous conclusions as to the probable outcome of a general election. The generation of loyalists which had welcomed the King back in 1660—the familiar faces that greeted him in the Cavalier Parliament—had long since passed away. From the Cabal onwards, ministers had shrunk from an appeal to the country. When the appeal was finally made in February–March 1679 the electorate was in the throes of the panic engendered by the Popish Plot. In these elections, and those subsequently held in August–October 1679, and January–March 1681, the Whigs held a decided majority.[2] Religious violence directed itself specially against the Catholic heir-presumptive to the throne. The Cavalier Parliament had petitioned for his removal from the royal councils.[3] Its successor voted in April 1679 that the prospect of his accession had been a chief inducement to the Plot, which was supposed

---

[1] Costin and Watson, i. 43–6.

[2] On the elections of 1679–81, see E. Lipson, *The Elections to the Exclusion Parliaments, 1679–81*, 28 E.H.R. 59, and E. George, *Elections and Electioneering, 1679–81*, 45 E.H.R. 552. These elections were the first to be fought on definitely party lines.    [3] Ogg, 589.

to aim at the King's assassination to make way for his brother. Uninfluenced by the King's promise—of dubious value, indeed— to assent to a bill safeguarding religion and property under his successor, it proceeded to consider an Exclusion Bill, disabling James from succeeding, making it treasonable for him to exercise any act of sovereignty, and directing that after Charles's death the succession, omitting his brother, should pass to the next heir.[1] In 1680 a new Exclusion Bill made even James's presence in England treasonable.[2] When the Lords refused to pass the bill the Commons declined to grant supply. In 1681 a new Parliament, still holding to exclusion,[3] also demanded annual Parliaments and the abolition of the standing army.

*The King's success*   Against this onslaught the King fought with determination and skill. The Parliament of March 1679 was prorogued in May and dissolved in July. That elected in the following autumn was seven times prorogued before its dissolution in October 1680. That of 1681 was dissolved in a week. Charles's hand had meanwhile been strengthened by a French subsidy. His final success was due to the consolidation, against Shaftesbury and his Whig followers, of a Royalist and Tory party, gathering strength as reaction arose against the horrors for which the Popish Plot was made the pretext. During the long prorogations of 1680, Tory sentiments had been revealed in memorials "abhorring" the action of the dominant Whig "Petitioners" who encroached on the Prerogative by addresses urging the King to assemble Parliament.[4] By 1681 Whig excesses had aroused a Tory loyalism on which the King might venture to rely. Henceforth his government could rest on Tory support, and on that basis proceed to the destruction of the Exclusionist Whigs.

*His surrenders*   In these critical years the King had on the whole preserved the Prerogative intact, though such individual points as the tenure of the judges, placemen in Parliament, intermission of parliamentary sessions, and the standing army had all been assailed. He had indeed made two surrenders. Not only had his pardon to Danby been set aside, but the Lords had resolved that an im-

[1] Ogg, 588-9; Christie, 329-32; D. W. Furley, *The Whig Exclusionists*, 13 *C.H.J.* 19.            [2] Costin and Watson, i. 183-4.
[3] Ogg, 615-19; Christie, ii. 672-86.
[4] Feiling, 177. The devices of petitioning and presenting counter-petitions of "abhorrence" were repeated later; see Christie, ii. 443, and Feiling, 231.

peachment was not terminated by a prorogation or a dissolution.[1] Since the impeachment had been dropped, this point was not perhaps serious. What was of greater importance was that an Act, prepared but not passed by the Cavalier Parliament, was enacted in the first Exclusion Parliament under which the procedure in Habeas Corpus proceedings was improved.[2] The government had hitherto been able to evade the writ by moving prisoners from place to place. In *Jenkes's Case* (1676) the writ had been denied by the Chancery on the ground that it was only issuable in term time.[3] These and other defects were now cured. Gaolers were required to produce their prisoners within three days. The place of confinement was not to be changed in order to defeat the writ. Any judge of any superior court was required to issue the writ as of right, and refusal to do so in vacation was punishable by fine. Persons accused of treason or felony were to be remanded for trial at the first opportunity, and, if that were omitted, were entitled to release on bail, and to be finally released if a second occasion for trial were allowed to go by. On lesser charges bail was available at once, and unconditional release followed if no trial took place at the earliest opportunity. Even if the Habeas Corpus Amendment Act left some loopholes it substantially diminished the coercive power of the Crown. Everywhere else, the King's legal power still stood in 1681 where it had stood in 1678.[4]

Charles had done more than preserve the Prerogative. He *Defeat of* had maintained the right of his dynasty to rule. The furthest *Exclusion* limit of his concessions—the Expedient of 1681—had involved York's banishment; the education of his son, if he left one, as a Protestant; and, if necessary after Charles's death, a Regency to be conducted through a Privy Council approved by Parliament.[5] He never yielded up the right of the reigning house to rule. He prevented monarchy from degenerating into a mere elective magistracy with a parliamentary title. His ultimate success left York as heir with no conditions imposed.

Yet it is to be remembered that Charles's battle was purely *Charles* defensive. He did not add to the sum of royal powers. Institu- *and the* tionally, there could be no "second Stuart absolutism" akin to its *Tory Party*

[1] Costin and Watson, i. 180-83.  [2] Costin and Watson, i. 46-54.  [3] Ogg, 511.
[4] Note, however, his temporary acceptance of Temple's scheme for a remodelled Privy Council (below, 261), and of Shaftesbury as Chancellor.
[5] Ogg, 615.

predecessor. Charles's success was based on a correct appreciation of the relations which must subsist between the Crown and the Tory party on which its ascendancy in the constitution was dependent. English government for the moment involved the acceptance of the Tory constitutional thesis. This admitted Divine Right, hereditary and indefeasible, royal control of administration and policy, executive and judicial appointments and the armed forces, and royal discretion in the summoning of Parliaments. While maintaining Parliamentary supremacy over legislation, it did not deny a dispensing power; and while preserving that supremacy over taxation, it permitted the Crown to control expenditure. A King who left the Anglican monopoly intact and refrained from a foreign policy which affronted the religious susceptibilities of the Anglican Church, need expect no further formal encroachments on his right to govern as he pleased.

*Over-*
*throw of*
*the Whigs*

For the time at least, the protagonists of Whig limited monarchy were routed. Shaftesbury, acquitted by a London jury on a charge of treason for which he was lodged in the Tower, indulged on his release in designs, possibly treasonable, for promoting the claim to the throne of Charles's illegitimate son James, Duke of Monmouth, fled to Holland to escape arrest or enlist support, and died there in exile.[1] His political associates Russell and Sidney paid the penalty—the first by suicide, the second by execution—for their implication in the Rye House Plot, aimed at the life of Charles and his brother.[2] The Whig organisation they had built up, assuming its most militant and dangerous form in the London "Green Ribbon Club", was attacked in the boroughs, where its main strength lay, by rigid enforcement of the Corporation Act and by attacks on borough charters under writs of *Quo Warranto*.[3] London's temper had been shown by its association with Exclusion, and by the refusal of its grand jury to find a true bill against Shaftesbury. It was the first to suffer. Assailed on technical points regarding the imposition of tolls and the presentation of a petition "in the nature of an appeal to the people", the corporation saw its charter forfeited by the King's Bench

---

[1] Christie, ii. 445 ff.
[2] The views of Sidney are discussed in Gooch, *English Democratic Ideas*, 284-7, and J. W. Gough, *The Social Contract*, 120-22.        [3] Ogg, 517-19.

in 1683. A new charter reserved to the Crown a veto on appointments to civic office. Other charters were attacked, and many were surrendered even before the attack fell. New charters were issued which like that of London aimed at subordinating municipal government and borough elections to royal control.[1] It might well have been supposed that Whiggism, expressing constitutional doctrines reducing monarchy to a kind of elective magistracy exercised on contractual terms had been effectually destroyed.[2] Government was firmly in the King's hands. Setting aside a scheme devised in 1679 by Sir William Temple for placing administration in the hands of a remodelled Privy Council of thirty members,[3] Charles continued to conduct it through an informal inner committee, of which indeed Temple himself was for some time a member, and of which the Tories Clarendon and Rochester, sons of his old Chancellor, were the leading figures.[4]

Thus master of his kingdom, Charles ruled from 1681 onwards *Apparent* without a Parliament. There was little in contemporary Tory con- *triumph of* stitutional theory to oblige him to summon one. The remodelling *the Crown* of borough charters seemed to assure that when elections were again held the result would be entirely different from 1681. It is possible that towards the end of his life the King was considering such an experiment. When attempted by his successor in 1685 it was entirely successful. In the Commons of that year, it was reckoned that not more than forty members could be considered hostile to the Crown.[5] At his accession the new King told his Privy Council that he had "been reported to be a man for arbitrary power, but that is not the only story that has been made of me. I shall make it my endeavour to preserve this government in Church and State as it is now by law established." [6] On this basis he could confidently expect the support of a Church which held non-resistance as its main political tenet, and of a Parliament dominated by Tories from which Whiggism seemed to have been eliminated. His life revenues, collected without parliamentary grant

---

[1] Costin and Watson, i. 254-0, 332-9.

[2] For a discussion of the republican views attributed to the Whigs by their opponents, see Gooch, 279-81.

[3] Costin and Watson, i. 329. The extent to which Temple was responsible for this innovation has been fully discussed by Turner, *Privy Council*, i. 439-48.

[4] On this period of Charles's government, see G. Davies, *Council and Cabinet, 1679-88*, 37 *E.H.R.* 47.  [5] Feiling, 205.  [6] Feiling, 204.

since his accession, were renewed by statute.[1] Additional duties were granted for eight years on wine, tobacco, and sugar.[2] In a second session the alliance of Crown, Church, and squirearchy was even more strikingly proved. The rebellions of Monmouth and Argyll led the Commons to offer £700,000 for the upkeep of a standing army.[3] In providing a Catholic King with a largely increased permanent revenue and a standing force, Toryism gave the final and complete demonstration of its reaction against notions of limited monarchy and a diminished Prerogative.[4]

*Limits of Tory loyalty*     Yet there were bounds to this apparent relaxation of constitutional rigour against the Crown. Even the Tory Parliament of 1685 was the legitimate heir of that Cavalier assembly which had forced the withdrawal of two Declarations of Indulgence and enacted the Clarendon Code and the Test Act. In partnership with it the Crown might continue to be stronger than at any date since 1660. But the partnership was conditional, as Charles II had come to appreciate, on the maintenance of the Anglican monopoly and the avoidance of effective commitments towards France. To these implied conditions his successor was blind.

*James II's Catholicism*     Certain changes naturally followed the accession of a Catholic King and Queen. Catholic worship was celebrated at Court. Catholic sermons were preached there. The coronation service, though conducted by Protestant clergy, omitted the Anglican communion. All this was acquiesced in. There must be at least a necessary minimum of public and external change. James's religion could not remain purely private. There was a more disquieting note in his refusal to allow Lord Powys to open a Catholic chapel. Powys, he said, could not legally do so, but "to transgress the law was no doubt proper for him, the King, for he was above the law".[5]

*Repeal of the Test Acts refused*     Some relaxation of the civil disabilities imposed by the penal laws might perhaps have been looked for from Parliament. James's action showed that this would not be enough. The con-

---

[1] Shaw, *C.T.B.* viii. Part I. x-xi. Note that this was the last grant of the kind ever made.

[2] Shaw, *C.T.B.* viii. Part I. xiii-xv.          [3] Shaw, xv-xviii.

[4] It is doubtful, however, whether Tory opinion is best judged by reference to its more extreme exponents, such as Sir George Mackenzie in his *Jus Regium*. The opinions of the Tory, Sir William Temple, for example, are "impregnated with liberal thought". See Gooch, 278, 281, 287, 291-2.

[5] Ranke, *History of England*, iv. 220.

stitution itself must bend, and the Test Acts, excluding Catholics (and scrupulous Dissenters) from service under the Crown and place in Parliament, must be removed or nullified. Particular importance attached to the army created in Charles's later years and now expanded. But for the Test Acts, it could be officered by Catholics. Here was a danger at which even the loyalist Parliament of 1685 drew back. Declining either to abrogate the Test or even to regularise the position of Catholic officers already commissioned, it was prorogued in November 1685, and though not dissolved until July 1687 it never met again. James indeed could hardly have made his request at a less favourable time. The "Dragonnades" which preceded Louis XIV's recent revocation of the Edict of Nantes illustrated the use to which a Catholic army could be put, and the arrival of numerous Huguenot refugees created a religious panic not less compelling, better justified, and wider in its appeal than that of the Popish Plot. The doubtless accidental conjuncture between Louis's intolerance towards his Protestant subjects and James's attempted toleration of his Catholic subjects assumed a sinister meaning in the minds of Englishmen.

As his father had done from 1629 to 1640, James now turned to *Attitude of* the courts of law for judicial endorsement of those powers which *the judges* his Parliaments denied him. Though no separate administrative *towards* jurisdiction any longer existed, the courts of the Restoration *the executive* period, it must be remembered, were staffed by judges still holding *durante beneplacito regis*, whose political temper had hitherto been trustworthy and whose legal learning was sufficient to protect their administration of the law from popular contempt.[1] Among them the high Prerogative traditions of their predecessors were not yet extinct. The judgment in *Thomas* v. *Sorrell* (1674) had reaffirmed the accepted doctrine regarding the dispensing power.[2] In *Harris's Case* and *Carr's Case*, Chief Justice Scroggs had in 1680 maintained—in an interval during which the Licensing Act had lapsed and his decision had therefore to be based on Common Law alone—that no man had a right to publish without leave any matter bearing on government, and that even if the matter published were innocent, the act of publication was itself wrongful.[3] Juries, it is true, had been protected by the decision in

---

[1] See H. G. Havighurst, 66 *L.Q.R.* 62 and 229, and 69 *L.Q.R.* 522.
[2] Costin and Watson, i. 249-51.
[3] Costin and Watson, i. 252-4. See also P. Fraser, *The Intelligence of the Secretaries of State, 1660-1688*, 121.

*Bushell's Case* (1670) from being punished by a judge for giving a verdict with which he disagreed.[1] This immunity mattered little when, according to the law laid down by Scroggs, only the fact of publication, and not the nature or intention of the matter published, fell within their purview. Decision on that point was reserved to the Bench. With the Common Law judges "matter of State", no longer the concern of conciliar courts, seemed to have found a new home.

*Godden v. Hales*    To the judges, disciplined from time to time by the dismissal of those whom Chief Justice Jeffreys described as "snivelling trimmers", the King turned in order to overthrow the Tests. In 1686 a collusive action was brought against Sir Edward Hales, an officer who had, without qualifying under the Test Act, received command of a regiment. His servant Godden sought to recover a penalty awarded to him at assizes as a common informer. Hales relied for his defence on a dispensation under the Great Seal. Such a dispensation undoubtedly fell within the rule lately reaffirmed in *Thomas* v. *Sorrell*. The Exchequer Chamber, with only one dissentient, rightly held it valid, at the same time, like the judges in *Bates' Case* and *Hampden's Case*, plentifully overlaying its decision with *dicta* as to the absolute nature of the royal discretionary authority.[2]

*Catholics appointed to office*    Penal laws in matters ecclesiastical now lay at the King's mercy. Catholics, hitherto consulted by the King only in an informal camarilla, entered the Privy Council and the Treasury Commission. A Catholic became Lord Privy Seal. The Catholic Strickland took command of the fleet and presently caused a mutiny by ordering the public celebration of mass. Hales became successively governor of Dover Castle, lieutenant of the Tower, and Master of the Ordnance. The Catholic Tyrconnel took command of the Irish army. The Catholics Melfort and Perth displaced the Protestant Queensberry in Scotland, where Edinburgh Castle was committed to the Catholic Gordon. Protestants were correspondingly displaced. In October 1685 Halifax, notable a few years before as an opponent of exclusion, was dismissed from the

---

[1] Costin and Watson, i. 245-9.

[2] Costin and Watson, i. 256-8; Keir and Lawson, 96. For a valuable discussion of the legal points involved, see P. Birdsall, *Non Obstante*, in *Essays in History and Political Theory Presented to C. H. M'Ilwain*, 69-75.

Presidency of the Council for his defence of the Tests. In 1687 Clarendon and Rochester lost their offices. Rear-Admiral Herbert was cashiered, and a number of Household officials were likewise deprived.

It is perhaps unlikely that the King intended so general a displacement of Protestant by Catholic advisers and officials. He found, however, that in practice the two could not be combined. The ever-present risk, alike of Tudor and Stuart rule, of refusal by the governing class to co-operate with the Crown was again decisively manifested, and with it the solidarity created since 1660 between the governing class and the Anglican Church. Here again it is unlikely that the King contemplated a direct attack on the Establishment, or on the Universities which were its educational strongholds. Yet his Catholicism had inevitable corollaries. The multiplication of conversions, the return of Catholic monastic orders to England, and the presence at Court of the papal nuncio d'Adda awakened an anxiety naturally expressed in sermons which the King tried to restrain by the issue of injunctions in virtue of his ecclesiastical supremacy and by the creation in 1686 of a Court of Ecclesiastical Commission.[1] Overt breach of the Act of 1661 was avoided by vesting the Commission with jurisdiction over the clergy alone. Its legality was not apparently seriously impugned. Nevertheless the active exercise of the ecclesiastical supremacy by a Catholic King clearly involved the Church in a dilemma which no appeal to the strict letter of the law nor even to its own oft-asserted principle of non-resistance could satisfactorily resolve. The Commission was utilised first to suspend the Bishop of London, Compton, for his refusal to take action against a London rector who had publicly upheld the catholicity of Anglican orders. It was employed to suspend the Vice-Chancellor of Cambridge for his refusal to admit a Benedictine monk, Alban Francis, to a degree without taking the statutory oaths. Meanwhile at Oxford a Catholic, Massey, became Dean of Christ Church and thus head of the college as well as the chapter. The Commission set aside the election of the Protestant Hough as President of Magdalen by the Fellows in preference to the King's nominee. A special body of commissioners, violating the college statutes, deposed Hough and all but two of the Fellows,

*The Church, the Universities, and the Ecclesiastical Commission*

[1] Ranke, *History of England*, iv. 293-300. E. Carpenter, *The Protestant Bishop*, 158-60.

9a

imposing a Catholic head, Bonaventura Giffard, under whom twelve Catholic Fellows were presently elected. Such measures as these perhaps aimed at no more than opening a limited entry into the Universities for Catholics. They were thus akin to the partial removal of the Tests in individual cases by the dispensing power.

*The Declarations of Indulgence* A more challenging demonstration of the Prerogative in ecclesiastical causes was provided by the Declarations of Indulgence which, undeterred by the failures of 1662 and 1672, the King published in April 1687 and May 1688.[1] In general substance they were alike. With safeguards for the Anglican establishment and secularised Church lands, they suspended penal laws in ecclesiastical matters, the obligation to take the Tests and the oath of supremacy, and restraints upon liberty of worship. Where the second differed from the first was that an order in Council commanded bishops to distribute the Declaration and have it publicly read by their clergy. They were placed in a deeply embarrassing position. To refuse to carry out the order was to deny the principle of non-resistance. To obey it was to recognise the legality of acts by which the King could destroy the safeguards of the Establishment. Only in one way could the dilemma be escaped. Sancroft, Archbishop of Canterbury, and six diocesan bishops were commissioned by their colleagues to present to the King a petition praying to be relieved from the duty imposed on them.[2] The King, treating the petition as a "standard of rebellion" and those who presented it as "trumpeters of sedition", ordered them to fulfil their obligation. When their petition was found circulating in print he had them arrested and put on trial for seditious libel.

*The Seven Bishops* The *Seven Bishops' Case* is from a strictly legal point of view curiously unsatisfactory. A multiplicity of issues were raised, including the right of petition and the privilege of bishops as lords of Parliament. The suspending power itself was not the main question. It arose incidentally to a charge of seditious libel.[3] Counsel for the bishops contended that their action in reminding the King, by a petition neither false in content nor malicious nor seditious in intention, that known laws existed in the ecclesiastical sphere

[1] Costin and Watson, i. 343-6.    [2] Costin and Watson, i. 346-7.
[3] Though of course it might be urged that if there was no suspending power, there could be no libel in saying so.

among which the suspending power found no place, could not be punishable. For the King it was argued that the proper place for presenting a petition was Parliament; with more force, that the only presumption against the suspending power was found in resolutions of the Commons which had no legal effect, while a proclamation was at least a legal instrument issued by virtue of the Prerogative; and that the imputation that the King was a lawbreaker must be regarded as seditious. The court was weak, divided, and outweighed by the counsel arrayed for the bishops. Two judges summed up for, two against the Crown. Exceptionally, the question of motive was left to the jury. Their verdict was unanimous for the bishops. But, however confused and unusual the case was, it was the first of the kind which had gone against the Crown since the days of Coke.[1]

In truth, the issue between King and people had escaped the arbitrament of lawyers. To James, the decision enhanced the necessity of summoning a Parliament. Preparations had for some time been on foot. Against the Anglican ascendancy James endeavoured to mobilise the ranks of Dissent. Lords-Lieutenant were directed to submit lists of Nonconformists suitable to hold the Commission of the Peace. Those who refused to do so were dismissed. Justices of the Peace were required to pledge support for the abrogation of the penal laws. London was compelled to receive a Presbyterian mayor. Nonconformists and Catholics were appointed as sheriffs.[2] A like urgency filled the minds of James's opponents. There must be a Parliament, and the birth of a son to the King in June 1688 made it essential, if he were not to be educated as a Catholic and surrounded by Catholic officials, that the Parliament should not be one packed by the King so as to ensure its recognising a *fait accompli*, but one freely elected. Seven peers, three Tory and four Whig, invited James's nephew and son-in-law William of Orange to intervene against the King.[3] A free Parliament might give Dissenters toleration on the firm basis of statute instead of the precarious basis of a disputable Prerogative. It would defend and preserve

*The Revolution of 1688*

---

[1] Costin and Watson, i. 258-71; Keir and Lawson, 99.

[2] Ranke, iv. 333-5, 337-40.

[3] Ranke, iv. 397. For the text of the Invitation, see Costin and Watson, i. 352-4.

the Tests. Before this danger James retreated. A proclamation of September 1688 confined itself to freedom of conscience and a partial repeal of the Act of Uniformity.[1] This had always been the only reasonable policy. It was now too late. By the end of the year James was in exile and William in possession of his capital and, *de facto*, of his government.

iv

*Statutory aspect of the Revolution Settlement*  The constitutional settlement effected by the Revolution is contained, so far as enacted law is concerned, in the Bill of Rights of 1689, the Triennial Act of 1694, and the Act of Settlement of 1700. It is far from easy to recognise that any of the three made any substantial change in the law of the constitution. The first of the three traversed much old, but entered on little new ground.[2] It abolished the suspending power outright, but its validity had always been doubtful. It condemned the dispensing power only "as it hath been used and exercised of late", and intended a statutory regulation of its exercise which was never carried out. It swept away the Ecclesiastical Commission. It condemned the levying of taxation save by parliamentary grant, but this provision was hardly more than declaratory of existing law. Of all the powers unquestionably belonging to the Crown in 1660 only one was destroyed—that of raising and keeping a standing army in time of peace. This power was henceforth based on statute. An annual Mutiny Act fixed the size of the military establishment and authorised the maintenance of military discipline by courts-martial.[3] The Triennial Act obliged the King to summon Parliament at least every three years, but annual sessions had in any case begun. More serious, perhaps, was the limitation of Prerogative imposed by the rule that Parliaments could not continue longer than three years, yet it cannot be regarded as a damaging blow.[4] As originally enacted, the Act of Settlement was the most far-reaching of the three.[5] Making an exception of the reign of Anne, it provided that future kings must not evade the control of the Privy Council by transacting business of State through other channels, that persons holding places of

---

[1] Ranke, iv. 422; Steele, *Tudor and Stuart Proclamations*, i. 469.
[2] Costin and Watson, i. 67-74.          [3] Costin and Watson, i. 55-7.
[4] Costin and Watson, i. 33-4.          [5] Costin and Watson, i. 92-6.

profit under the Crown should be ineligible for membership of the Commons, and that judges were to hold office during good behaviour. But the first two of these clauses were repealed before they ever came into operation, and the third only made statutory the practice regularly followed by William III. Of the purely constitutional clauses of the Act—that is to say, those which determined the distribution and exercise of power—nothing innovatory remained after 1707 but the rules that England must not without parliamentary consent be involved in war for territories not belonging to the English Crown; that foreigners were to be incapable of membership of the Privy Council and Parliament and of receiving offices or grants of land from the Crown; and that a pardon under the Great Seal cannot be pleaded in bar of an impeachment. The explicit and permanent limitations on the power of the Crown imposed by the Revolution Settlement are incomparably less than those enacted by the Long Parliament, and even the Petition of Right seems to surpass them. The years 1688–9 were no time for constitution-mongering. Republicanism was out of fashion,[1] Whigs who would have liked to grasp the opportunity of imposing new checks on royal authority had to work with Tories who had no such object. The new sovereigns, William and Mary, were armed on their accession with a panoply of undoubted legal powers as ample as that borne by their two immediate predecessors.

This fact does not detract from the fundamental constitu- *The true* tional importance of the Revolution Settlement. It inaugurated *importance* a monarchy as different from that of Charles II and James II *of the Re-* as the essential continuity of English constitutional development *volution* permitted it to be. Sovereignty in 1688 was for practical purposes grasped by the nation. No Parliament existed nor was there any valid means of convoking one, since James had destroyed the writs prepared for that which he contemplated, and had removed the Great Seal. William, still merely Prince of Orange and therefore an alien without any constitutional standing, was invited by an informal assembly composed of peers, members of the Commons in any of Charles II's Parliaments (mostly, in the nature of the case, former members of the Exclusion Parliaments) and the City authorities of London, to send out writs summoning

[1] On its decline, see Gooch, 292-4.

a Convention.[1] This equally irregular assembly condemned in a Declaration of Right the alleged illegalities of James, and asserted that his flight was equivalent to abdication, thereby reconciling Whig and Tory views of that event. More startlingly, it declared that the throne was vacant. Legally, this statement, even if made by a valid Parliament, was devoid of substance, for there can, in strictness, never be a vacancy on the throne. As a practical measure it was necessary in order to bar the claim of James's son, and practical necessity triumphed over law. Passing by all legitimist claims and repudiating allegiance owed to Catholics or persons married to Catholics, the Convention, though its Tory members vainly tried to save the principle of legitimacy by attempting an offer of the throne to Mary alone, finally asked William and Mary to accept it jointly. The offer was accepted. William and Mary became King and Queen, and the Convention a Parliament.[2] William was vested with the exercise of royal authority during their joint lives. The succession was entailed, after the death of the survivor of the two, first on the heirs of Mary, then on her sister Anne and her heirs, and finally on those of William by any second marriage. Allegiance to Roman Catholics or persons married to Roman Catholics was repudiated. Future sovereigns were required to make the declaration against transubstantiation.[3] A new form of coronation oath, imposing specific obligations to "govern according to the statutes in Parliament agreed on", and to maintain them, was prescribed to William and Mary and all their successors.[4] New oaths replaced the ancient oaths of supremacy and allegiance.[5]

*Extinction of monarchy by Divine Right*   Thus perished, at the hands of an assembly animated by an authority which can hardly be otherwise regarded than as popular sovereignty in action, the idea of sacred and inalienable governmental powers, inherent in kings possessing a divine, indefeasible, hereditary title, which had lain at the basis of the Restoration monarchy. Thus also were dissolved moral obligations, fortified in many cases by oath, incurred towards a kingship so constituted. As the Restoration statutes had demolished the moral and religious sanctions underlying the Solemn League

---

[1] Costin and Watson, i. 186-8.

[2] For the statute by which it declared itself to be so, see Costin and Watson, i. 54-5, and compare that of 1660, Costin and Watson, i. 1.

[3] Costin and Watson, i. 72, 73.          [4] Costin and Watson, i. 57-9.

[5] Costin and Watson, i. 60-61. On the Succession since the Revolution, see C. d'O. Farran, *The Law of the Accession*. 16 *Modern Law Review*, 140.

and Covenant, so now did the Revolution statutes destroy those underlying kingship by Divine Right. The subjects of William and Mary, except for the tiny if resolute handful of Non-Jurors inspired by a like spirit to that of the Covenanters,[1] repudiated an allegiance hitherto regarded as sacred, and assumed an equal duty towards the Revolution dynasty. This duty might in certain cases be reinforced by oath. Yet its basis was to be found not in the imperious voice of conscience but in the law of the land in which the will of the community was enshrined. The new monarchs and their successors might, and did, staunchly defend their Prerogative. They could hardly invoke the old sanctions in its defence, or treat its existence as a matter of conscientious scruple either for themselves or their subjects. Prerogative became henceforth merely a department of the Common Law, comprising those of its rules which were peculiar to the King and not shared by the subject. Its recognition becomes a matter of expediency. Its content is such as Parliament and the courts may define. Its justification is a purely utilitarian conception of the public good, laid down not by the King but by his subjects. Royal powers might be regarded either as the outcome of an original contract between King and people, which James "by the advice of Jesuits and evil-disposed persons" had violated; or, if contract seemed to assure too much to the Crown, then simply as a revocable trust conferred by the people, such as Locke presently enunciated in his *Second Treatise on Civil Government*. This inevitably leads to an essentially practical and largely secular notion of monarchy. Not for nothing had England been kingless for two months in 1688-9.

If William and Mary could not hope to hold the exact position *Legal* of their two predecessors, it was not so much because the *powers of* powers of the Crown had been curtailed as because their whole *still intact* basis had been transformed. The Bill of Rights was not, in substance, a serious limitation on the powers of the Crown. William indeed may have intended to displace James but he had no intention of dissipating the authority which James had validly exercised and which he required for his own purposes. Nor did the framers of the Bill of Rights intend the annihilation of monarchy. On its new basis, it must be preserved so that the

1 On the position of the Non-Jurors, see N. Sykes, *Church and State in England in the Eighteenth Century*, 28-9.

nation might have "a real, working, governing King, a King with a policy".[1] With a title based on popular consent and not on Divine Right, he succeeded, in substance, to the position of the last two kings.

*The Crown and the political parties*

He also succeeded to their difficulties, in a form which soon became acutely accentuated. Charles II had forged, and James II destroyed, an alliance between the monarchy and the Tory party which had held some promise of maintaining the predominance of the Crown in the constitution, with Parliament as its occasional and subordinate partner. It is doubtful how long this system could have been maintained. Tory support had wide limits. None the less, it was not unlimited, and within its limits the Crown must move. Nor, perhaps, would Tory ascendancy have lasted for ever. Though routed in 1681, the Whig party, expressing the ideals and interests of so large a section of the nation, could not be doomed to permanent extinction. James II's later policy had recognised the latent political strength of Dissent. With the Revolution, the Whig party re-emerged strong and revengeful. Temporarily united to achieve the Revolution, Whigs and Tories soon fell into bitter mutual animosity, fed largely by the religious divisions to which their existence was in great part due, and reinforced by the conflicts of the commercial and landed interests, and conceivably also by corresponding social antipathies.[2] The Indemnity Bill introduced by the Whigs in the Convention Parliament threatened to become, like that of 1660, a bill of pains and penalties, directed against all who had aided James II in governing according to principles now for the first time formally condemned.[3] Their Corporation Bill menaced with loss of office for seven years all who had taken part in the surrender of the charters.[4] On the other hand, the strength of Toryism prevented any large measure of relief for dissent. That division of the nation into Anglicans and Dissenters which the Clarendon Code had implicitly recognised was stereotyped by

[1] Maitland, *Constitutional History of England*, 388.

[2] Lecky's analysis of the Whig and Tory parties is here adopted, but it would seem that the real distinction between the two parties corresponds to a profound divergence of political thought, as well as on—perhaps rather than on—religious differences. It is perhaps doubtful whether economic rivalries had as much place as has been thought. Well-to-do and enterprising landowners were connected with the business world, and commercial men, as always, tended to become landowners.

[3] Ranke, iv. 576.                    [4] Ranke, iv. 577.

the Toleration Act of 1689, in which the principle of comprehension, urged by William, was finally and emphatically rejected. The grant of toleration to Protestant Trinitarian Dissenters, enabling them to worship in meeting-houses to be licensed by the bishops, was a grudging measure. It was unaccompanied by the final repeal of a single penal statute. It expressed, so far as it was politically safe, the continued detestation of Anglicans for Nonconformists. It sharpened rather than allayed the hatred of Nonconformists for the privileged and arrogant Establishment.[1] In the heated atmosphere of these various and complex dislikes, religious, economic, and social, party bitterness waxed fast. The omission to renew the Licensing Act when it lapsed in 1694 enabled publication to be carried on subject only to the Common Law rules regarding blasphemy, sedition, and the like. In printed and spoken word, sermon, speech, pamphlet, broadsheet, and petition, an era of intense partisan strife began. In neither party could William find assured support for the Crown. A foreigner and a Calvinist, he could not draw on the springs of Tory loyalty, which turned mainly towards Mary and often towards the exiled Court at St. Germains. All he could expect from Tories was a grudging support born of emergency, and notably weakening after Mary's death in 1694. The Whigs, though more fully committed to William as the embodiment of the Revolution Settlement, were by tradition and principle inclined to further diminution of royal power. He had therefore to reckon with a Tory party unsympathetic towards the person of their King, and a Whig party intent on weakening the powers of the Crown. It was inevitable that sooner or later both should turn, even if they did not co-operate, against him.

Inexorable necessity prevented him from imitating his predecessors in dispensing with the Parliament in which the strife of *Annual Parliaments* parties and their latent ill-will towards the Crown were expressed. Once again constitutional development was hastened by the pressure of war. From 1689 to 1697 the conflict with France necessitated annual sessions of Parliament and annual grants of supply. With regard to the frequency of Parliament, the Bill of Rights had merely laid down a general principle which might have meant no more than strict adherence to the Act of 1664. In 1694

[1] Costin and Watson, i. 63-7.

that statute was re-enacted, after a bill for the purpose had been
vetoed by the King in 1692, and rejected by the Commons in
1693 on the ground that it had been introduced in the Lords, who
ought not, as a non-elective body, to interfere with the elective
branch of the legislature.[1] It authorised the issue of writs under the
Great Seal when three years had elapsed without a Parliament.
But practical reasons had already led to annual sessions. The main
importance of the Act was indeed that by limiting the duration
of Parliament to three years it disabled the Crown from retaining
a favourable Parliament; obliged it to continue the technique
begun by Danby of influencing members through its patronage;
compelled it to conform its policy to the need for winning
electoral and parliamentary support; and complicated its task by
ensuring, through triennial elections, that party feeling was kept
at a high pitch.

*Increased
financial
control
by the
Commons*    To some extent, however, the war, for which national feeling
was almost universal, facilitated the business of government.
Money was abundantly provided for the war, to the amount of
four or five millions yearly. It was largely raised by a land tax of
four shillings in the pound, the incidence of which further embittered the relations of the Tory landed class who paid the tax, and
the Whig moneyed class which lent to the government and drew
the interest on their investment from the proceeds of taxes paid
by the landowners. By an astonishing financial effort, three-fourths
of the cost of the war was met by current taxation. For this lavish
financial support there was a serious constitutional price to be paid.
It involved the foundation of a permanent system of estimate,
appropriation, and audit. In 1690 the Commons—for the first
time—considered the army, navy, and ordnance estimates, and the
accounts of expenditure and loans for these services since 1688.[2]
In 1691 they appointed a number of their members as Commissioners of Public Accounts, rejecting the claim of the Lords to
participate in this work. This body, though its efficiency improved
with experience, was handicapped by not working, like the
modern Committee on Public Accounts, in conjunction with the
Treasury. Preparation of accounts by means of its own inquiry

---

[1] Costin and Watson, i. 79. For the Triennial Bill debates, 1693-5, see A. S.
Turberville, *House of Lords under William III*, 170-75.

[2] Shaw, *C.T.B.* ix. part I. Introduction, cxxxvi-cxxxix.

involved a wasteful and unpractical duplication. Nevertheless it opened to the Commons a department of government hitherto withheld, except on rare occasions, from their investigation.[1]

Appropriation, hitherto unusual and of doubtful constitutional propriety, became regular. It was particularly useful in the negotiation of loans. To lend on a fund appropriated by statute was infinitely more attractive than lending on the King's security alone, by which public creditors had suffered at the Stop of the Exchequer—those losses now, however, being partly made good by the decision in the *Bankers' Case*.[2] The creation of annuities encouraged lenders to leave their capital in the hands of government and be content to draw interest alone. This new departure is reflected in the weakening of the system by which taxes were voted to the sovereign himself. Obviously a grant terminating at his death provided inadequate security. In 1693 an additional excise was imposed for a term of 99 years, to guarantee the payment of annuities.[3] Negotiable Exchequer bills enabled the government to arrange short-term credits. Lending to the government was the main function of the Bank of England, founded in 1695 and from 1709 associated by statute with the issue of Exchequer bills.[4] Government was henceforth able to command a supply of borrowed money which obviated the old difficulty that money from taxation came in irregularly and slowly. The effect was to consolidate parliamentary control over its finances. Only on such terms would Parliament venture to put large sums of money in the hands of the executive. *Government borrowing facilitated*

It might perhaps be supposed that the complete assumption of control by Parliament over the raising of money by tax or loan—and its expenditure as well—were expedients applying only to extraordinary revenue. In theory, this is true. Yet even the "ordinary" revenue of the Crown entered on a new phase of its history after 1688. The Convention Parliament accepted the old principle of a permanent endowment of the Crown, and resolved that an annual income of £1,200,000 should be *Beginning of the Civil List*

[1] Shaw, *C.T.B.* ix. part I. cli-cliv: cf. S. H. Baxter, *The Development of the Treasury, 1660–1702*, 235-6.

[2] Costin and Watson, i. 271-8.

[3] Shaw, *C.T.B.* ix. part I. clxxxiv.

[4] A. Andreades, *History of the Bank of England*, 72-5, 121-2; E. L. Hargreaves, *The National Debt*, 18.

provided.[1] Experience had shown the danger of this system
without suggesting that the true principle was to provide for
strictly governmental services by recurrent grants, and endow
the Crown for purposes only of strictly household expenditure.
A series of short-sighted and ineffective devices followed. The
hereditary revenues were deemed to have lapsed—though it
is difficult to see how they could, and William denied it—and
were renewed.[2] With them the Crown obtained an excise for
the joint lives of the sovereigns, with remainder to the survivor, and the customs for four years only, a grant renewed in
1694 for five years more.[3] In all this, no account was taken of the
King's real needs. He was driven into an indebtedness made deeper
by the power given him to borrow for war purposes on the security
of the excise and customs, thus burdening himself with obligations
which Parliament ought to have defrayed. Officials, ambassadors,
persons receiving salaries, pensions, grants, and even charity from
the Crown all had to go short, as had the King himself. By 1695
he was £1,300,000 in debt.[4] Parliament's only remedy was to
authorise him to borrow further. After 1697 he sought a permanent
settlement, and got a Civil List of £700,000.[5] On this the fighting
services were no longer a charge. Full financial responsibility for
them had been taken over by Parliament. Even for his purely
civil expenses the sum allotted was inadequate. The drift into debt
continued, and with it the need for further recourse to Parliament.
The Revolution ended any possibility that the King should "live
of his own".

*The Treasury and the Commons*    The inevitable result of the new relation between King and
Parliament was to change the whole connexion between executive
and legislature. Any idea of separating the two was impracticable.
The financial powers of the Commons began to draw the Treasury
into the parliamentary sphere. Theoretically an instrument for
controlling the King's finances in his interests alone, it tended to
become a link between him and Parliament, informing it of his
needs, suggesting methods of meeting them, and giving account

[1] See Shaw, *C.T.B.* ix. part I. Introduction, xvii-xxxviii, for the debates
leading to this resolution.
[2] Shaw, *C.T.B.* ix. part I. Introduction, xxiv, lxxii, lxxx.
[3] Shaw, *C.T.B.* ix. part I. lxxxi, lxxxiv.
[4] Shaw, *C.T.B.* xi-xv. Introduction, x.
[5] Shaw, *C.T.B.* xi-xv. Introduction, xxvi.

of how grants had been spent.[1] The King was obliged to consider his ministers not solely as heads of departments responsible to himself, but as politicians also, capable of presenting and defending his policy before Parliament and gaining for it the support of a majority, particularly in the Commons who held the purse-strings.

The task of dominating an assembly sharply divided on party *The* lines and in which preponderance passed from one side to the other *appoint-* at triennial elections was always difficult. Party feeling ran deep. The *ment of* *ministers* Whigs dominated the Convention Parliament, the Tories that of 1690. The election of 1695 gave the Whigs a majority again, those of 1698 and 1701 restored and confirmed Tory preponderance. That the King should accept as ministers the leaders of a party which had succeeded in snatching a majority on a three years' tenure would have seemed a monstrous constitutional perversion. Yet the permanent division on party lines had to be reckoned with. Alliance with one party alone was no longer possible as it had been to Charles II, nor had William any idea of figuring only as the leader of one party even if he could. The most natural way of dealing with Parliament was to maintain his prerogative to appoint ministers, set the Crown above party feuds by selecting both Whigs and Tories for office, and use their influence over their respective followers as a means of uniting all in support of his government.[2]

Such ministries suffered from radical defects. Ministers of differ- *Defects of* ent political opinions found it hard to work together and "support *mixed* *ministries* the Crown rather than oblige their party". Those belonging to one party sustained attack from the parliamentary forces of the other. Neither side could wholly control its own nominal followers, for if party feeling was high, party discipline was weak. Ministers were detached from their parties, and leadership fell rather to influential private members heading local or personal followings, whose co-operation could not easily be ensured.[3] Until Mary's death in 1694 the system of "mixed ministries" worked after a fashion, though individual ministers like the Tory Nottingham and the Whig Shrewsbury found their position impossible and resigned. From

---

1 D. M. Gill, 46 *E.H.R.* 6, 13. In Anne's reign the connexion between the sovereign and the Treasury was much weakened. William III kept it close.

2 G. M. Trevelyan, *Blenheim*, 108–9; Feiling, 275–7.

3 Trevelyan, *Blenheim*, 196–7.

1694 Tories, including ex-ministers, no longer actuated by loyalty towards a Stuart queen, turned into overt antagonists of a ministry becoming mainly Whig. While the war lasted, the crisis was delayed and the ministry maintained its hold. In 1696 an assassination plot led both Houses to declare their resolve to defend William, legalise an Association to protect him[1]—membership of which the Whigs would have liked to impose as a qualification for office—temporarily suspend the Habeas Corpus Act, enact that Parliament should not be dissolved by his death, and condemn by attainder a Jacobite conspirator, Sir John Fenwick, against whom the two witnesses necessary under statute to prove his treason could not be found. This not wholly disinterested solicitude for the King's person was quite compatible with further inroads on the Prerogative, such as the recoinage ordered by statute in 1696,[2] the attempt by the Commons to nominate the members of a newly appointed Board of Trade,[3] and their revocation of grants made by the King out of Crown lands to the Dutchman, William Bentinck, Earl of Portland.[4]

*The attack on the Prerogative*

Thus, even in the later war years, a Whig ministry could not entirely control a Whig House of Commons. After Ryswick it drifted helplessly amid a storm of attack, which the Tory electoral success of 1698 made only more vehement. It fell first on the military establishment. The combined effect of the Bill of Rights and the Mutiny Act made it impossible for the Crown to maintain in time of peace a standing army unauthorised by Parliament. Its existence, number, pay, and discipline all were subjected to statute. The Whigs of 1697, and the Tories of 1698, agreed in demanding its reduction to 7000. An increase was authorised only on condition that no troops were placed on the naval establishment. The King's Dutch guards were sent home. His pleas for an adequate military force were disregarded. His grants of forfeited rebel lands in Ireland to his foreign generals and advisers were investigated by a Committee of the Commons, and, despite the Lords' attempt to support him, William was obliged

---

[1] Costin and Watson, i. 87-9. In 1700, an Act attainting the Pretender was passed, and also a peculiarly ferocious Act against Catholics; Costin and Watson, i. 90-91.

[2] Shaw, *C.T.B.* xi-xv. Introduction, cvii. ff.

[3] For a similar attempt in 1689, see R. M. Lees, *Constitutional Importance of the Commissioners for Wool*, 13 *Economica*, 147, 264.    [4] Ranke, v. 102-3.

to consent to their cancellation by statute.[1] His prerogative in the conduct of foreign affairs was the next object of attack.[2] From 1698 he carried on through a few confidential advisers and in a highly informal and irregular way a negotiation with France and the Dutch Republic which issued in the First and Second Partition Treaties. In 1700 Louis XIV repudiated his treaty obligations. The Tory majority resolved not to be dragged into war for the Partition Treaties, and investigated and attacked the procedure by which they had been made as well as the policy they embodied. The Secretary, Lord Jersey, admitted that he had concluded the First Treaty on oral instructions from the King and without consulting other members of the Privy Council, and it was revealed that Somers, as Lord Chancellor, had affixed the Great Seal to a commission authorising the acceptance of the Treaty by persons whose names were left blank.[3] An attempt was now made to impeach him with his ex-colleagues of the Whig Junto, Orford and Montagu.

After these extremities, when two ungovernable parties seemed to vie with each other in making the conduct of government by the King and his ministers impossible, that united support for which he had vainly sought was suddenly restored. The succession question became urgent with the death in 1700 of Anne's last surviving child, the Duke of Gloucester. Against Jacobites who desired the recall of the exiled dynasty and doctrinaire Whigs who hoped to end monarchy altogether, it was possible to rally moderates of both parties and enact the Act of Settlement. Its terms reflect the constitutional conflicts of the years since 1697. But it repudiated legitimism even more directly than had the Bill of Rights, by enacting that on Anne's death without direct heirs, the Crown should pass to the Hanoverian descendants of James I's daughter Elizabeth. Zeal for the Protestant succession gave a sharper edge to the hostility to France awakened by Louis XIV's occupation of the Spanish Netherlands in the summer of 1701.[4] On James II's death in September of that year the French King in violation of the terms of the Treaty of Ryswick, recognised his son as *de jure*

*The Act of Settlement*

---

[1] M. E. Grew, *William Bentinck and William III*, 374-5.

[2] M. Thomson, *Parliament and Foreign Policy, 1689–1714*, 38 *Hist.* 234.

[3] T. Merz, *The Junto*, 30-32, 35-8, 122-3, 143. It is to be noted that again impeachment failed owing to the attitude of the Lords.

[4] M. Thomson, *The Safeguarding of the Protestant Succession 1702–18*, 38 *Hist.* 39.

sovereign of England. That the temper of the constituencies was turning against the extremist Tories in the Commons had been indicated by such petitions as that presented by the Grand Jury of Kent, praying the House to "turn their loyal addresses into bills of supply".[1] Though the Commons voted the Kentish Petition a breach of privilege and imprisoned those who presented it, the King had got his cue for a dissolution. The general election returned a House which, if still mainly Tory, was prepared to support a mixed ministry, predominantly Whig, committed to the war for which William had engaged himself by the Grand Alliance of the Hague.

*Constitu-*
*tional*
*position of*
*Anne*

William III thus transmitted to his successor a control over government which had been seriously menaced but was still intact. Notwithstanding her sex and her mediocre capacity, Anne was well qualified to defend her heritage. The restrictions imposed on the Crown by the Act of Settlement were only to become effective when another foreign King ascended the throne. She herself, a scion of the Stuart line, whose adherence to the Anglican Church was not, as that of the Hanoverians would be, a duty imposed by the Act, but the expression of a genuine and ardent affection, whose heart, unlike theirs and William's, was "mere English", had a powerful hold over Tory loyalty. On the other hand, she never countenanced her more extreme Tory and Anglican supporters by denying that she "stood on a Revolution footing".[2] While she emphasised her connexion with the pre-revolutionary monarchy by reviving the practice, abandoned by William, of "touching for the King's evil",[3] she never claimed that her royal powers were of divine origin. However strong her Tory and Anglican sentiments, which were well known, she was unlikely to throw herself unreservedly into the hands of Tory zealots. Her abilities might be modest. They were compensated for by a strong common sense, a tenacity of purpose, and a vigorous patriotism which combined to form a character at once practical, decided, and steadfast to the duties of an English sovereign.

Queen Anne must therefore be regarded, within the limitations

---

[1] Costin and Watson, i. 191-2.
[2] Trevelyan, *Blenheim*, 172-7.
[3] Among the persons she thus "touched" was Samuel Johnson.

imposed on her by her sex, her intellectual powers, and the *The* military and diplomatic stresses of her reign, as the effective *Queen and her* head of her own government. Notwithstanding the censure *Cabinet* passed by the Act of Settlement on the practice of substituting for the authority of the Privy Council that of a small informal group of important ministers and advisers, the continued evolution of the "lords of the Cabinet Council" during her reign showed that this detested innovation had come to stay. The Regency Act of 1705 largely repealed the prohibition against it.[1] Meeting, usually weekly, in the Queen's presence, the nascent Cabinet, including such officials as the Chancellor, Privy Seal, Lord President, Secretaries of State, and Lord Treasurer or First Commissioner of the Treasury, decided all questions of policy, relegating the Privy Council to the formal transaction of routine business and administrative duties for which no separate departmental organisation existed.[2] The Cabinet was as yet an inchoate body. Relations between its members were ill-defined. Private conferences between leading members, such as the Lord Treasurer Godolphin, and Marlborough, who sat as Master of the Ordnance, occurred regularly apart from their deliberations with their colleagues.[3] Their political opinions, though there was a necessary minimum of agreement, were diverse. They were primarily the Queen's servants, and she was the arbiter between them. Her personal preference was for Tory ministers, who on her accession replaced the Whigs employed by William. In 1702 the Tory party predominated in the Commons. In the elections of 1705 the Whigs gained largely, and in 1708 they obtained an electoral triumph. Yet Anne stubbornly refused to admit that any group of men could force themselves on her as ministers and advisers merely because their adherents formed a majority in one House of Parliament or even in both.[4] The ministry altered much in composition from 1702 to 1710, but it always remained nominally that which had originally assumed office. No general election, no degree of parliamentary pressure, ever obliged her to part with the whole of a ministry or accept a wholly new one.

---

[1] *Statutes of the Realm*, viii. 502.

[2] E. R. Turner, *The Cabinet Council, 1622–1784*, i. 440 ff., describes its work, and derives it from the "Foreign Committee" of the Privy Council—a view suggestive of greater precision of form than probably existed at this period. See J. H. Plumb, *The Organisation of the Cabinet in the Reign of Queen Anne*, 5 *T.R.H.S.* vi, 137.

[3] With Robert Harley, these ministers were described as the "Triumvirate".

[4] Costin and Watson, i. 359.

And when at last the ministry fell in 1710, it was, to all outward appearance, because the Queen dismissed it.

*Ministers and Parliament*

The reign of Anne was not, then, a period of cabinet government in the modern sense. It was, however, one in which the relations of ministers and Parliament were incessantly drawn closer. More than ever was it clear that ministers must cultivate the dual function of conducting executive business and winning parliamentary support for what they did. The Commons in particular possessed, in their exclusive control over the raising of taxation, in appropriation and its corollary of audit, a power attracting the executive out of the sole orbit of the Crown and into their own. In this process the necessities of war finance had a leading part. Over half of the fifty million pounds which the Spanish Succession War cost was met by taxation, as to the raising and spending of which the Commons were persuaded, guided, and informed by the Treasury. Its business was not as in modern times to draw up a single comprehensive Budget, but nevertheless to present each individual branch of revenue, and the purpose for which it was intended, in what approximated to a national financial plan.[1] It was in this period that the phrase "ways and means" was given currency by William Lowndes, Secretary to the Treasury. By the end of Anne's reign the direction of the government over matters of finance had been fully accepted. Standing Order No. 66 of the House of Commons, adopted in 1713, provided and still provides that no money can be voted for any purpose except on the motion of a minister of the Crown. It followed naturally that the leading position in the Cabinet came to be associated with the Treasury, and to Godolphin, Lord Treasurer until 1710, the name of "Prime Minister" was occasionally applied.[2] The repeal of the clause in the Act of Settlement prohibiting office-holders from sitting in the Commons enabled the ministers and the Lower House to continue in an association which was increasingly to become the essential characteristic of English government.

*The use of Crown patronage*

It did even more than this. The Regency Act divided offices into two classes—"old" offices existing before 1705, and "new" offices subsequently created, to which the disqualification, in default of statutory provision to the contrary, continued to apply.

---

[1] Gill, 46 *E.H.R.* 614 ff. Dr. Shaw's Introductions to the *Calendars of Treasury Books* for the reign of Anne show that her administration suffered the same financial hardships as William III's. Estimated revenue fell short of the supply needed, revenue received enormously more so.   [2] Trevelyan, *Blenheim*, 188 *n.*

The result was not only that ministers could continue to sit in the House of Commons, but holders of other "old" offices and places of profit could likewise do so. By command of this patronage, ministers were enabled to create a body of "Queen's servants" sufficiently numerous to give the government effective support and sometimes to hold the balance between Whigs and Tories.[1] While the Commons' control of finance enabled them to draw the ministry closer to themselves, conversely the ministry's control of patronage enabled it to ensure the solid nucleus of a governmental party. The process was attended by the danger that official appointments, whether "old" or "new", if used mainly for political ends, should become the "spoils" of party warfare. This must in the outcome have been fatal to efficient administration. The Queen's determination to maintain her prerogative to appoint to office under the Crown, that of capable ministers, notably Godolphin, to have governmental business competently done, averted the danger for the time.[2] During this generation and the next, professional competence rather than political allegiance continued to be the essential qualification for administrative office.

The relations thus established between executive and legislature *The strife* necessarily precluded any rapid adjustment of the composition of *of parties* the ministry to that of the legislature. But political strife showed no signs of abating, if during the first half of the reign the prosecution of the war provided at least one question on which a measure of agreement existed. Even this great national enterprise presently contributed to the exacerbation of party feeling. As in the preceding reign, the burden of war finance fell heavily on the Tory landed class. While the great Whig landowners paid the land tax which was its mainstay, the failure of an attempted income tax in 1703 demonstrated the difficulty of getting the moneyed men who constituted the bulk of the Whig party to pay their share.[3] The widening horizons of the war as it turned into a world conflict, the need for maintaining military efforts on several fronts simultaneously, and the acceptance as an essential war aim of the ejection of the Bourbon King Philip V from the Spanish throne inevitably

[1] Trevelyan, *Blenheim*, 213.
[2] Trevelyan, *Blenheim*, 206-7; Hughes, *Studies in Administration and Finance*, 269-72.                    [3] Trevelyan, *Blenheim*, 292-3.

tended to alienate the Tory party from the government, and led ministers to rely on the more thorough-going support of the Whigs. Nor did the policy and finance of the war stand alone as provocations to party rancour. Religious animosity made its baneful contribution. The indignation of Anglican Tories was specially aroused by the growing practice of occasional conformity. Dissenters, debarred from office by the Restoration statutes, qualified by intermittently taking communion under the Anglican rite, remaining for all other purposes members of their own communions. A notorious example of this breach of the whole intention of the law had occurred towards the close of William III's reign. The Lord Mayor of London, Sir Humphrey Edwyne, proceeded to a Presbyterian chapel in his mayoral robes with the civic insignia borne in front of him.[1] Politics were mingled in the problem of occasional conformity. If the practice could be stopped, Tory and Anglican control would be restored over municipal government and borough elections. Hence, in Anne's reign, when Anglican zeal might have hoped for satisfaction on this point, bills directed against the practice began to be promoted in the Commons, meeting with rejection in the mainly Whig House of Lords.[2] By 1705 another contentious issue of the same kind was raised by the demand of the Tories for a Schism Act, intended to destroy the Academies which the Dissenters, excluded from the Universities by the Act of Uniformity, had founded during the last half-century, and which had attained a modest prosperity and filled a useful place in English education.[3] If the Occasional Conformity bill menaced the voting strength of Dissent, the Schism bill threatened its very existence.

*Party propaganda and organisation*    These and other various causes of mutual hatred were vigorously inflamed by party propaganda. The pulpits of the Anglican parson and the dissenting minister reached the masses who blended their politics with their religion. For the educated classes, newspapers were now supplanting the news-letters of former days. Periodicals commenting on the news began to appear, for example in Defoe's *Review*, Addison and Steele's *Spectator*, Swift's *Examiner*, and the

---

[1] Trevelyan, *Blenheim*, 277-8.
[2] Trevelyan, *Blenheim*, 277 ff.; *Ramillies*, 14-16.
[3] Robert Harley had been a pupil at a Dissenting Academy. On these Academies, see C. E. Whiting, *Studies in English Puritanism, 1660–88*, 455. E. R. Cragg, *Puritanism in the Period of the Great Persecution*, 186-91. For the idea that the Academies were seminaries of republicanism, see Gooch, 295.

like. Political pamphleteers such as Defoe, and Swift in his famous *Conduct of the Allies*, were enlisted in a war of words in which the parties rivalled each other and the government itself participated. All the conditions, in short, existed to tempt ambitious and masterful men to mobilise popular support for their own interests and beliefs. Systematic party organisation did not yet exist. Its place was taken by the activities of great territorial magnates. Among the Whigs, a minority faced by the powerful combination of Tory squirearchy and Anglican parochial clergy, the art had necessarily to be cultivated to a high degree. Under the Junto of Somers, Halifax, Sunderland, and Wharton it received a strong impetus both in Parliament and in the constituencies. Freeholders, well aware of the value of the franchise as a piece of property, were in the market to get the best terms. Other voters, less independent, were exposed to the pressure of intimidation as well as of bribery, though both were forbidden by a statute of 1696 which remained very much of a dead letter.[1] Elections could be manipulated and the results falsified by returning officers who rejected votes cast for political opponents. In cases of dispute as to the return, the Commons exercised a final jurisdiction, determined on purely party lines.

A classic illustration of the whole system is afforded by the *The Aylesbury Election Cases* Aylesbury election of 1700.[1] The Tory mayor, White, rejected as returning officer the votes of a number of Whig electors. Under the patronage of Wharton, one of them, a cobbler named Ashby, successfully brought an action against him at assizes. The decision was reversed by the Queen's Bench in 1704, on the ground that the case, since it affected parliamentary privilege, was one in which the Common Law courts had no jurisdiction, as the Commons alone could adjudicate on the qualifications of electors. This view was not unnaturally upheld by the Tory House of Commons. It was clearly open to the criticism that the Commons jurisdiction existed only where the result of an election was disputed, and there was no dispute as to the result at Aylesbury. Thus no question of privilege arose, and it was proper for the courts to protect Ashby in his right to vote. Such was the line taken by Chief Justice Holt, dissenting from his colleagues in the Queen's Bench, and by the Lords in reversing their

[1] Costin and Watson, i. 83.    [2] Trevelyan, *Ramillies*, 20-25.

decision.[1] Encouraged by Ashby's success, five other aggrieved electors of Aylesbury began similar actions, were committed for contempt by order of the House of Commons, and on seeking release by habeas corpus were remanded into custody by the Queen's Bench, Holt again dissenting. In this second case—*Paty's Case*—he was, however, as clearly in the wrong as he had been right in *Ashby* v. *White*, for the right to commit for contempt was an undeniable privilege. The attempt to bring this decision before the Lords by writ of error created a constitutional crisis. Both cases seemed to bring the privileges of the Lower House within the jurisdiction of the Upper.[2] A prorogation, followed by a dissolution, was the only way out of the deadlock.

*Tories and Whigs in the government*    It was no easy matter for the Queen's ministry to ride this whirlwind of party strife. Yet Anne's determination not to accept a ministry imposed on her by a party majority never wavered, and the leaders of her Tory ministry of 1702 were resolved to preserve their detachment from the feuds which envenomed political life and threatened national unity in a period of crisis. Their governing objects were the successful prosecution of the war and the maintenance of internal harmony. By 1704 the High Tory ministers Nottingham and Rochester, unable to sympathise with the policy of continental intervention, and eager to press on the bill against occasional conformity, had been discarded. After the Whig electoral gains of 1705 the ministry, reconstituted on a moderate Tory basis, began to draw closer to the Whig Junto and its well-disciplined party following, among whom the staunchest supporters of the war were to be found. With their help, the Regency Act of 1707 was passed, providing *inter alia* for the continuance of the Privy Council and Parliament after the Queen's death, the immediate proclamation of her Hanoverian successor, and a Regency under Lords Justices to govern until the new sovereign's arrival.[3] With their help, again, the Act for Union with Scotland had been accepted in the same year by the English Parliament.[4] It was with difficulty, however, that the Whig leaders forced even one of their number, Marlborough's son-in-law Sunderland, into the ministry as Secretary of State in 1706.

---

[1] Costin and Watson, i. 278-9; Keir and Lawson, 264.
[2] Costin and Watson, i. 279-84; Keir and Lawson, 266.
[3] Costin and Watson, i. 111-16.      [4] Costin and Watson, i. 98-111.

By 1708 they had driven the moderate Tory leader Harley out
of the ministry, and after their triumph in the general election
of that year they succeeded in capturing the main offices for
themselves. Even with the backing of their large majority their
tenure of office was insecure. Their failure to make peace when
a favourable opportunity occurred in 1709, and their ill-advised
impeachment in 1710 of an Anglican clergyman, Dr. Sacheverell,
for a sermon setting forth the doctrine of non-resistance in a
form which seemed to attack the Revolution, the Act of Settlement, and the Hanoverian succession,[1] gave the Queen her
opportunity for ridding herself of a ministry which, though
still ostensibly headed by the nominal Tories Godolphin and
Marlborough, had in fact been captured by the Junto. The secret
promptings of Harley, conveyed to the Queen by her confidant
Abigail Masham, whose influence had ousted that of Anne's old
intimate, Sarah, Duchess of Marlborough, led to the piecemeal
destruction of the ministry. The change of ministers was
followed by the general election of 1710 in which the Whigs
were routed.

At first sight, the closing years of Anne's reign would appear
to be a period of unqualified party government. A Tory ministry,
backed by a Tory majority renewed in 1713, held office continuously. Discarding the policy of its predecessor, it negotiated
peace with France by the sacrifice of its partners in the Grand
Alliance. Whig opposition in the Lords, which in earlier years
the Tories had tried to overcome by "tacking" obnoxious provisions of a non-financial character to finance bills so that the
Lords could not amend them,[2] was now directed against ratification of the Peace. It was overcome by the use of the royal
prerogative to create twelve new peers.[3] Another Act, intended
to consolidate the parliamentary ascendancy of the Tories,
enacted that members for shires must in future be qualified by
possession of landed property to the annual value of £600, and
borough members similarly to the annual value of £300.[4] The
Occasional Conformity Act passed into law in 1712,[5] the Schism

*Tory
ministry,
1710–14*

---

[1] Costin and Watson, i. 197-207.

[2] Costin and Watson, i. 192. For the origins of "tacking", see Turberville,
*House of Lords under William III*, 194-5.

[3] Trevelyan, *The Peace and the Protestant Succession*, 196-8.

[4] Porritt, *Unreformed House of Commons*, i. 166-72. Costin and Watson, i. 117.
The last traces of payment of members had long since gone: see R. C. Latham's
article in 66 *E.H.R.* 27.                [5] Costin and Watson, i. 118-21.

Act in 1714.[1] Moreover, in the Tory ministry, the ascendancy passed from the moderate Harley, elevated to the Earldom of Oxford in 1711, to the extremist St. John, created Viscount Bolingbroke in 1712, whose inclination, with that of the Tory right wing, the "October Club", veered towards a restoration of the Old Pretender. The prospect divided the Tory majority. But it did more, for it restored control to the Queen. Until 27th July, 1714, she maintained Oxford, the partisan of the Hanoverian succession, in office. His dismissal left Bolingbroke in supreme power. With him were a group of men ready to bring about the return of the exiled House. In their hands lay command of the powers and resources of government. Yet it was the weakness of the nascent Cabinet that it was still informal and embryonic, and the strength of the obsolescent Privy Council that it still preserved historic form and function. In these circumstances Bolingbroke's government had insufficient coherence to carry through the impossible policy to which it was committed. On 30th July, when the Queen's illness took a fatal turn, a Privy Council assembled at Kensington Palace and recommended her to confer the Treasurership just vacated by Oxford on the Whig Duke of Shrewsbury.[2] The Tory ministers, including Bolingbroke himself, submitted, and even co-operated in the measures taken to ensure the accession of George of Hanover. On the following day, with her government again in the hands of a mixed ministry including leading Whigs with leading Tories, the Queen died. Her last act as Queen had been once again to grasp with her failing hands the power of an English sovereign to control the government conducted in her name.

[1] Costin and Watson, i. 121-3.
[2] On these events, see W. Michael, *England under George I*, i. 51-5.

# CHAPTER VI

## THE CLASSICAL AGE OF THE CONSTITUTION,
### 1714–1782

### i

FOR three-quarters of a century before 1714, England had been *Contrasts*
a byword for political instability. She had passed through the *between*
crucible of civil war, executed her King, abolished and then re- *the seven-*
turned to monarchical government, expelled the restored dynasty *eighteenth*
and repudiated its hereditary right to the Crown, and placed first *centuries*
a Dutch and then a German sovereign on a throne held by a
purely parliamentary title. Her constitution had successively taken
the forms of personal monarchy, of republicanism under parliamentary and later under military direction, and finally of an
ill-defined dualism between a Crown theoretically supreme in
matters of administration and policy and a Parliament sovereign
in matters of legislation and finance. Internally, the country had
been convulsed by rebellion, conspiracy, and a war of parties the
"mercilessness" of which gave evidence of their inability to agree
on the fundamental principles underlying the organisation of
either State or Church. Though England had survived the ordeal
of recurrent warfare abroad, to emerge the dominant European
power of the early eighteenth century, her security within the
island system itself had been impaired by conflicts, both military
and political, with her Scottish neighbour. The recovery of
Ireland had, in 1649 and again in 1689, twice to be undertaken.
England's weakness and instability had, at these moments of crisis,
impaired her control over her colonial possessions. Yet, improbable as such an outcome might have seemed, the accession in 1714
of an elderly and unprepossessing German prince, ignorant alike of
the language and character of his new kingdom and profoundly
attached to his Hanoverian electorate, ushered in an age of almost
unbroken internal tranquillity and external progress. The Jacobite

10                          289

risings of 1715 and 1745 only demonstrated the security of the Revolutionary settlement of the succession. Half a century elapsed before any acute party differences disturbed the serenity of English political life. Apart from the execution of the Scottish Jacobite lords, Lovat and Balmerino, as traitors for their share in the Rising of 1745, no political offender paid for his activities with his life after that penalty was exacted from Fenwick in 1696. Even the milder pains of impeachment passed into desuetude.[1] An atmosphere of moderation and tolerance, which the reign of Anne had scarcely even presaged, pervaded the relations of Englishmen of different political and religious opinions. If English habits of life were still rough and violent, order imperfectly maintained, popular outbreaks not uncommon and the *mobile* or "mob"[2] a recurrent anxiety to government, such disturbances never attained more than local dimensions or assumed political significance. The symptoms of social revolutionary tendencies which had very occasionally been apparent in the preceding century almost wholly vanished among a "stolid, homekeeping, and reasonably contented" population. The rudimentary nature, indeed, of the machinery for maintaining internal order, and the efficacy with which, on the whole, its work was done, testify to the inherent simplicity of its task.

*Scotland, Ireland, and the overseas possessions*   Beyond the northern border, Scotland, still under Anne an independent kingdom in a mood to break away from her English connexion, was drawn by the slow but effective working of the economic advantages procured by the Act of Union of 1707 into the position of an active and loyal if not highly congenial partner. The Catholic masses of rebellious Ireland, exhausted by their efforts and sufferings in the previous century and deprived of their national leaders by the substitution for the ancient nobility of an alien garrison of English and Protestant landlords, remained passive and inert until towards the close of the century this new ascendancy class itself began to respond to

---

1 After the impeachment of the "Jacobite" lords, Bolingbroke, Oxford, and Ormonde, in 1715 (Michael, *England under George I*, i. 125-9) the only other case in this period was that of Lord Macclesfield in 1725 for corruption as Lord Chancellor.

2 The first recorded use of this word is about 1688. See the instances given in the *Oxford English Dictionary*. See also, M. Beloff, *Public Order and Popular Disturbances, 1660-1716*, 9.

interests which, if conceived of in its own terms, were at least national in that they challenged English domination. Overseas, the colonies and plantations, attached by loose political but powerful economic ties to the mother-country on which their commerce and defence seemed to depend, entered upon a period of vigorous and profitable expansion, the benefits of which were not unequally shared by both sides. Meanwhile, through the East India Company—transformed from a purely commercial organisation into one with territorial and governmental responsibilities—Eastern trade continued to enrich the nation and the foundation of a vast new empire was laid. In 1763, by the Peace of Paris, the fabric of English world-power had been raised to its highest point. Based on undisputed command of the seas and on a small but well-tried and capably-led professional army—in which the House of Hanover had by 1760 succeeded in enlisting the Highland valour hitherto generally opposed to it in the cause of the Stuarts [1]—and supported by abundant revenues, easily raised and not altogether inefficiently administered, the predominance of the island kingdom seemed impregnably assured.

The peace and prosperity which reigned within its borders were *Internal* reflected in its economic progress, its social well-being, its intel- *progress* lectual vigour and the brilliance of its civilisation. Husbandry *and* *stability* was advanced by the improved methods advocated by Jethro Tull and put into practice on a large scale by such enlightened landowners as Lord Townshend. Stock-breeding at a later date similarly profited by the experiments of the Leicestershire farmer Bakewell. Capital flowed plentifully into the land,[2] and the marketable surplus of production proved capable of maintaining a population which, long stationary, started to increase during the second half of the century. A similar application of capital and technical skill to industrial production substituted for the old system of domestic industry carried on by hand-workers new processes employing power-driven machinery. Inland transportation began to be facilitated by the construction of improved roads and the system of canals laid out from 1760 onwards by Brindley. During most of the period, however, internal communication was

---

[1] See E. M. Lloyd, *The Raising of the Highland Regiments*, 17 *E.H.R.* 446.

[2] Eighteenth-century agriculture seems largely to have capitalised itself from profits. The influx of capital from industry and commerce was less important.

still slow and hazardous, and the life of each district was contracted within its own narrow limits. Towns were closely linked with the agrarian and pastoral countryside which they served as markets and governmental centres. The county town was something of a local capital, to which the gentry of the shire resorted for such duties as those connected with quarter sessions or assizes, and for the social occasions which from time to time enlivened a rural existence lived for the most part in the halls and manor houses where in patriarchal fashion they conducted the business of their estates and their functions as Justices of the Peace. In town and country alike the course of an economic routine depending on a largely hereditary succession to particular trades tended to immobilise labour and even capital, and engraved on English society the imprint of an agelong process of growth. Fixity of abode, of occupation, of social status, created a corresponding fixity of associations and loyalties, and invested local families with an unquestioned ascendancy and the prerogatives of an accepted leadership. Though there was a darker side to the picture, the mass of the population were comparatively comfortable, well-fed, and well-housed. Social gradations in this mainly rural, localised, and immobile society were sufficiently sharply-drawn and unalterable to be accepted as natural, and therefore not to engender that war of classes which a less well-defined system seems to arouse.

*Eigh-*
*teenth-*
*century*
*civilisation*
Social harmony was promoted by the tolerance which came to be the habit of the age. In no European country save Holland were freedom of discussion and intellectual liberty more complete or individual rights so adequately protected. A cultivated and liberal upper class, highly cosmopolitan in its culture, created a world in which literary, artistic, philosophical and scientific pursuits could flourish. Its political as well as its social hegemony was readily accepted. As had been the case since the Restoration, the principal offices of State and a predominant position in local affairs seemed to fall to its members as of right. The quality of their rule vindicated the pretension on which their ascendancy was founded. In this Augustan age of wealth, success, self-confidence, and enlightenment, the problems of organising society and government which had vexed previous ages seemed under the direction of a capable and energetic aristocracy to have been triumphantly solved.

The institutions which enabled the nation to excel alike in *Venera-* the arts of war and peace attracted the admiration of intelli- *tion for the* gent observers at home and abroad and evoked the attachment *tion* and pride of those whose regard, if less reasoned, was no less firmly grounded on advantage and sentiment. As decade succeeded to decade of external progress, domestic tranquillity, and increasing wealth and refinement, the constitution which maintained these happy conditions came to be the object of a deepening veneration which the comments of such foreign eulogists as Montesquieu and Voltaire flatteringly confirmed.[1] English government, based on the political philosophy expounded by Locke, seemed to illustrate the truth that the rules necessary for the conduct of human society, like those of the human intellect itself and of the external universe within which it worked, were ascertainable by rational process. The enquiry seemed to form part of that general examination into the laws of Nature with which the mind of the age was preoccupied. The constitution could be regarded as the result of a successful investigation into the natural laws underlying government.[2] Such a conception involved the danger that any attempt at alteration or improvement would be deemed as mistaken and wrongful as opposition to Divine Hereditary Right had been in the not very remote past. Reverence for the established order became, in fact, a veritable stumbling-block to progress. It was particularly professed by the lawyers of the eighteenth century. Nor was their influence confined to professional circles. Blackstone, whose lectures on law delivered at Oxford from 1750 onwards formed the basis of his famous *Commentaries*, presented to successive generations of students drawn from the governing class a conspectus of English law in which he took up, though less indiscriminately than has often been supposed, the rôle of apologist of the established order.[3]

It is somewhat startling to find that the system of government *The Rule of Law*

[1] See E. Lavisse, *Histoire de France*, viii. (2), 170-75, and L. Stephen, *History of English Thought in the Eighteenth Century*, ii. 188-90. De Lolme may be added to the list. On him, see Stephen, ii. 209.

[2] Holdsworth, *History of English Law*. x. 8-10.

[3] Holdsworth, xii. 727-31; *Gibbon, Blackstone and Bentham*, 52 L.Q.R. 46; *Some Aspects of Blackstone and his Commentaries*, Cambridge Law Journal (1932), 261.

fashioned in the heat of seventeenth-century constitutional conflicts should thus have come to be regarded as the supreme and
ultimate embodiment of dispassionate political wisdom. Yet it is
evident that the permanent and valuable result of these conflicts
had been the establishment of a well-defined relationship between
government and law. Nowhere in the constitution did there exist
an arbitrary power, capable of imposing its commands on the
subject, carrying them out by its own executive action, subjecting
their meaning and effect to its own exclusive jurisdiction. Parliament possessed unquestioned legislative sovereignty, but neither
executive power nor, save within the narrow spheres occupied
by its two Houses separately, judicial authority. To carry out the
law was the office of the King and his servants and other public
officials. The executive administered the law but, except for a
narrow proclaiming power, did not make it, nor—again subject
to very slight qualification—interpret it. From the King down-
wards, every executive official derived his authority from the
law, common and statute, though the King and his own servants,
it is true, possessed in the Prerogative a peculiar range of Common
Law powers special to the Crown. So far as the ordinary subject
was concerned, no purely administrative jurisdiction existed.
Though there was duality between Chancery and the Common
Law courts, the judicial system formed a single comprehensive
entity, the courts at Westminster controlling subordinate jurisdictions and being themselves controlled by the appellate powers
of the Lords.[1] Made independent of the executive by the Act of
Settlement, the judges were almost equally so of the legislature,
which could obtain their dismissal only by a joint address from
both Houses to the Crown.

*The*            Each fulfilling its appropriate function, Crown, Parliament,
*separation* and Bench were considered as operating in mutually exclusive
*of powers* spheres, maintaining a separation of powers which effectively
guaranteed that individual liberty which was the hallmark of an
essentially legalistic constitution. Government was subordinated

---

[1] Three qualifications seem necessary in this general view of the eighteenth-
century judicial system. First, the Privy Council was a court as well as an
administrative body. Secondly, there are traces of an administrative jurisdiction
exercised by the commissioners of Excise (Hughes, *Studies in Administration and
Finance*, 328-35). Thirdly, the list of courts needs to be completed by mention
of the ecclesiastical and Admiralty jurisdictions.

to a law it could not transgress, which it was the business of the courts to uphold through the plentiful remedies at their disposal and which could be changed only by the popular consent which Parliament accorded. It was of course undeniable, in final analysis, that Parliament, in which legislative sovereignty resided, held the position of ultimate supremacy. Even here the idea of limitation was discernible. Theoretically, neither lawyers nor political theorists were quite prepared to accept the full implications of its legislative sovereignty, the first being inclined to regard the Common Law, the second, natural human rights, assumed as an element in the fashionable contractualist theory of government, as being in some way fundamental. These reservations, however, possessed little practical importance. No statute was ever challenged, though its interpretation might sometimes be affected, by reference to any legal or moral standard to which it failed to conform.[1] Much more important was the application to Parliament of the system of checks and balances which characterised the constitution as a whole. Its action involved the co-operation of the three interconnected but independent authorities of King, Lords, and Commons. The merits of monarchical, aristocratic, and popular government were thus combined, and the demerits peculiar to each avoided.

Such was the classical precision and proportion in which the eighteenth-century constitution presented its outlines to admiring contemporaries. To some extent, their praise for the rule of law and the separation of powers which preserved it was justified. The law of the land was supreme. The units of government were divided. Yet it is plain that the emphasis laid on this latter point was over-stressed. Interconnexions abounded. The Crown was an organ common to the legislature and the executive. Ministers sat in both Houses. Both Houses had judicial powers, and the Lords were as an appellate tribunal an integral part of the judicial system. Local courts of justice possessed administrative functions which the central courts supervised. There undoubtedly was check and balance. But there was no complete separation. Indeed, the experience of the preceding century strongly suggests that separation led, between organs of government at all equal in power, only to deadlocks in which the executive quarrelled with

*Theory and fact in the constitution*

<hr>

[1] Holdsworth, x. 526-31.

the legislature, and judges were either deprived by the Crown or impeached by Parliament. To produce harmony, the strict letter of the constitution must be supplemented by constitutional conventions such as the seventeenth century had failed to devise. In the sixteenth century, these conventions had assured the predominance of the Crown in government. In the nineteenth, they were to ensure, through the Cabinet system, the predominance of the House of Commons. In the eighteenth, they aimed at preserving the checks and balances which seemed the very foundation of liberty, without so over-emphasising them as to throw government into confusion and weakness.[1]

*Conventions of the constitution*    The object to be sought was therefore the maintenance of unity among divided authorities. Thus the Crown must be closely linked with its ministers, they with the Houses of Parliament, the Houses one with the other, the judges with both executive and legislature, and even, it may well be added, the governing authorities of Church with those of the State. Towards this general end, the principal means employed was what was described as "influence". Later to be stigmatised as "corruption", it nevertheless formed for three-quarters of the century a necessary and in many ways defensible ingredient in the constitution. Of its many forms, which included the influence of great landowners over county and borough elections, and therefore ensured to a large extent the harmony of the Lords with the Commons,[2] the influence at the Crown's disposal through appointments to office civil, military, and ecclesiastical, and the grant of honours, pensions, and contracts for the public service was easily the most important. With these instruments of persuasion the Crown endowed its chosen ministers, though what it entrusted to them it could also revoke. The influence of the Crown was used to build up ministerial ascendancy in Parliament, particularly in the Commons, and in the electorate, and to draw together

[1] Holdsworth, *Conventions of the Eighteenth-Century Constitution*, 17 *Iowa Law Review*, 161.

[2] Holdsworth, *H.E.L.* x. 628-9; *The House of Lords, 1689-1783*, 45 *L.Q.R.* 432-8; Turberville, *House of Lords in the Eighteenth Century*, ch. xvii. Two points need emph.sis. (i) Though the majority of members sat for boroughs, they were genera   ountry gentlemen and not townsmen. (ii) Notwithstanding the influence of the peers as borough-owners over elections to the Commons, the theory of the eighteenth-century constitution plainly recognised the superiority of the elective House.

institutions otherwise divergent. Generally stated, therefore, the assumptions which connected themselves with the eighteenth-century constitution were that ministers were primarily the King's servants, conducting his government and policy and dispensing his patronage, in which task his authority underlay theirs; that Parliament ought not to impose on him ministers he found distasteful; that the creation of a "formed opposition" was disloyal and factious; that it was the duty of members who could with good conscience do so, to support the King's government, even if they had to be stimulated by material or social rewards to vote according to their consciences; that no impropriety attached to the use of "influence" towards this end; and that the judiciary and the Church ought to be regarded, as far as they could be enlisted for the purpose, as instruments available for the support of the government.

The whole system operated with remarkable effect. No king *Their* had to resort to the royal veto, never employed after Anne in *effective-* 1708 refused assent to a Scotch Militia bill. No government *ness* ever lost a general election,[1] nor did any government, until the ill-success of that of Lord North in the American War caused its overthrow in 1782, ever fail to sway Parliament so long as it possessed the King's confidence. Collective resignations were rare, and generally due to withdrawal of royal support. The formation of an opposition party intending to overthrow the ministry and force on the King advisers whom he would not have chosen for himself was in disrepute. No effective challenge was made before 1782 to the use of "influence" as a means of government, or to the anomalies in the administrative and electoral systems which made it practicable. To a large extent, therefore, the constitutional conventions of the age were recognised and operative. Yet it is important to recognise their limitations. To work smoothly, they required continuous mutual trust between King and ministers. There must be unity of interest and purpose within the group from which ministers were drawn. Contentious questions which might arouse acute party feeling against them in the Houses and the nation at large must not be allowed to emerge

---

1 An exception ought perhaps to be made for the election of 1741. Walpole gained a majority, it is true, but it was too narrow and unstable to enable him to command the Commons.

10*a*

or, if they did, to continue unabated. Social and economic conditions must so far remain static that no general demand could arise for reform of the administrative and parliamentary systems on which "influence" rested. Finally, to justify itself at the bar of parliamentary and public opinion, a government based on "influence" must attain a high level of success in action.

*The Whig monopoly, 1714–60*   Under the first two Hanoverian kings these conditions were largely satisfied. George I considered the Whig leaders, supporters of the Hanoverian alliance and the Hanoverian succession, the only appropriate instruments of his rule. From them he had chosen the temporary regents whom he was empowered to nominate under the Regency Act.[1] Into their hands he committed his government. Ignorant of the English language and of English domestic problems, and interested mainly in diplomacy and military affairs, he left his ministers to decide in informal consultations from which he was generally absent the measures to be taken in his name, and to exercise the means of influence at his disposal. His example was in general followed by his son. The Whig ministers they maintained in office were held together by the necessity of preserving the dynasty during its prolonged early unpopularity, and unity was imposed on them by the rigid discipline on which Walpole insisted during his long ascendancy from 1721 to 1742. The succession crisis of 1714 destroyed Tory unity. Though probably representing a majority of the nation, the Tories in Parliament were always in a minority, and a minority divided into opponents and supporters of the Hanoverian Succession. Popular acquiescence in Whig rule was promoted by a policy of peace and low taxation, and by cautious withdrawal from courses against which public opinion might be aroused. Social and economic change was so largely obscured that the essential foundations of Whig power remained unimpaired. And the conduct of government by the Whigs seemed to justify itself by reference to every practical test.

*Decay of the eighteenth-century constitution*   Under George III these harmonies were broken. The new King was not content passively to accept the tutelage of the Whig oligarchy. That body could no longer justify their monopoly by posing as the defenders of a dynasty now unchallenged, or of Revolution principles now generally accepted by Tories as well

---

[1] Trevelyan, *Peace and the Protestant Succession*, 279, 311; Michael, i. 57-8.

as Whigs. No longer united by the need for defending these principles, they had become resolved into a multitude of mutually hostile factions each held together mainly by personal loyalties. It was natural that the King should attempt to end their outworn domination and create a government depending, as indeed strict constitutional theory implied, on himself alone. The methods he employed, however, drew attention to the anomalies of the electoral and the perversion of the administrative system through which "influence" was made possible. Both systems were in fact already becoming obsolescent, and a public opinion again aroused to active interest in political questions was expressing itself in demands for their reform. Finally, the practical success which alone could have preserved his government from attack was denied to the King. In the disasters of the American Revolution the eighteenth-century constitution sustained its death-blow. The collapse of the King's attempt at personal government inaugurated an age of constitutional reform.

## ii

The central administrative system of the eighteenth century was the preserve of the Crown. Even William III had successfully resisted the creation of an administrative department by Parliament. Anne, supported alike by Godolphin after 1702 and Harley after 1710, had tried to preserve administrative appointments from becoming the spoils of party warfare. "New" offices created after 1705 were to some extent detached from politics by their incompatibility with a seat in the Commons. Acceptance of the principle of separation of powers involved the consequence that the executive branch of government belonged to the King alone. In practice, this meant for a long period after 1714 that administrative appointments were treated as the "spoils" of the Whig ministry, but in principle they belonged to the King, and George III's career was to show how effectively this principle could be translated into fact.

The system which the Crown had successfully defended from parliamentary encroachment was the product of centuries of growth. Almost every period of English administrative history

*The Crown's control over the central executive*

*Complex-*
*ity of the*
*central*
*govern-*
*ment*

was recorded in its complex and archaic organisation. Offices like that of Earl Marshal had long since become hereditary and honorary, and had ceased to play any part in government. Others, attached to the Household, such as those of the Lord Steward, Lord Chamberlain, and Comptroller, were still efficient for their own purpose of dealing with the King's domestic business. Others again had in process of time moved "out of court" and become established as independent departments of State. Of this kind were those of the Lord Chancellor, the Lord Treasurer, the Lord Privy Seal, and the Lord High Admiral. Others again, of more recent origin, had similarly acquired a separate existence, such as those conducted by the Secretaries of State, the Secretary at War and the Postmaster-General.[1] Certain offices, like the Treasury and the Admiralty, were permanently or intermittently held by bodies of commissioners, but the greater number remained under individual ministers.

*The*
*Household*
*offices*

First place among the administrative departments must naturally be accorded to those connected with the royal Household itself. Here archaic survivals from the Middle Ages were most plentiful. Its numerous offices included those of the wardrobe, the robes, and the jewels of the Crown, an accounting department called the Board of Green Cloth, a Board of Works charged with the upkeep of royal residences and property, a Court of the Marshalsea for the trial of cases between members of the Household, and a multitude of sinecure posts of minor importance. Moreover, superadded to this antiquated and expensive system were the separate organisations connected with the King in his other capacities as Prince of Wales, Duke of Lancaster, Duke of Cornwall, and Earl of Chester. It was in the complex and cumbrous structure of these various offices, standing closest to the Crown, and furthest removed from public inspection, that the inefficiency, waste, and corruption of the central government reached their worst point.[2] But since the central government was everywhere within the exclusive control of the Crown, the same characteristics were reproduced to a greater or less degree in every depart-

---

[1] The Post Office, inherited from the Protectorate, was confirmed by a statute of 1660. Two Postmasters-General were created in 1691. In 1711 the English and Scottish Post Offices were combined (G. Evelyn Murray, *The Post Office*, 2–11).     [2] Holdsworth, x. 492–3.

ment. Nothing, indeed, could be more remarkable than the contrast between the classical ideals of order and proportion beloved by the England of that age and the Gothic eccentricity of its administration.

The departments dealing with the raising and spending of *The Treasury* revenue exhibited the same general aspect as those of the Household. Here the centre of the ancient system was the Exchequer. From this office, however, the Lord Treasurer—its original head— had since the reign of Elizabeth been increasingly dissociated. In commission regularly after 1714, the Treasury Board was during the eighteenth century an active body, meeting frequently for the transaction of financial business, and imposing its control both over the officials concerned with receipts and those concerned with payments.[1] On this board sat the First Lord, the Chancellor of the Exchequer—who since the reign of Henry VII had also been Under-Treasurer—and the junior Lords to whom were committed the Financial and Patronage Secretaryships between which the duties of the Secretary of the Treasury were after 1714 sub-divided.[2] The administrative routine of the Board caused the development of a complicated system of Treasury warrants and other papers by which its wishes were signified to executive officials.

The financial system over which the Board presided was of *The* the most heterogeneous character. The recesses of the Exchequer *Exchequer and* concealed offices dating from every period in its history, preserv- *revenue* ing its connexion with the Chamber, established under Elizabeth, *offices* and recording the association with it of revenue departments originating at various dates and serving many different purposes. A Clerk of the Pipe, originally an assistant of the Treasurer, kept the Pipe Roll, of which a duplicate was kept by the Comptroller of the Pipe, originally an assistant of the Chamberlain. The Clerk of the Rolls recorded issues and receipts, a writer of the Tallies audited receipts, each of four Tellers was custodian of a chest into which he received money and from which he paid it out, but of which he had only one key, the two others being held by different

---

[1] The best account of the work of the Treasury in the eighteenth century is to be found in the introductions by W. A. Shaw to the *Calendars of Treasury Books*, 1729 to 1745.

[2] On this office, see D. M. Clark, *The Secretary to the Treasury in the Eighteenth Century*, 42 *A.H.R.* 22.

officials, one of whom, the Clerk of the Rolls, had originally been a deputy of the Chamberlain. By virtue of this historic connexion, indeed, the Chamberlain of the Exchequer was as integral a part of the whole organisation as the officers whose authority was derived from the Lord Treasurer. The complexity arising from this dual organisation was enhanced by the survival of numerous offices, such as those of Clerk of the Escheats, Clerk of the Hanaper, and Surveyor-General of Green Wax, made necessary by the development in former times of new financial business but now wholly useless. Moreover the staff of the Exchequer had been swelled by including that of the Court of Augmentations and First-Fruits and also that of the Surveyor-General of Crown lands. From the former of these two sources the Exchequer received in particular the functionaries known as Auditors of Imprests. In more recent times new sources of revenue had been placed under special bodies of commissioners—of excise, of customs, of land tax, of stamps, of salt duties, and the like—all working under Treasury supervision.[1]

*Defects of the revenue system*    It will be obvious that this system was necessarily expensive and inefficient. Inefficiency was increased by the perpetuation of such obsolete practices as the use of court-hand instead of ordinary script, of the Latin language and numerals, and of the medieval system of tallies. Money, instead of being placed in the Bank of England, was kept in the Tellers' chests. Sums handed out to the spending departments and officials were allowed to remain unaudited in their hands for many years, the recipients meanwhile drawing the interest on them, though public-spirited men like Chatham and Burke declined thus to profit at the public expense.[2]

*Work of the eighteenth-century Treasury*    Some general co-ordination of national finances could naturally be expected from a Treasury Board so active as that of the eighteenth century. Its miscellaneous functions gave it a constant interest in all departments of government. It ordered the preparation of estimates, examined, passed, or disallowed accounts, reviewed expenditure on public services, dealt—often in a quasi-judicial capacity—with questions arising out of contracts and with petitions for financial redress, supervised the conduct and discipline

---

[1] Holdsworth, x. 487-91. On the relation between the Treasury and the Excise office, see Hughes, *Studies in Administration and Finance*, ch. vii.

[2] B. Williams, *Life of William Pitt*, i. 152-7; J. Morley, *Burke*, 93-4.

of public employees. Its work was seriously hampered by the defects of the whole system of receipt, payment and audit. It sometimes had to admit lack of knowledge, particularly with regard to outlay incurred in remote places or under pressure of emergency, and its records suggest that it was heavily over-burdened with responsibility and deficient in means of imposing its will. Its main purpose seems often to be merely to ensure that formal constitutional safeguards regarding receipts and payments are maintained, and, within this framework, to satisfy rather than to restrict or co-ordinate the demands for money which poured in from all sides, and not least from the King himself.[1] It did demand the preparation of estimates by the fighting services. But the King could augment military establishments, and go directly to the Commons for money for this purpose through the Secretary at War.[2] Over the navy it had even less control. Expenditure was divided into two heads—ordinary and sea service—the first comprising harbour and shore expenses, pensions, half-pay and hospitals, while the latter included the maintenance of ships, ordnance and personnel.[3] The Treasury had some little authority over the ordinary expenses, but the sea service was dealt with by King in Council, Admiralty and Navy Board in concert, omitting reference to the Treasury, and moving their own financial business in the Commons.

With regard to civil government, the Treasury had as little *The Civil* opportunity of control, since the expense was defrayed from *List* the Civil List.[4] As this sum was voted at the beginning of each reign for its duration, and regarded as entirely at the King's disposition, estimates were not considered necessary and none were prepared. An attempt by the Commons on Walpole's resignation in 1742 to have his administration of the Civil List investigated was defeated by the King's refusal to permit his accounts to be produced.[5] Supervision by the Treasury over this branch of revenue and expenditure could not be maintained with the strictness which

---

[1] Shaw, *C.T.B. 1742-5*, Introduction, xli.
[2] Shaw, *C.T.B. 1742-5*, Introduction, xviii.
[3] Shaw, *C.T.B. 1742-5*, Introduction, xxvi.
[4] For the fullest account of the history of the Civil List, see *Return of Public Income and Expenditure, 1869*, Part II, Appendix 13, pp. 585-607. There is an excellent summary in T. Erskine May, *Constitutional History of England* (ed. Holland), i. 156-66.    [5] Shaw, *C.T.B. 1742-5*, Introduction, xxxix.-xl.

accountability to Parliament alone would have ensured. Some relatively fixed outgoings existed, such as judges' salaries. Other services were roughly rationed, for example the Board of Works and the Treasury of the Household, but if they overspent the King merely directed the accounts to be declared and passed. Overspending was habitual, and the Civil List failed by a large margin to cover its expenses. Its amount was fixed at £700,000 annually for George I as it had formerly been for Anne, and in 1697 for William III. But Anne incurred £1,200,000 of debt and George I £1,000,000, and the position was made worse by discharging the debt by a loan secured on the Civil List itself.[1] Under George II the Civil List was raised to £800,000, any deficiency to be made good by Parliament, any surplus to be retained by the King, yet in 1745 it had again to be cleared of debt.[2] George III gave up his hereditary revenues and got a fixed Civil List of £800,000, increased by other sources of income to over a million.[3] Even so, appeal had to be made to Parliament in 1769 and 1779 to discharge arrears.[4] While the conception held that government was the King's sole concern, this unsatisfactory practice of running into debt on the Civil List continued. The distinction, which at the present day seems obvious, between the King's personal and domestic expenditure and that which he must incur in paying officials, judges, and government servants, was slow to develop. It was natural for the Crown to cling to the two principles, inconsistent though they must ultimately prove, that the Civil List was its own preserve, and that, if it could not make ends meet, Parliament must, without inquiry, supply the deficit.

*Military organisation*    The underlying cause of the failure of the Treasury, despite its best efforts, to relate all public expenditure to a coherent scheme was the sense among the other departments that all were in principle equal, that their heads were similarly connected with the King, and that none could assert superiority over the rest.[5] This idea naturally prevailed most strongly in the administrative organisation of the fighting services. Supreme command of the military forces was vested in the Crown, and over military

[1] Holdsworth, x. 483.                               [2] Erskine May, i. 157.
[3] Burke's estimate, quoted by Holdsworth, x. 483; Costin and Watson, i. 138.
[4] Erskine May, i. 160-61.
[5] See the remark of Lord Stormont quoted in Keir, *Economical Reform*, 50 L.Q.R. 376.

affairs even George I and George II manifested an interest which they seldom showed elsewhere. The ancient militia, expressing the Common Law principle that every able-bodied adult male ought to serve for national defence—though not, except in case of invasion, outside his own county—which had been reorganised by statute under Mary and again under Charles II, fell into decay in the early eighteenth century. After the 1745 rebellion and in face of the alarms of the Seven Years War, it was reconstituted by statute in 1757.[1] Each county had to produce its quota, selected by ballot from a list of eligible men, to serve for three years under the Lord Lieutenant, his deputies, and other officers. More important, however, and forming a new feature of English government, was the permanent existence of a regular army, which by the middle of the century had a strength of about 19,000,[2] and rose to about twice that strength after 1763. Impressment for the army was illegal at Common Law, but statutes from time to time gave power to magistrates to compel the enlistment of disorderly, idle or criminal persons.[3] A series of statutes recognised and provided for the existence of a force with which the wars of the period gradually familiarised a nation inheriting the anti-military traditions of the preceding century. A Mutiny Act of 1702 besides re-enacting the statutory powers of the Crown for the maintenance of discipline acquiesced in its power to do so by Articles of War. In 1715 its statutory powers for this purpose were drastically increased, and in 1717 authority to issue statutory Articles of War was confirmed.[4] A clear distinction was thus gradually established between the ordinary law of the land and the special code applicable to soldiers, to which branch of law— known in later times as military law—the term "martial law" continued to be applied in a confusing way which obliterated its essential difference from "martial law" in the sense of military jurisdiction over civilians in time of crisis.[5] Thus recognised, placed under a special legal code, and financed by Parliament on annual estimate, the army became "engrafted on the constitution", and developed its own administrative system. The reluctance of

[1] Clode, *Military Forces of the Crown*, i. 38-40; Costin and Watson, i. 135-8.
[2] Exclusive of about 12,000 on the Irish establishment.
[3] Clode, ii. 12-19.
[4] Clode, i. 146-7; Costin and Watson, i. 212 (Lords' Protest).
[5] For instances of this indeterminate use, see Costin and Watson, i. 211; and Keir and Lawson, 224-25.

Parliament to admit this fact, and the King's resolute hold over his military prerogatives, combined to prevent its organisation from attaining much real coherence. Related to the King rather than to Parliament, the Secretary at War formed the channel through which passed administrative orders relating to the army and warrants for the payment by the Treasury of the sums allocated by Parliament for military purposes, these sums being controlled and expended by the Paymaster of the Forces. A Board of General Officers dealt with army clothing but a department of the Treasury was charged with the commissariat, and the two Secretaries of State controlled the movements of troops at home and abroad. No more confusing or dislocated system could well have been devised. It was hard to induce coherence or unity of direction among so many intermixed authorities or to fit army organisation into a co-ordinated executive system, and still more so to subordinate it to control by any other department.[1]

*Naval organisation*      The navy, though equally independent of external administrative control, was at least more simply and rationally organised within itself. Naval discipline had since 1661 reposed on a statutory basis, remodelled in 1749.[2] Impressment, denied to the military authorities, was permitted to the navy and upheld in the case of *Rex* v. *Broadfoot* (1743).[3] Here the King's Bench recognised its validity provided that it were exercised only over seafaring men, and that warrants of impressment were executed by a commissioned officer, though holding on the facts of the case— in which a sailor who had resisted a press-gang and killed one of the party was charged with manslaughter—that the warrant was invalid because no officer was present at its execution. The naval forces, even if enlisted by such methods, were not unpopular either with the public or with Parliament. In place of the diffused control, due to the mutual jealousy of executive and legislature, which hampered military organisation, the navy was administered on a well-defined plan. Under the Admiralty, in commission throughout the century from 1708 onwards, the Navy Board dealt with supply except for victualling—for which a separate

[1] On military organisation in the eighteenth century, see J. S. Omond, *Parliament and the Army*, 60–72; Hampden Gordon, *The War Office*, 35–41. The subject is fully dealt with in Clode, vol. ii. chaps. xix, xxi, xxiii, xxv, xxvii, and in A. Forbes, *History of the Army Ordnance Services*, i. 79 ff. 134 ff.
[2] Holdsworth, x. 381.          [3] Costin and Watson, i. 289–90.

board existed—and ordnance, provided for by an Ordnance Office which held a position almost co-ordinate with the two fighting services which it supplied with arms and munitions, and was largely independent of Treasury control.[1]

Serving as a link between the fighting services and the civil *The* administration, besides being responsible for the miscellaneous *Secretary-* duties of their own offices, were the Secretaries of State.[2] The *ships of* rise of this office (in theory, whatever the number of Secretaries, *State* their office was, as it still is, all one) to a position of importance was slower than that of the Treasury. Under William III the Secretaries had been of little significance. He could and did act without them, as in the Ryswick negotiations and the formation of the Grand Alliance, while in the Partition Treaties the Secretary had played a small and most irregular part. In the reigns of Anne and the early Hanoverians, the Secretaries became the acknowledged channels for the conduct of diplomacy, even if in that period foreign ambassadors occasionally addressed themselves rather to the Lords of the Treasury. Each Secretary established a well-defined authority over his appropriate geographical sphere of action among European states. Irish affairs (with colonial) belonged mainly to the Southern Secretary, acting in conjunction with the Lord Lieutenant. For Scottish affairs a separate Secretaryship of State existed at intervals from 1709 to 1746, when its failure during the 1745 Rebellion caused its abolition.[3] In colonial affairs, where control belonged nominally to the Privy Council advised by the Board of Trade and Plantations, the Secretaries intervened almost at pleasure. In 1768 a separate Secretaryship of State for the Colonies came into being, to be suppressed by the administrative reform of 1782.[4]

It is obvious that the Secretaries of State, as principal instru- *Their* ments of the royal will in matters of diplomacy and war, and as *importance* linking various departments together, were bound to take a leading place among the King's ministers. Had not Pitt been Secretary of State, it has been said, he could not have taken the full charge

[1] On the Ordnance Office, see Clode, ii. ch. xx; Forbes, i. ch. v.

[2] M. A. Thomson, *The Secretaries of State, 1681–1782*, 18–28, gives a useful sketch of the holders of the office from 1702 to 1782. For a description of the Secretaries' duties in 1761, see Costin and Watson, i. 393

[3] Thomson, 29–38.

[4] On this office, see A. M. Basye, *Secretary of State for the Colonies, 1768–82,* 28 *A.H.R.* 17, and Thomson, 56–64.

he did of the operations of the Seven Years War.[1] The attendant risk was of course that the duties of the office might become too multifarious, and that its two holders might fail to work in harmony. The geographical division of their duties which persisted until 1782 was conceived on no really rational basis, and the inconvenience of a dual control was bound in the end to bring about a redistribution of duties. When that was accomplished, it took the form of a severance between home and foreign affairs. During the greater part of the century, however, the purely domestic business attached to the office was of very minor importance.

*Mainten-ance of public order*

In the main this business, shared between the two Secretaries, related to the preservation of public order. For this purpose, they exercised powers of ordering the arrest of suspects, searching private premises, intercepting and examining correspondence, seizing papers, and, in moments of acute stress, ordering out the militia and the regular forces as the ultimate safeguards of public security.[2] In the eighteenth century, as has been said, the problem of maintaining internal order was not on the whole a serious one. Popular outbreaks with political aims in view and unrest arising from social discontent were equally uncommon, and political conspiracy, except for that connected with the '15 and the '45, became unknown. The causes of disturbance were few, and disturbances tended to be purely local, connected with scarcity and high prices, or rapid fluctuations of price, which were almost more grievous in their effect; with changes in the system of taxation, such as the abortive Excise Scheme of 1733, by which Walpole tried to turn the customs duty levied on wine and tobacco on importation into an excise on their consumption;[3] with abuses arising from billeting or the press-gang; and with the excitement attending elections. The duty of suppressing disorders belonged primarily to the local magistrates, relying mainly on the ancient system of an unpaid local constabulary, reinforced by the militia, and on many occasions by regular troops.[4]

The law available for the preservation of order was exceedingly

[1] Thomson, 88.
[2] Thomson, 107, 111, 112-18; B. Williams, *Stanhope*, 180-83.
[3] E. R. Turner, *The Excise Scheme of 1733*, 42 *E.H.R.* 34; C. S. Emden, *The People and the Constitution*, 41-5.
[4] S. and B. Webb, *The Parish and the County*, 488-9 n.

antiquated. It provided no really reliable local force for keeping *The law* the peace. Serious outbreaks tended almost at once to get out *connected* of control and to need repression by force of arms, and it was *order* fortunate for the authorities that they were of rare occurrence. Against these offences the law, in its weakness, tended to be correspondingly severe. Riot was penalised, notwithstanding a statute of Mary's reign which seemed to treat it as a felony, by a straining of the treason law which made it constructively treasonable. In support of this view there was, besides the authority of certain cases of the sixteenth century, that of the decision in *Messenger's Case* (1668) when the offence of leading a band of rioters to pull down all houses of ill-fame in London had been held treasonable on the ground that the intention was general and therefore amounted to levying war against the King.[1] This forced interpretation was followed in *Dammaree's Case* (1710) arising out of the riots attending the trial of Dr. Sacheverell, when a waterman who had led a mob with the purpose of destroying dissenting chapels in London was held guilty of treason because his action must be construed as intending war against the Queen, in that he aimed at destroying not one but all chapels. The defects of the law were rectified by the Riot Act of 1715, which enacted that an assembly of twelve or more persons threatening the public peace must on pain of conviction for felony disperse within an hour of being ordered to do so by a magistrate, and that, if force were then used to disperse them, those using it should be indemnified from the consequences.[2] While this statute clarified the law, it did not add to the machinery for enforcing it, and indeed in some ways it did harm by creating a doubt whether force could be used unless the magistrate had read the order set out in the Act. Thus when troops were used to suppress the Wilkes riots in 1768-9, a criminal indictment was lodged against a soldier who had fired.[3] In 1780 the riots stirred up by Lord George Gordon encountered a paralysed authority which feared to use military force until the King prevailed on the Privy Council to give the necessary orders.[4]

---

[1] Referred to, though not mentioned by name, in the judgment in *Dammaree's Case*, Costin and Watson, i. 286, 287.    [2] Costin and Watson, i. 123-6.
[3] Lecky, *History of England*, iii. 321.
[4] Lecky, iv. 322-3. But compare Thomson, 108-9. And see also J. P. de Castro, *The Gordon Riots*, 61, 114, 126-7.

*General*
*warrants*

The connexion of the Secretaries of State with such police arrangements as existed was, as will be evident, of the very slightest nature. For action which they could themselves take directly, a small body of King's messengers, some forty strong, constituted the only available force.[1] In one important respect their powers rested on a somewhat unsatisfactory legal basis. Though the Licensing Act had expired in 1695, the Secretary of State continued, by ill-defined custom, to exercise the powers of search and seizure of papers of a seditious or objectionable purport with which that Act had vested him. By an even more uncertain title he claimed authority to arrest and interrogate their authors, printers and publishers. The question did not for a long time assume practical importance, since the Whig governments of the period showed themselves remarkably tolerant of the criticism they incurred. After 1760, however, rising political excitement gave the question a new aspect and evoked a challenge to the powers which had long been tacitly ascribed to the Secretaries of State. Among a number of scurrilous attacks on the government in various papers, particular scandal was caused by an article in No. 45 of the *North Briton*, offensively criticising the King's speech at the close of the preceding session of Parliament. The Secretary of State, Lord Halifax, authorised in 1763 the issue of a warrant for the arrest of the authors, printers and publishers of the offending number. Among those arrested was John Wilkes, the suspected author, who refused to answer the questions put to him by the Secretary, and brought an action against Halifax's subordinate, Wood, for trespass in entering his house and seizing his papers. On habeas corpus proceedings, Wilkes recovered his liberty by virtue of his privilege as a member of the Commons,[2] though he had to leave the country when the House by resolution declared that the privilege of freedom from arrest afforded no protection against a charge of seditious libel.[3] More significant was his success in *Wilkes* v. *Wood* (1763), where the Court of Common Pleas directed the jury that general warrants of the kind issued by Halifax were illegal, and Wilkes accordingly recovered damages.[4] In the similar case of

---

[1] Thomson, 142, shows that until 1772 the Messengers were all under the Chamberlain but that thereafter sixteen were appointed to serve under the Secretaries. See also P. Fraser, *The Intelligence of the Secretaries of State, 1660-1688*, 116-17.    [2] Costin and Watson, i. 219; Thomson, 118-19.

[3] Costin and Watson, i. 220.

[4] Costin and Watson, i. 294-5; Thomson, 120-21.

*Leach* v. *Money* (1765), the plaintiff sued three King's messengers for his arrest and the seizure of his papers. Here, after the jury had contingently awarded damages, the legal aspects of the case were reviewed by the King's Bench, which in a first hearing rejected the contentions that the Secretary of State had similar powers of commitment to a Justice of the Peace, that the King's messengers were to be regarded as constables, that they or the Secretary were covered by the Acts protecting magistrates and constables in the execution of their duties, and that the warrant was legal. In a second hearing they took the narrower line, on which the case was decided, that Leach was not within the terms of the warrant, since it could not be proved that he was the author, printer or publisher of No. 45.[1] The decision, for all its narrowness, destroyed the value of general warrants as a means of laying hands on a miscellaneous collection of suspected persons and discovering the real culprit by examining them, for which purpose the executive had chiefly found them useful. Their value as a means of seizing suspected papers was demolished by the decision in *Entick* v. *Carrington* (1765), arising in circumstances almost exactly analogous to those connected with the *North Briton*. Here the Court of Common Pleas directly rejected the validity of a general warrant for the seizure of papers belonging to the alleged author of a seditious libel. Under the analysis of Lord Chief Justice Camden the whole structure of the Secretary's powers for this purpose collapsed. Camden denied—as indeed might have readily been inferred from the judicial opinion of 1591—that an individual Privy Councillor such as the Secretary had any power to order arrest save in cases of treason, or that he possessed the authority of a Justice of the Peace with regard to commitments. He equally refused to countenance the arguments that long acquiescence in the practice could invest it with any legal sanction, and that public policy required such a power of arbitrary arrest to be vested in some executive official.[2] Four years later Wilkes himself recovered damages from Lord Halifax for his arrest and the seizure of his papers.[3]

These decisions, which stripped the Secretary of State of the

---

[1] Costin and Watson, i. 295–7; Thomson, 123–4.
[2] Keir and Lawson, 312; Costin and Watson, i. 297–310; Thomson, 121–3.
[3] Erskine May, ii. 127.

*Legalistic spirit of the constitution* last vestige of this discretionary power, were very typical of the legalistic age in which they were delivered. At no period of English constitutional history has the notion of public policy had less meaning as applied to the internal government of the kingdom. The power of the State in this sphere was effectively limited by the universally accepted principle that all administration was essentially the mere fulfilment of duties imposed by Common or statute law. Such a principle left little or no room for the imposition of direct administrative control by the central government over local authorities. For all practical purposes, moreover, the machinery of control had been demolished when the Privy Council was stripped of its coercive powers in 1641. The eighteenth century was an era of almost complete autonomy for the local institutions of the country. Their duty was to carry out the law, and not to obey the commands of the central executive. The only compulsion available against them was that applicable by judicial process on the ground that their legal obligations had not been fulfilled or that their legal powers had been exceeded or abused.

*Local administration: the Justices of the Peace* Their legal duties and powers tended to increase. The Justices of the Peace, still predominant in the conduct of local administration, acquired in addition to their judicial functions a great variety of administrative responsibilities. The eighteenth-century Justice found that there were few topics on which the law omitted to invest him with powers and obligations.[1] He was concerned with the revenue, the armed forces, trade, poor relief, food supply and prices, wages, and many other topics; and, as in earlier times, the practical experience thus gained made a valuable ingredient in the training of the class from which members of Parliament were generally drawn. For these multifarious purposes, the Justices acted either individually, or in groups of two or more, or in Quarter Sessions, each method of action being appropriate to a particular type of business.[2] The increasing weight of their administrative work had led to a differentiation in procedure between judicial and administrative sessions, most clearly defined with regard to Quarter Sessions, where judicial business was dealt with publicly and administrative business in privacy.[3] Highway sessions and

---

[1] See the list of powers and duties in Holdsworth, x. 161-2.
[2] S. and B. Webb, *The Parish and the County*, 387-400.
[3] Webb, 437-46, 480-81.

licensing sessions had already become well established.[1] The work of the former, entailing general supervision over the upkeep of roads, was regulated by an Act of 1766 which lasted until 1835. An Act of 1753, arising from the alarming increase in spirit-drinking, was intended to strengthen the hands of Justices in brewster sessions. Their supervision over gaols began in 1700 when they were empowered to build and maintain these institutions, and subsequent statutes conferred powers of management.[2] In 1744 they got power to confine lunatics, and in 1774 to license and control the asylums in which they were placed.[3] A series of statutes increased the responsibility of the Justices for the administration of the vagrancy law. Most characteristic, perhaps, were their powers in connexion with the administration of poor relief. Here the cessation of central control in 1641 had left them free to administer a system made additionally oppressive by the Settlement Act of 1662 and the Act of 1697 requiring persons in receipt of relief to wear a pauper's badge. No very successful effort was made to distinguish between the deserving and the undeserving poor. Methods of relief, characterised everywhere by this unfortunate lack of discrimination, varied greatly from district to district. An Act of 1723 empowered parishes or groups of parishes to set up workhouses, relief being denied to persons who refused it in this form.[4] Gilbert's Act of 1782 gave similar powers to parishes with regard to their impotent poor, requiring them to set the able-bodied to work or relieve them otherwise.[5] Much commoner, however, was the practice of outdoor relief, which often coexisted with the system of workhouses. In the operation of this whole irregular and ill-conceived plan, from which every vestige of Tudor and Stuart paternalism was vanishing, the work of the eighteenth-century Justices is seen in its least favourable aspect, particularly when it was associated, as it came to be, with non-fulfilment of their ancient duties as to the fixing of wages and prices and similar parts of the Elizabethan social code.[6]

[1] Webb, *The Parish and the County*, 397.
[2] Webb, *English Prisons under Local Government*, 10, 29. For the legislation inspired by Howard, see Webb, 38 ff.    [3] Holdsworth, x. 179.
[4] Sir George Knatchbull's Act: parishes could build workhouses in which the able-bodied could be employed, and others maintained.
[5] Webb, *English Poor Law History*, Part I, *The Old Poor Law*, 151.
[6] This remark is subject to the qualification that many parishes continued to treat their poor benevolently, though others did not. The result of this was an

*Lesser administrative officials and areas*

The increased administrative duties of the Justices naturally entailed additional powers, of which the most important were increased authority to levy rates and to appoint subordinate officials. Various statutes had since Tudor days empowered them to levy rates, dividing their incidence in a rough-and-ready way among parishes by writs of assessment. In 1739 they were empowered to levy a general rate in place of the numerous separate rates hitherto existing.[1] Their duties with regard to highways involved the appointment of surveyors. But, for the greater part, the work of the Justices was performed through the ancient local organisation of which the most important component was the parish. The parish, governed either by an "open" vestry or general meeting of all parishioners, or by a "select" vestry of principal inhabitants, had thriven amid the decline of other local authorities such as the hundred, township, and manor, the responsibilities of which it had largely absorbed into its own organisation, along with the officials, fulfilling compulsory and unpaid duties, who discharged them.[2] Its churchwardens, overseers, constables and others, formed an active governmental authority, animated by the corporate spirit of the parish, and controlled by the Justices, who with the Lord Lieutenant and his deputies, the sheriff, and the coroners gave similar visible form to the corporate activity and organisation of the shire. The urban areas, unlike the counties, which on the whole resembled one another in the general outline of their government, were of the most heterogeneous types. Many boroughs were subject to the restricted and oligarchical government imposed on them by the charters of Charles II's reign. In others, like London, there existed an electoral body of freemen with rights in the appointment of mayors and other officers.[3] Elsewhere, the whole body of freemen themselves might exercise governmental powers.[4] Certain boroughs possessed their own independent commission of the

influx of paupers to parishes of the former kind. It may be noted that Justices do not seem everywhere to have given up the assessment of wages. See E. L. Waterman, *Some New Evidence on Wage Assessments in the Eighteenth Century.* 43 *E.H.R.* 398. See also, E. G. Dowdell, *A Hundred Years of Quarter Sessions,* 149-52, and E. Lipson, *Economic History of England,* iii. 263-4, where a number of instances of assessment are collected. Also R. Keith Kelsall in 52 *E.H.R.* 283 and 57 *E.H.R.* 115.

[1] Webb, *Parish and County,* 528.
[2] Webb, *Parish and County,* 173-5, 178; Holdsworth, x. 130.
[3] Webb, *The Manor and the Borough,* 368, 382-3.
[4] Webb, *Manor and Borough,* 366, 369.

peace.[1] Some embraced a parochial organisation.[2] Other towns developed a governmental system evolved out of a lord's court leet, and were in a greater or less degree of subjection to the lord of the manor. Such were Birmingham, where leet organisation retained importance to 1776, and Manchester, where it was still at work as late as 1846, after incorporation had come.[3]

On the whole it may fairly be said that the eighteenth-century system worked best when in the hands of the class of substantial gentlemen who for the most part conducted it. Where this class was absent the results were apt to be unsatisfactory. In this respect the London area presented sharp contrasts. The parish of St. George's, Hanover Square, was admirably governed by a vestry which undertook lighting, paving, policing, and cleaning of the streets, and pursued a liberal-minded policy of poor relief.[4] Adjoining districts were less fortunate, and Middlesex was notorious for its "trading justices", men of mean position and low standards of public obligation whose corruption and inefficiency were a serious detriment to public well-being and security.[5] *Contrasts in local administration*

Certain general characteristics of the system of local government are evident amid all its local diversities. It reposed on the ancient and fundamental basis of compulsory and gratuitous service, and formed a useful means of training even the humblest classes in the work of government. It preserved, by blending judicial and administrative duties and utilising the judicial machinery of presentment and indictment for administrative as well as judicial purposes, the principle that all government was essentially a matter of law, and that administrative duties must be performed in a judicial spirit and should be subject to the control of courts of justice.[6] But it had the defects of its better qualities. It involved as its chief requirement the mere fulfilment of bare legal duties, and it did not lend itself to progress. Moreover a purely judicial control over administration was apt to be lax, spasmodic and costly. *Characteristics of local administration*

There is much evidence that English society was outgrowing

---

[1] Webb, *Manor and Borough*, 280.    [2] Webb, *Manor and Borough*, 290.
[3] Webb, 99-113, 157-60, 202-11. In Birmingham the Court Leet continued to sit until 1854. On the municipal history of Sheffield, "a remarkable example of unco-ordinated local jurisdictions", see Webb, *Manor and Borough*, 201-3 *n.*
[4] Webb, *Parish and County*, 240-1.
[5] Webb, *Parish and County*, 329-36.    [6] Holdsworth, x. 155-8, 332-6.

*The rise of new authorities*

the administrative organisation which had so long served it. New needs as they arose were apt to be committed to the care of new authorities, supplementing the old. To some extent, indeed, the older authorities armed themselves by statute with additional powers for such objects as paving, cleansing, lighting streets, regulating markets, and the like.[1] More characteristic was the development, which advanced rapidly from the middle of the eighteenth century, of new statutory authorities, such as the turnpike trusts for the improvement of roads whose duties were consolidated by statute in 1773;[2] corporations, which existed in London and Bristol, for the administration of the poor law;[3] and above all improvement commissioners for a large variety of purposes connected with the better government of particular localities.[4] Though sometimes directly connected with these bodies by participating in their membership, the older authorities tended to be overshadowed by them in local government. Their powers filled an increasing part of the statute book, in which local Acts, numbering only three in 1701, rose to twenty-nine in 1751 and sixty-five in 1770, as against only forty-nine general Acts. Their development presaged the impending decay of the historic system of local government bequeathed by many previous centuries.

## iii

*Relations of executive and legislature*

The conception, axiomatic in the eighteenth-century constitution, that administration and policy were the business of the Crown and its ministers and servants, whose actions were authorised, supported and restricted by the law, involved a peculiar and characteristic relationship between the executive and the legislature. Parliament alone could amend or amplify the law on which the validity of governmental action depended. Parliament supplied all but an insignificant fraction of the revenue by which the executive performed its work. Parliament could and did criticise governmental acts and policy, and in extreme cases attempt to impose responsibility by a revival of im-

---

[1] Holdsworth, x. 190-95. For a specific example, see E. S. de Beer, *Early History of London Street-lighting*, 25 *Hist.* 311.

[2] Webb, *Statutory Authorities for Special Purposes*, 152-3, 159-61, 172.

[3] Webb, *Statutory Authorities*, 107-9.

[4] Webb, *Statutory Authorities*, 235-6, 238-46; Costin and Watson, i. 394, 405.

peachment. It could not go further without transgressing the King's control of his own administration, and violating the fundamental principle of the separation of powers. Under the Hanoverian Kings as under Anne, the notion that in choosing his ministers and determining his policy, the sovereign must accept the leaders of the party which held a majority in the Commons or in both Houses together, and govern by the advice they gave him was inadmissible. Government was still the King's. He chose his servants as he saw fit, even if his range of choice was to some extent limited by the number of those who could be trusted to administer their offices competently, and also by the real necessity in which he found himself of entrusting his affairs to men whose influence over Parliament could be depended on to ensure their being successfully carried on. But the responsibility of his ministers, after their responsibility before the Courts if they acted illegally, was not unequally divided between himself and the two Houses. Their hope of continuance in office depended on their acceptance of the King's policy, or their skill in prevailing on him to accept their own, and on their value to him as instruments for bringing Parliament into line with the Crown. If they should fail in their duty or serviceableness to the King, he need not and did not hesitate to dismiss them if he could find others in their place. This close association between King and ministers made it impossible, or nearly so, for any organised opposition to the ministry to be formed in either House. Opposition partook of the nature of faction, and was tainted with disloyalty. In times of crisis this conviction might lose its effect. On other occasions, the patronage of the heir to the throne, generally on bad terms with his father, protected opposition from these imputations. These special cases might, however, be regarded merely as exceptions which tested the rule and proved its substantial truth.[1]

Throughout this period, therefore, it is important to recognise that successive Kings occupied identical constitutional positions, employing their powers differently only to the extent that their personal qualities and political aims varied. Their constitutional authority, essentially based on the Revolution settlement, authorised them to make a free choice of their ministers. George I and George II gave their full support to the Whig magnates who had

*The King as head of his government*

---

[1] This view of monarchy in the eighteenth-century constitution is brilliantly expounded by Sir Lewis Namier in his Romanes Lecture, *Monarchy and the Party System.*

held fast to the Hanoverian succession when the Tory leaders had seemed to desert it. George III, quite consistently with the same principle, inaugurated his reign by dismissing a ministry of which he disapproved, and entered upon a career of building and destroying cabinets which continued even beyond the period now under discussion.

*Council,*
*Com-*
*mittee of*
*Council,*
*and*
*Cabinet*
*Council*

For the conduct of the King's business, both through administrative processes and in Parliament, three organs of advice, co-ordination and control existed. Of these, the Privy Council had, mainly on account of its size and unwieldiness, long been in decline. At the moment of Anne's death it had acted effectively in ensuring the Hanoverian succession. After this temporary revival it relapsed again into being a merely formal means of registering the royal will by such instruments as orders in Council, which it neither framed nor debated.[1] The Committee of the Council which in recent years had superseded the former standing committees of Privy Councillors exercised more active functions with regard to the colonies, the Channel Islands, and other matters, not generally of great importance, which might be referred to it.[2] It preserved to an abbreviated extent, capable, however, of subsequent development, the connexion of the Privy Council with actual administrative business.[3] In practice, the circle of the King's advisers and ministers took on a form wholly detached from the Privy Council. The informal conferences between the King and his leading ministers from which the Cabinet Council developed had been a feature of government both under William III and Anne and earlier. Sir William Temple's scheme in 1679 and the Act of Settlement in 1701 had been attempts to arrest their development and draw the proceedings of the King and his advisers into a fuller light. The attempt was now abandoned. In the proceedings of the Cabinet Council one important change began early in the Hanoverian period. After 1717 George I ceased to attend its meetings.[4] His absence may be mainly ascribed to his ignorance of the English language. It was also due in part to

---

[1] On the activities of the Privy Council from 1714 to 1782, see Turner, *The Privy Council,* ii. 29, 74, 86-90. Its membership rose from 52 in 1714 to 63 in 1752 and 106 in 1782. The attendance might rise as high as 59 (in 1714 on George I's accession) or fall to 4 (in 1752). The quorum was 6. The King was very frequently present.

[2] It is to be noted that the Council still preserved judicial powers over the colonies and the Channel Islands.    [3] Turner, *Privy Council,* ii. 382-401.

[4] On this process, see Turner, *Cabinet Council,* i. 356-61, 384-9, 423; ii. 92-7.

his ignorance of English affairs, which made his participation in discussions of little value, and induced him to be content with reviewing the decisions taken by his ministers rather than sharing in their formation. The example thus set by George I was imitated by his successors. George II throughout his reign occasionally took part in Cabinet proceedings, having already done so as regent during George I's absence in Hanover.[1] By the middle of the century, nevertheless, the presence of the King, except at the meeting preceding a session of Parliament when the speech from the throne was under discussion, was regarded as unusual though the difficulty arising from difference of language no longer existed. George III, though his interests were as wholly English as his speech, did not revive a practice now largely disused. Only twice, in 1779 and 1781, did he personally summon and preside over a Cabinet meeting.[2]

The King's absence had less effect than might have been expected. Since ministers were primarily the King's ministers, they considered themselves related to him rather than to one another. Eighteenth-century Cabinets were large, loosely-knit, and ill-organised. Besides the heads of great administrative departments, they included leading household officials, and sometimes the Lord Chief Justice and—in the Archbishop of Canterbury, at least a nominal member—the leading ecclesiastical dignitary of the realm.[3] Even among the holders of strictly political office cohesion was imperfect. They considered themselves servants of the King rather than colleagues in a united ministry, whose members, agreeing on a common policy and giving one another mutual support, accepted the leadership of a parliamentary chief. It is perfectly possible to make a list of the various ministries which held office from 1714 onwards, and to associate with each the name of one, or usually more, dominant ministers. Thus in

*The eighteenth-century Cabinet*

---

[1] Turner, *Cabinet Council*, ii. 97-8; H. W. V. Temperley, *Inner and Outer Cabinet and Privy Council, 1679-1783*, 27 E.H.R. 693. Queen Caroline also attended as Regent. Costin and Watson, i. 371-5, 383.

[2] Temperley, 27 E.H.R. 694; E. T. Williams, *The Cabinet in the Eighteenth Century*, 22 *Hist.* 244-5. But see also the instances quoted by Turner, *Cabinet Council*, ii. 98-100.

[3] See, for example, the lists drawn up by Turner, *Cabinet Council*, ii. 1 (1717), 2 (1729), 7 (1744), 9 (1761), 18 (1778), 19 (1782). Others than holders of offices were often members of the Cabinet, Turner, ii. 30. The Archbishop of Canterbury seems to have been present at a Cabinet meeting as late as 1763, Turner, ii. 80.

the reign of George I the Cabinet of 1714 may be linked with the names of Lords Halifax and Townshend, that of 1717 with Lords Stanhope and Sunderland, that of 1721 with Lord Townshend and Sir Robert Walpole. In the reign of George II similar positions seem to be held by Walpole until 1742; Wilmington and Carteret from 1742 to 1744; Henry Pelham from 1744 to 1746, and again from 1746—after the collapse of an ephemeral ministry under Bath and Granville—until 1754 when his brother Thomas Pelham-Holles, Duke of Newcastle, succeeded him; and by Newcastle and Pitt from 1756 onwards. In the earlier years of George III successive ministries were in the same sense headed by Lord Bute (1762-3), George Grenville (1763-5), Lord Rockingham (1765-6), Lord Grafton and William Pitt, now Earl of Chatham (1766-70), and Lord North (1770-82).[1] Yet it would be a serious misapprehension to regard any of these ministries except Walpole's as being constituted on a recognised basis of political solidarity, collective responsibility, or acceptance of common leadership.[2] In their essence they were the outcome of the King's choice of advisers whom he considered well qualified to conduct his business in their respective offices and in Parliament. Their tenure, in principle, depended on the continuance of royal confidence. With it they could maintain themselves. Lacking it, they fell. Such a generalised statement, true in principle, needs qualification in detail. The King's freedom of choice was obviously restricted by several conditions. He must discover men who found one another at least tolerable as colleagues, who possessed at least some capacity for administration, and who were able to hold their own in Parliament. They might none the less be divided in purpose, insubordinate to their nominal chief, disloyal in their relations with each other, rivals for royal favour rather than partners of the King's trust. Moreover, beyond the circle of office-holders to whom the conduct of affairs was formally committed, the King could find unofficial confidants and advisers by whom his decision might in the last resort be swayed.

[1] It may be noted that the names of these ministers are generally connected with either the First Lordship of the Treasury or the Secretaryship of State. The sole exception is that Chatham in 1766-8 held the office of Lord Privy Seal. After 1760 it seems evident that the leading position came to be accorded to the First Lordship. It should be noted that Chatham resigned in 1768 and the ministry was thereupon reconstructed.

[2] An opinion confirmed by J. H. Plumb, *Sir Robert Walpole, The Making of a Statesman*, and Costin and Watson, i. 369.

Constitutional arrangements by which the King could select his *Effective-* ministers for himself, share with them the framing of policy so *ness of the* far as he was able or felt inclined, and impose his control by their *Crown's control* dismissal, made it necessary to ensure that Parliament was content, *over* as a general rule, to follow the lead of the Crown and its advisers. *Parlia-* For this purpose, special care had to be taken to recapture the *ment* control once held by the Crown over the electoral system and over the two Houses themselves. In this respect the success achieved by the Tudors, which the Stuarts had failed to maintain, was to a remarkable extent repeated. During the seventeenth century, as the Stuart Kings and even William III had found, elections could go adversely to the government, and its ministers might find their parliamentary position untenable. The experience of Anne's reign had shown that the position was not irretrievably lost, and, like Anne, the Hanoverian Kings never failed to carry a general election, nor, until 1782, did their ministries have to face Parliaments whose opposition could not be placated save by a general change of the King's advisers.

This good fortune cannot be ascribed, like that of Anne, *Its causes* or that of Elizabeth in earlier times, to any profound sense of harmony and mutual affection between sovereign and subjects. It was due to the gradual appeasement, after 1714, of the quarrels which had embittered English politics during the preceding hundred years. During the twenty-five years' peace of 1714 to 1739, no fundamental problems provoked party conflict. The Whig ministries ruled with the utmost possible circumspection. Their Nonconformist supporters, with the sympathy of a few liberal Anglicans, hoped for a removal of their political disabilities, and Stanhope carried the repeal of the Occasional Conformity and Schism Acts in 1718, providing, however, against the repetition of such imprudences as that of Sir Humphrey Edwyne.[1] Despite an attempt at repeal in 1718, the Test and Corporation Acts remained, weakened in their effect by the passing from 1727 onwards of annual Indemnity Acts, relieving from penalty persons who had omitted to qualify for the offices they had assumed.[2] No proposal for total repeal of these two

---

[1] B. Williams, *Stanhope*, 384-95.

[2] On the operation of these Acts during the eighteenth century, see Webb, *Manor and Borough*, 391-3; Porritt, *Unreformed House of Commons*, i. 55, 134.

Acts was acceptable to Parliament. If Dissenters were in many instances admitted to public functions, Anglican apprehension was stilled by the retention of the statutes against them. The Whigs were at equal pains to recommend their rule on the grounds of economy and good management. The land tax imposed in 1692 and frequently attaining four shillings in the pound dropped by 1731 to one shilling.[1] Thriving import and export trade, abundant and cheap money, and the increasing value of land all betokened the growing prosperity of the country, and the creation of a Sinking Fund reduced the burden of a National Debt which in 1714 had risen to £36,000,000.[2] Before serious manifestations of popular opposition, the government cautiously withdrew, as it did over the proposed repeal of the Test and Corporation Acts in 1718; over the excise scheme in 1733; and again over a Jewish Naturalisation bill of 1753.[3] Towards political criticism its guiding principle was leniency and tolerance. Except for an Act of 1737 requiring stage plays to be licensed by the Lord Chamberlain, no new repressive powers were sought by the executive, and those which it had inherited were seldom put into use.[4] During these long years of political stagnation, the successive Whig ministries were able to fasten on the electorate and on Parliament a degree of control which demonstrates how exact was their judgment of the nation they governed.

*Necessity of managing Parliament*    It must none the less be said that their ascendancy did not rest solely on the acquiescent temper which they thus endeavoured to cultivate. Indeed had any attempt been made to base English government at this stage in its history on the opinions which prevailed among the mass of the people, the chances of survival of a party which embodied, even if under the leadership of a landed aristocracy, the forces of Nonconformity and the com-

---

1 S. Dowell, *History of Taxation*, ii. 50-53, 71, 81, 96-100. The loss was recouped by a renewed salt tax, see Hughes, *Studies in Administration and Finance*, 303. Also W. R. Ward, *The English Land Tax in the Eighteenth Century*. The local commissioners were not civil servants but remained parliamentary nominees.

2 E. L. Hargreaves, *The National Debt*, 20, 22 ff. The operation of the Sinking Fund and of Conversions is shown by the fact that though by 1739 the principal of the debt exceeded £46,000,000, the annual charge had been reduced as compared with 1714 from just over £3,000,000 to just over £2,000,000.

3 H. S. Q. Henriques, *The Jews and the English Law*. 171: B. Williams, *Life of William Pitt*, i. 174-6; Emden, 45-6

4 On this point, however, see L. Hanson, *Government and the Press, 1695-1763*, 68-73.

mercial classes would have been slight in a country where the Anglican Church and the squirearchy still enjoyed a substantial predominance. But there existed two mechanical means of controlling the parliamentary machine which could be relied on to work efficiently so long as no crucial issues on which popular opinion divided sharply were suffered to arise or persist. In the structure of the electoral system and the extent of Crown patronage the parliamentary manager found invaluable adjuncts for his task.

The electoral system restored in 1660 still remained the basis of *Distribu-* the eighteenth-century House of Commons, with the addition *tion of* in 1707, by the Act for Union with Scotland,[1] of 30 county *representa-* *tion* members, one burgess representing Edinburgh and 14 others each representing a group of burghs. Among the 558 members of the Commons an overwhelming majority, numbering 432, sat for borough constituencies as against a total of 122 for the counties, and 4 for the English Universities.[2] The disproportion was accentuated by the disparity in population between the boroughs and the counties, and among the boroughs themselves. Yorkshire had about 16,000 electors, Rutland about 600, and the average in the English counties was about 4000. The electorate of even the largest boroughs fell far below this figure. Only 22 boroughs had more than 1000 electors and only 33 more had over 500, while in the vast majority the electorate numbered less than 200.[3] The size of the electorate bore no necessary relation to the population of the borough. For example, Portsmouth with 20,000 inhabitants had 80 voters, while Winchester with only 3400 inhabitants had half as many again.

These anomalies reflected the diverse history of the boroughs, *The* where no statute had ever created a uniform electoral qualification *boroughs* and where different courses of evolution had created a variety of different types. In about a dozen a wide franchise existed, including in some cases every adult male resident who had not been in receipt of poor relief, or who had borne "scot and lot" in local church and poor rates, or who enjoyed economic independence as a "potwalloper" with a dwelling of his own and a hearth

[1] Costin and Watson, i. 103; Porritt, *Unreformed House of Commons*, ii. 24-5, 116, 143.

[2] Porritt, i. 17. Note that all counties and most boroughs in England returned two members.

[3] L. B. Namier, *Structure of Politics at the Accession of George III*, 100-102.

there at which to cook his food. More numerous, perhaps some eighty in all, were the "freeman" boroughs, where by apprenticeship, inheritance, marriage, purchase or nomination persons became qualified for the freedom of the borough and the vote attached thereto. In about forty more the franchise belonged to the holders of lands by burgage tenure. These tenements being saleable afforded an easy means by which a rich man might acquire control of a borough. Some of the most notorious "rotten boroughs", such as Old Sarum, fell into this category. The last class of boroughs was composed of those in which the charter restricted the franchise to a close corporation, excluding any popular electorate. While this classification is clear enough in its main outline, the boroughs included in each category might vary, though a statute of 1729, the Last Determinations Act, giving force to the decision as to the right to vote made by the House of Commons in disputed election cases, stabilised the position in each borough so affected.[1]

*Importance of control of the boroughs*

The immense preponderance of borough constituencies and the small size of the electorate in most boroughs, including some of the most populous, made manipulation of the electorate relatively easy in a period during which political excitement was seldom aroused. The counties, where the electorate of forty-shilling freeholders—in which yeomen freeholders were reinforced by the owners of other qualifying properties such as rent-charges and annuities, leases for life and freehold offices—constituted an electorate so numerous, so independent in temper, and so widely dispersed as to be difficult to control by purely mechanical means. It was otherwise in the boroughs. Some were recognised to be at the disposal of the Treasury.[2] In the seaports, the granting of naval contracts and of nominations to a numerous Customs staff created an amenable body of voters.[3] But in general the influence which prevailed was that of the great aristocratic patron. About the middle of the century, it has been calculated, 51 peers and 55 commoners made or effectively influenced the return of over 190 members of the Commons.[4] Extensive regions of England,

---

[1] Renewing an Act of 1696; Porritt, i. 8-9.

[2] Porritt, i. 340-41. See Namier, *Structure of Politics at the Accession of George III*, ch. vii. for a study of the Treasury boroughs of Harwich and Orford; Porritt, i. 299. See also Costin and Watson, i. 366-8.

[3] On the Admiralty boroughs, see Namier, 173-4. On the Treasury's capture of customs appointments, see Hughes, 312.    [4] Namier, 181-2.

counties and boroughs alike, became the electoral preserves of great families which could procure the return of whole batches of borough members, and generally of at least one of the members for the county. Thus Sussex became the domain of the Duke of Newcastle, who shared control of Nottinghamshire with the other ducal houses of Portland and Norfolk, while Cambridge-shire fell to the Rutlands, Huntingdonshire to the Montagus of Sandwich and Manchester, Gloucestershire to the Beauforts and Berkeleys, Westmorland to the Lonsdales.[1] To be able to carry elections became an even more valuable asset to these political managers when the Septennial Act of 1715 raised the value of seats by extending their tenure from three to seven years.[2] It need hardly be said that this control was not universal, nor always, where it existed, complete and unconditional. Some great popular constituencies, such as Westminster, and some small close boroughs such as Bath, were highly independent in temper.[3] Else-where, electors made it clear that they expected something in return for their votes. In 1754 Tewkesbury required candidates to consent to advance £1500 for the improvement of roads, and Oxford in 1768 intimated that offers to pay off part of the debts owed by the Corporation would predispose voters in favour of those who made them.[4] Constituencies would even invite rival candidates to come forward, in order to enhance the value of the favour they had to offer.

It was in negotiations of this kind, rather than the actual conduct of elections, that the art of electioneering in the eighteenth century mainly consisted. Election contests were rare, since the result of these preliminaries usually made it clear which of several possible candidates would be returned. In the counties the cost of contest-ing an election mounted so high that recourse to the polls became a formidable prospect.[5] Even in the boroughs polling was infrequent. In the general election of 1761 only 48 constituencies actually went to the poll.[6] Where polling did take place, the possibility of swaying the result by influence was everywhere present. Voting was open. No register of voters existed, for none was necessary. In the counties the elector might have to establish

*Eighteenth-century election-eering*

---

[1] Turberville, *House of Lords in the Eighteenth Century*, 459-60.
[2] Costin and Watson, i. 126-7; Porritt, i. 356.      [3] Namier, 96.
[4] Porritt, i. 158-64. For this action Oxford was censured by the House.
[5] Porritt, i. 190.                                    [6] Namier, 196.

his identity by producing a receipt for the payment of his land tax.[1] In the boroughs the electors were sufficiently known in person. Interference with elections had been prohibited by statute in 1696 and 1729. The former Act disqualified candidates if they were guilty of bribing electors after the issue of election writs, but did not provide against such malpractices if they had occurred earlier. The Act of 1729 required voters to take an oath that they had received no reward for casting their votes, and returning officers that they had taken none for making a particular return.[2] There was no provision against the taking of rewards at any later time, the offering of other inducements than money or its equivalent, or the corruption of persons other than voters and returning officers.

*The use of Crown patronage*    So long as political differences were in abeyance, opposition to the Crown regarded as factious, and the government quick to recognise and capitulate to popular unrest, a system under which mere manipulation could obtain the return of a favourable House of Commons put the King and his ministers at an immense advantage. Their task, besides maintaining control of the thirty or so Treasury boroughs over which they had a direct hold, lay mainly in ensuring that the support of the aristocratic patrons who nominated the majority of the borough and about half the county members was thrown on their side.[3] For this purpose the principal nexus was the patronage of the Crown. While the electoral manager might have to draw heavily on his own resources in order to satisfy the obligations he incurred towards those who supported his candidates, and the candidate might have to do the same, all concerned looked in the last resort to the Crown to consolidate the bonds of common interest which drew patron, member, and constituency together.[4] The means available to the Crown were almost inexhaustible, and, skilfully utilised to satisfy these demands, almost proof against failure. The prerogative to create peers, employed by Tory ministers of Anne's last years to carry the Peace of Utrecht against the Whig majority in the Lords, narrowly escaped restriction in 1719 when a Peerage Bill disabling

---

[1] Porritt, i. 25-8.

[2] C. Seymour, *Electoral Reform in England and Wales*, 168.

[3] Namier, 89-90. There is plenty of evidence that the intrusion of sons of peers into county constituencies was much resented.

[4] Porritt, i. 292-4, 302-3, 329-30, 334.

the Crown from creating new peerages in excess of six above the number then existing was passed in the Lords but lost in the Commons.[1] It was thereafter on the whole sparingly employed. The strength of the Upper House, which numbered—after the inclusion by the Act of Union of sixteen Scottish representative peers—a little more than two hundred, rose very slightly between 1714 and 1782, though the quantity of new creations was disguised by the fairly regular extinction of old peerages.[2] More important than the granting of titles was the use made of appointments to office. Every position, civil, military, or naval, every emolument or pension in the gift of the Crown could be utilised to enlist the support of members of the two Houses and enable them to reward their political adherents. The whole system supported by the Civil List, into which parliamentary inquiry was denied or at best resentfully and incompletely accorded by the Crown, abounded with offices which involved no duties whatever or duties which could be performed by ill-paid deputies while the titular holders drew the salaries attached to them. For example, the Registrarship to the Commissioners of Excise, carrying a stipend of £450, was executed by a deputy who was allowed only £30.[3] Even if salaries were small, the office might involve the right to allowances and the right to exact fees. Thus while the Secretaryships of State carried a nominal salary of £100, their real value was estimated at nearly £2000.[4] Offices were frequently regarded as pieces of freehold property, and they had a further value in that the recruitment of subordinates belonged to the officeholder, whose powers could be used to benefit his relatives or political clients. Lastly, it is to be remembered that the holding of office frequently carried with it the right to draw the interest on the large sums of cash which the unreformed Exchequer procedure left for long periods in the hands of the departments.[5]

[1] E. R. Turner, *The Peerage Bill of 1719*, 28 *E.H.R.* 243; Turberville, *House of Lords in the Eighteenth Century*, 169-85: Costin and Watson, 213.

[2] Turberville, 4-5, 416-19.

[3] See the list of sinecures in the Customs and Excise compiled for Lord Shelburne, in Holdsworth, x. 502-3.

[4] Thomson, *Secretaries of State*, 145-7. In addition, the fees taken in the Secretary's office amounted to much more. But of course each Secretary had to pay his own staff.

[5] For Henry Fox's record of his own practice as Paymaster, see T. W. Riker, *Henry Fox*, ii. 292-4.

*Extension of the spoils system*

Even the least important appointments in the gift of the Crown were gradually drawn into this system for inducing political support by offering material rewards. To treat subordinate executive positions as political spoils was obviously detrimental to efficient administration. There is evidence that the process met with resistance. The tradition dating from the days of Godolphin and Harley that administrative patronage ought not to be used for political ends proved tenacious, and the departments put up a long fight before surrendering to the Treasury a control over their inferior officers which could be used to buy the adherence of important politicians. From 1729 onwards their defences were breaking down.[1] By the middle of the century the encroachments of the Treasury were constant. With the use of existing offices for electoral purposes went the wholesale creation of new offices. In 1734 it was said that "the revenue officers created since the Revolution are in danger of upsetting the balance of the Constitution".[2] Under the Pelham ministries the control of the Treasury seems to have been well established. Later still, North's government is reckoned to have created 12,000 new revenue appointments, mainly, it may be presumed, for political objects, though it is possible that increased taxation needed a larger staff.

*Parliamentary and administrative systems of Scotland*

The parliamentary and administrative systems of Scotland offered ample opportunities for organising support for the government of the day. Except for the years after the Revolution, the northern kingdom had never known any vigorous and independent parliamentary life. Originating in the same period as the English Parliament, its unicameral legislature, comprising the three estates of the nobles, the barons—composed of representatives of the lesser tenants-in-chief of the counties and other freeholders—and the representatives of the burghs, had not before 1689 acquired either a constitutional status or a political importance in any way comparable with those of its English counterpart.[3] Its liberation from the control of the Crown in 1690, when the Lords of the Articles were abolished, inaugurated a period of rapid development, modelled largely on English parliamentary practice, in which

---

[1] Hughes, *Studies in Administration and Finance*, 311 ff.

[2] Hughes, 315. See also W. R. Ward, *The English Revenue Commissioners. 1754-98*, 70 E.H.R. 25.

[3] A. V. Dicey and R. S. Rait, *Thoughts on the Union between England and Scotland*, 70-74.

it became for the first time a true expression of Scottish national sentiment.[1] Its resolute defence of Scottish interests against English dictation, shown above all in the Act of Security of 1703— by which on Anne's death the Scottish succession was to pass to a member of the royal house and a Protestant, but not, unless England meantime agreed to remove the trade barriers between the two countries, the Hanoverian successor designated by the Act of Settlement—demonstrated the dangers inherent in the system of having co-ordinate sovereign Parliaments under the same Crown, and forced on the English ministry and Parliament the concessions to Scotland embodied in the Act of Union.[2] Signal as the services were which the Scottish Parliament rendered to Scotland during its brief period of independence, that period was too brief to establish a tradition of parliamentary life sufficiently strong to preserve the Scottish Parliament from an incorporating union with the English Parliament into a Parliament of Great Britain—in favour of which all idea of a merely federal union was set aside[3]—or to stimulate either the Scottish peers and commoners in the Westminster Parliament or the Scottish electorate into any really independent action. From the moment of their appearance, the Scottish members, apart from their vigilant care for purely Scottish interests and their desire to prevent taxation from falling on Scotland, had hardly any motive except to support whatever ministry was in office.[4] Scottish members shared the appetite of their English colleagues for place-hunting and, managed by the Lord Advocate of Scotland,[5] constituted a solid body of voters on which the government could generally depend. Governmental influence predominated in the election of the representative peers.[6] Even more than in England was the electorate of the Scottish counties and burghs small and easily controlled. In the counties the number of electors fell as low as eight in Bute, with an average of about eighty. In the burghs,

[1] Dicey and Rait, 62–70, 152–60.    [2] Costin and Watson, i. 98–110.

[3] Dicey and Rait, 209–10, 222–3; for the detailed arrangements proposed by the Scottish publicist Ridpath, see W. L. Mathieson, *Scotland and the Union*, 121 *n.*

[4] Porritt, ii. 4, 7; Mathieson, *The Awakening of Scotland*, 21–3. Scottish opposition to legislation affecting Scotland was not always effective. See Turberville, *House of Lords*, 147.

[5] Porritt, ii. 8.    [6] Turberville, 158–9.

self-electing councils had since 1469 controlled the return of representatives to Parliament and formed a burgh electorate collectively hardly more than twelve or thirteen hundred strong.[1] It is evident that in counties and burghs alike the Scottish electoral system lent itself perfectly to the establishment of a régime of patronage and influence. The Scottish magnates were even more completely at the disposal of the ministry than the great English electoral managers, and Scottish seats never came on the market for sale.[2] Beyond the narrow limits of the electorate, the mass of the Scottish people dwelt remote from political affairs, taking greater interest, so far as the Presbyterian majority were concerned, in the Church courts of kirk-session, presbytery, synod and General Assembly, in which the democratic principle of election obtained.

*The Scottish administrative system*

If a popular principle prevailed in the Church, it did so nowhere else. Like the parliamentary system, Scottish administration was far removed from any sort of popular participation or control. Outside the burghs with their oligarchical magistracies, the country, Lowlands as well as Highlands, was until 1747 covered with the heritable jurisdictions attached to feudal superiorities, the abolition of which, paid for by a grant of £152,000 to their holders,[3] merely removed from the path of the government a powerful and ancient rival, and enabled it to reduce Scotland still more completely to the position of a ministerial preserve. With regard to Crown appointments, the administrative system of eighteenth-century Scotland fell from the outset under the sway of a "spoils system", and it has indeed been conjectured that this blight spread territorially southwards from the northern kingdom to England itself.[4]

*Limits of government through influence*

With all due emphasis laid on the universality of "influence" in the eighteenth-century constitution, it is evident that the system had its practical limitations. The machinery was undeniably powerful. The King seemed to have effective control

---

[1] C. S. Terry, *The Scottish Parliament, 1603–1707*, 56–7, 168. In rather over half the burghs, the trade-guilds had a share in the election.

[2] Porritt, ii. 140. It may be noted that Scots members needed no property qualification. On the Scots members in the House of Commons, see R. Pares, in 39 *Hist.* 233. The relationship of Scots electorates to their M.P.s needs re-examination. Though smaller than the English ones, these electorates may have been more independent. See W. L. Burn in 52 *L.Q.R.* 103.

[3] Grant Robertson, *Select Statutes, Cases and Documents* (5th edn.), 221–3; G. W. T. Omond, *The Lord Advocates of Scotland*, ii. 34–41; Mathieson, *Scotland and the Union*, 372–7.     [4] Hughes, *Studies in Administration and Finance*. 338

over the choice of his ministers. The government could directly or indirectly control a majority of elections. Its majority in the Commons, voting without much regard to the merits of the case, could decide disputed elections without appeal. Its ample patronage ensured steady support in both Houses, and the numerous personal links which patronage formed between the Lords and the predominantly aristocratic Lower House created a long and profound harmony between them. In an age when parliamentary proceedings were at least in theory secret, what took place in Parliament went for the most part unregarded by the mass of the electorate. It might well appear that these conditions gave the King a free hand in making and unmaking ministries, ensured to the men who enjoyed his confidence secure command of a parliamentary majority, and protected King, ministers and Parliament alike from all effectual criticism and opposition. In reality, the system never worked with quite so mechanical a perfection. And from the middle of the century, there were indications that its vitality was ebbing. Several processes were already at work towards this end both under George I and George II. Groups of ministers tended to draw further away from the King, and to acquire, though not always to the same extent and never very perfectly, a coherent and independent character. While a "formed opposition" was theoretically indefensible,[1] in actual practice elements of opposition revealed themselves and acted together in Parliament. However skilful the manipulation of patronage, there remained an undercurrent of antagonism to its systematic use as an instrument of power. Finally, the habit of tacit popular acquiescence in the conduct of government and policy was disturbed and broken as the prolonged political calm of early Hanoverian times was troubled by a rising tide of public interest in parliamentary affairs, the growth of journalism and parliamentary reporting, and the re-emergence of contentious questions on which political passions could be aroused.

When George I began his reign by putting his affairs in *The Inner* the hands of the Whigs, he did so advisedly, and with no *Cabinet* intention of creating a government dominated by them and independent of the Crown. In theory, his cabinets were composed of individual ministers selected by himself, if all drawn from one party. But within the large and loose-knit group of

[1] Costin and Watson, i. 388.

those who served in the outer or "nominal" Cabinet, an inner ring of ministers, closely united in mutual confidence, gradually tended to form. The formal and regular consultations of an "inner cabinet" or *conciliabulum* cannot with certainty be discerned before the years 1739–41, when, as has so often been the case, the need for greater concentration was revealed by the emergencies of war.[1] Yet throughout the long period of Walpole's ascendancy that development was so plainly foreshadowed as to have induced the common belief that Walpole was the first of English "Prime Ministers"—a belief indeed held by the peers who in 1741 framed a protest against the development of such an office.[2]

*Walpole as Prime Minister*

If the term is invested with its modern meaning, its use is certainly based on a misapprehension. Walpole did not, as his insecure position on George II's accession shows, enjoy any tenure independent of royal favour.[3] He did not choose his colleagues. When he fell from office, they did not resign with him. On the other hand, he seldom convoked a meeting of the whole formal Cabinet, preferring to work with a few intimate associates. He endeavoured to infuse a certain discipline among ministers. In 1729 he forced the resignation of Lord Townshend, whose position in the ministry had hitherto overshadowed his own, as in 1725 he had obtained the dismissal of Roxburgh from the Scottish Secretaryship. On the failure of his excise scheme in 1733, there was a further removal of dissentients such as Lords Chesterfield, Clinton, and Marchmont.[4]

*Later ministries of George II*

No such unity as that imposed by Walpole's strong personality existed in the ministries which held office in George II's later years. The government formed in 1742 under the nominal

---

[1] On the developments of these years, see R. R. Sedgwick, *The Inner Cabinet, 1739–41*, 34 *E.H.R.* 290; E. R. Turner suggested 1745 as the earliest date at which the existence of an Inner Cabinet could be traced. On the whole question, see W. R. Anson, *The Cabinet in the Seventeenth and Eighteenth Centuries*, 29 *E.H.R.* 56, 325; H. W. V. Temperley, *Inner and Outer Cabinets*, 31 *E.H.R.* 291; E. T. Williams, *The Cabinet in the Eighteenth Century*, 22 *Hist.* 240, and note in the same vol. 332-4; D. A. Winstanley, *George III and his First Cabinet*, 17 *E.H.R.* 678.

[2] Morley, *Walpole*, 164. See also the extract from the speech of Sandys on the preceding page. For the full text of the Protest, see *Lords' Protests*, ii. 176-7.

[3] On Walpole's position in 1727, see Morley, *Walpole*, 85-9.

[4] Lecky, *History of England*, i. 400-401; Mathieson, *Scotland and the Union*, 330-31.

headship of Lord Wilmington was rent with discord between Carteret, the Northern Secretary, and his colleagues. After Carteret's dismissal in 1744, discipline was still feebly maintained by Henry Pelham, who may be regarded as Prime Minister during the ensuing years. The imperfect coherence of the Cabinet in this period did not, however, mean that the King was able to assert complete control over its composition. The test came in 1745-6. At this time, the King thoroughly disliked his ministers. They had opposed his policy in Germany, turned out Carteret who sympathised with it, and tried to bring into office William Pitt, who had described Hanover as a "beggarly German electorate". But his attempt to fall back on Carteret, now Lord Granville, and his ally Bath failed completely. Learning of his consultations with their rivals, the Pelhams resigned. Within two days Granville and Bath had to admit their inability to form a government, and the Pelhams returned in triumph, bringing the obnoxious Pitt with them.[1] Nor were matters any better for the King when Henry Pelham died. The ministry of Newcastle was, indeed, weakened by the feud between the nominal premier, who refused to part with Crown patronage, and his colleagues Henry Fox, Secretary at War, and Pitt, now Paymaster of the Forces. The outbreak of the Seven Years' War brought on a crisis. Pitt resigned, Fox followed, and finally Newcastle, unable to hold any ministry together, took the same course. Still the King was impotent as a Cabinet-maker. His efforts to instal a government under Fox came to nothing. With the Duke of Devonshire, Pitt, distasteful as he was to the King, resumed office. George in despair turned to Newcastle, exclaiming "I do not look upon myself as King while I am in the hands of these scoundrels."[2] But Pitt's position proved impregnable. His dismissal in April 1757 led to an eleven-weeks interval in which no administration whatever was in existence. Finally, in June 1757, Newcastle was prevailed upon to come to the King's rescue. He consented to do so only on condition that Pitt served with him as Secretary of State.

Reviewing the whole period from Walpole's fall to the end *Decline of* of George II's reign, it may be said that the King's ability to *the King's* form and maintain ministries was steadily on the decline. The *control* prerogative to choose his ministers and to retain them in *ministries* *over his*

---

[1] Lecky, ii. 34-5.                    [2] Lecky, ii. 372.

power was restricted by the increasing ability of great political leaders to prescribe their own terms for accepting office, and to make impossible the position of any alternative government which he might hope to rely on. The King's favour was no guarantee of security of tenure. In theory he might retain full control over appointments to the Cabinet. In practice there was developing within the Cabinet an inner *Conciliabulum* of ministers, united by links which he could not break, prepared to conduct his business on their own terms, and to resign if these proved unacceptable to him. It was from this inner *Conciliabulum* and not from the larger nominal Cabinet, that the modern Cabinet system was to grow.[1]

*Ministers and Parliament*
As ministers thus drew apart from the King, they necessarily drew nearer not only to one another but to Parliament. By 1742 Walpole had won the royal confidence which he did not possess in 1727. Yet it did not avert his defeat in the Commons and his resignation. The failure of Carteret and the success of Pitt similarly proved the value of parliamentary as distinct from merely royal support. Ability to manage this body was essential. For this purpose, the mere manipulation of "influence" was not enough.

*Formation of an opposition*
No doubt the stresses of war in 1742, 1744, 1746, and 1757 played their accustomed part in hastening the pace of constitutional advance. At no time, however, even under conditions of complete external peace, did Parliament present that appearance of disciplined unanimity which a too rigidly mechanical conception of the system of "influence" would suggest. "Formed opposition" might be repudiated, yet opposition of a sort was never lacking.[2] It might be led by Whigs out of office, like Walpole and Townshend from 1717 to 1720, Walpole's ejected colleagues during the next two decades, and the "Boy Patriots" who under Pitt challenged the Wilmington-Carteret ministry. Moreover, if Whigs might be, Tories must be in opposition, and the Parlia-

[1] Williams, 22 *Hist.* 333.
[2] Lecky, i. 438-48. While organised opposition may not have existed in the eighteenth-century Parliament, opposition as such was by no means discredited, and the tradition of a "Country" party as against the "Court" party—inherited from the seventeenth century—still persisted. Many constituencies, e.g. Northamptonshire, always returned Tories from 1689 and throughout the eighteenth century. Many members prided themselves on not being placemen or intriguers for patronage.

ments of the early Hanoverian period were never so entirely dominated by the Whig ministers of the Crown that the Tory party was threatened with extinction. Led in the Commons by Sir Thomas Hanmer and Sir William Wyndham, in the Upper House by Lords Harcourt and Trevor, and outside Parliament by Bolingbroke,[1] who returned to England in 1723 after nine unsatisfactory years at the Court of the Pretender, and was restored to his estates but excluded from the Lords, the Tory party, except for a dwindling minority of Jacobites led by William Shippen, became reconciled to the new dynasty, abandoned its outworn belief in Divine Right, and prepared to challenge the Whig monopoly of government. The connexion of government with party was still sufficiently weak to enable Tories from time to time to be admitted to minor offices.[2] The majority, allied with the malcontent Whigs, kept steadfastly to opposition.

It was an increasingly divided and difficult body that assembled *Attacks* in Parliament during the middle years of the century, less amen- *on the* able to "influence", more inclined to look askance at the means *system of influence* by which it was maintained. Critics of the Septennial Act advocated triennial or even annual Parliaments.[3] A motion in favour of the latter was in 1745 defeated by only 145 to 113 votes. The old jealousy of "placemen" had never wholly abated. Bills for their exclusion from the Commons had been frequently introduced—for example in 1730, 1734, and 1740—though rejected in the Lords.[4] An Act of 1743 disqualified commissioners of the Irish revenues and the navy and victualling offices, and officials in a large number of other departments, from being elected.[5] This measure, it is true, effected only a very inconsiderable reform. The private interests of too many members weakened their concern to maintain the purity of public life. But it is indicative of a sense that the independence of the legislature was being endangered by executive encroachment.

Outside the walls of Parliament, in fact, movements of public *Develop-* feeling were evident to which the most self-interested of members *ment of* could not be quite indifferent, and against which even a govern- *public* ment fully equipped with every device which "influence" afforded *opinion*

---

[1] For Bolingbroke's views on party, see H. N. Fieldhouse, *Bolingbroke and the Idea of Non-Party Government*, 33 *Hist.* 41.

[2] For the relations between the Tories and the "Broad-Bottom Administration" of 1744, see R. W. Greaves, *A Scheme for the Counties*, 48 *E.H.R.* 630.

[3] Lecky, ii. 63-5.   [4] Porritt, i. 215-17.   [5] Costin and Watson, i. 131-2.

could not stand. Under the tranquil régime of Walpole, indeed, indications of political restlessness could be seen in the popular demand for more frequent Parliaments. Occasional assertions were made in the larger and more politically active constituencies such as London and Westminster that members should act on the instructions of their constituents.[1] In his periodical, the *Craftsman*, Bolingbroke addressed himself to the task so successfully performed by the pamphleteers of the last generation of educating public opinion on political questions, and in his *Idea of a Patriot King* attacked the constitutional perversion by which the Whigs had imposed themselves as virtually perpetual ministers of the Crown. Public interest in the proceedings of Parliament was stimulated by the steady growth of parliamentary reporting. Though the reporting of debates was treated as a breach of privilege, and a London bookseller named Cave was imprisoned and forced to apologise for having thus offended, his *Gentleman's Magazine* founded in 1731 began from 1736 to make the reporting of debates a regular practice, which the rival *London Magazine* also adopted.[2] Both persisted in their course although the Commons condemned it by resolution in 1738 and the Lords brought the editors of both magazines before their bar to make apology in 1747. How high the tide of political feeling outside the House could rise was shown when Pitt was dismissed in 1757. "It rained gold boxes",[3] and these tokens of public confidence in the fallen minister demonstrated that "influence" alone was unable to keep a popular minister out of office at least in time of crisis, though Pitt's subsequent alliance with Newcastle, the most skilful political manager of the age, proved that it might be necessary to keep him in.

*Personal control asserted by George III*
The contest between the conception of a government wholly depending on a Parliament dominated by royal "influence", and one in which ministries mainly independent of the Crown governed by virtue of their own parliamentary strength came to a

---

[1] Emden, *The People and the Constitution*, 10.

[2] Hanson, *Government and the Press*, 76-83; Costin and Watson, 1. 217; D. M. Ford, *The Growth of the Freedom of the Press*, 4 *E.H.R.* 1. Such unauthorised reports were commonly open to the objection of being garbled to suit party interests. Samuel Johnson, in his reports for the *Gentleman's Magazine*, took care, as he said, "not to let the Whig dogs have the best of it".

[3] Williams, *Life of William Pitt*, 1. 311-12.

head in the efforts of George III to recover for the King in person that power, which the Revolutionary settlement had seemed to preserve to him, of controlling the composition of ministries and maintaining their parliamentary position. In many respects, he seemed in a stronger position to do so than either George I or George II. English by birth and predilection, he "gloried in the name of Briton".[1] Unlike his two predecessors, whose interests had for the most part been confined to foreign policy, and to the military forces (though not the navy, to them a wholly unfamiliar service), he was prepared to concern himself with every department of government. Still in early manhood, he was not embarrassed by the presence of any successor around whom an opposition could with constitutional propriety be formed. He took the duties of kingship conscientiously. The whole force of his simple and stubborn nature was thrown into the fulfilment of his mother's injunction to be a King. He made it his ideal to emancipate the Crown from the trammels which the Whig oligarchy had fastened on it and raise it above party to the elevated and disinterested position depicted by Bolingbroke in his *Patriot King*. Conditions seemed to favour the attempt. His effective range of choice was enlarged as the Tories, among whom Jacobitism had since the '45 become extinct, rallied to a King Hanoverian by descent indeed, but by descent alone. Meanwhile the Whig groups, no longer able to justify their monopoly by posing as the saviours of the Protestant succession, had become resolved into a swarm of mutually jealous cliques, uniting and dividing with no worthier motive than to bargain effectively for the spoils of office.[2] There was, moreover, plenty of support for a policy which aimed ostensibly at setting the national interest above the squalid aims of rival political factions, and the hungry followers who craved the "loaves and fishes" which office provided. The feeling that it was wrong to cabal in order to force on the King advisers he would not otherwise have chosen was still

---

[1] Possibly he meant to include the Scots in this description. And possibly he said "Britain". For a detailed study of the role of George III, see R. Pares, *George III and the Politicians*, 5 *T.R.H.S.* i. 127, in which the contrast between his constitutional action and that of George II is clearly drawn. The same point is made by H. Butterfield, *George III and the Constitution*, 43 *Hist.* 14; see also his *George III and the Historians*.

[2] The composition of the House of Commons in 1761 has been analysed from this point of view by L. B. Namier, *England in the Age of the American Revolution*, i. 234-47; see also his article, *The Circular Letters, an Eighteenth-Century "Whip"*, 44 *E.H.R.* 588.

strong. Men so eminent as Carteret in the last generation and Pitt in the present concurred in accepting the ideal of a ministry chosen freely by the King without regard to party.

*George III's earlier experiments*

The twenty-two years of George III's personal government proved beyond doubt that the object he set before himself was unattainable. The reasons for his failure were partly inherent in his character and training. He had been bred in the backstairs atmosphere of his mother's Court and was wholly inexperienced in political affairs. He came to require from his ministers not an independent intelligence and initiative, but literal compliance with his directions even against their own better judgment. These defects were not long in being revealed. It was natural enough that the new reign should begin with the displacement of the ministers who had served in the old. Within a few months a number of fresh appointments to office were made, including that of the King's confidant, Lord Bute, as Secretary of State. Some of the existing ministers were displaced. Pitt and his brother-in-law Temple resigned in October 1761, and their posts were conferred on Lord Egremont and the Duke of Bedford. In the following May Newcastle followed his former colleagues into political exile. It soon appeared that this re-shuffle, by which the King played off one group of Whig leaders against another, left him very much where he had been. The link of common loyalty to the Crown was inadequate, and the King found it impossible to hold any ministry together in the relationship with himself which he desired. Isolated among his colleagues, Bute found his position untenable and gave it up in April 1763. With George Grenville, his successor as first minister, the King found it impossible to get on, but no satisfactory alternative could be found. Grenville was succeeded by Lord Rockingham, whose administration, badly led and weakly supported, never obtained the confidence of the Houses or the King. The ministry which followed, nominally led by Pitt, now Earl of Chatham, and the Duke of Grafton, proved feebler still. Uncontrolled by Pitt, whose illness made him a perpetual absentee, the ministry exhibited dissensions which incapacitated it alike for the framing of a coherent policy and for establishing its influence in Parliament. Grafton's resignation in 1770 placed in power the one politician of the day, Lord North, who combined readiness to carry out the King's constitutional ideas and the political adroitness necessary to guarantee the security of his own parliamentary position. While he held office, the King realised his ideal of a "departmental" ministry, each great officer of state being directly related to the King, and to his colleagues only through their common service.

It is necessary to insist on Lord North's skill as a parliamentary *Technique* leader, his deft handling of the Commons, his aptitude for finance, *of North's* his conciliatory disposition, and his ability in debate as essential *government* factors in his long tenure of office, which lasted until 1782. None *ment* the less is it true that his position did not rest on these qualities alone. Since his accession, the King had availed himself of every instrument by which the Whig ascendancy had for so many years been maintained. Royal displeasure and royal favour were part of the essential technique of government. Newcastle's fall had been accompanied by the dismissal equally of great Whig noblemen like Rockingham from their Lord Lieutenancies and of the humblest clients who had owed administrative appointments to Whig patronage.[1] On the other hand, the number of placemen and pensioners steadily grew. A solid and useful core of ministerial supporters, composed of officials under the Crown, took shape, as in Anne's reign, under the name of "King's Friends", of whom the best that can be said is that they were ready to lend their help and experience in promoting the King's business, whatever government he might choose to put in office.[2]

It was natural that the dispossessed Whigs in Parliament *The Whig* should resent the thoroughness with which their own use of *opposition* influence had been turned against them. A nobler expression was given to their self-interested discontent by the genius of Edmund Burke. The hitherto prevalent conception of party as a mere factious confederacy to obtain or preserve the spoils of office was transformed into that of "a body of men united, for promoting by their joint endeavours, the national interest, upon some particular principle in which they are all agreed".[3] Thus inspired, the

[1] For details, see Namier, *England in the Age of the American Revolution*, i. 468-483.

[2] Namier, i. 257-62, places at 43 the number of civil servants as distinct from mere sinecurists with seats in the Commons. But about 250 in all had some material inducement to vote for the administration.

[3] Burke, *Thoughts on the Present Discontents*, in *Select Works* (ed. E. J. Payne), i. 82; Costin and Watson, i. 396-7.

Whigs of the Rockingham connexion found themselves gradually assuming the rôle of critics of the whole principle on which the ascendancy of the party had in former years been founded. Among the reforms they advocated were the rights of electors to make a free choice of their representative even if the Commons should declare him incapable of sitting, a more impartial adjudication on disputed elections, publication of division lists, the acceptance of parliamentary reporting, and above all, the reduction of those means of influence which the patronage of the Crown provided.

*Demo-* Outside Parliament there were more radical movements
*cratic ideas* for reform, going beyond any goal which the Rockingham Whigs considered desirable. Doctrines of popular sovereignty emphasising the dependence of Parliament on the electorate and the subordination of the individual member to his constituents continued the democratic tradition of seventeenth-century Puritanism into this more secular and political age.[1] As in the preceding century, it implied the pretension that the people could assert superiority over the three estates of the legislature. During the crisis of the Seven Years' War, George II had truly remarked to Pitt, "You have taught me to look for the sense of my subjects in another place than the House of Commons".[2] Pitt's whole career, indeed, curiously combines an implicit acceptance of the predominance of the King in government with an equally acute perception that popular support was the substantial basis of his own political power. To Dr. Johnson, the position seemed to be that whereas Walpole had been a minister given by the King to the people, Pitt was a minister given by the people to the King.[3] It is paradoxical but not surprising that, while Pitt on the one hand sometimes rejected the principle of party government and subscribed to that of royal predominance in a "departmental ministry", he inclined on the other hand to support schemes for remodelling the parliamentary system in order to bring the legislature and the nation into closer contact.

*The* This question was raised in an acute form by the events con-
*Middlesex* nected with the election of 1768 in Middlesex.[4] Returning from
*Election*

---

[1] On instructions to members in the eighteenth century, see Porritt, i. 266-72, and Emden, 16-22.     [2] Williams, *Life of William Pitt*, i. 301.
[3] *Boswell's Life of Johnson* (ed. Birkbeck Hill), ii. 195-6. Dr. Johnson added the words, "as an adjunct".     Costin and Watson, i. 229-35.

the exile into which he had been forced to flee by the general warrant proceedings, when the Commons declared that his privilege as a member of Parliament did not protect him from arrest for seditious libel, John Wilkes came forward as a candidate for the county and was returned at the head of the poll. Meanwhile, however, the proceedings against him with regard to No. 45 were concluded by a sentence of fine and imprisonment. The result was an outbreak of popular rioting in the name of "Wilkes and Liberty", to which the government retaliated by inducing the Commons to vote Wilkes's expulsion. An intervening by-election had demonstrated the temper of Middlesex by the success of his supporter, Serjeant Glynn. In that following on Wilkes's expulsion, Wilkes himself again headed the poll. The House thereupon declared him incapable of sitting. In a third contest, when he was again triumphant, his election was pronounced void and his opponent Luttrell held to have been duly returned. The action of the House seems at first sight constitutionally indefensible. Going apparently beyond its admitted jurisdiction to suspend or expel a member, it had declared an individual incapable not merely of taking his seat, but also of being elected thereto. Yet it might be argued that expulsion, as distinct from suspension, involved incapacitation from being re-elected, and there were precedents for such a declaration of incapacity to sit. On this reasoning, it might be urged that votes given to Wilkes had been thrown away, and Luttrell had obtained a majority of those validly cast. On the other hand, it seems clear that incapacity for election ought to be grounded on law, and not on resolutions of the House, and, moreover, since *Ashby v. White*, it was sound law that the right of the elector to vote was a piece of property of which he could not be deprived save by a Common Law court.[1]

Whatever be the correct legal view regarding this difficult case, the line taken by the Commons was an affront to the notion of popular sovereignty, and it engendered an agitation for radical constitutional reform. Numerous petitions from counties and boroughs protested against the violation of the rights of free-

*Agitation for reform*

---

[1] See Holdsworth, x. 540-44, for a full discussion of this whole question. In K. Feiling, *The Second Tory Party*, 108-9, the suggestion appears that there were actually *four* contests in Middlesex.

holders. Large political meetings made their first regular appearance as an element in English public life, and with them came the birth of political societies, the first of which was the Society of Supporters of the Bill of Rights, formed in 1769 in order to uphold Wilkes and to promote electoral reform, annual Parliaments, the exclusion of placemen, the subordination of the member to his constituents and similar objects.[1] In this society, and the Constitutional Society formed by a schism in its ranks, a radical party came into being.[2]

*The Press*     This rising popular interest in parliamentary and political affairs is well illustrated in the history of the press. The increase in the number of publications can be indicated by reference to the stamp duty imposed on periodicals in the reign of Anne. Between 1753 and 1774 their issue rose from seven and a half to twelve and a quarter millions annually.[3] Governmental control by means of general warrants had gone by the latter period. The question whether the intention or nature of publications was libellous was still reserved to the judges in prosecutions for libel. Juries were still confined to the questions whether authorship and publication had been proved against the persons accused of them. In these circumstances, government could hope by the aid of the judges to repress criticism, while refractory juries might thwart authority by returning such verdicts as "guilty of publishing *only*", and in some cases refusing even to do that.[4] Comment on political matters was increasing, mainly in the form of public correspondence, of which the *Letters of Junius* are the most famous example. Arising from these letters came the prosecution of the publisher and printers of *Junius*—Woodfall, Almon, and Miller—in 1770. Almon was found guilty of publishing, and fined, Miller was acquitted by a London jury at Guildhall, and Woodfall found guilty of printing and publishing *only*, a verdict which in the end secured him against the threat of a fresh trial.[5] Meanwhile the right of parliamentary reporting had been at least *de facto* obtained. By 1777, despite the increase of the stamp duty

---

[1] G. S. Veitch, *Genesis of Parliamentary Reform*, 29–34; Lecky, *History of England*, iii. 372–5.

[2] Veitch, 31; Lecky, iii. 374.

[3] Lecky, iii. 441. This duty was reduced in 1836 and abolished in 1855.

[4] On the function of the jury in libel cases, see Hanson, *Government and the Press*, 18–23, Lecky, iii. 441–4.          [5] Lecky, iii. 476–83.

by one halfpenny in 1776, seven daily newspapers appeared in London.[1] The practice of reporting debates was growing. In 1771 the question was raised in the Commons by Colonel Onslow, and a brisk struggle ensued between the House and the City authorities. The latter placed a number of printers collusively on trial before Wilkes and another City magistrate, who naturally acquitted them. An attempt to execute the Speaker's warrant for the arrest of the printers was defeated by invoking against it the exclusive jurisdiction of the City within its own precincts. The Commons replied by ordering the commitment of the Lord Mayor and another City magistrate, and by summoning Wilkes to the bar of the House, where he steadfastly refused to answer. The proceedings aroused further popular outbreaks, and the printers who were the central figures in the whole episode remained at liberty throughout. Thenceforward no attempt was made by the House to interfere with freedom of reporting.[2]

To some extent Parliament gave way before the popular *Modifica-* pressure evidenced during these years. In 1770 a statute enabled *tions of* actions to be brought at any time against persons entitled to *privilege.* parliamentary privilege, and deprived members' servants of their *Act* immunity from arrest.[3] The jurisdiction of the House over offenders who had injured members in their private capacity was allowed to fall into disuse. More important was the Act of 1770 which substituted for the jurisdiction of the whole House over disputed elections that of a committee of fifteen, thirteen chosen by ballot and two by the rival candidates.[4] Though this device was to some extent weakened by the revisory power of the House over the composition of the tribunal—the removal of able opponents being described as "knocking the brains out of the Committee"—it was so far an improvement on the old system that in 1774 a further Act made it perpetual.[5] Beyond these points advance hardly proceeded. Reform of the electoral system, advocated by Chatham in his proposal of 1770 to give one additional member to each county, and the proposal for shorter Parliaments to which he became converted in the following year, made no headway

---

[1] Lecky, iii. 476.
[2] Lecky, iii. 483; Costin and Watson, i. 236, 311.
[3] Porritt, *Unreformed House of Commons*, i. 571.
[4] Porritt, i. 540-41. The Act was passed against the opposition of the King and his ministers. Costin and Watson, i. 140.    [5] Porritt, i. 542.

even under such august patronage.[1] More representative of the
average Whig view was Burke, the opponent of shorter Parliaments, of electoral mandates to members, which he condemned
in a speech at Bristol in 1774,[2] and of any alteration in the framework of the electoral system. By degrees, however, the abuse of
"influence" by the Crown slowly urged the Whigs along the path
towards an administrative reform. A Place Act, often but unsuccessfully moved for in the past, was foreshadowed in the famous Whig
resolution of 1780, moved by Dunning, that "the power of the
Crown has increased, is increasing, and ought to be diminished",[3]
and became the programme of the party when it assumed office in
1782. Its aim was only to eliminate the influence of the Crown
from the legislature, and not to weaken that of the great political
patrons, still less to strengthen the influence of the people. Even
to accomplish this limited purpose only proved possible when the
pressure of war had broken the government based on "influence"
by which North enjoyed his twelve years' tenure of power.

## iv

*Beginnings of overseas expansion*  A new chapter in the history of English government had begun
in the seventeenth century, on lines originally laid down by exist-
ing tradition and practice, but destined to pursue a course which
differentiated them with increasing sharpness from those of constitutional development in the mother-country. Under the Tudors
the last fragment of English territory on the European mainland
was lost with the capture of Calais in 1558. Since that date, the
Crown had held no similar European possession except Dunkirk, acquired by Cromwell in 1658 but ceded to France by
Charles II four years later. In the reign of Elizabeth, the kingdom
of Ireland, the Channel Islands, representing the last fragments of
the ancient Norman duchy, and the fief of Man constituted the
only overseas possessions of the English Crown. Their coming
expansion was presaged by the grants made to English mariners
during the Elizabethan age, giving authority to acquire lands to
be governed under the Queen by laws and ordinances "as near as

[1] Williams, *Life of William Pitt*, ii. 267. For Pitt's views on reform in 1742,
see Williams, i. 90.
[2] Burke, *Works* (ed. 1826), 18-22; Costin and Watson, i. 392; Emden, 22 ff.
[3] Lecky, v. 96.

conveniently might be to the laws of the nation".[1] No permanent
settlement was effected under Elizabeth, but in 1606 her name and
the earlier schemes associated with it were perpetuated in the
foundation of the colony of Virginia, a term meant at first to
apply to the whole region of the North American seaboard intended for occupation by English emigrants, though subsequently
confined to the settlement based on Jamestown. During the
seventeenth century the remainder of this vast domain and the
adjacent Atlantic and Caribbean Islands came to be planted with
a large number of separate colonies, exhibiting forms of government of diverse kinds.

These settlements of English subjects in territories overseas *Earliest*
were not due primarily to the initiative of the Crown, which *types of*
was indeed too weak and impoverished to embark upon distant *govern-*
and dangerous enterprises calling for a large initial outlay and *ment*
likely to yield a delayed and hazardous return. They were, like
the contemporary foundations of English commercial establishments in Asia by the East India Company, the work of private
enterprise. The Crown's sole function was, in the first instance, to
confer on the grantees authority to govern lands acquired in its
name. For this purpose it could avail itself of one or other of two
prerogative powers—the prerogative to grant a fief, and the prerogative to grant a charter.[2] So far back as the reign of Henry VII
the former had been used to authorise the Cabots to acquire and
hold land as vassals of the Crown, enjoying a monopoly of trade
and paying to the Crown one-fifth of the profits. A similar grant
was made to Ashurst and his associates in 1501–2, and to Sir
Humphrey Gilbert in 1583, under which he temporarily held
Newfoundland.[3] In the seventeenth century such grants were
made to the Calvert family—first, and ineffectively, for Newfoundland, and then for Maryland—and to other grantees for Barbados
and the Caribbean Islands.[4] Later foundations on the same model
were established by the grant of the Carolinas to Clarendon and
a group of associates in 1663; to James, Duke of York, for the
colony of New York conquered from the Dutch in 1664; and to

---

[1] H. E. Egerton, *Short History of British Colonial Policy*, 17.
[2] A. Berriedale Keith, *Constitutional History of the First British Empire*, 3.
[3] Keith, 37.
[4] *Cambridge History of the British Empire*, i. 143-6, 168-70; V. T. Harlow, *Barbados, 1625–85*, 7-10.

William Penn for Pennsylvania in 1680.[1] Elsewhere the model
tended to be the grant to a chartered company. Of this type were
the original Virginia Colony of 1606, the Bermuda Company of
1615, the Plymouth Company of 1620, and the Massachusetts Bay
Colony of 1628 founded by grants made under the Plymouth
Company's charter setting up a Council for the planting of the
"northern regions now styled New England in America", and
acquiring a separate charter of its own in the following year.[2]
Beyond these colonies, whose origin was due to charter, fresh
waves of emigration created new settlements elsewhere in New
England, such as Connecticut and Rhode Island, which possessed
no charters, were not the result of enfeoffment, and represented
in the fullest form the wholly independent initiative of groups
of pioneer settlers owing only the slenderest obligation towards
the Crown.[3]

*Tendency
towards
local
autonomy*

On first impression, the fundamental constitutional difference
between the main types of colony would appear to be that
between colonies originating as fiefs and those originating by
charters. In the former, for which the palatine organisation of
Durham was the general model, the grant of authority to the
proprietor or proprietors might be so extensive as to preclude
the development of local self-government. In the latter that
system made an early appearance. The Virginian Charter centred
authority in a Council in London, but in 1619 its remote and
unsatisfactory control was supplemented by the formation of a
General Assembly in the colony itself, comprising the Governor
with a Council and a Lower House of two burgesses from each
town or hundred. This institution, surviving the vacation of
the Company's charter in 1624, remained a permanent element
in Virginian government while the British connexion lasted.[4] The
Massachusetts charter of 1629 contained no provision requiring
the governing body to remain in England, and in 1630 the
General Court sat for the first time in the colony itself.[5] In practice,

---

[1] *C.H.B.E.* i. 248-50, 252-3, 254-5.

[2] *C.H.B.E.* i. 78-9, 85, 147-8, 157-61; for the first Massachusetts Charter, see
W. A. MacDonald, *Documentary Source Book of American History*, 23-6.

[3] *C.H.B.E.*, i. 162-4. These colonies received royal charters in 1662 and 1663
respectively, lost them under James II and recovered them under William III.
But their charters virtually confirmed existing government arrangements.

[4] *C.H.B.E.* i. 152.          [5] *C.H.B.E.* i. 160.

however, it proved difficult to maintain too sharply this distinction between proprietory and chartered colonies. If settlers were to be attracted to the former, it must necessarily be difficult to give them a constitutional position comparing too unfavourably with that existing elsewhere, even in democratic commonwealths like Rhode Island which had virtually set up such governmental arrangements as they pleased. Most of the colonies tended therefore in their earliest days to assume a popular self-directing authority which removed them from the orbit of royal power. Among the Puritan settlers of New England the spirit of popular sovereignty manifested itself strongly. The Plymouth colonists during their voyage to America on the *Mayflower* had indeed by a species of social contract formally constituted themselves a body-politic,[1] and the autonomous principle thus expressed came to characterise to a greater or less degree all the communities of English subjects settled on American soil.

Against this centrifugal tendency, facilitated by distance and slowness of communications, the authority of the home government at length began to assert itself. During the first two Stuart reigns, the Crown, if unable to direct effectively the affairs of the nascent colonies, at least succeeded in preserving colonial business within the exclusive domain of the Prerogative. Parliamentary interference, which might perhaps have been theoretically justified on such grounds as that certain statutes like the Act of Supremacy had been made applicable to all the Queen's dominions, was denied.[2] The collapse of royal authority in 1642 opened the field to parliamentary intrusion. In the colonies, it is true, the opportunity was taken to attempt to eliminate all external authority. In 1643 Massachusetts, Connecticut, New Haven, and Plymouth formed the Confederacy of New England to co-operate for such common concerns as defence, migration and Indian policy, under a body of eight commissioners, two from each province. The claim of Parliament to legislate for the colonies was rejected. Three other colonies combined in 1644 to

*Parliamentary sovereignty imposed on the colonies*

---

[1] *C.H.B.E.* i. 158; W. A. MacDonald, *Documentary Source Book of American History*, 19.

[2] *C.H.B.E.* i. 148, 151; Keith, *Constitutional History of the First British Empire*, 4-5.

obtain a parliamentary patent enabling them to erect their own form of government. In 1649 Virginia, supported by Barbados, Bermuda, and Antigua, rebelled against the regicide Republic. But the Long Parliament, which had established a commission on colonial affairs in 1643, reduced the rebels to obedience, and gave effect to its authority by passing legislation applying to them all, such as the Navigation Act of 1651.[1]

*Legislative restrictions on colonial trade*

The doctrines of parliamentary sovereignty thus enunciated were fully applied after the Restoration. Valued rather as sources of supply than as areas for immigration and settlement, except by the least desirable members of English society, the colonies found themselves enveloped in a network of imperial commercial regulation reposing on statute. The Navigation Act of 1660 restricted colonial trade to ships owned in England, Ireland, or the colonies and manned by crews three-fourths of whom must be subjects of the English Crown, and forbade the export of certain commodities except to England, Ireland, or an English colony.[2] Later Acts forbade the import of foreign goods into the colonies save as re-exports from England burdened with English dues and customs, and proscribed the manufacture in the colonies of certain commodities which might compete with English products.[3]

*Administrative system*

The imposition of this legislative control naturally involved the creation of an appropriate administrative machinery. In principle, responsibility for commercial regulation fell on the Governor, whose duties were in practice performed, or omitted, by an official styled the naval officer or clerk of the naval office.[4] From 1673 there developed a revenue staff, comprising one or more collectors for each colony, a comptroller and surveyor-general, and subordinate officials, in receipt of salaries borne on the home customs establishment.[5] Reinforcing their activities were

---

[1] On the constitutional history of the colonies during the Civil War, see G. L. Beer, *Origins of the British Colonial System*, 340 ff., and H. E. Egerton, *Short History of British Colonial Policy*, 57-66. For the Navigation Act, see Gardiner, *Documents* (5th edn.), 268-71.

[2] Grant Robertson, 3-13; G. L. Beer, *The Old Colonial System*, i. 58-77. 130-38, 167-8.

[3] G. B. Hertz, *The Old Colonial System*, 37; Beer, i. 77-9. For a convenient résumé, see the document printed by S. E. Morison, *Documents and Sources for the American Revolution*, 74-83.

[4] L. W. Labaree, *Royal Government in America* 104-5, 120-1.

[5] Beer, i. 280-92.

the Admiralty Courts—sometimes commissioned by the Lord High Admiral directly, elsewhere by the Governor as Vice-Admiral, and dealing with revenue cases without a jury—whose jurisdiction could ultimately be made effective by the power of the Royal Navy itself.[1] In these ways the Treasury and the Admiralty were brought into connexion with colonial administration.

Under the Restoration monarchy it seemed possible that the *Colonial* links between the home government and the colonies would be *government in* drawn even closer. Though charters were granted by which *the* proprietary governments were established in Carolina, New *Restora-* York, New Jersey, the Bahamas, and Pennsylvania, and companies *tion period* in Connecticut and Rhode Island, the Council for Plantations pressed on the Crown in 1661 the desirability of converting all colonial governments into direct governments by the Crown, as Virginia had been since the forfeiture of its charter in 1624.[2] In New Hampshire the governor began to be a royal nominee, and the Crown reserved the right to disallow legislation and to hear appeals.[3] In 1684 the charter of Massachusetts was forfeited, and it became, and thenceforth remained, a royal province.[4] Under James II this plan achieved a wide though somewhat illusory success. Already proprietor of New York, the King converted it into a royal province, administered by the Crown's officials, with an ample standing revenue, complete control over expenditure, and full legislative authority exercised through a nominated Council. There existed no popular assembly, and the Crown reserved the right of disallowance and of hearing appeals.[5] In 1685 the governor of Massachusetts was empowered to apply the same system to that colony and to New Hampshire, and in 1686 the forfeiture of the Connecticut and Rhode Island charters enabled them to be included. In 1688 New York and New Jersey were added to what was now styled the Dominion of New England.[6]

---

[1] Beer, i. 292-300. On the connexion of Privy Council, Treasury, and Admiralty with the colonies, see Beer, i. 264-5.

[2] Keith, 62.                                    [3] Keith, 108.

[4] Keith, 107-8. On the government of Massachusetts after 1684, see Egerton, 97-8.

[5] Under proprietary rule, New York had a small representative assembly, deficient in financial power, and subject to the negative voice of the proprietor and governor. Keith, 92-6; compare 109.                    [6] Keith, 109-18.

*The Re-*
*volution of*
*1688 in the*
*colonies*

Such an absolutist system, even if it had the merit of co-ordinating civil and military government efficiently under the Crown, had no great chance of survival. Its control of taxation, its enforcement of the trade laws, its supervision of grants of lands, and its efforts at religious toleration all awakened colonial hostility, and the Revolution of 1688 in England was accompanied by a collapse of the colonial administrative system.[1] The post-Revolutionary monarchy proved itself unable to stay completely the tendency towards colonial autonomy. In Massachusetts the new charter of 1691 vested the appointment of the governor in the Crown, gave him a veto over the legislation of the General Court, and reserved a power of disallowance, but it provided the royal authority with a seriously inadequate basis of support. There was no sufficient standing revenue. The General Court, chosen by the freeholders of the colony, elected the Governor's Council and appointed to executive and judicial office, while the governor's military power was circumscribed by his inability to exercise martial law without his Council's consent or to compel men to serve beyond the bounds of the colony. The subordination of Massachusetts, more apparent than real, was just sufficiently evident to remind the colonists of what they had lost and tempt them to seek to recover it.[2] Elsewhere the progress towards autonomy proceeded to a similar or even greater extent. New York obtained a representative assembly, the New Jerseys reverted to the control of their proprietors (which in the western half of the province meant the whole body of freeholders) and Connecticut and Rhode Island resumed full enjoyment of their former free constitutions.[3]

*Attempts*
*at unifica-*
*tion by*
*the Crown*

Against this tendency, which meant the decline of royal authority and the negation of colonial unity, the Crown did what it could by unifying colonial administration and substituting royal for proprietorial or company government. Thus Lord Bellomont was in 1697 commissioned as governor of New York, New Hampshire, and Massachusetts, and Captain-General of Connecticut, Rhode Island, and New Jersey.[4] Pennsylvania was

---

[1] On the effects of the Revolution of 1688 on the American colonies, see
C.H.B.E. i. 280-83.
[2] Keith, 143-7; for the text of the charter, see MacDonald, 84-90.
[3] Keith, 150.                                      [4] Keith, 148-9.

included from 1692 to 1701 within the sphere of the governor of
New York. Maryland passed for twenty-three years under a royal
governor.[1]

The number of royal governors slowly increased. They had *Increase in*
existed in Jamaica from 1661, in Barbados from 1663, the Leeward *number of*
Islands from 1671, and Bermuda from 1684. When the proprietors *Royal Provincies*
of the Carolinas got into difficulties and surrendered their grants, a
royal administration was set up—in South Carolina from 1719, and
in North Carolina, separately administered since 1712, in 1729.[2]
Georgia, founded in 1732 as a proprietary colony but with an
administrative system largely subject to royal control and dependent for supply on grants from the British Parliament, became
formally a royal colony in 1754.[3]

Newly annexed territories were subjected to royal control from *Conquered*
the beginning. Yet extreme diversity marked their constitutional *and ceded colonies*
character. Nova Scotia, ceded by France in 1713, had, owing to
the influence of British settlers, been allowed to follow the same
line as the older settled colonies and obtained an assembly in
1758. Prince Edward Island, separated therefrom in 1769, did the
like in 1773.[4] Certain royal governments founded on conquests
were not so organised. The general rule in fact was that while
colonies ceded by a civilised state retained their own private
law, their public law was created by the Crown. Gibraltar,
acquired in 1713, remained under military rule until 1720, and
though English law was introduced by letters patent in 1721, the
colony continued to be strictly controlled by the Crown, as also
did Minorca, where Spanish law was suffered to remain in force.[5]
A more important example of this kind was Canada. The Crown's
original intention of founding a government of the normal type,
announced in 1763, proved unsuitable to Canadian conditions since
the large French population of the province was wholly unfamiliar
with the representative system and knew only the working of a
despotic monarchy.[6] The Quebec Act of 1774 entirely discarded
the original proposal. It created a governor and a nominated
Council with authority to legislate but not to tax—endowed,

---

[1] Keith, 152-9.                       [2] Keith, 167-8.
[3] Keith, 170. For the Georgia Charter, see MacDonald, 95-103.
[4] Keith, 168-9.                       [5] Keith, 170.
[6] For the proclamation of 1763, see Morison, 1-4; R. Coupland, *The Quebec Act*, 35-9.

however, with a standing revenue by a British statute, the Quebec
Revenue Act. Control of the military forces was entrusted to the
governor.[1] The constitutional difference between the two varieties
of colony established by conquest was made clear in 1774 by the
decision in *Campbell* v. *Hall*, which laid down that where the
Crown had set up a representative legislature it could not fall
back on its prerogative power to tax, which otherwise remained
unfettered.[2]

*Variety of colonial constitutions*

The colonial empire of the middle eighteenth century thus
comprised many types of government. There were the royal
provinces, with or without elective legislatures and councils.
Interspersed with the royal provinces, there still remained the
archaic survivals of proprietary government in Maryland and
Pennsylvania, and of chartered government in Connecticut
and Rhode Island. In the former two the Crown retained some
control, in the right of approving governors nominated by the
proprietors and in the disallowance of legislation. In the latter
royal control was reduced to a shadow. They elected their
own governors and refused to submit the election for royal
approval. They enacted laws repugnant to English law, declined
to recognise Admiralty jurisdiction or the right of appeal from
their own courts, neglected to provide quotas for defence, and
encouraged trades forbidden by imperial legislation. They were
in fact republics owning only a vague allegiance to the British
Crown. It is true that they were territorially insignificant. But
their constitutional emancipation offered a seductive example to
their larger but less independent neighbours.

*Legislative control over the colonies*

Over this miscellaneous assemblage of colonial possessions the
British government attempted a fitful and ill-organised control.
Where there existed a strong royal government, unhampered
by any local assembly, and possessing full power over executive
and judicial appointments, imperial control was raised to a high
point. Where this condition did not exist, imperial relations
involved ceaseless friction. The legislative sovereignty of the
British Parliament, exercised at least since the Long Parliament
and quite unmistakably since 1688, was employed without formal

[1] Morison, 103-4; Coupland, 92, 119-20; 208-17.
[2] Keir and Lawson (4th edn.), 487-92; I. Jennings and C. M. Young, *Constitutional Laws of the Commonwealth*, 57-61.

denial by the colonies, mainly with reference to commercial topics. Thus the Molasses Act of 1733 imposed prohibitive duties on foreign sugar, rum, and molasses imported into the colonies.[1] Other Acts prohibited the manufacture of pig-iron, and forbade that recourse to a paper currency which the interests of debtor-communities like the colonies so frequently suggested. Statutes also dealt with the production of naval stores, the establishment of a postal service, and other miscellaneous topics.[2] The possibility presented itself that British and colonial legislation might conflict. Here the right of disallowance was called into play, mainly perhaps in order to preserve the Prerogative intact, but also to maintain the trade laws, and to guard vested interests and the liberties of the subject, particularly freedom of conscience, which intolerant colonial statutes sometimes attempted to infringe.[3] Disallowance created much grievance, and colonial assemblies showed considerable ingenuity in rendering it inefficacious, by such devices as passing temporary Acts, constantly renewed when they lapsed.[4]

Executive control over the colonies likewise presented serious difficulties where local elective legislatures existed. Supervisory power over colonial affairs was vested in a large number of departments and officials forming part of the home government, —the Privy Council, the Board of Trade and Plantations, the Treasury, the Secretaries of State, the Admiralty, and the War Office. Among these the Privy Council possessed in theory the most extensive general concern with colonial matters. From 1660 to 1696 authority was exercised either by a committee or committees of the Council itself, or by committees into which a non-conciliar element of expert members was introduced.[5] In 1696 a reorganisation was effected on lines which were to be permanent. Repelling a parliamentary encroachment on the Prerogative in a bill setting up a Council of Trade nominated by Parliament and equipped with statutory powers, the King created a Board of Trade to which the great officers of State nominally belonged,

*Executive control over the colonies*

---

[1] Beer, *British Colonial Policy, 1764-5*, 33-4. The text is in MacDonald, 103-5.
[2] On the Colonial Post Office, see Beer, *British Colonial Policy, 1754-65*, 34-5. It is of some importance as furnishing an argument for the Stamp Act.
[3] Keith, 296.                              [4] Labaree, 247-54.
[5] E. R. Turner, *Privy Council, 1603-1784*, ii. 268, 274, 276-8, 316-31; R. P. Bieber, *British Plantation Councils, 1670-74*, 40 E.H.R. 93.

but the effective personnel of which lay in its eight salaried members, one of whom acted as President.[1] Besides dealing with strictly commercial matters, it prepared Instructions for governors, corresponded with them, and reported on colonial matters generally. The Board varied greatly in activity and usefulness, falling to its lowest point under George I and George II after doing valuable work under Anne, reviving under the energetic presidency of Lord Halifax from 1748, losing its control of patronage in 1761, and finally being overshadowed from 1768 by the existence of a Secretaryship of State for the Colonies. At every stage, however, and even when it was most active, it was hampered by one radical defect. It lacked executive power, and merely considered and reported on colonial business for the guidance of the Privy Council, with which it was connected through a committee of the latter body.[2] While the department which thus possessed the fullest information regarding colonial affairs was denied executive power, that power was held by others to which colonial affairs were merely subordinate elements in their work. The Treasury, acting mainly through the Commissioners of Customs, maintained and extended over the colonies a network of commercial regulations, carried out by officials provided for on the home establishment.[3] The Admiralty, with its subordinate departments, conducted business relating to naval defence, supply, and operations.[4] Military affairs were dealt with by the Secretaries of State, the Secretary at War, the Ordnance Board, the Board of Trade, and the Treasury.[5] The salient features of the whole system were that no single authority with executive power was primarily responsible for imperial relations, and that, besides the governors, the only direct representatives of the Crown in the majority of the colonies were customs officials, soldiers and sailors.

*Position of colonial governors*  Governors of royal provinces (the most numerous class) were appointed by the Crown on the recommendation of the Secretary of State, or, from 1752 to 1761, on that of the Board of Trade,

---

[1] E. R. Turner, *Privy Council, 1603-1784*, ii. ch. xxvii; Beer, *Old Colonial System*, i. 232 ff.; M. P. Clarke, *The Board of Trade at Work*, 17 *A.H.R.* 17. For the detailed history of the Board, see A. H. Basye, *The Board of Trade, 1748-82*.
[2] Turner, ii. 381 ff.
[3] Beer, i. 262-90; Keith, 278-80.  [4] Beer, i. 292 ff.; Keith, 281-2.
[5] Keith, 271, 282, 313-19; Thomson, *Secretaries of State*, 84-7. For the governors' military powers, see Keith, 216-20.

and those of proprietary provinces by the proprietors subject to the Crown's approval. In the chartered colonies the governors were elected.[1] A governor might find himself under a dual or even threefold obligation—to the Crown, the proprietor if there were one, and the colonial assembly. Dependence on the Crown was shown by the tenure of royal governorships during good behaviour, and by the commissions and instructions under which these governors acted. On the other hand, they were required to govern according to the reasonable statutes passed by their assemblies, against which a governor sometimes found it impossible to protect his own authority. Moreover, he was usually dependent on the assembly for finance. His salary normally was derived from a grant by the legislature, save where, as in Virginia, Maryland, North Carolina, and the West Indian Islands, it was derived from Crown revenues, or, as in Nova Scotia and Georgia, it was provided by the British Parliament.[2] If, therefore, the governor was empowered by his commission to supervise administration, appoint to offices, enforce the trade laws, and the like, his power of doing so was in practice miserably deficient. The colonial legislatures of the eighteenth century, by the devices of appointing commissioners to carry out their statutes, legislating with regard to qualifications for offices, and using their control of the purse, were enabled in large measure to bring executive appointments under their own control. So also, by appropriation of supplies, they encroached on the governor's right to control expenditure. At every point, indeed, the governor's authority was circumscribed. The grant of lands, the reservation of quitrents to the Crown, control over Indian affairs, military and naval defence were all nominally within the sole sphere of the executive. In effect, none of these powers could be effectively used against the resistance of the assemblies. The executive power of the Crown tended in colonies where elective assemblies existed to become something of a figment. In its place emerged the *de facto* sovereignty of the assemblies them-

---

[1] Keith, 187-8. The nomination of royal governors (except from 1748 to 1761) belonged to the Southern Secretary; Labaree, 44; Basye, 73-6, 109-10. For an interesting account of the royal governors, see Labaree, 27-34.

[2] On the governor's salary, see Labaree, ch. viii. It might also be supplemented by the constitutionally objectionable method of gifts from the Assemblies, against which the Home government always protested.

selves, exercised in the executive sphere by commissioners or committees, whose work was unco-ordinated and who were joined in no common responsibility.[1]

*Lack of influence by executive over legislature*

In contemporary English government, the relations of executive and legislature were adjusted by the habitual use and general acceptance of the system of "influence". No like system existed in the colonies. It is true the electorates were not large. In Virginia, for example, only 9 per cent of the whole population voted, in Massachusetts only 2 per cent.[2] But over these oligarchies the Crown had no control and no resources with which to acquire it. As in the preceding century in England, aggressive assemblies claimed authority over the electoral system, the frequency and duration of sessions, parliamentary privilege and procedure. Governors had little power of initiating legislation, and not much more of withholding assent. As a constituent part of the legislature, they tended to lose significance, as also did their councils, which in no way achieved the constitutional status of the Lords in the British Parliament. The careers of the majority of governors in this respect degenerated too frequently into a series of squabbles with the elective assemblies, in which the latter prevailed.

*Position of the colonial courts*

The sovereignty of the assemblies began to extend itself also to the judicial sphere.[3] Governors nominally appointed judges, and themselves, either alone or in Council, exercised judicial functions. In the West Indian colonies, these powers were a reality, and in Virginia also the governor in Council possessed an original jurisdiction. Elsewhere, however, jurisdiction belonged to courts in which he had no seat. In Massachusetts he did not possess even appellate jurisdiction, which belonged to a Court of Assistants. Nor did the governor of Pennsylvania possess any judicial powers. If governors in theory appointed judges, and could remove them for adequate reasons, in practice the judges, being dependent for their salaries on grants from the assemblies, tended to escape executive control, and to be exposed to a pressure from local opinion which put the executive at somewhat of a disadvantage

---

[1] Keith, 198-201. For similar processes in the West Indies, see H. E. Egerton, *Colonial Administration in the Seventeenth and Eighteenth Centuries*, 4 T.R.H.S. i. 190. It is only fair to add that an able governor (they were the exception) could get his own way, even in Massachusetts. On royal quitrents, see B. W. Bond, *Quitrent System in the American Colonies.*          [2] Keith, 233.
[3] On this process in the royal provinces, see Labaree, 374-82.

in litigation. The main exception to this rule was provided by the twelve colonial Admiralty courts, to which were committed jurisdiction over offences committed at sea, maritime cases such as charter-parties, and evasions of the trade laws.[1] On this latter point it was natural that friction should arise. The Admiralty courts were attacked by the local courts through such means as prohibitions, and colonial statutes attempted to introduce into them the system of trial by jury.[2] Thus handicapped, the efforts of these courts to enforce the system of commercial regulation attained no high degree of efficiency.

Summing up, it may be said that the defects of colonial govern- *The need* ment in the first half of the eighteenth century were lack of *for reforming* effective imperial control, disunion between the colonies them- *colonial* selves, the weakness of the colonial executive, the means of *govern-* aggression possessed by colonial elective assemblies, the anomalous *ment* position of the judges—secure neither against the executive nor against the legislature—and the unpopularity of Admiralty jurisdiction. At the close of the Seven Years' War, the need for reconstructing the system had become plain. During the war, the incoherence and inefficiency of the defensive system of the colonies, the evasion of the trade laws, and the prevalence of trading with the enemy had all been constant sources of anxiety. To eradicate the defects of the existing system, and provide the colonies with a centralised, coherent and effective machinery of government, presented itself as an obvious necessity.

Successive governments in England after this date addressed *Attempts* themselves to the task. Customs organisation was overhauled, *at re-* and the performance of duties by deputy, a main cause of in- *organisa-* efficiency and corruption, was forbidden.[3] The duties of the navy *tion* in the enforcement of the trade laws were put on a statutory basis.[4] A new Vice-Admiralty court was set up at Halifax, before which, at the option of the prosecution, cases arising out of the trade laws could be heard.[5] More important, because more innovatory,

---

[1] Keith, 261.
[2] Keith, 263. For early colonial opinion of these courts, see H. Crump, *Colonial Admiralty Jurisdiction in the Seventeenth Century*, 164.
[3] Beer, *British Colonial Policy, 1754-65*, 232-5.
[4] Beer, 229.
[5] For the reorganisation of Admiralty jurisdiction in 1764, see Beer, 249-251.

was an effort to organise systematically the defence of the colonies.

*The problem of defence*    Only three times since the century began—in 1709 for the campaigns in Acadia and the St. Lawrence, in 1745 for the campaign against Louisbourg, and in 1754 when Governor Shirley of Massachusetts, as commander-in-chief in America, had planned the Ohio expedition—had there been even a partial co-ordination for active service purposes of the forces in the colonies. A conference held at Albany in 1754 in order to obtain greater unity in colonial government achieved no success, and brought nearer the prospect of imperial intervention for that purpose.[1] The plan of maintaining a standing army in the colonies by means of taxation levied in America under authority of the Imperial Parliament was not new. The Seven Years' War and the outbreak of the Indian rebellion led by Pontiac in 1763 emphasised its desirability, and the continued presence of the French in the West Indies and of their Spanish allies in Louisiana meant that the problem was not one of past history alone, but must be provided for with regard to the future. It seemed inequitable that the home taxpayer, burdened with four millions of interest on a National Debt swollen by war expenses to £130,000,000, should bear the whole burden. A new Molasses Act of 1764 reduced the prohibitive tariffs of 1733 to a moderate tax designed to bring in revenue, and placed the proceeds of the duty at the disposal of the British Parliament for colonial defence.[2] The Stamp Act of 1765 was intended for the upkeep of a regular military establishment on American soil.[3]

*The problem of expansion*    At the same time, the question of relations with the Indians, closely connected both with the economic and the defensive problems of the mainland colonies, was undertaken afresh. In addition to Indian diplomacy, already conducted by royal commissioners, the Imperial government proposed to control westward expansion, the acquisition of lands, and trade with the

---

[1] J. T. Adams, *Revolutionary New England*, 76-83, 180-85, 214-17, 234-44. The article on *Attempts at Imperial Co-operation during the reign of Queen Anne*, by W. T. Morgan, in 4 *T.R.H.S.* x. 171, shows, as does Adams, that the responsibility for failure might largely lie with the Imperial authorities.

[2] Keith, 243-5; Beer, *British Colonial Policy*, 276-80; MacDonald, *Documents*, 117-22.

[3] Beer, 285-6; Grant Robertson, *Documents*, 240-43.

natives.[1] After a period of experiment, the Quebec Act of 1774 closed the door against any westward expansion by the seaboard colonies by annexing to Canada the hinterlands on which their eyes were fixed.[2]

Besides commerce, defence, and native affairs, there remained *Internal* the general problem of the internal government of the colonies. *government.* In 1767 the Stamp Act, withdrawn in 1766 in face of a determined *The* colonial opposition inspired by Massachusetts and manifested in *Town-* the Stamp Act Congress,[3] was replaced by a still more compre- *shend* hensive scheme, drafted by Charles Townshend, Chancellor of *duties* the Exchequer in the Pitt-Grafton ministry. A series of import duties, intended avowedly to raise revenue and not merely to regulate trade, were imposed by imperial legislation in order to provide for the permanent endowment of the colonial executive and judicial establishments, any surplus to go to colonial defence. The machinery of collection was improved. Writs of assistance, akin to general warrants, were made issuable by the superior courts of each colony. New Vice-Admiralty courts were set up. A separate body of customs commissioners for America was created. Finally, the molasses tax, reduced to one penny per pound, was converted frankly into a revenue duty.[4]

Nothing could have been better intended, or worse conceived *Strong and* and executed, than this series of measures. At every point the *weak* British Government had a strong case. The colonists, professing *points of* acceptance of the principle of commercial regulation, had in *policy* practice made it largely illusory. Their record in war, though redeemed by one or two of the New England colonies, was blemished by parsimony, mutual jealousy and refusal to co-operate effectively. In dealing with the natives, they had showed a violence, ruthlessness and lack of scruple to which the constant danger of an Indian rising must largely be attributed. Their assemblies had continuously sought to bring the executive and judicial branches of government into complete subservience to

---

[1] See the proclamation of 1763 in Morison, *Documents*, 2-3, and compare the Board of Trade Report of 1768, Morison, *Documents*, 62-73.

[2] There is a good short account of the frontier policy of the British Government, 1763-74, in C. W. Alvord, *The Mississippi Valley in British Politics*, ii. ch. viii.    [3] For the resolutions of this Congress, see Morison, 32-4.

[4] Text of the Townshend duties, in MacDonald, 143-6. See also Keith, 358, 361. For a writ of assistance, see MacDonald, 106-9.

local and not always highly respectable interests. On these counts, the imperial government was largely in the right. Yet this policy was clumsy in the extreme. To resort to a stamp duty on legal and commercial documents, newspapers and pamphlets, enforceable in the Admiralty courts, was to arouse the hostility of two strong vested interests—the law and the printing trade—well able not only to defend themselves but to conduct counter-propaganda. The repeal of the Stamp Act was coupled with a Declaratory Act reaffirming the competence of the Imperial Parliament to tax the colonies, which only sharpened the point of principle at issue.[1] Townshend's scheme was a masterpiece of misapplied ingenuity. Avoiding the objection to an *internal* tax revealed in the opposition to the Stamp Act, it perverted *external* taxation, hitherto used as a means of commercial regulation, into an instrument of supply. The mercantile interest in the colonies, already made restive by the Stamp Act, set itself solidly against the new duties, which in 1770 Lord North's government was forced, with the sole exception of the tea duty, to withdraw.[2] These concessions themselves were ill-devised. Five of the six duties were abolished. The tea duty was retained, not because any revenue was expected from it, but because its continuance preserved the principle contended for in the Declaratory Act, and that despite the fact that when levied in England it had produced more than it did in colonial ports. The crowning error was perhaps the well-intentioned Quebec Act, which frustrated western expansion, created in Canada a non-elective government, recognised an alien system of French law, and affronted colonial Protestantism with the spectacle of an established and endowed Roman Catholic Church.

*Colonial resistance organised*    Antagonising both the most radical and even the more conservative elements in American society, the government found itself faced with an opposition in which, for the first time, and ominously for the future, the colonies found it possible to combine. At the time of the Stamp Act in 1765 the resolutions of the Stamp Act Congress asserted, as part of the colonists' birthright of common and statute law, their right not to be taxed save with their own consent given in their own assemblies, and to be tried by jury instead of by Admiralty jurisdiction. In the resistance

---

[1] Grant Robertson, 244-5.        [2] Keith, 365.

to the Townshend duties a reorganised opposition, again stimulated by Massachusetts, extended the denial of any imperial right
to tax from internal taxation to external taxation for revenue, protested against financial independence being accorded to governors
and judges, and boycotted trade with the mother-country by
non-importation agreements. North's concessions of 1770 did
something to disarm conservative opposition, but the lead was now
taken by other disaffected elements who lost no opportunity of
keeping the popular movement of opposition alive. For this
purpose the friction created by the trade laws proved invaluable.
Incidents such as the seizure of the sloop *Liberty* by customs
officers in 1768, and the burning of the naval cutter *Gaspée* by
Rhode Islanders in 1772 caused direct conflicts between the popu-
lace and the revenue and defence forces of the Crown. In 1770 a
mêlée attended by bloodshed occurred between the military and
the townspeople of Boston. Given these conditions, the incident
of the "Boston tea-party" was easily produced and led to
momentous consequences. The East India Company, in grave
financial straits and suffering serious loss from the American
boycott of taxed tea, was permitted by Lord North's government
to sell direct from its own warehouses, and relieved of the
duty on re-export from England. Had it succeeded, this device
must have broken the boycott. The Boston radicals prevented
it by force.

The failure of the punitive measures now adopted by the British *Failure of*
government plainly revealed that weakness in executive authority *punitive*
which had so long marked colonial administration. In Massachu- *measures*
setts the constitution was remodelled by the Massachusetts
Government Act.[1] The elective council was replaced by one
nominated by the Crown, which also resumed control, directly or
through the governor, of the appointment of judges and sheriffs.
Jurors were to be appointed by the sheriffs. The town-meetings
which in this province gave effect to the principle of local self-
government, and moreover extended their attention to the affairs
of the province at large, were suppressed except for formal business
done with the governor's leave. The governor was empowered to
change the venue of trials, if necessary to Great Britain itself. A
Quartering Act, on the model of one already applied in 1768 to

---

[1] Morison, 100–102.

New York, required the colony to provide barracks for troops.[1] Another Act closed the port of Boston until reparation had been made for the tea outrage.[2] But the new administration could not get to work. The executive authority of the Crown collapsed before the resistance organised by the Committees of Correspondence which since the non-importation agreement of 1768 covered the provinces with their closely-connected chain.[3] For Massachusetts did not resist alone. Once more the unity already created by common opposition was reforged.

*The Continental Congress*

In September 1774 a Continental Congress assembled, including representatives from every province save Canada, Georgia, and Florida.[4] Its resolutions, like those of its predecessors, seemed to contemplate the maintenance of imperial unity, and appealed to fundamental rights which might be regarded as based on English law—no taxation or legislation by any authority unrepresentative of the subject, no standing armies, the restoration of trial by jury, affirmation of the right of petition. Place was still found for the trade laws in force before 1764, but it was plain that a mere return to the situation of that year would not go to the root of the difficulty. It could not have been accepted in England, and it is at least highly doubtful whether it would long have satisfied the colonies. Not even the most sympathetic advocates of the colonial case in Great Britain were prepared to abandon the whole system of control except for the trade laws which experience had shown to be inefficacious. Chatham, with more common sense than logic, would have excluded taxation from the sphere of imperial legislation and left the colonial assemblies to settle the extent of their contributions for themselves, but he would admit no protests against the presence of a standing army, and he retained ultimate authority in the legislative sphere for the British Parliament.[5] Burke's eloquent panegyrics on the value of liberty as the essential unifying principle of empire involved no abandonment of the principle of imperial sovereignty—" as

[1] For a Quartering Act of 1765, see MacDonald, 131-6. See also Keith, 360-61, 368-9.
[2] For the text of the Boston Port Act and the Administration of Justice Act, see MacDonald, 151-4, 159-62; Keith, 368.
[3] Morison, 122-5. On the Committees of Correspondence, see C. H. Van Tyne, *Causes of the War of Independence*, i. 373-6, 427-8.
[4] Morison, 118-22; Keith, 369-72.    [5] Williams, *Life of Pitt*, ii. 307-12.

an instrument of empire and not a means of supply"—to be tempered in its exercise only by considerations of expediency.[1] Neither Chatham nor probably even Burke could have averted a process which had since the foundation of the colonies tended to draw them outside the range of imperial authority for practically every purpose. The colonists themselves, for all their outward acceptance of a limited imperial control, had put forward claims to which no logical or legal bounds could be set. The North ministry and its parliamentary majority, lagging far behind the limit of concession suggested by Chatham and Burke, and going no further than an offer—such as had already been made by Grenville in 1764—that the colonies should, in any manner they chose, fulfil defensive obligations imposed on them by the home government, obstinately but feebly prepared to meet the colonial challenge.

That challenge had at first been invested with strictly constitutional forms. The colonies, urging the fundamental nature of the Common Law and of their royal charters, which seemed to suggest a limit on parliamentary legislative authority, had argued their case as British subjects. Their case was fatally impaired by the undeniable fact that the authority of numerous British statutes (including some, like the Bill of Rights, which might almost be regarded as integral to their own case) had long been accepted by them as binding.[2] Their only course was an appeal to natural justice, which removed the question from the sphere of constitutional law. The appeal was backed by force of arms. In April 1775 fighting broke out. In August a royal proclamation declared the colonies to be in a state of rebellion, and a statute forbade trade with them. In the following year, when Congress recommended the establishment of State governments[3] and issued its Declaration of Independence,[4] the appeal to the colonists' rights as British subjects was finally abandoned, and the principles of natural law were taken as the basis of a new state wholly independent of the British Crown. *The Declaration of Independence*

Responsibility for the failure of the eighteenth-century con-

---

[1] Burke, *Select Works* (ed. E. J. Payne), i. 157.

[2] For a full discussion of this question, see C. H. M'Ilwain, *The American Revolution—a Constitutional Interpretation*, and the contrary view expressed in R. C. Schuyler, *Parliament and the British Empire*.

[3] Morison, 148.                                    [4] Morison, 157-60.

Responsibility for the failure of the old colonial system

stitution to find any means of harmonising imperial unity and colonial self-government may be not unequally divided between British and American politicians, the former for their lack of realism in dealing with the problems involved, and the latter for their irresponsible repudiation of imperial obligation. That British statesmanship might be induced to accept an imperial constitution markedly different in principle from that which had collapsed seemed to be indicated in the British peace proposals of 1778. Two statutes renounced taxation of the American and West Indian colonies save for the purpose of trade regulation—the proceeds to be given to the colony where the duties were levied—removed the tax on tea and repealed the Massachusetts Government Act.[1] Commissioners to negotiate peace were empowered to make large concessions on such points as the amendment of colonial constitutions, the Declaratory Act, defence, the appointment of judges and officials, Admiralty jurisdiction, the enforcement of the trade laws by colonial officials, and the surrender of royal quit-rents.[2] Coming at so late a date, and from the detested North government, these proposals had little chance of acceptance. They at least suggest the recognition of basic facts in the relationship between colonies and mother-country, and their subsequent acceptance constitutes one of the many reasons why the Empire has not again been broken asunder by such shocks as tore the Thirteen Colonies from the Britain of George III.[3]

[1] Keith, 383.                    [2] Morison, 186-203.
[3] On the whole problem of eighteenth-century colonial policy, reference may usefully be made to H. H. Bellot, *The Mainland Colonies in the Eighteenth Century*, 17 *Hist.* 344, and R. A. Humphreys, *British Colonial Policy and the American Revolution*, 19 *Hist.* 42.

# CHAPTER VII

## ADMINISTRATIVE AND PARLIAMENTARY
## REFORM, 1782–1867

### 1

THE face of Britain, for many centuries unaltered in its general *The trans-* aspect, bore in 1782 many indications of profound impending *formation* change. A long and gradual process of transformation, converting *of Britain* what hitherto had been a predominantly agricultural country into the "workshop of the world", had over many decades and almost imperceptibly been gaining impetus. The rise of the industrial village presaged the rise of the industrial city. A manufacturing system operating under capitalistic ownership and control was emerging. Although the work was still largely carried on in the homes of the workers there was an increasing tendency towards factory organisation.[1] The factory system was indeed no novelty. In the seventeenth century, certain industries, such as soap and glass and certain branches of the textile and metal trades, were thus being organised, though these experiments had been neither numerous nor perhaps very successful. The expanding markets of the eighteenth century and the influx of wealth gained in overseas trade created conditions highly favourable to this new form of enterprise, and stimulated the development of a new manufacturing technique, which utilised the many mechanical inventions of the age. Likewise the continuous application of capital to the land, directed to the improvement of the quantity and the quality of both crops and livestock, led to an agricultural revolution which proceeded simultaneously, though more slowly, during the change in the old industrial system. It led to an acceleration of enclosure, effected in the earlier stages mostly by agreement, though later in the century by the compulsive power of statute. Farms were consolidated and enlarged. The number of

[1] On the evolution of capitalist industry, both domestic and factory, see E. Lipson, *Economic History of England*, 3rd edn., ii. 1-10, iii. 208 ff.

small freeholds, after an early tendency to increase, gradually diminished. The mass of the rural population found themselves in process of surrendering their never very secure hold on the land they cultivated. If the social and economic arrangements of Britain about 1782 still retained many traits of the ancient order, the outlines of a society constructed on entirely dissimilar lines were rapidly appearing. While the image of the past could still be discerned, its lineaments were becoming distorted and blurred.

*Agrarian and Industrial Revolutions*

By 1867 the picture once so firmly and almost indelibly imprinted had wholly dissolved. The green fields of England had themselves been redrawn after a new fashion. By the progress of enclosure the old open fields had been replaced by the now familiar hedgerows, banks, and walls. The application of capital to agriculture had long since ended the old communal system of husbandry, concentrated the ownership of land in the hands of a relatively small number of wealthy landlords, eliminated the formerly numerous class of small proprietors, deprived the villager of his small plot of arable land and his grazing rights, and turned the mass of the rural population into a landless proletariat. English agriculture had assumed its modern and characteristic form of substantial tenant-farming. Displaced freeholders, and village labourers doubly affected by the agrarian revolution and the collapse of domestic industry, had in large measure been driven off the land altogether, and obliged either to emigrate to overseas colonies like Canada, Australia, and New Zealand, or to the rising industrial towns, where densely clustered factories and dwelling-houses chequered with dark patches the verdant expanses of the older England on which from year to year they steadily encroached. The industrialised England which had sprung into existence maintained a much larger population, and one which, unlike that of earlier Hanoverian times, rapidly increased. Rising very slowly during most of the eighteenth century, the population of England and Wales, numbering some eight millions in 1780, amounted to thirteen millions in 1831, nearly eighteen millions in 1851, and by 1871 was to attain twenty-two and three-quarter millions. At this date it had become to a large extent urban. The earliest stages in the industrialisation of England had not tended to swell the number of town-dwellers. In the search for water-power, manufacturers had established themselves in

Pennine valleys where a fall could be utilised without impeding inland navigation. The effect was rather to diffuse than to concentrate population. But a second revolution in the application of power, following so soon after the first as to obscure that effect, had led to the general adoption of steam, the preliminary experiments of Watt and Boulton which introduced it beginning about 1780. Steam-power created the urban factory, situated on or near the coal-fields. The result was a large displacement of population, by which the North gained immensely, partly at the expense of the South, partly by immigration, particularly from Ireland, and partly because of a steady natural increase. While the urban population rose everywhere, older cities like London rising from one to three million in the first half of the nineteenth century, Liverpool from 82,000 to nearly 400,000, and Bristol from 61,000 to 137,000, the increase was most marked in such towns, originally only large villages, as Bradford, which rose to 103,000 by 1851. This process involved the relative decline of the older centres of English industry such as those of East Anglia and Gloucestershire, and the slow destruction of the domestic industry which in earlier times had been diffused over the countryside in the homes of village labourers whose families carried on the occupation of spinning as an adjunct to their agricultural pursuits. Linked together by vastly improved means of communication, the new industrial areas formed a system within which the interchange of commodities and the movement of labour were progressively made easier. The work of Macadam and Telford revolutionised the road system, the latter amplified the series of canals begun by Brindley, but the effects of improved road and water transport proved insignificant before those achieved by the coming of the railway. From 1825, when the Stockton and Darlington line was built, the efforts of the railway engineer, particularly during the 'forties, covered the country with an intricate network of high-speed power-driven transport. On the sea, steam began slowly to displace sail, and the increased size of ships and the improvement of internal communications combined to cause the decay of many older harbours serving local markets and to concentrate traffic in the great seaports. Brought into ever closer contact with a world-market for which she formed the principal workshop, banking centre, and headquarters of commercial exchange, mid-nineteenth-century England had reorganised her life on a basis substantially different from that of her simpler and stabler past.

*Their
political
effects* Changes so fundamental in her economic and social organisation involved a slow but radical alteration in the machinery of government. The predominant influence in national affairs inevitably passed from the landed to the industrial and financial class. Their rivalry had already appeared, it is true, during the earlier part of the eighteenth century. Yet even towards its close the landed interest still preserved its ascendancy in a nation still largely agricultural. During the nineteenth century it was forced step by step to give way before the rival claims of the factory-owner and the commercial capitalist. To both of these, the need for plentiful supplies of raw material, cheap food, and unimpeded access to every part of an expanding world-market where they might buy and sell as widely as possible, prevailed over every argument in favour of fostering English agriculture or conserving a system of tariffs and trade restriction. Since Parliament was the essential instrument of political power, control of which was necessary to any interest desirous of serving its own purposes, the early nineteenth century witnessed a violent conflict between the landed class which wished to maintain its monopoly and its industrial rivals who intended to capture that instrument for their own ends. In the Reform Bill of 1832 the latter came within sight of their goal. In 1834 the Poor Law Amendment Act broke down the authority of the landed gentry in a department of local affairs which for almost two centuries had been under their unfettered control. In 1846 another mainstay of their position was removed by the repeal of the Corn Laws. In 1849 the repeal of the Navigation Act freed overseas trade from the trammels of the old colonial system, and opened the British market without restriction to the inflow of commodities from whatever source. Meanwhile, by a long series of measures spaced out over the whole period, the tariffs which restrained British commerce were simplified and finally, by Gladstone's 1860 Budget, in large part swept away to admit the principle and system of free trade.

*The age of
laissez-
faire* Freedom of enterprise was indeed the prevalent maxim of the whole century from the younger Pitt to Gladstone. The practical considerations which seemed to justify it were fortified by a

generally accepted philosophy. This was the age of *laissez-faire*.[1] In the pages of Adam Smith classical expression was given to the already familiar view that the condition of national greatness was the liberation of individual energy, unhampered by anything more than an irreducible minimum of social restraint. The pursuit by every man of his own interest as he conceived it would result, it was assumed, in harmonies which would make regulation of national affairs by governmental action needless, and, if persisted in, harmful. The main business of government, on this view, was to clear away obstructions which impeded the free play of individual enterprise. This task, though theoretically a purely negative one, must involve, at least in its earlier stages, a certain amount of positive action. The removal of encumbrances ought to mean the demolition of ancient forms and institutions seen to be incompatible with strict *laissez-faire* principles. Everything inherited from the past must, as it were, be put on its trial. Not only the economic institutions of the past, like the mercantile system and the inherited organisation of industry, but also political institutions such as Parliament, the administrative system, and the law and the courts of justice had to face examination and subject themselves to reform. Thus Parliament should be transformed so as to reflect the interests preponderant in the nation and, with these given their proper weight, the representative system would afford, through the processes of reason and discussion through which it operated, the ideal way of attaining those natural harmonies which, according to the predominant school of thought, were inherent in the social order though hitherto thwarted by the frustrating grasp of the past. So also the administrative system needed to be overhauled and stripped of its antiquated survivals and useless accretions. The law and the courts attracted the close and unfriendly scrutiny of the reformers of the late eighteenth and early nineteenth centuries. Their dilatoriness and expense, their technical and antiquated procedure, the duality of Common Law and Equity, and the rigours of the penal code all evoked criticism and prompted the desire for amendment. The opinions which became fashionable

[1] The removal of restraints from trade had many advocates from the Restoration onward. Adam Smith's *Wealth of Nations* owed its success partly to works by predecessors like Sir Josiah Child and Charles Davenant. See Lipson, *Economic History of England*, iii. 15-16.

in this age required that every institution should justify its existence on practical grounds. The Utilitarian school deriving its inspiration from Jeremy Bentham reinforced the demand for the removal of obstructions, as put forward by the classical economists who followed Adam Smith, by making the maintenance of existing institutions depend primarily on their success in serving "the greatest good of the greatest number".[1]

*Criticism and Reform*    This current of destructive criticism, which did not visibly abate until the appearance of J. S. Mill's *Principles of Political Economy* in 1848, constituted a force wholly dissimilar from any force effective in the earlier part of the eighteenth century. The complacency with which English institutions had then been regarded had now to be modified to suit the sceptical temper of the new age. Even the Tories who enjoyed a half-century of power under George III and George IV found themselves obliged to initiate reforming processes which, if they did not include—and for the Tory party, representing as it did the landed interest, could not include—a remodelling of the parliamentary system, yet embraced a long sequence of reforms, financial, administrative and judicial. Perhaps most radical of all was the dissolution, by the repeal of the Test and Corporation Acts and the passing of the Act for Roman Catholic Emancipation, of a unity integral since Restoration times between the State and the Anglican Church. In 1832 the attack of their opponents upon the parliamentary system itself succeeded. Their Whig rivals, supported by a radical group professing the doctrines of Bentham, came into power, and the progress of reform proceeded at an accelerated pace. Its first-fruits were to be seen in the new Poor Law of 1834 and the reform of municipal corporations in the following year. Taking into account the whole ensuing period to 1867, it achieved among other things a further approach to complete religious toleration and the abolition of confessional tests, revision of the criminal law, prison reform, the beginnings of social legislation with regard to conditions and hours of labour, and the establishment of free trade. The advance, it is true, was delayed by the powerful conservative influences at work in both parties, and its final stages lie beyond the period now under

---

[1] On Bentham's career and teaching, see L. Stephen, *The English Utilitarians*, i. ch. v, vi; particularly pp. 276 ff. for Bentham's criticism of English law and its political applications. A. V. Dicey, *Law and Opinion in England*, 126 ff.

discussion. But the last innovation of the period, the enlargement of the franchise in 1867, opened the floodgates to further change.

As a matter of strict theory, much that was accomplished during this long period of reform could be regarded merely as the removal of antiquated and useless institutional lumber. Yet experience showed that the doctrine of *laissez-faire* could not remain a merely negative and destructive one. Such a doctrine proved untenable, and it is questionable whether any of its exponents ever held it in its abstract simplicity. Destruction must necessarily be followed by an attempt to create. Moreover, even the theoretical assumptions of *laissez-faire* did not go unchallenged. While on the one hand conservative opinion declined to accept the universal validity of the appeal to reason and utility as justifying or condemning institutions, on the other the early English socialists pointed out with much force that the results of this appeal were barren and repulsive. The principle that the good of all was best attained through the pursuit by each of his own interests untrammelled by social control did not in practice yield those harmonies which its advocates anticipated.[1]

*The challenge to laissez-faire*

Here the facts of social evolution substantially justify the criticism. The pursuit of individual self-interest led not to harmony but to anarchy. The problems of poverty, disease, and ignorance instead of vanishing only became increasingly acute. For these maladies, the gospel of *laissez-faire* held no healing message. It proved impossible to fulfil with literal strictness the plan of removing all external regulation and restraint on the individual. The effects of such an abdication could only be disastrous. Thus whether the fashionable philosophy justified or condemned it, the State was again obliged to intervene, for example, to permit the organisation of labour by the repeal in 1824 of the Combination Acts passed in 1799 and 1800,[2] to regulate working conditions, to make at least a modest beginning in providing for popular educa-

*State intervention*

[1] K. B. Smellie, *A Hundred Years of English Government* (2nd edn.) 13-15.

[2] Costin and Watson, ii. 40. Even so, the Unions were under the Common Law disability that they might be held illegal as being associations in restraint of trade. This disability continued until removed by the Conspiracy and Protection of Property Act of 1875. In 1867 the Queen's Bench held in *Hornby* v. *Close* that a Trade Union, as an association in restraint of trade, was not entitled to the protection of the law against a defaulting official. This was remedied by an Act of 1871, but the Act practically forbade picketing. The Act of 1875 permitted "peaceful" picketing. See G. Wallas, *Life of Francis Place*, 197 ff.; S. and B. Webb, *History of Trade Unionism*, 97-109, 262, 276-83, 290-92.

tion, to combat disease and the insanitary conditions which bred it. Here again, particularly in the domain of local government, the process long ante-dated the Reform of 1832. During the preceding half-century, the more ancient institutions of local administration had been in course of renovation, while their efforts were ceaselessly being supplemented by the creation of *ad hoc* authorities for special purposes like drainage and sanitation, lighting and paving, and other forms of improvement. After 1832 the central government began, if slowly, to adapt itself to these needs, which the rapid and chaotic growth of an urban and industrial society made even more urgent. Government had to enlarge its sphere beyond the maintenance of the elementary services to which it had, at least since 1640, been mostly confined. Besides national defence and foreign relations, it had to undertake to an increasing extent the provision of what may by anticipation be called social services, connected with industry, trade, transport, health, and education. Its structure and organisation assumed new forms. New departments began to emerge, staffed by a professional administrative personnel, among whom proficiency rather than patronage came to be the necessary qualification for appointment, and to whom were committed an increasing number and variety of statutory powers, some purely executive, others involving subordinate legislation and even the performance of functions as to which they exercised a discretion, and which therefore acquired a quasi-judicial character. Nor was the amplification of the sphere of government confined to wholly domestic concerns. Scotland, indeed, followed in a less paternalistic fashion much the same general course of social and economic evolution as England, its urban areas growing with the progress of industrialism while its rural areas were similarly, and by even more ruthless means, depleted of their population. But Ireland, united with Great Britain in 1800, presented to the government a very different problem, with its predominantly rural society, its acute difficulties of poverty, religious division, and its separate if not yet separatist national feeling. Overseas the creation of a new empire, including with Canada and the older possessions of the Crown recent colonies like the settlements in Australia and New Zealand, the territorial gains, such as Cape Colony, made by the peace treaties of 1815, and the dominions of the East India Company brought in 1773 under the joint and in 1858 under the sole control of the Crown, caused a further extension of the machinery of the State.

A government thus remodelled to deal with new needs at home *Parlia-* and overseas could no longer be regarded as a mere emanation *ment and* from the Crown, armed in the main with prerogative powers, *the* and preserved as the personal concern of the sovereign. It became *Executive* the business of Parliament to assert over the executive a control much more systematic than that afforded by its legislative sovereignty and its power to grant and appropriate supply. To set up new departments of State and define their powers by statute, to finance them by annual grant where formerly provision had been made by permanent revenues or by fees due to officials, formed a natural line of advance. The process by which the central executive was subjected to investigation and reform by Parliament was begun in 1782 not in order to increase administrative efficiency, but to diminish the royal influence based on patronage which threatened to impair the balance of the constitution and the independence of the legislature. Once begun, it continued as a means of improving the machinery of government, of which in every part a more vigorous and business-like spirit becomes perceptible. The more ancient departments of State, it is true, tended to remain, as they always had been, a kind of Crown preserve. New departments as they were added, however, took their place somewhat outside that province. If it was natural for the Crown to continue to regard, for example, the army and the navy as in some sense its own exclusive affair, the same could hardly be said of the departments which arose to supply new public needs as they developed. Government, in short, came less and less to be considered the personal concern of the sovereign, more and more as the business of the leaders of the dominant political party in Parliament and especially in the Commons.

This process was intensified when the Reform of 1832 largely *Parlia-* destroyed the control over Parliament which the Crown had for *mentary* more than a century possessed through the use it made of influence *reform and* and patronage. It gradually became plain that the Reform, if in *its results* many ways limited and conservative, had had at least two really revolutionary effects. The first was that the King could no longer choose his ministers at his sole discretion and furnish them, so long as they retained his confidence, with a parliamentary majority generally reliable under normal conditions. The second was that the Lords, hitherto so closely linked with the Commons that constitutional conflicts between the Houses were of rare occurrence, had lost their former position, that the ascendancy had now passed to the Lower House, which found in its own popularly-elective character a basis for resisting the claims of a non-elective assembly to act as an independent and even rival force. The collective effect of these two changes was momentous. Ministers henceforth were increasingly to derive their strength from the support of the electorate, and less and less from that of the Crown and the Lords. It is true that this change came about slowly. Party divisions and organisation, both in Parliament and in the country, long remained so amorphous that the influence of the Crown over the composition and the policy of its ministries, and the pretensions of the Lords to an authority co-ordinate with that of the Commons, were maintained for more than a generation after 1832. The conventions of the eighteenth century were not easily dissolved. But by 1867 the changes were becoming visible. Ministries, backed by parties organised both in Parliament and in the constituencies, and elected to carry out a precise political programme, stood secure in the support of the Commons alone.

*The Electorate and Parliament*    Developments after 1832 reveal the gradual education of the electorate to take a part in the constitution which the conventions of the eighteenth century had not allowed to it. To capture the parliamentary machine as an instrument by which the will of the nation could be put into effect was one of the principal objects of the Reform movement before 1832, and though for purposes economic rather than political, of the Chartists thereafter. The massing of a great artisan population in the cities and towns made urgent the claim of the manual worker to the vote—and therefore to the control of the Commons and of national policy—which was conceded in 1867. By this date the long empire of *laissez-faire* was drawing to a close. The newly enfranchised masses, intent on using their newly acquired power, tried from the outset to utilise Parliament as an instrument for applying and extending the regulative power of the State to their own advantage. A new sovereign manifested his presence and grew to a realisation of his power. Personal sovereignty and even parliamentary sovereignty yielded place to the sovereignty of the people.

## ii

Though the personal share of the sovereign in government *Functions* steadily lessened after the fall of Lord North's ministry in 1782, *of the* the process was slow. The monarch did not degenerate, and in- *Crown* deed never has degenerated, into a functionless appendage of the constitution. His action has always been necessary for the performance of a large number of acts of governmental routine. Apart from this, he has always preserved, though to a degree increasingly limited by the hardening of new conventions, a discretionary power, exercised in a purely personal way over the choice of ministers and the conduct of government and policy, which may be regarded as the ultimate reserve force in the constitution. The sovereign's duties, both formal and discretionary, have therefore always required that he should be capable of transacting the business which law or convention requires of him.

In strict legal theory, the sovereign is deemed always to be *Theoretical* capable of doing so. He never dies and is never so situated that he *attributes* cannot carry out his duties. So abstract and artificial a concep- *of King-* tion of kingship, attributing to it qualities which cannot without *ship* absurdity be predicated of a natural man, is of necessity contradicted by the incidents and vicissitudes of human existence. The law itself, indeed, witnesses to the fact that the King is a man like other men. By statutes of William III, Anne, and George III, an attempt was made to dispel some of the results of the demise of the Crown by enactments prolonging the life of Parliament beyond the term which the sovereign's death would otherwise have imposed on it, and giving the judges a permanent tenure unaffected by that event.[1] Though an Act of 1797 revived the Parliament last in existence in the event of the sovereign's death immediately after its dissolution,[2] the law remained substantially unaltered until the Reform Act of 1867 finally made the life of Parliament wholly independent of that of the sovereign. Not until a still later date, however, was the tenure of office under the Crown similarly dealt with.[3]

---

[1] Anson, *Law and Custom of the Constitution*, ii. i, *The Crown* (ed. Keith), 278-9; Costin and Watson, i. 84, 112, 139.    [2] Costin and Watson, ii. 16.
[3] By the Demise of the Crown Act, 1901, Costin and Watson, ii. 136.

*Royal*
*incapacity*    The law has had to find further devices for reconciling the abstractions connected with kingship with the practical inconveniences resulting from the fact that the office is held by a human being liable to various incapacities. Already under William III, the King's absence from the realm had necessitated some provision being made for his duties to be discharged by others. During her lifetime, Mary was given statutory powers for this purpose. After her death, Lords Justices were appointed to act in the same way, and the Regency Act of Anne's reign contained a clause appointing Lords Justices to conduct the government in the event of her Hanoverian successor being out of the realm at the time of her death.[1] The Act of Settlement prohibited the new King, when he succeeded, from leaving his dominions without consent of Parliament, but this clause was soon repealed, and provision had again to be made for the King's absence. Thus in 1716 the Prince of Wales was made Lieutenant and Governor of the kingdom, and a similar position was accorded to Queen Caroline during the absence of George II.[2] The appointment of Lords Justices during the King's absence recurred even in the early nineteenth century—in 1821, and again in 1837 to provide for the possibility of the young queen's death while her heir-presumptive, the King of Hanover, was overseas.[3] The improvement of communications during ensuing years rendered it unnecessary to make special provision for her absence from the realm.

*Regencies*    More important have been the provisions necessitated by incapacity due to infancy. Here again statutory enactments have been passed to establish a regency in the event of the accession of a minor. An Act of this nature was passed in 1751 on the death of Frederick, Prince of Wales, whose son, the future George III, was then only thirteen years of age.[4] In 1765 George himself on recovering from a serious illness gave the royal assent to a bill empowering him to nominate as Regent, in the event of his death, either the Queen, the Dowager Princess of Wales, or any descendant of George II, his own eldest son being then only an

---

[1] E. R. Turner, *The Lords Justices of England*, 29 *E.H.R.* 453.
[2] Turner, 29 *E.H.R.* 457-8. After 1716 the Prince was not again appointed, and recourse was made to Lords Justices. Caroline held the position in 1729, 1732, 1735, and 1736. Lords Justices were appointed after her death.
[3] Anson (ed. Keith), ii. i, 274; Erskine May (ed. Holland), i. 151.
[4] Erskine May i. 114.

infant of three.[1] Similar provision was made on the death of George IV in 1830, when the Duchess of Kent was empowered if necessary to act as Regent for the heir-presumptive, her daughter Princess Victoria, then aged eleven,[2] and in 1840, when the Prince Consort was to act as Regent for his still unborn son Edward should he succeed as a minor.[3]

The most acute difficulties have been those created by illness. *Physical* They arose in a peculiarly intractable form in 1788, when George *and mental* III was afflicted by a prolonged period of insanity. The machinery *the* of the constitution seemed likely to be thrown out of action, for *Regency* Parliament stood prorogued, must be opened by the King or by *Bill of* royal commission, and must have its bills made effective by the *1788* signification of the royal assent. The King was capable of performing none of these acts, and no legal provision existed for their performance on his behalf. The simplest solution would have been to invite the Prince of Wales to assume the regency with unrestricted powers. Party considerations intervened to prevent its adoption. The Prince was known to be a partisan of the Whig opposition led by Fox, and the Prime Minister, Pitt, feared his advent to power, and contended that he had no right to assume the regency save by parliamentary authority, and on terms to be fixed by Parliament. The Whigs found themselves forced to take up the position, seemingly inconsistent, as Pitt incisively pointed out, with their traditional principles, that the Prince had a right which Parliament could not deny or limit. Thus succeeding in his intention to "unwhig" Fox, Pitt carried a complicated proposal authorising the Lord Chancellor under resolutions of the Houses to affix the Great Seal to a royal commission for opening Parliament, and thereafter to a Regency Bill, defining the Prince's authority as Regent, when it had passed both Houses. It may be remarked that if Fox and the Whigs were driven into the position of defending a conception of indefeasible right not subject to parliamentary control, Pitt himself was no less guilty of a violation of Tory principle by introducing the dangerous expedient—capable of being turned against the monarchical principle of which the Tories were the ostensible defenders—of creating a means of supplying a purely fictitious

---

[1] Erskine May, i. 116-8.
[2] Erskine May, i. 149-50.      [3] Erskine May, i. 151.

royal assent by the action of the Houses alone. In 1788 the device thus invented was not employed owing to the King's recovery. When in 1811 George III relapsed into an insanity which proved incurable, it was utilised in the same form as the basis of the regency henceforward exercised by the Prince of Wales.[1]

*Personal share of Sovereign in government*

At that date, the Prince's connexions with the Whigs had been weakened, and his advent as Regent did not cause any interruption of Tory rule. But the inner significance of what may appear a pedantic quarrel over constitutional niceties lies in the fact that throughout the period preceding the Reform of 1832, the King's share in government was not limited in the main to the performance of purely routine duties. So long as the unreformed parliamentary system, the extensive use of Crown patronage, and the conventions which justified that use still persisted, so long must the King remain in the same degree the real head of the government carried on in his name. Such a degree of direct and continuous supervision of administration and policy as that in which Lord North had acquiesced was, indeed, after its disastrous results in America, too dangerous to repeat. During the remaining years of George III's reign and that of George IV it was not again attempted. Yet the end of the personal system of 1760–82 did not mean the withdrawal of the King from all intervention in the business of government. On first impression, indeed, royal intervention seems to continue during the next half-century little affected by the reverse of 1782. The King's support had not availed to maintain North's declining majorities from 1780 to 1782, to induce him to remain in office, to avert his fall, or to exclude the Rockingham Whigs from power. Yet the change of ministry was not complete, nor was the new ministry wholly united. Lord Thurlow, retaining the office of Chancellor, shared in the deliberations of a Cabinet whose measures he disapproved, and of whose leader he said, "either he or the King must go, to settle which of them is to govern the country". In this same Cabinet, Lord Shelburne

---

[1] On the Regency Bill of 1788, see Costin and Watson, ii, 154-9; Erskine May, i. 118-31; Lecky, v. 379 ff.; J. Holland Rose, *William Pitt and National Revival*, ch. xviii. For the Act of 1811, and the form of royal assent to it, see Costin and Watson, ii. 34-8, 164-6. On the King's illnesses of 1801, 1804, and 1810, and the Act, see also Erskine May (ed. Holland), i. 132-46.

acted as a vigilant observer of business in the King's interest.[1] The government which he himself formed on Rockingham's death in 1782 was avowedly based on royal influence and support.[2] Though this failed to prevent its overthrow by a coalition headed by Fox and North, at least the King, stubbornly defending his freedom to choose his own advisers, refused his confidence to these self-imposed ministers, and ultimately brought about their downfall by inducing the Lords to reject Fox's India bill.[3] Much as he had done twenty years earlier, he demonstrated that no government could survive unless it possessed his confidence. Again, as in that day of youthful and self-confident kingship, he gathered control into his own hands and undertook, with a success apparently greater than ever before, the construction of a ministry at once acceptable in his own eyes and capable of conducting his government with parliamentary approval. The younger Pitt, to whom he had first appealed on the fall of Shelburne, consented to form an administration on the dismissal of Fox and North.[4] From December 1783 to March 1784, the opposition, commanding a majority in the Commons, tried vainly to bring about a dissolution. The King, supported by the Lords, kept firm hold on his Prerogative. In the Commons the adverse vote against the government, originally nearly two to one, fell away to a margin of only a single vote. Here was the signal for a dissolution at the King's own choice.[5]

During the months of this sternly-contested defensive action, *The General Election of 1784* every device of eighteenth-century electioneering had been utilised to ensure that the King's appeal to the electorate should succeed. The papers of John Robinson, whose experience as Secretary to the Treasury in North's government fitted him better than any other man in England for the task, contain clear evidence that the result of the general election of March 1784 was made, so far as was humanly possible, a foregone conclusion, and that Pitt, before accepting office, was fully aware of the extent of royal support on which he might count. He won an overwhelm-

[1] See the letters in Fitzmaurice, *Life of Shelburne*, ii. 104-9.

[2] So at least said Horace Walpole, quoted by Erskine May, i. 43. But Walpole is not very good evidence. Compare Fitzmaurice, ii. 246-8.

[3] Turberville, *House of Lords in the Eighteenth Century*, 409-15. Costin and Watson, i. 403.

[4] See K. Feiling, *History of the Second Tory Party*, 151-62, for the attitude of Pitt towards the acceptance of office in 1783.    [5] Feiling, 157.

ing triumph. His opponents were routed, over one hundred and
sixty of "Fox's Martyrs" losing their seats.[1]

*George III
and his
later
Cabinets*

Throughout Pitt's long ministry, George III continued in count-
less ways to rule as well as to reign. He criticised and even opposed
the policy of his ministers, discussed legislative proposals, and controlled appointments to office.[2] His opposition to Catholic emancipation, which Pitt had coupled, whether intentionally or not,
with the Irish Union of 1800, obliged his prime minister to
resign in the following year.[3] When Pitt, having dropped the
Catholic question, came back into office in 1804, the King was
able to insist both on the exclusion of Fox from the Cabinet and
on the inclusion of Addington, who had been premier since
1801.[4] After Pitt's death in 1806, the Grenville ministry which
succeeded him found itself in the same relation with a King who
in old age had not forgotten the constitutional conventions in
which he had been bred during his youth. The Cabinet's attempt
to grant some statutory relief to Catholics and Dissenters serving in
the army and navy led the King to compel them to abandon their
policy and to exact from them a written pledge never again to
raise the Catholic question. This gave them no alternative to
resignation.[5] Like Pitt in 1784, Portland and Perceval, who took
office on the fall of the Grenvilles, seemed to find that royal
favour was the passport to success in the general election of 1807.[6]

*George IV
as Regent
and King*

When, in 1811, the King's mental breakdown removed him
from the scene, the same part was enacted, though with less
interest and pertinacity, by the Regent. It had been generally
expected that his accession to power would be followed by a
change of Cabinet. Such hopes and fears were disappointed, not
only at the moment itself, but also when Perceval's assassination in 1812 offered another opportunity of change.[7] The existing

1 On the general election of 1784, see Lecky, *History of England*, v. 244-60;
J. Holland Rose, *William Pitt and National Revival*, 169-74; Feiling, 160-61;
W. T. Laprade, *Public Opinion and the General Election of 1784*, 31 E.H.R. 224,
and C. E. Fryer, *The General Election of 1784*, 9 Hist. 221.

2 Erskine May, i. 60-63.

3 Feiling, 221-3; Holland Rose, *William Pitt and the Great War*, 435-9. Costin
and Watson, ii. 349-52.                4 Erskine May, i. 67-71.

5 See M. Roberts, *The Fall of the Talents*, 50 E.H.R. 61

6 Erskine May, i. 79-80; Feiling, 256-7.

7 Costin and Watson, ii. 353. For an examination of the Prince's part in the
reconstruction of the ministry in 1812, see M. Roberts, *The Ministerial Crisis of
1812*, 51 E.H.R. 466.

ministry was merely reconstructed under the leadership of Lord Liverpool, and the confidence thus bestowed by the Regent was continued when in 1820 he became King. Even in his relaxed grasp, the influence of the Crown was still strong enough to evoke in 1822 a motion drafted in terms very similar to those used by Dunning, that it was "unnecessary for maintaining its constitutional prerogatives, destructive of the independence of Parliament, and inconsistent with the well-governing of the realm".[1]

The conclusions which this evidence suggests need qualifica- *Decline of* tion. In the precise form in which it had been used before 1782 *royal* personal government was incapable of being resumed. Pitt's *control* triumph in 1784 must not be misconstrued. It may have been due, as was once maintained, to a genuine revulsion of popular opinion against the Coalition.[2] The eighteenth-century electoral system was never so mechanical in operation as to frustrate all expression of spontaneous public feeling. It is at best doubtful whether the royal manœuvres of 1783-4 would have achieved so much in the cause of any other man. What is certain is that there was no one else to whom the King could at that moment have committed his affairs. The choice lay between Pitt and surrender to a "formed opposition". No politician besides Pitt, it is safe to say, could have retained by royal support alone the ascendancy he commanded during the rest of his political career.[3] Where he and his successors in office enhanced their strength, it was due to their increasing sway over Parliament and public opinion, and where they failed in a contest with the Crown it was due to the coincidence against them of royal antipathy, popular mistrust, and dissension within the ranks of their colleagues.[4]

While, therefore, considerable allowance must be made for the *Develop-* continuance of royal influence after 1782, it is more important to *ment of* think of the Cabinet in its development as a coherent entity in- *the* dependent of the Crown. In this development, it is significant *Cabinet* to note the mental derangement which afflicted George III, the contemptible personal character of George IV, and the negligible

---

[1] Erskine May, i. 90.

[2] See on this point the views of Lecky, v. 255 ff., which receive some support in Feiling, 161-2.

[3] It is true that to retain it, Pitt had, like Walpole, sometimes to give way before opposition.

[4] See, generally, A. S. Foord, *The Waning of the Influence of the Crown*, 62 E.H.R. 484.

qualities of William IV. Particularly in the crucial years of the war and its aftermath, such sovereigns were unfitted to sustain the former relationship between the Crown and its ministers. But after 1782, that relationship was in any case incapable of being preserved.

*Its growing solidarity*

In the precise form practised by George III before 1782, this system had broken down. North himself declared his opposition to the principle of "departmental" ministries, whose members were connected more closely with the King than with each other, and was justified in asserting that he had not been its inventor.[1] It was indeed a practice derived from the earlier part of the century, when Cabinets had been loosely compacted bodies lacking in unity, definition, and solidarity.[2] After 1782 the distinction between the titular and the efficient Cabinet disappears. The dominant personality of Pitt gradually ensured that Cabinet deliberations must be confined to persons actually holding office and in agreement with the views of their colleagues. It was no longer open to former ministers to regard themselves as still of the Cabinet, or to the King to seek advice from or extend his confidence to others than his responsible ministers. In 1792 Pitt obtained the dismissal from office of Lord Thurlow, who, though Lord Chancellor, opposed him in Parliament.[3] In 1801 the claim of an ex-minister to take part in Cabinet proceedings was decisively rejected by Addington. Under him the Chancellorship had been conferred on Lord Eldon. Lord Loughborough, its holder under Pitt, attempted to

[1] Moreover, North rejected the title of "Prime Minister". On the other hand, he is credited with an unusual degree of control over his Cabinet. See Lecky, v. 283 and note; Costin and Watson, i. 398.

[2] How far doctrine had changed by 1779 is suggested by the following extract:

"Every expedition, in regard to its destination, object, force, and number of ships, is planned by the Cabinet, and is the result of the collective wisdom of all his Majesty's confidential ministers. The First Lord of the Admiralty is only the executive servant of these measures ; and if he is not personally a Cabinet minister he is not responsible for the wisdom, the policy, and the propriety of any naval expedition. But if he is in the Cabinet, then he must share in common with the other ministers that proportional division of censure which is attached to him as an individual. In no situation is he more or less responsible to his country than his colleagues for any misconduct which flows from a Cabinet measure."

(1779, *Sandwich Papers*, vol. ii. 255. Navy Records Society.)

[3] Holland Rose, *William Pitt and the Great War*, 33-4. Costin and Watson, ii. 345-6.

retain membership of the new Cabinet. He was obliged to desist by Addington's warning that "the number of cabinet ministers should not exceed that of the persons whose responsible situation in office obliges their being members of it".[1]

Even admitting the persistence of royal influence after 1782, *Eco-* the growing solidarity and independence of the Cabinet, and *nomica* therefore the substitution of the authority of the Prime Minister *reform* for that of the King, are thus evident. The King was slowly, but quite unmistakably, losing the effective headship of his own government.[2] From 1782 a process of reform set in which emphasised this tendency by drawing a clear distinction between his personal and household expenses on the one hand and those which, though still defrayed from his Civil List, were treated as more public in character and thus brought under some degree of parliamentary control. The Rockingham Whigs, so long excluded by the King's extensive command of patronage, came into office in that year as the avowed enemies of the system once the very foundation of Whig ascendancy but now condemned in their eyes through its perversion by George III. Their challenge had already been made in Dunning's resolution of 1780, and in the Civil Establishment bill introduced by Burke in 1780 and 1781.[3] In 1782 the reformers signalised their victory by placing on the statute-book a number of measures embodying the policy known as "economical reform". These included Burke's bill, now passed in a somewhat modified form, Crewe's Act, disfranchising revenue officers, Clerke's Act, disqualifying government contractors from sitting in the House of Commons, and an Act regulating the office of Paymaster-General.[4]

Burke's Civil Establishment Act was the most radical and far- *The Civil* reaching of the four. Opportunity for this measure was provided *Establish-* by the recurrence of over-expenditure on the Civil List, which *ment Act* involved recourse to Parliament for the debt to be cleared. Such over-spending was nothing new. Under George I and George II Parliament had had to come to the rescue of the Civil List. George

[1] Anson, ii. i. (ed. Keith), 116.

[2] The process is examined in some detail in Professor A. Aspinall's Raleigh Lecture on *The Cabinet Council, 1783–1835* (Proceedings of the British Academy, 1952).

[3] Erskine May, i. 161-2. Burke brought in four other bills, but this was the only one read.    [4] For these Acts, see Costin and Watson, i. 145-50.

III, beginning his reign with a surplus of £172,000 inherited from George II, and accepting, on the surrender of the hereditary revenues, a permanent income of £800,000 annually, had found himself in the same difficulties as his predecessors. In 1769 and again in 1777 he had applied for relief to Parliament. On the second occasion, though the debt was discharged and the Civil List raised to £900,000, the government had met with serious opposition, in which Burke and Wilkes were prominent.[1] The King was blamed for his inability to keep his implied promise to live within his income, for failure to produce a comprehensible account of how the deficit had occurred, and for abuse of the Civil List as a means of corruption. Burke's celebrated speech in support of his bill of 1780 had taken wider ground. He criticised the antiquated and wasteful organisation of the royal household, the maladministration of royal property, the inefficiency of the Exchequer, the retention of large balances by paymasters and other public accountants, and alleged the uselessness of certain offices and departments of state.[2] These ideas underlay the Act of 1782. It abolished the Secretaryship of State for the Colonies and the Board of Trade, as also a large number of official positions connected with the Household, and introduced a new classification of charges on the Civil List. These were now arranged in the following order of priority: the Privy Purse, the judicial establishment, ministers to foreign courts, bills of royal tradesmen, wages to servants, pensions and annuities, and fees and salaries in government offices, those of the Treasury and Exchequer coming last in order to encourage the Treasury and Exchequer officials to insist on due economy in all the prior charges.[3]

*Results of economical reform*  In considering these reforms it must be borne in mind that their main object was not so much to increase parliamentary control over the executive as to diminish the extent to which royal influence could be utilised in order to control Parliament. Their sponsors aimed primarily at restoring the balance between legislature and executive, which seemed to them to have been disturbed by the encroachments of the latter. It may be doubted

[1] Cobbett, *Parliamentary History*, xix. 114-26.
[2] For Burke's speech, see *Works* (ed. 1826), iii. 231.
[3] R. H. Gretton, *The King's Government*, 92.

whether either the Civil Establishment Act, or any of the measures accompanying it, was highly successful for this purpose.[1] The end in view could be achieved only by some scheme of reform in the electoral system itself, widening the franchise and eliminating rotten boroughs. The advocates of economical reform were inclined for the most part to avoid any such larger scheme, and expected that their proposals would make it unnecessary. Not only was that expectation disappointed, but even as a practical administrative device, economical reform was disappointing in its results. The Board of Trade could not be dispensed with, and re-appeared within four years.[2] In 1793, shortly after the outbreak of war with France, a third Secretaryship, for War, was easily established, in that Dundas, as Secretary of State, simply transferred those of his powers which related to the armed forces to the Duke of Portland.[3] The Act of 1782, in short, did not prevent the creation of new Secretaryships of State, though it did of course debar more than two of their holders from sitting in the Commons. The Act regulating the office of Paymaster-General proved so defective that it had to be repealed in the following year and replaced by a new measure. Above all, over-spending on the Civil List went on as before. In 1786 £210,000 more was needed, and in 1802 a fresh application for relief was made to the Commons.[4]

Yet the movement for economical reform produced valuable *Later* results, even if these were somewhat different from those intended *reforms* by its movers. In 1780 North had so far yielded to his critics as to appoint a body of commissioners to examine into the public accounts. Their reports, which embraced the whole system whereby public money was expended and accounted for, gave Parliament for the first time a complete and detailed view of the subject, and prompted a series of reforms, for which Pitt was mainly responsible, in the fiscal administration of the State.[5] In 1785 the reforms already applied to the Paymaster of the Forces

---

[1] On the results of these measures, see Keir, *Economical Reform*, 50 L.Q.R. 368.
[2] H. Llewellyn Smith, *The Board of Trade*, 33-7.
[3] For the debates on this appointment, see Cobbett, *Parliamentary History*, xxxiii, 963 and 1141.
[4] See Erskine May, i. 164 n., for a list of grants to clear the Civil List of debt, 1769-1816.
[5] For a summary of these reports, see Keir, 50 L.Q.R. 382-3.

13

were extended to the Treasurer of the Navy.[1] The Exchequer was reformed by the abolition of the useless office of Auditor of the Imprests, and salaried commissioners for auditing the public accounts were created.[2] Commissioners were appointed to inquire into Crown lands, woods and forests.[3] Investigation began into the fees paid to holders of offices.[4] Above all Pitt adopted in 1787 one of the main recommendations of the commissioners on the public accounts, by substituting for the system under which separate heads of revenue were segregated into distinct funds each with its own items of expenditure charged against it, a new system based on the pooling of the entire public revenue in one Consolidated Fund, from which all branches of public expenditure were met.[5]

*The Secretaryships and the Board of Trade*    The outbreak of war in 1793 did not interrupt, though in some ways it retarded, the process of administrative change. To the two existing Secretaryships of State—which since March 1782 had been transformed so as to deal respectively with foreign and with domestic and colonial affairs [6]—was added the Secretaryship for War in 1794. In 1801 colonial business was transferred from the Home Secretary to his new colleague, who from this date until 1854 became Secretary of State for War and the Colonies.[7] The duties remaining to the Home Secretary after this change had been effected were at first small, including such functions as acting as a medium of communication between King and subject, advising the King on the use of certain prerogative powers, and issuing instructions to local officials like Lords-Lieutenant and Justices of the Peace. At the close of the war, indeed, it was proposed to revert to the former system of having only two Secretaries.[8] New fields of work, however, were already opening up to the Home Secretary through the enlargement of his powers by statute. A series of Acts beginning in 1793 brought aliens under the control of the Home Office. Post-war statutes began the process of placing prisons and police under its supervision. The way was

---

[1] 25 Geo. III, c. 31.    [2] Costin and Watson, ii. 1.    [3] 26 Geo. III, c. 87.
[4] 25 Geo. III, c. 19; 26 Geo. III, c. 99; 27 Geo. III, c. 35; 28 Geo. III, c. 4.
[5] Costin and Watson, ii. 2-4.
[6] The change was made by Fox in the Rockingham ministry of 1782.
[7] In 1782 the duties of the Secretary of War had been amplified, and in 1793 the office of Commander-in-Chief, only in occasional existence since 1670, was revived.    [8] Gretton, 117.

thus prepared for the transformation of the Home Office into the greatest of internal administrative departments.[1] The Board of Trade, restored in 1786 after its temporary disappearance in 1782, occupied itself at first with mainly advisory duties, relating to the exploitation of new markets, the encouragement of new industries, and the negotiation of commercial treaties. The war hastened its development from a mere consultative committee into an administrative department, dealing with such matters as contraband, enemy trade, food supplies, and the like. The President, acting alone and assisted by a salaried staff, acquired executive powers. The Board itself became merely formal and its business of the old advisory kind increasingly slight.[2]

Most important of all, however, was the progress made during *Financial* the war in the transaction of financial business. In 1802 the *reforms* practice was inaugurated of preparing an annual survey of the national finances, leading up in 1822 to the provision of an annual balanced statement of accounts.[3] From 1802, moreover, another stage is to be traced in the separation between the expenses incurred on behalf of the King and his household and those which, though charged on the Civil List, arose from matters of strictly public concern. The plan adopted in 1782 had failed. In 1802 the Civil List was once more in debt. On this occasion the Prime Minister, Addington, abandoned the line taken by his predecessors, that the expenditure of the Civil List was entirely the King's affair, and fully informed the Commons of the disbursements made under the various heads. It appeared that the King's personal and household expenses had been rigidly retrenched. The deficit had arisen partly through the rise in prices, and partly from the development and extension of civil government.[4] Parliament had thus to endeavour to distinguish, as it had never done or been encouraged to do before, between the domestic and the public expenditure of the Crown, and to assume, as was right, a larger responsibility for the latter. It was only with reluctance that it faced this unwelcome prospect. The antiquated principle that the King should "live of his own" was once more sounded, even at

---

[1] E. Troup, *The Home Office*, 18-22.
[2] Gretton, 118-20; Llewellyn Smith, 37-51.
[3] Anson, ii. ii. (ed. Keith), 180.
[4] For Addington's speech, see Cobbett, *Parliamentary History*, xxvi, 372 ff.

the opening of the nineteenth century. Yet each application for a supplementary grant to the Civil List strengthened the case for relieving it of burdens of which the King ought to be relieved, and involved examination of alternative means for doing so.

*Civil List* The main alternatives were three in number. To charge
*and Supply* additional expenses on the Consolidated Fund was open to the
*services* objection that, once granted, they tended to become fixed and permanent, and thus defeated attempts at economy and excluded the Commons' control over finance.[1] A second alternative was to try to make civil government self-supporting on the basis of the fees paid to officials. If the King could not live of his own, at least the departments of state might; and one of them, the Post Office, in fact already did so. Some progress was made along this line. For example, in 1808, the Privy Council Office began to pay all fees into a single fund, from which officials drew standardised salaries reckoned in round figures. This process led inevitably to the cutting away of much dead wood. Lucrative sinecures were exposed and salaries tended to become a fair return for work done. Departmental scales of pay afforded a standard for computing subsequent parliamentary provision for administrative expenses.[2] Such provision was the third, and, as it proved, the most satisfactory method of financing the requirements of the civil government. Dependence on fees was suited only to the needs of a fixed system serving a static society. As the necessity of elaborating governmental services revealed itself, it became plain that a revenue derived from fees would not permit of sufficiently rapid expansion. Therefore the practice developed of asking for annual parliamentary grants to supply the deficiencies of the income from the Civil List and the fee funds. In 1802 a new head of public finance makes its appearance—"Miscellaneous Civil Services out of Supply". These included public works and buildings, salaries of public departments, law and justice, education, science and art, colonial, foreign, and consular services.[3] In 1816 a great advance was made when the Civil List Act removed certain payments altogether from the Civil List, charging them on the Consolidated Fund, and allotted to each of the remainder a specified annual allowance. On George IV's accession his Civil List of

[1] On this point, see Gretton, 105.

[2] Gretton, 110.                                    [3] Gretton, 104.

£850,000 was again charged with specified categories of expenditure, but a milestone was reached in 1830 when William IV accepted a Civil List of only £510,000, based on the recommendation of a Select Committee that "the Civil List should be applied only to such expenses as affect the dignity and state of the Crown, and the personal comfort of their Majesties", and that these should be removed from the other expenses of government.[1] The Crown was now relieved from any financial responsibility for the conduct of civil administration. It remained only for Parliament to accept full responsibility, placing certain heads of expenditure permanently on the Consolidated Fund, and providing for others by annual supply based on detailed Civil Estimates. When that step had been taken, civil government, so long the preserve of the Crown, would fall wholly under parliamentary supervision, to be conducted by ministers as heads of departments, subject to the guidance of the Treasury.

Reaching beyond the executive machinery of the State, the reforms of the half-century beginning in 1782 covered also the machinery of the law. For this purpose, as for the procedural and substantive amendment of the law itself, the prevalent influence of Benthamism determined the direction and to some degree the pace of change.[2] Thus in 1792 the system of paid or stipendiary magistrates, originated at Bow Street, was largely extended, a supplementary Act of 1800 drafted by Bentham himself still further amplifying the system.[3] In 1829 a similar system was connected by Sir Robert Peel with the newly created Metropolitan Police. Manchester had followed the example of London in 1813, though the system was not copied elsewhere for upward of twenty years thereafter.[4] The police system itself was introduced into the boroughs in 1835, and the counties were in 1837 enabled and in 1856 compelled to have police forces.[5] A local jurisdiction for petty civil cases was meanwhile being evolved by the

*Reform of the legal and judicial system*

---

[1] *Report on Public Income and Expenditure, 1868-9*, Part II, Appendix 13, pp. 603-5; Erskine May, i. 165-6.

[2] See on this point, Redlich and Hirst, *Local Government in England*, i. 86-7.

[3] Holdsworth, *History of English Law*, i. 147-8.

[4] Holdsworth, i. 148; Webb, *Manor and Borough*, 754. It has never spread widely, perhaps because no part of the salary is paid by the central government. See Redlich and Hirst, i. 415.

[5] Redlich and Hirst, i. 171. J. Hart, *Reform of the Borough Police, 1835-0*, 70 E.H.R. 411.

creation of numerous courts of requests.[1] From 1750 Middlesex possessed a County Court, established by statute, which was the precursor of the County Courts exercising civil but not criminal jurisdiction set up in 1846.[2] The same period witnessed the beginnings of a reform of the Common Law courts. In 1810, and again from 1818 to 1822, the offices attached to these courts were investigated, and a great number of sinecures were abolished.[3] As in the administrative departments of government, a serious blow was struck at the ancient conception of office as a freehold, and official positions began to be regarded as implying primarily efficient and salaried service to the State. In this process the judges themselves were affected. In 1826 their income from fees was abolished, and their salaries, charged on the Consolidated Fund, raised to £5500 per annum.[4] Even more than the Common Law courts, the Chancery stood in need of reform. Its delays and congestion led in 1813 to the appointment of a Vice-Chancellor, but the remedy proved defective, and the obstinacy of the Lord Chancellor, Eldon, blocked until 1830 the way to any thorough-going attempt at improvement. The Chancery was, in a fashion, subjected to critical examination from 1826 to 1828, as were the ecclesiastical courts in 1823 and 1824, the Court of Admiralty and the Court of Delegates in 1824, and the Common Law courts again from 1829.[5] It is true that little definite action was taken before 1832, and that action only followed slowly thereafter. The clash of jurisdictions, especially between Common Law and Equity, the technicality, costliness and delay of English litigation were defects difficult to remove, even if some simplification was effected by an Act of 1830 which amalgamated the two Courts of Exchequer Chamber, and constituted a single Court of the same name for appeals, comprising the judges of the two Common Law courts other than that whose decision it was sought to reverse,[6] subject to the final appellate jurisdiction of the Lords.[7] Yet it may be said that already by 1832 at least some preliminary steps had been taken on the thorny path towards judicial reform. The main

---

[1] On these see W. H. D. Winder, *The Courts of Requests*, 52 *L.Q.R.* 369.

[2] Costin and Watson, ii. 94. Holdsworth, i. 191. For earlier attempts to bring about the creation of local courts, see Holdsworth, i. 189-90.

[3] Holdsworth, i. 262-3.              [4] Holdsworth, i. 255.

[5] Holdsworth, i. 635-6.              [6] Holdsworth, i. 245.

[7] On the jurisdiction of the Lords in this period, see Turberville, *House of Lords as a Court of Law, 1784-1837*, 52 *L.Q.R.* 189.

obstacle was that lawyers alone knew how to frame adequate reforms, and were not generally anxious to do so.

Finally, in the domain of local administration, the years from 1782 to 1832 saw the crumbling of the old system and the founding of the new. Here the primary cause was the social transformation accomplished by the changes in agriculture and industry, which impaired the efficiency of many ancient organs of government and imposed an intolerable burden on others. As population deserted the countryside and massed in the towns, the rural units of government lost vitality, and those dealing with urban areas were overwhelmed by their responsibilities. Among the problems which faced them, two rose to outstanding importance—the problem of crime and the problem of poverty. During the earlier eighteenth century, neither had been acute except perhaps for the recurrence of disorders in London.[1] The new distribution of population, and the creation of a new class of poor labourers who, unlike their predecessors, were not limited in numbers and well known to the relieving authorities, presented a wholly different question. Nor was the assessment and collection of rates on new kinds of property an easy matter. The system of relief which had hitherto answered well enough tended to become unworkable. Many magistrates in the southern and eastern counties followed the example set by the Berkshire magistrates at Speenhamland in 1795, and adopted the plan of indiscriminate outdoor relief, making up wages out of rates to a minimum level determined by the price of bread.[2] The Speenhamland plan contributed to a rapid increase in the burden of the poor rates, which, stable at about one million pounds annually over the eighteenth century as a whole, reached four millions in 1800, and eight millions by 1818.[3] With poverty went crime, hitherto a serious menace only in London. The new urban areas came to offer much the same difficulties as the metropolis. Everywhere disorder tended to take on a novel and alarming aspect. It

*Decline of the old system of local administration*

---

[1] On the problem of order in London, see M. D. George, *London Life in the Eighteenth Century*, 82-4, 118-19, 132-3, 180.

[2] On the Speenhamland system, see Lipson, *Economic History of England*, iii. 481-4.

[3] Other causes contributing to the growth of the burden of poor relief were a rise in prices (due partly to a depreciated currency), bad harvests, and the economic dislocation due to the war.

assumed the form of disturbances connected not only with local and passing grievances, but with deliberate challenges to constituted authority. The old governing class found itself inadequately equipped for its new tasks, and was moreover weakened as its members began to withdraw from districts where industrialisation destroyed the amenities of rural life.

*The demand for reform of local administration*

Further, a new element in the class of moneyed men was coming into existence which threatened the monopoly hitherto enjoyed by the ancient oligarchy. The product of recent industrial development, this class was generally drawn from a wholly different section of the population, whose resentment at exclusion from the county and municipal magistracies was often sharpened by the religious animosity between Dissenter and Churchman. To some extent, the desire of the Dissenters to control administration was met in the creation of the *ad hoc* authorities, to which the disqualifications of the Test and Corporation Acts did not apply.[1] But men of this type were naturally inclined to press for wholesale reforms of local administration, and for its reconstitution on a different basis. The demand was reinforced as the movement for political equality and for a more even distribution of political power gained ground, and with it the utilitarian idea that institutions however venerable which served no useful purpose should be swept away.

*Beginnings of the new system*

Under the impact of these forces, the old local administrative system neared collapse. Institutions began to appear which rested on new principles such as paid instead of unpaid service, expert instead of amateur direction, democratic instead of oligarchical control, a legal basis in statute instead of Common Law and local custom, and centralisation instead of local autonomy.[2] The first two of these principles had indeed manifested themselves earlier, in the occasional appointment of salaried officials, for example, parish clerks, and surveyors of highways. The technical requirements of administration in the later eighteenth and early nineteenth centuries made it necessary to increase their number. During this period innumerable local statutes amplified the powers of existing local

[1] G. D. H. Cole, *Town Life in the Provinces* in *Johnson's England* (Ed. A. S. Turberville) i. 207.
[2] For a full discussion of this change of principles, see Webb, *Statutory Authorities*, ch. v-vi.

authorities such as Justices of the Peace, borough magistrates, and vestries, and added multitudes of new *ad hoc* bodies. All of these, whether old or new, came to rely on paid experts as engineers, surveyors, and the like. Inevitably, the function of the ordinary citizen in local government ceased to involve unpaid and compulsory service, and implied principally the obligation to pay rates. The consequence was the gradual application of the elective system at least to the composition of the *ad hoc* bodies, in which there came to exist, side by side with *ex-officio* or nominated members, a number of representatives elected by ratepayers qualified by their ownership of a requisite minimum of property. The multiplication of separate local statutes conferring specific powers on particular authorities slowly gave place in the early nineteenth century to Acts prescribing general rules, sweeping away local variations, and tending towards uniformity in the administration of poor relief, roads, prisons, and other services, all hitherto regulated by the varying practice of individual controlling bodies. From the general statute passed by Parliament it was only a short step to the general administrative supervision exercised by the central government. For this purpose the Home Office was naturally utilised. The Prisons Act of 1823, though not quite universal in its application, is noteworthy as "the first measure of general prison reform to be framed and enacted on the responsibility of the national executive".[1]

It will be evident that for half a century before 1832 administration was ceasing to be in the main the personal concern of the sovereign, or to be carried on in the main by virtue of prerogative and Common Law powers. The sovereign's control over his Cabinet was declining. The Cabinet was acquiring greater homogeneity with its greater independence. The functions and organs of government were rapidly multiplying and extending. A process of reform was at work, affecting both the administrative and the judicial system, and aiming at the substitution of efficient salaried public servants for sinecurists owing their appointment to patronage. The monopoly so long enjoyed by the Anglican landed gentry in the central and local government of England was being undermined. In 1828 and 1829 it was breached by the repeal of the Test and Corporation Acts and by the Catholic Emancipation Act,

*Administrative changes, 1782–1832*

---

[1] S. and B. Webb, *The English Prisons under Local Government*, 73.

13a

which, with a few exceptions, freed the service of the Crown, municipal office, and membership of Parliament from religious disabilities.[1] Changes so profound as these, touching the very foundations of government, inevitably extended to the one great political institution which so far had been unaffected. Every argument which had led to the reforms already achieved could be applied to a reform of the parliamentary system. Such a reform would eliminate "influence" and replace it by democratic principles, would end the ascendancy of the landed class and introduce that of the industrial capitalist, would enable surviving abuses to be dealt with effectively, and liberate the forces of free individual enterprise from the dead hand of the past.

### iii

*Tardy rise of the demand for parliamentary reform*      The reformers of 1782 had deliberately preferred to concentrate their attack on the abuse of "influence". Believing that the infirmities of the parliamentary system were due to this cause, and not to any radical defects in its structure, they had refrained from, and even been hostile to, any scheme for remodelling the electoral franchise or the distribution of seats, or for bringing the Commons into closer contact with the constituencies by shortening the duration of Parliament. Yet fundamental criticisms, of the kind which they thus refused to admit, had already been frequently raised, and schemes for parliamentary reform had been propounded. The main defect of the electoral system was considered to be the immense preponderance in the Commons of members representing rotten boroughs. A century earlier, Locke had advocated reform by recourse to the Prerogative. But the Prerogative had for this purpose been long disused. Reform must therefore depend on the recognition by Parliament itself of the need for change. Recognition could in the nature of things only be slowly and grudgingly accorded by a body itself constituted under a system which it was to be invited to condemn. It is moreover to be remembered that almost until the close of the eighteenth century the electoral system, for all its anomalies, did succeed in representing very fairly the nation whose mind it purported to express. "Influence" no

[1] Costin and Watson, ii. 42-53.

doubt deeply affected it, but did not so entirely dominate it as to divorce the Commons from those who exercised the franchise. No one conceived that the purpose of the electoral system was to elicit the views of a numerical majority of the nation. It was intended to voice the opinions of those "interests" which had a right to be consulted, and of which the landed interest was still the greatest. Commerce, the universities, and even the democratic masses of large cities and towns such as Westminster or Preston[1] also found opportunity to make their views heard in Parliament. So long, in fact, as England continued to be, as it had been, a stable and mainly agricultural society, its unreformed House of Commons was no inadequate embodiment of its principles, interests, and prejudices.

The easy-going toleration of anomalies and abuses to which *The first* this general identity of interest between electors and elected *remedial* naturally led was coming to be interrupted, long before the end *measures* of the century, by criticisms uttered both inside and outside Parliament. An attempt was made by statute in 1762 to check bribery at elections by imposing a fine on offenders,[2] but the investigation of elections at Shoreham in 1771, Hindon in 1775, and Cricklade in 1782,[3] carried out by committees appointed under the Grenville Act of 1770, revealed how inveterate were the old evils. The increasing venality of the electoral system, often attributed by contemporaries to the efforts of "nabobs" enriched by Indian trade to buy entry into Parliament, evoked a series of proposals to legislate against bribery and excessive expenditure in elections. In 1786 one such bill, intended to apply to county elections, actually passed the Commons and was only wrecked by the opposition of the Lords.[4] A bill of 1809, penalising corrupt agreements for the return of members, succeeded in reaching the statute-book, though in practice it produced little result.[5] There was indeed no adequate machinery giving effect to measures

[1] For all its size, the Preston electorate was, however, generally controlled by the influence of the Stanley family, until won for radicalism by "Orator" Hunt in 1830.

[2] Erskine May, i. 226.

[3] Erskine May, i. 228-9; Porritt, i. 16. Shoreham was enlarged by the addition of the freeholders of the Rape of Bramber. Similar measures were taken with regard to Cricklade, and later at Aylesbury (1804) and East Retford (1828).

[4] Erskine May, i. 230.          [5] Erskine May, i. 232-4.

against electoral corruption. The committees created under the Grenville Act were an improvement on the former system by which election disputes came under the jurisdiction of the House as a whole. Yet their value was diminished by the method by which they were appointed, and they tended to become partial and incompetent, giving their decision on strictly party lines with little regard to the merits of the case.[1] The deep-seated evils inherent in the electoral system were hardly to be eradicated by penal statutes which it was difficult to enforce. Nor could much be hoped from the plans for holding general elections more frequently, like those brought forward annually from 1771 by Alderman Sawbridge, member for Hythe.[2] The remedy must be more drastic. It could hardly become effective unless it remodelled and enlarged the electorate to such an extent that the accustomed means of corruption were no longer applicable.

*Early proposals for parliamentary reform*     Such remedies had already been propounded, for example, by the Supporters of the Bill of Rights in 1767. In subsequent years both a redistribution of seats and an enlargement of the franchise found advocates. In 1770 Lord Chatham, who condemned borough representation as "the rotten part of the constitution", proposed to counterbalance it by adding a third member for each county.[3] Wilkes in 1776 proposed a more sweeping change, giving additional members to London and to the more populous counties, disfranchising rotten boroughs and merging them in their counties, and providing for the separate representation of such large towns as Manchester, Leeds, Sheffield, and Birmingham.[4] In 1780 a still more radical scheme, for annual Parliaments, universal suffrage, and equal electoral districts, was produced by the Duke of Richmond, but rejected by the Lords without a division.[5] Plans of a more moderate kind commended themselves to the younger Pitt, who moved in 1782 for a committee of inquiry into the state of parliamentary representation, brought forward in the following year resolutions against corruption and in favour of additional representation for London and the counties, and, as Prime Minister, tried to introduce a reform bill, intended to ex-

---

[1] On the defects of these committees, see Porritt, i. 540.
[2] G. S. Veitch, *Genesis of Parliamentary Reform*, 34–5.
[3] Williams, *Life of Pitt*, ii. 267; Veitch, 37–9.
[4] Veitch, 44–6.      [5] Veitch, 70–1.

tinguish by purchase the right of fifty boroughs to return members, to distribute the hundred seats thus made available, and to enlarge the electorate by admitting copyholders to the franchise.[1] He found himself unsupported. The King was hostile to the bill, the Cabinet divided, and the Commons unfriendly. Leave to introduce the bill was refused, and Pitt allowed the subject to drop. In 1790, though still professing support for the principle of parliamentary reform, he opposed a motion for the addition of one hundred county members to the House.[2] The outbreak of war with France in 1793 ended any prospect of electoral reform on governmental initiative.

However adverse the attitude of the government, or even of the nation at large, to tampering with parliamentary institutions during the critical period which now began, the question could not be shelved completely or for ever. Public interest had very clearly been already aroused with regard to the relations between the nation and its representatives in the Commons. Petitions to Parliament formed one important means of impressing on the House that it must bear in mind the views of electors, and had been used, by the voters of Yorkshire and other counties, to strengthen the hands of the economical reformers.[3] Other petitions dealt with such topics as parliamentary reform, the war against the American colonies, and slavery, and the number of petitions annually presented increased twentyfive-fold between 1780 and 1830.[4] They culminated in the monster petitions for electoral reform in 1830–32. Public meetings, in the past an uncommon though not unknown political device, became unprecedentedly frequent after 1780, and it was in these meetings that petitions were usually framed and approved.[5] During the period of the French war, when the extension of revolutionary movements to England haunted the mind of a government poorly equipped with means of keeping order, statutory limitations were imposed on the

*Growth of petitions and public meetings*

---

[1] Holland Rose, *William Pitt and National Revival*, 131-2, 197-207.

[2] Holland Rose, *William Pitt and the Great War*, 11-12.

[3] Veitch, 60-1, 63-4. Representatives of the petitioning counties were assembled in London in a Convention. Note their analogy to the American Committees of Correspondence.

[4] Emden, *The People and the Constitution*, 77-8.

[5] On the organisation of public meetings in the eighteenth century, see Veitch, 57-60.

right of public meeting, except for meetings of county gentlemen summoned normally under the auspices of the Lord-Lieutenant or sheriff. Parliament strengthened the law for the preservation of order by a suspension of the Habeas Corpus Act,[1] and by a Treasonable and Seditious Practices Act (1795) which, besides re-enacting the customary list of treasons, made it treasonable to use force to coerce the Houses and penalised spoken or written words intended to create disaffection towards the King and the established government.[2] It also passed in 1795 a Seditious Meetings and Assemblies Act prohibiting meetings held for seditious purposes and imposing severe restrictions on meetings of every kind.[3] Yet in the years of distress which followed the war, political meetings multiplied, and the tumults attending the dispersal of that held at St. Peter's Fields, Manchester, in 1819, caused the law to be reinforced by the Six Acts, which included, *inter alia*, an Act further adding to the law on this point.[4] Meetings of more than fifty persons for political or similar purposes were prohibited except when convened by Lords-Lieutenant or sheriffs, mayors, five or more Justices of the Peace, or held by parishioners within their own parishes. The agitations preceding and accompanying the passing of the Reform Bill of 1832 again indicated plainly that this new technique for imposing the will of the electorate on the legislature could not be frustrated.

*Political societies*      A further instrument for the same purpose was found in the formation of political societies. The Society of Supporters of the Bill of Rights proved the precursor of a long series of such associations, examples of which were to be found in the Yorkshire Association; the Society for promoting Constitutional Information founded by Major Cartwright [5] (1780), and others also advocating administrative and parliamentary reform; the Protestant Association of the same year whose activities led to the Gordon riots;[6] the society of moderate reformers, mainly of the middle and

---

[1] It was suspended from 1794 to 1801. During the century after 1689 there were only nine instances of suspension; Erskine May, ii. 131-4. For a suspension Act for Ireland, in 1803, see Costin and Watson, ii. 32-4.

[2] Costin and Watson, ii. 10-12.

[3] Costin and Watson, ii. 12-16. It lapsed in 1799 and was renewed for a short period in 1800.

[4] On the Six Acts, see Erskine May, ii. 81.

[5] Veitch, 71-5. Cartwright helped later to found the Hampden Clubs.

[6] On the Protestant Association, see J. P. de Castro, *The Gordon Riots*, 14-17.

upper class, formed in 1792 under the name of Friends of the People;[1] and the more radical working-class London Corresponding Society, formed a few weeks before, and later linked with kindred societies elsewhere.[2] Associations for political purposes were suppressed by statute in 1799.[3] Even before the war ended, however, political activity of this character was resumed. From 1812, the Union and Hampden Clubs agitated for universal suffrage and annual Parliaments,[4] the Anti-Slavery Association of 1823 demonstrated the force of organised opinion in achieving a humanitarian end through the exercise of influence on Parliament.[5] Finally, the development of the press, even if retarded by restrictive statutes in 1798 and 1817-19,[6] provided yet another means of bringing Parliament into closer relation with public opinion and the popular will. An important point was gained in Fox's Libel Act of 1792,[7] which for the first time left the decision as to the intention and the nature of published matter, hitherto reserved to the bench, to be made by the jury, though the *Case of Sir Francis Burdett* (1820)[8] showed with what strictness the law of libel could be defined by judges in their summing-up for the guidance of jurymen.

If therefore a majority of both Houses continued during all these years to be hostile to reform, forces were in process of creation outside Parliament which, in one way or another, implied the necessity of conforming the legislature to the will of the people. In the war period itself, the small Whig minority left after the majority under Portland had seceded to the side of the government continued to raise the question of reform. During this agitation, in which the names of Grey, Erskine, and Burdett

*The reform agitation.*

---

[1] Veitch, 196-200; P. A. Brown, *The French Revolution in English History*, 54-9.  [2] Veitch, 191-6. See also Brown, 63, 66, 111, 136.
[3] For the Act, see Costin and Watson, ii. 18-20.
[4] J. R. M. Butler, *Passing of the Great Reform Bill*, 27. On the Hampden Clubs, see H. W. C. Davis, *The Age of Grey and Peel*, ch. viii. The name was suggested by Hampden's refusal to pay taxes.
[5] On the Abolition Society of 1787, see W. L. Mathieson, *England in Transition, 1789-1832*, 65-6; Erskine May, ii. 27-8; for the Act abolishing the Slave Trade, see Grant Robertson, 295-9. For the Anti-Slavery Society of 1823, see Emden, 91, 259.
[6] Erskine May, ii. 60-62, 74, 82. See also W. H. Wickwar, *The Struggle for the Freedom of the Press, 1819-32*, 5 B.I.H.R. 51, and his book of the same title, in which ch. iv deals with the Six Acts in this connexion.
[7] Costin and Watson, ii. 6-7.   [8] Costin and Watson, ii. 251-6.

were prominent, schemes were put forward in 1793, 1797, 1809, and 1810.[1] On the conclusion of peace, the advocates of reform, now reinforced by Bentham—who had taken up the question in 1809, published a Plan of Parliamentary Reform in 1817, and prepared a draft bill in 1819 [2]—and by Lord John Russell, returned to the attack. Plans for reform came before Parliament in 1818, 1819, 1820, 1821, 1822, 1823, and 1826.[3] These proposals it is true were all rejected. But a number of instances of corruption threw a revealing light on the decay of the unreformed system. Some piecemeal cure was attempted. In 1821 the notorious borough of Grampound was disfranchised and its two seats allotted to Yorkshire.[4] Corruption at Northampton and Leicester in 1826, though unattended by the same penalty, gave strength to the case for reform.[5] Finally the issue was precipitated by the abuses disclosed at Penryn and East Retford. In both cases the Opposition urged disfranchisement, and the transfer of the seats thus made available to the large unrepresented boroughs of Manchester and Birmingham.[6] In each case the proposal was wrecked either in the Commons or in the Lords. The result was to end any chance of gradual readjustment by the transfer of seats from decayed or corrupt constituencies to unenfranchised towns whose claims to representation were daily growing with the increase of their wealth and population, and to throw the ancient constitution of the House of Commons into the melting-pot.

*General character of the Reform Act of 1832*

The Whig government which assumed office in 1830 and passed the Reform Bill in 1832 pledged itself from the outset to correct those defects in the representative system "which had been occasioned in it by the operation of time", in order to restore "that confidence on the part of the people" which it no longer enjoyed.[7] The resulting Act was the first which had ever dealt with the system of parliamentary representation as a whole. Its title "an Act to amend the representation of the people" was in itself the admission of a new principle, since the elective principle throughout its history had been applied to the representa-

---

[1] G. M. Trevelyan, *Lord Grey of the Reform Bill*, 47-8, 75-6, 94-6; M. W. Patterson, *Sir Francis Burdett and his Times*, i. 233-5; see generally, Erskine May, i. 270-3.

[2] Butler, 29-30.   [3] Erskine May, i, 273-6.

[4] Erskine May, i. 275. For Lord Liverpool's objections to the disfranchisement of Grampound, see Costin and Watson, ii. 362.

[5] Erskine May, i. 277.   [6] Erskine May, 278-9.   [7] Erskine May, i. 282. For the text of the Act, see Costin and Watson, ii. 55-68.

tion not of "the people" as such, but of communities and interests among them which appeared, by prescriptive right or from considerations of expediency and without regard to their numerical weight, to be entitled to have their views expressed.[1] The Act, differing profoundly at first sight from the measures for parliamentary reform proposed in the eighteenth century, did not limit itself to readjustments within the existing system, but introduced organic changes which reflected the increasing ascendancy of the radical thought stimulated by Bentham and reinforced by the democratic impulse received from the doctrines of the French Revolution. It did in fact owe much to these influences, quickened into even greater vigour by the example of the July Revolution in France, which showed the possibility of introducing sweeping political changes without destroying the established social order.[2] Yet it is plain that the reform of 1832 was not wholly based on contemporary radical theories, and that it implicitly accepted certain historic principles of English government, though giving them a fresh application. It continued the traditional connexion between property and political power, insisting only that property other than land was entitled to be taken into account for this purpose. While introducing new types of franchise, it preserved the old. Though destroying many decayed boroughs, and enfranchising populous towns unrepresented in the past, it was far from equating representation and population. Its chief object was to end that overwhelming preponderance of the landed interest which the unreformed system had secured, but which social and economic changes had rendered out of date and intolerable.

The main achievement of the Act was the redistribution of seats. *Redis-* It was in the smaller boroughs that the strength of the territorial *tribution* interest had most firmly been entrenched, and the Whig minis- *of seats* ters of 1830 described nomination as the worst evil of the constitution, though they regarded it with more indignation when patronage was in the hands of their opponents than when it belonged to their own adherents.[3] They set themselves to eliminate it by disfranchising the smaller boroughs, enfranchising new

---

[1] Note the criticisms made by Disraeli in the extract from *Coningsby*, Costin and Watson, ii. 377-79.

[2] See on this point, Butler, 85-9, and E. Halévy, *Histoire du peuple anglais au xixᵉ siècle*, iii. 1-5.

[3] C. Seymour, *Electoral Reform in England and Wales*, 62-8.

boroughs, and opening the borough franchise everywhere. Fifty-seven boroughs, all but fifteen of which were in the South, lost their representation entirely, and thirty more, twenty-one of which were in the South, lost one of their two seats. Twenty-two boroughs hitherto not represented, five being metropolitan, and the remainder mostly situated in the North, obtained the right of returning two members, and twenty-one, again mostly northern, that of returning one. Of the 141 seats forfeited by boroughs, 103 were lost by southern constituencies, and of the 65 of these used to enfranchise new boroughs London and the North gained 45. Sixty-five more seats were used to increase county representation. Twenty-six counties were divided into new constituencies, seven English and three Welsh counties were allotted one additional member each. The thirteen seats still available were transferred to Scotland and Ireland.[1]

*The reformed franchise*    Like the historic franchise, that introduced in 1832 preserved the distinction between counties and boroughs. In the former the ancient forty-shilling freehold qualification was retained, subject to the condition of residence, but three new qualifications were added by the enfranchisement of copyholders, leaseholders having leases for specified periods, and tenants-at-will paying rent of not less than £50.[2] This last addition, created by an opposition amendment known as the "Chandos Clause", was incomparably the most important, bringing into existence a large number of voters who, as tenants-at-will, were specially open to influence from their landlords. In the counties the predominance of the landowning class was fortified during the next half-century by the operation of this clause, only partially off-set by a provision that freeholders in boroughs who did not occupy their freehold should vote in the county where the borough was situated. This sometimes enabled urban

---

[1] Fifty-five boroughs returning two members each and one (Higham Ferrers) returning one are listed in Schedule A of the Reform Act, and thirty returning one each in Schedule B. These yield a total of 141 seats available for redistribution. The remaining two were obtained by throwing the "double" borough of Weymouth and Melcombe Regis into one, by s. 6 of the Act (Costin and Watson, ii. 55-6). See generally N. Gash, *Politics in the Age of Peel*, 64 ff.

[2] Copyholders of £10 clear annual value; leaseholds of £10 for at least 60 years; leaseholds of not less than 20 years, and of not less than £50 (Costin and Watson, ii. 57). The "reformed" franchise was even more complicated than the unreformed (Gash, 86).

voters to sway county elections. So Birmingham voters could carry one seat in Warwickshire, and Leeds voters one in the West Riding of Yorkshire.[1] In the boroughs the existing qualifications were retained subject to the voters being resident, but with few exceptions all save the freeman franchise became non-heritable, so that they terminated with the lives of those holding them. The new qualification now created was that of the £10 occupier, which served in general to enfranchise the middle and lower middle, but not the artisan classes. As a whole the electorate was increased by 217,000, or 50 per cent.[2] In the counties little difference in its composition was made. Most of the electors continued to be forty-shilling freeholders, a quarter or a fifth were tenants-at-will, and a negligible number were copyholders or lease-holders.[3] In the boroughs the change was more drastic. A majority of the electorate was now qualified by the £10 franchise. About half the ancient-right voters were immediately excluded by the new requirement as to residence, their number falling at once from 188,000 to 108,000, and continuing to fall until by 1865 they formed only one-tenth of the borough electorate and controlled at most twenty-five seats. The results of this disfranchisement were specially severe on the old class of artisan voters, who everywhere lost ground to the middle classes.[4]

The effects of the Reform Act seem, on the first impression, to constitute a veritable revolution. To peruse the schedules in which such ancient constituencies as Old Sarum, Bossiney, Tregony, Wendover, Midhurst, Castle Rising, and St. Germain's are sentenced to extinction, after so many centuries in which they and their members had figured in the history of Parliament,[5] while others such as Manchester, Birmingham, Leeds, Sheffield, Wolverhampton, Bolton, Warrington, Whitehaven, and Merthyr Tydvil advance to take their places, is like witnessing the end of an old civilisation overborne by the *" The end of an auld sang "*

[1] Seymour, 13 and n., 14-15.   [2] Seymour, Appendix I.   [3] Seymour, 78-9.

[4] Seymour, 83-5. The reformed system was a reflection not of social but of economic status, Gash, 88.

[5] It is not perhaps without interest that among these condemned boroughs Peter Wentworth had sat for Tregony, as did Harley later, Sir John Eliot for St. Germain's, Hampden for Wendover, as did Burke and Canning later, Ashley Cooper for Downton, St. John for Wootton Bassett, Walpole for Castle Rising, the elder Pitt for Old Sarum, the younger for Appleby, and Fox for Midhurst.

tumultuous forces of its aggressive and triumphant adversary. With all its defects and anachronisms, the parliamentary system which succumbed in 1832 had been tried and not found wanting during centuries of proof. The men who had sat for boroughs now no longer to survive had fought the battles of the nation against an alien Church, a despotic Crown, subversive movements in politics and religion within the realm, and innumerable foreign enemies without, from Philip of Spain to Napoleon. The rotten boroughs themselves had partly justified their existence by providing an easy avenue into Parliament for capable young men brought forward by enlightened patrons. It was to the unreformed Parliament that the reforming achievements of the last half-century were due. That it consented to its own extinction is perhaps the culminating proof that, despite its faults, it succeeded not imperfectly in representing the will of the nation. It is impossible to close the record of the unreformed House of Commons without a tribute to the wisdom, courage, loyalty and success with which it had to the last discharged its trust to the people of England, and a regret that its end should have been effected in such a way as to leave on it the stigma of corruption and decay.

*Similarities between the reformed and unreformed Commons*
Some contemporaries indulged in the gloomiest prognostications about the character of its reformed successors. Yet the event was to show that, for all the apparent breach of continuity which the Act had accomplished, the new House of Commons was surprisingly like the old.[1] So long indeed as the property qualification for members was in existence, the House necessarily reflected in its composition the propertied classes, and, if the preponderance now passed to the moneyed as distinct from the landed class, there was something in common between the two, and much between them both and their predecessors of pre-Reform days. What the landed interest consented to in 1832 was, in short, not a surrender, but a partnership in power. The reform had not substantially altered the personnel of the Commons, nor did it lead to the emergence of any new and more democratic party. The diminished effect of the artisan vote produced by the enlargement of the franchise was seen when the radical, Orator

---

[1] On this point see Halévy, iii. 57-9, and S. F. Woolley, *Personnel of the Parliament of 1833*, 53 E.H.R. 240. For a tentative appraisement of the position in the next decade, see W. O. Aydelotte, *The House of Commons in the 1840's*, 39 Hist. 249. Cf. A. Aspinall, *The Old House of Commons and its Members*, in *Parliamentary Affairs*, xiii-xv.

Hunt, lately elected for the borough of Preston, lost his seat. A handful of Radicals, hardly more than a dozen in number, was returned. A separate Irish party came into being under O'Connell as a result of the Roman Catholic Emancipation Act. But, as in former years, the main forces in the House were to be found in the two great parties of Whigs and Tories, between whom the pendulum was to alternate, the Whigs dominant after 1832 and the Tories after 1841.

Such revolutionary effects as the Act of 1832 actually had were demonstrated only so slowly as to make it doubtful whether *Revolu-* the Act made any real "revolution" whatever. Yet, if sufficient *tionary* time is allowed for these effects to reveal themselves, it will be *effects of the* seen how profound was the constitutional transformation it caused. *Reform* By diminishing, if not wholly destroying, the system of patronage and nomination it deprived the Crown of the principal means it possessed of determining the composition of ministries and securing for them adequate parliamentary support, and enhanced the growing independence of the Cabinet and the supremacy of the Prime Minister. Though making no overwhelming addition to the electorate, it sufficiently changed the electoral system to ensure that the decision of larger and less easily manageable constituencies should determine which party obtained an effective majority in the Commons and therefore oblige the sovereign to accept that party's leaders as his ministers. Thereby it led directly to a thorough organisation of parties in the constituencies and in Parliament. By ensuring the ultimate supremacy of the electorate, it vindicated that of the House of Commons over the Lords and destroyed the convention of a constitutional balance between Crown, Lords, and Commons. Finally, it provided an example of wholesale electoral reform which stimulated the demand for further change, to be carried out by similarly sweeping methods and based on the democratic principle of numerical preponderance which had not been fully recognised in 1832. By this example it made certain that though it was the first, it would not be the last statute dealing with the representative system as a whole.

The effect of the Reform on the King's prerogative to choose his ministers was clearly shown by the events of the first ten years after 1832. "How", Peel had asked during the debates on the bill,

*Decline of royal control over the Cabinet*

"could the King thereafter change a ministry?"[1] His own career was soon to illustrate the difficulty. In 1834 the Whig ministry had to be reconstructed on the elevation of one of its members, Lord Althorp, to the Upper House. The Prime Minister, Melbourne, suggested that Lord John Russell should be the new leader of the Commons, but the King was unwilling to accept him, and gave Melbourne a hint, which was acted on, that the ministry might resign. The King now attempted, much as his predecessors might have done, to construct a ministry under a premier of his own choice. Peel, who accepted his invitation, failed to obtain a majority at the ensuing general election or to maintain himself in Parliament without one. Such a situation had seldom arisen in pre-Reform days, and Peel's assumption of responsibility for what the King had done did not conceal the fact that the Crown might now be exposed to the risk of having its acts, and its advisers, disapproved by the electorate. Only by a complete withdrawal of any claim to control the composition of the ministry, except when the verdict of the electorate was indecisive, could the dignity of the sovereign be preserved.[2]

*The Bedchamber question*

Another illustration of the new position occurred in 1839. Lord Melbourne's government was defeated in the Commons, and he advised the young Queen Victoria to send for the leader of the Opposition in the Lords, the Duke of Wellington. Wellington, pointing out that he had no authority in the Commons, advised her to entrust the task of forming a ministry to Peel as head of the Tory party in the Lower House. Peel consented to do so only if he might have evidence of the Queen's confidence by being allowed to nominate the ladies of her household. This condition the Queen refused to accept. Melbourne accordingly returned to office. There could be no doubt of his having the entire trust, and even affection, of his sovereign. It gave him no command over Parliament. Two years more in office found him still facing a hostile House of Commons, and Peel moving that "it was at variance with the spirit of the constitution for a ministry to continue in office without the confidence of the House".

[1] Smellie, 41-2.

[2] On the fall of Melbourne and the appointment of Peel, see Costin and Watson, ii. 383-8; W. I. Jennings, *Cabinet Government* (3rd edn.), 403-6; G. Kitson Clark, *Peel and the Conservative Party*, 191 ff.; N. Gash, *Peel and the Party System*, 5 T.R.H.S. i. 47; Keith, *The King and the Imperial Crown*, 66-8.

The general election of 1841, in which a Tory majority was returned, again indicated decisively that royal favour alone no longer enabled a ministry to remain in office or win an election.[1]

Yet the conventions of a former age stubbornly persisted. The *Survival* Queen derived from Melbourne the principle that a dissolu- *of royal* tion should be accorded only if the ministry had a real prospect *over the* of success in the elections, a view which clearly implied that *choice of* ministers were primarily her servants, and that an adverse majority *a Prime* against them would be an affront to the sovereign.[2] Moreover *Minister* the notion survived, particularly among Tories, that there was a serious difference between, as Wellington phrased it, "willingness to serve the Crown if called upon", and pursuing "a course of measures which are to have for their object to force the administration to resign, and the sovereign to call for the services of others".[3] Ministries, again, still regarded themselves as primarily charged with administrative responsibility, and not with the execution of a political programme endorsed by the electorate, and were inclined to refuse to resign after an adverse general election, to await the verdict of the House, and expect that they should be given a fair chance there before being voted down.[4] It is further to be remembered that, for over twenty years after 1846, when the Tory party split irreconcilably over the repeal of the Corn Laws, no general election gave expression to a decisive verdict by the constituencies which the Crown must feel bound to accept. After that date, on the contrary, the multiplicity of parties, which comprised Whigs, Tories, Peelites, Radicals, and Irish, forced on the Crown the duty of endeavouring to build cabinets and choose Prime Ministers. The importance of the part which the Queen played and had to play in making ministries during these years is indicated by the fact that minority governments held office from 1846 to 1852, 1858 to 1859, 1866 to 1868, and a coalition from 1852 to 1855,[5] and that never in this period was there any strong case for the resignation of a government as a result of a general

---

[1] On the events of 1839–41, see Kitson Clark, 416–26; Halévy, iii. 227–31, 321–30; Smellie, 44–5; Emden, 157–9; Miss B. Kemp, *The General Election of 1841*, 37 *Hist.* 146.          [2] Keith, 140–42.          [3] Smellie, 53.

[4] Not until 1868 (Derby and Disraeli Ministry) did a government immediately resign after an adverse general election: and as late as 1892 Lord Salisbury awaited a defeat in the Commons before resigning.

[5] See C. H. Stuart, *Formation of the Coalition Cabinet of 1852*, 5 *T.R.H.S.* iii. 45. Jennings, 31.

election.¹ With rare exceptions it was the Queen's duty, taking such advice as she could obtain, and where she could obtain it, to find a Prime Minister and, if necessary, help him to find colleagues to carry on her business in Parliament. These facts are to be borne in mind when her later interventions in politics are considered, and they do in some degree at least weaken the censures which her action on these occasions has subsequently incurred.

*Over composition and policy of ministries*

The influence of the sovereign extended not only to the choice of a Prime Minister, but also to the choice of his colleagues and the conduct of policy. The principle that royal approval of the composition of the ministry was necessary had been laid down by Melbourne, and to it the Queen adhered.² Thus in 1851 she showed reluctance to accept Disraeli as Secretary of State, and exacted a promise that Palmerston should not have the Foreign Office.³ In later years she criticised other ministerial appointments. She endeavoured, with varying success, to discover the personal opinions expressed by ministers in Cabinet meetings, raised matters for discussion there, and insisted on being consulted before major questions of policy were publicly raised by the government.⁴ In the work at least of those departments most largely concerned with the use of prerogative powers the Queen was accustomed to take a close personal interest. This was particularly so with regard to the Foreign Office, where from 1847 onwards she complained of Palmerston's failure to submit despatches to her.⁵ In 1850 she defined the rules with which her Foreign Secretary must comply. He must inform her of the action he proposed to take, he must not depart from what she had agreed to, and she must be kept informed of diplomatic correspondence and given time to consider it. These rules may seem to imply only a formal and conventional control, based mainly on standards of courtesy between sovereign and minister, which Palmerston's impulsive action in recognising Louis Napoleon's *coup d'état* of 1851 manifestly neglected. Yet the Queen held with determination to the principle involved, and used

---

¹ Costin and Watson, ii. 405, 407-9.

² Jennings, 62. But compare, on the same page, the view expressed by Peel in 1850.

³ Jennings, 63. The Queen's objections were, however, based not on political but on personal grounds of suitability for office.

⁴ Jennings, 351-364.                            ⁵ Costin and Watson, ii. 396.

it to indicate her own views on foreign policy to the Cabinet.[1]
On at least one occasion, the personal act of her husband, the
Prince Consort, in modifying the terms of a despatch to the
United States government during the American Civil War directly
and beneficially affected English diplomatic relations.[2] The same
tendency for the Crown to interest itself in the work of the departments of state can be illustrated elsewhere, particularly with regard
to the fighting services. Nor was the Queen's intervention limited
to dealings with her ministers. On occasion she was to be found
serving as mediator between government and opposition, endeavouring to obtain the latter's consent to non-contentious
measures such as the bill settling the precedence of the Prince
Consort in 1856, and even to conciliate the opponents of contentious measures like Russell's Reform bill of 1866.[3]

When all due allowance has been made for the Queen's right *Limits of*
to intervene in the formation of ministries and their conduct *royal*
of business, it has none the less to be recognised that, in dealing *control*
with a determined Prime Minister supported by a unanimous
Cabinet and a decisive majority in the Commons, she had no
option but to give way. During the years 1832–67, it is true, the
lines of division between parties, and the organisation of parties
both in Parliament and in the country, were still so ill-defined as
to create a fluid situation in which the Crown still retained the
power, and indeed was under the duty, to take a strong line. Yet
during those years, the Cabinet, especially under Peel's masterful
control, was becoming a more disciplined and homogeneous body;
and if some of Peel's successors, like Russell and Palmerston, lacked
his capacity for supervising every department of state and his
ability to dominate his colleagues,[4] at least they possessed authority
enough to control appointments to office, to defend or dismiss
their colleagues, and sometimes even to commit them to a policy
of which they disapproved. Loyalty to a common leader, to common principles, and to party ties took the place in the action of
the Cabinet formerly held by the obligation of common service
to the sovereign. For the period witnessed the formation of a
party organisation on the strength of which any ministry must
ultimately depend.

[1] Jennings, 367.     [2] J. Morley, *Life of Gladstone*, i. 707–8.
[3] Jennings, 382     [4] Jennings, 177 ff.

*Electoral
morality
after the
Reform
Act*
This process originated with the Reform Act itself, which, for the first time, laid down a statutory procedure for the registration of voters.[1] In practice the procedure proved exceedingly defective. The apathy of persons who did not trouble to register, the laxity of the overseers charged with compiling the lists, and other causes combined at first to defeat the intentions of the Act. Moreover, if aristocratic influence was largely diminished, the bribery and intimidation which were still carried on hardly demonstrated any improvement. Direct money gifts, tickets entitling electors to kegs of beer, appointments to remunerative jobs like committee man, messenger, or musician, and intimidation by landlords, by employers, and by creditors continued as part of the new technique of electoral management.[2] There was a prevalent impression that electoral morality had suffered as a result of the reform. An increasing number of elections, particularly in boroughs, were declared void, and some boroughs, such as Sudbury in 1844 and St. Albans in 1852, were disfranchised.[3] Various remedies were suggested. During the 'thirties the radicals, led by Grote, member for the City of London, advocated vote by ballot.[4] Acts of 1841 and 1842 attempted to check corruption.[5] In 1852 an Act provided for the appointment, on an address from both Houses, of commissioners, with power to examine on oath, for the investigation of electoral abuses in the boroughs where they occurred. A year later a Corrupt Practices Act for the first time defined bribery and undue influence, penalised these offences, and required an audit of election expenses. The remedy was imperfect. Vote by ballot, the real cure, was not yet adopted; there was no attack on intimidation; the audit of election expenses was useless so long as their amount remained unlimited. So long as the Commons retained their jurisdiction over elections, disputes were committed to a tribunal which, though improved by an Act sponsored by Peel in 1839—reducing the membership of committees under the Grenville Act to six and providing

---

[1] Costin and Watson, ii. 62-4; Seymour, 108-14.      [2] Seymour, 172 ff.

[3] Seymour, 97, 222. The four seats made available were given to Birkenhead and to Yorkshire and Lancashire county divisions. See also E. Temple Patterson, *Electoral Corruption in Early Victorian Leicester*, 31 *Hist.* 113.

[4] S. Maccoby, *English Radicalism, 1832-52*, 155. Seymour, 209-11. In 1838 200 M.P.'s voted in its favour.

[5] Seymour, 216-18 (Act of 1841), 220-22 (Act of 1842).

an improved method for their nomination—was still nevertheless imperfectly judicial in temper.[1]

Depressing as the picture of electoral conditions in the post-Reform era is, it is not without its brighter side. The passing of the Reform Bill itself had involved a reference to public opinion on a major political issue after a fashion for which there was no precedent, and the habit of making such references was to grow. With its Radical allies, the Whig party stood for a systematic attempt at ameliorative legislation, including the abolition of slavery in the colonies, reform of the poor-law and municipal government, and the like; and the Conservative party, re-created by Peel and fully accepting the changes effected by the reform, emerged as the defender of interests such as the land and the Church, for which, on their merits, electoral support could be invited.[2] The manifesto to the electors of Tamworth issued by Peel during his brief premiership of 1835 was, in intention if not form, an appeal to the new electorate as a whole.[3] If it failed then, the electorate in 1841 rallied to a party which stood for economy, remedy of abuses, and resistance to further proposals for organic change. Defective, limited, and corrupt the new electoral system might be, but it could be applied to the purpose of enlisting reasoned public support for a coherent party programme. An impressive example of the uses to which electoral organisation might be put was afforded by the activities of the Anti-Corn-law League, skilful and unscrupulous in turning to account the defects of the electoral law by the manufacture of spurious qualifications for its supporters and the raising of frivolous objections to those of its opponents, but remarkable in its power of forming and directing a great mass of popular feeling.[4] It was in imitation of its example that the great political parties undertook the task of local electoral organisation.[5]

The increasing strength of parties energised by their reliance on the public opinion revealed by elections operated not only to diminish the influence of the Crown but also that of the Lords. In the eighteenth century the Upper House had been ascribed

*Organisation of public opinion*

*The Lords before the Reform Act*

[1] 2 and 3 Vict. c. 38.          [2] Kitson Clark, 298-9, 379-80, 451.
[3] Emden, 203, 206-7; Kitson Clark, 209-15.    [4] Seymour, 127-9, 135-6.
[5] On this, see below, p. 469. On party organisation in the Commons, see A. Aspinall, *English Party Organisation in the Early Nineteenth Century*, 41 E.H.R. 389; J. A. Thomas, *The System of Registration, . . . 1832-70*, 35 Hist. 81 ff.

a constitutional position not, except in respect of its financial powers, very seriously inferior to that of the Lower. It is, of course, true that conspicuously able statesmen like Walpole had preferred to spend their active political life in the Commons, thereby recognising, at least for certain purposes, its superior importance. Yet, it was also thought that the Lords acted as an effective counterpoise to the popular House in a balanced constitution, as a "a check on the people in the interests of the King and upon the House of Commons in the interests of King and people".[1] Generally in sympathy with the Commons, they felt on occasion able to stand against them. Thus it was that in 1778 Lord Shelburne could appeal to them against a servile House of Commons, and in 1783 George III relied successfully on them to wreck Fox's India Bill and overthrow the Fox-North coalition.[2] It would, however, seem that the constitutional status of the Lords entered on a slow decline during the half-century before the Reform Bill. Their peculiar accessibility to royal influence tended to underline their non-representative character. Even to such a conservative as Burke the House was by 1793 "the feeblest part of the constitution".[3] During Pitt's ministry its numbers, though not perhaps its authority, increased by the inclusion of four bishops and twenty-eight temporal lords under the Act of Union with Ireland and by the creation of ninety-two new peerages.[4] Liverpool added as many as fifty-six more.[5] It may be urged that many, if not most, of these new creations could have been justified by the public services of their recipients. Unquestionably certain others were due to the desire of the Crown and the ministry to exploit the principal form of patronage left intact by the economical reform of 1782, to the desire to enlist the support of borough-owners, and, though to a far less extent, to the need for recognising the claims of the new propertied class created by the Industrial Revolution. Their col-

---

[1] Holdsworth, *The House of Lords, 1689-1783*, 45 *L.Q.R.* 448.
[2] For Shelburne's declaration in 1778, see Turberville, 378-9, and Holdsworth, 45 *L.Q.R.* 450.
[3] In *Observations on the Conduct of the Ministry*; *Works* (ed. 1826), vii. 275. Burke did not, however, imply that it was becoming weaker.
[4] Costin and Watson, ii. 21. G. C. Richards, *Creation of Peers by the Younger Pitt*, 34 *A.H.R.* 44. A. S. Turberville, *House of Lords in the Age of Reform*, 55 ff., 103 ff.
[5] Turberville, 163 ff.

lective effect was unfortunate. The House lost the weight attaching to it when it was a smaller and more coherent assembly, its membership diminished in value when it came to be so generally thrown open, and, as a body, it seemed to stand too plainly for the interests of property and privilege and to lose its former character as a close-knit group of hereditary counsellors of the Crown.

Moreover, this too rapid expansion inevitably suggested a ready *The Lords* means of overcoming the opposition of a majority in the Upper *and the* House. Hitherto the only instance of the wholesale creation of *Reform* peers for this purpose dated back to the proceedings on the Peace *Bill* of Utrecht. From 1830 to 1832 the Lords fought a stubborn battle against the Reform Bill. In its first form the bill had been wrecked in committee by the Commons. After a dissolution the Whigs returned to power with an immense majority. The Commons passed the bill, but it was rejected in the Lords. A third bill passed the Commons, and before it went to the Lords the ministry obtained from William IV a conditional promise to create enough new peers to pass the bill if it were rejected in the Upper House.[1] When opposition showed itself there, the King tried to withdraw from the obligation to create peerages to so large a number as was seen to be necessary. The ministry resigned, the King tried to form another through Wellington, and failing to do so, he surrendered. Before the threat that the House would be swamped, a sufficient number of opposition peers absented themselves to permit of the bill being passed.[2]

The effect of the Reform Act was to deepen the cleavage thus *The Lords* manifested between the Houses. That harmony which had been *after the* naturally created when so many members of the Commons were *Reform* nominees of the Lords was destroyed with the abolition of so *Act* many nomination boroughs and the enlargement of the franchise. If members of the Lower House were, in the political confusion which preceded the hardening of party organisation and discipline, largely free to oppose ministers, they were even more free to oppose the Lords. The Radicals—though not the Whigs—would readily have proceeded to their abolition as a part of Parliament.[3]

---

[1] Butler, *Passing of the Great Reform Bill*, 328-38, 371, 409-12.
[2] Butler, 414-15; Trevelyan, *Lord Grey of the Reform Bill*, 349.
[3] Miss E. Allyn, *Lords versus Commons*, 29-30.

The Lords responded to the challenge. It was under difficulties only overcome by Wellington's influence that they yielded to the repeal of the Corn Laws. They regularly opposed measures threatening vested interests.[1] In 1861 they rejected the repeal of the duties on paper, which formed a component bill in the Budget of that year.[2] It might be argued that they were within their rights in doing so, for their action did not impose a new but merely retained an existing tax, and moreover the remaining bills in the Budget were allowed to pass. Their success was short-lived. A Select Committee of the Commons pronounced against their right to reject a money bill except on purely financial grounds. The Commons resolved in favour of their own exclusive power of remitting as well as imposing taxation.[3] And Gladstone, as Chancellor of the Exchequer, proceeded to combine all finance bills forming parts of the Budget into one single comprehensive measure, to be accepted or rejected as a whole. By denying, in the *Wensleydale Peerage Case* (1856), the prerogative of the Crown to create life peerages conferring a seat in Parliament,[4] the Lords rejected the chance of being "tacitly reformed", and entered upon a period in which their antagonism to the Commons was to provoke the demand that they should be "mended or ended" and lead ultimately to the statutory restrictions imposed on them by the Parliament Act of 1911.

*Renewal of the movement for parliamentary reform*
That principle of popular sovereignty which the Reform Act had grudgingly but irrevocably accepted was bound in the end to do more than merely diminish the weight of the Crown and the Lords in government, and enhance the power of a ministry reposing on a properly organised majority of votes. It must, given the social changes still progressing with accelerated pace, presently challenge the electoral system established in 1832. Those changes produced, even within the restricted framework of the Act itself, a further increase of about 400,000 in the electorate during the next generation.[5] The larger the electorate grew, the more unreasonable did the restrictions imposed by the Act appear. The dissentient peers of 1832 pointed out, with much force, that

[1] Allyn, 32, 34-5, 44.        [2] Allyn, 51 ff.
[3] Costin and Watson, ii. 187.
[4] Allyn, 44-9; L. O. Pike, *Constitutional History of the House of Lords*, 372-9. Costin and Watson, ii. 403.
[5] The figures were 652,000 in 1833, 1,056,000 in 1866; Seymour, Appendix I.

the Act could not be a final adjustment of the representation of the people, that the franchise was unjustly and unevenly distributed, that it created as many incongruities as it attempted to correct, and contained within it the elements of further change.[1] The property qualification for voters was too arbitrary to survive. There was no magic in the figure of £10 as the qualification in boroughs. It did not even qualify any uniform social class, since in small towns it enfranchised a smaller proportion than in large towns where rents ruled higher. As national wealth increased, the £10 franchise, declining in real as distinct from nominal value, qualified a growing number of persons, and made the contrast between those who could and those who could not vote even more indefensible. Popular opinion showed itself in favour of further democratisation. The Act, so largely a disfranchising measure as far as the artisan was concerned, engendered a bitter discontent which found expression in the demands of the People's Charter for manhood suffrage, secret ballot, equal electoral districts, annual parliaments, abolition of the property qualification, and payment of members.[2] To some extent these demands were supported by the Radicals in Parliament, but the two dominant parties were equally opposed to further electoral change. Some little progress was made in 1838, when the property qualification for members was extended to include personal property, and in 1858 when the qualification was wholly abolished.[3]

The electoral system, though long remaining intact, presently *Reform* began to come under review. In 1852 appeared the first ministerial *bills,* proposal for a new measure of reform. Between that date and *1852–1867* 1860 four bills were brought forward, three of them by Russell, whose previous assertion that the Act of 1832 had attained the limit of desirable change had earned for him the nickname of "Finality Jack".[4] With variations in detail, these proposals aimed on the one hand at lowering and therefore widening the property

---

[1] Grant Robertson, 344-6.
[2] The Charter was a draft in the form of a bill, divided into 13 sections. See M. Hovell, *The Chartist Movement*, 1, 2.
[3] 1 and 2 Vict. c. 48; 21 and 22 Vict. c. 26.
[4] Earned on account of a speech made in 1837. For Russell's bills of 1852, 1856, and 1860, and the Conservative bill of 1859, see Seymour, 241-6.

qualification for voters, and on the other at balancing the influx of poorer and presumably less educated classes to the electorate by creating what came to be derisively described as "fancy franchises"—additional votes to persons of education and property.[1] In 1866, after the death of Palmerston, whose influence had told steadily against reform,[2] the question was revived, but the bill was wrecked by a revolt of disaffected Liberals known as the "Adullamites" against their own government's measure. The short-lived Conservative government of Derby and Disraeli, however, "dished the Whigs" by enacting a reform bill of its own.[3] The county franchise was left unchanged except that the qualifying leasehold or copyhold was reduced from £10 to £5 annual value, and an occupancy franchise introduced in respect of premises of £12 rateable value, the county electorate being thus increased from 540,000 to 790,000. More fundamental were the changes in the borough franchise, where a household franchise conditional on the payment of rates and a lodger franchise in respect of lodgings of £10 annual value were introduced. Except in London, the latter was of little or no importance. The effect of the other change was startling. A clause inserted in the Act permitted the registration as voters of householders who paid rates through their landlords as an addition to the rent.[4] These "compounders", who had not been within the original contemplation of the Act, swelled the electorate in the boroughs to gigantic dimensions, the number of voters being doubled, and the artisan masses placed in a clear majority. The increase was most striking in the new industrial boroughs, and the boroughs as a whole, with a population two millions less than the counties, now had 50 per cent more voters.[5] The sole counterpoise to the strength of the industrial vote lay in the disparity between the number of electors and the number of seats. Four million people living in the larger towns returned only 34 out of 334 borough members, and two-thirds of the constituencies were still situated south of the Wash and Severn.[6] In most of the projects of reform put forward before 1867 some measure of redistribution had been proposed. In 1867 and 1868 a number of

[1] See W. L. Burn in *Parliamentary Affairs* (1955), 240.
[2] See H. C. Bell, *Palmerston and Parliamentary Representation*, 4 *J.M.H.* 186.
[3] On the Liberal bill of 1866 and the Act of 1867, see Seymour, 247 ff., 257 ff.; Costin and Watson, ii. 103-7.   [4] Seymour, 268-71.
[5] Seymour, 282-4.   [6] Seymour, 285, n. 1.

small boroughs were partly or wholly disfranchised, and of the 52 seats thus made available 25 were allotted to the counties, 19 to the boroughs, one to London University, two to the Scottish Universities, and the remaining five to Scottish constituencies. But no attack was made on the problem as a whole.[1]

The use to which the industrial masses would turn their newly acquired predominance in numbers if not in representation might have been inferred from the expansion of the sphere of government during the years since the Reform Act. While the principle of *laissez-faire* still commanded theoretical acceptance, practical difficulties led inevitably to its piecemeal abandonment as a guide to governmental action. It was effective only in slowing the rate at which government accepted new responsibilities, and in rendering the extension of State control unsystematic and illogical, towards which results it combined with the tenacious resistance to change produced by the continuity of political and legal tradition, the spirit of amateurism and the distrust of the professional expert still inherent in English administration and the prejudice in favour of individual freedom and against arguments from public policy which was ingrained in the Common Law.[2] *Reform and expansion of the administrative system, 1832–6*

One impulse towards reform, already in operation before 1832, was derived from radical and utilitarian zeal for renovating the machinery of administration and finance. The Exchequer, even after and largely because of Pitt's reforms, served no useful purpose either for the receipt, disbursement, or audit of money. Money could most conveniently be kept in the Bank of England. The army and navy had their own pay offices and the civil establishment drew only a part of its income from the Exchequer. The system of payment on Treasury warrants rendered the intervention of the Exchequer superfluous, and its audit system was cumbrous and inefficient. In 1834, therefore, the old Exchequer office was abolished. The departments collecting revenue thereafter paid it directly into the Bank, where an account was opened for a Comptroller-General, whose salary was charged on the Consolidated Fund. Issues were to be made to paymasters no longer by imprests *Financial reforms*

---

[1] Oxford and Cambridge received representation in 1603. Trinity College, Dublin, enfranchised by James I, received representation in the Parliament of Great Britain under the Act for Union with Ireland (Costin and Watson, ii. 21).

[3] Smellie, *A Hundred Years of English Government*, 56–8.

or advances, but by authority of Treasury warrants whose legality it was his business to verify.[1] The method of audit was still defective, since there was no adequate check in the interests of Parliament on the use to which paymasters (whose offices were consolidated into that of Paymaster-General in 1836) put the funds thus placed at their disposal. Such audit as existed was only between superiors and subordinates in the same spending department. From 1832 an effective system of Appropriation Audit existed in the navy, enabling Parliament to see how money granted was actually spent.[2] Ten years later it was extended to the Army and Ordnance Votes.[3] There remained to be dealt with only the Civil supply, an item which had grown as the financing of the Civil Service by annual supply came to displace the older plan of financing it from Civil List, Consolidated Fund, and fees—a process completed when in 1849 Civil Estimates were for the first time laid as a whole before the Commons.[4] The final stage of reform began with a Select Committee on Public Moneys in 1856, whose recommendations were given effect to in the Exchequer and Audit Departments Act of 1866.[5] With the office of Comptroller-General was now combined that of an Auditor-General whose business it was to ensure first that expenditure had been approved by Parliament, and secondly—reporting for this purpose to a Select Committee on Public Accounts—that it had been duly spent on the objects to which it had been appropriated.[6]

*Reform of other offices*

Sir James Graham, the reformer of Admiralty audit, was responsible in 1832 for a thoroughgoing reform of naval organisation as a whole.[7] The separate Navy and Victualling Offices both became departments of the Admiralty, each dealing with a separate branch of business under a Lord who represented it on the Admiralty Board.[8] Everything except the supply of munitions, which continued to be controlled by the Ordnance Office,[9] thus

1 R. G. Hawtrey, *The Exchequer*, 12-14.
2 A. J. V. Durell, *Parliamentary Grants*, 107.
3 Durell, 107, n. 1.
4 Gretton, *The King's Government*, 123; Durell, 46-7.
5 Costin and Watson, ii. 101. T. W. Heath, *The Treasury*, 36, 59-61.
6 On this Committee, see Durell, 103 ff.
7 C. S. Parker, *Life and Letters of Sir James Graham*, i. 147, 151-5, 165-8.
8 Smellie, 61-2.
9 After the abolition of the Ordnance Office, the Navy built up its own Ordnance Department.

came under unified control. Progress in the reform of military organisation was slower. Control was divided between the Secretary at War, mainly, though rather vaguely, responsible for finance, the Secretary of State for War and the Colonies, responsible for determining the size of the establishment and theoretically for the conduct of operations in war, a Commander-in-Chief responsible for discipline, a Commissariat Department responsible for provisioning, and a Board of General Officers responsible for clothing, with the Ordnance Board responsible for munitions, while the Home Office was responsible for the use of the military in Great Britain and for the organisation of the militia and yeomanry. The dangers and defects of this divided control need no emphasis, and they were lamentably revealed by the Crimean War, when a process of reform had to be undertaken.[1] In 1854 the Secretaryship for War was separated from that for the colonies, and under it were placed the Board of General Officers and the Commissariat. Control of the yeomanry and militia was transferred from the Home Office. In 1855 the Board of Ordnance was dissolved, and its functions were divided between the Secretary for War and the Commander-in-Chief. Finally in 1863 the Secretaryship at War was abolished, and its duties merged with those of the Secretary of State for War.[2] Army organisation was still afflicted by the duality of control between the latter and the Commander-in-Chief, whose position, independent of Parliament and connoting the direct authority of the sovereign over the army, was obstinately defended by its holder and by the Queen.[3] In the Foreign Office, efficiently reorganised by Canning, there was less need for reform, but the growth of business required a gradual increase of personnel, which in the 'sixties comprised the Secretary of State, the Permanent and Parliamentary Under-Secretaries, an Assistant Under-Secretary, and a clerical staff.[4]

It is not, however, in the reform but in the expansion of the *Home* administrative services that the most significant feature of the *Office and* period 1832–67 is to be found. The growth of industry, of banking, *Board of Trade*

---

[1] Hampden Gordon, *The War Office*, 49-50; A. Forbes, *History of the Army Ordnance Services*, i. 257-74.

[2] Gordon, 51-2; Forbes, ii. 4-5.       [3] Smellie, 60.

[4] Smellie, 62-4. J. Tilley and S. Gaselee, *The Foreign Office*, ch. iii.; E. Jones Parry, *Under-Secretaries of State for Foreign Affairs, 1782-1855*, 49 E.H.R. 308.

of joint-stock enterprise, of maritime transport, of inland communications, especially railways, of town-life and the consequent
need for police, sanitation, water-supply, education, and poor-
relief created problems which, whatever the theoretical merits of
*laissez-faire*, could not be disregarded. In response to these demands a vast system of administration, central and local, had to
be improvised. Antipathy to the principle of public control in
general, and to central control over hitherto autonomous administrative units, led to the situation being dealt with in a short-
sighted and grudging fashion which produced results strangely
in contrast with the traditions of urban civilisation in Western
Europe and still harmfully affecting national life to the present
day.[1] Even if action was timidly and unsystematically taken,
it could not be omitted. The Home Office, to which many
of these duties were appropriate, would have been overwhelmed
had the whole burden been allowed to fall upon it. While it
continued to acquire powers regarding aliens, police, labour and
factory conditions, mines, industrial and reformatory schools, and
agriculture,[2] other departments were adapted to the task of internal
administration. Thus the Board of Trade, acquiring from 1826 a
salaried President who after 1853 ceased even in theory to preside
over an actual Board, was turned in 1867, when the office of
Vice-President was abolished, into an executive department. It
thenceforth stood clearly apart from the Privy Council, any Committee of which should in theory have been presided over by the
Lord President. Under the presidency of Huskisson (1825–7) and
Gladstone (1841–5), it had taken a leading part in the tariff revisions
consequent on the adoption of free-trade. Though in later years
its functions in commercial negotiations declined in importance,
those relating to internal administrative business developed rapidly
as innumerable statutory powers enabled it to deal with transport, harbours and shipping, gas and water supply, weights and
measures, patents, and bankruptcy.[3]

*The Education Department*
    Another emanation from the Privy Council was the Committee,
comprising the Lord President, Lord Privy Seal, Home Secretary,
and Chancellor of the Exchequer, established in 1839 to "super-

[1] J. L. and B. Hammond, *The Age of the Chartists*, chs. ii. and iv.
[2] Troup, *The Home Office*, 22–5.
[3] Llewellyn Smith, *The Board of Trade*, 55–67; Smellie, 64–5. The Board's
responsibility for railway transport has just been examined in H. Parris, *Government and the Railways*.

intend the application of any sums voted by Parliament for the purpose of promoting public education".[1] These sums, first voted in 1833 when £20,000 was granted, were meagre enough. There was strong objection both to the assumption by the State of educational administration, hitherto left to private and charitable enterprise, and also to education being brought into the field of party politics. Here again the State could not escape its responsibility. By Order in Council of 1856, an Education Department was created, within which was included the establishment for the encouragement of science and art lately developed by the Board of Trade. A subsequent Act gave the department a paid head responsible to Parliament and holding the office of Vice-President.[2]

Elsewhere, new departments were brought into being for the relief of poverty and for the closely related subject of the prevention of disease. The Act of 1834 ended the Elizabethan organisation of poor relief, lately vitiated by the Speenhamland system, formed a body of three Poor Law commissioners, with power to group parishes into unions for the purpose of poor relief, and with detailed executive control over local Poor Law administration.[3] The reports of the Poor Law commissioners drew attention to the grave defects of sanitary conditions and the consequent prevalence of disease, and urged legislation on this topic.[4] Their recommendations, to which urgency was given by recurrent outbreaks of cholera and by the report of a Royal Commission on the Health of Towns and Populous Places (1843–5), led to the enactment of the first Public Health Act in 1848.[5] It set up a General Board of Health and gave power to establish local Boards of Health. Neither of the two new central departments so created managed to survive unchanged. Both were unpopular because being unrepresented in Parliament they were not responsible to public opinion, because they necessarily encroached on local independence, and because their extirpation of abuses was accomplished with too rigorous and unsympathetic a hand.[6] In 1847 a new Poor Law Board, responsible to Parliament, was established. In

*New departments*

[1] L. A. Selby-Bigge, *The Board of Education*, 2.          [2] Selby-Bigge, 6-7.
[3] Costin and Watson, ii. 69-79. Redlich and Hirst, *Local Government in England*, i. 103-10.
[4] Redlich and Hirst, i. 134-6.          [5] Redlich and Hirst, i. 139-43.
[6] For the opposition to these bodies, see Redlich and Hirst, i. 110, 143-7, and Webb, *English Poor Law History*, Part II, vol. i. ch. ii.

1858 the General Board of Health, deprived of most of its powers in 1853-4, was abolished, its functions being divided between the Home Office and the Privy Council.[1] If the apparatus of central supervision over public health was thus dismantled, the statute-book ceaselessly witnessed to the necessity for some such authority, in Acts, both general and local, dealing with vaccination, sanitation, the removal of nuisances, and the prevention of disease. In 1867 the day for the restoration of central control was not far distant. The needs of agriculture called forth a further series of new departments—a Tithe Commission in 1836 appointed by the Tithe Act of that year and charged with the duty of commuting tithes of produce into rent-charges, a Copyhold Commission created in 1841 to deal with the enfranchisement of copyhold lands, and an Enclosure Commission appointed under the General Enclosure Act of 1845 which obviated the need for obtaining separate Acts of enclosure.[2]

*Reforms in local government*    The development of the central administrative system was meanwhile being paralleled in the domain of local government. Here the dissolution of the traditional order, begun before 1832, went on rapidly thereafter. Parishes were under the Poor Law of 1834 grouped into unions, in each of which a Board of Guardians, partly composed of Justices of the Peace sitting *ex-officio*, partly of members elected on a franchise giving special weight to property, administered poor relief through a salaried relieving officer who, like the Guardians themselves, fell under the rigid control of the Poor Law Board.[3] In the following year a Municipal Corporations Act, based on the report of a Royal Commission, drastically reformed the government of boroughs.[4] Highly radical in temper, the commissioners condemned the existing system in terms which strongly suggest that they had prejudged the issue before making their inquiry.[5] They investigated 285 towns, of which 246 were held to be boroughs, 67 were left untouched on account of their insignificance—as was London on account of its size—and the remaining 178 were brought within an Act designed also to be applied

---

[1] Redlich and Hirst, i. 111, 147, 149-50.
[2] F. Floud, *The Ministry of Agriculture and Fisheries*, 10.
[3] Webb, *English Poor Law*, Part II, vol. i. 119-21.
[4] Costin and Watson, ii. 79-91. Webb, *Manor and Borough*, 712 ff.
[5] Webb, *Manor and Borough*, 718-19, 721.

to towns not as yet incorporated. The old oligarchies, with their merits as well as all their faults, were swept away.[1] Borough government was committed to councils elected by ratepayers, which were given authority to legislate by by-law, required to appoint town clerks and treasurers, subjected to Treasury control with regard to loans and the sale of assets, and given administrative powers over police, finance, and property. Jurisdiction was separated from administration, and judicial appointments in boroughs were put under Crown control. Later legislation enabled borough councils to be used as local boards of health. This new system was extended throughout the boroughs, and by degrees copied for other local administrative units, so that, with results both good and bad, "local government was entirely municipalised" in modern England.[2] Meanwhile other local governmental entities were coming into existence. In 1835 parishes were enabled to combine for the maintenance of highways, appointing a joint surveyor, and in 1862 Justices of the Peace in quarter sessions were empowered to group them compulsorily for this purpose.[3] In 1852 parishes were empowered to elect Burial Boards for the maintenance of local cemeteries.[4]

The broad result of all these innovations was to cover the *Complex-* England of the 'sixties with a multiplicity of local authorities, *ity of the* administering different areas for different purposes, often levy- *local adminis-* ing rates separately, conforming to no coherent scheme either *trative* territorial or financial, and constituting by their complexity a *system* challenge to further reform. Certain ruling features can be distinguished amid the chaos—the tendency to adopt the elective principle in their constitution, the tendency to subordinate them to some species of central control, and the tendency to place that central controlling department in a position of responsibility to Parliament. In the central and local organs of government which had emerged, the new democracy of 1867 was to find a powerful instrument of social and economic amelioration.

It will be evident that such reforms, carried out to so large an extent by statutes, which in turn were often based on pre-

[1] For examples of the best of the unreformed boroughs see Webb, *Manor and Borough*, 406 ff. (Penzance), 481 ff. (Liverpool).
[2] Redlich and Hirst, i. 213.
[3] Webb, *Story of the King's Highway*, 201-4, 208-10.
[4] A. L. Lowell, *The Government of England*, ii. 134.

*Parlia-
mentary
procedure
and
privilege*

liminary inquiry ordered by Parliament or by the Crown at
Parliament's request, implied a substantial change in the functions
and work of Parliament itself. The business of legislating, and
especially of dealing with legislation promoted by the government, occupied an increasing share of its attention. Procedure had
to be adapted accordingly. Committees, during the eighteenth
century usually nominated by the member of Parliament who
sponsored a bill, were being converted into bodies nominated
mainly by the government. The time allowed to committees was
increased (1833), printed questions were introduced (1835), debate
on petitions ceased (1839), as did debate on a first reading (1849);
the "rule of progress" was adopted, under which the principles of a
bill having been accepted on its second reading could not be later
discussed in the committee stage; and the time allotted to government business and to Committees of Supply and of Ways and Means
was defined and enlarged.[1] Parliament constantly busied itself
with acquiring and disseminating information relating to matters
of public concern.[2] While the decision in *Stockdale* v. *Hansard*
(1839),[3] following Lord Holt's judgment in *Ashby* v. *White*, rightly
affirmed that the Commons could not by resolution assert a
new privilege by authorising the publication of libellous matter
included in a report made to the House, the Parliamentary
Papers Publication Act of 1840 enabled reports prepared for
Parliament to be placed before the public without the risk of
legal proceedings ensuing.[4] Immediately afterwards, however, the
ability of the House to vindicate its own view of its privileges,
if it chose to do so, by commitment for contempt, was shown in
the *Case of the Sheriff of Middlesex* (1840). With the successful
plaintiff in *Stockdale* v. *Hansard* and his solicitor, the sheriffs of
Middlesex were committed for seeking to give effect to the decision
in the earlier case and failed to obtain release by habeas corpus.[5]
While a continuous flow of Parliamentary papers enlightened
the electorate on public matters, parliamentary reporting became

[1] Redlich, *Procedure of the House of Commons*, i. Part II, ch. i.
[2] Redlich, i. 82 n., ii. 47-50.
[3] Keir and Lawson, 270; Costin and Watson, ii. 264-73.
[4] 3 and 4 Vict. c. 9.
[5] Keir and Lawson, 283; Costin and Watson, ii. 273-5. These cases illustrate the distinction between cases where the point at issue is the existence of a
privilege (*Stockdale* v. *Hansard*), and those where the mode of its exercise is at
issue (*Sheriff of Middlesex*).

fuller and better. From 1803 regular reports of current debates were begun by Cobbett in his *Parliamentary Debates*, to which the name of Hansard was attached from 1812 when the latter bought Cobbett's interest in the publication. In 1855 a measure of public recognition was given to these reports, hitherto entirely a private enterprise, and Hansard received a subsidy from public funds. In 1868 the decision in *Wason* v. *Walter* was to show that the publication of words uttered in parliamentary debate, even if defamatory, and of comments thereon, was not actionable if done *bonâ fide* with a view to the public interest.[1]

In the work of government, the services of the expert were now *The Civil* displacing those of the amateur both in the central departments *Service* and to a less extent in local affairs. It was natural, as government came increasingly within the sphere of parliamentary control, that appointment to the public services should take on a more public character, that proficiency should replace patronage as the means by which entrants were recommended, and that the administrative staffs of ministers should no longer be within their sole power to appoint. The Treasury attempted reform by examining candidates for entry, and placing them on a year's probation if accepted. Other departments adopted a plan either of examination or of probation.[2] Examination and probation might alike be of the most perfunctory kind. In 1853, however, Sir Charles Trevelyan and Sir Stafford Northcote, who had been requested by Mr Gladstone to report on conditions in the Civil Service, condemned patronage, urged the merits of open competition, and suggested different methods of recruitment for the superior and the merely routine branches of administration.[3] In 1855 the Civil Service Commission was established, to inquire into the qualifications of candidates and issue certificates to those suitable for employment.[4] At first the Commission suffered from working too closely under the control of the departments; competition was seriously restricted and the reign of patronage lingered on.[5]

<hr />

[1] Keir and Lawson, 295; Costin and Watson, ii. 287–94.

[2] On conditions of appointment in the earlier half of the century, see A. L. Lowell, *Government of England*, i. 155–6; T. L. Heath, *The Treasury*, 160–61.

[3] Heath, 165–9, and see in particular the valuable survey by E. Hughes, *Civil Service Reform, 1853–5, 27 Hist.* 51.

[4] The Commission was established by Order in Council, in order to obviate the risk of parliamentary opposition, recourse to Parliament being made only for the necessary appropriation.

[5] Heath, 170–71.

14a

Finally, by Order in Council of 1870, the principle of open competition by written examination was made universal throughout the home Civil Service, except for a few appointments made by the Crown, or by the head of a department where special reasons for dispensing with an examination existed.[1] In local government, though the expert element increased, no substantial progress was made, or indeed has yet been made, towards throwing appointments open to general competition.

*The Constitution in 1867*   It will be evident how powerful was the mechanism which the Reform Act of 1867 placed at the disposal of the new electorate. Parliament reflected with increased accuracy the will of a majority of the electors. Ministers and policy were in consequence being removed from the control of the Crown. The Lords no longer dominated the Commons. Legislative action, which was coming to be the main concern of ministers and Parliament, had created by degrees a powerful professional administration. Measures such as the Factories and Mines Acts, and the Acts dealing with railways, joint-stock companies and banks, had everywhere fortified the principle of State intervention. In local affairs the elective principle was slowly gaining acceptance. Both centrally and locally the traditions of *laissez-faire* were perforce being discarded. In the new age inaugurated by the Act of 1867 the prevalent ideas were to favour State intervention. Further restriction of the influence of the Crown and the authority of the Lords, the more complete democratisation of Parliament and local government, and the development of a still more centralised and efficient administrative system seemed to be indicated as the probable lines of future progress.

iv

*The decline of Convocation*   By 1867 the integral association between Church and State established at the Restoration had been largely dissolved. In 1660, and still more completely after 1689, royal supremacy over the Church had been invested with a parliamentary rather than a personal form. The quarrel between Parliament and Convocation caused by the pretensions of the latter to legislate with royal approval but without regard to the wishes of Parliament—lately

[1] Lowell, i. 157-8; Heath, 171-2.

shown by the Canons of 1640—ended in Parliament's favour
when the validity of the Canons of 1640 was formally condemned
by statute in 1661.[1] In 1664 the clergy surrendered their right of
voting taxes in Convocation, and the main safeguard for its regular
future assembly disappeared. Its independence could only be
revived by a closer alliance of Church and Crown than existed
under Charles II and James II. During these two reigns, Convocations, though summoned, were normally prorogued without
having transacted any business.[2] In 1689 Convocation was
again allowed to deliberate, but the antagonism of its Lower
House to proposals for comprehension supported by the Upper
House, by the Crown, and to some extent by Parliament,
only demonstrated the dangers of granting authority to a body
regarded by so many of the clergy as a bulwark against lay control
over the Church.[3] From 1701 to 1717 the proceedings of Convocation were marked only by quarrels on this fundamental
issue between the theocratically-minded Lower House and the
bishops, who stood firmly for Erastian principles. In 1717 the
controversy came to a head, and the Whig government reimposed
the principle of lay control by proroguing the assembly before
any business could be done.[4] Except in 1741, when, with unsatisfactory results, the deliberations of Convocation were once
more permitted, the practice of prorogation before any business
was transacted continued. The pretensions of the Church to a
legislative authority co-ordinate with that of Parliament were
thus suppressed.

On the whole, the eighteenth-century Church accepted this *Church*
situation with resignation, and even contentment. As the sway of *and State*
Latitudinarian ideas extended, questions of ecclesiastical organ- *in the*
*eighteenth*
isation and independence came to excite little interest among the *century*
clergy. The episcopate was content with its place in Parliament,
and bishops usually associated themselves with the political
parties to which they owed their elevation. For, after 1702, the
ecclesiastical patronage of the Crown began to fall into the hands

---

1 13 Car. II, c. 12.
2 N. Sykes, *Church and State in England in the Eighteenth Century*, 300-301.
3 On the Convocation of 1689, see W. H. Hutton, *History of the English
Church from Charles I to Anne*, 247-51.
4 Sykes, 310-14.

of its ministers. The Calvinist William III had left it to a com‑ mission of Anglican divines. Anne made a resolute but only partly successful attempt to resume it, in appointing Dawes to Chester and Blackhall to Exeter in 1706‑7, but had to surrender to her Whig ministry ᵗhe nominations to St. Asaph, Norwich, and Chichester.[1] The early Hanoverians permitted this patronage to escape them. From 1723 nominations were mainly controlled by Bishop Gibson of London, against whom even the able Queen Caroline was unable to prevail.[2] Though George III here as else‑ where attempted to recover the Crown's authority, the tradition of his predecessors was not easily overcome. The bishops of the eight‑ eenth century, appointed on political grounds, generally formed a solid block of governmental supporters. Locally, they were active in elections to Parliament, and used their patronage for this and cognate purposes.[3] The rank and file of the clergy found them‑ selves in the same way gradually assimilated to the governing class of country gentlemen. They took their share in every side of the work of each of the two fundamental organs of English local government, the parish and the county. On the county bench the clerical Justice of the Peace was a prominent figure during the eighteenth century, often acting as chairman of quarter sessions, and displaying not only an unusual knowledge of the law, but an even more unusual humanitarian spirit, though his zeal as a magistrate was apt at times to outrun his charity as a Christian minister.[4]

*Growth of religious toleration*   So harmonious a blending of the spiritual estate with the government of the realm had hardly been seen since Elizabethan days, and to a far greater degree than in that age was the Church content to accept subordination to the State. Yet at one point the two situations were radically dissimilar. Under Elizabeth the Church had dealt with a government intent on making it com‑ prehensive. Since the Restoration the notion of comprehension had been abandoned, and the Church found itself in partnership

---

[1] Sykes, 37-9, and his article, *Queen Anne and the Episcopate*, 50 *E.H.R.* 433. This article records the picturesque episode when the Bishop of St. Asaph responded to the Commons' order that his sermons should be burned by instructing his cook to burn the order of the Commons.

[2] N. Sykes, *Edmund Gibson*, 141-2.

[3] See, for an example of clerical electioneering, Sykes, *The Chapter of Exeter and the General Election of 1705*, 45 *E.H.R.* 260.

[4] Webb, *County and Borough*, 350 ff.

with a dominant ruling class, which, while it penalised dissent, implicitly, and after 1689 avowedly, accepted its existence at least in its Protestant form. With the abandonment of comprehension came the concession of a toleration at first relating only to matters of private life, but ultimately extending also to public rights and duties. Penal statutes against Dissenters and even Roman Catholics came during the eighteenth century to be attacked as unnatural and indefensible, and the demand arose for the removal not only of disabilities affecting civil status but likewise of the constitutional disabilities imposed by the Test and Corporation Acts.[1] If the contention were ever to be accepted that the religious profession of the subject should not affect his public rights and capacities, the way would be opened up for a dissolution of the links which so closely connected the government of the kingdom and the established Church. No longer committed to upholding Anglican privilege and political monopoly, government would naturally assume a more secular aspect. As that happened, the Church would begin to attempt to shake off the secular control over its affairs exercised by Parliament, and to revive long dormant claims to autonomy.

Throughout the eighteenth century, and until well into the nineteenth, the statute-book still contained an immense mass of penal legislation on religion inherited from every reign since the Reformation. On Roman Catholics this legislation fell with special severity. If strictly applied, it would have made the presence of Roman bishops and priests in England and the offence of converting or being converted to the Roman faith treasonable. To harbour a priest would have been treated as a felony, and to conduct a service under Roman rites would have been punishable by fine or imprisonment, or both. Roman Catholics laboured under serious personal and private disabilities, and were debarred from service under the Crown and place in Parliament.[2] Dissenters were less seriously penalised, but legislation against them, while modified by the Toleration Act of 1689, remained on the statute-book. Their ministers and schoolmasters continued until 1779 under an obligation to subscribe to the Thirty-Nine Articles, and were then required to make an alternative declaration not

*The Penal Laws in the eighteenth century*

---

[1] For the debates of 1787 and 1789, see Erskine May, ii. 190-94.
[2] See the summary in Stephen, *History of the Criminal Law*, ii. 491.

abolished until 1811.[1] Not until 1812 were the Five-Mile Act and Conventicle Act repealed and toleration formally accorded to non-Trinitarian Christians. A large batch of penal laws, including a part of the Act of Supremacy of 1559 and two statutes of 1581 and 1593 against sectaries, were still left in existence until 1844 and 1846.[2] The public disabilities inflicted on Dissenters by the Corporation Act had from 1729 been removed by annual Indemnity Acts, but the statute itself, like the Test Acts, nevertheless survived intact until 1828.

*Removal of religious disabilities*    The removal of religious penalties was congenial to the mind of the eighteenth century, particularly since Dissent in its new Wesleyan form was, unlike the older Dissent, conservative and not radical in its politics.[3] Penal laws, so far at least as they merely affected private rights, fell into decay through non-enforcement. In this process the courts of law took their part. In 1767 the House of Lords upheld a decision in which the Court of Delegates reversed one given by the city magistrates of London approving a perversion of the Corporation Act practised by the city authorities—that of electing Dissenters as sheriffs and fining them for refusal to qualify.[4] As to Roman Catholics, the Attorney-General stated in *Lord George Gordon's Case* that he could recall only one prosecution, and both Camden and Mansfield were distinguished for their efforts to protect recusants.[5] Nevertheless, so long as the penal laws remained they could be utilised by unscrupulous persons as means of blackmail, and, among the Whigs at any rate, efforts for their repeal frequently occurred in the later eighteenth century. Even before the Act of 1779 relieving Protestant Dissenters, Sir George Saville's Act of 1778 removed the penalties of the Act of 1700 against Catholics who would swear allegiance, disclaim the Stuarts, and repudiate various political doctrines ascribed to the Catholic Church.[6] Notwithstanding the disorderly outbursts, led by Protestant Associations,

---

[1] Erskine May, ii. 186, 214.          [2] Stephen, ii. 483.
[3] W. J. Warner, *The Wesleyan Movement in the Industrial Revolution*, 86, 98, 124; but compare 128 ff.
[4] Erskine May, ii. 183-4.
[5] Erskine May, ii. 187; C. H. S. Fifoot, *Lord Mansfield*, 40-41. On the other hand, Camden seems to have felt some sympathy with Lord George Gordon, but Mansfield did not.
[6] Erskine May, ii. 188; Stephen, ii. 492.

against this Act and a similar Act affecting Scotland, further progress was made in an Act of 1791 abolishing certain penalties imposed by Elizabethan and Jacobean legislation.[1]

There still subsisted, both for Catholics and Dissenters, the public disabilities imposed by the Test and Corporation Acts. From 1787 the Whigs made repeated efforts to procure the repeal of these statutes, and after 1800 the Irish Union raised in an acute form the problem of Roman Catholic disabilities, which had been largely removed in Ireland by an Irish Act of 1793, but still subsisted in England. Pitt's implied undertaking that Union should be followed by a measure of Catholic emancipation was made nugatory by George III's scruples at giving his assent to legislation which he considered inconsistent with the coronation oath. The King's opposition later frustrated the proposal to open commissioned ranks in the army and navy to Catholics and Dissenters. Under Lord Liverpool, English opinion veered in favour of the abolition of religious tests. An Act of 1817 permitted Irish Roman Catholics to hold such offices in England as they had been enabled to hold in Ireland under the Act of 1793.[2] In the Cabinet it was agreed that Catholic Emancipation should remain an open question.[3] With the relief of Protestant Dissent, it was dealt with in 1828-9.[4] The Commons carried against the government a motion for the repeal of the Test and Corporation Acts. The government, unwilling to resign, negotiated with the bishops to get an agreed bill, which, substituting a statutory declaration for the sacramental test, passed into law.[5] Catholic emancipation presented a more contentious issue. The King— George IV—and many ministers, were hostile. Wellington and Peel, faced by the agitation of O'Connell's Catholic Association in Ireland and doubtful of the fidelity of the Irish troops, saw the necessity of surrender. The Act of 1829 admitted Roman Catholics, on making a declaration in lieu of the oath of supremacy, to both Houses of Parliament, all corporate offices, all judicial positions

*Repeal of the Test and Corporation Acts: the Roman Catholic Emancipation Act*

[1] Costin and Watson, ii. 4; Erskine May, ii. 194; Stephen, ii. 493; J. H. Hexter, *Protestant Revival and Catholic Question in England, 1778-1829*, 8 *J.M.H.* 297. In Parliament, at least, the Acts passed before 1800 were non-contentious.

[2] Erskine May, ii. 219.      [3] Costin and Watson, ii. 371.

[4] See the article by Hexter for an account of the relations between the two movements for emancipation.

[5] Costin and Watson, ii. 42-5.

except in the ecclesiastical courts, and all political offices except
Regent, Lord Chancellor of England, and Lord-Lieutenant or
Lord Chancellor of Ireland.[1]

*Restric-
tion of
ecclesi-
astical
jurisdic-
tion*

The principle that adherence to the Anglican communion was
necessary for the enjoyment of full legal rights both private and
public had thus been rejected. Succeeding years saw the remaining
links between the temporal and ecclesiastical organisations gradually removed. The jurisdiction of the ecclesiastical courts which
had so long occupied an important place in the judicial system
was whittled away.[2] In 1823 perjury ceased to fall within their
cognisance, in 1836 suits relating to tithe, and in 1855 suits
for defamation. Finally a statute of 1857 deprived them of
jurisdiction over divorce and matrimonial causes, vested in a
Divorce court, and over wills, vested in a Court of Probate. Such
jurisdiction as still remained related to questions of a purely
ecclesiastical nature and even from this diminished sphere
of competence suits regarding Church rates were removed in
1868.

*Control
maintained
by the
State over
the
Church*

While the Church thus lost jurisdiction to the State, the
State did not relax jurisdiction over the Church. In 1832 the
Court of Delegates was abolished, and its jurisdiction transferred
to the Privy Council, to be in the next year vested in the Judicial
Committee of that body, in which bishops might sit but which
was essentially a lay court.[3] Parliament, too, continued actively
to exert a legislative authority no longer morally justified by its
necessary connexion with the Church through the Test Act of
1678. Among the Radicals in particular there seemed many indications of a determination to use parliamentary control over the
Church as a means of extensive interference.[4] In 1833 the proposal of the government to suppress ten Irish bishoprics by act of
the civil power alone called forth Keble's famous Assize Sermon
on National Apostasy and the *Tracts for the Times*. It was plain
that a secularised State could no longer hope to wield the same

---

[1] Costin and Watson, ii. 45-53.
[2] On this process, see Holdsworth, i. 620, 622-4, 630.
[3] Holdsworth, i. 518-19, 605. During the eighteenth century, bishops had
ceased to be summoned to the High Court of Delegates. Under the Act of
1833, archbishops and bishops who were Privy Councillors could sit. The
Appellate Jurisdiction Act of 1876 excluded them, except as assessors.
[4] For the Whig theory of relationship between State and Church see G. F. A.
Best in 45 *Hist.* 103. But the extent to which agreement existed as to Church
reform see, generally, O. J. Brose, *Church and Parliament . . . 1828-60*.

authority over the Church as had existed while Church and State were deemed to be inseparably united. In 1850 the *Gorham Case* showed how the appellate jurisdiction of the Privy Council could be employed to encroach on ecclesiastical independence even in strictly ecclesiastical cases. The Bishop of Exeter having refused to institute a clergyman whose doctrinal views he disapproved, institution was nevertheless enforced by a Privy Council decision.[1] Presently, however, the Church recovered an instrument by which its mind might, in a fashion, be expressed. In 1852 the Canterbury Convocation reassembled. In 1855 it was permitted not only to meet and transact business but also to hold debates. In 1861 that of York was likewise revived. The Church had at least set itself at the beginning of the path leading to independence and autonomy.[2]

v

From 1782 to 1867 the geographical horizons of British gov- *Ireland* ernment were widely expanded. At the former date, the imperial *and the* authority of the Crown and the competence of Parliament as an *colonies,* imperial legislature seemed to have reached their nadir. Control *1782-1867* over the thirteen North American colonies had been lost, and in the following year their independence was to be formally recognised. At the same time the Irish Parliament, profiting from these embarrassments, declared its legislative sovereignty. At the close of the period, however, the Crown again held sway over a vast empire, within which the Parliament at Westminster was the supreme legislative authority and the Judicial Committee of the Privy Council the supreme appellate tribunal. The Irish Union of 1800 had united the Parliaments and Churches of England and Ireland, restored the appellate jurisdiction of the British House of Lords over Irish courts, and turned Irish administration into a departmental concern of the British Cabinet, following policies for which it was responsible to a non-Irish majority in the legis-

[1] On this case, see F. Warre Cornish, *History of the English Church in the Nineteenth Century*, i. 321-30.

[2] For a useful summary, written from a High Church point of view, of the relations of Church and State down to the Enabling Act, see E. P. Chase, *The Struggle for the Autonomy of the Church of England*, in *Essays . . . presented to* C. H. McIlwain, 109.

lature. Under the same parliamentary control the government of British India had been annexed to the Crown. That of many Crown colonies had been refashioned so as to reduce them to fuller subordination to the Crown. British rule had in various forms been introduced to new tropical dependencies. Finally, the means of preserving an effective voluntary connexion between the Crown and colonies settled by men of British race and tradition inheriting or acquiring representative institutions and preserving them in their integrity, which had eluded the statesmen of the first British Empire, seemed at last to have been discovered in Lord Durham's Report on Canada, and successfully applied there and elsewhere in the subsequent evolution of responsible self-government. A generation later than Durham, another problem which eighteenth-century statesmanship had likewise found insuperable, that of combining neighbouring colonies under an effective common government, was dealt with by the British North America Act of 1867, providing a constitution for the first federal union within the Empire. It was not the least of the achievements of this remarkable period in the history of British government that an imperial fabric so impressive and so skilfully designed should have been brought into existence.

*Failure of the Irish Union*

In one case only was the work of British statesmanship imperfectly done. By the Act of Union of 1800 Ireland, hitherto occupying a status which for all practical purposes was colonial, was drawn into an integral connexion with Great Britain. In 1867 the experiment stood condemned by its results.

*Irish government, sixteenth to eighteenth centuries*

The kingship into which Henry VIII in 1536 transformed the medieval English lordship of Ireland was wholly different from that conjoined with the English Crown by the Anglo-Scottish Union of 1603. The latter was until 1707 a purely dynastic bond between two mutually independent sovereign states. The Irish kingship was inseparably annexed to that of England, and Ireland, though possessing a Parliament, executive, and courts of its own, was unquestionably subject to English sovereignty. By Poynings' Law, in 1495, the Irish Parliament itself made applicable to Ireland all statutes lately made in England, and enacted that it should in future meet only when the King's Lieutenant and Council in Ireland should under the Great Seal of Ireland certify the causes and considerations for holding it, and that the king, in his Council in England, should approve all bills to be introduced when it met.[1] It thus possessed no legislative initiative. The wars of the sixteenth and seventeenth centuries, which extended English authority in Ireland—confined under Henry VII to the district round Dublin known as the Pale—throughout the country, created a new ruling class of English and Protestant origins. They were, however, unaccompanied by any important increase in the powers of the Irish Parliament, even when these were inherited by what was intended to be a loyalist garrison. The Irish Parliament indeed obtained a limited legislative initiative, but its bills had still to be successively approved by the Irish and the English Privy Councils, and it had no power of altering or rejecting bills sent to it by the latter body. The Parliament at Westminster continued to enact laws affecting Ireland. The most important class of these was commercial. A series of statutes excluded Ireland from the benefits of colonial trade, forbade the export except to England of staple products such as wool, and penalised Irish agriculture and industry in order to safeguard those of England.[2] Conversely, many important English statutes did not apply to Ireland, nor was their place permitted to be taken by Irish enactments. There was no Habeas Corpus Act in Ireland before 1781, and until 1782 Irish judges were dismissible at pleasure.

The Irish Parliament, besides being constitutionally almost impotent, was also in a peculiar degree subject to the executive. *Constitutional subordination of Ireland to England* Irish revenue was two-thirds hereditary, and therefore beyond parliamentary control. Irish patronage, utilised as an adjunct to the system of "influence" in England, created an executive system in which many lucrative sinecures were held by Englishmen, and which was costly, inefficient and corrupt. Before 1793 no statute restricted the number of placemen and pensioners who could sit in Parliament. By this means the subservience of the Irish Parliament to the executive was assured. Not until the Octennial Act of 1768 was there any limit on the duration of an Irish Parliament save that imposed by the demise of the Crown. The narrow-

---

[1] Perhaps it was meant rather as a check on the Viceroy than on the Parliament; Grant Robertson, 205-6, and explanatory statute of 1556, 206-7. A. F. Pollard, *Reign of Henry VII*, iii. 298-9.

[2] Lipson, *Economic History of England*, iii. 128, 200-205; Keith, *Constitutional History of the First British Empire*, 72.

ness of the franchise, from which Catholics were excluded, and
the vast preponderance of borough members in the Commons,
rendered the task of the government in controlling Parliament
exceedingly easy. English control was equally complete over the
Irish courts. In *Annesley* v. *Sherlock* (1719) the House of Lords
at Westminster denied the final appellate jurisdiction asserted
by its Dublin counterpart.[1] In the same year the British Parliament
reaffirmed by statute its right to legislate for Ireland and rejected
the claim of the Irish House of Lords to review the decisions of
the Irish courts.[2]

*Rise of an*
*opposition*
*in the*
*Irish*
*Parlia-*
*ment*

Constitutionally, therefore, Ireland seemed with singular in-
felicity to combine the disadvantages both of subordination and of
autonomy. From the Revolution of 1688 onwards, however, a
movement of revolt against English control can be discerned
within the Irish Protestant ascendancy itself. Under William III
the Irish Parliament disputed the competence of the English
Parliament to legislate for Ireland. Stimulated by the writings of
Molyneux and Swift, the discontent due to commercial restrictions, to the decision in *Annesley* v. *Sherlock*, and to such abuses as
the issue of Wood's halfpence[3] gradually created an opposition
which became numerous and active in Parliament by the middle
of the eighteenth century. Its objects included such reforms
as larger financial control by Parliament, a place bill, limitation
of the duration of Parliaments, security of tenure for judges, and
a Habeas Corpus Act.[4]

*Achieve-*
*ment of*
*legislative*
*independ-*
*ence*

The Octennial Act of 1768 formed the only substantial gain
achieved before the American Revolution. That event both
quickened the desire of the Irish to throw off their colonial
status and diminished the power of the British government to
continue to impose it. As the military forces in Ireland were
depleted by the war, a volunteer force for Irish defence came into
being which presently developed a political programme. This included, besides the claim for legislative independence and free-
trade, more radical demands put forward by Protestant Dissenters
for the repeal of the Irish Test Act which debarred them from

---

1 Lecky, *History of Ireland in the Eighteenth Century*, i. 447-8
2 Costin and Watson, ii. 128.
3 See A. Goodwin, *Wood's Halfpence*, 51 E.H.R. 647.
4 Lecky, *History of Ireland*, ii. 52-3, 70-77.

office, and for parliamentary reform.[1] Under a pressure which even the government's majority of "Undertakers"[2] did not enable it to withstand, a series of reforms were rapidly carried. England conceded free-trade, the repeal of the Test Act, a Habeas Corpus Act, security of judicial tenure, and an Irish Mutiny Act.[3] Full legislative independence followed. In 1782 the British Parliament repealed the Act of 1719, and the Irish Parliament did the same for Poynings' Law and conferred supreme appellate jurisdiction on the Irish House of Lords. In 1783 the British Parliament abandoned British legislative and judicial supremacy over Ireland. For eighteen years Great Britain and Ireland constituted two independent kingdoms under the same Crown.[4]

These years, during which Ireland was governed by what has *The age of* generally been described, after its most influential member, as *Grattan's* "Grattan's Parliament", have been regarded as a golden age of *Parliament* Irish government. The constitution was liberalised by the admission of Catholics to the parliamentary franchise in 1793, and by the removal of at least a number of Catholic disabilities.[5] The abolition of commercial restrictions promoted a revival of economic well-being. But the constitution of 1782 suffered from the incurable defect that while the legislature was sovereign, it possessed no sort of control over the executive. Though King of Ireland, the King must in the last resort act on the advice of British ministers. The Irish administration, headed by an English Lord-Lieutenant and an English Chief Secretary, conformed to English direction. British ministers might in theory favour reform in Ireland. In fact, the maintenance of their control over the Irish Parliament forbade any real advance. Parliamentary reform and the complete removal of the religious disabilities of Catholics and Dissenters remained unfulfilled ideals. It is therefore not surprising that when Irish discontent, embodied in the Society of United Irishmen, betrayed dangerous sympathies with the Revolutionary government in France and broke out into rebellion in 1798, a legislative union between Britain and Ireland, frequently advo-

---

[1] Lecky, ii. 241-3, 282-5, 346-7.    [2] Lecky, ii. 54.
[3] Lecky, ii. 242-3, 246, 254-9, 274-5, 315.
[4] Lecky, ii. 307-8; Grant Robertson, 255-8 (Irish statutes), 258-60 (British statutes).
[5] Lecky, iii. 163-8; Erskine May, ii. 197-8.

cated from 1782 onwards, should have appeared to British and even to Irish ministers the only satisfactory safeguard for the interests of both countries.

*The Act of Union* The Union which came into force on January 1, 1801, abolished the Irish Parliament, introduced into the British House of Lords twenty-eight Irish representative lay peers elected for life and four Irish bishops sitting according to a scheme of rotation, and into the Commons one hundred members from Irish constituencies. Irish judicial independence was extinguished, and the House of Lords became the supreme appellate tribunal from Irish courts.[1] Unlike the Scottish Union, the Act of 1800 had been obtained not through negotiation but by methods of intimidation and bribery. Notwithstanding the means by which it was achieved, and its ill-starred later history, it was in many respects an equitable and well contrived measure. The representation given to Ireland was fairly adjusted to its wealth, though not to its population. Irish peers, more fortunate than those of Scotland, were, if not elected to the Lords, permitted to seek election to the Commons in Great Britain. Financial relations between the two countries were not unjustly arranged. The two Exchequers were to be kept separate until the National Debts of Great Britain and Ireland formed a proportionately equal burden on their respective financial resources. Above all, free-trade was conceded and commercial disabilities imposed on Ireland by British statutes disappeared.[2]

*The question of Catholic emancipation* The initial cause of the failure of the Union is to be found in the inability of Pitt to carry the measure of Catholic emancipation which had come to be regarded in Ireland as the necessary corollary of the scheme for union. Apart from Emmet's rising of 1803, a last flare-up of the embers of '98, Irish opposition first became organised in the Catholic Associations formed from 1805 onwards to support the cause of emancipation by petitions to Parliament. After 1823, under the leadership of O'Connell, the movement assumed a new form and embraced wider aims. Largely popular in composition, extensively supported by the Catholic lower clergy, it looked beyond emancipation to repeal.[3]

---

[1] Costin and Watson, ii. 20-28.
[2] J. O'Connor, *History of Ireland, 1798-1924*, i. 121.
[3] O'Connor, i. 164, 170, 172-4; Lecky, *Leaders of Public Opinion in Ireland*, ii. 59. It was, however, the Protestant middle-class of Dublin who had begun the repeal movement in 1810; O'Connor, i. 207.

The case for repeal rested on broader grounds than merely *The* the delay in carrying emancipation. O'Connell's election to the *Repeal* Commons in 1828—as member for Clare, for which he was as a *movement* Catholic not qualified to sit, but was returned by a majority of more than two to one—indeed directly caused the Emancipation Act of 1829. That Irish agitation led on from emancipation to repeal may perhaps be partly attributable to no better reason than the personal ambition of the "Liberator", but in the main the demand for repeal was deeply rooted in the conditions under which Irish government was being carried on. Pitt's utopian dream of successfully ruling Ireland through a British Parliament deriving impartiality and wisdom from its detachment from Irish affairs, and supplying the needs of the poorer country from the superabundance of the wealthier, had in practice been entirely dispelled.[1] Though plentifully supplied with information regarding Ireland by administrative departments and by royal commissions, Parliament had neither purpose nor interest sufficient to act promptly or intelligently. To make even emancipation itself anything more than a paper concession proved difficult. Long after 1829 Protestants still largely monopolised offices, both administrative and judicial, central and local.[2] An Act of 1829, accompanying that of emancipation, had weakened the Catholic electorate by raising the qualifying freehold from forty shillings to ten pounds.[3] The Irish Reform Act, though opening some of the larger and disfranchising sixteen of the smallest of the Irish boroughs, had made no such radical changes as in Great Britain. Only through a restored and reformed Irish Parliament could the opinion led by O'Connell become effective. Nor was this all. The Catholic peasantry demanded relief from the burden of paying tithes and Church-rates to the Protestant establishment. The needs of education, communications, industry, and public services of every kind had to be supplied. To almost every aspect of Irish government a Parliament at Westminster showed itself largely indifferent. It almost seemed that its principal concern was merely to keep order. In Ireland the Habeas Corpus Act was usually suspended. In 1833 popular resistance to tithe led to the passing of a Coercion Act, the precursor of many.[4]

[1] Lecky, *History of Ireland in the Eighteenth Century*, v. 234.
[2] O'Connor, i. 227, 233-4.    [3] Costin and Watson, ii. 53-5.
[4] 3 and 4 Will. IV. c. 4.

*Attempts to provide for Irish needs*

It would be misleading to say that nothing positive was done In 1831 a system of national primary education was introduced. A series of statutes culminating in 1838 dealt—though with undue delay, and after much disorder had taken place—with the problem of tithe, reducing its amount and commuting it into a rent-charge.[1] In 1838 an Irish Poor Law was passed.[2] In 1840 Irish municipal corporations were reformed so as to facilitate the entry of Catholics.[3] The Church Temporalities Act of 1834 diverted part of the revenues of the Establishment to the relief of poorer benefices.[4] In 1845 an increased grant was made to the Catholic theological college at Maynooth. Queen's Colleges, of university standing,[5] were established at Belfast, Cork, and Galway. During the Under-Secretaryship of Thomas Drummond an enlightened temper prevailed in Irish administration. While reorganising the constabulary system and firmly repressing disorder, he wisely adopted the policy of employing Catholics in official positions, and attempted to provide for such elementary Irish needs as the construction of railways.[6]

*The land problem*

While sometimes acting too late, and sometimes, as in the establishment of the non-sectarian Queen's Colleges, with a certain disregard of Irish opinion, the English government acted on one important question entirely harmfully. Throughout the period after the Union, the evils of the Irish land system revealed themselves with alarming clearness. Except in the North, the Irish landlords were severed from the peasantry by barriers of race and religion. Too commonly absentees, they were for the most part interested in their properties solely as sources of income. On Irish estates, generally much larger than those of England and Scotland, much less capital was expended on improvements by either landlord or tenant. Leases were rare, rack-rents the rule, and rents rose as a rapid growth of population sharpened the appetite for land of a population which had no industrial system

---

[1] O'Connor, i. 224-6.    [2] O'Connor, i. 232.

[3] O'Connor, i. 234. Hitherto there had been only 200 Catholic municipal electors in all Ireland.

[4] O'Connor, i. 226.

[5] O'Connor, i. 30-33, ii. 33. Collectively, these constituted The Queen's University in Ireland.

[6] See generally J. F. M'Lennan, *Memoir of Thomas Drummond*, chs. xiv.-xviii. There is a useful sketch in R. B. O'Brien, *Fifty Years of Concession to Ireland*, ii. 429-55.

to absorb it. Holdings were meanwhile infinitely sub-divided. Dependent mainly on the potato-crop, the peasantry lived on the brink and sometimes in the midst of famine. The principal contribution of the British Parliament to the solution of this problem was to facilitate eviction, which successive statutes made easier and cheaper than before the Union. In the great Famine of 1846 the whole crazy system collapsed. The government, which had lately investigated the Irish land question through the Devon Commission,[1] took no positive ameliorative action. Apart from the repeal of the Corn Laws, it still adhered to its earlier policy. During the decades after the Famine Ireland was a land of evictions and agrarian crime. An Encumbered Estates Act,[2] intended to introduce new capital into Irish agriculture, merely created a new class of absentee landlords even less closely linked by interest and sympathy to their tenants than the old. Judged by the ultimate test that a peasant population can apply to its government, English administration in Ireland was hopelessly found wanting. Among the Irish emigrants to America, animated as they naturally were by implacable hatred of the government which they considered responsible for their exile, there arose the Fenian Brotherhood formed for the purpose of destroying English rule in Ireland.

Ireland itself was meanwhile quiescent. The repeal movement, *The origin of separatism* never able under the new franchise of 1829 to command more than forty of the hundred Irish seats, and suffering a setback in the general election of 1841, had split thereafter between O'Connellites and Young Irelanders. The impact of Fenianism revived and transformed it. O'Connell, loyal to the Crown and an instinctive conservative, would have been content with a federal union with Great Britain.[3] The constitutional aims of the new nationalism were to tend rapidly towards a separatism, relying if necessary on violence, which paid either lip-service or none at all to the principle of imperial unity.

With this unhappy failure to contrive an efficient and acceptable government in Ireland is to be contrasted the remarkable progress achieved in the overseas Empire. That progress, it must

---

1 See R. B. O'Brien, *Parliamentary History of the Irish Land Question*, 68-71.
2 O'Brien, *Fifty Years of Concession to Ireland*, ii. 149-51.
3 Lecky, *Leaders of Public Opinion in Ireland*, ii. 210-14.

*The
American
Revolu-
tion and
colonial
govern-
ment*

be admitted, was at first exceedingly slow.[1] The American Revolution seemed to instil into English statesmen only the lesson
that, if it was unwise to tax the colonies through the Imperial
Parliament and the practice must be abandoned, it was nevertheless equally unwise to permit in the colonies the growth of democratic institutions which would inevitably follow the same course
as those of the thirteen lost colonies. It was perhaps not unwelcome
to the British government that Canada, the largest remaining
British province in North America, contained a population devoid
of any tradition of representative institutions or self-government.
Though in Nova Scotia, and in New Brunswick detached from it in
1784, representative institutions of the conventional colonial type
existed, the executive was too strong and democratic forces too
weak to threaten at first any repetition of the American disaster.[2]

*British
North
America*

The influx of exiled Loyalists from the United States wholly
transformed the political position in these remaining provinces.
The Loyalists, while honourably distinguished by their fidelity
to the Crown, were the heirs of the colonial tradition in
which they had been nurtured, nor was it reasonable to expect
them to accept an inferior constitutional status because their
fidelity had led them into exile. Hence a Radical party, highly
critical of the government, appeared in the Nova Scotian
Assembly. A similar development occurred in New Brunswick,
where the majority of the settlers were from the outset drawn
from the lost provinces. The settlement of the United Empire
Loyalists was most numerous in Canada proper, both in the
French districts on the Lower St. Lawrence and more densely
still on the north shore of Lake Ontario. In 1784 these settlers
petitioned for the establishment of representative institutions in
Canada.[3] In 1791 an Act was passed separating Upper Canada, with
its mainly English population, from the mainly French Lower
Canada, and setting up representative institutions in each, but
counterbalancing the elective Lower House by a nominated
Council. The appointment of the executive Council also lay
in the hands of the governors.[4] Thus the British North Ameri-

---

[1] H. T. Manning, *British Colonial Government after the American Revolution*,
12-15.
[2] *Cambridge History of the British Empire*, vi. 188, 214.   [3] *C.H.B.E.* vi. 195.
[4] For an account of the Act and the difficulties attending its operation, see
Manning, 332 ff.

can colonies all came to possess constitutions generally similar to those existing during the earlier stages of colonial history. The main differences were that since colonial revenues, partly derived from the Quebec Revenue Act and partly from the income of Crown property, was not wholly covered by grants from the Assemblies, the executive did not, as in former times, tend to fall under the domination of the legislatures; and that a permanent, if small, British military establishment was at its disposal.

The system thus given a new lease of life worked no better than before. In Lower Canada the Assembly, predominantly French, and wholly inexperienced in government, entered on a long and sordid quarrel with an executive which Crown patronage made mainly English, and the utility of which, to the Crown and the colony alike, was impaired by the lack of departmental ministries, so that the governor, a stranger to the colony, fell into the hands of secret cliques of irresponsible and self-interested advisers. In this contest, sharpened by every sort of personal, racial, and religious animus, the Assembly resorted to such devices as impeachment and attempts to control and appropriate supply, and the governors to punitive dissolutions.[1] Various attempts at compromise by the British government, and the visit of a Royal Commission in 1835 under Lord Gosford, led to no result. In 1837 a revolt broke out. It synchronised with a rising in Upper Canada which demonstrated the defects of the Act of 1791 even in a province where racial dissensions played no part. Here the executive and legislative Councils, membership of which was practically identical, found themselves at issue with an Assembly representative of a growing democratic society violently opposed to the predominance of what came to be known as the "Family Compact".[2] The ability of Governor Colborne (1828–36), and the government's success in the election of 1830, staved off a crisis for the time. Defiance of Canadian opinion by his incompetent successor, Sir Francis Head, kindled rebellion in December 1837.

*Constitutional difficulties in Lower and Upper Canada*

---

[1] *C.H.B.E.* vi. 209–10, 246, 269. For a general survey of the Canadian situation in 1837, see C. W. New, *Lord Durham*, ch. xvi.

[2] *C.H.B.E.* vi. 207, 260–61. The phrase was coined in 1828.

*The Maritime Provinces*

Analogous conditions, not, however, leading to rebellion, prevailed in the maritime provinces.[1] Executive power was strengthened, and that of the Assemblies weakened, by the division of Nova Scotia into four parts. While New Brunswick and Nova Scotia possessed representative Assemblies, Cape Breton had none, and Prince Edward Island was for a moment in danger of being reduced to the same status. In these provinces the movement for responsible government was led by the Nova Scotian Assembly, and, after a contest the moderation of which sharply contrasts with the violence of the outbreaks in Canada, the Crown conceded full control over revenue in 1837, and the governor later proceeded to add to the Executive Council persons commanding the confidence of the legislatures.

*The Durham Report*

The Canadian rebellions led by more stormy courses to the same result. In 1838 Lord Melbourne commissioned Lord Durham as Governor-General of the North American provinces with special authority to investigate conditions in the Canadas.[2] His Report, the landmark dividing the constitutional histories of the first and second British Empires, "arrested men's attention throughout the Empire in 1839 and has kept its pages fresh and influential to the present day".[3] Its comprehensive review of every aspect of Canadian affairs contained practical recommendations which have become ingrained in British colonial policy. Lord Durham's plan for dealing with French-Canadian nationalism by reuniting the two Canadas—based as it was on fashionable but fallacious radical theories as to the solvent effects of political experience, education, and reason—was indeed foredoomed to the failure made evident in the renewed division between the provinces of Quebec and Ontario carried out in 1867 by the British North America Act. The supreme merit of the Report lies in its recognition of the necessity for conceding responsible government—not through an undifferentiated Council but by heads of definite departments—as the corollary of representative institutions. His proposals would, as he recognised, "place the internal government of the colony in the hands of the colonists themselves", while reserving imperial control over "the form of government, the regulation of foreign relations, and of trade with the Mother Country, the other British colonies, and foreign nations, and the

[1] *C.H.B.E.* vi. 276-81.

[2] The scope of the Report was extended to cover all the North American Provinces.          [3] *C.H.B.E.* vi. 301.

disposal of the public lands".[1] The whole subsequent evolution of the Imperial Constitution exemplifies and forms a commentary on Durham's principles. They have become "the standard by which colonial constitutionalists have regulated their claims".[2] Responsible government has been increasingly made effective, the subjects reserved by Durham have gradually passed within its ambit, and the self-governing colonies have assumed, under the British Crown, the essential attributes of sovereign states.

The Colonial Secretary, Russell, who in June 1839 had pro- *First ex-* nounced responsible government in the colonies unworkable, *periments* declared in a despatch of the following October that office under *in respon-* *sible* the Crown in the colonies need not any longer be during good *govern-* behaviour but was subject to such considerations of expediency *ment* as governors accepted.[3] It remained to discover by experiment how governors would interpret this power. It did not necessarily imply—any more than in England itself—the acceptance by the Crown of the leaders of the predominant party as its ministers. In Canada, Sydenham (1839–42), dominated by Russell's instruction that his chief business was to maintain the influence of the Crown, tried unsuccessfully to govern through a Council chosen from men of moderate party views. His successor, Bagot (1842–3), relaxed control so far as to admit French-Canadians and Radicals. Metcalfe (1843–6) adhered with greater resolution to the policy which virtually made the Governor his own Prime Minister. After the brief rule of Lord Cathcart (1846–7), the decisive step was taken in 1848 by Durham's son-in-law, Lord Elgin. With the approval of the Whig Colonial Secretary, Lord Grey, he frankly accepted party as the basis for the Canadian ministry.[4] From that date the question descended from the constitutional to the political level, and the history of Canadian self-government was merged in that of Canadian parties.

Of the Durham Report, Edward Gibbon Wakefield had said,

[1] Durham Report (ed. Sir C. P. Lucas), ii. 281-2.
[2] C.H.B.E. vi. 307.
[3] C.H.B.E. vi. 284-6; J. L. Morison, British Supremacy and Canadian Self-Government, 1839-54, 74-6. See also Russell's despatch to Poulett Thomson (Lord Sydenham) in October 1839, in Keith, Letters and Speeches on British Colonial Policy, i. 173.
[4] Morison, 198-200.

*Responsible government in the Maritime Provinces and Newfoundland*

"It has now gone the round from Canada through the West Indies and South Africa to the Australias, and has everywhere been received with acclamations".[1] In Nova Scotia, the policy of introducing responsible government by degrees, in conformity with the movements of Sydenham, produced a further constitutional conflict, ended like that in Canada by Grey's despatch, which led to the establishment of the first fully responsible government in the colonial Empire. In 1851 Prince Edward Island followed suit, and in 1854 a party ministry took the place of coalitions in New Brunswick.[2] Newfoundland, long a mere fishing settlement with a naval governor, acquired a representative assembly in 1833. This turbulent body, whose pretensions to the same privileges as the House of Commons in Great Britain were rejected by the Privy Council in *Kielley* v. *Carson* (1838), was suspended in 1840, being replaced for a time by a partly nominated single-chamber legislature. In 1854 fully representative government, to be coupled with ministerial responsibility, was introduced.[3]

*Constitutional evolution in Australia*

Under very different conditions from those in North America, British colonisation in Australia had begun in 1786 with an Order in Council appointing the eastern coast of New South Wales, or adjoining islands, as a place to which offenders might be transported. The Governor of the new colony was empowered by statute to establish a government. The circumstances of this settlement naturally did not admit of any elective assembly, and the governor received wide powers for all necessary purposes of administration, defence, and jurisdiction.[4] As population grew and free settlers entered, it became impossible to continue this rudimentary system. Besides the free settlers, ex-convicts—many of whom had been guilty of no offence which could reasonably be regarded as criminal—rose to fortune and importance, and a sharp conflict arose between these "emancipists" and the official class known as "exclusives".[5] The grievances of the former at first

---

1 *C.H.B.E.* vi. 307.                                 2 *C.H.B.E.* vi. 357-60.
3 *C.H.B.E.* vi. 433. Responsible government was initiated in 1855. On *Kielley* v. *Carson*, see C. Wittke, *Parliamentary Privilege in the Empire*, in *Essays in History and Political Theory presented to C. H. McIlwain*, 320; Keir and Lawson, 263 n.
4 *C.H.B.E.* vii. Part i. 59.
5 *C.H.B.E.* vii. Part i. 106-7, 146-4, 162-4.

related solely to their legal status, and an Act of 1823 remedied these, introducing trial by jury and a supreme court.[1] Leaving executive power intact with the governor, it also created a nominated Council, without, however, any legislative initiative or taxative power. In 1828 the governor lost his special legislative powers and the non-official element in his Council was increased. Representative government was still withheld. But the emancipist agitation in its favour steadily grew. In 1842 an elective element, amounting to 24 was introduced into the Legislative Council, as against 12 nominated members.[2] As in North America, the result was only to produce conflict between executive and legislature. By this time, Canadian experience was beginning to exercise its powerful influence on colonial constitutional development. Australian opinion like Canadian demanded the surrender to the legislature of the Crown's independent revenues, and the appointment of responsible ministers. By this time also, the adoption of free-trade by Great Britain and the repeal of the Navigation Act had signalised the end of the Old Colonial system on its economic side, and destroyed one of the main arguments for restricting colonial self-government. An Imperial Act of 1850 gave to New South Wales a limited power of constitutional amendment, used by the Legislative Council to draft measures for giving complete financial control to a wholly elective Lower House, which were enacted with the approval of the Imperial government in 1855.[3] Ministerial responsibility followed as a matter of course. In Tasmania, South Australia, and Victoria, separated from New South Wales in 1825, 1836, and 1850 respectively, the powers given by the Act of 1850 were used to create, simultaneously with the new constitution of New South Wales, schemes of government modelled on the same lines. Queensland, separated from New South Wales in 1859, was similarly treated.[4]

In New Zealand, where colonisation under the sovereignty of the Crown had been undertaken from 1840 by a Company, government began with a governor and an official Legislative Council, replaced by an elective Assembly in 1846. An elaborate

*New Zealand*

1 C.H.B.E. vii. Part i. 150–51.
2 K. Bell and W. P. Morrell, *British Colonial Policy, 1830–60*, 53–61.
3 C.H.B.E. vii. Part I, 273–7; Bell and Morrell, i. 123–9.
4 C.H.B.E. vii. Part I, 283–91; Bell and Morrell, 129.

constitution on a provincial basis was enacted in 1852, and large powers of amendment were conferred on the Assembly.[1] Two years later the British Government, having wholly abandoned the notion of introducing responsible government by degrees, assented to its adoption in the colony forthwith.

*Further developments to 1867*

From this point, the constitutional development of the self-governing colonies was to proceed towards two further goals; closer integration with each other, and further emancipation from imperial control. By 1867 Canada had already begun to mark out the line of progress. The British North America Act divided Canada into the two provinces of Quebec and Ontario, federated with them the provinces of Nova Scotia and New Brunswick, and enabled other provinces already existing or still to be formed to join when they wished.[2] In Australia, however, geographical separation, diversity of interest, and the absence of any powerful neighbour delayed any such process.

*Enlargement of colonial authority*

The restrictions on colonial autonomy which the Durham Report had laid down had already become impaired. Thus control of unoccupied lands in Canada had been turned over to the provinces by Acts of 1840 to 1852. The legislative authority of the colonies over commerce had been acquiesced in when a Canadian tariff imposing duties on English goods was enacted in 1858.[3] In 1865 the Colonial Laws Validity Act laid down the principle that the validity of a Colonial Act could not be impugned except so far as it was repugnant to an Imperial Act intended to apply to the colony in question.[4] Even the power of the home government to make treaties affecting the colonies had become an object of criticism with regard to the fisheries of the Maritime Provinces (1854).[5] After 1867 the movement towards complete autonomy moved along a predestined course.

*Some exceptions*

Other colonies, however, either stood still or moved constitutionally in the reverse direction. In the Cape of Good Hope,

---

[1] W. P. Morrell, *The Provincial System of Government in New Zealand, 1852-76*, 47 ff.

[2] H. E. Egerton, *Federations and Unions within the British Empire*, 121 ff.

[3] *C.H.B.E.* vi. 349-50.

[4] The Act is printed as an Appendix to K. C. Wheare, *Statute of Westminster and Dominion Status*. For the important sections, see A. V. Dicey, *Law of the Constitution*, 101-2.

[5] *C.H.B.E.* vi. 363.

acquired in 1815, racial divisions and the presence of a large native population with whom frequent wars broke out made the Imperial authorities reluctant to concede responsible government, since it would mean the withdrawal of Imperial control and protection.[1] Colonies such as Jamaica, originally possessing a constitution with a wholly elective legislature, lost it, and had to accept either actual or potential official majorities in their legislatures. As the nineteenth century advanced, only three colonies of all those founded in the period before the American Revolution—Barbados, Bermuda, and the Bahamas—still had constitutions based on the ancient model, fully representative, but not involving responsible government. In the numerous colonies acquired by conquest or cession since 1814, the creation of this classic type of colonial constitution has been altogether given up. The government of masses of non-European subjects precluded the acceptance of any principle of representation and of any responsibility of the executive save to the law, and to the Imperial government and Parliament through the Secretary of State for the Colonies.[2]

This experiment in the government of non-Europeans was tried on the largest scale in India. The constitutional history of this vast dependency has passed through three well-defined stages. Until 1773 the East India Company was invested either by charter or by statute with governmental powers over the settlements which it acquired whether by agreement with native princes, or, in the case of Bombay, from the English Crown. From 1773 control was dual, shared between the Company, which in 1833 lost its commercial while retaining its political privileges, and the Crown, acting from 1784 through a newly-founded department called the Board of Control. In 1858 the Company ceased to exist,[3] and its territorial possessions, now widely extended, passed under the exclusive sovereignty of the Crown, responsible to the Imperial Parliament through the newly created Secretary of State for India.

*Constitutional development of India*

[1] C.H.B.E. viii. 367 ff.
[2] See C. Jeffries, *The Colonial Office*, 105 ff., for its organisation and work.
[3] Its trading functions were finally wound up in 1863.

15

*The East India Company*

The East India Company had been incorporated by charter in 1600[1] under an annually elected Governor and twenty-four "committees",[2] to trade with the East Indies, Asia, Africa, and America, to exercise legislative powers appropriate to its functions, and to enforce its own rules. Unlike the Companies formed to settle America, the Company was not considered to need authority to govern newly discovered countries. Its settlements were to be formed on territories belonging to native rulers. Even this involved carrying out certain governmental activities. A subsequent charter granted by Charles II conferred on it authority to send ships, munitions and men to guard its stations, to commission officers, appoint governors and other officials, make peace and war with non-Christian rulers, and govern its own servants and persons living under its control according to the laws of England.[3] The sphere of the Company's operations became, through the competition of foreign rivals elsewhere in the East, confined to the Indian mainland. Commercial stations were conceded to it by the Mogul Emperor at Surat and other ports. On the east coast, Masulipatam and Armagaon were acquired, the latter being in 1640 abandoned for Madras. The local ruler gave the Company the right to fortify and govern this city, which now displaced Masulipatam as its centre in southern India, and was held directly under the Mogul Emperor from 1687 onwards. In the later seventeenth century the Company extended its posts into Orissa, Bihar, and Bengal. In 1690 a settlement was made on the Hugli, fortified in 1696 and named Fort William in honour of the reigning king. Here, in addition to its other privileges, the Company acquired from the native ruler the right of collecting taxes from the neighbouring district.[4] Unlike the Surat, Madras and Bengal settlements, made by arrangement with native rulers and involving no acquisition of territorial rights under the English Crown, Bombay was conferred on the Company by Charles II. In a charter of 1668, the King, who had obtained it from Portugal as part of

---

[1] For this charter, see Prothero, *Statutes and Constitutional Documents*, 448-55.

[2] I.e. a committee of twenty-four members.

[3] Keith, *Constitutional History of India*, 8-9. The charter of 1676 gave authority to strike a coinage, and those of 1683 and 1686 enlarged military and judicial authority, but also made it clear that the Company used it only under the Crown.          [4] Keith, 25.

his wife's dowry, granted it in common socage at a yearly rent and conceded rights to govern the inhabitants of the territory as well as the Company's servants.[1]

The extension of the Company's settlements, and the need *Enlarge-* for providing it with governmental powers in regions where *ment of* the Crown itself was unable to exert direct authority, naturally *the Com-* enhanced its political attributes. Successive renewals of its charter *govern-* placed it in possession of such powers as those of maintaining *mental* discipline by martial law, raising naval forces, acquiring territory, *powers* administering justice, coining money, setting up municipal government, and the like.[2] In the early eighteenth century government was exercised by the three co-equal presidencies of Calcutta, Madras, and Bombay, equally subordinated to the overruling control of the Company itself. In this complex of powers, those arising from grants by the Crown and those derived from native princes were curiously interwoven. But everywhere native authority receded before that of the Company, which, with the decay of the Mogul Empire, became a competitor for political ascendancy in India. That ascendancy it won by its remarkable victories during the Seven Years' War. Under Mogul suzerainty, now reduced to the shadow of a shade, it became ruler of Bengal, and in particular acquired the right of diwani or collection of taxes, which from 1771 it administered through its own servants and not through the existing native officials.[3]

Nothing could have worked worse than this combination on *Abuses of* so great a scale of commercial and political functions. Miserably *Company* underpaid and inadequately controlled, the Company's servants *rule* used their governmental authority solely as a means of enriching themselves. Moreover, despite the Company's prohibition, they were tempted to indulge in private trading, carried out with the utmost lack of scruple. Meanwhile, as its servants throve on these nefarious gains, the Company, overburdened by its political and military responsibilities, got into financial straits, and could not meet the financial obligations which under its charter it owed to the Crown.

---

[1] Keith, 9-10.    [2] On these charters, see Keith, 13, 14, 18, 20, 44, 51, 73.
[3] Keith, 54-5. For the grant itself (1765) see Keith, *Speeches and Documents on Indian Policy*, i. 20-27.

*North's Regulating Act*    The result was the intervention of Parliament by statute in 1773 One Act dealt with the Company's financial position. Another remodelled its governmental system. The latter, the Regulating Act, was preceded by a resolution which asserted that the acquisitions made by the Company belonged to the State, but was not pressed to its logical conclusion of ending the Company's government altogether.[1] Besides refashioning the organisation of the Company in England, and providing against abuses by its servants in India, the Act created a new constitution for Indian government. This centred in a Governor-General and Council at Calcutta, exercising control over the other two presidencies at least to the extent that, except in emergency or on receipt of special orders from the Company, they could neither make war nor conclude treaties. The Governor-General and Council were in their turn controlled by the Court of Directors, and the latter was supervised by the Treasury and the Secretaries of State. A Supreme court was set up at Calcutta, with jurisdiction in Bengal, Bihar, and Orissa, extending primarily over British subjects, but for certain purposes over natives also. Ultimate jurisdiction over the Governor and Council and the judges of the supreme court was conferred on the King's Bench.

*Indian Government, 1773–1784*    It was under this constitution that Warren Hastings carried on his memorable administration. He achieved the triple success of preserving India intact during the disasters of the American War of Independence, restoring the Company's finances, and establishing a strong machinery of government and law in India. He ended native participation in the Diwan, centralised it, and created sound administrative and judicial control over the revenue, set up effective courts, attempted to combine jurisdiction over private litigation and over revenue questions, and codified native law.[2] Yet the system revealed radical weaknesses. Unlike a colonial governor, he was not merely advised but actually controlled by his Council, which during most of his career was dominated by men whom he had not appointed and could not override or

[1] Keith, *Constitutional History of India*, 69. For the Act, see Keith, *Speeches and Documents*, i. 45–59.

[2] See Keith, *Constitutional History of India*, 76–92, for an account, highly favourable in tone, of Hastings's work as Governor-General.

displace, and who were his personal enemies. Not until 1777 was he fully its master. His relations with the other presidencies were unsatisfactory, and their policy towards native rulers provoked friction and war. Serious difficulties arose as to the jurisdiction of the Supreme court over the Governor and his Council, whose subjection to strict rules of English law under conditions in which their application would have made government impossible was not to be tolerated. It was indeed a grave flaw in the constitution that a jurisdiction based on English principles should have been set up in 1773 with an ill-defined sphere of competence.

These difficulties, and the arbitrary dealings of Hastings with native rulers, led to his recall and impeachment,[1] and to an attempted reconstruction of Indian government. In 1783 Fox's India Bill sought to divide the governmental from the commercial business of the Company, placing the former under a board of commissioners, whose proceedings were largely immune from parliamentary supervision, and who were to exercise full control over the Company's revenues, territories, and patronage.[2] This last item was fatal to the bill. It awakened mistrust of the vast additional source of influence which would be placed at the government's disposal. This mistrust, and George III's pressure on the Lords to oppose the bill and destroy the Fox-North coalition, caused its rejection. *Fox's India Bill*

Pitt's Act of 1784 successfully avoided this danger.[3] The Board of Control composed of six Privy Councillors, including the Chancellor of the Exchequer and a Secretary of State, which he established to supervise the government of British India, had no control over patronage, nor did it directly exercise administrative power, which was left to the Company and its servants. Unlike the commissioners proposed by Fox, the Board was responsible to Parliament. Its supervisory powers were secured by its right to issue orders to the Company regarding government and revenue, to have access to all papers, and to remove from revision by the Proprietors any decision by the Directors which it had approved. *Pitt's India Act*

[1] Costin and Watson, ii. 159-60. For the main portions of Burke's speech on the impeachment, see Keith, *Speeches and Documents*, i. 114-55.

[2] Keith, 94-5. The main objection to Fox's bill was that it implied perpetual control over Indian patronage by the Whigs.

[3] Grant Robertson, 261-72; Keith, *Speeches and Documents*, i. 95-114.

The government in India itself was reconstructed. A Governor-General was created in Bengal, and governors in the other two presidencies, each with a Council. Over the governors the Governor-General obtained additional authority in matters of peace and war and relations with native states. Only if they received from the Directors, or the "Secret Committee" of three of that body which dealt with political affairs, orders different from those of the Governor-General were they justified in disobeying him. The Governor-General himself was limited by the necessity of obtaining similar consent for making war except when the Company's territories or those of native states guaranteed by treaty were attacked. As a general indication of policy it was laid down that "to pursue schemes of conquest and extension of dominion in India are measures repugnant to the wish, the honour, and policy of this nation".[1]

*Indian government under Pitt's Act*  Such, with slight subsequent alterations, was the scheme under which Indian government was conducted until 1858. From 1793 the Board had a salaried president, Dundas, who, with a seat in the Cabinet, conducted its business.[2] In India the detailed application of the Act was worked out by Cornwallis, whose main achievements were the permanent settlement of the Bengal revenue, reform of the courts, the institution of a police system, and the beginning of a codification of law in which English rules gradually superseded native custom and the way was prepared for the ultimate amalgamation of the Supreme court presided over by royal judges and the Sudder courts conducted by the Company's servants.[3] In 1833, when the Company's commercial privileges were abolished, the Governor-General of Bengal became Governor-General of India. The most significant change discernible in these years is the steady growth of the powers of the Crown over the Company. In 1853 it acquired power to nominate some of the Directors and to recruit the service by competitive examination.[4] Even had there been no Mutiny the assumption of full sovereignty by the Crown was clearly foreshadowed.

1 Keith, *Constitutional History of India*, 97.
2 W. Foster, *The India Board*, 3 *T.R.H.S.* xi. 61.
3 Keith, 106-9.
4 *C.H.B.E.* v. 16; A. L. Lowell, *Government of England*, i. 156.

At the time of the Mutiny, which led to the extinction of the *Establish-* Company's government and the substitution of direct rule by the *ment of* Crown, the dominions of the Company had been vastly extended *govern- ment by* through the acquisition of Lower Burma, Scinde, the Punjab, *the Crown* Nagpur, and Oude. Moreover, in effect though not formally, the Queen succeeded to the position of the Mogul Emperor. Hence, outside British India proper, the Crown claimed allegiance from the Indian princes, and the process of absorption of territory into British India came to an end. For British India a new era of government began, more Western in its conceptions and methods than that of the Company, which had always been "deeply saturated with old-world prejudices and habits" derived from the Mogul Empire.[1] At home, a Secretary of State, advised by an expert Council, assumed responsibility to Parliament for Indian affairs.[2] The first-fruits of the new era were seen in the Indian Courts Act of 1861 amalgamating the Supreme and Sudder Courts, and the Indian Councils Act.[3] Distance, however, removed Indian affairs from the effective supervision of the home government, and committed them to the direction of a Governor-General in Council largely independent of its control until the laying of the Red Sea cable in 1870. Within India, distance was annihilated even earlier through the improvement of communications, especially by telegraph. Thus, normally immune from interference from above, and increasingly in control of the provinces below him, the Governor-General was able to undertake the task of creating a reformed governmental system throughout a great sub-continent.

[1] V. A. Smith, *Oxford History of India*, 736.

[2] See Keith, *Speeches and Documents*, i. 370-82, for the Act of 1858.

[3] The Indian Councils Act set up a Governor-General's Council of five members—one military, two civilian administrators, one finance member, and one legal member. In practice, the Commander-in-Chief was an additional member.

The dual system of Supreme and Sudder Courts—the former royal courts, dealing with the affairs of Europeans and with suits against European officials, the second appointed by the Company and dealing with ordinary civil and criminal cases on appeal, had in practice long proved cumbersome and inconvenient.

For the Indian Councils Act, see Keith, *Speeches and Documents*, ii. 20-46.

# CHAPTER VIII

## PARLIAMENTARY DEMOCRACY SINCE 1867

i

*General conditions of development*

It is not easy to summarise the complex conditions and experiences which have determined the evolution of the British governmental system since 1867. Yet at the risk of over-simplification by the omission of much which may justly be regarded as relevant, certain factors may be accorded primary importance. The industrial and commercial development which by 1867 had transformed England and Scotland into predominantly urban and manufacturing countries proceeded at an accelerated pace. Agriculture, now left unprotected against the external competition which unrestricted free trade permitted, entered during the 'seventies into a major depression followed by a recovery which never became more than partial, and maintained itself with difficulty in an expanding industrial society. Except in Ireland, population mounted regularly, from the 26 million of 1871, to 33 million in 1891, nearly 41 million in 1911, and over 51 million in 1961.[1] This growth accentuated an increasing disparity between the urban and the rural populations. To a steadily diminishing extent was this mainly urban society able to feed itself from supplies produced at home. Its life became bound up with its ability to develop its export trade in manufactured goods.

*Decline of Britain's industrial predominance*

Britain's industrial predominance, however, began to be challenged by powerful and efficient rivals. The industrialisation of continental states like France and Germany, of the United States, and in later years of the Dominions and India and of Japan, destroyed beyond hope of recovery the virtual monopoly she had formerly enjoyed. While her industrial output increased, and with it her export trade, its proportion to the whole volume of international commerce fell away, and the home market itself began to

[1] These figures are for England, Wales, and Scotland combined: the figures for Northern Ireland rose from 1,243,000 in 1931 to 1,425,000 in 1961.

be encroached upon by manufactured imports. In days when British industry held the leading position in the market at home and abroad, no effective demand could arise for governmental intervention in its interests. The task of government was confined within the narrow limits of seeking, by commercial negotiation, to break down such barriers as prevented the universal acceptance of free trade. Faced by less advantageous conditions, in which other states strove to create and organise industrial systems of their own, expand their sphere of operation, and protect them by tariffs and bounties, the advantages of *laissez-faire* became less evident. The maintenance of free trade came to mean the endeavour to prevent a deliberate exclusion of British goods from foreign markets. British industry, suffering the disadvantages as well as deriving the benefits of private control, drew nearer invoking State support in its struggles against competitors supported and directed by their respective governments. At first in an advisory capacity but with a necessary bent towards regulative control, the government was obliged to intervene in the conduct of the economic activities of society.[1]

Internal conditions tended to produce the same result. *Laissez-* *Internal* *faire* in industry had caused or aggravated social evils which even *problems* during its period of unquestioned theoretical acceptance had obliged the State occasionally to interfere. After 1867 this need became even more peremptory and its fulfilment ceased to be regarded as inevitably harmful, futile, or improper. Social and economic inequalities arising from increased specialisation of labour, and poverty sharpened by unemployment and by the competition, at least in certain industries, of low-paid foreign producers, were degrading large sections of the population to a position in which they could neither maintain health and efficiency, nor enjoy the amenities of human existence.[2] The new

---

[1] See K. B. Smellie, *A Hundred Years of English Government* (2nd ed.), 86-91. It may, however, be suggested that the continued *increase* of the British export trade is more important than the fact that its *proportion* of the world output declined; and also that its expansion was largely due to the stimulus of competition. But this does not of course affect the point that it could derive benefit from State encouragement and help.

[2] On the other hand wages ruled lowest in trades such as dressmaking, where no foreign competition existed. They were also low on the railways, where obviously the same was true. Overall, *real* wages tended to fall after 1900, having risen since 1867.

15a

working-class electorate, among whom, after 1867, the leaven of Trade Unionism was strongly at work, expected remedial State action.[1] It became the function of the State to regulate the labour market, to deal with the conditions and remuneration of work, and finally with the problem of unemployment itself. It took an increasing interest and part in the protection of public health, introduced universal and compulsory elementary education, provided secondary education, and partly financed and controlled higher education. For many of these purposes responsibility was in large measure devolved on local authorities, which also acquired powers for the supply of public services supplementing those supplied by private enterprise.[2]

*New conceptions of the functions of the State*

The functions of the State, whether exercised centrally or locally, were carried far beyond the maintenance of a general framework of rules within which uncontrolled private initiative moved without check. Political theory was revolutionised with changing political practice. The last manifestoes of the old individualism found utterance in John Stuart Mill's *Essay on Liberty* and Herbert Spencer's *Man versus the State*. Significant of the new direction in which opinion was to set were the writings of Francis Herbert Bradley and Thomas Hill Green, where the assumptions of *laissez-faire* were destructively criticised, and the conception appeared that State intervention, so far from destroying, might promote, and even perhaps be necessary for, the achievement of individual freedom and the fulfilment of human personality. The function of the State, as henceforth conceived, was to ensure that where individual enterprise promoted the well-being of the citizen and of society, its creative impulses should be allowed free course, but where it did not, it should be restrained or supplanted by the action of government itself.[3] More radically, the Fabian Society, founded in 1884, studied the means of transforming society on collectivist lines by legislative action, though Socialism as such made little impact on the electorate and none on Parliament.[4]

*Democracy and Empire*

The imposition in practice, and the acceptance in theory, of

[1] The decision of the Queen's Bench in *Hornby* v. *Close* (1867) was reversed by legislation in 1871 and 1874. The Trades Union Congress met annually from 1871.    [2] Smellie, 100-107.    [3] Smellie, 108.

[4] The process is traced in juridical terms by A. V. Dicey in his *Law and Opinion in England* and reflected—in the Introductions rather than the text—of the later editions of his *Law of the Constitution*.

public control over a steadily enlarging area of the national life
had already progressed far on the eve of the first World War:
that cataclysm itself proved that yet another of the main conditions
under which British government had since 1867 been carried on
no longer held, exposed its shortcomings and hastened change.
In the age of Disraeli and Gladstone the expansion of Empire
had continued. The Suez Canal, opened in 1869, linked the
United Kingdom more closely with its Asiatic possessions; in
1871 Disraeli bought the Canal shares belonging to the Khedive
of Egypt. During the 'eighties, Upper Burma, North Borneo,
and New Guinea came under British rule. It was, however, in
Africa, the last of the continents to yield up its secrets, that
British explorers, traders, administrators, and soldiers penetrated most rapidly and widely. The prospect of an "all-red
route" from the Cape to Cairo gleamed before the vision of Cecil
Rhodes and the men he inspired; merging into the still brighter
dream of a world under Anglo-Saxon control and at peace. The
*Pax Britannica* which enfolded the late Victorian world might well
seem to justify such hopes. Under the sure shield of the Royal
Navy, the ships of the nations traversed the seven seas on their
lawful occasions. A succession of "little wars" on distant frontiers
guarded the gates of civilisation and kept bright the sword of the
Queen-Empress's armies, professional, highly skilled, yet too
small to rival the conscript hosts of Europe. Never had the
world been so effectively and economically policed. It was little
wonder that the mind of the age responded to the Imperial vision
in its nobler as well as its baser aspects; thought of Empire as an
enduring organisation with potentialities even greater than had yet
been seen; tried, as did the Imperial Federation League from 1884,
to invest it with coherent institutional forms. Britain's supremacy
in the world was accompanied and justified by the perfection of
her governmental arrangements and their universal applicability.
But the bright visions faded. Imperial expansion, even though
reluctantly undertaken or accepted, awakened external jealousies
revealed by the friendlessness of the British Empire in the South
African War. The "splendid isolation" that had been possible
from 1867 to 1900 had to be replaced by a search for alliances
which involved the Kingdom and Empire in the mazes of
European diplomacy. The Royal Navy, its strength justified by a

British mercantile marine which was the largest in the world, began to be rivalled by the German Navy, for which no such case existed. More disturbing, however, than the hostility which Empire aroused from without was the doubt it sowed at home, where the ideas of Imperialism and democracy came into conflict. Colonial peoples of European stock were progressively accorded a self-governing independence which must also in the end be claimed by non-Europeans in subject-territories. How could an Imperial constitution be devised which would hold such disparate elements together, still less unite them for common defence?

*Domestic crises before 1914*

Prospects looked most ominous nearest home. The unity of the Kingdom itself was imperilled by the threat of civil war in Ireland. Recourse to violence discredited and delayed the movement for women's suffrage. Economic agitation began to wear syndicalist aspects incompatible with parliamentary democracy. In Britain, as elsewhere, forces making for revolution advanced along with those making for war. Though in 1914 the latter prevailed, the margin was narrow; and the adjustment of our institutions to the ordeal of war strongly accelerated the change which domestic circumstances already demanded.

*The first World War and its sequel*

From 1914 to 1918 war compelled regulation of every activity capable of being organised as a means of victory. Man-power, industrial production, food supplies, and shipping, to take only the leading examples, were brought under governmental direction. Authority was concentrated in an inner or "War Cabinet" detached from administrative routine and charged with the framing of a policy to which the action of every department was related. Much of this machinery was dismantled when the emergency ceased. But post-war conditions did not relax the rate at which public control thrust itself into the affairs of the nation, though they partly diverted its course. The pre-war social services, besides being amplified, came to be supplemented by a complex system of economic regulation, for such purposes as industrial and agricultural production, currency and foreign exchange, and overseas trade and investment. In the principle of *laissez-faire* and the interests and the habits of mind which still invoked it, there remained only sufficient vitality to make the intervention of the State unmethodical and imperfectly co-ordinated. It formed a series of expedients dealing piecemeal with particular needs which it was hoped were transitory, rather than a plan intended in successive stages to transform society in accordance with conditions which had fundamentally and permanently changed. Even when the economic crisis of 1931 had made it bitterly plain that this had happened, the need for any such transformation was not generally accepted, nor were its implications systematically worked out even by those to whom the need seemed clearest.

This precarious balance was destroyed by the second World War. More rapidly than in the first, because so much earlier experience was available and so many more preliminary measures had already been taken, the State gathered to itself every power requisite for a total mobilisation of national resources and national effort. The nature and duration of the emergency required these powers to become increasingly extensive and effective. The technique of exercising them developed with constant practice, as did their acceptance by those on whom they were exercised. When the war ended the State stood possessed of such a range of authority as the constitution had never previously conferred. *The second World War*

Circumstances during the years after 1945 might have deterred any government from sweeping surrender of the authority so acquired. In fact the government which, supported by an overwhelming parliamentary majority, then came into office found such a heritage by no means unwelcome. The party it represented, more fully committed to State intervention than any other, and regarding it not as an occasional expedient but as an essential principle of action, was resolved to apply it to the remodelling of society on a collectivist basis. The legislation of ensuing years removed from private to public ownership such essential industries as coal, transport, gas, electricity, iron and steel, established State control over the Bank of England, and devised various methods of imposing it, usually in a highly centralised form, both in the economic sphere thus invaded, and also over such social services as medical and hospital treatment. If some of the powers acquired by the State for war purposes were allowed to lapse, many were retained and others added. In all this there was more than an attempt to meet an exceptional or temporary situation. The notion now seemed to have prevailed that the primary function of the State was by such measures to promote the welfare of the community, and thereby the welfare of the individual citizen. *The "Welfare" State*

Whether these two interests were, as now re-stated, identical; whether, if they were, the means taken to promote them were wisely judged; above all, whether such projects could be pursued in isolation from the wider issues involved in international affairs, all tended to escape critical examination. Yet the "Welfare" [1] State thus constructed is now taken in its main outline to be an issue on which fundamental disagreement no longer exists. Its acceptance seems to sum up a process extending over nearly a hundred years which has changed, at first almost imperceptibly and later at headlong speed, the current of British political thought and practice.

*Trans-formations of Parliament*    In conformity with these dominant forces the institutions of government have evolved as the instrument for imposing the will of a democratic electorate intent on using its sovereignty to effect comprehensive schemes of social and economic amelioration. Successive statutes enlarged the electorate so as to include ultimately the entire adult population. Only the slightest vestiges of the ancient system of "influence" survived the statutes abolishing open voting and penalising what came to be stigmatised as corrupt practices. The representation of "interests" was abandoned in favour of proportioning representation to population, new and largely artificial units were constructed for this purpose, comprising aggregations of population reckoned on a purely numerical basis, existing only for parliamentary elections, and often possessing no other principle of life. As a result of redistribution on this plan, the old preponderance of the agricultural districts over the urban, and of the smaller and mainly non-industrial boroughs over the large manufacturing towns, was destroyed. The voter's freedom of choice between candidates widened; for religious tests disappeared;[2] poverty ceased to be a bar against entry to a House of Commons, membership of which became a salaried occupation,[3]

---

[1] A term not of British but German origin, made current here, it would seem, by Archbishop William Temple.

[2] By the collective effect of the Roman Catholic Emancipation Act (1829), Costin and Watson, ii. 45-53, and Acts of 1858 and 1866 relieving Jews and other persons unable to take an oath as Christians; 21 and 22 Vict. c. 48, 49; 29 and 30 Vict. c. 19.

[3] Under the Appropriation Act of 1911 and each subsequent year. See Erskine May, *Parliamentary Practice* (ed. Lord Campion and T. G. B. Cocks), 17-19. No less important, particularly for the rise of the Labour Party, was the repeal by legislation of *Osborne* v. *Amalgamated Society of Railway Servants*, (1909), which had decided that a political levy by a Trade Union was illegal. Costin and Watson, ii. 320.

the sex restriction was removed in 1919, and women could thereafter be elected to the House and appointed to ministerial or even
Cabinet rank.[1]

As the electoral system became democratised, the House of *The*
Commons was drawn into closer contact with the constituencies. *Commons*
The number of contested elections multiplied until to-day almost *and the electorate*
every constituency is the scene of a contest in every election.
Party leaders have developed the habit, presaged by Peel's
Tamworth Manifesto of 1834 and impressively illustrated in
Gladstone's Midlothian campaign of 1879, of appealing to the
electorate as a whole, like one gigantic constituency.[2] In recent
times, broadcasting has converted the entire electorate into a
single audience. It seems to constitute a unit, and the aggregate
vote cast in the constituencies is considered almost as significant as
the distribution of voting strength in the House of Commons. The
decision of the electorate in a general election came to be accepted
as mandatory, and a Government against which it decisively
pronounced no longer needed to await an adverse vote in the
Commons before resigning, or expected to be given a period of
trial before being condemned.[3] Conversely, a favourable decision
by the electorate would invest the leaders of the victorious party
with the right and indeed the duty, of forming an administration,
and be increasingly accepted as an endorsement of the legislative
programme and the administrative policy which they—rather
than the individual candidates supporting them—put forward for
public approval. Their position in dealing with their own supporters has become stronger and the Commons transformed into
an organ of power put at the disposal of a political group to whom
the electorate majority has for a term of years accorded its confidence in the expectation that election promises will be adequately
redeemed.

A House thus regarded primarily as a means of giving effect *Supremacy*
to the will of the people must naturally be regarded as the *of the*
supreme power in the State. Though becoming weaker in relation *Commons*
to the Cabinet, to which reforms in procedure gave increasing

[1] 8 and 9 Geo. V. c. 47.
[2] Morley, *Life of Gladstone*, ii. 195-6, 216-20; Smellie, 124; Emden, *The People and the Constitution*, 2nd ed., 203-4, 288-90. On the other hand, Disraeli scrupulously avoided making political speeches, otherwise than in Parliament, outside his own constituency.      [3] Emden, 162. And see above, p. 407 n. 4.

control over its time and its business, it developed immense power against the Lords. They could claim no popular mandate and their whole position was impaired by the rejection of "interests" in favour of mere numbers as the basis of Parliament. More than ever before ministers found it possible to acquiesce in having relatively few spokesmen in the Lords, and necessary to mass their main strength in the Commons. The Monarchy itself, recognising the authority with which the electorate asserts its will, has been obliged progressively to withdraw from direct participation in the actual conduct of government.

*Development of the administrative system*   Using the power of Parliament as the instrument of its own purposes, the electorate has approved courses of action which require the creation of a highly complex administrative system, both central and local. The Cabinet, itself in touch with a number of expert advisory bodies, presides over an ever-expanding series of departments staffed by expert professional administrators. To this bureaucracy have been committed powers not of enforcing only but of making the law, and even of deciding cases where public policy and private interests conflict. In the eyes of its critics it has come to acquire a dangerous pre-eminence in the constitution, while the means of reducing it to control have been unwisely neglected. The Courts cannot adequately control it, and Parliament, becoming a mere reservoir of powers on which it draws at will, thus loses effective control over their use. Similar problems arise in relation to the bodies established to conduct nationalised industries and the other *quasi*-governmental authorities variously styled Commissions, Committees, and Corporations, to which have been entrusted such public services as marketing, industrial development, the control of monopolies, broadcasting, and the creation of new towns. Their relationship with the legislature and the judiciary has become indefinite and unsatisfactory and in consequence the Executive has apparently achieved an unhealthy predominance in the Constitution. The interest of the citizen has been subordinated to an alleged public interest. Further confusion has arisen from the failure to bring within the Constitution the manifold activities of the bodies controlling nationalised industries and is not diminished by the evident trend in modern society, irrespective of political belief or tradition, to require for most of its purposes larger rather than lesser units of organisation, and to prefer dealing with the mass rather than the exception.

The disquieting tendencies inherent in these developments need *Dangers* no emphasis. In the electoral system intelligent opinion seems *inherent in* swamped by an uninstructed mass vote. Legitimate interests may *develop-* be denied effective utterance. The art of political leadership may *ments* seem to lie in technical proficiency in appealing to the electorate through means as dubious in their way as those employed in the eighteenth century, and differing therefrom mainly in that there has been substituted for the corruption of individuals the collective bribery of the electorate by appeals to class interest. Politics, instead of being the vocation of a privileged minority called to it by social status and education but not making their living by it, may become only one form of business among many, and the concern not of the aristocratic amateur but of the professional huckster. There is a further risk that Parliament may cease to be regarded as an assembly in which the various interests in the nation are represented and safeguarded, and in which by process of discussion they are harmoniously and peaceably adjusted, and the Commons degenerate into a mere automaton exploited by an Executive manipulating the accumulated powers of the administrative leviathan. Alternatively, the parliamentary process may seem too antiquated and slow to meet contemporary needs, a brake on progress or an irrelevance. So far as such fears are justified, they suggest conditions in which the maintenance of British constitutional tradition will be impossible.

Even graver has been the apparent failure of the constitution *Empire* as an instrument of Empire. After the War of 1914–18 there could *into* be no return to arrangements by which the United Kingdom took *Common-* responsibility for foreign affairs and their tremendous implica- *wealth* tions for peace and war. The Dominions advanced from self-government to sovereignty. After that of 1939–45, India was followed by the dependent territories in an uneven progress towards the same goal: proclaimed, however remotely, for them all. Such progress could be evolutionary; with the Monarchy as the source of lawful authority, and the Westminster Parliament and Courts, even British local government, providing models for its distribution and use. Experience since the second War has shewn that such ideas have sometimes been fulfilled, if at all, in strangely altered forms. The evolution of the Commonwealth has had among its results the assertion of popular sovereignty, the transformation of monarchical into republican government and Presidential dictatorship, and of democracy into the one-party State, the erosion of civil and political liberties, attacks on the independence of the Bench and other perversions.

*An episode of disillusionment*
So confidence in parliamentary democracy has waned. The British constitution has not retained the authority at home or overseas so confidently anticipated when the Second Reform Act ushered in the great age of Gladstone and Disraeli or even when that great age ended. Ours is indeed a changed world from that in which Dicey first proclaimed in 1885 the doctrines set out in his *Law of the Constitution*: the sovereignty of Parliament, the Rule of Law, the dominant rôle of custom in the working of government. It has changed also in that the contemporary mind often believes economic institutions to be more relevant than political to the health of nations. Yet if it may be doubted whether British parliamentary democracy has offered the easiest or aptest lessons in the art of government, it should never be forgotten that fewer than a half-dozen governmental systems in the world which are more than sixty years old to-day are of other than British origin.

ii

*Electoral reform*
The reform of 1867 made an immensely larger addition to the electorate than the Act intended. Even so, the process of change was far from being arrested at the point now reached. The new democracy in the first place had to emancipate itself from the coercion and bribery still prevalent in the electoral system. Secondly, defects in the method of registration, which impeded many voters from establishing their qualifications, had to be eliminated. Thirdly, the electoral franchise itself had to be made simpler and more uniform, and the qualification lowered. Finally, the discrepancies between population and representation which the redistribution of 1868 had served rather to emphasise than to cure still called for remedy. Towards these ends the progress of the ensuing years until 1885 was directed.

*Election petitions*
An initial step was taken towards purifying the electoral process itself when by a statute of 1868 the jurisdiction over disputed

elections exercised by committees set up under Grenville's Act was transferred, on the recommendation of a Select Committee, to the Queen's Bench. Disputes were henceforth to be tried, normally at least, in the constituency from which the petition arose, and before a single judge, who dealt both with the law and the facts involved, and whose decision was final. In 1879 jurisdiction was vested in two judges, who must be in agreement if an election were to be voided. Not unnaturally, the courts showed some hesitation at being concerned with a subject so intimately connected with party politics and not everywhere considered appropriate to their jurisdiction. The experiment vindicated itself. A diminishing number of election petitions failed, for it was less easy to bring a petition on frivolous or vexatious grounds. Stricter observance of the law relative to elections was forced on candidates and their agents.[1]

Meanwhile that law was itself becoming more stringent. Some- *Vote by* thing had been gained by the Act of 1854. But bribery during *ballot* and between elections was still rife, and the auditors appointed to scrutinise election expenses had been so useless that in 1863 their duties were made over to the returning officers, who did little better. The provisions against intimidation had remained a dead letter. The obvious cure was to render both intimidation and bribery futile by introducing secrecy of voting. Little had been heard of the demand for vote by ballot since the days of Grote in Parliament and the Chartists outside it. Occasional motions on the topic were, it is true, moved in the House of Commons, and a Ballot Society tried to interest the public in it. But secret voting lacked powerful advocacy, and encountered an opposition strongly based on principle. To its critics, who were found in both parties, it made an undesirable breach between the privilege and the responsibility of being a voter, and was open to the objection that "the motives under which men act in secret are as a general rule inferior to those under which they act in public".[2] The gross evils revealed by a parliamentary inquiry into the conduct of the election of 1868, however, won many converts to the idea of secret voting. Mr Gladstone's government of 1868–74 introduced a bill which, rejected by the Lords in 1871, was finally carried in

[1] Costin and Watson, ii. 107-11; Seymour, *Electoral Reform in England and Wales*, 419, 423-7.                     [2] Seymour, 428.

1872. The agelong practice of public voting now came to an end.[1]

*Corrupt practices*

Though the immediate effects were salutary, and disorder at elections was perceptibly reduced, it would be idle to contend that the Ballot Act eliminated all the inveterate ills of the voting system. Human nature could not be changed by an Act of Parliament, and in various forms pressure could be brought to bear on venal or timid electors. Voting by ballot of course reduced the market price of votes the exact use of which by the voter could not be verified, and thereby diminished bribery. Intimidation could no longer be so successfully practised, and it is perhaps significant that no petitions alleging intimidation were upheld after 1872. Yet neither corruption nor coercion could be altogether destroyed so long as the ethical standards of those who sought and those who disposed of votes remained tainted by the traditions of the past.[2] Four boroughs, returning six members, were disfranchised for corrupt practices between 1867 and 1885.[3] Further parliamentary inquiry in 1881 revealed the persistence of undue influence and suggested the need for curbing the outlay on electoral expenses. In 1883 Mr Gladstone's second government passed a statute which proved remarkably efficacious in restraining the grosser forms of corruption.[4] Election expenses were proportioned to the size of the constituency. The objects on which money might be spent were specified, and accounts required from election agents. Corrupt practices were more closely defined and the list of such offences amplified. A candidate, if proved personally to have broken the law, was for ever disqualified from election by the constituency in which the offence occurred. Breach of the law by his agents disqualified him for seven years. Convictions for corrupt practices were made punishable by imprisonment or fine, and the Director of Public Prosecutions was required to see that the law was enforced.[5]

*Success of the Act of 1883*

In the debased form in which they survived until this Act, the practices now penalised represented the traditional methods by which the electorate had long been organised. Their origins lay in devices for controlling the Commons which had been practised

[1] Seymour, 430-32; Costin and Watson, ii. 111-12.

[2] See W. L. Burn, *Electoral Corruption in the Nineteenth Century*, in *Parliamentary Affairs* (1951), 437.

[3] Beverley and Bridgwater in 1870, Macclesfield and Sandwich in 1885.

[4] Seymour, 442-5.          [5] 46 and 47 Vict., c. 51; Seymour, 445.

in one way or another since the Middle Ages. For the future they could persist only in a highly attenuated form. No doubt minor evasions of the Act have remained possible, and the advantage possessed by a wealthy candidate prepared to spend large sums in "nursing" a constituency cannot be discounted. Yet it is on the whole true to say that the Act of 1883 demolished a system of electoral management by that time thoroughly depraved and cleared the way for new methods.

In the principle those new methods embodied lay the future of electoral organisation. The activities of such bodies as the Anti-Corn Law League offered a congenial example for adoption by party organisations as, during the interval from 1832 to 1867, party alignments founded on clear political differences and no longer mainly on "influence" and on personal loyalties began to manifest their existence in the Commons and the country.[1] From 1832 the Carlton Club began the practice of scrutinising electoral rolls through local Conservative registration societies. After 1852, when the organisation of the party was overhauled, the Central Office, an extension of that of the Whips, kept a list of approved candidates. In 1868 the local committees were linked in a National Union, and effective organisation helped to win the Conservative triumph of 1874.[2] A parallel development occurred in the rival party. In 1835 the Radicals had set up a registration office. By the redistribution of 1868 the cities of Birmingham, Manchester, Liverpool, and Leeds were given three members apiece, each voter being allowed only two votes. It was evident that the majority must make every effort to carry all three seats, for if only two were won, one would be cancelled out by that gained by the minority, and the constituency would carry no more weight in the Commons than a single-member constituency of much smaller size. Careful distribution of votes, however, was certain to ensure three successes, and in Birmingham the Radicals organised so thoroughly for this purpose as to win all three seats in 1868. The system was now applied with similar results in the field of local government by the mayor, Mr Joseph Chamberlain,

*Electoral organisation*

---

[1] The transition from eighteenth to nineteenth century electoral practices is described by G. R. Kitson Clark, *The Electorate and the Repeal of the Corn Laws*, 5 T.R.H.S. 409.

[2] Smellie, 33, 126-7; A. L. Lowell, *Government of England*, i. 497-504.

and the secretary of the Birmingham Association, Mr Schnadhorst. If open to the objection that it introduced politics into local administration, it justified itself in the eyes of its creators by giving them complete control over municipal affairs and enabling them to undertake extensive schemes of improvement. The pursuit of similar purposes in national politics led to the adoption in many boroughs (and after 1884 in many counties also) of associations based on the Birmingham model. In 1877 these local organisations were combined in the National Liberal Federation. England and Scotland came to be covered with a complex network of local political associations, employing paid agents, for party organisation and propaganda.[1] The Trades Union Congress created for similar purposes the Labour Representation League, which put forward thirteen candidates in 1874.[2] Direction was given by the various central organisations in the choice of candidates. They helped with financing election expenses and with distributing political publications. To some extent party organisation ceased to be localised and independent, and the formulation of a programme and the choice of men pledged to support it fell under central control. The harmful results of local activity in raising objections to the qualifications of voters assumed to be unfriendly were obvious. A parliamentary committee reported in 1868 in favour of removing the registration of voters from the inefficient hands of the overseers of the poor, to whom, subject to the scrutiny of revising barristers, it had been committed in 1832, and entrusting it to new registration authorities. Acts of 1878 and 1885 introduced this system in boroughs and counties respectively, and the local party organisations were confined to more useful tasks.[3]

*The franchise*    Registration had not been made easier by the complexity of the franchise after 1867. Alike in the boroughs and the counties a variety of different qualifications existed. In the former, besides a surviving remnant of ancient-right franchises, there were both

[1] Lowell, i. 483–97; Emden, 137–9.
[2] Two were elected in 1874, 3 in 1880, 11 in 1885, 9 in 1886, 15 in 1892, 11 in 1900, 56 in 1906. Until 1900 none were put forward by Trade Unions, Lowell, ii. 25; Emden, 96. The first working-man elected to the House (Thomas Burt, elected in 1874 for Morpeth) was, however, elected as a Liberal. For the later history of Labour representation, see Lowell, ii. 35 ff., and G. D. H. Cole, *History of the Labour Party from 1914*; H. M. Pelling, *Origins of the Labour Party, 1850–1900*; S. C. Roberts, *The Trades Union Congress*, 59.
[3] Seymour, 375, 380.

the £10 occupancy qualification of 1832 and the householder and lodger franchises of 1867. In the latter, besides a substantial proportion of ancient-right voters, amounting to a fifth of the aggregate county electorate, and those qualified by the various franchises introduced in 1832 and modified in 1867, there were also those qualified by the new £12 rateable value franchise created in the latter year. These complications were perhaps less effective in stimulating the demand for reform than the anomaly that the franchise was notably less democratic in the counties than in the boroughs. The Liberal Reform bill of 1884, inspired by Radical pressure, was championed in a divided Cabinet by the Radical leader, Mr Chamberlain, and supported by monster public demonstrations. Mr Gladstone himself, though he had in 1864 announced his conviction that every man who was not naturally incapacitated had a moral right to come within the pale of the constitution,[1] was reluctant to sponsor a large electoral reform in the closing year of his ministry. Yet there were few direct opponents in either party of the principle that the household franchise should be introduced into the counties.

Here, however, unanimity ceased. Liberals hoped, and Conservatives feared, that the agricultural vote in the counties would *Redistribution* be swamped by that of their industrial inhabitants, such as miners. Thus redistribution was immediately linked with any change in the franchise, and could not be postponed to become the work of a predominantly Liberal and Radical House returned by an enlarged electorate. Failing in the Lower House to connect reform and redistribution, the Conservatives relied, and not in vain, on the Upper. The opposition of the Lords, and the intervention of the Queen to avert a conflict between the Houses, produced agreement that redistribution was to be coupled with reform.

Thus two statutes resulted. In the Franchise Act—into which *The Act* the Radicals unsuccessfully sought to insert clauses against plural *of 1884* voting, university representation, and ancient-right votes, and in favour of women's suffrage—the main provision was the extension of the householder franchise to the counties, where the electorate was immediately tripled, rising from 900,000 to 2,500,000. In counties and boroughs alike, the householder franchise was now predominant. A great variety of others lingered on—in the

[1] J. Morley, *Life of Gladstone*, i. 760.

boroughs the £10 occupancy franchise and the lodger franchise, in the counties the £5 copyholder and the £50 and £5 lease-holder franchises, and in both counties and boroughs the surviving ancient-right voters.[1] It could hardly be doubted that further simplification would some day become imperative.

*Anomalies of the electoral system*    Even apart from its adventitious connexion with the franchise question, that of redistribution demanded attention as democratic principles came into fashion. Additional representation was needed for the industrial areas, in counties as well as boroughs. The disparity between population and representation had since 1867 been further emphasised by the massing of a huge artisan population in county areas where, before 1884, they were not usually qualified for the vote. When they acquired it, that disparity must at once be reflected also in the electorate. Great industrial regions such as the North-East and South Wales would appear more than ever grossly under-represented. Among the boroughs the greatest diversity persisted. The Commons still abounded in representatives of small boroughs, saved in 1832 and unthreatened in 1867. In Liverpool the proportion between representation and population was 1 to 155,000, in Calne 1 to 5,000. In 1884 seventy-three English parliamentary boroughs had less than 15,000 inhabitants. Those of Cornwall, Devon, and Wilts with a gross population of 100,000 could outvote the two million inhabitants of boroughs in the industrial Midlands, Lancashire, and Yorkshire.[2]

*The Act of 1885*    Obviously a House constituted on the lines laid down in 1867 continued to be largely dominated by territorial and aristocratic influence, exerted through a restricted county electorate and a preponderance of small agricultural boroughs. The Act of 1884 demolished the first, that of 1885 the second of these buttresses of aristocratic power.[3] Various schemes for adjusting representation to population had been canvassed. Proportional representation was mistrusted. The system of multiple-member representation introduced into certain constituencies in 1868 had not justified itself. Opinion came round now to the single-member constituency.

---

[1] Seymour, 465.                    [2] Seymour, 348-50, 490-92.
[3] Costin and Watson, ii. 126-8; Seymour, 508-10. Boroughs of 50,000 to 165,000 received two members. Those of larger size received three members, and one more for each additional 50,000 inhabitants. All constituencies except the two-member boroughs (23 in number), Oxford, Cambridge, and Dublin Universities and the Scottish Universities were single-member constituencies.

The Act merged all boroughs of less than 15,000 inhabitants in their counties, those of larger size retaining separate representation. Boroughs hitherto not separately represented having 50,000 inhabitants received one member each. Larger boroughs received more members in proportion. Seventy-two boroughs disappeared altogether, and 36 more lost one member. From these and other disfranchisements 142 seats were available for redistribution. Counties and boroughs were for the most part carved into single-member constituencies. Sixty-four new members were allotted to counties or divisions of counties in England and four to Wales. Seventy-four seats were allocated to boroughs or divisions of boroughs. The result was not to proportion representation perfectly to population; though an average of one member to 54,000 inhabitants was fairly well maintained, Durham City with only 15,000 and the Romford division of Essex with 217,000 returned one member each. But it meant the destruction, for all practical purposes, of the agelong predominance of the southern over the northern constituencies and of agriculture over every other interest in the English parliamentary system.[1]

Further changes in the distribution of population naturally *The need* suggested in later years a further redistribution of seats; in 1905 *for further reform* when the average population of Irish constituencies was 44,000 and of English 67,000, the government of Mr Balfour was attracted by the idea of transferring seats from Ireland to England.[2] Nothing of the sort was carried out, however, until the Representation of the People Act of 1918 entirely remodelled the electoral system as a whole, both by redistribution and by enlarging the franchise. The highly complicated nature of the franchise after 1884, the anomaly that the law regarding the payment of rates as between owner and occupier was different in England and Scotland, the undue stringency of the residence qualification which prevented many persons from acquiring a vote who were well equipped to exercise it, and the existence of plural voting, all seemed to need amendment. Meanwhile, in practice, the system had produced something so nearly approaching manhood suffrage that the overt adoption of that principle could hardly be regarded as a radical change.[3] With it, however, came the revolutionary step of admitting women to the franchise.

[1] Seymour, 513-18.     [2] Lowell, i. 201.     [3] Lowell, i. 212-13.

*The Acts*
*of 1918,*
*1928, and*
*1948*

The Act of 1918 gave the vote, in counties and boroughs alike, to all adult males resident or occupying premises in the constituency, and to women of at least thirty years of age, who, or whose husbands, occupied premises or lands to the annual value of £5 under the law relating to local government elections. An Act of 1928 at last produced a virtual uniformity. All adults could vote who were resident in a constituency, or occupied premises there to the annual value of £10, or were married to persons thus qualified. The qualifying period of residence, in the constituency itself or an adjoining one, was reduced to three months. Electors might in respect of business premises qualify, but not vote, in more than one constituency. The only form in which plural voting still existed was that university electors[1] could also vote in the constituencies where they were qualified by residence. Subject to certain legal disabilities, affecting a limited number of persons, the electorate now included the entire adult population of the country, so that women constituted a majority.[2] The surviving relics of plural voting lingered for twenty years more, until the Representation of the People Act of 1948 abolished the University constituencies and the so-called "business vote". Along with these relics went also the surviving two-member constituencies. In Parliamentary elections, therefore, the principle of "one man, one vote" has been achieved. The redistribution effected under the Redistribution of Seats Act of 1949 has now produced a House of Commons of 630 members, of whom 511 sit for English, 36 for Welsh, 71 for Scottish, and 12 for Northern Irish constituencies.

*Votes and*
*Seats*

The latest redistribution approaches even more nearly the principle of equal electoral districts, and four Commissions have been established to keep the size of constituencies under review in England, Wales, Scotland, and Northern Ireland and to report at stated intervals. This may correct the disparity between the total number of votes cast as compared with seats won; as for example when the Conservatives in 1922 and 1929 obtained 38 per cent of the votes cast but only 260 seats in 1929 as compared with 347 in 1922; while the Labour party, polling 36 per cent in 1929

[1] To those Universities already mentioned were in 1918 added London, the combined English Universities (other than Oxford, Cambridge, and London), the University of Wales, and The Queen's University of Belfast.

[2] For a summary of the Acts of 1918, 1928, and 1948, see Wade and Phillips, *Constitutional Law* (7th edn.), 104 ff.

returned 287 candidates (27 more than were returned by the 38 per cent of Conservative votes), and polling 33 per cent in 1931 returned only 52.[1] Such disparities, which are inseparable from any plan of single-member constituencies with only one vote for each elector, reinforce the plea for proportional representation, specially attractive to third and minority parties which see in it a chance to make their opinions felt in a House more accurately representative of the various shades of national opinion. If the advocates of this device have so far failed to persuade their fellow-citizens, it is perhaps because of the fear that it would prevent any party from achieving a clear majority, lead to the creation of unstable coalition ministries divided in policy and lacking in energy, and stultify the representative system by paralysing its ability to communicate vigour and continuity to the conduct of government.

The desire to promote the efficiency of Parliament for this *Procedure* purpose which emerged after 1867 led to extensive reforms in its rules of procedure, which like its privileges are entirely subject to its own authority. Procedure is governed for the most part by standing orders supplemented by temporary sessional orders. Their effect, during the last century, has been to economise time and increase the speed with which business can be transacted. Various stages once incidental to the discussion of bills have been omitted or curtailed. Besides the Committee of the Whole (termed for financial purposes Committee of Supply and Committee of Ways and Means), numerous standing and sessional committees came into being, to which particular measures, or all measures of a particular kind, would be referred, and much business thus be transacted apart from formal meetings of the Commons, and the work of the Speaker supplemented by that of the Chairman of Committees and his deputy.[2]

Procedure in the House was still further simplified by the adop- *Closure* tion of the system of closure, the immediate occasion of which

[1] These examples now appear to have been abnormal, and recent General Elections produced a closer correspondence between votes cast and seats won: but the fundamental point made in this paragraph is unchanged.

[2] See J. Redlich, *Procedure of the House of Commons*, ii. 203-12, for a general sketch of the history of Committees. Parliamentary Committees are described by K. C. Wheare in his *Government by Committee*, 119 ff. On Standing Committees see D. Pring in *Parliamentary Affairs* (1958), 303.

was the organised obstruction offered by the Irish members in 1881 to a Coercion bill. Several all-night sittings were followed by forty-one continuous hours of debate, brought to an end by the action of the Speaker in putting the question forthwith. There was no precedent for this action. Authority for the future was soon supplied, in the form of an urgency resolution empowering the Speaker, on the motion of a minister supported by a three-to-one majority in a House of not less than 300, to assume unrestricted control over business. In 1887 a new Standing Order enabled any ordinary member, subject to the Speaker's veto, to move a "closure" of debate forthwith. In the form of the "guillotine", closure enables all undiscussed clauses to be carried without debate. The risk of important clauses being excluded from debate by the guillotine, while time was wasted in discussing others of less importance which happened to occur early in a bill, was averted by a modification called "closure by compartments", which prescribed a time-limit for successive groups of clauses. Again, by the "Kangaroo closure" (1909), the Speaker could select various clauses and amendments for discussion at the Report stage, omitting the rest.[1] Further reform of parliamentary procedure was intermittently discussed during the inter-war years, but no important changes were effected, and indeed existing devices such as the closure and the guillotine were seldom invoked. Some elements among the then Opposition, however, made no secret of their intention to take drastic measures when their party came to power. In 1945 the moment arrived. A Select Committee on Procedure was appointed. Its proposals, moderate in their scope, apparently failed to satisfy the new Government, which imposed measures the Committee had rejected. Restrictions were imposed upon debate on the Budget, but more far-reaching was the increase in the number of Standing Committees, to which bodies the Government proceeded to refer bills which according to previous practice would have been dealt with by the House as a whole. The protests to which this innovation gave rise were reinforced by those evoked by another new device, the application of the guillotine to bills dealt with in Committee. It is not surprising that important

---

[1] Redlich, i. 155-8, iii. 55; Erskine May, *Parliamentary Practice* (ed. Campion and Cocks), 457 ff. P. Bromhead, *The Guillotine*, in *Parliamentary Affairs* (1958) 443.

legislation rushed through by such untried methods, discussed inadequately and by too small a number of members, proved defective in practice and did little to commend the procedural reforms which brought it about.[1]

The efficient transaction of business in the House also requires, *Parlia-* as it always has, that its proceedings should be protected by *mentary* Parliamentary privilege. This means that whatever is said or done *privilege* in the course of its proceedings lies within its own jurisdiction, exercised primarily by the Speaker, and is not actionable elsewhere: it also means that persons unprotected by such privilege who act in violation of it are liable to become subject to its jurisdiction if they fall into contempt of the House—and of this the House remains sole judge and the offender has no right to be legally represented. Here, as in such earlier instances as *Stockdale* v. *Hansard* and the *Aylesbury Men*, lies a still unresolved problem of the constitution: it involves on the one hand the right of members to debate and on the other the right of the public to criticise.

Leaving on one side as too slight for discussion certain recent *Recent* attempts to treat published criticisms of the conduct of members *privilege* as breaches of privilege in order to gain a political advantage, the *cases* most important recent test of parliamentary privilege occurred in 1957. A Member of the Commons, Mr. G. R. Strauss, was threatened with an action for libel because of a letter written by him to the Paymaster-General criticising the affairs of a Department for which that Minister was answerable to Parliament. The questions so raised—was the letter "a proceeding in Parliament", and was it, even so, removed from the area of privilege by the Parliamentary Privilege Act of 1770—remained unsettled; a proposal to seek the opinion of the Judicial Committee of the Privy Council on the general issue being set aside as striking at the very root of parliamentary privilege. So the issues remain unsettled, and in this there is nothing to regret, even if it leaves the House to be judge in its own cause. How it can enforce this jurisdiction was demonstrated in the case of Mr. John Junor, editor of the *Daily Express*, summoned before the House in January 1957 to receive its reprimand for statements appearing to impugn the

[1] Difficulties arose most acutely at the Report stage with bills that were often found to need considerable amendment.

good faith of its members in their collective capacity.[1] Summing up, it seems best to say that parliamentary privilege is primarily intended for the protection of the House as a whole and not of its individual members; that it is solely intended for the proper conduct of its business: that it is not intended to suppress criticism published *bona-fide* in the public interest: that it would not be wise to lay down its exact limits: and that the House, acting through the Speaker and the Committee for Privileges, should be left to bear the onus of responsibility.

*Relation of Cabinet and Commons*    Procedural change greatly strengthened the control of the Cabinet over the Commons, the private member being the main sufferer. Notwithstanding the increased length of sessions private members on both sides came to have less time at their command, their motions and bills tending to be sterile. Government business took precedence. Legislation became mainly sponsored by ministers. The main business of the private member became criticism and putting questions. The value of these functions is undeniable, but the Cabinet has ample means of protecting itself against the embarrassments and dangers which even the most pertinacious opponent can present. Yet the measure of its control over the Commons must not be exaggerated. Though the private member has kept little or no time of his own, and is hard driven by the government's time-table, the proportion of time available to the Opposition has undergone little change. Besides sustaining systematic attack from the Opposition, the Cabinet has constantly to accommodate itself to the opinions of its own supporters, and may at times be open to the risk of a revolt of its own "back-benchers", tempered only by their disinclination to press opposition to the point of overthrowing the government and precipitating a dissolution.[2]

*The Speaker*    The application of procedural rules to the business of the Commons lies in the hands of the Speaker. His duties must not, however, be limited to knowledge of procedure and memory of precedent and the case-law arising from earlier decisions by the chair, though these technical skills are important and usually make it advisable to elect a practising lawyer to the Speakership.

[1] In 1947 *Allighan's Case* demonstrated the authority of the Commons to expel one of its own members adjudged to have been in contempt. Wade and Phillips, 159-60.

[2] On the relations of Cabinet and Commons, see Jennings, *Cabinet Government* (3rd ed.), 472 ff.; Lowell, i. ch. xvii-xviii.

Personal qualities are supremely important. A Speaker must have the House's confidence. Occasions when his rulings are challenged are as embarrassing as they are infrequent. His aim must be to ensure that parliamentary democracy means "majority rule tempered by minority rights". He is chosen by the House as a whole, not on party lines or with an eye to party advantage. He is not the nominee of the Government: nor is he the creature of a party.

The non-partisan character of his office is a nineteenth-century *Non-* development. Under the Tudors, and indeed until the reign of *partisan character* Charles II, the Speaker was virtually a royal nominee. To serve *of the* two masters, the Crown and the House, involved, as the Tudor *Speaker-* constitution broke up, an impossible contest of loyalties, ex- *ship* perienced for example by Finch at the adjournment of 1629 and Lenthall in 1642 when Charles I attempted the arrest of the five members. Lenthall's famous reply to the King, that he had "neither eyes to see nor tongue to speak in this place but as this House is pleased to direct me, whose servant I am here", was in significant contrast to that of Finch in 1629, when he said to the House, "I am not the less the King's servant for being yours".[1] It clearly points to a new status for the Speakership, which, though not achieved in 1660, emerged in 1679 when in order to save Danby from impeachment the King tried, but failed, to impose as Speaker his nominee Sir Thomas Meres instead of Sir Edward Seymour, on whom the choice of the House had fallen. In this case both the King and the House gave way and a third nominee was appointed.[2] The advantage, however, lay with the House. Though royal influence was to be occasionally used thereafter in the choice of a Speaker, the King had lost the controlling voice. If subsequent Speakers were no longer partisans of the Crown, they were still active party politicians. During the long tenure of the Chair by Arthur Onslow (1727–61), the office came first to be set above party. He safeguarded his independence by declining to hold office under the Crown, and strictly enforced the rules of debate so as to preserve the rights of minorities.[3] George III's intervention in politics, and the acute differences of political opinion which sharpened party divisions during his reign, arrested the development towards a non-partisan Speakership.

[1] Gardiner, *History of England*, vii. 71, x. 140.
[2] Porritt, *Unreformed House of Commons*, i. 437-43.    [3] Porritt, i. 448-54.

In 1780 the King was able to prescribe the choice of a Speaker in the person of Cornewall. His predecessor Sir Fletcher Norton had been an adherent of the opposition. His successor Addington was a partisan of the government. Speakers Abbot and Manners-Sutton took an active part against Catholic Relief in 1813 and 1825 respectively. Manners-Sutton did likewise against the proposals of 1834 to admit Dissenters to the universities. It was as late as the Speakership of Abercromby (1835–39) that the Speaker's participation in debate was abandoned. Shaw Lefevre (1839–57) established a standard, maintained by all his successors, of strictly impartial conduct both inside and outside the House.[1] The non-partisan character of the Speakership was henceforth preserved. The election and re-election of Speakers by voting on party lines in the Commons ceased.[2]

*Opposition to the Speaker in his own constituency*

There is one vulnerable point in the Speaker's position. He must be a member of the House, elected, like all his fellow-members, by a constituency. To help him preserve his non-partisan character, he has generally been returned unopposed.[3] He issues no election address, makes no political speeches, and undertakes no party propaganda. The rule that he is returned unopposed, which had only once, in 1895, been departed from since 1832[4]— was again challenged when opposition was offered to Speaker Fitzroy at Daventry in 1935, on the plea that the rule amounted to a virtual disfranchisement of his constituency. In ensuing discussions it was suggested that a nominal constituency, without voters, should be created for the Speaker. It was more commonly felt, however, that his authority would be weakened if he ceased to be qualified as a member of the House in exactly the same way as the rest. There is at least a risk that if the practice of opposing the Speaker's return is persisted in, the office might resume its historic partisan character, and that a partisan Speaker might con-

---

[1] Porritt, i. 480.

[2] The election of Speaker Morrison on a division at the opening of the 1951 Parliament probably represents only an incidental departure from the general rule, which had remained unbroken since 1895. When Sir Harry Hylton-Foster became Speaker in 1959, the Leader of the Opposition, Mr. Gaitskell, though expressing the opinion that the procedure was not satisfactory, did not divide the House.

[3] He stands not as a party candidate but as "the Speaker seeking re-election".

[4] Porritt, i. 461. See W. S. Livingston, *Security of Tenure of the Speaker*, in *Parliamentary Affairs* (1958), 484.

ceive himself to be the servant of the sovereign electorate as his predecessors of long ago were servants of a personal sovereign.

While the Commons began to lose ground to the Cabinet, *Commons* it was more successful in establishing its own ascendancy, and *and Lords* therefore that of a Cabinet which it supports, over the Lords. Since 1867 the membership of the Upper House largely increased without the principle of its composition being seriously changed. Before that date the last remnant of connexion between land tenure and peerage had been destroyed in the *Berkeley Peerage Case* (1861),[1] and ancient peerages can only be revived by proof that a lineal ancestor of the claimant received and acted on a writ of summons. Such a summons, preceded by the issue of letters-patent creating the peerage, is the principal basis of membership. The introduction of a limited number of life peers (at first, however, qualified to sit only during tenure of office) was effected by the Appellate Jurisdiction Acts of 1876, which created law lords to exercise the appellate jurisdiction of the House, hitherto, and most unsuitably, vested in its members at large.[2] Other life peers were of course the archbishops, with the bishops of London, Durham, and Winchester and the next twenty-one diocesan bishops in order of seniority of election to their sees. The right of women who hold peerages in their own right to receive a writ of summons was denied in *Viscountess Rhondda's Case* (1922).[3]

The pretensions of this non-elective assembly—numbering by *Conflicts* 1914 over 700, of whom only a fraction ever attended debates— *since 1867* to exercise an authority co-ordinate with that of the Commons became ever less easy to defend. That rivalry which after 1832 replaced the ancient harmony of the two Houses was further emphasised after 1867. With a Conservative majority in the Commons the two Houses could be tuned into unanimity. With a Liberal majority there they came into repeated conflict. Either situation was detrimental to the status of the Upper House. The first made it a mere appendage of the Lower, the second placed it in the invidious position of seeming to challenge the will of the electorate. As before 1867, the Lords resisted measures

[1] Wade and Phillips, 97.
[2] L. O. Pike, *Constitutional History of the House of Lords*, 304-7.
[3] [1922] 2 A.C. 339. The Sex Disqualification (Removal) Act of 1919 was held not to have removed this disability. Cf. p. 463 above.

16

removing the disabilities of non-Anglicans. They opposed the disestablishment of the Irish Church in 1869 as in 1838 they had opposed the diversion of its surplus revenues to secular purposes. They resisted the Ballot Act, the Reform Act of 1884 unless accompanied by redistribution, and the Home Rule Bill of 1893. These and other instances of opposition, and their amendments to local government and employers' liability bills—in the latter case so drastic that the measure was withdrawn—created the demand among supporters of the Liberal ministry that the House should be "mended or ended".[1] With a Liberal government once more in office in 1906, the opposition of the Lords to the Commons began anew. By 1909 they had destroyed bills abolishing plural voting in parliamentary and in London County Council elections, four bills dealing with land and housing in Scotland, and a Licensing bill, and had mutilated an Education Act.[2] In 1907 the Commons carried a motion that "in order to give effect to the will of the people as expressed by their elected representatives, it is necessary that the power of the other House to alter or reject bills passed by this House should be so restricted by law as to secure that within the limits of a single Parliament the final decision of the Commons shall prevail".[3] The introduction of payment of members was soon to reinforce the Lower House by men whose antecedents and interests sharply opposed them to the propertied and privileged classes predominant in the Lords, and made them less patient of their opposition.

*Rejection of the 1909 Budget*    It is possible that so long as the Lords had confined their opposition to non-financial measures such as those hitherto rejected, the resolution of the Commons in 1907 would have been barren of result. In 1909, however, the Lords were tempted into occupying a less defensible position. After 1671 they had been formally denied the right of amending money bills, the uncertainties as to the nature of which—facilitating the eighteenth-century practice of "tacking"—had long since been dispelled. They still preserved power to reject such bills outright. Since their opposition to the repeal of the paper duties in 1860, all money bills had been combined in a single budget. Piecemeal rejection of individual money bills was no longer possible. The budget must now be accepted or

---

[1] E. Allyn, *Lords versus Commons*, 91-5, 100, 113-17, 151, 156.
[2] Allyn, 172-3, 178.          [3] Allyn, 174; Emden, 226.

rejected as a whole. Its rejection must obviously be attended by serious risk of a life-and-death struggle with the Lower House. That risk the Lords, in view of the principles of taxation involved in the 1909 Budget, finally decided to take.[1] Their decision had few precedents even before 1860, when the rejection of a money bill was easier, and none later.

The general election which followed their rejection of the Budget was intended by the Lords as an appeal to the electorate against the Commons, and so accepted by the Government. The Lords' resistance was based less on the ground of their constitutional parity with the Commons than on their assumed right to ensure that the Commons really represented the will of the nation. Such an appeal had avowedly been made in 1895 on the issue of Home Rule, when the Lords were vindicated by the decision of the electorate. The result of the appeal made in January 1910 was less fortunate. The Government, though it lost heavily, retained a majority. This composite body depended on the adherence of the Irish Nationalists, who wished to diminish the power of the Lords in order to force through a Home Rule Bill. In the new Parliament, the Lords accepted the electorate's decision and passed the Budget. They now found themselves threatened by a Parliament Bill, for which the Nationalists were specially insistent, designed to extinguish their power over finance bills and limit it over others. The Government announced that rejection of this measure by the Lords would mean another dissolution, and the adoption of measures for overcoming the Lords' resistance. As their opposition did not weaken, a second appeal to the electorate was made in December 1910, with results which varied little from the first. When the Parliament Bill reached them, the Lords, without rejecting, attempted to amend it. Their amendments were rejected in the Commons, and the two Houses were irreconcilably at odds.

The constitutional practice of the past provided only one expedient likely to be of help to the government in this dilemma.

*The Parliament Bill introduced*

*The Lords' resistance overcome*

[1] Emden, 228-9. The Lords' objections to the Budget of 1909 were directed mainly against the proposal to tax the profits derived by landlords from the increased value of their land. This plan, involving compulsory registration of land and embodying what appeared to be a social policy adverse to private ownership of land, was not regarded as solely or even mainly financial. Its inclusion was therefore regarded as tantamount to a renewal of "tacking".

The ancient devices of conferences between "managers" appointed by the Houses—disused since 1851—and of interchange of messages between the two Houses,[1] could not be expected to do any good. The precedent of 1832, based on that of 1712, exercised a compelling influence. In the debates on the Parliament Bill in the Commons, the Prime Minister, Mr Asquith, made public a promise given before the election by King George V to create a sufficient number of peers to overcome the resistance of the majority.[2] Before this threat the "die-hard" Lords gave way, and the bill passed into law.

*Provisions of the Act*    The Parliament Act contained four main elements.[3] It defined money bills, and in case of doubt made the Speaker's certificate that a bill is of this nature final and unappealable in a court of law. It provided that such bills should, if not passed without amendment by the Lords within a month of their being received, forthwith receive the royal assent without the Lords' concurrence. With regard to other bills it enacted that if passed in the same form by the Commons in three successive sessions they should receive the royal assent even if not passed by the Lords, provided that not less than two years had elapsed since their second reading in the first session and their final reading in the third session in which they passed the Commons. Finally, the enhanced authority thus given to the Commons was partly counterbalanced by the increased control conferred on the electorate through the shortening of the duration of parliaments from seven to five years.

*Its effects*    Though intended to readjust the balance between the two Houses, and to form a prelude to a reform of the Upper House, the outcome of the Act was to reduce almost to vanishing-point its power to defeat the authority of the Lower House. It would do no more than impose delay on legislation other than money bills. Since 1911, in fact, no government has needed to rely on the Lords' support, or regard their opposition as endangering its existence. This was the essential purpose of the Act rather than the infliction on the Upper House of a legislative impotence. In the inter-war years, the power of amendment could be employed so as to force into a bill clauses largely altering its character, so that ceas-

[1] Redlich, *Procedure of the House of Commons*, ii. 82-3. For discussions on the relations of Lords and Commons in 1893 and 1907, see Costin and Watson, ii. 204-7.    [2] Jennings, 437 ff.
[3] For the Act, see Costin and Watson, ii. 140-43; also Allyn, 196 ff.

ing to be substantially the same it might lose the procedural protection of the Act. Again, the reduction in the life of Parliament, taken in conjunction with the fact that, except during the Wars of 1914–18 and 1939–45, only one Parliament lasted its full five years, might in theory have made the procedure set up under the Act virtually inoperative throughout the second half of the life of an average House of Commons.[1] And finally, the maintenance of opposition by the Lords for two years might make a bill in its original form no longer applicable to changing circumstances, and therefore lead to its withdrawal. The Lords occasionally contrived after the Parliament Act to delay and force the withdrawal of legislation. Only two Acts were, up to 1939, passed under the procedure it laid down—the Home Rule Act and Welsh Disestablishment Act of 1914—and the effect of both was suspended by legislation in which the Lords shared.

The power of the Lords to delay non-fiscal legislation was *The Lords* reduced from two years to one by the Parliament Act of 1949, a *from 1914* measure which was itself passed under the procedure laid down *to 1951* by the 1911 Act. This diminution in the power of the Upper House seems, however, less important than the fact that a party traditionally opposed to the Lords' veto in any form should have implicitly renewed that recognition of the authority of the Upper House which appears in the earlier Act, an authority which was again used when in 1951 a bill for the abolition of capital punishment was rejected by the Lords. The true importance of the 1949 Act was that it reflected an awareness that the House of Lords has become a different body from that of half a century ago. Its debates attain a high level. Its members, many of whom are widely experienced in a great variety of affairs, share effectively, and for the most part dispassionately, in the legislative process. Further, as a practical point, the Government of 1945–50 in its haste to get legislation on to the statute book found the additional time and facilities available in the Lords constantly useful. Modern criticism of the House of Lords has been constructive as well as negative.[2] It is evident that a Second Chamber can help the Lower *Functions* House to economise time by dealing with legislation, preferably *of the Upper House*

[1] The Act did, however, depart from the normal rule that the dissolution of a Parliament automatically terminates the career of all bills not yet passed.

[2] See the special number of *Parliamentary Affairs* for 1953–4 on The Future of the House of Lords.

of a non-contentious kind, to be sent down to the latter after being discussed in the former. It can revise and improve the form of legislation generally. It can lend useful assistance with private bills. It can supply independent criticism of administration. It can provide a place in Parliament for ministers, and for persons whose counsel is useful to the State but who do not care to immerse themselves in party politics. Its proceedings impose a second stage on the legislative process which may give time for reflection, and in itself be valuable as eliciting new points of view. And it is conceivable, though highly unlikely, that this might lead to the appearance of so much support for the Upper House that it would feel able to force an appeal to the electorate. As there has been since 1895 no instance of the Lords successfully appealing to the electorate against the Commons, the latter, for better or worse, may not unjustifiably regard themselves as embodying a limitless sovereignty, against which the Lords have no right to contend. Until this position had been accepted, no comprehensive plan for reforming the Second Chamber could succeed.

*Projects of reform* — Ever since 1832 schemes had been mooted for reforming at least the composition of the House. In 1834 it was proposed to deprive the bishops, who had nearly all opposed the Reform bill, of their legislative and judicial functions,[1] and further plans of reform were put forward by Russell in 1869, and by Rosebery in 1884 and 1888.[2] Such schemes generally aimed at diminishing the powers of the House. It was also possible that reconstruction might leave them intact or even increase them.[3]

*The Bryce Committee* — The preamble of the Parliament Act declared the intention of

[1] Allyn, 30-32.

[2] See Allyn, 96-7, 147-50, for these and other proposals for reform.

[3] This latter possibility did not escape the Lords themselves. In 1907, though rejecting a reform bill moved by Lord Newton, they appointed a committee to consider the subject. In 1910 they resolved that a reformed and strong Second Chamber was necessary, and, following the lines of Lord Newton's bill, that a distinction should be drawn between peers and lords of Parliament; that the latter should be chosen partly by the former, partly by the Crown, and partly by outside bodies; and that other lords should sit *ex officio*, as bishops, law lords, and past or present holders of office. In 1911 Lord Lansdowne proposed a House of rather over three hundred members, sitting for twelve years, but a quarter to be renewed every three years. One-third were to be nominated by the Crown in proportion to the numerical strength of parties in the Commons, one-third elected by the other lay peers, one-third by the House of Commons, to act as representatives of large regional constituencies.

reconstructing the House on an elective basis. In 1917 a committee for this purpose was set up under Lord Bryce. Its report advocated a double system of appointment. Besides *ex-officio* members such as law lords, there were to be 246 members elected by the Commons, voting in thirteen constituencies, and by proportional representation. Eighty-one were to be elected from the hereditary peers and spiritual lords by a joint committee of ten drawn from both Houses. Both categories of elective members were to sit for twelve years, subject to the renewal of one-third every fourth year.[1] This scheme, like its predecessors and all suggestions subsequently advanced for the total reconstruction of the Lords, was still-born. The Commons, it became obvious, would never create a House which by virtue of its elective character could rival themselves.

With diminished powers, however, and safe against any major *Life* reconstruction which might increase them, the Lords at length *peerages* became subject to a reform directed at constitutional rather than political ends. In 1958 the conferment of life peerages, for which women were equally eligible with men, was authorised by a statute which also provided for the payment of expenses to all peers attending the House and the granting of leave of absence to those who did not. In 1963 further changes were made. Peeresses in their own right, and all Scottish peers, could receive writs of summons and sit in the House. The decision in *Viscountess Rhondda's Case* was thus reversed: and Article XXII of the Act of Union with Scotland repealed.[2]

These results were, however, not the primary purpose of the *Renuncia-* Act, which was to enable a peer to renounce his peerage. The *tion of* constitutional importance of the point arose from the incapacity *peerages* of a peer to sit in the Commons, so that when a Member of Parliament succeeded to a peerage he had to give up his membership. This rule, always in the past accepted, however regretfully by men whose political careers it interrupted or broke, was not acceptable to the second holder of the Stansgate peerage, Mr. Anthony Wedgwood Benn, who, when he succeeded to it, was member for South-East Bristol. He sought unsuccessfully to

[1] Allyn, 224-5; Emden, 306.
[2] The rights of representative peers for Ireland had already ended through lack of the prescribed means of electing them.

renounce his peerage, stood as a candidate at the ensuing by-election, was returned by a large majority, but was held on petition to have been ineligible and the seat awarded to his opponent, who did however resign when Lord Stansgate could legally renounce his title.[1]

*Effects on the House of Lords*  Renunciation is for life, and is complete and irrevocable and it disqualifies from subsequent acceptance of a hereditary though not a life peerage. It is too soon to judge what its constitutional results will be. On first impression, it would seem still further to depress the status of the Upper House, but this may well be doubted, and nothing much has so far happened to confirm the doubt or dismiss it. As for the future of the Lords, it seems reasonable to expect that a body which has gained rather than declined in reputation in the exercise of its revisory functions since 1911, and has hitherto succeeded in avoiding any irreconcilable quarrel with the Commons, is in no immediate danger of change or destruction. The history of the Lords has made it plain that their functions must in the main be revisory. They cannot pretend to mirror electoral opinion more accurately than the Commons. The theory of "checks and balances" in the constitution, so justly emphasised in the eighteenth century, has ceased, as far as the Upper House is concerned, to have any validity.

*The Electoral Mandate*  The Commons thus asserted a clear supremacy. Yet that supremacy has begun to be qualified by a theory which, though by no means new, has gradually gathered influence and now subtly interpenetrates much contemporary constitutional thinking; that of the electoral mandate. The notion that such a mandate places the individual member in the position of a delegate from his own constituency—or even from the majority who vote for him—has never won acceptance. The doctrine laid down by Edmund Burke in his speech to the electors of Bristol is still the orthodox one.[2] Somewhat inconsistently, however,

---

[1] Unexpected results followed. Lord Stansgate's example was followed by other peers, including the Earl of Home and Viscount Hailsham. As the bill came into force, against the intention of the Government, immediately on receiving the Royal Assent, it enabled these two to be taken into consideration, as commoners, for the succession to Mr. Macmillan when he resigned as Prime Minister.

[2] "*Authoritative* instructions, *mandates* issued, which the member is bound blindly and implicitly to obey, to vote, and to argue for, though contrary to the clearest convictions of his judgment and conscience—these are things utterly unknown to the laws of this land, and which arise from a fundamental mistake

the electorate as a whole has been placed in a different relationship to the House of Commons as a whole. Regard is paid not only to the numerical strength of the parties in the House but to the aggregate vote obtained by each in a general election. By endorsing the programme of a party returned to power, the electorate appears to confer on it a mandate to execute that programme— no less, but also no more. Two consequences are made to follow. The first is that if a particular measure did not find a place in the election programme of the successful party, it ought not to be subsequently introduced, for there is no "mandate" for it. The second is that the mandate is to be judged by reference to the amount of votes cast in the election rather than by the size of the resultant majority in the House. A government may, as we have already seen, have a majority quite disproportionate to the actual distribution of voting—the voting may even show a preponderance for the opposition parties. The consequence is drawn that its constitutional as well as political authority is open to doubt. In other words, a general election comes near to being regarded as a kind of referendum. Nothing could be more at variance with the essential principles of the constitution. The Commons as a body holds no delegated authority any more than its individual members do. There is no power in the electorate to prescribe the actions of Parliament, for if there were its essential function, that of discussion, would be stultified, and policy would tend to be imposed by irresponsible bodies outside.[1]

It now remains to examine the functions of the Crown as the third partner in the system. Bagehot in his celebrated analysis of the constitution in 1868, though rightly pointing out that the supposed checks and balances no longer existed, seems to relegate the Crown, as he then found it, to an unduly formal position in the State. Granting that the Queen's prerogative powers were still extensive, he yet invested monarchy as an institution with attributes suggesting dignity rather than independent authority. To him it was indeed the *dignified* rather than the *efficient* part of British government, presenting sovereignty in an easily understandable form, imparting to it a personal and domestic interest,

*The Crown: Bagehot's view*

of the whole order and tenour of our Constitution."—*Speech at the conclusion of the Poll.* For the earlier history of the doctrine, see Emden, 22–5.
[1] For a full discussion of this important topic, see Emden, 297–324.

16a

connecting with it the sanctions of religion, and enabling the standards of conduct and morality to which society is expected to conform to be influenced by a compelling example. He concedes that a constitutional sovereign has, besides his formal functions, three personal rights—to be consulted, to encourage, and to warn. It is equally clear that Bagehot considers that only rarely would a monarch be able or adequately qualified to exercise these powers with effect.

*The Queen and her ministers before 1885*   The history of the monarchy after 1867, though in general confirming Bagehot's judgment, subjects it to serious revision. Much is now known of the personal use to which Queen Victoria put her prerogatives, and at least something about their use under her successors. Down to 1868, it will be remembered, while the Queen never made a purely personal choice of a Prime Minister or any of his colleagues, the complexity of party politics as well as the survival of old conventions enabled and indeed required her to intervene in other ways in the making of Cabinets. The habit thus formed was not to be easily given up. From 1868 to 1880 the solid majorities supporting the ministries of Mr Gladstone (1868–74) and Mr Disraeli (1874–80) naturally determined the choice of a Prime Minister and strengthened his power of choosing his colleagues. But during these years the Queen had learned to distrust Mr Gladstone and to trust his successor. When to her dismay the Conservatives were defeated in 1880, she tried to evade accepting Mr Gladstone as Premier, offering the position to Lord Hartington, who refused it.[1] During Mr Gladstone's second Premiership the Queen strongly criticised his choice of colleagues, showed herself overtly antagonistic to her ministers, and tried to foster dissensions among them between Whigs and Radicals.[2]

*Her actions from 1885 to 1894*   In the later years of this ministry there was added to the cleavage between Whigs and Radicals a schism between Home Rulers and anti-Home Rulers. It appeared that the multiple-party situation of the recent past had returned. This was the Queen's opportunity, as it is to some extent her justification, for attempting to determine the composition of her ministry. The general election of 1885 was inconclusive. The Conservatives were not sufficiently numerous, the Liberals too divided, to compose a stable ministry.

[1] Jennings, *Cabinet Government* (3rd edn.), 56, 518.
[2] Jennings, 332–3, 354–5.

Hence when the Conservative Lord Salisbury took office, the Queen first tried, without success, to enlist for him the support of Mr Goschen's anti-Home Rule Liberals, then to induce Goschen to form a government.[1] Her action is capable of defence. Mr Gladstone, to whom on the advice both of Salisbury and Goschen she had finally to turn, proved unable to command a majority for his first Home Rule Bill in the Commons and resigned, and the ensuing general election returned an anti-Home Rule majority of Conservatives and Liberal Unionists which kept Salisbury in power until 1892. In 1892, when the Liberals with the help of the Irish Nationalists obtained a majority, the Queen tried without avail to secure Rosebery as Premier. Though obliged to accept Gladstone, she refused to have Sir Charles Dilke as a Cabinet Minister.[2] On Gladstone's resignation in 1894 she again asserted her discretion by sending for Rosebery, the Liberal leader in the Lords, rather than Sir William Harcourt, the leader in the Commons.[3]

Queen Victoria's actions have been very variously judged, and often acrimoniously criticised. Her political bias cannot be denied. Yet, judged by the appropriate constitutional standards, her use of the Prerogative was by no means indefensible. It is not wholly to be wondered at if throughout her long reign she continued to be dominated by the traditions she inherited, which all confirmed the authority of the Crown to choose its ministers. She recognised, as was inevitable, that later circumstances obliged her to accept a ministry which had a clear electoral majority and a solid party backing. If those conditions were not fulfilled, her freedom of action assumed the aspect of a duty almost as much as a right. And it is to be noted that they were fulfilled very intermittently throughout her reign. Only Peel's government of 1841–6, Gladstone's of 1868–74 and 1880–85, and Disraeli's of 1874–80, were based on clear majorities, and of these Gladstone's second depended, as events proved, on an unstable Whig-Radical combination. The canons of constitutional propriety cannot, under these conditions, have prescribed themselves to the

*Constitutional aspect of her actions*

---

[1] Jennings, 34-7, 41, 520. F. Hardie, *Political Influence of Queen Victoria*, 92-5. It is to be remembered that Goschen had just been elected in Edinburgh against a Gladstonian Liberal Home Ruler.     [2] Jennings, 64-5.

[3] Keith, *The King and the Imperial Crown*, 102-4. She did not consult Mr Gladstone as to the choice of his successor. Had she done so, he would, it appears, have suggested Lord Spencer. Compare Hardie, 104-5.

Queen with the simplicity or precision they have assumed in the eyes of her modern critics.[1]

*The pre-rogative of dissolu-tion*      Granted the cardinal principle, which neither theory nor prac-tice completely contradicted during so large a part of the Queen's reign, that the choice of a Premier and the composition of a Cabinet had not been wholly removed from the sphere of Prerogative, it naturally followed that she was reluctant to allow other prerogatives to escape from her control. She had begun her reign with the view that the prerogative of dissolution lay solely at her disposal, and referred to it in 1846 as "a most valuable and powerful instrument in the hands of the Crown, but one which ought not to be used except in the extreme cases and with a cer-tainty of success".[2] On this view it rested with the sovereign to decide whether to give or withhold a dissolution. The underlying theory, that dissolution is a personal appeal to the electorate by the sovereign, on whom an adverse result would inflict a personal humiliation, gradually weakened as it became clear in practice that the risk was one from which the sovereign ought altogether to withdraw. Yet the Queen always maintained her right to accept or reject the advice of her ministers on this point. She refused to pledge herself to Stanley in 1851 and 1858. The opinion that she was free to do so was reaffirmed by Russell in 1866, Disraeli in 1868, and Salisbury in 1886, though Salisbury added that it would be "natural and ordinary" for the Queen to give Mr Gladstone the dissolution he then sought for.[3] The right of the sovereign to force a dissolution, which had seemed natural to the Queen in 1859, was discussed between her and Lord Salisbury as late as 1892, when she was strongly dissuaded from compelling a dissolution against her ministers' advice. The same counsel was given her in 1895.[4]

*The Queen and the Cabinet*      Holding as she did that it lay within her just sphere of authority to give her confidence to or withhold it from her ministers, and to permit or prevent an appeal to the country, the Queen clearly conceived it was her right and duty to interfere in matters of policy, and to form an independent view by consultation with such private advisers as she chose to refer to.[5] On the questions of foreign relations, India, Ireland, the reform of the Lords, and

[1] Cf. Jennings, 30, 330 ff.          [2] Jennings, 420.
[3] Jennings, 413-14; Keith, *The King and the Imperial Crown*, 152, 155-9.
[4] Jennings, 423-4; Keith, 154.          [5] Jennings, 343-6, 283; Keith, 220.

others of less importance, she formed strong convictions, which she not only communicated to her ministers but allowed to be known outside. Continuously from the time of Sir Robert Peel, she received reports on Cabinet meetings from the Prime Minister, endeavoured with varying success to become informed of the personal views of ministers, and complained if the information which reached her was inadequate.[1] She steadfastly asserted the right—on which so late as 1894 she founded a reprimand to Lord Rosebery over a speech on Lords' reform—that no major change of policy should be publicly announced without its first being submitted to the sovereign.[2] In Lord Salisbury's opinion, expressed at this time, the sovereign's disagreement would oblige the Cabinet to resign. This principle, which would enable the sovereign to veto even a unanimous Cabinet decision, is too far-fetched to be convincing, and the Queen never acted on it.[3]

A study of Queen Victoria's interpretation of the constitutional functions of the monarch suggests that Bagehot's analysis was at the time inaccurate. It was nevertheless prophetic. The Queen herself found it difficult, and sometimes impossible, to give rigid effect to her theories as to the relations of Crown and ministry. Her successors have abandoned the positions she defended so obstinately. Though King Edward VII helped Mr Balfour to reconstruct his Cabinet when it broke up owing to its differences regarding free trade and protection, tried to induce him to dissolve rather than resign, and rejected the contention that the Commons could require a dissolution, he wholly dissociated the Crown from any partisan attitude towards the ministry. On its resignation he did not hesitate to send for Sir Henry Campbell-Bannerman as Opposition leader to form a new government, accepted readily his choice of colleagues, and granted him a dissolution.[4] As far as he expressed opinions on points of policy, he did so exactly as he had done with the outgoing Conservative ministry. To Mr Asquith, whom he accepted as Campbell-Bannerman's successor in 1908, he conceded a dissolution in 1909 when the Lords rejected the Budget. But he strongly insisted on his name being kept out of the controversy between the two Houses.[5]

*Edward VII and his ministers*

[1] Jennings, 356 ff.      [2] Jennings, 365; Smellie, 124, 144; Hardie, 108.
[3] Jennings, 366; Hardie, 109-12.      [4] Keith, 107-9.
[5] Keith, 161. It should be noted that Edward VII took an active interest—not, however, in opposition to his ministers—in diplomatic affairs. Jennings, 372-3.

*George V and the crisis of 1910–11*

To this embarrassed position, which set the most stringent possible test on the conventions governing the use of the Prerogative, King George V succeeded. To grant a second dissolution within the year, as he did, was not enough to solve the question. The Lords, rightly or wrongly unwilling to accept the decision of the electorate as conclusive, prepared to resist the Parliament bill. The King had to decide whether or not to accede to a request from the Premier to create sufficient peers to ensure a majority in its favour. The question had already been raised before his predecessor's death, for though Mr Asquith stated that no pledge had been asked for, a private gathering presided over by the Archbishop of Canterbury at Lambeth Palace had discussed how the King ought to act if it were.[1] On his accession King George V summoned a conference of party leaders to seek an agreed solution.[2] When it failed, he consented to a dissolution on condition that the bill should at least be submitted to the Lords. As regards the creation of peers his position was less easy. Mr Balfour had in the Lambeth talks pointed out the possibility of King Edward declining to give such a pledge, refusing a dissolution to Mr Asquith, and inviting the Conservatives to form a ministry. This tempting but perilous course the new King would not follow. Before granting the dissolution, he had, with much hesitation, privately promised to create sufficient new peers if the ministry, having won the general election, were still faced by intractable opposition in the Upper House. When that manifested itself, the King's pledge was for the first time made public. It was effective. By Conservative abstentions, the bill passed the Upper House by a majority of seventeen and without recourse to new creations.[3]

*Features of the King's action*

The salient features of the King's action may be briefly summarised. He required the bill to come before the Lords for discussion after its approval by the Commons. On its rejection there he consented to a dissolution requested by his ministers and did not invite the Opposition to assume office and then dissolve on their request. The ensuing election was fought on the bill, and he accepted the electorate's decision. His promise to create peers was not made public before the election, nor indeed afterwards until

---

[1] Keith, 162.                [2] Keith, 198.
[3] On the constitutional crisis of 1910–11, see Jennings, 435 ff., H. Nicolson, *George V*, 128 ff., 145 ff., and R. Jenkins, *Asquith*, 199 ff. and 218 ff.

the bill had again gone to the Lords and been so seriously amended that the Commons could not accept it. It cannot be said that he put himself and his Prerogative unreservedly in the hands of his ministers, to be used as they pleased. His action, however it was prompted, was independent. It was the application of a reserve power in the Constitution, employed, at his own discretion, when all other means of carrying on government were exhausted.

The King's qualifications for the wise use of this reserve of authority developed with experience. Monarchy in the modern constitution did not become an empty formality, merely lending dignity to government, appealing to sentiment, and making the sovereign authority more personal and more easily "understanded of the people". Nor was its practical utility to be summed up in the performance of routine tasks however important and necessary.[1] But the abstract attributes, the non-governmental functions, even the routine duties of the King were, and must be, less significant than his personal influence on government and his reserve power of acting for the public good. By his mediation in political crises, such as those created by the Parliament Act and by the Home Rule controversy of 1913–14, and by his ability to co-operate with ministers of all political opinions, King George V achieved a personal position the strength of which was well indicated in 1931. *Function of the Crown in the modern constitution*

The government of Mr MacDonald, though recognising that the public finances had become unbalanced and must be restored, had been unable to agree on the measures necessary for this purpose. The King, returning from Scotland, was advised by the Premier to consult the Conservative and Liberal leaders, with whom the Government had already been in communication. It was announced that he was doing so in order to ascertain the views of their respective parties. Soon after, the Cabinet resigned. *The crisis of 1931*

---

[1] *Ad hoc* arrangements had to be made if the monarch could not personally transact them. Thus the absence of Edward VII (and also of the Prince of Wales) in 1906 had to be provided for by the appointment of the Lord Chancellor, Prime Minister, and President of the Council to act for him, that of George V by the appointment of four Councillors of State in 1911–12, and his illness in 1928 necessitated the appointment of a commission composed of the Queen, the Prince of Wales, the Duke of York, the Lord Chancellor, the Archbishop of Canterbury, and the Prime Minister. The position was later regulated by the Regency Acts of 1937 and 1943.

The Premier appears to have been asked by the King to join with the Opposition leaders in forming an emergency government. This request was acceded to by Mr MacDonald, who may have expected a large section of his supporters to follow him. His action has been strongly attacked. In some quarters there has been a tendency to censure the King's also. It seems, however, to have been entirely correct. His consultations with the Opposition leaders had been undertaken on his Premier's advice. His invitation to them and to Mr MacDonald to form an emergency government was in accordance with the strictest constitutional propriety. For it was his responsibility to ensure that his government was carried on. If no single party could form an administration, he might, and must, find ministers by combining party leaders and indeed urging them to serve together.[1] The action of the King had to be raised above the conflict of parties and aim at the national interest for which his was the final responsibility. The Prerogative, however circumscribed by conventions, must always retain its historic character as a residue of discretionary authority to be employed for the public good. It is the last resource provided by the Constitution to guarantee its own working.

### iii

*The Cabinet*

The central administrative system of the State is controlled by the Cabinet. At the Cabinet table the activities of the principal administrative departments are co-ordinated and directed in conformity with a common policy determined by their responsible political heads. Summons to the meetings of this body lies entirely at the discretion of the Prime Minister. The size of the Cabinet, except during the two Wars, has varied within the fairly narrow range of 16 to 23 members, averaging about 20.[2] The apparent uniformity of these figures over the half-century conceals, however, some important changes. Offices once of Cabinet rank have ceased to exist; others have lost it; more important still, many new ministries have been established, so that to-day a Cabinet the same in size as that of a couple of generations ago excludes

[1] On the crisis of 1931, see Jennings, 45 ff.; Keith, 133-7, Nicolson, 460-69.
[2] The tendency has been to increase, but even so the number 23 has not yet been exceeded.

the holders of many offices whereas its predecessor excluded few. A modern Prime Minister therefore undertakes a complicated task when he exercises his discretion in choosing a Cabinet. Some choices are self-evident, such as the Chancellor of the Exchequer or the Foreign Secretary. Others arise from the need to ensure that at least some ministers are free from departmental routine and consequently available for new or specialised tasks. Normally the Prime Minister will himself hold nominal office only as First Lord of the Treasury, and similarly no specific duties attach to the office of Lord President of the Council, of Lord Privy Seal—the latter's department was in fact abolished in 1884 —and Chancellor of the Duchy of Lancaster: in recent years such titles as Minister without Portfolio and Minister of State have been used to designate additional appointments of the same *ad hoc* kind. If, however, it is convenient to have non-departmental ministers, the notion of a small inner Cabinet composed of ministers without departments or definite duties and free to indulge in what Mr Churchill called an "exalted brooding over the work done by others" failed to commend itself, though powerfully advocated.[1]

If the Cabinet is to be generally composed of departmental ministers, which should be chosen? This problem, complicated by considerations of personal prestige, political tactics, and the relative status and influence of great and powerful departments, also involves important administrative problems. A Cabinet composed of the heads of all departments, while it would have the advantage of facilitating the co-ordination of policy and action, would be impossibly unwieldy. A Cabinet of about twenty, which experience seems to recommend, must therefore exclude about ten to a dozen ministers with pretensions to Cabinet rank, and though these are not necessarily the same at all times and the list of ministers enjoying Cabinet rank fluctuates, it seems clear that the newer ministries have a less secure tenure than the older.[2] Cabinet rank seems to be regularly attached still to the half-dozen offices already mentioned, and to those of the Lord Chancellor,

*Its composition*

[1] For example, by L. S. Amery in his *Reflections on the Constitution*.
[2] The most remarkable exception to this statement is afforded by the exclusion from the Cabinet after 1948 of the Secretaries of State for War and for Air, and the First Lord of the Admiralty, their places being taken by a Minister for Defence.

the Secretaries of State for Home Affairs and Commonwealth Relations, the Minister of Labour, and the President of the Board of Trade, but no such enumeration should be too definitely made. The Cabinet, like the Prime Minister himself, depend solely on convention.

*The ministry*    Outside the variable inner ring which constitutes the Cabinet, other office-holders, both executive and judicial, complete the ministry, and raise its total strength to about seventy, some of whom may be heads of departments, but most are subordinates. Apart from these administrative members, the ministry includes others who are almost entirely concerned with legal affairs, such as the Attorney-General, Solicitor-General and Lord Advocate, and in it are also to be reckoned the holders of five Household offices which have preserved their political character in that they change hands with a change of government.[1]

*The Premier's choice of his colleagues*    In making appointments to ministerial offices, as in determining which of their holders shall sit in the Cabinet, the Prime Minister has acquired an almost unrestricted discretion. He can appoint whom he pleases, or make no appointment at all. Not since Stanley in 1851 could not persuade Gladstone and others to serve has there been a failure to form a Cabinet. Invitations to serve are seldom refused nor are the Prime Minister's allocations or re-allocations of office called in question. His authority is virtually absolute. Parliament has no visible share in determining his choice. Nor has the Crown. Not since 1892 has there been a clear instance of successful opposition by the sovereign to any appointment.[2] The Prime Minister is not confined in his choice to members of the Commons and the Lords. During part of 1918–19 General Smuts sat in the War Cabinet though in neither House, in 1923–1924 the Lord Advocate was out of Parliament, and in 1935–6 Mr MacDonald and his son, though Cabinet ministers, were for a time without seats. Some restriction on the Premier's freedom of choice arises from convention. The absence of ministers from the Houses to which they are responsible is so plainly undesirable

[1] The numbers mentioned in this paragraph have later been increased by legislation to about ninety (instead of seventy), and the resulting total to one hundred and ten.

[2] In 1892 the Queen refused on personal grounds to accept Sir Charles Dilke and Mr Labouchere for any offices and Lord Ripon for any position connected with the government of India.

that arrangements of this anomalous kind are severely criticised. The convention is that ministers should sit in one House or the other, and that, if not elected to the Commons or raised to the peerage, they should resign. Since 1926 the law has been that a member, once elected to the Commons, need not resign on being appointed to any office under the Crown compatible with a seat in the House.[1]

A further restriction on the Premier's choice is that by law none but certain specified ministers, and a limited number of Under-Secretaries, may sit in the Commons.[2] Some ministers must therefore be chosen from the Upper House, and if a departmental head sits there, his subordinate must sit in the Commons, though the reverse is not true. Nineteenth-century Cabinets commonly included a large number of peers, but the House of Commons has come to insist on the more important departmental heads being chosen among its own members.[3] It seems almost to have been accepted as constitutional usage that the Prime Minister himself should sit in the Lower House, and this requirement may have influenced King George V's decision to invite Mr Baldwin instead of Lord Curzon to form a ministry in 1922.[4] *Distribution of ministers between the Houses*

With these qualifications it may be said that the composition of the Cabinet and of the ministry lies within the Premier's sole discretion. How far he is effectively in a position to impose his own choice is of course dependent on circumstances, personal and otherwise, which hardly lend themselves to constitutional analysis. *Authority of the Premier over the ministry*

[1] Re-election of Ministers Act, 1926. By a previous Act of the same name in 1919, members accepting an "old" office within nine months of the summoning of a new Parliament were exempted from the necessity of re-election.

[2] Modified by the Ministers of the Crown Acts, 1937 and 1951: House of Commons (Disqualification) Act, 1947; Ministers of the Crown (Parliamentary Secretaries) Act, 1960; and Machinery of Government Act, 1964.

[3] Omitting offices created solely for war-time purposes, several of which were held by peers, those which have since 1937 been so held include the Secretaryships for Foreign Affairs, Air, Dominions, India, and Burma, the Privy Seal, the Lord Presidency of the Council, and the First Lordship of the Admiralty, most of which have usually been of Cabinet rank. Others have been the Ministry of Civil Aviation, the Ministry of Works, the Ministry of Food, and the offices of Paymaster-General and Postmaster-General. There have been no striking contrasts between the practices of the different political parties.

[4] Lord Ronaldshay, *Life of Lord Curzon*, iii. 350-52. H. Nicolson, *George V*, 376-9. J. Wheeler-Bennett, *George VI*, 443-4, states that on the resignation of Mr Neville Chamberlain the King wished to appoint Lord Halifax rather than Mr Churchill.

It is equally in his power to force the resignation of any one of his colleagues, and to bring about their collective resignation by offering his own to the Sovereign. He is the sole channel of communication between the Sovereign and the ministry as a body, summons Cabinet meetings, controls their agenda, and, within uncertain limits, prescribes the policy which his colleagues are to follow. It seems clear that the ascendancy of the Prime Minister in the Cabinet has tended to increase. It has even been suggested that his position now resembles that of the President of the United States, and that in a British General Election as in an American Presidential Election the sovereign people exercise their choice between two or more rival candidates for supreme power. There may be superficial resemblances between the two processes: but their differences are fundamental; notably the Prime Minister's lack of that supreme executive authority which belongs to the President as such and of that control over his Cabinet which in a President appears to be complete.[1]

*Collective responsibility*    A Prime Minister's control depends on his ability to carry his colleagues along with him and on the solidarity which arises from unanimity. The doctrine of collective responsibility has become one of the strongest conventions of the constitution. On matters of policy as to which a majority of the Cabinet are in agreement, ministers who dissent from their colleagues have no option but to resign. There have been, since Catholic emancipation was left an "open question" in Lord Liverpool's government, a few instances when important questions remained undecided by the Cabinet, and ministers were therefore uncommitted.[2] There has also been an instance of open agreement to differ from a Cabinet decision without resigning. Lord Snowden, and Sir Herbert Samuel with his Liberal colleagues, accepted office in the National Government with leave to differ from their fellow-ministers on the tariff question. Their resignation in 1932, preceded by debates and divisions in which these ministers opposed the Government over the Ottawa Agreements, seems to show that the arrangement was quite unworkable.[3] It

[1] The topic is discussed by G. W. Jones in *Parliamentary Affairs* (1965), pp. 167 ff.
[2] E.g. the repeal of the Corn Laws (possibly), vote by ballot, the extension of the county franchise (in 1873), a militia scheme of 1905, women's suffrage; Jennings, 278-9. There are recent indications that the doctrine has taken a more flexible form, though Lord Longford's resignation in 1967 shows the true principle at work still.                    [3] Jennings, 280-81.

may in general be said that except in the rare instances where questions are of a kind in which Cabinet solidarity is not essential, ministers must stand or fall by one another and the Premier. They must not merely abstain from opposing, but must actively support the decisions of their colleagues.

For the individual acts of ministers in their own departments, it *Individual* is not so clear that the collective responsibility of their colleagues *responsibility* is necessarily engaged. On occasions—as when in 1873 Mr Lowe resigned the Chancellorship of the Exchequer on account of maladministration, or Colonel Seely relinquished the War Office in 1914 after the "Curragh Incident"—the minister stands unsupported by his colleagues or the House. A more difficult case arose in 1917 when Mr Austen Chamberlain, technically responsible, as Secretary of State for India, for the mismanagement of the Mesopotamia campaign, resigned over an issue on which, in normal times, the Cabinet as a whole would have been unable to evade sharing the blame. In 1922 Mr Montagu, holding the same office, had to resign when his colleagues declined to support his action in publishing on his personal initiative a despatch in which the Indian Government urged the revision of the Treaty of Sèvres. A curious instance of purely individual responsibility arose in 1935. Sir Samuel Hoare, empowered by the Cabinet to negotiate with the French Premier, M. Laval, accepted terms for the settlement of the Italo-Abyssinian War which it was plain neither the electorate nor Parliament would approve, was disowned by the Prime Minister, and had to resign.[1] While within almost indefinable limits the Cabinet, if it is undivided and can count on a majority of its supporters, may disclaim responsibility for the action of one of its members, recent experience suggests that the extent to which such individual responsibility can effectively apply has tended to contract. The miscarriages attending the schemes in East and West Africa for which as Minister of Food Mr John Strachey was answerable to Parliament might in strict constitutional propriety have involved his resignation. Cabinet support and the solidarity of the majority party in the Commons proved a sufficient protection.[2] It must of course be different if the

[1] For these various instances, see Keith, *The King and the Imperial Crown*, 165, 299; Anson, *Law and Custom of the Constitution* (ed. Keith), ii. ii, 241 n. 3.

[2] See generally, Wade and Phillips, 84-9. The doctrine of individual responsibility for maladministration was in 1954 carried to an extreme in the *Crichel Down Case*.

Cabinet is divided or the House of Commons turns against it.

*Conduct of*
*Cabinet*
*business*

It is the function of the Cabinet, and above all of the Premier himself, to co-ordinate the business of policy and administration. Though Prime Ministers have varied in the degree of their personal sway over their colleagues—which rose to its highest point under Peel, and receded under Palmerston and perhaps Disraeli also—it is essential that their authority should compel or induce sufficient agreement on at least the main lines to be followed and to be recommended to Parliament. Such agreement on general policy naturally involves the co-ordination of the activities of all the separate departments which are set in motion by Cabinet decisions communicated to them by their political heads. The complexity of government in the modern State has led to an increasing systematisation of the work of the Cabinet. The Prime Minister's letter to the King, formerly the only record of its transactions, has since 1916 been replaced by official minutes kept by a salaried Secretariat.[1] Before its regular meetings, agenda are circulated and memoranda prepared. Important points are referred to Cabinet committees for preliminary discussion. Such committees can now be regarded as having become more than mere administrative devices. They have constitutional significance. A Defence Council, formerly styled Committee, presided over by a Minister of Defence[2] apportions resources of all kinds between the fighting services, administers inter-service organisations, and deals with service matters in which common policy is desirable. The Committee system has spread to domestic affairs, especially economic,[3] and brings into close relationship with the Cabinet numbers of ministers who do not belong to it but whose participation in important if limited spheres of action is essential. A new kind of Cabinet system seems to emerge, in which the Prime Minister and a group of pre-eminent colleagues acquire superior importance as co-ordinating various groups of inter-related

[1] On Cabinet minutes and the Cabinet Secretariat, see Jennings, 242-5, 269-75 ff.

[2] From 1963, a Secretary of State for Defence presided over a unified Ministry of Defence (set up in 1946) in which the three Service Ministries have been absorbed, assisted by three Ministers of State connected respectively with the Royal Navy, the Army and the Royal Air Force. The three sets of estimates are, however, still presented separately to Parliament.

[3] There is a description of the Cabinet Committee system in H. Morrison, *Government and Parliament*, 16 ff.

departmental activities for each of which, taken severally, a departmental minister, who may not necessarily be a member of the Cabinet, is responsible. This works like a version of the inner Cabinet already mentioned, though the leading ministers who compose it are not necessarily free from departmental duties of their own. The possibility arises of individual responsibility becoming further blurred, though it is true that a Minister who disagrees with a Cabinet Committee can assert himself by raising the matter in the Cabinet.

Cabinet solidarity ensures that the administrative business of the State is co-ordinated by a unanimous collective will. Though itself only a deliberative body, it sets in motion the executive power stored up by Prerogative, Common Law, and statute in the great departments of state, decides disputes between them, and directs them unitedly towards the fulfilment of common purposes. The administrative machinery thus controlled has attained the highest point of complexity. A survey of administrative history since 1867 shows the further elaboration of pre-existing departments, the addition of new ministries, and the extension everywhere both of the range of their responsibilities and of the organisation and powers available for their discharge.[1] *The Cabinet and the administrative system*

There took place after 1867 a considerable enlargement of the diplomatic machinery of the State, but little substantial change of structure. In the Foreign Office, controlling the diplomatic and consular services, the Protectorates other than those administered by the Colonial and Commonwealth Relations Office, and the Anglo-Egyptian Sudan, the most important development, apart from internal changes of organisation due to increased pressure of business, was the merging in 1919 of the administrative and diplomatic services hitherto wholly separate. Though there had been from 1822 a salaried diplomatic service, its members were conceived of as belonging rather to the households of ambassadors than to the public service itself, and recruitment was based on patronage. A further amalgamation, carried out in 1943, united the Foreign Office and diplomatic and consular services into a single Foreign Service.[2] *The Foreign Office*

[1] The creation and abolition of ministries and the distribution and sharing of their functions were greatly facilitated by the Ministers of the Crown Acts of 1946 and 1964.

[2] S. T. Bindoff, *The Unreformed Diplomatic Service*, 4 *T.R.H.S.* xviii. 143 Lord Strang, *The Foreign Office*, 214 ff.

*The War*
*Office*

More radical changes were carried out in the War Office. Military organisation in 1867, though considerably simplified after the Crimean War, still retained many traces of its former inchoate character. A dual control existed, shared between the War Office in Pall Mall and the Commander-in-Chief at the Horse Guards, the first representing civil and parliamentary control, the other a military and royal control which the Queen and her cousin the Duke of Cambridge, who was Commander-in-Chief, were most reluctant to surrender, and which in any case seemed necessary to give due weight to professional opinion. The difficulty was resolutely taken in hand by Mr Cardwell, Secretary of State for War in Mr Gladstone's 1868 government.[1] By the War Office Act, 1870, the Secretary of State assumed an undivided responsibility. Under him, the Commander-in-Chief dealt with the raising, training, and discipline of the forces, military education, and intelligence; the Surveyor-General, in the Control Department, with transport, supply, and munitions; and the Financial Secretary with the preparation and presentation of estimates, and with appropriation, pay, accounting, and audit. The inefficiency of the Control Department during the Sudanese War of 1887 led to its suppression, and a twofold division of duties was arranged, the military side advising as to the requirements of the army and the civil side seeing that they were efficiently and economically provided for. Responsibility on the military side, which was vested in the Commander-in-Chief, proved too heavy for him to carry. A Royal Commission under Lord Hartington reported in 1889–90 in favour of substituting for his office a War Office Council, composed of heads of War Office departments, to advise the Secretary of State.[2] In a modified and most unsatisfactory form this recommendation was carried out, the Commander-in-Chief acting both as a member of a consultative council on administrative questions and also as the chief adviser of the Secretary on purely military matters. Once more on trial in the South African War, and once more breaking down, military organisation was again investigated by a Committee under Lord Esher (1904), on whose recommendation the office of Commander-in-Chief was at last suppressed, and the Secretary of State became the only

---

[1] See R. Biddulph, *Lord Cardwell at the War Office*, 54-5.
[2] H. Gordon, *The War Office*, 68-70; Lowell, *Government of England*, i. 95.

channel of communication between the Crown and the War Office.[1] The Secretary of State presided over an Army Council, composed of his Financial and Parliamentary Under-Secretaries, representing with himself the element of civilian control, of five military officers, and the Permanent Secretary. In the situation thus created, the army was directed by a civilian minister, acting on the advice of professional soldiers. Orders in Council of 1931 and 1947 completed his authority by making him solely responsible to Parliament for the Army Council, until in the reforms of 1963 that body disappeared along with himself.

The model taken for the War Office by the Esher Committee *The* was the organisation of the Admiralty, where dual control had *Admiralty* ended in 1832. After that date no point of principle caused difficulty in naval organisation. Yet there were disadvantages in combining in the same body the functions of administration and command. Subsequent reorganisations in 1869, 1887, 1929, and 1947 aimed at making a suitable redistribution of duties, until in 1963 the Board disappeared after nearly three centuries' unbroken history and the Queen became Lord High Admiral.[2]

The development of air power and transport showed the need *The Air* for a new defence department, under whose care civil aviation *Ministry* was, with somewhat unsatisfactory results, also placed at the outset. As a military weapon air power was at first developed independently by the navy and the army, in the Royal Naval Air Service and the Royal Flying Corps. Under the name of the Air Committee a consultative body was established in 1912 to co-ordinate air development by the Admiralty and War Office. Experience in the 1914–18 War suggested that the new arm required to be separately organised. After a short and unsuccessful experiment with a non-executive committee dealing with points referred to it by the Admiralty and War Office, a separate Air Board was set up in 1916. Hampered at first by lack of executive power and quarrels with other bodies—including by now the

[1] Gordon, 78-81; Lowell, i. 99-101.

[2] Wade and Phillips, 181, 379-81. Unlike the Board of Trade, the Admiralty actually met and transacted business as a Board: on the eve of its abolition it consisted of a First Lord (usually a civilian), five Sea Lords (respectively Chief of Staff, Director of Naval Personnel, Controller, Chief of Supplies and Transport, and deputy Chief of Staff for Air), the Vice-Chief of Staff, a Civil Lord, a Financial and Parliamentary Under-Secretary, and the Permanent Secretary.

Ministry of Munitions—it was of necessity transformed into a ministry. In the following year (1917) it was given a constitution modelled on that of the Army Council and placed under the charge of a Secretary of State.[1] It retained control over civil aviation until during the war of 1939–45 a separate Ministry of Civil Aviation with a minister of its own was established.

*The Com-mittee of Imperial Defence*   As defence became the affair of three separate service departments and further involved co-operation with the Foreign Office, India Office, and Colonial Office, the need was recognised for some permanent and strong link connecting with one another and with the Cabinet all the authorities concerned. After the self-governing colonies began to assume responsibility for their own defence, attempts to plan a coherent Imperial scheme led to a number of experiments—in 1885 a Colonial Defence Committee, in 1895 a Cabinet Committee on Defence, and during and after the South African War a Committee of Imperial Defence.[2] This body, constituted under the Prime Minister, and comprising the Secretary for War, the Commander-in-Chief, the First Lord, the First Sea Lord, and such other persons as the Prime Minister chose to summon, had consultative and not executive functions, but its systematic examination of every problem of defence underlay the organisation by which the first World War was carried on.

*The War Council and War Cabinet*   During the first World War it became a "War Council", including, besides representatives, civil and military, of the services, the Secretaries of State for Foreign Affairs and India, and the Chancellor of the Exchequer. Its constitutional position was embarrassing. The work of almost every department had in one way or another to be related to the exigencies of war. But the Cabinet as a whole, and particularly the Prime Minister, Mr Asquith, were reluctant to allow their authority to be superseded by that of the War Council. The difficulty of defining the relationship between Cabinet and War Council caused the formation, on Mr Asquith's resignation and under the premiership of Mr Lloyd George, of a War Cabinet of five members, with full executive powers but, except for the Chancellor of the Exchequer, without departmental duties.[3] Under the control of this body the departments were co-ordinated to carry out a national scheme, their work being aided

[1] Jennings, 135-8; Smellie, *A Hundred Years of English Government* (2nd edn.), 189-91.   [2] Jennings, 290 ff.; Smellie, 159.   [3] Jennings, 297-301.

by the creation of separate ministries for Munitions, National
Service, Shipping, and Food.[1]

The subordination of the departments to a body of which their *Reversion*
heads were not members, however desirable and indeed necessary *to the*
*pre-War*
as a war-time expedient, had to be abandoned with the restoration *system*
of peace. Departmental ministers would no longer acquiesce in the
severance of policy from administration and confine themselves
to purely administrative work under superior direction. Mr Lloyd
George's attempt to retain personal control over foreign policy by
establishing a kind of unofficial Foreign Office, in rivalry with the
department for which his Foreign Secretary, Lord Curzon, was
responsible, afforded a striking example of the evils which must
arise unless Cabinet government reverted to the accustomed
model.[2] In one matter, however, it still appeared necessary to
continue the co-ordination imposed by the War. The Committee of Imperial Defence was reconstituted in a larger form,
including the heads of a number of civil departments such as the
Treasury and the Home Office. Its enlarged size indicated the
truth that under modern conditions no branch of government can
be regarded as lying outside a national scheme of defence. Greater
unification between the service departments was attempted in
1936 by the creation of a Minister for the Co-ordination of Defence, having a seat in the Cabinet. It was an evident weakness
in his position that he was not primarily concerned to correlate
measures for the protection of the civil population, such as air-
raid precautions and the maintenance of food-supply, with those
taken by the fighting forces for their own special needs, and
that he had no separate department of his own.

The need for integrating every branch of government in the *Conduct*
task of national defence was peremptorily enforced by the second *of the*
*second*
World War. During the preceding decade, the Committee of *World*
Imperial Defence had through its sub-committees investigated *War*
the problems of material resources and man-power, of finance,
and of governmental organisation which would arise if war
broke out. When war came, the Committee was abolished but
its functions passed to a War Cabinet, served by a system of

[1] Jennings, 317-18; Smellie, 174-9.

[2] Ronaldshay, *Life of Lord Curzon*, iii. 260-61; H. Nicolson, *Curzon, the Last
Phase*, 57-61; Jennings, 220-21; an analogous position occurred between Mr
Neville Chamberlain and Mr Eden in 1937.

committees, some ministerial, some official, on such problems as food supply, civil defence, and military co-ordination. This organisation underwent a threefold evolution. The War Cabinet increased in size and ceased to be composed, as at the outset, of non-departmental ministers. The committee system, both ministerial and official, greatly expanded. Above all, the authority of the Prime Minister was increasingly emphasised. The post of Minister for the Co-ordination of Defence ceasing to exist in 1940, the Prime Minister became Minister of Defence and assumed general responsibility for the conduct of the war, and it was with him rather than with the War Cabinet as a whole that the Chiefs of Staff were related, and from him that the supreme directives issued. The continued existence of a Minister of Defence under the Act of 1946, even if separated from the Premiership, and the pressures leading to the major reconstruction effected in 1963, are reminders that under present-day conditions the fighting services must be a unity, held closely to one another and to the national strength and resources which sustain them and of which they are the ultimate safeguard.

*The Home Office*    The increasing burden of responsibility for domestic administration naturally began by falling on the Home Office.[1] When Parliament decided to bring some new topic of domestic concern under State regulation, the Home Office was naturally chosen for the purpose unless the matter clearly fell within the sphere of some other department. Its multifarious duties came to include those concerning aliens and naturalisation, factory inspection, workmen's compensation, children and young persons, magistrates and courts, police, prisons and treatment of offenders, the fire service, explosives, intoxicants, and dangerous drugs. Aerial navigation was in its infancy committed to Home Office supervision. In the course of 1938 the Home Office became responsible for air-raid precautions. Some relief, however, was afforded to a department which, as the area of State control widened, found itself under an ever-increasing burden, by the transfer of certain of its duties to new or to other departments, in addition to those already vested in them.

*The Board of Trade*    Among these the Board of Trade was already in 1867 a power-

[1] For the work of the Home Office, see generally, Sir Frank Newsam, *The Home Office*. In 1951 the Home Secretary was given the duties and additional title of Minister for Welsh Affairs. In 1957 the new post of Minister of State for Welsh Affairs was created, the first holder being a member of the House of Lords. In 1964 Wales acquired a Secretary of State of its own.

ful and active department, concerned with transport, industry, and commerce, but it too has by degrees been denuded of many of its powers. Its authority over railways, begun in 1840, originally intended to assert a control which might eventually lead to State purchase, and long including a supervisory power over the safety of the travelling public and of railway employees, was in 1919 transferred to the Ministry of Transport. The same happened during the second World War to the powers of the Board over shipping, created in 1850 and 1854, and amplified by the Merchant Shipping Acts, in order to ensure safety at sea. In 1942 it lost its powers in respect of gas and electricity to the Ministry of Fuel and Power. Its superintendence of industry remains largely in-direct, through the maintenance of standard weights and measures, and the protection of patents. The Board's control over policy has greatly relaxed before that of the Treasury; its work lies in examining and advising on the movement and development or recession of trade, on industrial trends, and the location of industry, and on the cost of living, in keeping contact with the com-mercial world, and in obtaining information, preparing statistics, and publishing, as it has done since 1890, the material contained in the *Board of Trade Journal*.[1] The connexion, once intimate, be-tween the Board and the Foreign Office on foreign trade and com-mercial treaties has weakened:[2] and its limitation to domestic concerns was emphasised when in 1963 the President also became Secretary of State for Industry, Trade and Regional Development.[3]

The administration of agriculture has during the last hundred years been drastically reorganised.[4] From 1880 opinion began strongly to favour the consolidation of all services relating to this industry, and an Order in Council of 1883 set up a committee of the Privy Council for the purpose. The effects of the prolonged agricultural depression of the later nineteenth century necessitated more radical action. In 1889 a statutory Board of Agriculture came into being, constituted on lines similar to the Board of Trade

*The Ministry of Agri-culture, Fisheries and Food*

[1] On the work of the Board, see H. Llewellyn Smith, *The Board of Trade*, chs. iv.-ix.

[2] Since 1945, however, the Department of Overseas Trade, once shared be-tween the Board and the Treasury, has been absorbed into the Board.

[3] The decline continued when in 1964 a Department of Economic Affairs was set up under a First Secretary of State.

[4] See F. Floud, *The Ministry of Agriculture and Fisheries*, chs. i.-ii.

and endowed with powers hitherto belonging to the Privy Council, the Lands Commission, and the Board of Works, to which others might by Order in Council be added. The powers of the Board of Trade in respect of fisheries were transferred in 1903 to what was now renamed the Board of Agriculture and Fisheries. By 1919 its burden had been lightened by the transfer of most of its duties regarding Scotland to the new Board of Agriculture for Scotland (1909) and regarding woods and forests to a Forestry Commission (1919), and it was reconstituted as a Ministry, possessing powers relating to the combating of disease, the improvement of livestock, crops, and land, agricultural education and research, marketing and statistics, besides the supervision of fresh-water and sea fisheries. To these were added in 1955 the duties previously fulfilled by the Ministry of Food.

*The Ministry of Education*     In the history of educational administration, the year 1870 was a landmark. The Education Department, hitherto mainly concerned with subsidising voluntary educational work from funds granted by Parliament, was transformed by the Elementary Education Act into an executive body, with powers to compel the local School Boards set up by the Act to provide efficient elementary schools, or, failing them, to appoint other persons to do so. It was not yet entirely detached from the Privy Council and had no independent and responsible spokesman in the Commons, nor were the relations of the Lord President of the Council and the Vice-President and members of the Board clearly defined. In 1899, after its work had been investigated by Select Committees and a Royal Commission had inquired into secondary education, the Board of Education Act was passed. It consolidated the Education Department and the Science and Art Department, set up a Board under a President of its own—a "phantom" Board which, like that of the Board of Trade, never met—gave it supervisory powers over education in England and Wales, and added to them others previously held by the Board of Agriculture and the Charity Commissioners. The Education Act of 1902 gave to the Board the power to enforce—as the Department had done —the duty of providing efficient elementary education. For this purpose it dealt with the 318 local education authorities which took the place of the old School Boards, deciding disputes between these authorities themselves, and between them and the managers of other schools, and administering grants of public money. With regard to secondary education, which local authorities might but were not obliged to provide, the Board's function was consultative. But the Act of 1918, laying on local authorities the duty of providing secondary education, required them to submit schemes showing what they intended to do, on the adequacy of which the Board was judge, and on which depended in turn the payment of the grants it controlled.[1] The Education Act of 1944, which changed it into the Ministry of Education, conferred on it greatly amplified, and indeed radically altered, powers over Local Education Authorities. Still more sweeping changes were effected in 1964, when the place of the Ministry was taken by a new Department for Education and Science under a Secretary of State. It comprises two main branches each under a Minister of State: one to deal with schools as the Ministry had done: the other with universities and with scientific research, hitherto the responsibility respectively of the Treasury and the Privy Council. The main effect of the legislation of post-war years has already been observed—the emphasis on centralisation. More completely subordinated to central control by a minister who may if he chooses intervene on his own initiative and not simply when his intervention is sought, Local Education Authorities seem relegated to the constitutional position of mere agents executing a prescribed policy framed by the central administration.

The creation of the Ministry of Labour in 1916 was a war-time measure for regulating the supply of labour and settling industrial disputes. Under its control were placed the Labour Exchanges set up in 1910, and it was empowered to administer the conciliation machinery established in 1907 and 1919 and the Trade Boards system. From the Board of Trade it took over the administration of the Factory Acts. In the "Welfare" State it has come to acquire increasing significance. It seeks to help both employers and employees in the settlement of industrial disputes, and in the recruitment, training and distribution of labour, it compiles registers of employment, collects and disseminates statistics and other information, administers the Disabled Persons Act, and deals with foreign workers and international labour problems.

*Ministry of Labour*

The Ministry of Transport came into existence in 1919 in order

---

[1] On the history of the Board of Education, see L. A. Selby-Bigge, *Board of Education*, ch. i., and B. M. Allen, *Sir Robert Morant*, Part III.

*Ministry of Transport*

to concentrate hitherto diffused powers concerning inland transport; civil aviation remaining, however, under the Air Ministry and coastal navigation under the Board of Trade. The functions of the new ministry therefore related in the main to railways and highways, to which in 1920, by transfer from the Board of Trade, electricity was added.[1] It was entrusted with the application of the Road Traffic Acts of 1930–62, and during the second World War with additional powers over merchant shipping. Civil aviation was added to its sphere from 1952 until 1959 when a Ministry of Civil Aviation was created.

*Local Government Board and the Ministry of Health*

Also in 1919 the department chiefly responsible for the oversight of local administration was wholly reconstructed and the Ministry of Health made its appearance. In 1868 when the machinery for central supervision of public health had for some years been partly dismantled, a Royal Commission was appointed to deal with the subject. Its report—to which weight was lent by a severe smallpox epidemic and a renewed threat of cholera—recommended an overhaul of sanitary administration and the formation in each district of a responsible public health authority—the Boards of Guardians in default of any other—to be controlled by a central department under a minister. Acts of 1871, 1872, and 1875 defined the constitution of the central and local authorities, and the last laid down rules which are still the foundation of public health law.[2] The Act of 1871 set up a "phantom" Board of the usual type, called the Local Government Board, under a salaried President by whom its work was actually done. On the Board were conferred powers hitherto belonging to the Privy Council, the Home Office, and the Poor Law Board with regard to public health, local government, and poor relief. Among its functions, those relating to the first topic gradually assumed the leading place. The Ministry established in 1919 was, unlike its predecessor, of full Cabinet rank. It possessed all the powers of the old Local Government Board, those of the Commissioners set up by the National Health Insurance Act of 1911, and certain powers previously belonging to other departments.[3] These it exercised with little change until the legislation introducing the

[1] Jennings, 318.
[2] A. Newsholme, *The Ministry of Health*, chs. ii., iv., vii.
[3] On the development of the Local Government Board and Ministry of Health, see also Allen, *Sir Robert Morant*, Part IV.

"Welfare" State exerted on it an effect more far-reaching than was sustained by any other Ministry. In 1945 it surrendered to the recently-created Ministry of National Insurance the whole responsibility for National Health Insurance and contributory pension schemes. In 1950 another new Ministry, that of Local Government and Planning, took over its functions with regard to local government, rating and valuations, housing, and public health.[1] These profound changes left it free to undertake duties, more closely according with its title than ever before, relating to the National Health Service set up by statute in 1946.

Scottish administration was until 1885 conducted by a number *The* of Scottish departments under an Under-Secretary at the Home *Scottish* Office. In that year a Secretaryship for Scotland was created, but *Office* the departments it controlled did not cover the entire field of Scottish administration, part being left to those which also dealt with England and Wales. In 1926 the Scottish Secretaryship was again raised to the dignity of a Secretaryship of State, responsible for a fairly complete range of administrative departments, dealing with Education, Health, Agriculture, Fisheries, and Prisons. Certain Scottish departments are linked with the corresponding English ministries by joint committees.[2]

The list of ministries may be briefly completed by mention of *Other* the Post Office, originally a prerogative department but in modern *depart-* times almost entirely regulated by statute; the Paymaster-General's *ments* Office; the Privy Council Office, concerned, *inter alia*, with the grant of charters, the regulations of professional corporations such as the General Medical Council, and medical and scientific research; the Ministry of Public Building and Works, successor to the former Office (later, Ministry) of Works, which was charged with the building and maintenance of government premises and historic monuments; the Duchy of Lancaster Office, administering the Duchy property, which has not, like other Crown revenues, been surrendered to the Treasury;[3] the Ministry of Pensions and Social Insurance; the Lord Chancellor's, Lord Advocate's, and Law Officers' departments, dealing respectively with the

---

[1] In 1951, Housing and Local Government were conjoined in a Ministry of that name, under a Cabinet Minister.    [2] Wade and Phillips, 209-10.
[3] The Duchy of Cornwall revenues have likewise not been surrendered. But the Duchy office is not separately represented in Parliament.

administrative business connected with the judicial system and with the English and Scottish legal business of the government. Imperial affairs once dealt with by the Colonial Office have passed to the Commonwealth Relations Office,[1] which was constituted in 1947 to fulfil the duties previously discharged by the Dominions Office set up in 1925, and subsequently on the abolition of the India Office assumed responsibility for relations with India, Pakistan, and Ceylon. All of these are represented in Parliament by responsible ministers. In addition there exists a group of departments which are not as such represented in Parliament, but for which one minister or another must answer. An enormous variety of autonomous and semi-autonomous administrative bodies exists, for which ministers are answerable so far as they have control. Finally, all government departments are surrounded by a constellation of advisory committees.[2]

*The Treasury*    Fundamentally, control and responsibility depend on the expenditure of public money. It follows that the Treasury is, from the administrative point of view, supreme in the whole system. Its authority extends over the personnel of the Civil Service—of which its Permanent Secretary is head—and covers establishment, appointment, salaries, and discipline, regarding which Treasury minutes and circulars are decisive. More important still, it conducts the national financial system. It collects revenue, arranges for the requirements of the departments to be formulated, supplies them with money from taxation or loans, and prescribes the form of their accounts. Subject to Cabinet decisions, by which it is of course bound but which it may do much to influence, it sanctions all departmental proposals for spending public money. Expenditure charged on the Consolidated Fund naturally escapes Treasury review, but what is voted by annual supply is based on estimates which the Treasury directs the departments to prepare and to submit to it for review. The work, begun about November in each year, is completed in time for the estimates to be laid before Parliament at the opening of the next financial year in the following April. Should the funds provided for a department prove insufficient and a supplementary estimate later become necessary,

[1] Renamed Commonwealth Office in 1966.
[2] On those advisory bodies, see Wade and Phillips, 219; Wheare, *Government by Committee*, 43-8; for departments unrepresented in Parliament, see Jennings, 104-5.

it rests with the Treasury to propose it. It rests with the Treasury also to approve the practice of *virement*, by which departments can transfer money from one sub-head to another within their estimates.[1]

These powers would naturally seem to suggest that the last *Treasury* word with regard to expenditure, and therefore, in effect, with *control* regard to any policy involving expenditure, must lie with the Treasury. There is certainly a widely-held belief that expenditure desirable on public grounds is often prevented by Treasury opposition. But certain qualifications must be made. Politically, the Chancellor of the Exchequer, though an influential member of the Cabinet, is bound by the decisions of his colleagues, and thus he may sometimes find himself compelled to find money for their schemes even if he disapproves and has opposed them. Administratively, Treasury control is apt merely to resolve itself into supervision of accountancy. In the technical services which the departments conduct, they are, by virtue of their expert knowledge, able to estimate their probable outgoings, whether strictly necessary or not, with greater accuracy than the Treasury is in a position to attain. The extent of "Treasury control" may be exaggerated. The main business of the Treasury is to provide money, see that it is legally and so far as possible economically expended, and give expert advice on what a particular policy is likely to cost. It may find difficulty in going further, for the focus of financial power really lies in the House of Commons, which, bringing new services into existence by legislation, automatically introduces new items of expenditure over which the Treasury has little or no control except of a formal kind.

Many government departments, if not all, necessarily perform *Local* much of their business locally. So, for example, the offices of the *govern-* Inland Revenue Commission, a sub-department of the Treasury, *ment* and the Labour Exchanges of the Ministry of Labour, exist in all important centres, and post offices everywhere. Other branches of administration, however, are to a large extent placed under direct local control. In 1867 an immense number of local administrative units existed for such purposes as health, highways, and poor relief. The Education Act of 1870 added to these the new School

[1] On Treasury control, see Jennings, 150 ff., and Wade and Phillips, 235-6. S. Beer's *Treasury Control* provides a detailed treatment. The relationship of the Treasury to the new Department of Economic Affairs does not yet lend itself to any precise definition.

Boards, and the Public Health Act of 1875 a series of urban and rural sanitary districts.[1] Confusion seemed to have reached its height, but the 1875 Act made some attempt to introduce order by utilising borough councils, where they existed, as sanitary authorities, and elsewhere using existing improvement commissioners, local Boards of Health and Boards of Guardians.[2] Borough government was dealt with in a consolidating statute of 1882, the Municipal Corporations Act, under which the Queen in Council was empowered to incorporate towns on the petition of their inhabitants, and the organisation and powers of municipal corporations were defined.[3] In 1888 an important advance was made in two directions.[4] The elective principle introduced by the Act of 1835 into municipal government and subsequently applied piecemeal elsewhere was extended to the counties, where the age-long reign of the Justices of the Peace in administrative business was ended. Secondly, the government of the counties, in which administrative complexity was worst, was greatly simplified. Each administrative county was placed under an elective council, modelled on that of the boroughs, to which almost the whole of the administrative powers of the Justices of the Peace were transferred, except licensing and police, the latter being shared with the County Council in a Standing Joint Committee. An attempt was also made to relate the lesser administrative units in the counties to the new councils. This latter process was carried further in 1894.[5] The urban and rural sanitary districts were renamed urban and rural districts. Highway boards were abolished and their powers transferred to the elective councils of the districts. The councils of rural districts were empowered to act as boards of guardians. In each rural parish of over three hundred inhabitants a council, and in those of less than three hundred a parish meeting, came into existence for parish business.[6] Outside the more or less symmetrical pattern so constructed the School Boards and Boards

---

[1] On the complexity of administration about 1870, see Lowell, *Government of England*, ii. 135-6.

[2] J. Redlich and F. W. Hirst, *Local Government in England*, i. 358, ii. 227-9. The first volume has been republished, edited by B. Keith-Lucas; references are here given, however, to the original edition.

[3] Redlich and Hirst, i. 221-7.          [4] Redlich and Hirst, i. 197-8.

[5] Redlich and Hirst, i. 211-13.

[6] A Council consists of elected members, a Parish Meeting of all ratepayers.

of Guardians still remained. In 1902 the School Boards were replaced by committees of the councils of counties and larger boroughs.[1] Boards of Guardians were transformed in 1929 into Public Assistance Committees of the same bodies.[2] Systematic organisation of local government under local democratic control seemed thus to be achieved. Yet neither the symmetry nor the local autonomy of these arrangements must be too strongly insisted on. It is impossible to construct an administrative map of England in which all units of local government form part of a uniform scheme.

In 1963 the government of London was entirely remodelled, *Adminis-* though its ancient Duchy persisted. While in the City authority *trative areas* remains with the Court of Common Council, the former London County Council, comprising twenty-eight Metropolitan boroughs, has been replaced by a Greater London Council composed not only of new boroughs replacing the old but also of four suburban county boroughs, and of the whole of Middlesex and parts of Essex, Kent and Surrey.[3] Its administrative services are organised on several different plans, the Metropolitan police, for example— though not the City police—being under a Commissioner controlled by the Home Office. Outside London there are over eighty county boroughs, from which the authority of the county councils is wholly excluded. What remains is divided into sixty-one administrative counties, these in turn into urban and rural districts, and the latter of these two into parishes. Besides the county boroughs, there exist within the county areas themselves a large number of noncounty boroughs which to a greater or less extent are subject to control by the county councils.[4] Side by side with these administrative organs in their varied professions, a multitude of other local bodies administer such services as land drainage, harbours, and so on.

Taking, however, the county borough and the administrative *The local* county with its sub-divisions as the normal type, its constitution *govern-* exhibits certain broad similarities. Except in rural parishes of less *ment* than three hundred inhabitants, which are governed by parish *electorate* meetings of all ratepayers, there exists in each area an elective

[1] Lowell, ii. 313-14, 322.

[2] H. Finer, *English Local Government*, 147, 338.

[3] On the government of London before 1965, see Finer, ch. xxi.: the new system is summarised in Wade and Phillips, 359-60.

[4] On the position of non-county boroughs, see Finer, 33-4.

council. Until 1945 the franchise was uniform, being exercised by all ratepayers, and the husbands or wives of ratepayers, over the age of twenty-one; in that year a second qualification, that of being on the Parliamentary Register, was added. The local electorate thus became larger than the parliamentary electorate; it is more immediately responsible for the cost of maintaining the public services; yet the proportion of local government electors who poll is far lower than in parliamentary elections, and uncontested elections are more numerous. Any ratepayer, owner of property, or other person qualified by a year's residence may be a candidate, if not an official under the council, or interested in one of its contracts, or in receipt of poor relief. In county and borough councils, two-thirds of the council are elected by the ratepayers, to hold office for three years, one-third retiring annually, the remaining one-third—the aldermen—being elected by the councillors to hold office for six years. Besides this instance of indirect election, certain boards such as the Standing Joint Committee are entirely constituted on this principle. There may be a wholly non-elective element in committees. Thus until 1947, the agricultural committee of a County Council contained certain members appointed by the Minister of Agriculture and Fisheries; and the executive committees which replaced them were nominated by the Minister and acted under his direction.[1] Elsewhere co-opted members may serve on committees: and in a number of instances the central government exercises control over the composition of specified committees.[2]

*Powers of local authorities*    The powers committed to local authorities are the creation of statutes, stating with some precision what they *must* do, and what they *may* do if they choose. Beyond this they can do nothing involving financial outlay. As illustrations of their powers may be mentioned those relating to the maintenance of order, health, education, libraries, housing, parks and cemeteries, sanitation, water-supply, slum-clearance, the provision of transport, and certain other forms of municipal trading.[3] In the county boroughs such of these powers as have been conferred or acquired are

[1] This is an extreme case, and virtually removes the committee from the sphere of local government.

[2] W. E. Jackson, *The Structure of Local Government*, 183-5.

[3] Such trading services included light, heat, and power till these were nationalised.

exercised by the council, in the counties they may be divided variously between the County Council itself and the non-county boroughs, urban and rural districts, and parishes. Normally the conduct of administration is entrusted to committees, subject to the control of the council to which they report, technical advice being given by paid officials such as clerks, treasurers, engineers, surveyors, and the like. Elective officials, excepting occasionally mayors, or chairmen of urban district councils, are, like other members of councils, unpaid.

Though dominated by the principle of democratic control by *Central* unpaid elective members assisted by expert advice and service, *control* local government is not wholly autonomous. The central government imposes in the national interest a minimum standard to which local authorities must conform. It encourages them to go beyond that minimum, provided they refrain from activities unauthorised by the law. In both ways, it exercises a supervision which implies a measure of control.

Legislation affecting local government may be based on the *Forms of* initiative of a central department. If it is embodied in a private *control* bill promoted by a local authority, it will none the less be subject to departmental criticism. A simpler procedure is to obtain a Provisional Order—made by a minister under the terms of a statute—perhaps made on his initiative and destined to be, with others, passed into law by a Provisional Orders Confirmation Act.[1] Ministers may have power to issue statutory rules and orders —e.g. the Home Office with regard to police—which local authorities must obey. Simplest and commonest of all is the ministerial order, authorised by statute, confirming a local authority's own scheme. Ministers may also have power to reconstitute or combine certain local authorities, or supersede them if they misuse their powers. Their by-laws need ministerial confirmation—those relating to public health by the Minister of Health, others by the Home Office. Ministerial approval is required for the appointment of certain officials, and disputes between local authorities themselves, or between them and private persons, may be settled by ministerial inquiry and decision.[2]

Above all local government is circumscribed in the sphere of *Finance of local government*

[1] Wade and Phillips, 369-70.
[2] See generally, Finer, Part IV.

finance.[1] The revenues of local bodies arise from four main sources: from revenue-earning property, from local rates, from grants by the national exchequer and from loans approved by the appropriate Ministry: and as local rating brings in only a quarter of the financial resources accruing to local authorities in England and Wales, it is not the principal element in the finance of local government. Local finance is to a large extent under central control. This extends to all four sources of income. The sanction of the central government is needed for sales of property and for raising loans; and more important still the distribution of revenues as between rating and exchequer grants has been substantially modified. In 1929 local authorities lost £24 million annually by the relief from rating then given to certain industries. This sum, together with certain grants hitherto made to local authorities on a percentage basis proportioned to their expenditure and with an additional £5 million subject to periodical revision, was henceforth allowed to them as a "block grant" to spend as they chose, grants for such services as police and education continuing to be reckoned on a percentage basis. It was laid down that the "block grant" should in the first instance be paid over to county and county borough councils: the latter, being the sole administrative authorities within their areas, keeping the whole of their part, while the former shared theirs with subordinate authorities, handing over to them fixed quotas per inhabitant and keeping what was left.

*Diminished scope of Local Authorities*    The next twenty years, however, while proving the value of the "block grant" system as a means of encouraging initiative among local authorities, effected so radical a transformation in their whole position as to relegate that advantage to relative insignificance. Two profound changes occurred. The first was that the sphere of responsibility of local authorities was greatly reduced. From the heavy burden of poor relief imposed by the economic distress of the 1930s, which had fallen on many of them harshly and unequally, they were freed partly in 1934 and finally by the National Insurance Act of 1948: and in the same year the National Health Service took over their responsibilities for hospitals, health visiting, and the care of mothers and young children. As these functions disappeared, expenditure correspondingly diminished. The second change was the loss of indepen-

[1] Finer, 373, 378, 380, 384 ff.

dent revenue from trading services such as gas and electricity as these became nationalised. The final financial result of a half-century of change is made evident by a comparison. In 1914 local authorities raised £71 million from the rates and received £22½ million from the Exchequer. In 1939 the corresponding figures were £290 million and £182 million. In 1960 they were £606 million and £754 million. It seems inevitable that a financial change so far-reaching must entail a similar redistribution of authority, both as between the centre and the local government units, and as between these latter themselves. The ratepayer democracy of late nineteenth-century local government is in its accustomed form ceasing to exist. Local expenditure rises at an even more rapid rate than central. Its increasing burden emphasises the defects of the rating system. Central control might take the form either of complete financial support or transfer of services. Either would be an admission that the ancient system no longer suffices. Neither has yet happened. But radical changes in the system of grants from the central government have further eroded the local independence and responsibility on which the ancient system was based. In 1948 "block" grants were replaced by "equalisation" grants related to an average national rateable value: and in 1958 these in turn were replaced by a "general" grant for a variety of particular purposes, and "deficiency" grants paid not on rateable value but on the actual product of rates. Local variations have thus yielded to the need to equate locally provided services.

An independent authority to levy rates belongs to county *Rating* borough councils, whereas in the counties the non-county boroughs and urban and rural districts receive a "precept" from the County Council ordering them to levy the "General County rate" in addition to their own. Rates still fall on owners of property, who may arrange with their tenants regarding their payment. They are based on the estimated letting value of premises, determined by the officials of the rating authority, revised by an Assessment Committee subject to appeal to Quarter Sessions and in some cases to the High Court and the Lords, and re-assessed at five-yearly intervals.[1] There is no upper limit to the

[1] Under the Local Government Act of 1948 this duty is laid on the officials of the Inland Revenue.

17a

rate which may be levied, and to that extent the local authorities are their own masters.

*Audit*   But, like their other revenues, the expenditure of the sums deriving from this source is subject to audit. All local authorities except boroughs must submit the whole of their accounts yearly to a District Auditor appointed by the Ministry, who may disallow items improperly incurred, and even surcharge them on the persons responsible. Even boroughs must submit for audit those parts of their expenditure which relate to certain specified services.[1]

*Inspection*   Wherever a grant is accepted, central supervision and control follow. Percentage grants for police and education are conditional on whether the central department is duly satisfied by the results of inspection. Even grants which seem more fully at the disposal of local authorities are largely controlled by Ministries, which under the relevant Acts are empowered to demand "a reasonable standard of efficiency".

*Quasi-governmental authorities*   Until the second quarter of this century, a sketch of the administrative system need have included no more than an incidental mention of governmental bodies lying outside the broad categories, central and local, hitherto described. It was not that such bodies had never existed, for the eighteenth-century constitution had abounded in examples of statutory authorities for special purposes, and the Poor Law Commissioners set up in 1834 formed a striking illustration of experiment on a larger scale along similar lines. The lesson which the history of such innovations served, however, to inculcate was that sooner or later they were absorbed into the normal administrative system and placed under democratic control, parliamentary or municipal. After the first World War this principle seemed rapidly to lose its vitality. As the social and economic activities of the State were enlarged, the need for creating new *ad hoc* authorities to deal with them became overwhelming, and these, unlike their predecessors, have shown little tendency to revert to conformity with the pre-existing administrative pattern. So profuse has been their growth that the task of enumerating them becomes impossible and that of classifying them difficult. All that can be attempted is to offer illustrative examples. Most obviously in line with earlier instances of the

---

[1] E.g. education, health and welfare.

creation of special bodies for administrative purposes are such bodies as the Central Land Board set up in 1947 to deal with the development and usage of land and the development charges and compensation payments arising therefrom, and the National Assistance Board, reconstituted in 1948 out of the Unemployment Assistance Board created in 1934, which administers relief to needy persons. More significant are the multitude of regulating authorities operating in the economic and industrial sphere, such as the Marketing Boards, the Cotton Board, and the Development Boards and Mortgage Corporations, all of which were intended mainly to assist various branches of industry, leaving ownership wholly and management largely unaffected. Most significant of all are the bodies set up to manage some great national service or industry, such as the British Broadcasting Corporation, the Boards of Governors, Regional Hospital Boards and local executive committees controlling the hospitals and health services, the National Coal Board, the Electricity Council, the Gas Council, the United Kingdom Atomic Energy Authority, the Transport Commission and the British European and British Overseas Airways Corporations.

It can hardly be said that any coherent constitutional doctrine *The* applicable to these newly-formed authorities has yet been fashioned. *constitu-* The case for creating them may be reasonably clear and the main *tional problem* principles underlying their operation as constituent parts of the government of the country can be defined at least in general terms. They exist in order to obviate placing on ministers and their departments an impossible burden of detailed managerial and technical duties. They do not relieve a minister from ultimate responsibility to Parliament. They do, however, ensure, at least in theory, that the responsibility, accompanied, as it must necessarily be, by a power to intervene in their affairs, shall not diminish efficiency of management, operation or financial control. The Minister has power to appoint or remove the members of the authority except where by charter, as in the British Broadcasting Corporation, they are appointed for a specified term. He may usually issue instructions on broad matters of policy, authorise the raising of loans and supervise the expenditure of funds provided by Parliament. For the use of these powers he is answerable to Parliament, as also he is on the annual reports which under the relevant statutes they must render to him. Yet it is questionable whether such an attenuated and tardily applied version of ministerial responsibility is really enough, and, in the more exact form of answering day-to-day questions in Parliament on the working of these vast concerns with their ceaseless impact on the life of the ordinary citizen, responsibility has been on the whole repudiated. It is easy to see why this should be so. It is less easy to be satisfied with the resulting situation or to discern what the ultimate solution will be. Administrative order has for the moment outrun constitutional progress.[1]

*General features of the administrative system*      Reviewing the administrative system as a whole, it is obvious that the period since 1867 has witnessed the development of an immensely powerful and intricate organisation of power. Its evolution has been the creation of statute, and as the sphere of public control has widened, and the subject-matter to be dealt with has become more technical, Parliament has been obliged to a great extent to confine itself to embodying in statutes a general expression of its purpose, leaving it to administrative bodies to fill in details. Ministers have been increasingly empowered to make rules, orders, or regulations for carrying out the intention of statutes.

*Delegation of legislative power*      "Delegated legislation" is no mere modern innovation. Side by side with the prerogative power of legislation by Order in Council, proclamation, or ordinance (still important in the army and navy, the Civil Service, and the colonial empire), instances occur in every century since the fourteenth of the grant of statutory powers of legislation to the King, the Privy Council, ministers, revenue commissioners, judges, Justices of the Peace and other local authorities.[2] There has been a notable increase in the grant of such powers during the last century. After 1832 the legislature lost its mistrust of the administrative system, hitherto used so often as a means of "influence", but now passing out of the Crown's sole control and under its own. By 1867 dislike of State interference was waning, and the new electorate sought to amplify public control and therefore the administrative power available for imposing it. During the eighteenth century additional administrative

[1] The present position is summarised in Wade and Phillips, 281 ff., and Jennings, 96-7.
[2] See the evidence of Sir W. Graham Harrison before the Committee on Ministers' Powers, in *Minutes of Evidence*, ii. 33-5, and J. Willis, *Parliamentary Powers of English Government Departments*, 11 ff.

powers were given by *ad hoc* statutes relating to particular cases. In the nineteenth, Parliament passed statutes of a more general kind, arming the administration with general authority to act not merely executively but legislatively as well. By 1925 nearly half the Public General Acts gave such power. The numbers of statutory rules and orders alone, to say nothing of other forms of law-making by the central government and by local authorities, increased from 168 in 1890 to over 800 in 1920. An abundant and confusing terminology had crept into use, in which, along with definable expressions such as Order in Council or by-law, are intermingled others far less precise, such as "regulation", "order", "rule", "directive", or even "scheme".[1]

So imperceptibly has this process gone on that its constitutional *The* implications have only slowly been realised. The danger is that *problem of* law comes to be laid down by an authority other than that of *control* Parliament, and that its formulation by discussion and consent is being replaced by the arbitrary fiat of officials. Against this no adequate safeguards exist. It is not easy for Parliament to find out what is happening. No General Act requires subordinate legislation to be laid before it, and though individual Acts may do so, they need not conform to any common procedure. The Rules Publication Act of 1893 provided that statutory rules and orders must be published in the *London Gazette* forty days before coming into operation, so that interested parties might have an opportunity of objecting. But there were serious gaps in this statute. It did not mention, and therefore presumably did not apply to, statutory *regulations*, and delegated legislation by certain departments was exempted from its operation, as also that made under statutes requiring such legislation to be laid before the House for a specified period before coming into force. This "laying provision" was exceedingly inadequate and confused. The "table of the House" where such rules and orders were to be laid was in fact the Library, where few members knew they were to be found, and still fewer troubled to examine them. The period of "laying" varied greatly. In some cases confirmation required a positive resolution by the House. In most, the absence of any negative resolution was enough, and here the dereliction of parliamentary

[1] See C. K. Allen, *Law in the Making* (7th edn.), 531 ff., for a critical survey of the process to date, and its acceleration since 1939.

CONSTITUTIONAL HISTORY OF MODERN BRITAIN

control was complete. Some drastic revision of the procedure for imposing parliamentary control over subordinate legislation had long been seen to be necessary, when the issue was forced on Parliament's attention in 1944. By an oversight the Home Secretary failed to lay before the House certain regulations he had made under a statute and doubt as to their validity consequently arose. The discussions on this question led to the establishment or a Select Committee on Statutory Rules and Orders, and in 1946 to the enactment of the Statutory Instruments Act and an appropriate change in the Committee's title.[1] The function of the Committee is to examine every statutory instrument involving action by the House which is laid before the House in final or draft form and to advise the House of any feature—those relevant being specified—which seems to require attention. The Act repeals the Rules Publication Act. It omits provision for antecedent publication, defines Statutory Instruments, standardises procedure after their publication, and requires those needing parliamentary action for their annulment, and having to be laid in draft on the table of the House, to be laid for a uniform period of forty days. Convenient though these reforms are, it should be noted that they do not touch one central problem, for whether a statutory instrument does or does not need to be laid depends on the terms of the Act under which it is made.

*The Judicial system*
In this extended executive Parliament created a rival not only to itself but to the courts of law. The history of the latter since 1867 begins with the entire remodelling of the English judicial system between 1873 and 1880.[2] By the Supreme Court of Judicature Act of the former year, the superior courts were amalgamated, and absorbed the courts of pleas of Lancaster and Durham, where only equity courts hereafter remained. Henceforth each of the former superior courts constituted a Division of the new Supreme Court, until an Order in Council of 1880 combined with the Queen's Bench division those of Common Pleas and Exchequer, another division being formed to deal with Probate, Divorce, and Admiralty. Equity and Common Law were so far fused as to allow both common law and equitable remedies to be applied and any judge to sit in any division, but

[1] Allen, 556 ff.
[2] Holdsworth, *History of English Law*, i. 638-45.

fusion of the two systems has not gone far. Judges normally deal with business singly, and in the Queen's Bench division usually with a jury. Criminal business is done on assizes or at the Central Criminal Court in London. For appeals from inferior courts, motions for new trials in cases already tried by jury, questions reserved by a judge, and proceedings under *mandamus*, prohibition, and *certiorari*, two or more judges sit together as a Divisional Court.

Appeals in civil cases were committed in 1873 to a Court of *Judicial* Appeal, composed of the Master of the Rolls and five Lords *appeal* Justices, with the Chief Justices of the three Common Law divisions, and, at the Lord Chancellor's option, ex-Lord Chancellors. It combined the functions of the old Exchequer Chamber and Lords Justices of Appeal in Chancery. In 1876, however, the Appellate Jurisdiction Act superimposed on the Court of Appeal the supreme jurisdiction of the Lords, the abolition of which in England had been intended in 1873, and vested it in Lords of Appeal in Ordinary, under the Lord Chancellor, conjoining with them other lords who have held high judicial office.[1] In criminal cases there was until 1907 no appeal, though a judge might reserve a point of law for consideration by the Court of Crown Cases Reserved, which could also be invoked if it could be shown that the indictment was bad or the sentence illegal. In 1907 a Court of Criminal Appeal composed of judges of the King's Bench division was established to hear criminal appeals on points of law, and, by its own leave or that of the trial judge, on points of fact also.[2]

The acts of governmental authorities, central and local, fall *Constitu-* like those of private persons under judicial control. The judges, *tional* though appointed by the Prime Minister or the Lord Chancellor, *status of the judges* have jealously guarded their independence of the executive. They have, like their seventeenth-century predecessors, looked askance on any proposals requiring them to give extrajudicial opinions on points which might subsequently come before them in litigation. In 1932, when subjected by the operation of an Order in Council reducing the salaries of servants of the Crown, they energetically repudiated that status.[3] True to the Common Law

[1] R. Stevens, *The Final Appeal, 1867-76*, 80 *L.Q.R.* 341.
[2] Holdsworth, i. 217-18. Under the Administration of Justice Act, 1960, appeal to the House of Lords can be granted if a point of law of public importance is involved.
[3] Holdsworth, *Constitutional Position of the Judges*, 48 *L.Q.R.* 25.

tradition, they have adhered to the principle that every governmental act must be capable of being justified by rules of Common
or statute law. In general this principle has led them to assume
the defence of private rights invaded by public authority.

*Judicial
control
over
adminis-
trative
authorities*
The task has not been easy. In times of crisis, when the ordinary
civil government has collapsed, it is probable that they would,
while requiring to be satisfied that its collapse should be proved
to their satisfaction if they do not take "judicial notice" of it,
acquiesce in the exercise of martial law, saving their right to
examine acts done under it once peace has been restored.[1] Under
normal conditions, their protection can be thrown over such
rights as those of personal liberty, vindicated by habeas corpus,[2]
freedom of speech and publication, the right of public meeting,
the right of property, and others which the Common Law
similarly regards as fundamental.[3] In these matters they are the
protector of the subject against the State, though recent decisions
may indicate, with regard to the right of public meeting, a new
bias in favour of authority.[4] However strongly the judges may
insist on the principle that all government must be carried on
according to law, the law itself does not enable them everywhere
to impose the same measure of control on public authorities as
on the ordinary citizen. The law does, and indeed must, differ-
entiate the position of the former and give them special rights and
immunities.

*Remedies
against
the
Crown*
Over the Crown itself and its servants, in the first place, is
thrown the protection afforded by a Prerogative incapable of
abridgement save by statute,[5] so that up to 1947 no proceedings
for crime or civil wrongdoing could be brought against the
Crown: the offender, to his own disadvantage and that of the
injured party, might be left by the Crown to bear the whole
consequence of a wrongful act done in the course of his official
duties, for the Crown can neither commit nor authorise nor be

---

[1] See, generally, Keir and Lawson, (5th edn.), 224-37.
[2] For the form of this writ, see Holdsworth, *History of English Law*, i. 660
Dicey, *Law of the Constitution* (9th edn.), 214.
[3] Dicey, *Law of the Constitution*, chs. v.-viii.
[4] See, for example, *Duncan* v. *Jones*, Keir and Lawson, 203, and 52 *L.Q.R*
158, 470.
[5] On the history of remedies against the Crown, see Keir and Lawson, 328-
337.

responsible for any wrongdoing: nor can a superior servant of the Crown be held responsible for the wrongdoing of his subordinate except where he has expressly ordered it, for superior and subordinate are not master and servant, but fellow-servants of the Crown. In civil actions other than tort the Crown could be impleaded only by its own consent, given in a *fiat* from the Attorney-General, and in the resulting proceedings, known as "petition of right", need neither disclose all relevant documents in its possession nor satisfy an adverse judgment. The Crown did not in fact misuse its advantages. It often assumed responsibility for the tortious act of its servant, and petitions of right proceeded much as ordinary actions do. So long ago as 1927 a committee proposed reforms which though generally approved did not result in legislation, and the enlarged scope of governmental action during subsequent years, at so many points involving the Crown, emphasised the need for bringing this department of public law up to date. In 1947 this was done by the Crown Proceedings Act. It abolished a large number of historic methods of procedure available to and against the Crown, and repealed the Petitions of Right Act of 1860 by which the most commonly used of these had been regulated by statute. It allowed civil proceedings to be taken by and against the Crown as though between subject and subject, either in the High Court or the County Court, enabled actions to be instituted by or against Government departments as such—or the Attorney-General if no appropriate department exists—and kept a number of existing types of action answering this purpose. The Court while unable to make an order against the Crown can in effect act equivalently by the issue of a declaration of the rights of the parties concerned, and disclosure of documents is subject only to considerations of public policy. The Act does not seem to apply to the Sovereign personally, and here presumably the old common law procedures must still be available.

Public authorities not emanating directly from the Crown, such *Other* as local authorities, have never of course been protected by the *public* Prerogative. But statutes like the Constables' Protection Act (1751) *authorities* and the Justices' Protection Act (1848) cover acts done *bona fide* but in excess of legal authority, and the Public Authorities' Protection Act (1893) gave these authorities, until its recent repeal, the advantage of a very favourable statute of limitations and penalised with heavy costs unsuccessful actions against them.[1]

*Control over delegated legislation*

It is elsewhere, however, that the courts find difficulties in controlling public authorities. Subordinate legislation may to a greater or less extent be removed from judicial control. Such legislation must be *intra vires* the statute by which it is authorised.[2] Over the by-laws of local authorities no serious impediment exists to the application of this rule, supplemented by the principle that by-laws must be "reasonable". It is otherwise with delegated legislation made by the central government, over which control by the courts has often been virtually ousted. Statutes conferring sub-legislative powers may be so widely drawn that ministers may legislate much as they please, so as, for example in the war-time case of *ex parte Zadig* (1917), to deprive the subject of the protection of the courts over such a fundamental Common Law right as personal liberty.[3] Elsewhere specific words in statutes have seemed deliberately to exclude judicial review. Subordinate legislation is to "have effect as though enacted in this Act", or its making is to be "conclusive evidence that the requirements of this Act have been complied with". In such cases, though the courts have made pertinacious efforts to assert the *ultra vires* rule, it may cease to have any applicability.[4]

*Control over discretionary authority*

Difficulties also arise over their control of administrative acts other than the making of subordinate legislation. Where a statute, or a rule of Common Law, imposes a precise and obligatory duty, —termed "ministerial"—on an administrative authority, the courts can compel its performance, for which purpose the prerogative order of *mandamus* is available, and can restrain any excess of authority. The law cannot, however, cover the field of governmental powers in so complete and rigid a fashion. Practical convenience makes it necessary to empower the administration to act if, how, and when it considers action expedient. In other words the law confers "discretionary" powers, similar in purpose to those once

---

[1] On these Acts, see Keir and Lawson, 339, 340, and C. S. Emden, *Scope of the Public Authorities' Protection Act*, 39 L.Q.R. 341. An Act of 1939 extended the period during which action might be taken against a public authority, in cases where the six months' limitation laid down in 1893 inflicted special hardship. Though repealed (as stated above) it has not yet been replaced.

[2] Keir and Lawson, 35-8.          [3] Keir and Lawson, 39 ff.

[4] Allen, *Law in the Making*, 563-8; Willis, 62 ff. Though such wordings as those quoted have ceased to be commonly used, the inherent difficulties remain.

so largely possessed by the Crown as part of its Prerogative, but founded on statute. The problem of imposing judicial control on such discretionary powers has proved as difficult as in the seventeenth century. Not only the *legality*, but also the *expediency* of such action has to be considered. The latter has to be measured in terms of a "public interest" analogous to what once was called "matter of state". Against this has to be weighed the consideration that action taken by an administrative authority on grounds of public advantage may infringe the rights, and particularly the property rights, of the private individual. A public authority armed with "discretionary" powers is thus in some sense placed in the position of a judge, balancing the competing claims of the community and of the individual subject. Its function becomes quasi-judicial, and many statutes have expressly conferred quasi-judicial authority on public bodies which are not, and do not pretend to be, courts of justice.[1]

That administrative authorities are in many ways unsuitable for this function is evident. In the first place they must obviously be to a large extent judges in their own cause, and incline to put the public interest, as they see it, above the rights of the individual. *Defects and merits of quasi-judicial powers.* Again, their procedure is such as they themselves determine, and may inadequately guarantee that private rights are duly weighed. It may, moreover, lead to arbitrary and capricious decisions, not made intelligible by reference to any acknowledged standard, or supported by reasons which are made public. On the other hand such bodies have at least the advantages that they are familiar, as a court of justice might not be, with the technical aspects of administration, and that their procedure is rapid and inexpensive. For example, an inspector under the Ministry of Housing and Local Government, holding an inquiry into a proposed slum-clearance scheme, and his superior, making an order on the subject, may both be presumed to judge better than could a court of justice whether buildings are or are not suitable for habitation. And the inquiry will certainly be a less costly business than litigation.[2]

The growth of such quasi-judicial powers has created a vast *Principles of control by the Courts*

[1] C. T. Carr, *Administrative Law*, 51 L.Q.R. 58.
[2] For examples of administrative action both central and local involving quasi-judicial elements, see F. J. Port, *Administrative Law*, 194.

administrative jurisdiction in modern Britain, attempting functions similar to those of the conciliar courts of earlier centuries.
Such an organisation is indeed an inseparable part of any system
of government. It may be used to regulate the relations of the
State with its own servants. So, for example, the military rights
and duties of soldiers and sailors have long been regulated by
courts-martial. Nor has such jurisdiction been solely confined to
servants of the Crown. Even in the eighteenth century, when
government seemed most rigidly confined within the framework
of law, there existed an excise jurisdiction, the arbitrary nature of
which led to complaint.[1] But it is on the whole true that the
general extension of administrative jurisdiction over the rights
and property of the subject is a comparatively modern growth. In
continental states like France, where administrative jurisdiction
has a longer history, its relation to the ordinary courts has been
systematically defined. Cases dealing with administrative acts have
been committed to properly constituted administrative courts,
headed by the *Conseil d'Etat*, which, while giving due weight to
administrative advantage, powerfully protect the interests of the
citizen.[2] In Britain, however, the traditional supremacy of the
ordinary courts has prevented the acceptance of such a dualism.
What the ordinary courts attempt is to ensure that administrative
jurisdiction is carried out, so far as possible, in a judicial spirit.
They treat administrative bodies making quasi-judicial decisions
as if they were courts, issuing to them the prerogative orders of
*certiorari* and prohibition by which they control inferior jurisdictions,[3] requiring them to give the subject an opportunity of
putting his case, demanding that no person whose own private
interests are affected by a decision shall have any part in making it,
and that no decision shall be based on extraneous considerations.[4]
It is perhaps right that the judges should refrain from further
interference, which would involve substituting their own judgment on technical points for that of experts. It cannot be pre-
tended that their control is wholly satisfactory. So far as applicable,
it may only impose an external conformity with the requirements

[1] See above, 294 n.

[2] See R. C. K. Ensor, *Courts and Judges in France, Germany and England*, 49–51;
J. Barthélemy, *Le Gouvernement de la France*, 195–209; Port, 296 ff.

[3] An Act of 1948 introduced these Orders, which have the same effect as the
ancient prerogative writs of the same names.        [4] Keir and Lawson, 492 ff.

of justice, under which the substantial merits of the case are to a greater or less degree disregarded by an administrative body more anxious to see its policy fulfilled than to deal fairly with those who suffer thereby.

On this as also on delegated legislation, a Committee on Ministers' Powers which reported in 1932 made some construc- *Reforms proposed by the Donough- more Committee* tive suggestions. They recommended that where impartiality is difficult for a minister acting alone a ministerial tribunal should be set up, that the reports on which decisions are made should be published, and that persons affected by decisions should be told the grounds on which they are made. They rejected any dualism between ordinary and administrative jurisdiction, or any regular appeal from ministerial decisions to the courts of law, though admitting the desirability of exceptional recourse to an Appeal Tribunal.[1] But no reform resulted, nor were even its principles agreed upon between those who favoured the assertion of judicial control and those who would displace it by an administrative jurisdiction. The arguments for judicial control seem to weaken as the defects of existing remedies against public authorities were revealed through the inability of the Courts in many cases either to compel them to do their duty or make them responsible for failure to do so. On the other hand, after a period of retreat, the Courts cautiously began to recover and extend the process of control, with a public opinion more inclined to support them in so doing than to see their jurisdiction ousted and that of some counterpart of the *Conseil d'État* substituted. After another Committee, appointed in 1953, had made a further but no more effective attempt on the problem, significant progress was at last achieved in 1958 in the Tribunals and Enquiries Act, based on *The Franks Report* the report of a Committee under Sir (as he then was) Oliver Franks' chairmanship. The lessons of experience helped to narrow and sharpen the Franks Committee's terms of reference, from which delegated legislation was excluded, and attention was directed to tribunals and enquiries deriving their existence and authority from statute law. That these were necessary and useful was not

---

[1] *Report of Committee on Ministers' Powers* [1932, Cmd. 4060], 99-107, 110-112. See, generally, D. M. Gordon, *Administrative Tribunals and the Courts*, 49 L.Q.R. 94, 419. The fullest recent study is to be found in S. A. de Smith, *Judicial Review of Administrative Action.*

in question: only how their activities could be governed by principles generally recognised even if not uniform in their application. They should be independent and not merely extensions of the Executive; their work should not be based on rejection of any fundamental distinction between administrative and judicial processes; they should be open and impartial; and they should give reasons for their decisions. To ensure that these principles should be followed, the Act placed such proceedings under the supervision of a Council on Tribunals, to be appointed by the Lord Chancellor and required to furnish to him an annual report.[1]

*Position of the executive in the modern Constitution*

So the problem remains that in the modern State an extended executive, able to make, enforce, and interpret law, has come into being, under imperfect parliamentary and judicial control.[2] The principle of the separation of powers has been violated. Considerations of "policy and government", as they would have been called in the seventeenth century, have been accorded a larger place in the constitution than they have held for three hundred years. To many critics the process is disquieting. It seems to threaten a more fundamental breach in the continuity of our constitutional history than has ever been effected in any previous age. It may in reply be suggested that the danger has been exagger-

[1] E. C. S. Wade, *Administration under the Law*, 73 *L.Q.R.* 470, and Allen, 593 ff. That difficulties remain is shown by the *Chalk-Pit Case,* Allen, 600.

[2] With the idea that parliamentary control would be supplemented and strengthened the Government appointed in 1967 a Parliamentary Commissioner (popularly known as an "ombudsman", after the Scandinavian example), whose position and authority were subsequently given validity by statute. This official—whose office was incompatible with membership of the House of Commons or of either branch of the Northern Ireland Parliament—was empowered to enquire, on complaint from any aggrieved subject, received through a Member of Parliament, into allegations of "injustice by maladministration" on the part of Government Departments or other authorities scheduled in the Act: provided that his complaint was received within twelve months of the action alleged, and that he had no recourse which he could reasonably have used to any court or tribunal. The Commissioner was empowered to require evidence on oath from ministers and their officials, and, since hearings are in private, under no rule of secrecy save for Cabinet proceedings. He is required to report to Parliament both generally and in individual cases. It is not yet possible to judge the value of this constitutional innovation: but, since of 2000 cases so far reported to him only 19 have shewed maladministration and in all these he approved the remedial action taken by the Department concerned, it may perhaps be judged that his jurisdiction is too narrow and that lack of authority to deal with the merits as well as the form of administrative action gives the subject less protection than had been intended.

ated. Numerous as are the statutes giving sub-legislative powers, no statute has yet created a general as distinct from a particular power to govern. All such powers are held by a tenure revocable at the will of Parliament. The number of instances in which quasi-judicial powers include the right to judge in matters of law as well as on the questions of fact to which administrative action relates is limited, and their existence is looked on askance. Quasi-judicial powers, with the restricted sphere where their existence is accepted, may be regarded not so much as an encroachment on the rights of the subject as an additional restriction on administrative action. They make the exercise of authority not an absolute power, but one to which safeguards and limitations apply. Neither sub-legislative nor quasi-judicial powers express the right of an omnipotent executive to do as it likes. Both express the power of a sovereign legislature to confer on a limited executive authority such functions as it may from time to time deem necessary.

## iv

In Ireland, as in Great Britain, the period after 1867 witnessed a *Ireland* rapid advance towards electoral democracy and a large expansion *after 1867* of the administrative services. In 1867 the Irish parliamentary franchise was still very restricted. Narrowed by the legislation of 1829, it had been cut down still further by an Act of 1850 raising the qualifying rateable valuation to £12 and reducing the electorate from 272,000 to 164,000.[1] The Act of 1867 made little difference. In fixing the borough franchise qualification at £4 and introducing the lodger franchise it enlarged the borough electorate only from 30,000 to 40,000. The effects of the 1884–5 legislation in a country still agrarian were, however, revolutionary. The Irish electorate rose at a bound from 200,000 to 700,000. Redistribution caused the disappearance of numerous small boroughs and gave a decisive supremacy to the rural constituencies. In 1898 the English Local Government Acts of 1888 and 1894 found their Irish counterpart in an Act establishing county, urban district, and rural district councils with control over local administration and

---

[1] J. O'Connor, *History of Ireland*, ii. 20.

patronage.[1] Parallel with this process a series of statutes aimed at adapting Irish institutions to Irish needs. An agitation for the disestablishment of the Irish Church, initiated in 1863, led in 1869 to the passing of a Disestablishment Act repealing what in 1800 had been declared to be an "essential and fundamental part of the Union".[2] At the same time the tithe question was finally settled by a scheme for paying off tithe rent-charge by a loan repayable to the Government over a term of forty-five years. A system of secondary education was introduced in 1878. In the following year university degrees were made still more widely available by the establishment of the Royal University of Ireland.[3] The fundamental problem of Irish life, that of the land system, was dealt with by a series of statutes from 1870 to 1903, intended at first to protect the interests of the tenant, but later transformed into a means of extinguishing agricultural landlordism altogether through land-purchase and of creating a landowning peasantry.[4] Under the Land Act of 1891 a Congested Districts Board was set up to deal with the barren and overpopulated regions of the West.[5] Early in the new century an Irish Board of Agriculture came into being, and, as the century advanced, British statutes applicable to Ireland covered the country with a network of administrative services.

*Decline of the old ascendancy*

The collective effect of these measures was to subvert the old ascendancy. Except in the northern Ulster counties, where a majority of all classes were united in race and religion, they destroyed its chief pillars. They brought into being among the Catholic Irish a new propertied class, invested it with an assured parliamentary predominance, and delivered over to it full control of local government. They created a large administrative system, staffed, in the main, by Catholic officials, except that the offices of Lord-Lieutenant and Chief Secretary for Ireland were never conferred on Irishmen, and that the heads of government departments, though usually Irishmen, were also usually Protestants. Taken as a whole, the implications of the policy pursued in Ire-

[1] 61 and 62 Vict. C., c. 37.
[2] 33 and 34 Vict., c. 42; Grant Robertson, *Select Statutes, Cases and Documents* (6th edn.), 597-600.
[3] O'Connor, ii. 33-4. The former Queen's University in Ireland with its three teaching colleges was thus replaced by a purely examining body.
[4] O'Connor, ii. 89, 136, 154, 161, 173.
[5] See W. L. Micks, *History of the Congested Districts Board*, 13-24.

land by successive British governments, both Liberal and Conservative, after 1867 rendered it impossible to continue to govern Ireland except, to an increasing extent, with the co-operation of the mass of the native Catholic population.

On what terms was such co-operation to be obtained? The *The Home* omens were not propitious. In the days of O'Connell the object *Rule* of Repeal was not separation from the British Crown, but the *movement* restoration of a Dublin Parliament co-ordinate with that of Great Britain, to which an Irish government should be responsible. At a later date the Irish leader, Isaac Butt, expressed in 1870 his readiness to accept federal devolution, with a Dublin Parliament in a subordinate position dealing with Irish affairs alone.[1] The newly enfranchised electorate of 1884–5 and after was impregnated with a very different spirit. The Famine, the evictions, Fenianism, the great agricultural depression which set in during the later 'seventies and affected agrarian Ireland more seriously than industrialised England and Scotland, agrarian crime, and coercion, had bred a bitter temper, which gave to Irish nationalism a separatist and republican aspect. The adoption of single-member instead of double-member constituencies in 1885 spelled the disappearance of the Irish Liberals, and the handful of Tory members returned were faced by a triumphant and implacable phalanx of Home Rulers whose attachment even to the Crown was highly dubious. It seemed impossible to reconcile the nationalist movement, which captured 85 out of 103 Irish seats in the elections of 1885, to the maintenance of the British connexion in any form, and hazardous even to attempt it. But in 1886 Mr Gladstone as Prime Minister resolved to make, while there was still time, the experiment of entrusting the government of Ireland under the British Crown to the Irish themselves. In this policy the Liberals persisted until 1914. So far as verbal professions went, the leaders of the dominant Irish party declared their willingness to accept a settlement by which a subordinate Parliament should sit in Dublin, exercising an authority limited to Irish affairs, though it is doubtful how far they would have felt obliged, or been able, thus to "set bounds to the march of a nation".

The Home Rule bill of 1886 proposed to set up in Dublin a *The Home* single-chamber legislature for the whole of Ireland. It was to *Rule bill* *of 1886*

[1] F. H. O'Donnell, *History of the Irish Parliamentary Party*, i. 48–51.

be composed of two orders, one non-elective, the other elective, sitting together but exercising certain constitutional checks on each other. To this body control over the Irish executive, except the police system, was to be conceded. Its competence was rigidly limited. Safeguards were inserted in the bill for the protection of Irish Protestantism. A wide range of topics, including the Crown, foreign affairs, defence, the colonies, and tariffs, was reserved to the Imperial Parliament, in neither House of which were Irish representatives any longer to sit. Local taxation alone was fully committed to the Irish Parliament, which was to pay over a sum of three and a quarter millions annually by way of an imperial contribution.[1]

*Opposi-
tion to
Home
Rule*

Devolutionary proposals had lately been in fashion. Both Mr Gladstone's second ministry and its short-lived Conservative successor under Lord Salisbury had discussed—the latter through the Viceroy Lord Carnarvon with the Irish leader Parnell himself —projects for an increase in local control over purely Irish affairs.[2] For some time Parnell and his followers voted on the side of Lord Salisbury's government, and by his instructions the Irish vote in England was in 1885 given to Conservative candidates. Among the Radical supporters of Mr Gladstone, headed by Mr Joseph Chamberlain, plans for Home-Rule-All-Round—contemplating the devolution of authority to councils established in the various parts of the United Kingdom, but subject to the control of the Imperial Parliament in which the whole United Kingdom was to be represented—were much favoured on administrative considerations.[3] Mr Gladstone's plan, however, involving an entire abandonment of control over Irish internal affairs, went far beyond anything that Conservatives or Radicals could be induced to support. The mere fact that Parnell and his followers were ready to accept it awakened their suspicion. Opposition was stimulated by the refusal of the population of the northern counties of Ulster, which had long held rigidly aloof from the political and agrarian movements of the rest of the country, to accept a scheme which seemed to imply perpetual subordination to what rightly or wrongly was

[1] For an abstract of the Home Rule bills, see Grant Robertson, 600-3, 607-13 J. L. and B. Hammond, *Gladstone and the Irish Nation*, 500 ff., 690 ff.
[2] Lady Gwendolen Cecil, *Life of Lord Salisbury*, iii. 155-64.
[3] N. Mansergh, *Government of Northern Ireland*, 47-50.

deemed to be an ignorant, priest-ridden, and disloyal majority of their fellow-countrymen. The risk may have been exaggerated. At the time, however, the objections of English and Irish Unionists prevailed. The Liberal majority in the Commons split, and the bill was rejected.

The bill of 1893 differed from its predecessor mainly in sub- *The bill* stituting a bicameral for a single-chamber legislature, both Houses *of 1893* being elective, and in retaining Irish representation, reduced to eighty members, in the Commons, at first only for Irish and Imperial affairs—under what was familiarly known as the "in-and-out" clause—but, in the bill as amended, for all purposes.[1] These modifications did not remove the fundamental difficulties connected with the cessation of English intervention in Irish domestic affairs and with the abandonment of the loyalist minority. It was perhaps of some importance that this time the measure actually passed the Commons, though it was defeated in the Lords. But its defeat was not followed by a dissolution, and Home Rule slumbered until 1912. By that date the question had somewhat altered in character. In the first place the Unionist policy of 1895–1906, first "resolute government" then what was described as "killing Home Rule by kindness", followed by the lenient administration of Mr Augustine Birrell, Liberal Chief Secretary from 1906, completed the last essential stages of the revolution which had broken down the Anglo-Irish garrison and raised up the new Catholic Irish claimants to power. English authority in Ireland had now shrunk into a bureaucracy and a semi-military police force, both almost entirely Irish, supported in the last resort by a military establishment. Its survival wholly depended, short of recourse to war, on the extent to which the bulk of the Catholic population was prepared to co-operate or at least acquiesce. Secondly the Home Rule movement, if it had lost something of its vitality, had also lost much of its danger. No doubt outside the ranks of the official Nationalist party there existed organisations, such as Sinn Fein, which still nourished doctrines of political and social revolution. The Nationalist party itself, long unopposed in Southern Ireland except where its own schisms created contests, had lost much of its former militancy.

[1] Mansergh, 52–3.

Its members were old hands at Westminster. Their leader, John Redmond, was something of an Anglophile, and the external support to which, by preference, he turned was not American as Parnell's had been, but Australian. It would seem, all things considered, that the grant of Home Rule was at once drawing nearer and becoming safer. On the other hand the anti-Home Rule sentiment displayed by Ulster since 1886 had developed in that region of the country a united, well-defined, and entirely self-conscious provincial nationality which would prove more than ever difficult to force into an autonomous Ireland.

*The bill of 1912*

It was on this reef that the final Home Rule scheme shipwrecked. In its essential features the third bill was much like its predecessors. It reaffirmed the supremacy of the Imperial Parliament, drew limits round the competence of an Irish Parliament constituted on a bicameral basis with a nominated Upper and an elective Lower House, and provided for Irish representation in the British House of Commons. Taxation, including Customs and Excise, was brought more fully than in any previous plans within the control of the Irish Parliament.[1] But it was to be an all-Ireland Parliament. By no scheme for safeguards or postponement was the North to be induced to accept subjection to such a body, and the government, on its side, lost every chance of excluding the four recalcitrant counties of Down, Antrim, Armagh, and Derry.[2] The conjunction of organised preparations for resistance in Ulster and the outbreak of the first World War caused the enactment of the bill in 1914 to be accompanied by a suspension of its effect until the war was over.[3]

*The Act of 1920*

At that moment the general expectation was that the war would be brief. When it ended, after more than four years, in the midst of which occurred the Sinn Fein rebellion of 1916, the Home Rule Act had long since ceased to be applicable. Irish nationalism had resumed its republican and anti-British tradition. Too late, a Government of Ireland Act, 1920, created separate legislatures and administrative systems for six of the northern

---

[1] Mansergh, 58-9.   [2] Mansergh, 98-101.

[3] 4 and 5 Geo. V, c. 88. Note that the preamble to this Act, unlike those of the Home Rule and Welsh Disestablishment Acts, recites the advice and consent of the Lords, and therefore makes no reference to the Parliament Act.

counties—the four referred to above, with Tyrone and Fermanagh—and the rest of Ireland, connected by a joint Council of Ireland, and both subordinate to the Imperial Parliament, in which Ireland was to continue to have representation.[1] The six counties unwillingly accepted the Act, thus coming to constitute a separate political entity as Northern Ireland. The rest of Ireland, where Sinn Fein had wrested control from Nationalism in the general election of 1918, rejected it, and set up in Ireland what was virtually a rival government at war with that of the Crown. The Anglo-Irish Treaty of 1921, which provided a new starting-point in the government of Southern Ireland,[2] linked its constitutional history with that of the self-governing Dominions, among which it took its place first as the Irish Free State, then as Eire until its secession in 1949.

In Northern Ireland there exists under the Act of 1920 a curious *Northern* and indeed unique constitutional experiment. The Crown has *Ireland* been represented, since the office of Viceroy of Ireland was *since 1920* abolished in December 1922, by a Governor. The Northern Ireland legislature comprises a Senate with 2 *ex-officio* members and 24 others elected by the Lower House. The latter has 52 members, elected until 1929 by proportional representation, and since then by simple majority vote, while a different series of constituencies return 12 members to the British House of Commons. A separate administrative system with seven departments is responsible to the Northern legislature, of one or other of the Houses of which their political heads must be members, and in either of which they may speak. A Northern Ireland judicial system has been constituted, with appeal on ordinary cases to the House of Lords, while those affecting the constitution may be referred by the Northern government or by the Home Secretary, who is its official channel of communication with the United Kingdom government, to the Judicial Committee of the Privy Council. Like the legislatures proposed by the Home Rule bills, the Northern Ireland Parliament is not a sovereign assembly. It can neither amend the constitution nor deal with certain excepted topics.[3] Again like the bodies proposed in the Home Rule bills, it

[1] 10 and 11 Geo. V, c. 67; Mansergh, 106-11; Grant Robertson, 603-6.
[2] For the text of the Treaty, see Grant Robertson, 587-91.
[3] On the other hand, the Government of Ireland Act, 1949, protects the Northern Ireland constitution from being changed otherwise than at the request of the Northern Ireland Parliament.

can impose only local taxation, the more important taxes being imposed by the Imperial Parliament. Imperial revenue raised in Northern Ireland is separately accounted for, and after deduction has been made for the cost of conducting imperial services there and for a fluctuating contribution to the Imperial Exchequer, the residuary share is handed over to the control of the Northern Parliament, which is thus in the anomalous position of being able to spend revenues over the raising of the greater part of which it has no authority.[1]

*Working of Northern Ireland government*

The Northern Government, spending about four-fifths of the money expended on the public services in Northern Ireland, has on the whole justified the belief that devolution would lead to greater efficiency. This has been specially evident in the spheres of agriculture, housing, health, and education, which have passed under its control, while Northern Ireland has benefited by the maintenance of non-transferred services still conducted by the Imperial government. Though on the administrative side the results of devolution have been encouraging, it is otherwise on the political side. The special circumstances of Northern Ireland have not produced a healthy alternation of parties in power. The minority tends to repudiate an authority it cannot hope to wield.[2] Its rejection of the whole basis and existence of the Northern Irish State has tended to make every election turn on this one fundamental issue. In such contests, parties concerned with other issues fail to flourish, sometimes even to survive. Thus the Unionist majority have monopolised government since 1920 and must do so until the constitutional question is set at rest. When that happens a more normal balance of political forces may begin to emerge.[3]

*India after 1867*

Presenting, in general, an agreeable contrast to the pathological conditions under which self-government was achieved in Ireland, both Southern and Northern, were those of its growth in India. From the assumption of authority by the Crown in 1858, there was little structural alteration in Indian government until the passing of the Indian Councils Act in 1892.[4] In London

---

[1] Mansergh, ch. x.
[2] Mansergh, chs. xi, xiii, xiv. See also T. Wilson (ed.), *Ulster under Home Rule*, 70 ff., and D. P. Barritt and C. F. Carter, *The Northern Ireland Problem*, 50-1.
[3] The Nationalist Party accepted in 1965 the rôle of Parliamentary opposition.
[4] Keith, *Speeches and Documents on Indian Policy*, ii. 76-81.

control over Indian affairs was vested in a Secretary of State, advised by an expert Council of India, the powers of which were, however, curtailed by a statute of 1869, so that the Secretary of State emerged more clearly as the centre of responsibility.[1] This responsibility, so far as it implied parliamentary control, was for many years more nominal than real. Though in 1858 it had been intended to inform Parliament annually of conditions in India, its interest in the topic waned, and policy passed to a very large extent under the Secretary's control. Such check as existed was provided not in Great Britain but in India. Theoretically the Secretary was, at the outset, only the representative of the Governor-General in the Cabinet and in Parliament. Executive power still lay, it was assumed, in India itself, as in the days of Company rule. But improved communications, and particularly the laying of the Red Sea cable in 1870, diminished the Governor-General's independence, and emphasised the authority of the Secretary of State. This process naturally brought about the increasing intervention of the Secretary of State, and ultimately of Parliament itself—as its interest and knowledge of Indian affairs increased—over the forms and working of Indian government.

In India government was vested in the Governor-General *Central* advised by a Council—whose business he was empowered to *and* regulate by the Indian Councils Act of 1861—which was now *provincial govern-* reorganised on a departmental basis and over which he asserted *ments of* a growing measure of control. For legislative purposes the Coun- *India* cil was enlarged by the inclusion of members, partly non-official, nominated by the Governor-General, who in addition possessed an emergency power to legislate personally, for reasons which he had to submit to the home government. Over the Provinces the central government possessed extensive authority. Each Province derived a portion of its income from the central government. Provincial budgets and schemes for expenditure required its sanction. The provincial Legislative Councils formed in Bombay and Madras in 1861, in Bengal in 1862, and in other Provinces at later dates were regarded as mere extensions of the central Legislative Council. That body legislated for the whole of British India. Its legislation circumscribed the sphere of the provincial Councils, dealing with matters which were by its action regulated on similar

[1] 33 and 34 Vict., c. 97.

lines within each Province. Certain topics could be covered by provincial legislation only under leave from the Governor-General in Council. Projects for legislation had to be laid before the Governor-General in Council and the Secretary of State, and every provincial Act needed the Governor-General's assent. Administratively the Governor of every Province and his executive Council were required not only to carry out his orders, but to report to him on its own conduct of administration. Provincial matters were the subject of commissions of inquiry set up by the central government, provincial governments were advised by its experts on subjects committed to provincial care, and by its decision was regulated everything relating to conditions in the public services. Though by practice the respective spheres of the central and provincial governments were approximately defined, the latter were in essence the mere agents of the former.[1] And, just as the improvement of communications with England tended to increase the control of the Home government over that of India, so in India itself, but at a much earlier date, the improvement of internal communications increased the control of the Governor-General over the Provinces. Collectively the influence of the Home government on that of India and of the latter on the Provinces resulted in the steady improvement of Indian administration in accordance with enlightened Western ideas.

*Character-istics of Indian adminis-tration*   Under these influences an ever-greater uniformity was imparted to Indian government, and the expanding public services were conducted with generally similar aims in view. The corps of about eleven hundred covenanted members of the Indian Civil Service, assisted by separately-organised bodies such as those in charge of police, medical, and forest services, carried out vast schemes of amelioration and development.[2] Both the Indian government itself and that of Great Britain were strongly possessed by the sense that British authority in India was a trust to be exercised for the advantage of India itself. To refer only to a few instances, famine relief, irrigation, the conservation of forests, the promotion of agriculture and education were all included in

[1] On the relations of the Government of India with those of the Provinces, see Keith, *Constitutional History of India*, 183-5.
[2] Keith, *Constitutional History of India*, 198-203.

the sphere of governmental action. The defects of the system, from an administrative point of view, were the excess of its good qualities. It tended to over-centralisation. There was, if anything, too much interference by the government of India with those of the Provinces, and subsequently by the Home government with that of India. Moreover, and still more important, zeal for efficiency led to an undue reliance on the services of Europeans in preference to Indians.

This latter feature of British rule, however explicable, was at variance not only with earlier practice, but with the express terms of the Royal Proclamation of 1858, which had held out the prospect that all the Queen's subjects irrespective of race and creed should be impartially admitted to such offices as they might be qualified to hold.[1] The rank-and-file appointments of the Indian government were of course largely committed to native hands, and even superior positions were theoretically open to them. They were, under the Indian Courts Act of 1861, eligible for appointment to High Court judgeships. They were also qualified to compete in the Indian Civil Service examination. But the rate at which they gained admission to the civil service was slow, and for many years only one Indian judge sat in any of the High Courts. If nominated to the legislative councils, they were liable to be out-voted by their more numerous European colleagues. *Position of Indians in Indian government*

Such a position of inferiority and exclusion was increasingly difficult to maintain or defend as an Indian educated class came into being. The extension of university education in India rapidly created such a class. At the same time, however, primary, secondary, and technical education lingered behind. The result was to throw up from among an illiterate lower class a body of persons who had received a literary or legal rather than scientific or technical education, among whom unemployment was rife, and who naturally turned to politics, which they regarded in the light of Western ideas inappropriate or at least premature in their application to Indian conditions.[2] During the latter half of the *Political aims of the educated class in India*

[1] For the Proclamation, see Keith, *Speeches and Documents on Indian Policy*, i. 382-6.
[2] *Cambridge History of the British Empire*, v. 353-6; H. H. Dodwell, *India*, ii. ch. vii.

18

nineteenth century the vernacular press of India came to rank as a new political force, with a marked tendency towards sedition. In 1878 the apparent need for a censorship evoked a Vernacular Press Act, requiring editors to give bonds that they would print nothing likely to excite disaffection, or to submit their proofs for censorship.[1] With results which may be variously estimated the Act was repealed three years later, and the experiment was presently begun of introducing an elective element into Indian government. For this purpose a beginning was made in 1883 with the establishment of a number of elective municipal authorities, and elective boards for rural areas. Except in large centres with a numerous British population, it proved a failure, making no appeal to the Indian educated classes.[2]

*The Indian Councils Act*    Their desire for a more important share in Indian government was manifested in 1885 by the foundation of the Indian National Congress.[3] Though immediately inspired by the grievance created by British opposition to the Ilbert Bill—which aimed at removing the incapacity of native district judges to hear criminal cases in which Europeans were involved[4]—it started with the intention of urging by strictly constitutional means the establishment of responsible government in India, even if under the leadership of Mr Tilak an extremist party came frankly to advocate a policy of violence.[5] Guided by Lord Dufferin, who before coming to India as Governor-General had held the same position in Canada, the British government decided to introduce, by the Indian Councils Act of 1892, an elective element into the legislative councils both of the government of India and of the Provinces.[6] To the central council were added members chosen by the non-official members of the provincial councils, to the provincial councils those chosen by local governmental authorities. This system involved no appointment of Indians to executive councils. It involved no process of popular election. And it gave the legislative councils no substantially enlarged functions, save the right of asking questions and that of considering finance.

*The Morley-Minto reforms*    Parallel with the extremist movement, which, in Bengal par-

[1] *C.H.B.E.* v. 548; Dodwell, ii. 193.
[2] *C.H.B.E.* v. 516-17, 534-5.
[3] H. V. Lovett, *The Indian Nationalist Movement*, 34 ff.
[4] *C.H.B.E.* v. 387, 539.
[5] *C.H.B.E.* v. 549-51; Lovett, 48 ff.        [6] *C.H.B.E.* v. 544-6.

ticularly, became identified with terrorism and assassination, the Congress continued to press for further advance towards representative and responsible government. Another stage was reached under Lord Minto, who arrived in 1906 as Governor-General— after previous experience, like Lord Dufferin, in the same capacity in Canada—and the Liberal Secretary of State, Mr John Morley. They brought about the introduction of Indian members to the Council of India, the appointment of an Indian, Mr Sinha, to the Governor-General's executive council, and the enlargement of the provincial executive councils to include Indians also.[1] In 1909 a statute provided for the enlargement of the legislative councils so as to include members representing a greater variety of Indian opinion and interests than had been contemplated in 1892, and in particular for the separate representation of the Hindu and Muslim communities.[2]

Notwithstanding these well-timed measures, which largely con- *The* tributed to the tranquillity of India during the 1914–18 War, the *Montagu-* goal of responsible government still seemed remote. The war *Chelms-* suddenly brought it close. In 1917 the Secretary of State, Mr *reforms* Montagu, announced the aim of British policy to be "the increasing association of Indians in every branch of the administration and the gradual development of self-governing institutions with a view to the progressive realisation of responsible government in India as an integral part of the British Empire", reserving to the British government and that of India the right to be "judges of the time and measure of each advance".[3] Under the scheme subsequently devised for this purpose in 1919 partially responsible government was established in the Provinces, in each of which certain subjects were transferred to ministers chosen from the legislatures, while others were reserved to the Governors advised by executive councils of two to four members of whom one must be Indian.[4] The legislatures were widely extended on an enlarged franchise, preserving separate communal electorates. At the centre an Indian Legislative Assembly, five-sevenths elective, and one-third of the remainder non-official, was set up in conjunction with a Council of State comprising 25 nominated and 34

---

[1] *C.H.B.E.* v. 570.
[2] Keith, *Speeches and Documents on Indian Policy*, ii. 100-105.
[3] Keith, ii. 133.        [4] Keith, *Constitutional History of India*, 247.

elected members. To this, however, the government of India was not to be responsible. Finance was, in respect of certain necessary services, made non-votable, and the Governor-General was empowered to pass bills even over the Assembly's opposition if he "certified" them as essential. Certain heads of taxation were made over from the central to the provincial governments, subject to their giving contributions to the expenditure of the government of India.[1]

*The Simon Commission*

The 1919 Constitution was to be reviewed at the end of ten years, and a Royal Commission under Sir John Simon reported on it in 1930. Its task was not made easier by the mistrust evinced by Indian politicians towards the commission as a purely European body, and their consequent refusal to assist it. Yet its report proved an immensely valuable document, not only for its acute analysis of the results of the 1919 experiment and of the difficulties, particularly that of defence, which beset further advance, but also for its constructive suggestions. Though the Provinces were, as their previous constitutional history showed, mere extensions of the central government, it was proposed to use them as the bases of a federation. The scheme was to be completed by the inclusion of the Indian States, with which since 1858 the British government, acting through the Governor-General as Viceroy, had dealt as states fully sovereign except only in their external relations, and as liable to direct internal intervention only in cases of gross and incorrigible maladministration. Their connexion with British India had been drawn closer in 1921 by the establishment of a Chamber of Princes to consult on matters of common concern. The Report recognised that the Indian States were so intimately interwoven with British India that, subject to their consent, their inclusion was necessary for the completion of the projected federal constitution. "The first essential", it was said, "for internal peace and prosperity for both parts of India is harmony between them."[2]

*The Act of 1935*

On these lines the constitution of India was redrawn in 1935. In the Provinces, elective legislatures returned by separate

---

[1] C.H.B.E. v. 595 ff.; Keith, *Constitutional History of India*, 260 ff.

[2] *Simon Commission Report*, ii. 10; Dodwell, ii. ch. ix. See generally, Holdsworth, *The Indian States and India*, 46 L.Q.R. 407, and L. Scott, *The Crown and the Indian States*, 44 L.Q.R. 267.

communal electorates were established with a defined sphere of competence. To these, saving the Governor's special responsibility "for the prevention of any grave menace to the peace and tranquillity of the province or any part thereof", the executive became fully responsible. At the centre, the executive responsibility of the Governor-General was divided. For certain topics, including defence, he remained responsible only to the Imperial Parliament. For all other topics responsibility to the Indian legislatures was introduced. Both chambers of the legislature were to include representatives of British India and of the States, the former elective, the latter nominated by the Ruling Princes. The adoption of federal government was necessarily accompanied by the creation of a federal court. Thus, save for the "special responsibilities" of the provincial governors and the reserved powers of the Governor-General, there began to emerge a new sovereign state under the British Crown.[1]

Insufficient time had elapsed to put these arrangements to the test when the second World War broke upon them. In most Provinces it proved impossible to form responsible ministries and government had to be conducted under the Governors' special powers. As the war went on the need for a new constitutional experiment was recognised and discussions entrusted to Sir Stafford Cripps had as their intention the establishment of a new Dominion constitution framed by Indians and including the right to end the imperial connexion and allegiance to the Crown. Later discussions, in 1964, indicated that fundamental divergences between Hindus and Muslims made the framing of such an all-Indian constitution impossible. The United Kingdom Government forced the issue by announcing in 1947 its intention to transfer authority in June 1948 to one or more successor authorities in India, and by enacting the Indian Independence Act. In August 1947, under this Act, the two new Dominions of India and Pakistan came into being, and the Crown's suzerainty over the Indian States was ended. Both Dominions were given constituent powers. The Indian Constituent Assembly used these to draft a constitution on republican and federal lines, into which most of the Indian States entered by acts of accession which at least in form were voluntary. In Pakistan until the new

*India and Pakistan*

[1] Keith, *Constitutional History of India*, 319 ff.

constitution was enacted creating an Islamic republic, the Act of
1935 still operated, but Pakistan legislation had already created
separate citizenship and ended appeals to the Privy Council.
These Asian Dominions thus took up Southern Ireland's example
in hastening constitutional advance.

*Develop-*
*ment of*
*the self-*
*governing*
*colonies*

Through processes unmarred by the friction and misfortunes
of constitutional development in Ireland and in India, the
colonies enjoying responsible government likewise moved after
1867. Their number was increased by the extension of that system
to Cape Colony in 1872, to Western Australia in 1890, and to
Natal in 1892. The Peace of Vereeniging which closed the Boer
War contained a promise that it would be introduced into the
newly-annexed provinces as soon as conditions permitted. The
undertaking was redeemed in the Transvaal in 1906 and in
the Orange River Colony in 1907. The Canadian federation was
enlarged by the admission of British Columbia in 1871 and Prince
Edward Island in 1873, and by the creation of the new provinces
of Manitoba in 1870 and of Saskatchewan and Alberta in 1905,
in territories which until 1869 had been administered by the
Hudson's Bay Company and later by the Dominion Government.
In Canada the example of the United States, and to some extent
the fear of its further expansion, strongly stimulated the movement towards federal unity. In Australia, where no powerful
neighbour moved the colonies to emulation or mistrust, the progress towards federation was slower. The need for a unified
Australian constitution had indeed long been recognised, and a
bill for the purpose was introduced in the Imperial Parliament in
1849.[1] Though Australian support for such a project was never
wholly lacking, the practical difficulties, accentuated by differences
of tariff policy in the two larger colonies of New South Wales
and Victoria, long proved insuperable. The Canadian example
inspired the appointment of a Royal Commission on federation
in 1870. Though there was agreement on the principle, radical
difference arose on the form of the new constitution.[2] In 1883 the
improvement of internal communications in Australia, and the
beginnings of foreign imperialism in the Pacific, prompted a
further effort. On Australian initiative, the Imperial Parliament

---

[1] H. E. Egerton, *Federations and Unions within the British Empire*, 169-84.
[2] *C.H.B.E.* vii. i. 431.

passed an Act setting up a Federal Council of Australasia, with limited legislative, but no executive or financial powers.[1] New South Wales and New Zealand held aloof, but the fact was that as the isolation of the Australian colonies from each other and the rest of the world decreased, the need for unity became increasingly plain. In 1891 a draft federal constitution was prepared. Though it accurately foreshadowed the future federal union, it proved unacceptable to the colonial legislatures. While they remained obstinate, however, a popular movement for federation came into existence, to the pressure of which the colonies finally responded.[2] In 1897 a constitutional convention assembled, and in 1900 its draft constitution passed into a statute enacted by the Imperial Parliament. Localism so far retained vitality that the framers of the Commonwealth of Australia Act rejected the Canadian model, in which defined spheres of legislation were specifically allotted to the provinces and to the Dominion. More closely following the American model, they reserved residual authority to the states themselves.[3]

While, in different ways, the Canadian and Australian constitu- *New* tions were planned on federal lines, those of New Zealand and *Zealand* South Africa became unitary. In the former the provincial *and South* councils created in 1851 were abolished in 1876.[4] In the latter, *Africa* though a provincial organisation was set up by the Union Act of 1909,[5] the country had long experienced the difficulty arising from the co-existence of four separate governments within its restricted and closely interconnected area, and all the provinces except Natal preferred union to federation. Under the new constitution, though the provincial councils could legislate and control local services and impose local taxation, they were strictly subordinated to the central government, and were denied control over the provincial executive, which was headed by an Administrator appointed by the Union government. Perhaps the only trace of the federal principle in South African Union was the equal representation granted to the four provinces in the Senate.

---

[1] W. Harrison Moore, *The Commonwealth of Australia*, 29-39.

[2] Harrison Moore, 40-52.

[3] Egerton, 185-230; Harrison Moore, 62-81. Note that the Australian "colonies" now become "states".

[4] W. P. Morrell, *Provincial System in New Zealand*, 231-40. *C.H.B.E.* vii. ii. 117.                              [5] Egerton, 231-91.

*Dominion status*

With the addition of Newfoundland, where again government was unitary, the self-governing colonies now numbered five. By decision of the Colonial Conference of 1907, the title of *Dominion* was conferred on them.[1] All, whether federal or unitary, possessed the common characteristic of possessing fully representative legislatures and fully responsible executives. Their constitutional development proceeded with the full approbation of the Imperial government and Parliament, but on lines chosen by the colonies themselves. Alike in New Zealand, Canada, Australia, and South Africa, progress had been marked by imperial statutes giving effect to their own expressly formulated desires. If unity between the Mother Country and the Dominions was to be preserved, there must be a limit, and one in which the latter acquiesced, to the extent to which Parliament surrendered its legislative authority over them and the Crown consented to be advised, in the conduct of Dominion affairs, by ministers responsible to colonial legislatures and not to the Imperial Parliament.

*Limits of legislative sovereignty*

Two limitations existed to the competence of these legislatures. The legislation they enacted, though embracing every topic included under the comprehensive head of "peace, order, and good government", was limited in its range of operation by the territorial boundaries of the Dominion. It was, moreover, restricted by the provision in the Colonial Laws Validity Act that it must not be repugnant to any imperial statute applying to the Dominion. In order to ensure legislative uniformity throughout the Empire, certain important matters such as merchant shipping were regulated by imperial statutes, but the total amount of such legislation was small, and did not greatly increase. The Imperial Parliament never legislated for any of the Dominions save at the latter's request or with its consent. Clearly, in each of the Dominions, the most important imperial statute specifically applying to it was that in which its constitution was embodied. In unitary states, and even in individual states or provinces included in a federation, the power of the legislature to effect constitutional amendment was not in doubt. It might be inferred from the Colonial Laws Validity Act itself, or might be expressly granted. The nature of the federal constitutions, embodying what were virtually agree-

[1] R. Jebb, *The Imperial Conference*, ii. 101, 374-5; *Cambridge History of the British Empire*, iii. 426.

ments between contracting parties, did not lend itself to any such easy process, but that of Australia contained provisions for its amendment without reference to the Imperial Parliament, and only the Canadian constitution, among all the five in the self-governing colonies, necessitated recourse to an imperial statute for its amendment. In essence, therefore, the legislatures of the majority of the Dominions were sovereign and even constituent bodies.

No attempt was made to confine the legislative powers of the *Imperial* Dominions within rigid limits. Subject to the provision as to *control* repugnancy contained in the Colonial Laws Validity Act, and to *colonial* the territorial limitation, their legislatures could make law as they *legislation* pleased. On the other hand there existed certain means by which an imperial control, more theoretical than effective, could be imposed on colonial bills and even Acts. Preserved from the earlier constitutional practice of the Empire was the Governor-General's right to give or refuse assent to legislation (his assent in fact was never refused); his power, or duty, to reserve certain bills before assenting to them, so that the King's pleasure, in expressing which he was guided by the advice of the British government, might be signified about them; and the King's right, similarly exercised, to disallow them even when they had received the Governor-General's assent. A power of reservation at the Governor-General's discretion was contained in the constitutions of New Zealand, Australia, and South Africa, and was later introduced into that of the Irish Free State.[1] Obligatory reservation of bills of a specified character was to be found in the Acts embodying the constitutions of New Zealand, Australia, and South Africa, and in certain imperial legislation such as the Merchant Shipping Acts.[2] Each of the constitutions of the Dominions contained a provision for disallowance, though it was to be excluded from that of the Irish Free State.[3]

Acceptance of the principle of responsible government clearly *The* implied that the Governor-General should act on the advice of his *Executive* ministers. But his was, in effect, a dual responsibility. He was *in the* *Dominions* appointed by the King on the recommendation of the Imperial

[1] K. C. Wheare, *Statute of Westminster and Dominion Status* (5th edn.), 62 ff., 261-2.

[2] Wheare, 66-7. Obligatory reservation might exist by virtue of the Governors' Instructions as well as under statute.

[3] Wheare, 70-74.

18a

government, though after consultation with the Dominion government in order to ensure that the choice would be acceptable. He was the channel of communication between the Imperial government and that of the Dominion to which he was appointed. So far as the Prerogative was committed to him, he was doubtless bound to exercise it in conformity with the conventions which determined its use by the King himself. It might, however, be regarded as doubtful whether the Prerogative had been committed in its entirety into his keeping. Apart from the explicit limitations imposed by provisions regarding disallowance, it was evident that there existed a large, though diminishing, sphere of governmental action in which the right of Dominion ministers to have their advice accepted was dubious. From this category defence soon disappeared. In 1862 the Commons resolved that, while the self-governing colonies had a right to imperial protection, they ought to assist in their own external defence.[1] By 1871, with minor exceptions, imperial military and naval establishments had been withdrawn from their territories. There still remained such important powers as the making of treaties, foreign affairs, peace and war, and neutrality, as to which it was uncertain how far colonial governments possessed any independent authority. From 1877 onwards the self-governing colonies were no longer included automatically in treaties made by the United Kingdom.[2] The right of separately adhering to treaties was amplified after 1898 by the right of separate withdrawal; after 1907 by that of separate negotiation of treaties; though not yet that of separate conclusion of treaties.[3] With regard to foreign affairs the self-governing colonies, while having no separate diplomatic or consular services, expected to be, and in fact were, taken into consultation by Great Britain in matters affecting their own interests, though not always to their own satisfaction. The final determination of foreign policy was left to the British government, and therefore also the issues of peace and war. In 1907 and 1911 the Dominions showed their desire for more intimate consultation with the United Kingdom on foreign policy and defence.[4] There was no indication

---

[1] Keith, *Sovereignty of the British Dominions*, 128.    [2] Keith, 279.
[3] Keith, 281, 285 ff. The first treaty to be separately concluded by a Dominion was that made between Canada and the United States in 1923.
[4] Keith, 139-40.

that they desired to stand aside. Apart from an occasional assertion of the right of neutrality, for example by certain Australians after 1870 and certain South Africans in 1899, it was nowhere contended that colonial self-government implied a right to refuse to be involved in wars declared by or against the British Crown.[1]

The sovereignty of the Dominions was limited in the judicial *The* sphere by the appellate jurisdiction of the Privy Council, put on *jurisdiction* a statutory basis by Acts of 1833 and 1844.[2] In Canada appeals *Privy* to the Privy Council from the Supreme Courts, Dominion and *Council* provincial, were unrestricted. In Australia, under the constitution of 1900, appeals lay as of right from the State Supreme Courts, and by special leave of the Privy Council from the Commonwealth High Court except in certain constitutional cases where its own leave is necessary. In South Africa appeals as of right were abolished by the South Africa Act, and the South African Parliament was given power, subject to reservation by the Governor-General of any bill for this purpose, to limit matters on which special leave to appeal might be sought from the Privy Council. In all three Dominions leave to appeal, being embodied in an Imperial statute, could not be abolished by their own act, and was further restricted by the territorial limit on their legislative powers.[3]

Such then were the principal marks of Dominion subordina- *The first* tion to imperial control before the outbreak of the War of *World* 1914–18. Once again, the stimulus given to constitutional develop- *Dominion* ment by the pressure of war has to be noted. Though the Imperial *status* War Cabinet and the British Supreme Command co-ordinated the war efforts of the Dominions, no encroachment was made, or was possible, on Dominion autonomy, and its rapid advance towards fuller control of external as well as internal affairs was shown in the peace settlement. The services rendered by the Dominions were recognised by their special representation at the Peace Conference for the discussion of matters in which they were concerned, while their representatives were also included in the British Empire Delegation. So also they participated separately in the signature and ratification of peace, and—with India but

[1] W. Harrison Moore, *The Commonwealth of Australia*, 28–9.
[2] On the Act of 1844, see Keith, 255.    [3] Wheare, 87 ff.

without Newfoundland—assumed separate membership of the League of Nations.[1]

*Separate diplomatic action*    Subsequent events emphasised the significance of these developments. In 1923 the Canadian government concluded a treaty with the United States by its own action, and without imperial intervention, and soon afterwards warned the British Government that it must understand that the extent of Canadian commitments under the Treaty of Lausanne was for the Canadian government and legislature to decide.[2] In 1925 the Dominions were not separately represented at the Locarno negotiations, nor did they separately sign the resulting Treaty.[3] It was becoming plain that the independent action of the United Kingdom and the Dominions in international affairs was reducing the diplomatic unity of the Empire to a fiction.

*The Irish Free State*    Meanwhile, the rate of advance was being still further hastened by the policy of the Irish Free State. In this, the youngest of the Dominions, the evolution of Dominion status was not achieved by a gradual process, in which the implications of responsible government were worked out piecemeal. It was attained at a bound, and by revolution. Even so Dominion status, so far as it implied imperfect sovereignty, was not the ultimate goal of the Irish leaders. Outside Northern Ireland, the Government of Ireland Act of 1920 had never become operative. In the Treaty of December 1921 which closed the so-called Anglo-Irish War, a constitution modelled so far as possible on that of Canada was promised. The Free State Constitution, as actually framed, bore certain resemblances to its prototype.[4] It set up a bicameral legislature (the *Oireachtas*), composed of a nominated Upper House (*Seanad*) and an elective Lower House (*Dáil*). The Crown was represented by a Governor-General, with power to reserve legislation, and the right of the Privy Council to give special leave to appeal was retained. On the other hand there were important differences. Sovereign authority was stated to be derived from the people. The Irish legislature was given constituent powers for

---

[1] Keith, 311 ff.; *Cambridge History of the British Empire*, iii. 645-65.
[2] Keith, 390-96.
[3] Keith, 398-401. On the separate diplomatic representation obtained by Canada, the Irish Free State, and South Africa, see Keith, 436-53.
[4] Grant Robertson, 591-6.

a period of eight years (subsequently extended by its own act), constitutional changes were thereafter to be effected by referendum. Ministerial responsibility was grounded in law rather than convention. The authority of the Crown was derived from the voluntary association of the Free State with the "British Commonwealth of Nations", and the Free State was not to be involved in wars affecting the United Kingdom except by consent of its own legislature. Two safeguards for imperial authority seemed to be preserved. By the Imperial Act confirming the Free State Constitution, the right of the Imperial Parliament to legislate for the Free State under the same conditions as for the other Dominions was affirmed. And the Treaty of 1921 was regarded as fundamental, so that the Constitution itself was subordinate to its authority.[1]

The ministers of the Free State made it their business to force to its furthest limits the autonomy which Dominion status, in the special form in which they had acquired it, could be made to yield. Their lead was followed, with varying degrees of readiness, by the other Dominions. South Africa, for reasons not dissimilar from those prompting the action of the Free State, pursued the same purpose. In Canada the refusal of the Governor-General, Lord Byng, to grant a dissolution on the request of the Prime Minister, Mr Mackenzie King, and his invitation to the Opposition leader, Mr Meighen, to form a government, to which a dissolution was at once granted, created in 1926 a constitutional crisis which caused the Dominion to wish to clarify at least the relationship between the Governor-General and his ministers.[2] The remaining Dominions were less anxious to undertake the delicate task of re-defining the constitutional system of the Empire. But they could not, in the general interests of the Dominions as a whole, stand in the way. These various problems came to a head in the Imperial Conference of 1926.

Since 1887 periodical consultations described as Colonial Conferences had been held between the British government and the

*Antecedents of the Imperial Conference of 1926*

*Colonial and Imperial Conferences*

[1] N. Mansergh, *The Irish Free State*, 45-9; Wheare, 100 ff.
[2] It should be added that Mr Meighen failed to obtain a majority in the ensuing general election. It has been strongly argued that Mr Mackenzie King was entitled to a dissolution and Mr Meighen was not. Only the result of the general election makes adverse criticism of Lord Byng's action possible. On the whole question, see Keith, *Sovereignty of the British Dominions*, 244-6.

Governors or Prime Ministers of the self-governing colonies. In 1907 this organisation was made more systematic. Under the new style of Imperial Conferences these meetings were to be held every four years. They remained purely consultative, and had no power of binding any of the participants. Yet their achievements up to 1914 led to a notable increase of co-operation within the Empire. General imperial or other special Conferences of 1894, 1897, 1902, 1907, 1909, 1910, and 1911, caused effective agreed action regarding such matters as defence, tariffs, emigration, communications, and the law regarding naturalisation, copyright, and Privy Council appeals. These conferences, it is true, had revealed the reluctance of the self-governing colonies to set up any federal authority within the Empire, but they had to a large extent corrected the weaknesses resulting from its absence.[1]

*Centri-*
*fugal forces*    When the first World War ended, their history was resumed under somewhat different auspices. By this time, while an Imperial War Cabinet had bound the Dominions and the Mother Country more closely together for war purposes, the autonomy of the Dominions had been recognised in the course of Imperial War Conferences, and was to be the subject-matter of discussion so soon as the return of peace permitted a normal Imperial Conference to be assembled.[2] The proceedings of the Conferences of 1921 and 1923 made it evident that the forces which tended to isolate and detach the Dominions from the Mother Country were in serious competition with those which before and during the War had tended to make imperial unity effective. Though questions of foreign policy might be discussed in common, and improved arrangements made for keeping the Dominions informed about the action of each other and of the Imperial government itself in this sphere, the sense of joint responsibility was hard to create, and proposals for the collective organisation of imperial defence were not sympathetically received. While asserting the right to be consulted, and to approve or disapprove British policy, the Dominions were

[1] For a general account of their history to 1907, and appendices of their resolutions, see Jebb, *The Imperial Conference*; thereafter, see Keith, *Governments of the British Empire*, 123-49.

[2] Jebb, *The Empire in Eclipse*, 4-9. The Imperial War Cabinet, comprising members from all the Dominions, is to be carefully distinguished from the War Cabinet mentioned earlier, though the latter included for a time General Smuts; Keith, 149-57.

not prepared to bind themselves to support, even if they approved, what the British government decided on.[1]

In the Imperial Conference of 1926 the centrifugal forces which *The* in varying degrees had manifested themselves attained a measure *Imperial* of recognition limited mainly by the fact that they were far from *Conference of 1926* being felt to the same extent by the various Dominions. The position and mutual relation of the United Kingdom and the Dominions was defined by a formula skilfully drafted by Lord Balfour. They were described as "autonomous communities within the British Empire, equal in status, in no way subordinate one to another in any aspect of their domestic or external affairs, though united by a common allegiance to the Crown, and freely associated as members of the British Commonwealth of Nations".[2] The declaration is notable as an admission that Dominion sovereignty, long accepted with regard to domestic concerns, now extended to foreign and even "inter-imperial" relations as well. On the other hand the declaration added in words equally authoritative, though less commonly remembered thereafter, that equality of status did not universally extend to function and that the distribution of functions between the Mother Country and the Dominions should be governed by the need for making imperial unity effective.[3]

The 1926 Conference may have intended to emphasise the need *The* for imperial unity as strongly as the principle of Dominion *Statute of* autonomy. But the practical implications of the former were less *Westminster* rapidly and systematically worked out than those of the latter. Its recommendation that legal restrictions on Dominion autonomy should be removed took effect within five years. After preliminary work by a Conference on the operation of Dominion Legislation in 1929, the results of which were reviewed by the Imperial Conference of 1930, a statute of the Imperial Parliament, passed in 1931 under the style of the Statute of Westminster, regulated anew the exercise of legislative powers by the Imperial and Dominion Parliaments.[4] The convention that the Imperial Parliament should not legislate for a Dominion except at the request and with the consent of its government was enacted as law. It

[1] On the Conferences of 1921 and 1923, see Keith, *Governments of the British Empire*, 163-70.
[2] Keith, *Sovereignty of the British Dominions*, 10.
[3] Keith, 11.     [4] Wheare, 122 ff.

may be that the legislative supremacy of the Imperial Parliament was implicitly preserved by the Statute, but it became a highly abstract conception. The test of repugnancy imposed by the Colonial Laws Validity Act was abolished. The extra-territorial limitation on Dominion legislation was removed. In every case the legislation of a Dominion Parliament now became fully enforceable in its own courts. The only, and natural, limitation existing on the legislative sovereignty of the Dominions was that applicable where, in federal unions, no one legislature could derive from the Statute any power to effect constitutional amendment by its own sole action. Thus in Canada—and in Australia with respect to the first eight sections of the Commonwealth of Australia Act—the Constitution Acts, and the means for constitutional amendment, remained unaffected.

*Application of the Statute in the Irish Free State*  With these exceptions, the competence of the Dominion legislatures was so expanded by the Statute as to seem to imply unrestricted sovereignty. Such topics as the reservation or disallowance of bills, appeal to the Privy Council, and even the Prerogative of the Crown were brought within their sphere. The Irish Free State, always in the vanguard of Dominion advance to independent sovereignty, proceeded to override the Treaty of 1921, the Imperial Act of 1922 which gave the Treaty statutory force, the Irish Act of 1922 to which were scheduled both the Treaty and the Irish Free State Constitution, and the Imperial Act confirming that constitution. It is true that the Statute of Westminster conferred no constituent power, in express terms, on the *Oireachtas*. But such a power might be inferred from the absence of any such limitation on its constituent powers as had been included in the Statute at the request of Canada and Australia, as also of New Zealand, with reference to their own constitutions. Free State Acts abolished reservation and the power of the Governor-General to refuse assent to bills, appeal to the Privy Council, the oath of allegiance, and the office of Governor-General itself (1936), finally by popular referendum the Free State Constitution was itself abrogated, and replaced by one of wholly independent origin (1937).[1]

[1] Wheare, 255 ff.; L. Kohn, *Constitution of the Irish Free State*, Appendix, showing amendments. In principle the unfettered authority of the Free State to enact a constitution entirely repugnant to the Treaty of 1921 was recognised by the Privy Council in the case of *Moore* v. *Attorney-General of the Irish Free State*, Jennings and Young, 450-58

In South Africa the Status of the Union Act, 1934, expressly *Its* denied the authority of imperial legislation in the Union except *applica-tion in* when enacted separately and additionally by the Union Parliament *South* itself. Disallowance was completely removed from the Union *Africa* Constitution, and reservation, whether obligatory or discretionary, which had by convention become disused since 1930, now survived only as regards bills dealing with Privy Council appeals and the government of native territories transferred to the Union. The discretion of the Governor-General was limited to giving or with-holding assent, and the Act required the King to act on the advice of his South African ministers, which implied that royal Instruc-tions would be issued in such terms as they might direct.[1] By a further enactment, the Royal Executive Functions and Seals Act, a separate Great Seal was created for South Africa, which enabled the Union Government to deal formally with foreign relations, dispensing with the intervention of the Foreign Secretary.[2] The Union Parliament further assumed authority under the Statute of Westminster to amend the so-called "entrenched clauses" of the South Africa Act[3] by ordinary legislative action, and in 1937 its right to do so was upheld by a decision of the Supreme Court.[4] As regards the very limited power of appeal to the Privy Council which existed in the Union no change was yet made.

Even discounting such extreme cases as those of the Irish Free *Weaken-* State and the Union of South Africa, it is difficult to avoid the *ing of Imperial* conclusion that imperial constitutional development after 1918 *unity* was mainly of a negative character. The legislative sovereignty accorded to the Dominions and the elimination of appeal to the Privy Council suggested the dissolution of the public law of the Empire and even of the unity which has hitherto, in essentials, pervaded its private law.[5] The position of the Crown as the vis-ible centre of allegiance, even apart from its destruction in the Irish Free State, was everywhere impaired, at least in appearance,

---

[1] Wheare, 243 ff., 320-23.          [2] Wheare, 250-51.

[3] Namely, those dealing with the proportionate representations of the pro-vinces in the legislature, the Cape coloured franchise, and the equality of the English and Dutch languages, and the clause protecting these clauses.

[4] *Ndlwana v. Hofmeyr*, Jennings and Young, 353-5; later reversed, however, in *Harris v. Minister of the Interior*, Keir and Lawson, 8; Wheare, 242, 339-47.

[5] But see R. T. E. Latham, *The Law and the Commonwealth*, in *Survey of British Commonwealth Affairs* (ed. W. K. Hancock), 571-3.

by the new status—detached from the Imperial government—
accorded after 1926 to Governors-General; while in South Africa
the legislation of 1934 transformed the monarchy into a mere
abstraction, by virtually creating a separate South African kingship. Everywhere, in fact, the point was reached when the King
might receive and be obliged to act on mutually inconsistent
counsels given to him by ministers whose views are irreconcilably
opposed.

*The abdication of King Edward VIII*    The first formal test of the relationship established by the
Statute of Westminster occurred in 1936. During the events pre-
ceding King Edward VIII's abdication, the British Prime Minister,
Mr Baldwin, after preliminary consultation with the Dominion
Prime Ministers, suggested that the Dominion governments might
each separately tender to the King their advice on the questions
involved. All, save that of the Irish Free State, did so. The King's
decision to abdicate could only be made legally effective by the
enactment of a statute, which under the terms of the Statute of
Westminster must, if it were to be effective in the Dominions to
which that Statute applied in its entirety, be enacted at their
request and with their assent. The request and consent of Canada
—to which the Statute of Westminster applied—and the assent of
Australia and New Zealand—where it had not been adopted—
were recited in the preamble to the Abdication Declaration Act.
In the Union of South Africa the view was taken that the legislation of 1934 admitted of a separate abdication of the throne in
South Africa, and the Union therefore, though assenting to the
Imperial Act (an assent recited in the preamble), did not request
and consent to its enactment. The Irish Free State, having passed
a Constitution Amendment Act omitting all recognition of the
King as sovereign, similarly refrained. By an Executive Functions
Act, it accepted King George VI for the purpose of acting in
external affairs to whatever extent he might be so advised by the
Executive Council while the Free State, now called Eire, remained
"associated" with the Commonwealth.[1]

*The problem of Imperial co-opera- tion*    While the machinery of consultation and legislation managed,

[1] On the legislation relating to the abdication, see Latham, 616-30; Wheare,
284-90. The South African government did not consider separate legislation
to give effect to the abdication. Newfoundland having in 1933 temporarily
lost its representative Parliament and being governed by a commissioner, was
constitutionally unable to act with the other Dominions.

though in an incomplete fashion, to get into motion, its partial success did not quiet the doubts which the recent constitutional development of the Empire had inspired. The salient features of that process were apparently to emphasise the possibility of separate and unrelated action by the governments of the Empire, to multiply the number of points on which disagreement and even mutual opposition were admissible, and to impede and render more cumbrous the means available for united and co-ordinated action. The inter-war period, moreover, while so deeply concerned with working out the corollaries of independence, was singularly barren in devising means for making common action prompt and powerful. It became more than ever plain that Dominion ministries, responsible to their own Parliaments, could never concede control over policy to a single Council of State or Secretariat in London or anywhere else, not merely in respect of commercial and defence questions where delay and discussion is possible and may be beneficial, but even over foreign policy where speed is essential and the unpredictable always occurring. As always, war would impose the most stringent tests on the structure and working of the constitution and hasten change.

The immediate answers given to this test were somewhat *The* incoherent. When on September 3 the United Kingdom Govern- *Domi-* ment declared war on Germany, Australia and New Zealand *nions and* *the war of* deemed themselves immediately involved, though in 1941 *1939-45* Australia issued its own declaration of war against Japan; South Africa decided by a small parliamentary majority to empower the Governor-General to declare war, which he did by proclamation on September 6; four days later, the Canadian declaration of war followed the acceptance by Parliament of an address from the throne; and Eire remained neutral throughout. The war, however, did give rise to effective *ad hoc* arrangements for mutual consultation and common action: besides communications, partly directly between Prime Ministers, partly through the Dominions Office, there were meetings of Dominion High Commissioners in London, interchange of visits between Prime Ministers, occasional attendances of the Australian High Commissioner at meetings of the War Cabinet, and other devices, including a conference of Dominion Prime Ministers in London in 1944—a prototype now commonly followed.

*Post-war developments*    Since the close of the war both structure and working have departed widely and rapidly from the pre-war model. The former system of Imperial Conferences has not been revived, and no formal organisation has as yet been substituted for it. A new mode of consultation has been found in conferences of Ministers. The conception of a common citizenship has been virtually abandoned, each Dominion defining its own citizenship; there is now no coherent system of reciprocity, for while it does exist between the United Kingdom, Canada, Australia, and New Zealand, it is almost wholly lacking elsewhere, each local situation being in effect governed by local legislation. Appeals to the Privy Council have been abolished save to a limited extent from Australia, New Zealand, and Ceylon. India and Pakistan, while remaining in the Commonwealth, became Republics; Eire, now renamed the Republic of Ireland, seceded in 1949, as Burma, detached from India by the Act of 1935, had already done in 1947. South Africa, becoming a republic in 1961, decided to apply for continued membership but later withdrew the application.[1] Newfoundland ceased to be a Dominion on being admitted as the tenth Province of Canada in 1950, and the term Dominion status has become so nebulous as to be discarded from constitutional usage. Beginning with India and Pakistan, independence has been conferred by separate Acts of the Imperial Parliament and not by enlargements in the application of the Statute of Westminster.[2]

*The New Commonwealth*    Constitutional change in the Empire since the second World War has not—as was once hoped, indeed assumed—been generated from within the system itself nor brought to fulfilment its inherent tendencies. The Crown is no longer the universal source of authority, for in most new constitutions sovereignty is expressly or implicitly derived from "the people", and a republican form of government preferred to a monarchy represented by a Governor-General, even if an interim arrangement on monarchical lines has sometimes and briefly been accepted. As Empire has been displaced by Commonwealth as a collective political term, the sovereign's role has diminished to a titular Headship devoid of power. The federal idea from which so much was once expected having already

---

[1] For the practice (or conventions) about admission to the Commonwealth see Wheare, *Constitutional Structure of the Commonwealth*, 117 ff. There has not been an exclusion.

[2] G. Marshall, *Parliamentary Sovereignty and the Commonwealth*, 124 ff.

failed to link the countries of the Empire together has succeeded little better as a means of preserving their own internal unity against the disruptive forces released by independence. Popular sovereignty has sometimes been misused to destroy minority rights, opposition parties, even "entrenched clauses" in constitutions, to undermine the public services, attack the independence of the Bench, stifle the Press and other forms of public criticism and establish dictatorial controls over every institution of government and every activity of national life. Such deformations present a sombre and repulsive contrast to the optimism which inspired liberal Imperialism. Parliamentary sovereignty and the Rule of Law, the first two articles of Dicey's creed, have seemingly lost their virtue when applied to the newly-fashioned Commonwealth. His third proposition holds only with sinister significance: since conventions and not laws are the ultimately decisive factor and as they derive from national character, no constitution can work better than it is made to work by those to whom it gives power. Only —so might the argument run—where the Crown continues to be the source of power or exercise it directly can British governmental institutions and principles be effectively perpetuated. To this defeatist opinion some support is given by recent events. The ordered gradualism which until lately characterised constitutional progress in the dependent territories proved impossible to maintain after the British collapse at Suez in 1956. That external catastrophe accelerated internal changes which would otherwise have taken decades to achieve and imparted to them a revolutionary aspect.

Independence came to fourteen countries of the Empire between 1956 and 1963: internal self-government to most others. While it would clearly be premature to discuss in any detail a process so rapid, far-reaching and erratic, a summary may furnish useful information and perhaps indicate some general features of constitutional progress. The African territories moved furthest and fastest. Ghana (a combination of the Gold Coast, Ashanti and the Northern Territories) became in 1957 the first African State other than the Union to attain independence within the Commonwealth, first under the Crown, since 1960 as a republic. Nigeria became self-governing, the Eastern and Western Regions in 1957, the Northern Region in 1959; a Federal Executive was

*The end of the dependent Empire*

established in 1958 in preparation for the Federation which began under the Crown in 1960 and became a republic in 1963. Sierra Leone became independent under the Crown in 1961. Even the minute riverine state of Gambia advanced to internal self-government in 1965. In the East African territories of Uganda, Kenya, Tanganyika and Zanzibar, where the foundations for constitutional progress were slighter and its coming was delayed by a resort to force by elements in the Kikuyu, Embu and Meru tribes in Kenya, the rate was much the same: increases in the elective membership of legislative Councils were made in 1957, elections held in the three mainland territories in 1958, internal self-government granted to Kenya in 1960, Tanganyika in 1961 and Uganda in 1962; independence came in 1963 and the supersession of the Crown's authority by republican forms of government everywhere in that and the following year; while the inter-territorial links hitherto maintained by the East Africa High Commission were with difficulty continued by its successor the East Africa Common Services Organisation.[1] The experiment, inaugurated in 1953, of federating the three Central African territories—Southern and Northern Rhodesia and Nyasaland—broke down in 1963. Nyasaland and Northern Rhodesia became independent, the first, as Malawi, under the Crown, the second, as Zambia, a republic from the outset. The sedater evolution of the West Indies was halted by equal if less expected difficulties. These ancient island possessions of the Crown, federated in 1956, broke up into their component units again in 1962, leaving Jamaica and Trinidad with Tobago as independent states under the Crown, a self-governing Barbados and the rest—the Leeward and the Windward Islands—still in search of a constitutional future. Similar but more serious uncertainties have beset the Asian territories: the Malayan Federation set up in 1957 and enlarged into a Malaysian Federation by the inclusion of North Borneo and Sarawak in 1961, lost Singapore by secession in 1965. Somewhat analogously, the attempt to unite the colony of Aden to the South Arabian Federation was impeded as much by the contrast between the interests of the great modern city and port and its

[1] The Sultanate of Zanzibar survived independence in 1963 only three weeks when it was forcibly overthrown and the country united in 1964 with Tanganyika to form the new state of Tanzania.

primitive hinterland as by hostile intervention from outside in their affairs. The Mediterranean island of Cyprus became an independent republic within the Commonwealth in 1960, and Malta became an independent state within the Commonwealth in 1964, as did Guyana, formerly British Guiana, in 1966.

The movement towards independence—in the constitutional *The process completed* sense, not necessarily any other—has in various ways extended to South Arabia, the High Commission Territories in South Africa, Mauritius, Fiji, and the Leeward and the Windward Islands, even British Honduras. Internal self-government as it extends to external affairs may bring about surrender by the Crown of its authority to rule and the total abandonment of British sovereignty, even if there be no need to assume that change will be pressed so far.

There is little force or comfort in the thought that the move- *Limits of decolonisation* ment cannot be universal. In the island territories, whether colonies or protectorates or protected states, scattered over the Atlantic, Pacific and Indian Oceans, separated from each other by vast distances and often themselves composed of widely-dispersed units, their land surfaces small, even minute, their populations scanty and difficult to sustain for lack of natural resources, it is difficult to see how the wealth or the manpower required even for internal self-government, still less independent sovereignty, can in all cases be generated from within; nor, it must be added, is either of these their hope or ambition. To this category belong a score and more of territories, measuring anything from two square miles to 11,500 and peopled by anything from 100 to 130,000 inhabitants, which still girdle the globe with British authority and responsibility.[1] Their significance will increase as air transport and air power develop, and so also will the stimulus they impart to alien cupidity or ambition and with it the prospect of their being swept into the orbit of other states. If this fate be averted, and their future like their past is one of

---

[1] In the Atlantic, Ascension, the Bahamas, Bermuda, the Cayman Islands, the Falkland Islands, Gibraltar, St. Helena, Tristan da Cunha, Turks and Caicos Islands, the British Virgin Islands; in the Pacific, the Gilbert and Ellice Islands, Hong Kong, the New Hebrides, Pitcairn Island, the Solomon Islands, Tonga; in the Indian Ocean, the Maldive Islands and the Seychelles. New Caledonia is a Condominium with France; the Sultanate of Brunei, a mainland territory of Borneo, is enclosed between territories of the Federation of Malaysia.

subjection to the British Crown, the traditional forms of British colonial rule may be self-contradictorily perpetuated without adaptation and growth save perhaps some slender form of "association" with each other and the United Kingdom itself.

*Tradition and innovation*

Not through such survivals—if in the event they do survive—will British constitutional forms and their historic principles transmit their value. That must depend on the new states of the Commonwealth. These may differ widely, often disconcertingly, from their prototype, which they may often seem to contradict rather than copy or adapt. They may seem to repudiate the basic ideas of British parliamentary democracy, and to make the Commonwealth appear as devoid of constitutional content as it is of political and economic cohesion or military might. Any traces of British institutions detected in such fragments may possess no more than antiquarian interest, hardly worth looking for in an age grown sceptical about tradition and seeking elsewhere the avenue to human progress.

*The transplantation of institutions*

Such pessimism loses meaning for the student who has observed over the centuries the challenges to which British institutions have been subjected, and their powers of response. It is natural that, when transplanted overseas, they have been more easily established in the older than the newer territories of the Commonwealth, and where race, language, religion, culture and private law all derive from British or European sources. It is such conditions rather than contrasts between peaceful and revolutionary processes of change that account for the differences between old and new. Revolution has had little part in the history of the Commonwealth, and change has characteristically been achieved, even when precipitate, by agreement and with mutual good feeling. Even the less attractive traits of certain new Commonwealth governments—the authoritarian executive, the controlled legislature, insecure political and civil liberties—reflect not so much alien notions of dictatorship as the devices to which in the past even the mildest of colonial administrations were sometimes driven; neither British rule overseas nor parliamentary democracy at home had in practice relied on them as a system. But the new regimes found them familiar, relevant and more easily copied than the remote and untried Westminster pattern of parliamentary and party rule.

Since peaceful change and transfer of power under forms of law have been the rule, authority to effect it lies in the Imperial Parliament and is expressed in statutes conferring partial or complete internal self-government or full independence. Like those establishing the Dominions, such statutes embody the results of discussion, negotiation, and mutual adjustment. Though the Imperial Parliament ceases to act as a constituent body once the Independence Act is passed, and constituent authority becomes vested in or is assumed by the newly-created local legislature, Commonwealth constitutions wear familiar aspects such as a cabinet system, a non-political Civil Service, an independent judiciary and judicial processes protecting rights which derive ultimately from the Common Law. All this may be a natural outcome of British precept and example; but equally, if less obviously, a reflection of colonial nationalist thought in the period of opposition to British rule, since it was an opposition more concerned with political than constitutional change. Constitutional thought, so far as it went, accepted familiar British patterns, only altered in detail to meet special local requirements. It could hardly have been otherwise; no pre-existing indigenous system could have been either generally acceptable (most have been abolished) or adequate to the tasks of modern government. Even if many new constitutions have presently moved away from British antetypes, these latter can still furnish a norm by which subsequent deviations will be critically judged. Contact with British rule and practice cannot be dismissed as an episode. It is a part of the experience of many peoples. It remains relevant and its results endure.

*Constituent legislation*

If then it be asked whether the nebulous and shapeless congeries of states and peoples into which the Commonwealth has resolved itself can either endure as a structure or even exert continuing influence, the answer no longer assumes a single central authority or any substitute for it; nor standard patterns for the distribution and exercise of power. There may never develop for the Commonwealth any common system of public law or common organs of government related thereto. In the failure to realise so many hopes, in the disappointments that change has brought, there is much to regret. But it will not matter, if the genius of the British constitution enters into all those which owe to it not merely their origins and forms, but also their vigilance for freedom and the legal safeguards which are its defence. There need be no regrets for the passage from Empire to Commonwealth if institutions the world over and the ideals they express testify to the resilience and continuity of the British tradition in government and prove that men and nations schooled in it do not forget the paths in which their feet have been set.

# INDEX

William III (of Orange), 255, 267, 268, 269, 270, 271, 273, 304, 307, 318, 321, 375, 428, 436
William IV, 382, 389, 413
Wills, Statute of, 132
Wilmington, Spencer Compton, Earl of, 320, 333, 334
Winchester:
  bishopric of, 480
  borough of, 323
  marquisate of, 137
Winwood, Sir Ralph, 176
Wolsey, Thomas, Cardinal, 14, 19, 55, 56, 57, 60
Women's suffrage, 460, 471, 474, 500 n.
Wood's halfpence, 436
Woodfall, 342
Worcester, battle of, 223
Worcester, county of, and Council of Wales, 25
Workhouses, 313
Works, Board of, 300, 304
  Ministry of, 409 n., 513
  Office of, 513
Wotton, Nicholas, 114
Writs:
  of assistance, 359
  of certiorari, 527, 532
  of consultation, 131, 152, 198, 200
  for election, 326
  of error, 210, 286

Writs—contd.
  under Great Seal, 26, 274
  of habeas corpus, 201, 230, 259, 549
  of mandamus, 527-30
  of privilege, 147
  under Privy Seal, 21, 119
  of prohibition, 198, 532
  of quo warranto, 260
  of subpoena, 130
  of summons to House of Lords, 137
Wyatt, Sir Thomas, 97
Wyndham, Sir William, 335

Year Books, 28
Yelverton, Sir Christopher, 149
York:
  archdiocese of, 49
  city of, 212, 217
  Convocation, 48, 61
  county of, 26, 125, 139, 323, 397, 400, 403
  Court of Chancery of, 48
York, Duchess of, 11
  Elizabeth of, 9
  House of, 5
    hereditary claims of, 8, 9, 101
  James, Duke of, 246, 252, 255, 257, 258, 259, 345; and see James II
Yorkshire Association, 398
Young Irelanders, 441

Zambia, 566
Zanzibar, 566